THE HISTORY OF
THE TIMES

VOL. IV
THE 150TH ANNIVERSARY AND BEYOND
1912—1948

PART II: 1921—1948

THE " FRONT DOOR " OF P.H.S. IN 1922

"I have asked Sir Campbell Stuart to have made a very large sign covering the whole of the building with gilt letters, including the Royal Arms in colours. *The letters should dominate the building*—not the building the letters. Do not delay. They can very easily dominate the street if brains and imagination are used. Chief."   (July 23, 1919.)

The "gilt letters," Royal Arms etc. were removed on the change of Proprietorship in 1922.

THE HISTORY OF
THE ✦ TIMES

DIEU ET MON DROIT

THE
150TH ANNIVERSARY
AND
BEYOND
1912-1948

PART II
CHAPTERS XIII - XXIV
1921 - 1948
APPENDICES AND INDEX

LONDON
WRITTEN AND PUBLISHED AT
THE OFFICE OF *THE TIMES*
PRINTING HOUSE SQUARE
1952

PRINTED IN GREAT BRITAIN

CONTENTS

LIST OF ILLUSTRATIONS

CORRIGENDA

Volume IV, Part II

973   footnote, line 4 : for " (August 19) " read " (August 12) ".

981   line 12 : for " July, criticized " read " July, 1939, criticized ".

983   line 5 : for " petifogging " read " pettifogging ".

986   line 27 : for " pride in him " read " pride in them ".

1020 line 7 from bottom of text : for " but of the " read " but the ".

1031 line 11 from bottom : for " crisis to head " read " crisis to a head ".

1033 line 28 : for " Friday " read " Thursday ".

1080 line 36 : for " the Allies could " read " the Allies should ".

1087 line 30 from bottom : for " assertions of " read " assertions on ".

1093 line 20 from bottom : for " col. 2354 " read " col. 2350 ".

1096 line 7 from bottom : for " *Meererungen* " read " *Meerengen* ".
      line 6 from bottom : for " *Aswärtige Angeletenheiten* " read " *Auswärtige Angelegenheiten* ".

1125 line 6 from bottom : for " newspapers each " read " newspapers are each ".

1133 under *Daily Mirror*, Editors : for " Alexander Kinealy " read " Alexander Kenealy ".

XIII

IRELAND, 1913-1921

THERE was much support in Printing House Square for " self-determination " before the President of the United States adopted it. The doctrine of national freedom that was sponsored by *The Times* after the invasion of Belgium, and applauded when it was made to inspire the Treaty, was fated to bring disaster to the policy which the paper expressed fifteen or twenty years after the Peace was signed. The country that accepted the doctrine in 1914 and supported it in 1919 maintained belief in it in 1936, 1938 and 1939. The doctrine had an immediate application to Britain, and, independently of Irish-American sentiment, *The Times* under Steed would have favoured the recognition of Irish Nationalism with the granting of self-government. The application of the principle of nationality to Ireland was implicit in Steed's attitude towards the separation, which he thought absolutely inevitable, of Czechoslovakia from Austria-Hungary. His attitude towards Ireland differed therefore in important respects from that of Dawson.[1] Moreover, the change in the international situation was bound to alter the policy towards Ireland that *The Times* had followed since the days of Barnes, Delane and Buckle.[2]

In the spring of 1914 Dawson was able to take a purely Empire view of the Irish crisis, and at the outbreak of war he felt justified in dropping the issue as far as possible. Steed, however, was compelled to adopt an attitude that corresponded with the immense change in European, Atlantic and Pacific relations. Both Japan and the United States were far stronger in proportion to the Western Allies than before 1914. Japan was a problem common, though for diverse reasons, to Britain and America. Steed was also bound to admit the change for the worse, in terms

[1] That Dawson was sensitive to the repercussions of Ireland upon Anglo-American relations is shown below (p. 543, 546). The basis of his concern was, rightly, the winning of the war, while that of Steed was, also rightly, the laying down of a new balance of power within the League of Nations, as a guarantee of peace.

[2] See Vol. I, Chapter XX, " O'Connell the Enemy "; Vol. III, Chapter III, " Parnellism and Crime."

of balance of power, in British financial, naval and military strength. The accretion of industrial and financial power, and her naval programme made America an arbiter of Anglo-Japanese and Anglo-Irish relations. That had been plain at the Peace Conference. It was a corollary that Britain could only adjust her existing Japanese agreement to an American agreement by first achieving an Irish settlement, in terms of self-determination.

It has been seen that Dawson had reasons, some of long standing and some of recent formulation, which induced him to adopt a waiting attitude. He had begun his duties as Editor in the middle of an Irish crisis, the real difficulties of which were soon apparent. Asquith's Ministry was dependent upon the Irish Nationalist Party, and during 1911 a Home Rule Bill had been framed. Lloyd George (Chancellor of the Exchequer) was personally desirous of excluding some part of Ulster from the Bill, but had accepted the Cabinet decision to establish one National Irish Parliament. In September, 1911, the Ulster Unionists announced the preparation of a Provisional Government for Ulster. In April, 1912, the Home Rule Bill was introduced into the House of Commons and in June Lloyd George, on behalf of the Government, rejected an amendment to exclude Ulster's four eastern counties from the Bill. On September 28, 1912, the "solemn League and Covenant," signed by Londonderry, Carson and Craig, declared that Ulster would never accept the Home Rule Bill drafted by the Liberal Government. Dawson's experience in South Africa warned him of the dangers of such a situation, but also encouraged him to hope and to work for a settlement which would preserve the unity of the Empire. Dawson's decision to support Ulster was confirmed by Northcliffe, who agreed that the question of Irish government must be reconsidered as a whole. Dawson, though favouring a conference on Irish affairs and prepared to consider the establishment of four provincial councils, argued that the first step must be the withdrawal of the existing Bill. Led by his first South African experience Dawson realized that to exclude Ulster would mean a Bill that divided Ireland. This was an obvious mischief.[1] Accordingly, he instructed John Healy, Editor of the *Irish Times* and " Our Own Correspondent " in Dublin of *The Times* : " I may tell you that the advocates of an immediate conference with the object of a ' settlement by consent ' are very hard at work. No doubt you know this better than I do. My attitude towards them is that I am not prepared

[1] For Dawson's scheme and its correspondence with the ideas of Lionel Curtis, F. S. Oliver and Philip Kerr, see Appendix II, Sources, XIII.

to support their proposals or to publish their articles under existing conditions. Our first object must be to kill the Bill, and we shall distract and confuse people if we make overtures for peace before that is accomplished."[1] Less than five months afterwards he made a dramatic exception to this principle : on September 11, 1913, a letter was printed in *The Times* from Lord Loreburn, hitherto regarded by all parties as one of the most staunch supporters of Home Rule. Loreburn's plea for a conference and settlement by consent caused considerable comment, and many concluded that it signified a Government weakening. From the preliminary correspondence with John Walter, however, it is clear that the ex-Minister's action was taken independently, though he believed that " if I was to write what is in the thoughts of many of those I know it might help to get other people to speak out."[2] His devotion to Home Rule was unswerving, for the words of his letter to Walter written later are firm enough: " If I have a further favour to ask it is that I should be regarded as a Home Ruler, which I am, and an All Round specimen of that class. I regard it as vital and am trying to get it if possible without friction beyond the necessary."[3] Dawson was on holiday when Loreburn's suggestion of a conference was first made to Walter, but he decided to accept it, though he did not approve the proposals: " As to the policy of ' conference, compromise, conciliation and consent,' I expect you agree," and, he put it to Walter, " it is not *our* business to press it now. I feel that it is the only course *in the end*, but not till the present H. R. Bill is withdrawn."[4] Events proved the Editor to have judged correctly; neither Redmond nor Carson would come to the Conference. At the end of September Dawson returned from holiday to find the situation rapidly developing. Carson and Craig had stiffened their opposition. A first-class leader-writer was needed, the Editor then saw, " to grapple with the political situation—that is primarily with Ireland." Dawson told Healy that " after taking a careful look round I have decided to detach Lovat Fraser for this work, and he has very kindly undertaken it. It is rather outside his line of country, but he is an absolutely first-rate man, writes quickly and forcibly to order, and is perhaps all the better for not having been involved in Irish affairs all his life."[5] Fraser was told to conceal his

[1] Dawson to Healy, April 21, 1913.

[2] Loreburn to Walter, August 30, 1913.

[3] Loreburn to Walter, September 13, 1913.

[4] Dawson to Walter, September 5, 1913. " Conference, conciliation and consent " was the slogan of the O'Brienites, formed in 1909 when O'Brien and eight others withdrew from Redmond's Parliamentary party.

[5] Dawson to Healy, September 29, 1913. Fraser had been writing on India.

identity and he took careful precautions ; carrying guide-book and camera, accompanied by his wife, he successfully posed as a tourist, on one occasion under the eyes of Redmond himself. Fraser's enthusiasm and interest were quickly roused and three days after his arrival he took up the pen to tell the Editor : " I feel I must unburden myself a little as I go along. In a short time I have seen and heard a good deal."[1] Thereafter, from both North and South, impressed with the significance of what was taking place, he wrote daily. In Ulster he saw the Unionist Volunteers drilling, obtained figures as to their strength and number of weapons, and gathered a good deal of confidential information. Carson, Fraser became convinced, was not moved by vanity or consumed by passion, but filled, rather, with a consciousness of " terrible " responsibility.[2] Fraser was struck by the sincerity and resolute determination of the Ulster Unionists, qualities he found curiously lacking in the South, where he heard Redmond, Dillon and Devlin speak at Limerick. His experiences convinced him that Ulster should not and could not be coerced. Healy was equally convinced that neither Redmond nor Carson would accept partition.[3] The Editor's plan of four provincial councils, after conference, appeared to be a possible solution, and he remained intent on defeating the Bill by demonstrating the strength of Ulster's resolution.

After the refusal, on March 20, 1914, of General Gough and a number of officers to serve against Ulster, troops were moved to the north in some strength and with naval support over the week-end of March 20-22. Repington was sent to investigate. On Monday, March 23, the bill page was given almost entirely to reports from various sources of what had taken place. The Unionists were convinced that more than merely precautionary measures were intended but they and Printing House Square were heartened by the evident disaffection in the Army. Repington wrote of gross mismanagement by Seely, Churchill and French, and concluded : " After this revelation of the sentiments of the Army the less said about the coercion of Protestant Ulster by His Majesty's troops the better for all concerned." But Repington's full account could not be completed for some time, and it was not until April 27 that *The Times* presented what it put forward as a " fairly complete analysis " of the attempted " *coup* against the Unionists." Publication

---

[1] Fraser to Dawson, October 5, 1913.

[2] Fraser to Dawson, October 5, 1913.

[3] For Healy's plan for a settlement, see Appendix II, **Sources, XIII.**

LOVAT FRASER

was timed to precede the debate in the House of Commons, and the account revealed beyond dispute the culpability of the Government. Evidence was not wanting that his Majesty's Ministers and not his Generals were responsible. The two-page analysis concluded with a section devoted to the evasive and contradictory explanations put forward by the Government. But as the Bill progressed the paper made the following statement :

We have consistently opposed the principle of Home Rule for Ireland and continue to do so. We should regard any form of settlement on the lines proposed, not with jubiliation but with sorrow. For us, too, it would spell defeat and not victory. Yet there are some defeats more honourable than victory and we place the preservation of the internal peace of these realms, and the salvation of the Empire from disaster, above the cause for a single Parliament for the United Kingdom for which *The Times* has battled so long. (April 30, 1914.)

Like Dawson, Repington was convinced that Ulster would rebel : Fraser and Repington had seen enough in Ulster to be certain on that point. The assumption that military resistance was the only, because final, means of opposition was far-reaching. The South was equally strong in- its conviction that the Bill, legally passed, should be enforced. Carson had already raised and maintained a private army : the South was bound to follow Carson's example. The Nationalist Volunteers were enrolled, dressed, armed, and drilled with a determination equal to Carson's, but their activities were not followed in the office with the attention that had been given to the Ulstermen. It was difficult for the paper to investigate the preparations, mainly secret, and almost impossible to obtain a contact with the most influential of the bodies, Sinn Fein, which supported the Southern movement.[1] *The Times* was naturally anathema to the ardent and implacable South, for Dawson's interest was in Ulster and Carson, and the office automatically supported Carson's armed rebels. On May 12, Asquith yielded so far as to offer an Amending Bill, the nature of which was not at first disclosed. Dawson thus instructed his leader-writer:

I do not want a " fighting leader." Our attitude is that the passage of the Home Rule Bill through the Commons is inevitable, and that attention must now be concentrated on the Amending Bill. We are prepared to wait for this and examine it upon its merits. But it is of no use unless it satisfies Ulster and averts civil war. That is its [the Bill] whole object.[2]

[1] Dawson was precluded from approaching Erskine Childers and John Chartres, who had both worked in P.H.S. before their Irish sympathies made this employment undesirable. See Appendix II, Sources, XIII.
[2] Dawson to Shadwell, May 18, 1914.

Meanwhile discussion in public and private concerned itself with compromises for the exclusion of the province of Ulster: permanent and temporary, whole and partial schemes were put forward by both sides and neutral intermediaries. Among those who interested themselves were Northcliffe and Rothermere. On June 30, two days after the murder of Francis Ferdinand and the Archduchess at Serajevo, Lord Murray of Elibank called upon the Nationalist leader and said that he had been unofficially invited to intervene by Rothermere, and had recently seen Carson and Bonar Law. Murray told Redmond that Northcliffe had started that morning for Ulster, but that Rothermere did not know then what significance to attach to his brother's journey.[1] Rothermere's scheme suggested a period of six years' exclusion, with a statutory poll every six years afterwards. Next day Murray again called on Redmond. He had spent two hours the previous night with Bonar Law and was to lunch with Carson. The Unionist leader was anxious to find a way to deal with the great difficulty of Tyrone, which had a Nationalist majority; and Carson only could decide this. Murray added that although these conversations were necessarily secret, and " Northcliffe was not aware of what was going on, yet he could be relied upon to support, through the *Daily Mail* and *The Times*, any settlement that was arrived at."[2] The European crisis was having an increasing effect upon responsible men of affairs, although the newspaper continued to give pride of place to the Irish crisis. *The Times* continued to criticize the policy of exclusion as included in the Amending Bill.[3] Dawson disliked the clause. " We do not like exclusion," he admitted to Fraser. Yet he realized that the Amending Bill corresponded with some, if not all, of the political facts about Ireland. There was no ideal solution, only a choice between evils. " It is a question now of averting a great disaster, and it is necessary to concentrate on what seems the best means of escape from civil war. One of our reasons for preferring the exclusion of the whole province is that this would facilitate the return of Ireland to a common system of Government."[4]

Within a week a surprising new move was made. Asquith decided in view of the European crisis to invoke the aid of the

[1] Redmond's memorandum of the same day (June 30, 1914) is printed in Denis Gwynn's *The History of Partition* (Dublin, 1949), p. 106.

[2] Denis Gwynn, *The History of Partition*, p. 107.

[3] By option of any counties in Ulster for six years. On June 20, Carson made his since famous reply: " We are to be sentenced to death but they are not to pull the rope round our necks till six years are expired. . . . I would rather be hanged to-day."

[4] Dawson to Fraser, July 9, 1914.

King. On July 18 the King summoned a Conference of representatives of the British and Irish parties, " to take place in my house, where I shall gladly welcome its members on Tuesday, the 21st instant, at an hour convenient to them."[1]

Meanwhile Northcliffe, in the interval of visits to Northern Ireland, was busy making vast preparations for a service of news from the areas of probable conflict, then viewed exclusively in Irish, and not in Balkan, terms. The Editor was a professed Unionist; Northcliffe's sympathies were with a solution, though not a solution that would automatically and immediately place the North under the authority of a Dublin Parliament. He either did not know, or decided not to interest himself in, the details of the numerous compromises by which it was hoped to bring the opposing sides into agreement. Nothing more was heard of the schemes of Plunkett, Rothermere or Murray, and it was more congenial for Northcliffe to concentrate upon the organization of a network of news-collectors. This, he decided, must be worthy of the best traditions of the paper. He himself headed the safari from Printing House Square and Carmelite House which descended on Northern Ireland, and included a corps of Correspondents, a tug chartered to ply between Larne and Stranraer, and a special train, kept in steam at Stranraer. Ernest Brain, who led the Printing House Square contingent, was perturbed by such extravagance; but the Editor was well content to disclaim responsibility for matters of finance. More serious, to his mind, was the threat of another sort of extravagance.

Belfast, as I know from my own experience, is one of the most infectious places in the world. We want all the news. On the other hand we also want in our Correspondents the power to rise above local infection and to present an unbiased account of things, proportionate to the real importance of events. There is another kind of infection—very prevalent in journalism—of which you will also have to beware, and that is the infection of other newspapers. The *Daily Mail*, etc., are deliberately, and I think rightly, trying to arouse the people of England to a state of affairs of which the public over here is only half aware. No one can accuse *The Times* of any

---

[1] The King read to the assembly an address, published in *The Times* of the next day. Asquith explained that it had not been written by him but " that every word of it was written by the King of his own motion; but that a copy had been sent to him before the opening of the Conference, and he did not feel it his duty to use any influence with the King to prevent him making the Speech. The Speech, therefore, was the King's own; but, of course, if any question was raised, he (the Prime Minister) would, so far as the public was concerned, take full responsibility for it in order to shield his Majesty." The authorship of the Speech (for the text see Appendix) needs to be borne in mind and related to the same monarch's Speech at Belfast in 1921, for which see below, p.575-7. The proceedings of the Buckingham Palace Conference were secret and unreported. The only published record is that of Redmond, in Gwynn, *History of Partition*, pp. 117-130

failure in this respect. We have insisted on the gravity of the position in Ulster for more than a year, day in, day out, but we have done it in our own way, and we must continue to do it in our own way. Anything like hysterics or screeching would undermine the great position of influence which I think the paper has achieved in this Irish business.[1]

The Conference broke down over the extent and definition of "exclusion." The King afterwards spoke sympathetically to the Irish leaders. This took place on July 24, the day after the Austrian ultimatum to Serbia and the armies of Correspondents came back from across the Irish Sea to face a crisis far greater than that they left behind. Four days after, Austria-Hungary declared war on Serbia and Asquith was preparing his speech on the Amending Bill. Bonar Law and Carson informed him that European events had made them decide to ask that the Amending Bill should be postponed. Redmond agreed to this course and the immediate occasion of rioting in Ulster was removed.

The paper on July 27 contained eye-witness accounts of the landing of the guns at Howth from a mystery yacht[2] and the subsequent shooting at Bachelor's Walk. The accounts were exciting reading, but grave in their implication, for the *coup* was successful.

The European crisis now mounted to its full height. When Germany declared war on Belgium, Carson rallied his supporters to the British cause. This was expected; what was surprising was Redmond's declaration on August 3, following Grey's speech, that the Government could withdraw troops from Ireland and leave the defence of the coasts to the Irish. " For this purpose armed Nationalist Catholics in the South will be only too glad to join arms with the armed Protestant Ulstermen in the North. Is it too much to hope that out of this situation there may spring a result which will be good not merely for the Empire, but good for the future welfare and integrity of the Irish nation?" Redmond said this, having taken it for granted that Asquith would forthwith put the Home Rule Bill on the Statute Book and postpone its application until the war was over. Carson held a similar belief, with a vital difference : " I am informed," he wrote to Dawson, underlining his words, " that what the Government are about to do is the price they are to pay to Redmond for the speech he made in the House."[3] In fact, Asquith at this time

[1] Dawson to Brain, July 21, 1914.

[2] Erskine Childers was the owner. He became a principal agent in arming the Volunteers. Reports in *The Times* did not disclose his name.

[3] Carson to Dawson, August 7, 1914.

gave a written undertaking to Redmond that his "intention to see the Bill on the Statute Book this session" was "absolutely unchanged."[1]

Dawson, writing on August 6 to a friend, had been non-committal: "I quite appreciate the difficulties and dangers in Ireland, but I am sure we must treat Redmond's protestations at their face value in the circumstances."[2] It was immediately apparent that Redmond's followers would not support him unless the Home Rule Bill was given Royal Assent. Asquith hesitated for several weeks. Carson was convinced, as he had already told Dawson,[3] of "the importance of presenting a united front to foreign nations," and declared his loyalty to the Crown. Carson's conviction was shared by the Editor: a united front was of the first importance. But the Editor was displeased in September when Asquith had overcome his hesitations and made the Home Rule Bill law, while delaying its operation until a year after the end of the war and dropping the Amending Act.

In a leading article on September 15, Dawson described the Government's action as "a particularly mean and dishonest plan," but he concluded: "We can deal with this internal matter of Irish government when we have crushed the common enemy without." There was, by this time, another aspect of the Anglo-Irish situation of which he was aware. It was the aspect that was, later, to change the traditional policy of *The Times* to which Dawson had, so far, been faithful. With the outbreak of war, as the office realized, a greater strain would be laid on Anglo-American relations than they had borne for over half a century. The Irish group in the United States was numerically superior to any other except the German; clearly a *rapprochement* between the two might be awkward and, in the case of an emergency, disastrous for the Allies. Even the average American was, by tradition and inclination, sympathetic with the principle of Home Rule. It was the same thing as the doctrine of "self-determination" and the "principle of nationality." That, too, was understood in the office. In all the circumstances the Editor was content to drop the controversy until the war was won. He wrote to the Correspondent in Washington on September 23:

[1] Gwynn, *The History of Partition*, p. 141.

[2] Dawson to Maurice Headlam, an official at Dublin Castle, who supplied Dawson with information on Irish affairs.

[3] Carson to Dawson, August 7, 1914.

You know now what has happened about Home Rule. The Government, in my opinion, behaved in an extremely dishonest fashion, though I fully recognise (a) the value of Redmond's initial speech in the House of Commons, and (b) the vital importance of conciliating Nationalist opinion in America. But you must not overlook the other side of the question—the feeling, not only in Ulster, but in a large part of our gallant Army, that they have been stabbed in the back while fighting the common enemy, and the broad principle that it is wrong to cart your friends in order to conciliate doubtful patriots. Personally, I contented myself with one strongish leader,[1] and I have no intention of reviving the controversy till the war is over. Let us hope it will all turn out better than one fears.

The controversy, unfortunately, was not destined to remain long in abeyance. Reassuring as Redmond's declaration was at the time he made it, events were soon to prove that he had only limited power to implement it. In May, 1915, the inclusion of Carson in the first Coalition Cabinet and the appointment of Sir James Campbell (a foremost Ulster Covenanter) as Attorney-General for Ireland made it obvious that the Irish Nationalist Party had ceased to exert influence at Westminster. Redmond's personal position had been virtually destroyed. In Ireland the Nationalist Volunteers, who had not been disbanded after August, 1914, split, and Sinn Fein, over whose activities Redmond had no control, enlisted fresh adherents. They demanded more than was offered by the Home Rule Bill, the operation of which was still suspended: their goal was a Republic; in 1916 they struck their first blow. To Dawson, already disturbed by the inefficiency of the Castle Administration and opposed to the aspirations of Sinn Fein, the Easter Rising of 1916 was, in a sense, a relief. It was not, he thought, a serious matter. It could be put right by sending the right man to Dublin Castle. This was hardly a penetrating view, though widely held among Unionists. They would have been firm with those of a seditious turn. He wrote to the Washington Correspondent that he was

very glad that this Irish business has come to a head. We have all known that the trouble was there, and it seems to have been more of a farce than it might have been. Birrell's administration has always been a scandal. He never goes near the place, lets his official residence in Dublin, and remains in England for the sole purpose apparently of extorting concessions in the Cabinet for the disloyal element in Ireland. I trust he may be sacked over it. If not, it will not be from want of pressure from Yours ever, etc.[2]

[1] That of September 15.

[2] Dawson to Willert, April 26, 1916. Birrell resigned on May 3.

Dawson had already made good his word : the leading article was outspoken :

> The whole miserable business is a sorry commentary upon the complete failure of Mr. Birrell to maintain respect for law and order during the nine years of his weak and callous administration. . . . Such are the fruits of truckling to sedition and making light of contempt for the law. This is not yet the moment for calling to account what is by common consent the worst Executive that was ever responsible for Irish affairs. The time will come when the reckoning must be made. (April 26, 1916.)

Details of the so-called " farce " were slow to reach Printing House Square. The rebels had cut the telegraph wires; but, more efficiently, Government censorship prevented the publication of news from other than official sources. Not until the Monday following the rising was *The Times* able to present a comprehensive record of the events. Healy's silence was explained. Since the evening of Easter Monday he had been virtually a prisoner in his own office, which at one time was in the line of fire. Two Special Correspondents had meanwhile been despatched, J. E. Herbert and Lewis Northend. Although the situation had been brought under control within the week, the reports of *The Times* Correspondents revealed that the rising had been anything but a " farce." On the other hand, it was not as serious as it might have been, in view of the support given to the rebels. The grand concern of *The Times* in 1916 was not with Ireland but with the European war; victory over the Germans was the one thing necessary. Much was made of the part, as proved, played by Germany in the rising. On Tuesday, the 25th, information was given by the Admiralty of an engagement between the afternoons of April 20 and 21. An attempt to land arms in Ireland made by a German auxiliary disguised as a merchant ship had been intercepted. Also announced was the capture of Sir Roger Casement, who had landed on the Irish coast from a German submarine on the night of the 20th-21st. With this in mind, the Editor decided that the leaders of the rising were traitors rather than rebels.[1] Their execution was justified.

> Thirteen rebels have been shot, and sentence is to be executed on two others. It is idle to represent this punishment as excessive or revengeful, or to pretend, with the Nationalist manifesto published yesterday, that it " shocks and horrifies " Ireland. Everybody will learn with relief that the necessity for further executions of a summary kind is now over, but a certain number of these executions were

---

[1] Flanagan's leading article on April 26 illustrates the attitude in the office. See Chapter IX above, " The Problem of America."

absolutely necessary to teach the traitors who take German money that they cannot cover Dublin with blood and ashes without forfeiting their lives. We think, however, the Government have been foolish in not stating plainly the reasons why these men were shot, and we welcome Mr. Asquith's promise that any future trials for murder shall be held with open doors. (May 12, 1914.)

The Prime Minister visited Ireland in person. But the Editor, writing under the compulsion of Verdun, remained detached from the problem of finding a settlement. " We shall all do well to remind ourselves daily that our first business is to win the war, with or without a contented Ireland. We cannot afford to play the German game by allowing the whole energies of the nation to be turned back at this moment upon a domestic problem which has distracted it for centuries. We have in any case to re-establish good order and security, which have almost vanished from Ireland under the late régime." (May 17, 1916.) The article won the general approval of Sir Horace Plunkett; but, although he wrote to congratulate the Editor, he added:

I daresay the line taken by *The Times* has some regard to what is at the moment by far the most important aspect of the Irish rebellion —its effect upon the Anglo-American situation. It was a ghastly business for us who saw it at close quarters, but it would be a very small price to pay for the breaking-up of the German-Irish alliance in the U.S. Willert evidently fears that the executions may have had the opposite effect, and I think you ought to use all your influence, as the leading journalist of the British Empire, to force the Government to give attention to this vital matter.[1]

The Editor, though still justifying the executions, was by no means unmindful of transatlantic reactions. *The Times*, in a leading article on May 22, urged that the Irish problem must not be allowed to complicate our relations with neutral countries, especially with America. Plunkett's sentiments were the Editor's ; and with Steed's approval some of Willert's cables were suppressed and the Correspondent asked to moderate his expressions. Willert thereupon replied that, as the executions were condemned by Americans, he genuinely feared the consequences should Casement be sentenced to death. The Correspondent acknowledged that American opinion was misinformed, and that his cables were justifiably suppressed. The Editor thought the most practical course was to obtain agreement between Carson and Redmond. A letter to Asquith, a copy of which Plunkett sent to the Editor, enlarged on this idea:

[1] Plunkett to Dawson, May 19, 1916.

546

A settlement blessed by Carson and Redmond and accepted enthusiastically (as it would be if you proposed it) by the House of Commons and English public opinion, might conceivably aggravate the trouble in Ireland. . . . Perhaps it might be well, instead of proposing a scheme, to invite Mr. Redmond and Sir Edward Carson to submit one, and if either or both failed to do so, to impose one of your own.[1]

The Prime Minister announced in the House of Commons on May 25 that Lloyd George would devote his energy to the promotion of an Irish settlement. This, said the Lobby Correspondent, was the one new fact that emerged from the Prime Minister's eagerly awaited statement, but " it marked the opening of a new chapter in Irish politics, and the Commons, with that sure instinct which rarely fails them in difficult times, gave the new conciliator the best possible send-off on his delicate mission." Meanwhile, the Commission of Inquiry into the causes of the Irish rebellion had been holding its first few sittings in London and the proceedings had been reported in *The Times* to the extent of many columns. The Commission now moved temporarily to Dublin, where Joseph Fisher covered the sessions as Special Correspondent to *The Times*.[2] Throughout Ireland martial law continued since " disaffection and unrest " prevailed and, according to John Healy, law-abiding Irishmen welcomed this measure. Lloyd George's Irish proposals, made public after a commendably short interval, were received with little enthusiasm in either Ulster or England. The Editor in a leading article observed :

Mr. Lloyd George, in his search for a temporary Irish settlement, seems to have committed his colleagues to an Imperial Conference or Convention to deal with larger problems immediately after the war. If so, that is a great step forward. . . . Whether the Dominions can help in practice to find a permanent solution of the special problem of Ireland is quite another question. The presumption is that Mr. Lloyd George has in mind some general notion of Imperial federation in which these islands, divided into appropriate provinces for purposes of local self-government, would form a Dominion or unit in the Imperial system corresponding with Canada or Australia. But the plain lesson of history, illustrated last in South Africa, is that each Dominion must first settle its internal problems for itself. (June 13.)

The negotiations for a provisional Irish settlement were apparently making progress in Ireland. The Ulster Unionists had

---

[1] Plunkett to Asquith, May 23, 1916. Printed from the copy in P.H.S.

[2] Joseph R. Fisher, formerly Editor of the *Northern Whig*, was an intimate of Sir James Craig and Sir Edward Carson. He was a partisan of a self-contained and self-governing Ulster united to the Crown, and was appointed by the British Government to the Boundary Commission of 1924-1925. See Appendix II, Sources, XIII.

already reluctantly accepted the exclusion of Ulster after Carson spoke in Belfast on June 6. From Belfast Withers reported on June 23 that the convention of Nationalists from the six Ulster counties excluded from the Government of Ireland Act under Lloyd George's scheme had accepted the proposals. But it soon became clear that the Lloyd George proposals were not to have any easy passage in England. While the trial of Casement on a charge of high treason was begun, the resignation on June 26 of Lord Selborne from the Presidency of the Board of Agriculture and Fisheries was announced. Selborne took this decision on the issue of the Irish proposals. *The Times* presently printed (with the *communiqué* and the War Correspondent's dispatches on the opening of the Battle of the Somme in which Irish soldiers were fighting, as gallantly as always, side by side with the English, the Scots and the Welsh) the report of the Royal Commission on the Irish rebellion. The report was a " plain straightforward and impartial record of facts and of certain conclusions to which they necessarily lead." From the report the paper said, " The main cause of the rebellion appears to be that lawlessness was allowed to grow up unchecked and Ireland for several years past has been administered on the principle that it was safer and more expedient to leave law in abeyance if collision with any faction of the Irish people could thereby be avoided." The Commissioners brought it home directly to Birrell indicating " very clearly that the responsibility is shared by the successive Governments which have kept Mr. Birrell in an office for which he was manifestly unfit."

As the Coalition Government was encountering pressure from the threatened resignation of Austen Chamberlain, Walter Long and Curzon, and Carson and Craig found their followers increasingly restive, so Redmond was embarrassed by opposition. Lloyd George's proposals had not been published, and all parties were mystified and suspicious. Redmond's destruction was certain when it was known that the British Cabinet had decided that the exclusion of the six counties of Ulster was to be permanent. Carson was acutely disappointed. He, too, wanted a United Ireland. Both Irish leaders had misread Lloyd George's intentions. When these were corrected they both withdrew. On July 25, the Prime Minister made a general statement on Ireland. The Home Rule Act should be brought into operation as soon as possible after Parliament had excluded the six counties and the three Parliamentary boroughs of Belfast, Londonderry and Newry from its operation. The Irish House of Commons was to consist of members returned at the present time, by the same constituencies, to the Imperial Parliament. The Appeal Court in Dublin was to consist of judges appointed by the Imperial Executive. Asquith explained that it was not the intention or desire of those who might form an Irish Executive to encroach in any way on the responsibility of the Imperial authority for the conduct of the war.

On August 1 *The Times* (Flanagan) was more pessimistic :

After three months of twisting and turning the Prime Minister announces that his Government cannot find any solution for the Irish question and that all they can do is to continue the system which he has so emphatically condemned.

A week later it was announced that Lord Wimborne had been re-appointed Lord-Lieutenant. As the Lobby Correspondent remarked, " So Ireland has come the full circle to the Castle Government which the Prime Minister said had broken down." He could have added that the influence of the Irish Nationalist Party and its leader John Redmond had been destroyed and that Sinn Fein was taking its place.

Roger Casement was hanged in Pentonville Prison on August 3. A leading article by Dawson on August 4 disclosed that *The Times* had received a great number of letters but had " absolutely refused during the last few weeks—in spite of some very curious pressure—to have the case re-tried in these columns." The article noted that the official statement issued on the previous night contained one new fact revealed since the trial—that Casement had made a definite agreement with the German Government for the use of his projected Irish Prisoners Brigade against the British Crown in Egypt—but the paper concluded:

We cannot help protesting against certain other attempts which have been made to use the Press for the purpose of raising issues which are utterly damaging to Casement's character but have no connexion whatever with the charges on which he was tried. Those issues should either have been raised in public and in a straight-forward manner or they should have been left severely alone.[1]

The year 1916 finished its course uneventfully so far as Ireland was concerned, the great event of the end of the year being Lloyd George's rise to power with the help of Carson.[2] With Lloyd George as Prime Minister the Irish question was again considered

---

[1] This refers to the attempts to discredit Casement's moral rectitude.
[2] In the circumstances described in Chapter VII, " Coalition."

as a matter of immediate relation to the prosecution of the war. Lloyd George, pressed by Carson to apply conscription to the whole of Ireland, assured Redmond that he would propose immediate Home Rule as a condition. The Irish leader knew that he could not guarantee the acceptance at home of such a measure. Redmond walked out of the House of Commons at the head of the Nationalists on March 7, 1917, to demonstrate their refusal to accept partition. The situation could not, however, be allowed to drift. Conscription or no conscription, the war made the maintenance of cordial American relations a first necessity. The Prime Minister suggested alternative plans for either an immediate settlement on a Home Rule basis, or the summoning of a representative Convention of all the Irish parties to consider the future government of the country. The second alternative found the more general favour. Although Sinn Fein at once declined to take part in it, preparations for the holding of the convention in Dublin were begun. These were timely, for on April 6, the United States entered the war. Northcliffe forthwith insisted on more prominence being given to Irish news. " Knowing the United States as I do," he told the office, " I greatly fear that the Irish canker will eat into the rose of the Alliance."[1] Events soon became pressing. At a by-election in East Clare, caused by the death in action of Major Willy Redmond, held in July, De Valera was easily successful on behalf of Sinn Fein. The size of his majority—much more than two to one over his Nationalist opponent—surprised even experienced political observers. John Healy, who had looked forward, with others, to a closer contest, analysed the influences that had been at work. Above all there seemed to have been an overwhelming revolt against the old Nationalist party machine—a fact which might not have been altogether unconnected with the new prosperity of the Irish farmers. The programme of the successful party was recognized as frankly anti-English and separatist, and *The Times* Correspondent pointed out that so open an expression of disloyalty imposed a fresh responsibility upon the Government— the leading article of the day adding that " it also absolves them from the last excuse for feeble administration." The leader proceeded :

For our own part we differ altogether from the prophets who have been predicting that a victory for Sinn Fein in East Clare must mean the end of any Irish Convention. That it will stiffen the refusal of the Sinn Feiners to take part is certain enough; but their refusal was already quite definite, and no one suggested on that account that the Convention should be abandoned.

[1] Memorandum, April 11, 1917.

In September Alison Phillips, formerly of *The Times* staff and then Lecky Professor of Modern History in Trinity College, Dublin, emphasized to the Editor the importance of better publicity methods on behalf of the Government, particularly in the matter of the war, about which there was a vast ignorance in Ireland. He ended some general observations on the disposition of the country with his opinion that " the one essential thing—which will not happen—is that Lloyd George should give a free hand to whoever is nominally responsible for the government of Ireland, and trust him." To this Dawson replied that he was sending the letter on to Carson privately, " since he now exercises a certain supervision over propaganda and may be able to do something for better publicity in Ireland." Later, Phillips was informed that Carson had been so impressed by the letter that he had read it to the Cabinet.[1]

The Irish Convention duly came into being. The chairman was Horace Plunkett, who for many years had been an unofficial counsellor of *The Times* on Irish affairs and had, it has been seen, corresponded with Dawson in the spring of 1916.[2] The Convention began as representing, and having the good will of, all the Irish parties except Sinn Fein, as well as the blessing of the British Government ; but before the end of December the prospects of its success were already becoming dim. Phillips wrote to Dawson suggesting that the Ulster rank and file were not likely to agree to the proposed compromise on the fiscal question, and Dawson replied :

Your news is always interesting and valuable. I only hope it is on the pessimistic side, though I believe it to be quite true, as you forecast, that the Convention is likely to break up in a division between the Nationalists plus Southern Unionists against the extreme Ulstermen. What will happen then ? You predict a strike in the Belfast munition works, and I daresay that is likely enough. Others tell me that there may be a considerable split in Ulster itself. As far as *The Times* goes I am as far as possible avoiding the subject altogether so long as the Convention is in being, and personally I feel that every day it sits is a day gained.[3]

The New Year opened badly in every sense. On January 8, 1918, a pronouncement from across the Atlantic bore heavily on the whole Irish controversy and, by implication, threatened intervention by the Peace Conference. The American President's announcement of his Fourteen Points brought with it acute and immediate embarrassment to the British Government. Willert

---

[1] Phillips to Dawson, September 27, 1917: Dawson to Phillips, October 5, 1917.

[2] For Plunkett's correspondence with Dawson, see above, p. 546.

[3] Dawson to Phillips, December 20, 1917.

outlined the possible consequences: if the Irish Convention failed Wilson might bracket Ireland with Poland in his peace policy; even if the Convention succeeded, he might still support Ireland if necessary to enable her to gain Dominion status.[1]   There seemed to be nothing that Lloyd George could do.   Late in January, 1918, Phillips had become so alarmed that, on the 21st, he wrote to Dawson begging him

for God's sake and the Empire's to do what you can to prevent the Press or people of influence in England from threatening, or seeming to threaten, the Ulstermen with coercion in any case. . . . The only result of any attempts to coerce Ulster would be to unite Ireland in solid hatred of England.   It is not love of England that makes the Ulstermen Unionists; and if they are driven from the Union by English action they will probably make common cause with Sinn Fein for an independent republic.

The Editor replied that all threats—to Ulstermen or anybody else—seemed to him a thoroughly stupid form of procedure. Meanwhile Carson resigned from the War Cabinet in order, among other reasons, to resume his freedom as an Ulster leader.

In the spring of 1918, the last mighty German offensive in France, as it turned out to be, though that could not then have been foreseen, led to the drastic Military Service Act.   This brought Ireland within the ambit of compulsory service.   Next John Redmond died, and the leadership of the Nationalist Party at Westminster fell to John Dillon, who further reduced the waning influence of the party by withdrawing altogether from the House of Commons for three months after the passing of the Military Service Act.   Simultaneously with the extension of conscription to Ireland appeared the report of the Irish Convention.   By a narrow majority it favoured what was broadly a Home Rule scheme.   The Government thereupon promised a measure of self-government and appointed a committee of Ministers to draft a Bill.   In Ireland, however, Sinn Fein had been winning elections on a frankly anti-British secessionist programme, and the strength of the movement had become so threatening that a number of its leaders were deported by Lord French, the new Viceroy in place of Wimborne, and the new Chief Secretary, Edward Shortt. Notwithstanding the passing of the necessary measures, conscription was not enforced in Ireland, but the mere threat of it had powerfully reinforced Sinn Fein.   The Coalition was left with the Home Rule Bill.   Repression of Sinn Fein coincided with

[1] Willert to Dawson, January 24, 1918.

fierce German attacks in the West and successful Allied counter-attacks. By July and August the end of the war was in sight.

At the General Election of December, 1918, no fewer than 73 Sinn Fein and Nationalist-elected Members decided to absent themselves from Westminster, and constitute themselves as a Dail in Dublin. They immediately sought Wilson's help to secure for them the freedom that had been held out in the Fourteen Points to small nationalities. The President was too well-advised to take any such step at the outset of the Peace Conference. It was inevitable, however, that with Britain at peace, secured at a Conference which brought together the nations that were, nominally at least, agreed on " self-determination," and on " rights of small nations," a movement should arise for settlement of the quarrel in Ireland. Since the previous July the Coalition Government had met the demand with gestures of despair, and *The Times* was satisfied that settlement could only be reached through talks and discussions, public and private, between both sides. This was the situation when Dawson retired from the editorship in February, 1919.

Conditions were then ripe for a reversal of the antipathetic attitude towards Ireland maintained under Delane and Buckle, and a change from the waiting policy of Dawson. The Paris Conference had decided Steed's mind, and he was determined on international grounds to press forward a measure of self-determination for Ireland. Printing House Square was brought the more easily to such a major revision of policy by the conviction that the Versailles settlement had rendered remote any resumption of the struggle by Germany or aggression by any Continental Power. Moreover, Steed had seen the efforts made by De Valera, Griffith and Count Plunkett to secure from the American delegation an Irish representation at the Conference. He could not fail to appreciate the significance of the Irish in the electoral mechanism of the United States. The Irish had even approached Wilson himself in the belief that "the apostle of liberalism " would aid them. Wilson refused, but the danger was not removed.[1]

[1] The " apostle " seems to have been considerably startled at the interpretation of his gospel. His reply was as follows: " When I gave utterance to those words (*i.e.* the right of small nations to self-determination) I said them without the knowledge that nationalities existed which are coming to us day after day. Of course, Ireland's case, from the point of view of population, from the point of view of the struggle it has made, from the point of interest it has excited in the world, and especially among our own people whom I am anxious to serve, is the outstanding case of a small nationality. You do not know and cannot appreciate the anxieties I have experienced as the result of these many millions of peoples having their hopes raised by what I have said." (Evidence of Frank P. Walsh. Hearing of the Peace Treaty, August 30, 1919. Quoted by Dorothy Macardle, *The Irish Republic* (London).)

Already in March, 1919, the House of Representatives had passed a resolution supporting Sinn Fein. Steed returned from Paris troubled by the pressure, not yet explicit, which the United States might exert to secure Irish independence. Such pressure would not be tolerated by British public opinion; the Irish " canker," as Northcliffe had prophesied, was threatening " the rose of the Alliance." Steed saw only one solution: that the Government should anticipate American intervention by settling the Irish problem forthwith. Steed's plan would entail a reversal of policy that Dawson and his predecessors would certainly have shrunk from initiating.

The new Editor first acted after, though not because, the Senate supported the House of Representatives which passed by sixty votes to one a resolution, that was, in Northcliffe's judgement, " the worst piece of news we have printed for many a long day."[1] The Washington Correspondent cabled that the resolution was a symptom of American suspicion of British power and, as such, directed at the League. (June 9.) The gist of the Editor's leading article was that Anglo-Irish relations were no concern of any other nation.

There have been determined attempts during the last few months to make the question of Ireland an international issue, and to place Great Britain in the position of a mere party to a dispute in which foreign states would act as advisers and intermediaries, if not as judges. It is as well to say at once that attempts of this kind are bound to fail. They will be wrecked upon the firm purpose of the British people to exercise for themselves the right of self-determination.

After an acknowledgment of American interest in Ireland, he continued :

Those who wish Ireland well—and we count ourselves among their number—could make no worse mistake than to treat the Irish question as a purely international problem, comparable with any of the new problems which the Peace Conference has essayed to solve. And it is precisely because of the British character of the problem that it is incumbent upon the British Government to address themselves, without delay and without thought of petty Parliamentary or electoral advantage, to its solution. (June 16, 1919.)

The Editor now determined to put pressure on the Government. In 1919 Campbell Stuart introduced to *The Times* as an expert adviser a young Irish barrister, Captain R. J. Herbert Shaw. He

[1] Northcliffe to the office, June 10, 1919.

RICHARD JAMES HERBERT SHAW

had served in 1916 as a soldier and later as a Press Censor in Ireland. In 1917 he became assistant secretary of the Irish Convention.[1] Afterwards he had served on the staff of Lord French when Lord-Lieutenant at Dublin Castle. Having thus gained an intimate knowledge of Irish affairs Shaw had clear and definite ideas about what must be done to bring peace to Ireland. He showed a draft of these ideas to the Castle authorities and then to the Cabinet. Both Castle and Cabinet rejected them. Shaw then showed his draft to the Editor, and it was in due course shown to Northcliffe who agreed that the Editor should go forward though he was far from certain of the right policy for Ireland, except for approval of the phrase, " Dominion of Ireland." Shaw's ideas were quite clear :

First, that the permanent exclusion of the whole or a portion of Ulster from any scheme of Irish self-government would not advance the pacification of Ireland, or settle the Anglo-Irish controversy.

Secondly, that the process of settlement of the Irish question should be by development from foundations well laid in accordance with the fundamental facts of the Irish situation.

Thirdly, that it is essential in the interests of the British Empire, and particularly so in its relation to the United States, that the Irish question should be concentrated in Ireland, and world interest focussed on Irish bickerings rather than on Anglo-Irish relations.[2]

The Editor concluded that in this scheme he had a possible answer to the Irish problem. But wishing to be reasonably sure of his ground, he pressed the idea that Healy and Henry Givens Burgess (later Senator[3]) should be jointly responsible with Shaw for any positive proposals. There was, indeed, a need for caution. Relations between Lloyd George and *The Times* were such that, were this scheme, or any other, put forward by the paper, it might instantly be quashed whether or not it was a good, or even the only possible, settlement. Steed therefore approached his object obliquely.

[1] Stuart had met Shaw in Dublin in 1916 when he was assistant Press Censor under Lord Decies and had corresponded with him on Crewe House business during 1918 and had thus been kept informed of the proceedings at the Irish Convention. Afterwards Shaw returned to the censorship rather than accept a post in the Crewe House organization. " I see clouds on the horizon in this country which make me think that we are in for very anxious times " (Shaw to Stuart, March 25, 1918). " Keep before your mind that propaganda in Ireland is propaganda in an enemy country. The majority of people in Ireland in their hearts would like to see England beaten " (May 27, 1918). Shaw's policy was based on the conviction that at the end of the war Britain would require " the establishment of a permanent alliance between Great Britain and the United States, with the removal of as much Irish grit from its smooth working as possible " (June 11, 1918). Thus Shaw was well fitted to serve Steed.

[2] Shaw's memorandum to Steed, June 13, 1919.

[3] A moderate Unionist, at that time General Manager of the London and North-Western Railway in Ireland.

On June 20 he mentioned to Northcliffe that " Our Irish scheme is now well afoot, and we should begin publication of a most important series of articles towards the middle of next week. I will tell you details when you are allowed [the " Chief " had lately undergone an operation] to see me." This series of ten articles (first entitled *Hibernia Pacanda* and later, at the suggestion of Thomas Marlowe, Editor of the *Daily Mail*, after much discussion, headed " Irish Peace ") appeared at the end of June and during the early part of July. The work of Shaw, Healy and Burgess, it examined every aspect of the problem; but did not then propound any definite scheme for a settlement. That was to come. Meanwhile, Walter Long, First Lord of the Admiralty, who had been a Chief Secretary for Ireland and now was one of the advocates of the Federal system for the United Kingdom with powers to each of the subordinate Parliaments suited to their individual needs, called on the Editor. Long asked if *The Times* had a scheme and whether it would be published. Steed said he had a scheme, and gave the reason why it was not put forward. The Editor offered to send Long and Lloyd George a copy of it and gave the following undertaking :

You may tell your colleagues in the Cabinet and the Prime Minister that, if the Government will take this scheme as it is, or improve upon it, they will be able to count upon the support of *The Times*, and, as far as I am able to answer for Lord Northcliffe, upon that of the *Daily Mail* and the other newspapers which Lord Northcliffe controls and that we shall never claim credit for having helped to promote a settlement, if a settlement is reached on such a basis.

The offer, Long admitted, was generous. Steed had protected himself, however; and when *The Times* was accused of girding at the Government though it had no scheme of its own, he wrote on July 22 to Long :

Both Sir Edward Carson's Belfast speeches and Mr. Lloyd George's references to the Irish question last night seem to show that it is hopeless to expect the Government to evolve an Irish policy of their own, or to make any adequate statement upon it before Parliament rises. Consequently, I have decided to publish very shortly the main features of the scheme for settlement which have been in our minds for some weeks and have formed the background of our articles. A copy of the scheme has already been sent to the Prime Minister. I enclose another copy for you.

Twenty-four hours later the Editor was writing to Northcliffe :

You will see by the time this reaches you that we have gone the whole hog to-night. If Healy is right, it may help to keep things from boiling over in Ireland. The credit for the work belongs to Shaw, who wrote an excellent memorandum as a basis for the leader.

The leading article of July 23 (by Sidebotham) laid it down that the significant feature of the previous Monday's debate on the Peace Bill was that the Government apparently had no policy for Ireland. Repeating what the Editor had told Long, the article said that if the Government would not make the first move, " others must."

Tomorrow, therefore, we shall attempt to lay down the principles and to suggest the outlines of a settlement. . . . Ireland is a problem for British statesmen. . . . Had the same spirit now shown towards the problem of Ireland been shown in the war, the Germans would long since have been in London.

The Editor now fulfilled the promise privately given to Long, and through him to the Prime Minister, that *The Times* would not embarrass the Government by publishing chapter and verse of its scheme. The next day's leader on " An Irish Settlement " was unique. It was the only leading article in that issue of *The Times* and, running to four columns, it was a monumental statement written by Steed and Shaw of the attitude of the paper. It deserves extensive quotation. At the outset *The Times* pronounced against partition.

Politically, there are acute differences between Ulster and the rest of Ireland; economically, they are closely interwoven. Economic bonds are stronger than constitutional devices. . . .

We have therefore sought a solution more in accordance with the fundamental factors of Irish economics, one which might lay sure foundations for future development. We have looked for a framework which Irish hands could adjust to Irish needs and desires. We have tried to face facts and to do even justice. . . .

The basis of our suggestions is that there should be created in Ireland two Provincial or State Legislatures. They should be set up by an act in substitution for the Home Rule Act—one Legislature for the three southern provinces, the other for the province of Ulster. The retention of the nine counties of Ulster as a unit would, we are convinced, give greater stability than if Ulster were reduced to six or four counties with an overwhelming Unionist majority. The arrangement of constituencies under the Act would ensure that there would be a Unionist majority in the province, while the existence of a powerful Nationalist minority in the whole province would give protection against disregard for minority rights and interests. . . .

Upon the two State Legislatures we suggest there would be bestowed full powers of legislation in all matters affecting the internal affairs of their respective States. . . . In each State there would, moreover, be constituted a State Executive responsible to the State Legislature. . . . The creation of State Legislatures and State Executives would be the first stage in the bestowal of self-government upon Ireland. There would be provisions for the eventual establishment of an Irish Parliament.

The basis of this Parliament should be that each of the two States in the Irish Federation would have equal representation in it. . . . Certain powers would be retained by the United Kingdom Parliament. . . .

The reservation to the Parliament of the United Kingdom of the powers not transferred to the Irish State Legislatures or to the Irish Parliament, and the latent sovereignty of the United Kingdom Parliament, necessitate the retention of an Irish representation at Westminster. (July 24, 1919.)

In Ireland this constructive article aroused commendation and condemnation. The article was read widely in America and the Dominions as Campbell Stuart had caused the text to be circulated to the newspapers which, in many instances, published it simultaneously with *The Times*. Friends of Britain who were disappointed with Lloyd George's half-heartedness were given fresh courage.[1]

At home the atmosphere became more favourable, and in the summer Parliamentary recess the Prime Minister appointed a Cabinet Committee to devise a definite scheme. In the last hours of the Session he announced proposals for the creation of two State Legislatures, one for Ulster and the other for the rest of Ireland, with a Council of Ireland as the national connecting link. Another helpful move was the appointment of a round-table conference to make agreed recommendations for a scheme of federal devolution for the United Kingdom.

But Ireland would have none of these things. Ulster showed no enthusiasm for the proposals while the South repudiated them. Sinn Fein was contemptuous. The year 1920 was not many days old when Sinn Fein demonstrated its power at the municipal elections. Also, early in the year it became plain that a murder conspiracy as ruthless as any in Irish history had begun, which forced the Irish Executive to realize the difficulties of vindicating the law. Evidence was unobtainable;

---

[1] *Cf*. Arthur Murray to William Wiseman, July 28, 1919: " This is one of my complaints about Lloyd George. . . . He fails or refuses to recognize that every day of delay in an attempt to settle the Irish question more and more endangers our Imperial and Anglo-American relations. He is inclined to take the view that the Irish question is a domestic question and concerns the United Kingdom only." Murray proceeds to say that " apart from Horace Plunkett's scheme which was recently issued, the only proposals that show some signs of forming the basis of a practical and reasonable system of government for Ireland are contained in a leading article in *The Times* of July 24th." (Arthur Murray, *At Close Quarters*, London, 1946, p. 79.)

public opinion was cowed or hostile, and the criminals invariably eluded the hand of justice. During January the Editor received a visit from a member of the Cabinet Committee set up in the summer, who told him that the proposals on which they had finally settled closely resembled those put forward by the paper. He feared that Lloyd George would reject them " on the ground that it would enable ' Northcliffe and *The Times* to shout victory '." The Editor repeated the undertaking he had given Long.

Early in February Parliament assembled with the new Irish Bill as the chief item in its programme. The shadow of bloody events in Ireland fell darkly upon its deliberations. News from across the Atlantic was not cheering. *The Times* had been in consultation with Grey and after many revisions a letter from him to the Editor was published on January 31, 1920, in the hope that it would assist the arguments of those in Washington who favoured a League even with reservations. But the outlook in February remained unhopeful. In Ireland things went from bad to worse. In the country there were raids on police barracks, increasing in frequency, and in Dublin conditions became so serious that on February 23 a curfew order was enforced. On February 28 the text of the Government of Ireland Bill was published. The formulated scheme followed closely Lloyd George's original statement, and Ireland gave it no better reception. *The Times* (Shaw writing), after criticizing the proposed area of Ulster, the constitution of the Joint Council, and the financial provisions, said:

For many months we have impressed upon the public the gravity of the Irish situation and our conviction that the only remedy lay in the immediate grant of self-government of Ireland. . . .

In three main particulars the Bill meets what we once stated in this journal to be the prime considerations affecting an Irish settlement. First, it is not inconsistent with the principle of federalization of the United Kingdom, nor with that of a greater centralization of the Government of the Empire. Secondly, it is essentially an embodiment of the judgment of Great Britain rather than an attempt to win consent from Irish political parties at an inauspicious moment. Therefore, in character, at all events, it is an imposed settlement. Thirdly, it is a measure based on the principle of evolution, even though that principle is not thoroughly applied. (February 28, 1920.)

In March Carson sought the opinion of the Ulster Unionists in regard to the Government's proposals. They gave a qualified approval, though the declaration involved the partition of their own province and the abandonment of three Ulster counties. Thus there was some hope of solution. But on March 20

MacCurtain, the Lord Mayor of Cork, was murdered. He was a prominent Sinn Feiner, and the Cork Correspondent in his messages mentioned local Sinn Fein allegations as to the identity of the murderers, who were not traced. At the same time Healy reported from Dublin his " deep conviction of the extreme gravity of the conditions in the south of Ireland." The murder of the Lord Mayor of Cork was, he wrote, represented as the work of admirers and supporters, or of " wild servants," of the British Government in Ireland. He also reported an affray in Dublin in which two people were killed. The immediate outlook appeared gloomy indeed and the Irish Executive was faced with a situation which demanded tact, firmness and intelligence of the highest degree. " Unfortunately," remarked the Correspondent, " no party in the country credits it with the possession of these qualities." In the midst of the depression caused by America's final rejection of Treaty, the Government of Ireland Bill, on March 31, passed its second reading by a majority of 254. While the debate was still in progress the appointment of Sir Nevil Macready as Commander-in-Chief in Ireland was announced, and a few days later Sir Hamar Greenwood succeeded Ian Macpherson as Chief Secretary. Almost at once came news of the burning of more than a hundred police barracks and many revenue offices. This was the boldest Republican demonstration of strength yet given. In the meantime a large number of Sinn Feiners in Mountjoy Prison maintained a determined hunger-strike. The Roman Catholic Bishops in Ireland protested, the Irish Trade Union Congress called a general strike, and the House of Commons debated the matter at length, Bonar Law speaking uncompromisingly. The Government gave way and the prisoners were released. Public opinion in England was deeply divided. The position of *The Times* was re-stated in April in a leading article :

In seeking a settlement of the Irish question and in commenting upon the Government of Ireland Bill we have consistently maintained that there should be no partition of the Province of Ulster. We have been and are convinced that the unity of Ireland—the only true solution of the Irish problem—must be sought in the eventual coalescence of the two States as similar in size, composition, and character as the admitted necessities of the case would allow. (April 26, 1920.)

On May 10 the House of Commons began the Committee stage of the Irish Bill. Almost simultaneously there were fresh burnings of police barracks in Ireland and a series of murders of policemen. Proceedings in Parliament soon showed that the

Government were determined to force their measure through
without important change; and this fact seemed to emphasize
the contrast between their professed Irish policy and their actual
Irish administration. There remained, nevertheless, reason to
believe that the new Chief Secretary contemplated new methods,
for there were drastic changes at Dublin Castle. The settlement
of Ireland continued to be the constant pre-occupation of
The Times. The topic was seldom absent from the columns
of the paper. It was the burden of frequent leaders; of
immensely long letters to the Editor; of special articles, apart
from the news messages from the resident and the Special Correspondents in the country itself. A striking series of special articles
written by Stephen Gwynn appeared in June and July. They
examined the background and the tendencies as well as the practical (apparently efficient) working of the Sinn Fein organization in
various quarters and districts in Ireland. The lawlessness and
violence of the Sinn Fein party made encouraging progress
increasingly difficult. The effort to impose law likewise inflamed
passion. The Government's answer to Sinn Fein's appeal to force
was a policy of reprisals. As police barracks were burnt down and
constables killed, so creameries were fired and town halls destroyed.
The Royal Irish Constabulary were in a difficult position for
they were reluctant to carry out such measures against their own
countrymen, but the Black-and-Tans and Auxiliaries had no
such scruples, and many instances of a gross lack of discipline
occurred.[1] Equally horrifying were the accounts of outrages
by the extremists and of reprisals by the military. The country
was closer to civil war than it had been in July, 1914; but, unlike
Dawson, Steed placed no restraint upon his leader-writers. The
thunder of many of the leading articles is to be paralleled only
by those of the period when Barnes was writing. Much of the
reverberation issued from articles that came from the pen of the
Editor. Censure of the violence on both sides was not spared;
but the Editor consistently attempted to keep united the moderate
men on both sides. He believed they existed in large numbers,
and it was they who must support the Government when some
effort was made to amend the Bill.

Meanwhile, the Editor watched the effect of Irish events on
American opinion with some apprehension. In the Presidential
election year of 1920, both parties were struggling to attract the

[1] There were three distinct Crown forces in Ireland at this time: the military (whose
reputation was good), the Black-and-Tans, recruits to the Royal Irish Constabulary,
whose members had resigned in large numbers, and the Auxiliaries, composed of
demobilized ex-officers. The term "Black-and-Tan" is commonly used to cover the
last two groups, though in some cases the use is incorrect and unjust.

Irish vote. The Irish case received excellent publicity (it was supported by Hearst), and De Valera himself conducted the Irish campaign. " Republicans," Willert cabled on June 9, " regard the Irish situation as desperate. They have scant sympathy for our treatment of it." The Democrats expressed sympathy with Irish aspirations in their party programme. But, though De Valera attended both party conventions, he accomplished less than he hoped. Willert told Northcliffe on July 8 :

> The Irish question went very well for us. Somebody asked me yesterday how much we paid Valera to keep him here. Certainly he has tremendously overplayed his hand trying to butt in on these conventions. Nor are the goings on of Sinn Fein liked, though I wish we could get more published here about them.

An event which aroused American opinion to a high pitch was the death of Terence McSwiney, Lord Mayor of Cork in succession to MacCurtain, who died in Brixton Prison on October 25. He had been arrested on August 12, charged with the possession of a police cypher and two seditious documents. By way of protesting against a sentence of two years' imprisonment he refused to eat. The course of his hunger strike, which lasted seventy-four days, was followed with anxiety by readers of newspapers throughout the world. The paper urged on the Government the wisdom of mercy, but in vain. The first leader in *The Times* recited the facts of the arrest and the stated offences. The leader continued:

> . . . with these only can he be justly charged. We therefore condemn as grossly unjust official suggestions that he was in reality guilty of other crimes. Particularly odious is the production on the day of his death by the Irish Office of a letter from Dublin alleged to have been found in the Cork City Hall at the time of the Lord Mayor's arrest, but upon which apparently no count in the indictment was based. Action of this kind can but intensify the feelings which his death will inflame among Irishmen the world over. When first we realized that he was indeed likely to persist in refusing to take food we urged upon Ministers the folly of permitting him to die, and counselled his release as an act of grace. Had he been clearly convicted of participation in any crime of violence we should not have done so ; but we considered that the offences proved against him were not sufficiently grave to warrant the Government in carrying the law to its strictly logical conclusion. We have never regretted, and do not now regret the advice which we then tendered. We felt that in some circumstances logic is a poor thing, a thing, moreover, out of keeping with our national political temperament. (October 26, 1920.)

The removal of the body of the dead Lord Mayor in his coffin
from St. George's Roman Catholic Cathedral, Southwark, to
Euston Station on the way to Cork for burial was made the
occasion of a remarkable procession of Sinn Feiners, including men
in green uniforms, and other Irish people and sympathizers,
while large crowds all along the route watched in silence. At
Holyhead there was some trouble, though no violence, when the
relatives and others accompanying the coffin were told that the
ship was going straight to Cork in order to prevent possible
disturbances in Dublin arising out of the planned procession
through that city. Special Correspondents of the paper
graphically reported all these events. Their effect on American
opinion was serious. On October 26 it was also reported in
the paper that Cox, the Democrat candidate, had promised to
use American influence in support of Ireland were he elected.
A leading article directed the attention of the Government to
this declaration as an instance of likely international repercussions.

In Printing House Square, Steed's conduct of the paper was
precipitating repercussions. Walter questioned the attitude
adopted towards the Lord Mayor of Cork, and particularly the
leading article of October 26. Both the Proprietors, as well as
the Editor, were personally menaced. Northcliffe was given an
armed guard of plain-clothes police. The head offices of the
newspapers under his control, notably *The Times* and the
Daily Mail, were considered to be in danger of being set on fire
or damaged by explosives, and armed police stood on duty at
the entrances day and night. A system of staff identity cards
was instituted and no one, however well known in the office, was
admitted without first showing the card and being scrutinized
by the policemen at the door. Northcliffe and Walter recognized
that the attitude of the paper did not please many of its readers,
a number of whom reproached the Editor or the Proprietors, or
cancelled their subscriptions. These dissentients belonged
mainly to the Unionist-Loyalist group, who saw *The Times*, so
long the opponent, now as the abettor of the separatist and
traitorous Irish; also the separatist and traitorous Irish themselves hotly resented the paper's refusal to countenance the
coercion of the Unionists. The sharp fall in the circulation
figures was watched by Northcliffe with uneasiness. He was
harassed by the protests of his mother and his family. Moreover,
he was accused of dictating the policy of the paper by his personal
animosity towards Lloyd George; though he strenuously denied
this, even Walter was not entirely convinced. The Editor was
between the upper and the nether millstone: he possessed,
however, private information which encouraged him.

There were numerous attempts to secure a settlement by secret negotiation. An envoy representing Arthur Griffith —Patrick Moylett, of a Dublin firm of importers—was in touch with Steed's former colleague at Crewe House, C. J. Phillips of the Foreign Office, with whose help Moylett was hopeful of approaching Lloyd George. The basis of these negotiations was to be a truce on both sides, followed by a conference between representatives of the Dail Eireann and the Government. Progress was slow: the Prime Minister was "interested" but reluctant to trust the envoy; Moylett lacked authority to offer definite assurances. A full account of conversations between the parties was kept in Steed's safe. The declaration by Lloyd George on November 9, that the Government had "murder by the throat", was not auspicious; nor was his assertion that "when he had invited Irishmen to speak for Ireland, no one had dared to speak, so great was the terror." *The Times* corrected him: "It is not true that there was no response to the Prime Minister's invitation. There was a response but he ignored it." On November 18 the prospect was more hopeful. A cryptic memorandum which recorded Moylett's activities thus describes the day:

Moylett returns London with letter from Griffith. . . . Definitely commissioned start peace negotiations. Saw Phillips 3 p.m. Saw Phillips who promised to take up at once with No. 10. Saw —— who impressed by letter as credential. Asked how far Griffith would go away from Republic. Told him no navy, no foreign affairs, might like militia; wanted finance and consulor [*sic*] representation. What about Ulster? Would give Ulster autonomy in Ireland and probably admit as third party to discussion.

Griffith was prepared to make the concessions *The Times* deemed necessary. But Lloyd George would not act precipitately; he demanded the week-end for reflection. Unfortunately, events moved too fast. Sunday, November 21, 1920, will be remembered in Dublin. On that Sunday gunmen murdered in cold blood fourteen British Army officers and ex-officers and wounded six. Afterwards, at a football match in Croke Park, twelve persons were killed and many wounded. The paper's leading article on the crime began with the strongest condemnation. "The leaders of political Sinn Fein see now the harvest of their own wicked folly. . . . The injury that Sinn Fein has wrought, not only to its own reputation but to the cause of Ireland, is incalculable. To murders such as these there is but one answer—the sternest and most unremitting vindication of the law." *The Times* proceeded to insist that justice most needs to be above reproach. We do not believe that, in normal circumstances, these murders could have met with aught but reprobation from the great mass of Irishmen. But an Army already perilously undisciplined, and a police force avowedly beyond control have defiled, by heinous acts, the reputation of England; while the Government, who are the trustees of that reputation, are not free from suspicion of dishonourable connivance. We, and all who have protested against indiscriminate reprisals, have been accused most foolishly of weakening the hand of the Irish Executive. Yet, in the light of yesterday's events, who can doubt that the strength of the Irish Executive would in this grave emergency be ten times greater had its record entitled it to appeal for the moral support of all those Irishmen to whom murder is an abomination ? (November 22, 1920.)

Moylett at once saw Phillips and reported that he had received from Griffith a message telling him to hold on and keep his head. Next day he added that Griffith agreed to do all in his power to prevent further shooting, but warned Phillips that if reprisals were taken Griffith could not expect to preserve control. The negotiations were only finally wrecked by the arrest of Griffith himself on the 26th. This act of criminal folly seems not to have been engineered by Lloyd George, who, in fact, knew nothing in advance. Moylett thus wrote to Shaw :

You may look out for a serious hardening of Irish opinion, which more than ever tends to become a solid block behind Arthur Griffith. The fact that the people of Ireland believe that he was put into gaol by Dublin Castle or the British Government for sinister purposes has greatly added to his prestige and this from all sides, and all sides have complete trust in Griffith, both as to political wisdom and to the fact that he is impervious to any soft soap from Downing Street or elsewhere.[1]

Since a reference to the negotiations had already appeared in the *Irish Independent*, and there was no further hope of Moylett's success, *The Times* judged it opportune to publish his account of what had taken place.[2] Soon afterwards martial law was proclaimed in four Irish counties and the death penalty instituted for persons who, after a fixed date, should be found with arms or wearing unauthorized uniforms. On December 12 the city of Cork was grievously ravaged by fire.[3] There were threats of incendiarism in England. The policy of *The Times* remained,

[1] Moylett to Shaw, December 7, 1920.
[2] See the communication of the London Correspondent of the *Chicago Tribune*, December 11; also the letter to the Editor signed " The Envoy," December 15, 1920.
[3] The result of General Strickland's inquiry was to inculpate the Auxiliaries. Steed refers to this report on p. 568.

of course, unchanged. Since the defeat of the Treaty and the rejection of the League, Ireland was more than ever the touchstone of cordial Anglo-American relations.

A change had, moreover, occurred in the Washington representation of *The Times*. It roughly synchronized with the coming into power of a new President. In November, 1920, Arthur Willert[1] gave up the Washington correspondence and was succeeded by Willmott Harsant Lewis, who had joined the staff in March. Lewis was born in Cardiff and was educated at Heidelberg and at the Sorbonne. He was a linguist and had a taste for the Orient. His first important position in journalism came to him in Shanghai where he became editor of the *North China Daily News*. He was in China during the Boxer Rebellion and in Korea during the Russo-Japanese War as correspondent of the *New York Herald*. Next he went to San Francisco, where he failed in a commercial enterprise, and returned to journalism, again in the Far East, as editor of the *Manila Times*. During the war he was in France handling American propaganda to Europe at the demand of Pershing whom he had known since their Philippine days; and at the Peace Conference he was the Paris Correspondent of the *New York Tribune*. Northcliffe, impressed by his familiarity with American journalism and his American methods, engaged him. His dual knowledge of the United States and the Far East well qualified him to assume the correspondence at this particular time. He was 42 when he became responsible for the treatment in *The Times* of the great Pacific and Atlantic issues, the efforts to establish connexion between Washington and Geneva, the prospective naval agreement involving Japan as well as Britain, and the immediate repercussions of the Irish problem—now the key to Anglo-American harmony.

Irish agitation in the United States was so effective that the state of American feeling by the autumn and early winter of 1920 was the reverse of encouraging to British plans for the settlement of all outstanding issues, including the naval ratio. The temper shown in many parts of the Union was so hostile to the policy, as it was represented, of British repression in Ireland, that the Editor communicated his views orally and by letter to Churchill, then Secretary of State for War. It appeared to the Editor that the promotion of an immediate Irish settlement was the supreme task of statesmanship and that it could not now be postponed without danger to the highest interests of the British Isles.

[1] Now Sir Arthur: he had been knighted in 1919 for his services with the British Mission. He resigned shortly after his return to London.

WILLMOTT HARSANT LEWIS
From a portrait in oils by Bjorn Egeli

December 28th, 1920.

I wanted to see you to-morrow (Wednesday) morning in order to put before you some views and information which I have received during the last 48 hours upon opinion in the United States on the position in Ireland. You will remember that I spoke to you on this point when I had the pleasure of seeing you last week. The head of one of the biggest news organizations in the United States, a man whom I know well and who has always been Anglophil, writes it as his firm opinion that " this country [i.e. the United States] is consciously and unconsciously preparing for war with Great Britain, whether it comes in twelve months or in twelve years." A Canadian friend who recently visited the States writes that the bitterness against England, chiefly on account of the Irish situation, is quite incredible unless it has been actually experienced. Dr. Charles Raton, now Editor of *Leslie's Weekly* and formerly the right-hand man of Charlie Schwab in the American shipping campaign during the war, warned me months ago that the feeling against England was being worked up to a very dangerous pitch—and he is as strong a friend as we have over there. To-day Bishop Kelley, the Roman Catholic Bishop of Chicago,[1] who is in this country on a special mission to the Vatican connected with American missionary organizations, spoke to me with real alarm on the situation. Bishop Kelley is a native of Prince Edward's Island and very friendly to this country. He said:

" It is a great mistake for people over here to think that the Irish vote was beaten in the Presidential election. In reality it won the election for Harding, not only by its own weight but by the weight of all the other votes which it controls. It deliberately voted against Governor Cox because he was thought to represent Wilson's pro-British policy of the League of Nations. It smashed the Democratic Party with which it had always been associated for that very reason. President Harding will not be able to get away from its influence. He does not want to build ships against England, but he will have to unless there is a settlement in Ireland. The people who elected him will see to that. The Catholic Church in the States is being slowly driven in the same direction by Irish pressure. I who edit a weekly Catholic journal that has a million-and-a-quarter readers feel that the current is irresistible. Burke Cochrane has completely lost his influence over the Irish because he supported Governor Cox. Judge Cohalan, of New York, a cousin of the Bishop of Cork, is in reality doing his best to stem the tide and to neutralize De Valera's movement. One of the biggest millionaires in the United States, a pro-English Irishman [Doheny], has recently subscribed a very large amount to the Sinn Fein fund, because he believes that only thus can England be goaded into making a settlement, and only through a settlement can an Anglo-American conflict be averted."

His principal object in writing [the Editor proceeded]

---

[1] This is inaccurate. Cardinal Mundelein was Archbishop of Chicago at this time, while Bishop Kelley was head of the Catholic Extension Society which he had founded in that city.

is to urge upon you with all the emphasis at my command to use your great influence in the direction of promoting a settlement in Ireland without delay.

I am very sorry that the Labour report on Ireland has been issued before the military report on the Cork burnings. However unfavourable the military report may be, it would have been better for it to have been issued promptly and for the Government to have accepted its findings. It is, I am convinced, time for the Government to prove that it is still in control of its agents in Ireland and that it is not subservient to any of them. If vindictive action like that just taken against the *Freeman's Journal* were avoided or, at least, corrected, and if Arthur Griffith and O'Neill were released, I believe that with the help of people like Archbishop Mannix and Archbishop Clune, the terms of peace could be arranged and that, after a truce of a month or six weeks, it would be possible to reach a basis of a settlement with members of the Sinn Fein Parliament.

But for this policy to succeed it would be necessary for the Government not to boggle, but rather to say: thus far and no farther will we go, and to state at once the maximum concessions that can be added on to the new Irish Act. I know that the question of Irish policy is trembling in the balance and that it may be decided for good or evil before very long. I wish every member of the Government could realize as keenly as I have been compelled to realize how much is at stake and how greatly the whole of the position of the Empire throughout the world would be strengthened were the British Government to do the bold and just thing, not out of any tactical considerations but because it is just.

Concluding, the Editor said that in his submission the British object

must be not merely the subjugation but the reconciliation of Ireland and the neutralization of Irish hostility towards us in the United States and in the Dominions. This cannot be accomplished by any administrative or military victory over murder. It can only be accomplished by bold and generous statemanship on our part. And it is because I regard you as the boldest and one of the most generous of our statesmen that I make you this appeal.[1]

The Editor was still resolved to do his utmost to see that *The Times*, so far as any newspaper could, assisted the cause of reconciliation in Ireland and the neutralization of anti-British agitation in America. The outrages committed on both sides were rapidly mounting in number and violence. The Government published during December an impressive statement of the outrages committed by the rebels in Ireland between January 1 and December 18, 1920. On December 28 the Labour Commission

[1] Steed to Churchill, December 28, 1920.

568

had published as the result of its investigations its report, strongly condemning the methods of Irish administration and bringing serious charges against the Crown Forces in Ireland. Yet, in the view of certain observers, the year was closing with signs, even though slight, of some improvement in the Irish situation generally. Martial law apparently was being substituted for the practice of reprisals, and the Prime Minister had announced his willingness to meet the Sinn Fein Members of Parliament at a conference to which all but certain notorious criminals were promised a safe conduct. The Editor's policy of pressing for an Irish settlement was again expressed in a letter to C. F. G. Masterman. Masterman had thanked him for publishing in *The Times* a letter replying to a personal attack by Hamar Greenwood in the House of Commons. Steed replied saying that no thanks were owing to him.

As to Ireland, we have done our best for the past two years to promote a just settlement and shall go on until we succeed. The Government have done their damnedest against us, but as all their attacks have been based on the false assumption that our policy was inspired by personal rancour, they have always failed and will fail. We have a good many faults and more difficulties to contend with than our readers know, but we are trying to be honest.[1]

The Times, of course, backed the Prime Minister's offer to Sinn Fein. Nevertheless it miscarried. Six men, two found guilty of murder, four of high treason, were under sentence of execution in Dublin. Large crowds knelt in the rain outside the gaol and public sympathy was expressed in a general stoppage of activity in the city and the closing of workshops and factories. The Editor made strenuous efforts to have the executions postponed if not stopped altogether. On March 13, 1921, he wrote to Northcliffe detailing the events and circumstances which had decided him not to print a short leader he had written about the executions:

Last week Mr. Arthur Vincent, a paraphrase of whose letter to the Prime Minister we published, went to Dublin with a request from Sir Basil Thomson[2] to do his utmost (1) to bring about a meeting between De Valera and Craig, the Ulster Premier-Designate, and (2) with a request to bring over somebody who could discuss a truce. Basil Thomson gave Vincent a written safe-conduct for *anybody* except Mike Collins, the head of the Irish Republican Army. The understanding was that anybody whom Vincent might bring back with him would at once see the Prime Minister.

[1] Steed to Masterman, February 23, 1921.
[2] Then head of the Special Branch at Scotland Yard.

In Dublin Vincent got in touch with De Valera, but found he would have to travel some distance in order to see him.

Meanwhile the atmosphere had become so tense, on account of the impending executions at Mountjoy and of the petitions for the reprieve of the condemned men, that Vincent felt it would be useless to start any negotiations until the question of the executions was settled one way or the other. On receipt of a telegram from Basil Thomson urging him to see Sir John Anderson at Dublin Castle, Vincent saw Anderson, who told him that the death sentences in the case of Wheelan and Moran had been confirmed on the strength of evidence obtained since the trial by the capture of a Sinn Fein dispatch. Vincent returned to London yesterday, when he received a letter from Basil Thomson saying that it would be useless for him to bring over anybody unless the Sinn Feiners were prepared beforehand to submit a " constructive " programme to the Government. This was completely at variance with Basil Thomson's previous undertakings. Vincent asked to see the Prime Minister, but Basil Thomson, after consulting J. T. Davies, told him that it would be quite impossible. Then Vincent came to us and gave us the information.

I rang up Basil Thomson telling him that I had the information about Anderson and would use it unless the execution of the men was postponed sufficiently to enable a new trial to be held, at which all the evidence would be publicly produced. He advised me to get on to the Irish Office, where, of course, there was no one. Hamar Greenwood was out of town and J. T. Davies had evaporated; but I got on to Miss Stevenson, told her the circumstances and said that Mr. Vincent was with me. She said the Prime Minister had been expecting him at Chequers all day. So I got from her the precise route and started Vincent off. He reached Chequers at dinner time and dined with the P.M. and Reading. They went into the case thoroughly, rang up the Judge-Advocate, Cassel and, in spite of all Vincent's endeavours and entreaties, decided that the excutions could not be postponed. In the meantime I had prepared a short leader upon the position for publication in case Vincent on his return should think it would in any way help matters. He returned at 11.30 and strongly urged that we should say nothing for the moment that might further inflame Irish feeling, which was already at boiling point. Our Dublin telegrams confirmed this, so we decided not to publish. . . .

At 10 o'clock Burgess rang up to say that the heads of the Irish Transport Workers' Union had come over and were with him, with everything ready for the arrangement of a truce. He urged us to do all we could to stop the executions, which would prevent any truce. We told him we had done everything humanly possible, and now unfortunately things must take their course for a while. The whole system is as damnable as it can be.[1]

[1] Steed to Northcliffe, March 13, 1921.

The executions were carried out on March 14. The Editor, however, was disinclined to " let things take their course," despite a difficult situation in the office—Northcliffe sulky, Brumwell and Flanagan in opposition—which made his position uncomfortable. The threat of American intervention on behalf of Ireland had lessened when Harding took office as President in March, 1921, on the slogan of " normalcy," but the satisfactory settlement of many questions was still uncertain. The Editor published letters from Lord Grey and Horace Plunkett, both well acquainted with the intricacies of Anglo-American relations. Plunkett warned Steed that the British war debt would be demanded to the last farthing if the Irish question remained unsettled. (March 14, 1921.) However, the retirement of Bonar Law enabled the Editor to make a fresh effort, for Austen Chamberlain at once got in touch with him. The Editor told Northcliffe of the circumstances.

Austen [Chamberlain] sent a man to me . . . to say that Austen hoped to be elected leader of the party, and to ask whether *The Times* would support him. I said *The Times* never supported any persons on personal grounds, but that there seemed to me to be no one else in the running, and that Austen was obviously entitled to the job, if he wanted it. I gather that L.G. had really been a good deal upset by the Bonar episode, and that he is not at all happy at the idea of having to work closely with Austen.

Austen's man also gave me a strange message. He did not give it formally in Austen's name, but he said it so emphatically that I think it was inspired. It was this: " For goodness sake, keep up your pressure about Ireland. You have no notion what good *The Times* has done. Keep it up and you will pull it off. Things are moving on the inside." . . . Things are now in such a position that if there were goodwill there would be a broad road open to a settlement in a very short time, but there may be many a slip. . . . It is a toss up whether there will be bad fighting at Easter or not. [1]

Next day he wrote again to Northcliffe :

You will be glad to know that—barring some tremendous outbreak at Easter—things are really shaping more favourably in regard to Ireland. I had a long talk with Austen this afternoon, really for the purpose of finding out his attitude towards a settlement and how much he knew of what four at least of his colleagues had been doing. He knew very little, but his attitude is distinctly satisfactory. Derby also is moving in a cunning underhand sort of way, doubtless in the hope of taking the wind out of L.G.'s sails by promoting a settlement. The main threads, however, are in the hands of

[1] Steed to Northcliffe, March 22, 1921.

Burgess. It was in order to be able to tell Burgess what Austen's line of country is that I saw A. this afternoon.[1]

Writing to Austen Chamberlain a few days later, the Editor recorded that

Captain Shaw, our Irish expert, received today a letter from Mr. George Russell (" A.E.") whose position will be known to you. It bears upon one point which I mentioned—that physically and militarily the Sinn Fein leaders are not afraid. My information was drawn from other sources, all of which we used to call Unionist. But this letter confirms it. I believe it is a pretty accurate analysis of the Sinn Fein state of mind.[2]

Austen Chamberlain referring both to that letter and the conversation of a few days before it, pointed out that

mistrust is, I am afraid, mutual. If they think they have reason to distrust us, I feel as little confidence in their good will to any settlement which would safeguard the vital national interests of this country, and until we get closer to some responsible body of men, I feel little would be gained by the firm offer of which " A.E." speaks, which must be, I take it, our last word in concession.[3]

To this letter Steed made a long rejoinder. "If we wait until we find a responsible body of Irishmen animated by good will towards this country," he wrote, " we may wait until it is too late to find any solution."

Good will can only grow very slowly after what has happened, but we as a nation simply cannot afford to allow the present position to develop, as it may easily develop, into a predicament that will oblige us to double the number of our forces in Ireland. You will probably have seen the " conclusions " of the so-called American " Commission of Inquiry." They will, nevertheless, carry weight in the United States, especially when supplemented by the reports of strongly Anglophil American writers like Mr. Hard, who has just returned from Ireland quivering with indignation and declaring that he can no longer tone down the truth, as he has hitherto done in the interest of Anglo-American concord. . . . A settlement with Ireland would, according to my information, bring us rapidly American ratification of the Treaty of Versailles, with one reservation about the League of Nations; a strong Republican movement for the cancellation of Allied debts to America ; and a much more friendly spirit in regard to the cables, oil and Naval ship-building.[4]

[1] Steed to Northcliffe, March 23, 1921.
[2] Steed to A. Chamberlain, March 27, 1921.
[3] A. Chamberlain to Steed, March 29, 1921.
[4] Steed to A. Chamberlain, March 31, 1921.

An exchange of letters at the end of March, 1921, between the Editor and General Sir Nevil Macready, G.O.C. in Ireland, illuminates the truth about Ireland and the state of feeling concerning the country. The General had written privately to the Editor on March 29, enclosing some official information which he described as exposing " the unreliability of some of your correspondents in Ireland." The Editor agreed to publish a correction, and proceeded :

I have sent from time to time to Ireland men who constantly risked their lives during the war as accredited correspondents in recording the deeds of the British and Allied forces in France and in other theatres of war. But though they naturally went with feelings of loyalty and admiration for the Forces of the Crown, they returned filled with loathing at the manner in which operations in Ireland are conducted on both sides. Besides, they cannot rid themselves of the feeling that the warfare in Ireland, on both sides, is being carried on by men who are their fellow citizens.

This journal has done its utmost during the past two years, and will continue to do its utmost, to promote an Irish settlement upon honourable terms. It is my conviction, based on extensive knowledge of imperial and international affairs, that unless there is soon a settlement in Ireland by negotiation, the Irish question will ruin the Empire and involve us in the most serious difficulties with the United States.[1]

As to the policy of the new American President, Lewis predicted a " middle ground between aloofness and injurious commitments." A forecast of the Harding Administration's foreign policy appeared on April 6, cabled by the New York Correspondent. The Peace Treaty would not be ratified and the United States would not join the League; either before or after the negotiation of peace with Germany steps would be taken to arrange some " association of nations " based on an international tribunal. The United States would always be ready to defend civilization but would make no military alliances; and she would claim her rights under the Armistice and the Peace Treaty although she had not ratified the latter. Next must come a naval agreement.[2]

The Times, encouraged by the consensus of opinion that Harding was not among the " irreconcilables " kept to its course : Ireland must somehow be settled. While the Sinn Fein ambushes and assassination in Ireland and arson in England continued with undiminished bitterness most strenuous efforts were being made to bring about a truce. It was believed that the King's

[1] Steed to Macready, March 30, 1921.
[2] For *The Times* and the British naval agreement with the United States, see Chapter XIV, " The Naval Treaty."

influence was being brought to bear.[1] Towards the end of April Lord Derby under the alias of "Mr. Edwards" paid a brief secret visit to Ireland. May 5 brought the news that Sir James Craig had engaged in an informal conference in Dublin with De Valera, the first hopeful sign for many months. Cardinal Logue had stated a few days before that a number of influential people in both England and Ireland had been working for peace. *The Times* confessed its knowledge of at least five such efforts as being in progress, but the Craig–De Valera meeting in Dublin offered the greatest hopes. Yet these faded when, in the middle of May, an election for the Southern Irish Parliament took place. It was held indeed without disturbance, but the Sinn Fein candidates were all unopposed, and they scored a complete triumph. Simultaneously outrages were renewed in England. There were shootings and burnings in London, Liverpool and St. Albans, followed soon by further incendiary fires on Tyneside. Late in May rebels set fire to and gutted the Dublin Customs House, and a number of the incendiaries were caught red-handed and killed by Crown Forces. It was then announced that the Cabinet had decided to send large reinforcements to Ireland.

To these outrages and threats that appalled decent people all over England and Ireland, Printing House Square offered a curious parallel, which, known only to few, placed the Editor in a position that was all but desperate. While the Editor was striving to place *The Times* in a position to influence an Irish settlement first for its own sake and secondly for the sake of a naval settlement with America, Northcliffe was secretly proceeding by devious means with a plan to evict the Editor and dispose of the paper. He made an open and general complaint of Steed's editorial capacity in March and demanded a reversal of policy towards the pooling of coal, threatened to sell the paper in April and began the arrangements by which he would leave Printing House Square in May. The collapse of this scheme[2] gave the Editor a promise of continuity in his position and policy. He was not long left unthreatened.

Hitherto Northcliffe, worried as he was about the Editor's Irish policy, had made no protest against the Editor, although

[1] The withdrawal of Lord French as Viceroy and the sending of Lord FitzAlan, a personal friend of the King, in his place was seen as evidence of Royal influence. FitzAlan was a Catholic and a special enabling Act of Parliament was required to hold an office from which members of that religion were debarred by law. It has been seen above, p.541, that the King had taken a keen personal interest in the abortive Conference at Buckingham Palace in 1914. It was at FitzAlan's house that Craig stayed on his visit to De Valera.

[2] The next Chapter describes some of Northcliffe's activities in the spring of 1921, and Steed's efforts to offset them while, at the same time, forwarding an American policy, the way for which was to be cleared by an Irish settlement.

the " Old Lady of Totteridge " continued to be greatly vexed by articles in *The Times* and protests from relatives and friends in Northern Ireland. Eventually Northcliffe, early in the summer, after a few preliminaries which Steed thought he could disregard, demanded outright that the policy be changed. Steed stood firm and, in an effort to avoid a complete rupture, asked Northcliffe to give him a month's grace. This was granted. Before the month had elapsed the announcement was made that the King would visit Belfast to open the Ulster Parliament. Steed had not known of the decision beforehand. The announcement was made on June 8, and immediately Steed was visited by two Irishmen, one Nationalist and one Unionist, who both advised him, independently, that it would be dangerous for the King to go. The Editor went to see Lord Stamfordham on the 10th with these warnings in mind. Being told that the King and Queen were determined to go, whatever the risk, he suggested to Stamfordham that if the King were to go as the King of All Ireland, equally ready to open a Parliament in Dublin, or even a united, central Parliament, the risk would be lessened. Were the King to do this, to encourage his people to call a truce to their quarrels and to work together as citizens of the Empire, the Editor promised that *The Times* " would go bail for him." Stamfordham pointed out that the Government were responsible for the King's speech, but, on the Editor's insistence, he agreed to beg his Majesty to consider the matter. Stamfordham also suggested Steed should see Grigg, then Lloyd George's political secretary. Steed did so. He repeated to Grigg what he had told Stamfordham, and added: " Tell the Prime Minister that whether he plays up or not, the leading article going bail for the King will appear in *The Times* on Monday morning; that if he doesn't play up, and anything happens to the King, *The Times* will denounce him."

Stamfordham was successful. The King expressed his dislike of the draft prepared by the Government, and with the help of Smuts, then in London for the Imperial Conference, he added his own corrections.[1] The amended draft was not to Lloyd George's liking, but before it could be altered at a Cabinet meeting the promised leading article had appeared in *The Times* of Monday. Stamfordham later told the Editor that " this leader enabled Balfour and Austen Chamberlain to write into

[1] Smuts, in his biography, claims he did not see the draft. But according to De Valera he did. Smuts, however, publicly acknowledged that he had had a hand in the final composition. The explanation may be that Smuts did not see (or disregarded) the original draft, while De Valera was referring to the amended version. Smuts was certainly interested, and had unofficial conversations with Tom Casement, De Valera's representative.

the King's speech certain passages against the will of the Prime Minister."

The leading article of this day, June 20, echoed the Editor's original words to Stamfordham : the King would have gone "with equal readiness and pleasure to inaugurate a Southern Irish Parliament, or to discharge the greater function of opening a united Parliament of Ireland." The Editor collaborated with Shaw in writing this leader. On the 22nd the paper included a supplement devoted to the city of Belfast and the first leader in the parent paper was properly devoted to the Royal visit to Ireland. The writer spoke for the United Kingdom in saying that, "Above all else its hopes and prayers are centred upon the King and Queen and upon their solemn mission of peace so dutifully and so generously undertaken. Meanwhile at Westminster," the leader continued,

The Irish question lies still in the dust of party politics. We learn therefore without surprise that the Cabinet has been sharply divided upon it : that division is one of the bitter fruits of the Government's failure. Too long have they preferred the inexperience of their own Ministers, soldiers, and officials to the advice of Irishmen long versed in the difficulties of the national problem. Serious and moderate opinion in Ireland has been consistently against them, and that opinion has beyond question been right. . . . The hopes of those who imagined that the Government might have chosen yesterday's debate in the Lords for the announcement of a change in their Irish policy are doomed to disappointment. To the moving appeal of Lord Desart, and the ripe wisdom of Lord Dunraven, the Lord Chancellor [Lord Birkenhead] had no reply save that the Government intended to go on. . . . If this indeed be the Government's last word we can but despair of an Irish peace in their lifetime. They hold out naught but a prospect of continued repression, and of force warring upon force until Ireland lies in ruins. This is not statesmanship nor Christianity. (June 22, 1921.)

The Royal visit to Ireland was a brilliant success, though marred by the blowing-up of the train by which the Royal escort of Hussars travelled southward from Belfast.[1] On June 23 *The Times* reported in full the King's Speech with his sincere appeal "to all Irishmen to stretch out the hand of forbearance and conciliation; to forgive and forget, and to join in making for the land which they love a new era of peace, contentment and good will." The leading article, entitled " Playing the Game," was widely quoted throughout this country and beyond. *The Times* (Shaw writing) first described the speech as " a triumph of tact and statesmanship—the statesmanship that is great enough

[1] The direct consequence, in Stamfordham's view, of the speeches made by Birkenhead and Worthington-Evans on the 21st.

to be human and obviously sincere. . . . To Ireland as a whole he spoke as her King and as head of the British Commonwealth of Free Nations; but still more appealingly as her friend and well-wisher. . . . All that the King can do the King has done. He at all events has played the game, nobly and right well." Recalling that on the day of his Majesty's departure Ireland was debated in both Houses of Parliament, the article continued :

Some clear word of God-speed to him on his mission; some effort to lighten his task would surely not have been misplaced. Yet in the House of Lords the Government by the mouth of the Lord Chancellor ruthlessly dashed all hopes that their heart might have changed and decreed intensified warfare in Ireland to the bitter end. In the House of Commons, Sir L. Worthington-Evans (Secretary of State for War) supplied details that were lacking to a full comprehension of the Chancellor's statement. Such action may be essential to the continuance of the Government's present policy. But [and from this point the Editor took a hand in the leader] it is astounding that it should be resolved and announced upon the very eve of the King's appeal for peace in Ireland, and indeed immediately after a very large section of the Cabinet had advocated the abandonment, or at least the postponement of a " war " policy until a policy of reconciliation had been tried. Truly those members of the Government who believe a " war " policy is wrong yet acquiesce in it rather than risk their offices cut a sorry figure. But the Government as a whole cut a figure still sorrier. They have failed to " play the game " towards a Sovereign who with high courage and sense of duty has played the game with them, with his peoples, and with the Empire. (June 23, 1921.)

The King returned to London on the afternoon of Thursday, June 23, the day on which *The Times* leader, entitled " Playing the Game," was published. On Saturday, June 25, Lord Stamfordham saw the Editor at Buckingham Palace. He then said he was commanded by the King to thank the Editor for the great help which *The Times* had given. "You may have noticed," Stamfordham said, " how closely some passages in the King's speech resembled *The Times* leader of last Monday." He added, " The King also read your leader, ' Playing the Game ' on his way back from Liverpool. He let the Ministers at Euston see that he was not pleased with them. But now the King would be glad if you would hold your hand for a while, and not censure the Government." Stamfordham would not say more except that something would happen. The Editor agreed to hold his hand against a fresh development in the Irish situation. This was not long delayed.

Hopes of peace in Ireland had been strengthened by the news of the dispatch of letters by the Prime Minister (Lloyd George) inviting Craig and De Valera to a conference in London, " to explore to the uttermost the possibility of a settlement." There was general and profound gratitude towards his Majesty. *The Times* observed :

The hour of peace has struck for Ireland, an hour charged with hope but heavy also with responsibilities. The Prime Minister's letter to De Valera has changed the atmosphere as swiftly as the lightnings of yesternight cleared the air of London. The King's prayer that his going to Ireland might prove " the first step towards an end of strife amongst her people " may be on the verge of fulfilment. (June 27, 1921.)

Craig accepted the invitation at once; De Valera temporized, stating that he was seeking a conference with the representatives of the minority in Ireland, but he invited Craig, with Lord Midleton and other Southern Unionists, to meet him in Dublin first. The former refused; the others accepted, and a conference was held on July 4 in Dublin, and adjourned. On July 5 General Smuts visited Dublin and met De Valera, and on returning to London said that the Irish problem was soluble. This was the upshot at which Stamfordham had hinted in advance. As a result of his discussions with the Southern Unionists, which had been resumed on July 8, De Valera wrote accepting the Prime Minister's invitation. With that acceptance the face of the whole situation was changed. On July 9 the terms of a truce by the British Army Headquarters and by De Valera were published in Ireland. Instantly peace reigned throughout the country. On July 12 De Valera with Griffith and other emissaries arrived in London, and were received by Lloyd George who met the Irish mission for informal conversations. On July 15 he again received De Valera and also conferred with Craig. This first stage of the negotiations continued for several days, and then the Northern Irish leader returned home, to be followed by De Valera on July 22. In the meantime the Editor of *The Times* had gone to the United States, where he joined Northcliffe, and at the end of that month occurred the " interview " in which Northcliffe was said to have made certain statements concerning the King's visit to Belfast.[1]

After the Irish leaders had returned home, in possession of the British Government's proposals for a settlement, it was announced early in August that the Northern Cabinet had

[1] For the details, see next Chapter, " The Naval Treaty."

communicated its observations to London and that De Valera had summoned a meeting of Dail Eireann for August 16. All the members of the Dail interned or imprisoned, to the number of thirty-four, were released and enabled to attend. On August 15 the text of the correspondence between Lloyd George and De Valera was published. The Government had offered full Dominion status subject to six conditions. These, De Valera declared, involved a control that Ireland could not admit, and he described the Dominion status offered as " illusory." Lloyd George replied that on the point of allegiance there could be no compromise. On the same day a letter from Smuts to De Valera urging acceptance of the Government's offer was published.

When the Dail met on August 16 De Valera refused to accept the British Government's proposals. For several days the matter was discussed in secret session, and on the 19th Parliament adjourned, after a statement by the Prime Minister. In *The Times* of August 17 the leading article—consistently understanding Sinn Fein—stated firmly the point of view and solid intention of the people of England standing behind their Government. It said:

Sinn Fein should understand beyond all doubt that the Government's offer to it has been received by an overwhelming majority of the English people with profound feelings of thankfulness and relief. . . . There is but one dominant feeling . . . that we in England have at last extricated ourselves from the morass. We stand, as we have not stood for centuries, on a firm rock. There may be, and must indeed be, Englishmen who think that the Government have gone too far; but even these recognize the superiority of an impregnable though straitened foothold over the treacherous insecurity of quicksands. But we Englishmen do not believe that the Government's offer outstrips public opinion. . . . Here, in English eyes, is an immeasurable advance in policy upon anything that has ever been transacted between Great Britain and Ireland before. The idea of self-determination, limited only by the sovereignty of the King, is a commonplace in the political thought of five confederate nations. For the first time in Irish history that status is within the grasp of Irishmen. . . .

But, *The Times* proceeded:

The British Commonwealth is determined that no jot or tittle of the Government's essential reservations shall be abated. . . . The English conscience is now clear; and the future rests solely with Ireland herself. On fundamental principles the English mind may be taken by Sinn Fein to be made up. No rhetoric, no sophistry, no appeal to violence will move the electors of Great Britain or the Dominions to yield on that one cardinal point upon which the constitution of the British Empire depends. (August 17, 1921.)

This leader (written by C. W. Brodribb), unlike so many others on the subject, won the approval of John Walter. The Deputy Editor, G. S. Freeman, wrote thus to him :

I took rather special pains over it because I felt that De Valera's swollen head gave us an opening to develop a point of view which our recent attitude may have led our readers to think we ignored. I fully agree with what you say about not recalling our previous utterances—it is what we say to-day that matters, and " I told you so " is always bad journalism. The leader has, I think, been well received. It was meant to define our position, and to make it clear that no further claims on the part of Sinn Fein would have any backing from *The Times*. I am not without hope that in this direction it will be useful.

Nevertheless, the Irish leader did not cease to press " further claims." De Valera wrote to Lloyd George on the 24th to say that the Dail rejected the Government's terms by an unanimous vote. More correspondence followed, to little purpose, and August ended with a fresh outbreak of rioting attended by shooting in Belfast. On September 7 the Cabinet met at Inverness. De Valera had suggested a conference on the principle of " government by consent of the governed." The Cabinet had answered that they must have a definite reply as to whether Sinn Fein was prepared to " enter a conference to ascertain how the association of Ireland with the community of nations known as the British Empire can best be reconciled with Irish national aspirations." De Valera intimated his acceptance, but his letter contained reservations as to Ireland's status which in the Cabinet's view made negotiations impossible. Thereupon the Prime Minister cancelled the proposed meeting, and the next move was with De Valera, who suggested a conference without prejudice. Telegrams were exchanged, and the Prime Minister once more invited Sinn Fein to a conference to be held in London in October on the basis he had previously suggested. This invitation was then promptly accepted by Sinn Fein, though De Valera refused to attend in person.

On October 11 the Irish Conference held its first meeting at Downing Street in secrecy. The Cabinet representatives were Lloyd George, Austen Chamberlain, Birkenhead, Churchill, Worthington-Evans, Hamar Greenwood and Gordon Hewart;

those of Sinn Fein were Arthur Griffith, Michael Collins, R. C. Barton, E. J. Duggan and Gavan Duffy. Childers and Chartres were secretaries to the Irish team. Parliament reassembled on October 18. On October 20 the Pope telegraphed a message to the King praying that his Majesty might have " the great joy and imperishable glory of bringing to an end the age-long dissension," and De Valera at once telegraphed to the Pope in terms virtually of reproof, denying that Ireland owed allegiance to the British Sovereign. British indignation was aroused and it seemed that the Conference might founder. Although it weathered the storm a section of the Unionist Party had been growing increasingly restless and a group of Unionists in the House of Commons put down a motion of censure on the Government. The Prime Minister, in one of the most remarkable speeches of his career, defended his policy in the debate on October 31, and the motion was heavily defeated.

Craig arrived in London on November 5, and two days later it became known that he had undertaken that his Government should consider the suggestions that would emerge from the conference. By this time it was generally understood that a basis of settlement agreeable to both the Government and Sinn Fein had been found. However, it was not acceptable to the Ulster Unionists. Reflecting Ulster's anxiety, the " Diehards " in the Unionist Party grew more restive and announced that they meant to raise the question of Ireland at the conference of National Unionist Associations at Liverpool on November 17, and were prepared, if necessary, to split the Unionist Party. On the day before the Liverpool conference a Unionist protest meeting took place in Belfast. At Liverpool the Unionist leaders submitted a resolution phrased to allay the doubts of their followers, and the result was an overwhelming vote for the Government's policy. It was admitted that there would be no coercion of Ulster. It was clear, too, that Ulster would not enter an All-Ireland Parliament.

This was the deadlock that the Irish Conference had to remove. On November 29 Craig told the Northern Parliament that either the negotiations would have broken down by the following Tuesday, December 6, or the Prime Minister would have submitted new proposals for the Ulster Cabinet to consider. In the early hours of that Tuesday, after prolonged and anxious discussion, agreement on a Treaty was reached. On December 5 Lloyd George's principal expert, Thomas Jones, had suggested to Arthur Griffith that Craig should be informed that if he remained in opposition the Area contemplated in the Bill would be revised by a Boundary Commission. By this Griffith understood that the greater part of two (Tyrone and Fermanagh, which had Nationalist majorities) of the six counties would be transferred to the new Dominion, in addition to large areas in Down and Armagh, thus depriving Ulster of economically valuable Catholic populations, and making it virtually certain that the Northern Province would not permanently remain outside the Dominion. Craig accepted Jones's Boundary Commission scheme on condition that the Northern Ireland Parliament and Government should at the outset retain separate jurisdiction. Thus the Anglo-Irish Treaty was made ready for signature by Griffith, Collins, Duggan, Barton and Gavan Duffy. Under heavy pressure from Lloyd George they signed on December 6, 1921. The terms were set forth in eighteen articles, the first of which declared that Ireland should have the same constitutional status as the British Dominions and should be styled and known as the Irish Free State. The Free State's relations to Imperial Parliament were to be those of the Dominion of Canada. The fourth article prescribed the oath of allegiance to the King to be taken by members of the Free State Parliament.

To some extent the terms were in advance of what the Government had offered after the first negotiations with De Valera; but the chorus of approval which greeted them in Great Britain showed that the Government had not gone too far. *The Times* of December 7 included a special Irish Section with photographs of all the chief personalities concerned in the long negotiations. A message from the King to the Prime Minister was reproduced.

The Times also printed a message from Wickham Steed, then in Washington, in which the Editor spoke of the general impression of " joyful surprise " among Americans.[1] The prospect of a settlement could not fail, he felt, to have a happy influence upon the Washington Conference, and also upon the British delegation at the conference. The part played by *The Times* in promoting an Irish settlement during the previous two years and a half was recognized and approved, he found, in responsible quarters in the United States. Shaw's leading article in this issue referred to the efforts of the paper and summarized the points made by *The Times* during the previous two years. He wrote :

The news that the conference had reached agreement was welcome in a special sense to this journal. Since the end of the war we have spared no effort to impress the urgent necessity of an Irish settlement

[1] The Editor was in Washington in connexion with the Naval Conference. See Chapter XIV, " The Naval Treaty."

upon the Government of the country. For months we failed to stimulate the action which we hoped Ministers would take. In July, 1919, we chose the unusual course of publishing concrete suggestions for a measure of Irish self-government in the hope, that by doing so, we might concentrate Parliamentary and public opinion upon the possibility of attaining an Irish peace at any time.[1] Our proposals were in advance of the current thought of British political foresight, and we incurred obloquy and criticism to a degree that no newspaper would lightly have courted. We acted, however, with good reason to believe that upon the lines we suggested prompt statesmanship would have achieved a settlement.... The Government of Ireland Act was based upon some of the principles that we sought to inculcate; but the Act was obviously inadequate for its professed purpose, and fell far short of the minimum requirements of the situation as it then was. Therefore, we felt bound persistently to press for its enlargement. That Act failed, as it was foredoomed to fail.... The King's Speech at Belfast expressed the growing conviction of the nation and of his Ministers that the Irish policy of the Government had been fundamentally wrong.

With an optimism as excusable as it was premature the leader-writer described the Treaty as an historic document.

The status that many of her best friends have hoped for has been accepted by the representatives of Southern Ireland. The vision of Lord Northcliffe, who ventured so long ago as June, 1919, to prophesy the coming of a " Dominion of Ireland," seems at last to be on the point of realization.... Great Britain has gone to lengths of generosity greater than many of her sternest critics have ever demanded. Viewed as the world will view them, these are indeed fitting peace terms to mark the close of an age of discontent and mistrust, and the beginning of a new era of happiness and mutual understanding.

The article concluded with a conventional recognition of the capacity of Britain to govern by consent. The articles of the Treaty proclaimed

that the genius of the British nation for government is not dead, and that our statesmen have not lost the ancient secret of our national greatness. If the signatories of the agreement have surmounted difficulties that have defied the statecraft of generations and have solved the problem that centuries found insoluble, Englishmen will thank them, one and all, and will rejoice with the King in the spirit of his message to the Prime Minister. (December 7, 1921.)

The signatories of the agreement, nevertheless, had not surmounted difficulties that had defied the statecraft of generations. With the publication of this leader *The Times* chronicled the

---

[1] The reference is to the Walter Long-Steed conversations and the subsequent leader of July 24, 1919. See above, p. 556-58.

instant decision of the Sinn Fein leader. De Valera said that the plenipotentiaries had exceeded their powers and left unfulfilled their promises to refer to Dublin before appending their signatures; and secondly that the Dail would not ratify

Nevertheless, the office saw the importance of the Treaty as lying less in the peace the Treaty might have brought in time to a single Ireland than in the transference of authority and responsibility from the British to the Irish leaders. Irish affairs were henceforth of local significance; they could no longer trouble the relations of Great Britain with other Powers. *The Times* had in 1921 the same general interest in Ireland as in 1832. From the point of view of Ireland, Wales and Scotland, *The Times* was what the Germans called it, the " *Weltblatt*," its policy towards Ireland was shaped by its sense of Imperial necessity. Under Steed the paper expressed no narrow Protestant, English, or Unionist policy. The paper had every reason to be proud of being the first influential voice to champion the raising of all Ireland to Dominion status; to have opposed partition and to have tried to open the way for the sister island to become a partner in the Empire, and through the Empire, in world affairs. It was an effort to bring Ireland directly, and not merely through Irish immigration, into the mainstream of responsibility; to rescue her from the provinciality that necessarily besets a country rendered subject by an aggressive and ambitious race; to appropriate and employ in behalf of peace and commerce, the talent of a great neighbouring people. *The Times* felt it had succeeded so far as its contribution was concerned and that circumstances outside the influence of any newspaper had intervened to perpetuate partition. But at least it may be said that by its leadership between 1919 and 1921 in the cause of Dominion status for Ireland *The Times* rendered compensation for its misjudgement in the case against Parnell in the years 1886-1890. After 1921 *The Times*, disappointed as it was, could face the Dominions and the United States with a clear conscience. Even domestically, as to Printing House Square, the fact that the Irish problem had been faced was of importance. Northcliffe was on his world tour, absorbed in Japan, Germany or the Empire; the Editor was occupied with Anglo-French relations and the war debts. It was immensely satisfactory that a constitutional form of government had been given to Ireland, and it remained for the Irish leaders to make a success of it. *The Times* would watch the progress of events, but henceforth the policy of the paper was one of detachment.[1]

[1] See Appendix II, Sources, XIII.

The Editor had succeeded in holding the paper to a clear and definite course in the face of Northcliffe's attitude, which was first one of toleration, next of scepticism and later of opposition. He had conducted the policy, and continued it, while the Chief was suddenly and subtly planning to sell *The Times*. How this unexpected and discouraging enterprise, begun in the new year of 1921, had been as suddenly abandoned in the spring, needs now to be told, in conjunction with an account of the paper's policy on the naval question.

585

XIV

THE NAVAL TREATY

ACCORDING to Northcliffe, The Times Publishing Company was at this period facing greater anxieties than at any time in its history. " If the paper is to continue under its present Proprietary, the existing scale of expenses is impossible." So ran the Chief's New Year Message of 1921 addressed to Stuart. It arrived at a time when Northcliffe was authorizing all manner of extravagances, an insurance scheme for instance. The Managing Director concluded that the Chief was out of sorts, and the Editor assured Northcliffe, in an appeasing letter on January 9, that he would not have him bothered with many communications. On the 13th, the Chief, then at Menton, wired him that he was now " perfectly fit despite rumours here." His sight certainly must have improved for he had his eye on the paper, and wrote to Stuart on February 25 that he was

looking forward to the announcement of the Insurance. Something is urgently needed to peg down the sale. I sent Steed an analysis of the figures yesterday—a steady diminution. As I told you before, I am not in the least afraid of the position. I wish that I were as sure about the cure of my throat as I am about the cure of The Times.

The necessity to find a cure for the Chief's throat and a " cure " for The Times coincided with the need for a revision of the paper's policy. Immediately demanding attention were the naval question, the Pacific situation and the Anglo-Japanese Alliance. These three matters, apart from Ireland which, it has been seen, was intimately related in the Editor's mind with them, demanded reconsideration. Versailles had thrust upon Steed's attention the naval question; it was a question that intensely interested Northcliffe.

In the Anglo-Japanese Alliance, renewed in 1911, a clause had been added which specifically exempted Britain from any obligation in the event of a Japanese conflict with America. This clause was inspired by, though not dependent on, an arbitration

Treaty then under negotiation between the United States and Britain. This Treaty the Senate had never ratified. In Printing House Square, however, the discriminatory clause was regarded as effective. Accordingly, Britain could afford to be foremost in scrapping battleships, battle cruisers and even dreadnoughts, and the country, in an epoch of reconstruction, could cut unproductive spending. But in July, 1920, Japan adopted a bill which gave her, or would give her when the ships were built, a Navy equal, or superior to, that contemplated by the American programme of " adequacy " announced four years earlier. Both the American programme of 1916 and the Japanese bill of 1920 were adopted in the conditions of war-boom, but as time passed these boom conditions were recognized as no longer obtaining. Japan and the other nations were ready to consider delaying or reducing their building schemes, but it was obvious that neither of the Pacific parties was willing to forego its ambition to become dominant in that ocean. In America, moreover, the large-Navy school led by Admiral Benson and the Secretary for the Navy, Josephus Daniels, was in the ascendent.

It was a surprise to Britain that while she was disarming steadily, new plans should be announced for augmenting the United States Navy in order to secure " world power." On December 19, 1920, Northcliffe in an interview with the United Press referred to a statement attributed to Daniels to the effect that the U.S. had to arm in order " to compete against any combination of Powers that might be formed against the U.S." If that had been said, Northcliffe hoped " some Washington journalist will give my love to Mr. Daniels and ask him to name his combination." In reply the Secretary instructed the United Press to " Give my love to Northcliffe. Tell him that I want agreement between all nations of the world and no competitive building. I want all the nations of the League to join." He added that he thought Northcliffe spoke on the strength of the fact that he intended to recommend another three-year building programme, and " I would not recommend that unless it were absolutely certain that we were going to stay out of the League, or any associations of the nations altogether." Upon this Northcliffe repeated his question about the possible combination; said that Daniels had not answered it; affirmed that there was no such combination; that " competitive building has no sense." He promised that his newspapers would investigate the question of big and small ships with a view to finding the best protection for our commerce " which is the sole object of British naval policy now and in future." The correspondence was printed conspicuously in *The Times* and backed by a leader on " England and American opinion " which emphasized the opposition that Australia, Canada (British Columbia) and other Dominions would offer to the slightest suggestion that Britain should at any time enter into a combination against the United States. It was natural that the Pacific Dominions should turn to the United States if the British Pacific squadrons were weak. *The Times* had no doubt that the people of the home country would offer no less opposition. The paper hoped that America would see her way to accept in the association of nations, or some modification of the League, the position to which she was entitled. The issue awaited further treatment. The Editor was moved to write a second leading article which discussed the past history of the Anglo-Japanese Alliance and re-affirmed in strong terms the impossibility for Britain to contemplate a situation in which she would be involved, as she would be, in hostilities against the United States.

At the end of 1920 *The Times* had already made clear its position towards Japan. It was understood that if Americans thought little about the Atlantic they were not thoughtless about the Pacific. *The Times* endeavoured to make it plain that " not only is it not true that our treaty stipulations with Japan bind us to join her against the United States, but we deliberately varied those stipulations in 1911 for the express purpose of excluding the possibility of this liability." (December 30, 1920.) By way of reassuring American opinion the paper secured for publication in the new year an authoritative statement from the Japanese Ambassador:

The basic idea of the alliance is to protect by common action the territorial rights and the special interests both of Japan and Great Britain in Eastern Asia and India. The United States of America has never been thought of by the contracting parties as a country which would ever take, or contemplate taking, any action likely to threaten their territorial rights and special interests in the Far East.

It was, therefore, never in the mind of the Japanese Government to fight the United States at all, and, moreover, in the most improbable eventuality of such a war, to which I refer merely for the sake of argument, Japan would not expect England to come to her help. Hence, the Japanese and the British Governments agreed to insert in the Agreement of the Alliance Article IV, which would absolve Great Britain from an obligation to join Japan in a war against America. Only a general phraseology was selected in the Alliance Agreement for the reasons of diplomatic nicety, but what the negotiators of the Agreement had in mind is obvious. (January 4, 1921.)

The Japanese effort to allay American suspicion was decidedly welcome but causes for alarm remained, as the Editor knew. At the beginning of the new year it was rumoured that a naval agreement between the United States and Canada was being considered in certain quarters. The British Ambassador in Washington, Sir Auckland Geddes, when approached, agreed that this might be a possibility. If it were, settlement without delay, said the Washington Correspondent, would become imperative; Canada had reason for anxiety. *The Times* was not yet prepared to abandon Japan, the Alliance with whom the paper had done so much to secure.[1] When McClure, the American newspaper proprietor, drew attention to Japanese expansion and even forecast war between East and West, in an article on January 15, he was ridiculed in a leading article. In point of fact, said *The Times*, " Japan wants room certainly but she denies vehemently, and we believe truly, that she has any desire to seek it across the Pacific." McClure, however, knew something of his own people, and to the extent he did so the prospect was disturbing. When Borah proposed some sort of naval holiday, the Washington Correspondent expressed his belief that there was little enthusiasm in Congress for disarmament, or that the programme would be much reduced (January 11, 1921). The American ambition was parity with Great Britain and superiority to Japan (February 7).

The Editor considered what could be done. In all the circumstances to press for increased British armament was not merely difficult, it was impossible; but to secure an agreed measure of disarmament had yet to be proved practicable. In February, 1921, the Editor reported to Northcliffe that he had recently had a long talk with Beatty on big ships. Beatty told him that all the technical men, including air and submarine experts, who had been examined by the Committee on National Defence were unanimous in recognizing the necessity of a moderate programme of big battleships. The politicians were sitting on the fence and trying to postpone any decision until the Imperial Conference in June. He said he must have a decision by March 31, and that even then we would still be behind the United States and probably behind Japan in 1924-25. His limited programme would cost £4,000,000 in 1921-22, £9,000,000 in 1922-23 and £20,000,000 in 1923-24.[2]

It was unfortunate for the Editor that at the moment when a matter of such importance demanded his undivided attention,

[1] See Volume III, Chapter XII, " The End of British Isolation."

[2] Steed to Northcliffe, February 23, 1921.

and he needed all the support he could obtain from his Chief, he was deprived of both. Northcliffe suddenly made up his mind that the office was out of date and *The Times* was as antiquated as ever. The paper, after seven years of the Chief's unremitting time and trouble, was still not a contemporary product. It was not " A1 " as he had said in 1919. In the spring of 1921 the Chief was intensely critical of its every column. Everything in the paper was good ; nothing in it was interesting. So wrote the Chief again and again in the first months of the new year. The Editor, in consequence, felt unsettled. The disquiet he felt in the autumn of 1920 deepened. Suddenly it became obvious that something more than another typographical change, or even a new " feature," was impending. A telegram to Stuart on March 14 read :

DO NOT THINK YESTERDAY'S FIRST LEADER VERY WELL WRITTEN. LONG[1] LATE FOREIGN EDITOR STATED REPEATEDLY THAT STEED DID NOT GIVE SUFFICIENT PREPARATION TO LEADING ARTICLES WHICH OF COURSE IS HIS CHIEF DUTY AND TO WHICH DELANE AND THE GREAT WALTER DEVOTED ALMOST THEIR WHOLE TIME. OUR LEADERS ARE NOW STRONGLY CRITICIZED NOT ONLY IN THE GREAT WORLD BUT ALSO FOR THEIR ALLEGED LACK OF SCHOLARSHIP DISPLAYED. CHIEF.

By sending such a telegram openly addressed to the office, it was clear that Northcliffe had not only turned against Steed and towards Long but wished the fact known. Soon there were rumours in Fleet Street that Steed was to be replaced, some said by Long, others said by Stuart. On March 22, Steed, in a letter to Northcliffe, ingeniously alluded to these and other stories:

You will be interested to know that I am to be dismissed and you are to be ousted from *The Times* by the end of the year. This secret information was brought to me on Saturday by a friend in the City— who is usually uncommonly well informed—who wished to warn me that there was " a deep-seated plot against you and me." I bade him be of good cheer, and remember that you were not dead yet, and that, as for me, there was plenty of fight left in me. But remember what I said to you here last week, and do not let them send you to the Pacific.[2]

---

[1] B. K. Long of the Imperial and Foreign Department in the confidence of Stuart. The word " Late " must mean that Long had been chosen by Northcliffe and Stuart to succeed Steed. Long resigned on July 15, 1921, to take up the editorship of the *Cape Times*. He died in 1941. See footnote on p. 605.

[2] The reference is to the plan of Northcliffe's medical advisers to send him on a health tour round the world. The tour began in July and the Pacific was included. See below, Chapter XV, " After Northcliffe's World Tour."

A week later Steed inadvertently admitted that a few days' holiday would do himself no harm. It was true that he was tired, but Northcliffe, delighted to think he was ill, seized the opportunity to advise a long holiday. Hence, in spite of the threatened coal strike and Northcliffe's plan to return at once, the Editor went to the Isle of Wight; but only for a few days, leaving Freeman, Brodribb and Gordon Robbins in charge. Northcliffe had more than one reason for wanting to return to London. In May the jubilee of the *Daily Mail* would be celebrated. Everybody who knew Northcliffe expected dramatic intervention on his part in that paper's affairs. Meanwhile the coal trouble was the pretext for a telegram to Steed.

SATURDAY, APRIL 2, 1921

THERE CAN BE NO COMPROMISE INVOLVING ANY SORT OF SURRENDER OF CONTROL AND DIVISION OF PROFITS OF MINES TELL MARLOWE. CHIEF.

He followed it with increasingly harsh criticisms of *The Times* and the *Daily Mail*. It seemed to Steed and Marlowe that the Chief was considering Carmelite House and Printing House Square rather than coal. Yet nothing happened. It was not until late in April that Northcliffe repeated to Steed what he had already told Stuart on New Year's Day. The financial condition at Printing House Square was such that " I really cannot put my hand into my pocket again for *The Times*. I have too many other responsibilities." The other " responsibilities " were, perhaps, those at Carmelite House that might be increasing shortly. However, nothing further was said about Printing House Square. Northcliffe's mind, after all, did seem to be genuinely exercised by the coal strike and the several solutions to it canvassed in the leading articles of *The Times*. No other explanation of his telegrams was necessary. But that innocuous explanation was soon to prove baseless. Stuart was summoned to Paris when Steed returned from his few days at Ventnor. In Paris the Chief and Stuart agreed upon drastic action. The latter, who was still in Paris on the 23rd, the day of the dispatch of a new telegram to Steed at his private address, was presumably aware of its contents and intention :

1.23 P.M., ARR. 2.8 P.M.

SATURDAY, VERSAILLES, APRIL 23, 1921

VERY URGENT THERE MUST NOT BE ADVOCACY OF ANY FORM OF POOLING. SHOULD I SEE ANY INDICATION OF IT I SHALL WITHOUT WARNING DISPOSE OF MY INTEREST

IN THE PAPER TO A VERY REPUTABLE PURCHASER
WITH WHOM I HAVE ALREADY ARRANGED THUS
CONFORMING TO THE URGENT WISHES OF MY MEDICAL
AND OTHER ADVISERS TO GET RID OF EVERY TRYING
RESPONSIBILITY THAT RENDERS IT DIFFICULT FOR ME
TO BE ABROAD. I BEG OF YOU AND THE STAFF NOT TO
BE SURPRISED AT THAT WHICH WILL TRANSPIRE NEXT
WEEK IF MY WISHES BASED UPON FAR GREATER KNOW-
LEDGE OF LABOUR AND ITS AIMS THAN THE WRITERS
OF THE LEADING ARTICLES ARE DISOBEYED. CHIEF.

Before Steed read this message (he was playing golf with Bernard
Darwin for *The Times* team all Saturday), Northcliffe wired a
second time, again to Steed's private house, the following:

8.40 A.M., ARR. 10.41 A.M.
SUNDAY, VERSAILLES, APRIL 24, 1921
SUNDAY HAVING RECEIVED NO EXPECTED ASSURANCE
IN REPLY TO MY TELEGRAM OF YESTERDAY MORNING
I HAVE DECIDED TO TRANSFER MY INTEREST.
MACKENZIE WILL HAND YOU FORMAL LETTER THIS
EVENING. I HAVE APOLOGIZED TO SIR ROBERT
HADFIELD FOR AN UNMERITED SNEER FOR WHICH I
AM NATURALLY HELD PUBLICLY RESPONSIBLE. CHIEF.

Crossing this telegram, Steed sent, on the same Sunday morning,
a message through the *Daily Mail*:

SUNDAY, APRIL 24, 1921
LORD NORTHCLIFFE. HOTEL DES RESERVOIRS.
VERSAILLES.
I WAS OUT OF TOWN FROM EARLY SATURDAY MORNING
TILL LATE EVENING. YOUR TELEGRAM ONLY HANDED
TO ME LATE LAST NIGHT. I TOOK IT AS EXPRESSION
YOUR WISH WHICH I WAS BOUND TO RESPECT NOT AS
ENQUIRY NECESSITATING IMMEDIATE REPLY. THERE
WILL NATURALLY BE NO ADVOCACY OF MATTER TO
WHICH YOU TAKE EXCEPTION. I DEEPLY REGRET YOUR
DECISION TRANSFER YOUR INTEREST. STEED.

It was too late to do more. Northcliffe was working at speed.
On the same day he wrote to Steed the " formal " letter referred
to in his telegram. The letter was marked

*Personal. To be delivered by hand (of Campbell Stuart) through
Mackenzie.*[1]

[1] Mackenzie was Northcliffe's accountant. It was in his office on February 4, 1908,
that Moberly Bell came to terms with Northcliffe. See Vol. III, Chapter XVI,
" *The Times* for Sale."

This was what the Editor read:

Hotel des Reservoirs,
Versailles.
April 24, 1921

My dear Steed,

After reading the last two issues of *The Times* that had reached me at Versailles, I sent you a telegram. As I received no reply I repeat it here: [*v.* telegram to Steed from Northcliffe, April 23, 1921, on preceding page.]

I wrote to you last week that I was not unmindful of the good work done by Freeman and Shadwell[1] up to that time. But the last three Papers that I have received make my position as controlling Proprietor quite impossible.

I am within one hour's telegraphic distance from the office, receive and reply to many telegrams from my business every day and yet I wake to find myself unconsulted, beginning to be committed to the policy of " pooling," which I know to be fatal to national efficiency. I am also responsible for an unmerited sneer at one of the proved best authorities on Labour in the world, Sir Robert Hadfield (whom I know personally).

You must have surmised that I have long wished to relieve myself of the continual series of burdens of *The Times*—financial, personal and social.

My doctors declare it to be essential for me to divest myself of some portion of the weight on my shoulders.

As the whole of the rest of my undertakings are intertwined with my great estate in Newfoundland, I cannot part with shares in them without dispossessing myself of the control of that beloved enterprise. *The Times*, therefore, is the only responsibility from which I can escape.

I am now hurrying back in order to get into cable communication with John Walter who, in justice, should be informed of my intention.

I shall provide *The Times* with a proper and entirely British substitute for myself able to take a more active part in its affairs. I have the choice of three aspirants, all of whom are well equipped financially.

I had a long talk yesterday with Campbell Stuart, who is about to make an important visit to Newfoundland. He raised many objections to my decision. But I think that I finally convinced him that the position is quite impossible. You will know, my dear Steed, that I have no personal feeling in this matter. We have worked together in various relations for many years without, as far as I remember, a single cross word or *arrière pensée*.

I dare say that I am to blame for having spread my butter on too much bread.

All my other affairs are growing at a pace with which it is very difficult to compete and *The Times* is just that last straw which makes the load unbearable.

Your affectionate,
NORTHCLIFFE.

[1] Arthur Shadwell, the expert on industrial and labour problems. See Chapter II, "' Revolution ' at Home."

This was the domestic situation of Printing House Square when the mind of the Editor was, as it should have been, engrossed with the urgent business of the newspaper. Harassed as he was by the " affectionate Northcliffe," the Editor was bound to give his best attention to the paper. He could not escape the task of formulating the paper's policy towards armament in general and the British, American and Japanese ratios. Steed, after his discussions with Beatty, understood that all measures of armament or disarmament were, for the United States, related to the Anglo-Japanese Alliance, the renewal of which came automatically under consideration in 1921. The Washington Correspondent was unequivocal about the unpopularity of the Alliance in America: his messages were published though the trenchancy of his phrasing was editorially minimized. He also advised the office that the Japanese factor must be borne in mind, though not unduly stressed. A point of danger was soon reached. In addition to possible eventualities underlying the Anglo-Japanese Alliance, the United States was immediately concerned with the mandate of Yap, an island given to Japan under the Treaty of Versailles. There was nothing eventual about this. It was actual: the United States had a cable interest in the island, and protested to the League against the mandate. Willmott Lewis saw the protest as a pistol held to the Allies' heads: " The character of American relationship to Europe will be determined by the nature of the European answers to the Yap Note " he cabled on April 14. He also added, privately for the office:

DIFFICULT TO EXAGGERATE IMPORTANCE YAP NOTE HAS FOR THEM STOP AM AUTHORITATIVELY INFORMED IF REPLIES THERETO JUSTIFY TAKING FURTHER FRIENDLY STEPS THEY WOULD ENDEAVOUR INITIATE CONVERSATIONS REGARD QUOTE APPROXIMATE DISARMAMENT UNQUOTE

The United States was ultimately able to settle the question peaceably, but in the eyes of Washington the incident lent the Anglo-Japanese Alliance a threatening character. There was much discussion behind the scenes of submarine and anti-submarine appropriations; the big-ships v. small-ships controversy had not been settled; and other technical questions continued to divide experts. The weight of opinion, as Beatty's conversation with Steed indicated, seemed to favour the laying down of some big ships. There was, therefore, a building programme to be settled; and it could not be settled without an understanding with the United States. The matter must come up for settlement without delay.

Northcliffe understood this but was not prepared to help *The Times* in pressing the fact upon the public, which was highly uncharacteristic of him; nor would he, at this time, act upon the obvious fact that the slightest doubt upon such a matter would have the gravest effect upon the conversations that were bound to be held in the near future. Northcliffe was still concentrating upon an entirely new " cure " for his own health, and for that of *The Times*, by giving up the newspaper. He had no time for even the gravest international considerations. Hence, the Editor, while intensely concerned over Northcliffe, was continually criticized over policy. He was called ineffective and his paper rejected as inadequate. The Editor's position as a whole was worse than his predecessor's in 1919. Steed, simultaneously, had to edit, to formulate policy and to deal with Northcliffe's new plan to provide *The Times* with a " proper and entirely British substitute " for himself; one " able to take a more active part in its affairs." Steed had no idea of the names of all three " aspirants," or Northcliffe's choice for the position, though he could guess that Rothermere was one; that Walter was a possible, and that Ellerman was not. After consultation with Freeman and Lints Smith the Editor thus replied to Northcliffe's letter:

April 25, 1921

My dear Chief,

This is not a formal answer to the letter which Mackenzie brought. We can discuss that when we meet.

This is only to express my deep sympathy with you in what I cannot help feeling is a great turning point in your life. No doubt this matter has long been in your mind. What I want you to remember is that you have the goodwill and affection not only of myself but, as far as I can judge, of the whole staff. Should you carry out the decision you announce, I feel sure you would feel sorry to the end of your days that you had vacated the premier position in journalism, in which you have done so much for England: and that, while relieving yourself of some financial and political responsibility, you would be acquiring a burden of regret that would weigh you down.

There is surely a way out of the difficulty if we only seek it diligently. Will you not let one or two of us who are devoted to you, wish to make nothing out of you, but are truly anxious to help you to help the country, seek the way with you ? At a critical moment like this, great as are your energy, your capacities and your resource, you need the help of true friends. You kindly say that we have never had a cross word nor an *arrière pensée*, and I am sure we shall have none. But I am seriously concerned for you, for the Paper and for the country, and I wish to do everything I can to help all three.

Yours affectionately,

H. W[ICKHAM] S[TEED].

On April 26, Northcliffe telephoned from Broadstairs to the Editor saying, in crisp words, that he had received his letter but that he was forced to relinquish *The Times* as he could no longer control it from abroad. The motives of Northcliffe's intention to sever his personal connexion with *The Times* are difficult to analyse. His health was not good; his doctors had urged him to conserve his strength by reducing his responsibility. Rothermere, on behalf of some members of his family, had pressed upon him the need to remain loyal to his own personal creations, the *Daily Mail*, the Amalgamated Press and the Newfoundland Development Corporation. Finally, he had recognized that while the degree of power he personally and directly exercised at Carmelite House was absolute, his power at Printing House Square was relative. In his state of health and mind he felt he could hardly hope to alter Printing House Square, at least while Steed was in the chair. Ill though he was he craved for more power. Steed was only another Dawson and worked with the obstructionist Freeman. Could he not make Long or Stuart, people he could work with, Editor in Steed 's place ?

It was not difficult for Rothermere, who disliked all strong Editors, to persuade Northcliffe that there was no financial future for *The Times*, and that he should give it up and return to his proper place at the head of the *Daily Mail*. Northcliffe said he would do this. He privately told Stuart, and its public announcement was to be the sensation of the semi-jubilee banquet that Carmelite House was organizing by way of celebration of the 25th anniversary of the first issue of the *Daily Mail* on May 4, 1896. The feast was to be served on May 1, a Sunday. There were not many days in which to clear up things at Printing House Square. Steed was to be got rid of before the change was effected, but it did not follow that because Northcliffe gave up the control that Walter or Ellerman should have an opportunity to secure it. Rothermere's motives are also not easy to distinguish. The wide political divergence between Northcliffe and Rothermere had not been bridged. Their attitude towards the Government of the day, and towards the Prime Minister especially, was far from identical; though Rothermere had long campaigned against Lloyd George's " policy of waste," he believed in the Coalition and hoped for its continuance. He thought it, incidentally, good journalism to season with criticism the support that the

Sunday Pictorial gave to the Coalition Government. Thus, the Rothermere formula was different from Northcliffe's for the *Daily Mail*. Rothermere could nourish no hope that Northcliffe's return to Carmelite House would mean a reversal of his policy towards Lloyd George. He did, however, himself cherish the ambition of changing the policy of *The Times*. That was, in all circumstances, to be wished. The paper had increased in political significance, even if it had decreased in circulation. To bring *The Times* round to the Government was immensely desirable. It was not impossible if he could persuade his brother to leave it and return to Carmelite House. It was good policy, therefore, for Rothermere to exaggerate the cost to his brother's health of the worry of Printing House Square.

In the meantime it was already being rumoured in Paris, and believed in many quarters, that Northcliffe had already either sold or half-sold *The Times*. Some alleged that the purchaser was Hugo Stinnes. Naturally, Northcliffe heard these stories. To certain intimates he replied that he had not sold his interest in *The Times* although a lot of pressure was being put upon him to limit and even reduce his responsibilities, and his doctors had been warning him to drop some of his more troublesome worries and go for a long sea voyage. But these tales about Stinnes were not likely to alter his course; he relished being the subject of the right sort of gossip, but not gossip about his health. The rumour at last got into type in London. Beaverbrook's *Daily Express* reported that "a great historic newspaper" had been sold. The *Morning Post* denied that the reference was to itself; the *Star* said the *Daily News* was not included in any sale. Fleet Street thought Ellerman had bought Northcliffe's interest in *The Times*. A later rumour was that Sir Davison Dalziel on behalf of a syndicate of Lloyd George's friends had acquired a controlling interest. Lord Iverforth's name was in many mouths and under this scheme Mr. Philip Kerr (later Lord Lothian) was to be the new Editor. Such was the "informed" gossip in London towards the end of April. At this time the Prime Minister, answering a question in the House of Commons, said that "If proceedings were instituted to refute every charge brought by *The Times* newspaper against His Majesty's Government the business of the courts would be hopelessly blocked."[1] Anything, indeed, might have happened between the 23rd and the morning of the 28th. On the evening of the 28th the whole scheme, for simple reasons, collapsed.

[1] April 25, 1921, answering Mr. Mosley.

When on Tuesday, April 26, Northcliffe came back to England he went from Dover straight to Broadstairs, and on the 28th went to Totteridge to report to his mother. He told her on the Thursday how and why he had adopted his brother's plan that he should give up *The Times*, return to the *Daily Mail*, and make the announcement at the banquet due to take place on the following Sunday, *i.e.* May 1. The " Old Lady of Totteridge " utterly disapproved. The idea of Harold supplanting her favourite son, Alfred, at Printing House Square was repugnant, and Mrs. Harmsworth spoke strongly against her son leaving *The Times*. If this were not enough, opposition had also been voiced by Lady Northcliffe and Sir Robert Hudson, whom Steed had warned on Monday the 25th. The combined opposition overwhelmed him. On May 1 Mrs. Belloc Lowndes wrote to Steed to say that Lady Northcliffe had just rung up to tell her that " there was no truth at all in the rumour which was being put about by a certain peer—and that there never would be."

The *Daily Mail* banquet took place without any sensation. It was, nevertheless, a remarkable affair. The jubilee was celebrated on Sunday, May 1, at Olympia, the " largest hall in London." The guests numbered 7,000. The plates laid in readiness numbered 40,000 and there were 75,000 pieces of cutlery. So it was reported. Preceded by Lady Northcliffe, Northcliffe walked in with his mother, aged 83. Grace was said by the Reverend Basil Bourchier, Minister of the parish church of Golders Green. Praying as one of the " frail creatures of Thy providence," he implored Almighty God to pour down " upon this company the dews of Thy heavenly blessing," thus enabling every man to be diligent in his task, " delivered from all selfishness " and governed by a spirit of " harmony, love and goodwill." This being said, the Minister, after a pause, besought the Almighty to be mindful that " Thou has endowed Thy servant Alfred with many singular and excellent gifts. Grant him health and strength, wisdom and power from on high, that he may continue to serve his time and generation, holding ever aloft the torch of Imperial faith, and guiding aright the destinies of this great Empire." This prayer being concluded with " God Save the King," there was sung " God Bless the People," while 945 waitresses, dressed in black and white, made their solemn entry with the dishes. While lunch was proceeding, special editions of Northcliffe's papers were sold outside by newsvendors showing bills lettered " The Chief at Olympia." His speech was delivered to the assembly from a prefabricated gramophone record amplified by five Stentorphone trumpets and a Marconi radio-microphone.

Responding to a toast proposed by the publisher of the *Evening News*, Northcliffe thanked the audience " on behalf of my wife and my mother " for their very cordial greeting. Everything passed off agreeably. The ordeal of *The Times* had not materialized. The paper had not passed into the control of Rothermere and Lloyd George.

The Editor thought the crisis as a whole had passed, and that he would now be able to edit without further interruption. He was wrong. Immediately the Editor found himself face to face with another obstacle. When he received Northcliffe's telegram and letter on April 25 stating that he had decided to sell his holding in *The Times*, he acted upon the counsel he had been given on more than one occasion. Steed had been instructed by Northcliffe to discuss any emergency that might arise with Hudson, who had Northcliffe's confidence. It has been seen that Steed had done this on the 25th. No doubt he guessed that Hudson would discuss Northcliffe's telegrams and letter with Lady Northcliffe, and imagined that she would take prompt action. But he had not approached her directly, nor had he at any time discussed Northcliffe's affairs with her. Nevertheless, the events of April 27-28 convinced Northcliffe that Steed had " talked," and he dropped all communication with him, which was at once a relief and an embarrassment.

All this time the Editor, it has been seen, was preoccupied with the actual Irish crisis and the impending American talks. In his mind the former, as it has been shown, was intimately connected with the latter. The situation, as the Washington Correspondent described it, was that America was not without hope in Japan, she had faith in England, but trust in a Navy equal to hers. In Lewis's phrase, America believed in faith, hope and parity. He put before the Editor the relevant strategical ideas, and measured the backing they were receiving in Washington and thus enabled Steed to clear his mind on the crucial subject of the Anglo-Japanese Treaty. Misunderstanding elsewhere than in Washington still existed about Britain's Japanese commitment. On April 30 the Editor was requested by Lord Derby to say why Northcliffe had made his statement in December, when he conducted the argument with Daniels in *The Times*. Steed explained that Northcliffe " was very anxious about the American belief that in case of hostilities between Japan and the United States, we should be bound to back Japan," and, he proceeded,

Only last Saturday [April 30] I heard from a well-informed Japanese source that the Japanese themselves were not aware of the position.

The matter seems to have been arranged between Sir Edward Grey and Inouye, but Inouye's memorandum to his Government on the subject seems to have been pigeon-holed in the Foreign Office at Tokyo, and to have been entirely overlooked by the successors to the Kato Cabinet. In fact, when *The Times* published last autumn a preliminary statement upon the position, and it was cabled out to Japan, there was a great stir in Tokyo, and Baron Kato telephoned to some of his friends in the Foreign Office to ask whether his administration had in reality been responsible for the arrangement. He was assured that it had. The Japanese were apparently under the impression that in case of hostilities with the United States, England would give them armed support. This impression may account for the persistent belief in Washington—a belief said to be founded upon dispatches from the American Ambassador in Tokyo—that England is in reality bound to fight by the side of Japan. I know that Lord Northcliffe's statement made a deep impression in official circles at Washington.[1]

Derby replied with a suggestion: " I think that if you could come out with some article in which you definitely stated that England would not side with Japan and if you could, in support of that, quote any answers of Ministers—and I expect there must be some statements on this subject by Ministers—it would I think do good."[2] The Editor answered that " We have repeatedly said in leading articles that there is no possibility of England siding with Japan in any armed struggle between Japan and the United States, but I do not think there are any definite statements by Ministers on the point."[3] The position of the Harding Administration toward Europe and disarmament was indicated in a long letter from Lewis:

The administration came to power with a general " practical " policy to fill the interregnum between League and Association—as close an association with Britain and France as a tender care for American interests would permit. If these three countries hang together just now, they can call the tune for the rest of the world. This will carry us over the bad days, until we can find time to work out a more durable relationship. Perhaps the development of such an association between the three powers will show us the way. If it doesn't, at least it will have brought present tangible benefits . . . and so on, and so on. This is the sort of thing Harding said from time to time. . . .

In the beginning, it was not at all desired to let Britain and France know too suddenly that this accord was to go beyond the formal

[1] Steed to Derby, May 2, 1921.
[2] Derby to Steed, May 5, 1921.
[3] Steed to Derby, May 6, 1921.

exchange of friendly assertions. The effect on Britain and France might have been, from the American point of view, unfortunate, to say nothing of the effect on the irreconcilables. An opportunity had to be found, out of which might come an invitation to take a hand, and (as one sees it now) for some time this comedy was played: Britain and France not caring to risk the refusal of an invitation to join them, and America not desiring to raise hopes too high by indicating that an invitation would be welcome . . .

The Correspondent proceeded to more general observations:

Here I hope you won't mind if I speak of Anglo-Franco-American relations as they seem to develop from this angle. Just at present they are (I don't mean on the surface, but actually) about as follows:

Anglo-American	...	...	...	good
Franco-American	...	...	...	dubious
Anglo-French	...	...	...	? ? ? ?

In such a situation, it seems to me clear that any one of the three powers friendly with both the others, will occupy the strongest position so long as the others are in less than complete accord. Now, it will take longer for American doubt of the propriety of French policy in Europe to wear off, than it should take us to freshen up the Entente. There is no doubt that, if the U.S. could arrange things to its own taste, it would be found serving as a sort of *trait-d'union* between us and France, playing one off against the other. Aren't we ideally cast for the part of the *trait-d'union*, however ? In any case, it is certain that the better our relations with France, the better they will be with America—just as it is certain that if we irretrievably broke with France, the whole structure built by " practical " American politicians on the basis of a working and informal accord with Britain and France would come down. This is why I believe that *The Times'* policy of unwavering loyalty to the Entente has been of the greatest service here.[1]

The arrival of this letter was preceded by Harding's " feelers " on disarmament. Lewis cabled the news that the question of disarmament was to be laid before the Supreme Council (June 3). A fortnight later he added :

Outside the region of conjecture . . . and standing solid whatever else may happen, is a plan for an agreement, or understanding, or arrangement—call it what you will so long as you do not call it a formal alliance—between the English-speaking peoples. I assert with the fullest confidence that this is the very backbone of the Administration's policy. (June 15, 1921.)

[1] Lewis to Steed, May 28, 1921.

This passage was quoted in the leading article, which went on to describe the Entente as " the pivot of the only practicable policy for the reconstruction of Europe." The article, in words reminiscent of Lewis's letter, recognized that any quarrel between Great Britain and France would " almost certainly result in a return of America to the policy of ' aloofness '." (June 15.) This, indeed, was the " pivot " of the paper's policy for several years, and was responsible in no small degree for the Editor's conclusion that Lloyd George's policy was dangerous.[1] A combination with America, however welcome, would not enable either Britain or France to dispense with the League. Meanwhile the tools nearest to hand must be used, and of them the best was disarmament. This brought the whole matter back to Japan.

The Far East was a subject that did not, as yet, interest Northcliffe, though within a few months he was to deluge the Editor with cables about the Japanese. In April and May, however, he held aloof, while Steed was occupied simultaneously with his decisions on the King's approaching visit to Belfast,[2] and his dispositions towards the new Administration in Washington. A situation had arisen that would have keenly touched Northcliffe in 1919 and 1920. The Editor, however, was still not favoured with the Chief's views though he received ample information from Lewis. The Washington Correspondent devoted the greater part of a long message to *The Times* to the Japanese problem:

No honest attempt to reflect the opinion of the administration in this matter [disarmament] would be complete unless stress were laid on the fact that no naval arrangement could keep house with an Anglo-Japanese Alliance or (I have ample reason to know) with any modification of our relations with Japan which should leave us formally allied. The matter is of such importance that I have been at pains to secure authoritative information of the official point of view. (June 18, 1921.)

The reasons he assembled were cogent. The United States Government was concerned at the policy of the Japanese militarist party towards China : Great Britain was prevented by her Alliance from supporting any protest the United States Government might make to safeguard the " open door," and the Alliance thus made possible a combination between Great Britain and Japan against the United States and China; the justification of the Alliance, the menace of Russo-German power in the Pacific, was now non-existent; the United States Government could, therefore, see no

---

[1] See Chapters XVI, " The Coalition Stands," and XVIII, " The Coalition Dissolves."
[2] See preceding Chapter.

necessity for renewal. This message was published during the same period as the report of a debate in the House of Commons, and two leading articles on the Alliance. *The Times*, despite a rapidly formed conviction that the Alliance was an embarrassment, was content in June to give general support to Chamberlain's opinion that it should be possible to reconcile the United States to it, and that there could be no question of offending an old friend and tried ally. Steed had no source of information other than the Washington Correspondent in whom he had complete confidence. He had found no substitute for Page and House; he had never been to the United States, and was cut off from Northcliffe.

In June and July there were many complications in the formulation of Anglo-American policy. The Government did much to increase these complications. On July 7 Lloyd George announced that he was awaiting replies from the United States and China before making a statement on the Anglo-Japanese Alliance. This was astonishing, since the United States Government had received nothing that demanded reply, and the phrase was deleted from Hansard on request by the Prime Minister. When Harvey, the American Ambassador, met the Editor next evening, he expressed his belief that the British Government intended anticipating the probable American invitation to a Conference in Washington by sending out invitations to a Conference in London. He warned the Editor that this would not do. Steed had no difficulty in perceiving that friction with a Power to whom Britain owed five million gold dollars on a few days' call was undesirable. He returned to the office to write a leader placing beyond doubt the British acceptance of an invitation to Washington. He emphasized the importance of a straightforward issue which transcended all merely subtle verbal solutions. The main point, the article said, was that the Empire " is certainly ready to discuss, in any form that may be expedient, suggestions for the limitation of armaments in the Pacific, and contingent questions, with the United States and Japan." On the day this appeared, July 9, Harvey asked Steed to visit the Embassy, and there told him that in view of its importance, he had cabled the leading article verbatim to Harding. He added that next Sunday evening he might have something important to say. Steed duly paid his call, and heard that the President had received the cable on a week-end cruise, and had immediately drawn up, with the approval of Hughes (Secretary of State), invitations to a Conference at Washington. Harvey had been instructed to deliver the text to the British Government at once, and had found the Prime

Minister at Chequers, with Curzon, conferring with the Dominion Prime Ministers and drafting the text of the invitation to a London Conference. It was apparent that the American initiative was not welcomed. However, the invitation could not be refused. With this news Steed returned once more to Printing House Square to dictate a leading article, which referred to the situation at Chequers in a manner that was appreciated by those concerned. The official announcement of Harding's proposal of a Conference was published the same day, July 11, 1921. The questions to be considered were, first, disarmament between Great Britain, France, Italy and Japan; and, secondly, Far Eastern problems, to which China was invited.

Next day the composition of the British delegation was under discussion, the names of Lloyd George and Curzon being put forward. In view of what he knew of their activities during the preceding four days, Steed argued that their presence would threaten the hope of agreement on these questions from the start, and he instructed Flanagan that evening to quash in emphatic terms the proposal to head the British Delegation with the Prime Minister and the Foreign Secretary.

The attendance of Mr. Lloyd George or of Lord Curzon at Washington seems particularly undesirable. The pompous and pretentious manner of the Foreign Secretary, his business incapacity, as exhibited in the present state of his Department, and his obsequious docility to the Prime Minister's behests, even when these do not commend themselves to his judgment, unfit him for the discharge of the responsible duties which the mission would impose upon him. The Prime Minister himself has many admirers at home, even among his opponents. The " magnetic influence " of the man, his courage in debate, and his humour appeal to them. But of all statesmen in Europe he is probably the most distrusted. It is notorious that no Government and no statesman who has had dealings with him puts the smallest confidence in him. In America he is widely regarded as the man who encompassed Mr. Wilson with his " wizardry " or, as Mr. Keynes—whose book [*The Economic Consequences of the Peace*] has been largely read in the United States—more brutally puts it, as the man who " bamboozled " the ex-President and was unable to " de-bamboozle " him. . . . The great qualification needed from the representatives of the Empire is a character for conspicuous straightforwardness and honour. We have many such men in our public life, but Mr. Lloyd George is not of them. (July 13, 1921.)

The week was exciting for the Editor. Northcliffe had decided to accept the advice of his doctors and to make a tour round the world. The first stage was to go to New York and Washington, and travel across the continent to Toronto and Vancouver. He was to make this tour unaccompanied by any competent adviser, although he would see political personages and journalists *en route*. A party was given by Lady Northcliffe for the Chief's fifty-sixth birthday on July 15. Steed was invited.[1] After the party Northcliffe returned to Printing House Square and, having dispatched some business with Steed, told him that he had been working hard, looked tired, needed a holiday. Northcliffe then announced that he was sailing next day on the *Aquitania* and pressed Steed to go with him to the United States and even to the Pacific if he liked. The Editor would, he said, have to go to the Washington Conference in any case, and ought to study the position in Canada and the United States beforehand. Suddenly, three days after Lloyd George met De Valera and Craig,[2] Steed saw himself forced to drop all detailed consideration of the Irish crisis and concentrate upon the American problem. The Editor was astonished. Northcliffe had swung himself, or been swung round, to Steed's side. For one thing the Irish problem had, after all, been rightly handled in *The Times*. The paper, in spite of Northcliffe's threats to " provide *The Times* with a proper and entirely British substitute for myself able to take a more active part in its affairs " had done well. Rothermere had not yet obtained the control. Finally, *The Times* had succeeded as a consistent critic of Lloyd George and the Government of the day. Rightly, therefore, in reflecting on his mother's advice, he was glad that he had not given up *The Times* ; nor would he now do so. Wickham Steed was, after all, the incarnation of editorial activity and was personally loyal to himself. The Chief knew that the Editor had his critics inside as well as outside the office. In the circumstances of his own ill-health and absence, the Chief was now prepared to think that Steed at Paris had worked prodigiously for *The Times* and the *Daily Mail*. He had the right idea about the United States and had won the confidence of Colonel House who had long been a close friend of the Chief's. Steed also appreciated the importance of Ireland in relation to America, and he had been right. The meeting of Lloyd George with De Valera and Craig was plain proof of the correctness of Steed's policy.

Northcliffe's lost faith in the Editor had completely revived. When he returned from the tour that the doctors ordered he would work harder than ever at the newspaper. Health came first. He

[1] Long (see footnote on p. 590) also attended this party, at which Smuts publicly invited him to Capetown. Long gave Northcliffe his resignation on their return to the office.

[2] As described in the previous Chapter.

would realize his ambition and renew his vigour by travelling round the world. The Editor would be left uninterruptedly to work out the paper's policy towards the controversies between Britain and America that had come to the surface at Versailles and had now become urgent. It would suit the Editor to accompany him to Washington where he could open doors for him. Together they would go to America, Steed for the first time. Such were the Chief's reflections before astonishing his Editor with the proposal. The office was not pleased. The Editor had only a few hours to get clothes and make the necessary arrangements. As the Manager, Lints Smith, had difficulty in getting a cabin on the *Aquitania* it is probable that Northcliffe had not given any previous thought to taking Steed with him; and Stuart, indeed, had told Northcliffe on April 23 that he declined responsibility for *The Times* if Steed were to remain in the editorial chair while the Chief was absent. Nevertheless, the Editor started with Northcliffe from Waterloo on the afternoon after the party. Among those on the platform were Lady Northcliffe and Lovat Fraser, who remained friendly to Steed while being Rothermere's literary and political henchman. He warned Steed: " Be on your guard. He [Northcliffe] doesn't mean well with you. Don't let him keep you away too long." On board the *Aquitania* at Southampton, just before sailing, Northcliffe had himself photographed with his arm around the Editor's shoulder, and gave instructions for the photograph to be published in the *Daily Mail* and in *The Times* of July 18, " not less than $4\frac{1}{4}$ inches square." He was pleasant to the Editor though he seemed weary; and he was considerably bothered by learning, while he was at sea, that Lord Curzon had instructed the Foreign Office to refuse news facilities to *The Times*, and the British Embassy at Washington to boycott him in revenge for the leading article written, as was thought, by the Editor.[1]

---

[1] A Prime Minister and a Foreign Secretary had not been thus manhandled in *The Times* since the period of Barnes and Delane. *Cf.* Barnes's " thundering " in the issue of July 19, 1834, on Lord Brougham's speech on the Coercion Bill, " It is not often that we feel justified in any strong concurrence of opinion with Conservatives in either House of Parliament, but really neither conscience as regards ourselves, nor justice nor sound policy towards other persons, will permit us to withhold our full acquiescence for the expressions of astonishment, and more than astonishment, which proceeded from some of the Tory Lords on Thursday evening at the contrast between Lord Brougham's vehement speech on the 4th instant in defence of those clauses of the Coercion Bill which aimed at the suppression of seditious meetings, and his contemptuous allusion on Thursday to those very clauses, which he declared he would get rid of if he could! We will venture to say that an inconsistency so palpable, that a levity of political principle so all but preternatural, that a forgetfulness of everything like public decency so wonderful, have never been exhibited by any man conscious of being exposed to the observation of his fellows." Also Delane in *The Times* of February 28, 1851: " What are Ministers or Cabinets to us ? A few months, or at most a few years, and they pass away, to be remembered or forgotten with the Ministers and Cabinets that have gone before them. This journal has survived innumerable public men and political reputations, and we see no reason to suppose that it is approaching the end of its career."

The news of this boycott caused some stir.[1] In the United States the Proprietor and Editor of the journal concerned received greater attention than would otherwise have been the case. This was to prove unfortunate, for soon after arrival in New York on Saturday, July 23, Northcliffe and Steed were involved in a faked interview that, besides gravely damaging *The Times* and the Editor, drew a repudiation, by the King, of words which the " interview " directly attributed to His Majesty.

The circumstances were these. The heat in New York drove Northcliffe out of the city. On Saturday evening a reporter of the *New York Herald* sought to interview him. Steed telephoned the request to Northcliffe who was golfing at New Rochelle. He replied : " You know my mind," and instructed Steed to give his known views. Steed dictated a statement to the *New York Herald* and corrected the proof. Then Adolph Ochs, proprietor of the *New York Times*, asked Steed to visit his office and to make a statement for publication in Northcliffe's name. On Northcliffe's instructions, Steed dictated the statement to a reporter of the *New York Times*. Naturally, the chief interest of both reporters was the Irish question,[2] in particular the King's attitude. There had been some American discussion of this topic since the disclosure in the Press of a divergence of opinion between the King and the Prime Minister. At the time, Madame de la Panouse, the wife of the French Military Attaché in London, who moved in " court circles," had collected a great deal of gossip which she communicated regularly to André Géraud (" Pertinax "), former correspondent in London and then Foreign Editor of the *Echo de Paris*. From London, she sent Pertinax in Paris an account of an exchange between the King and the Prime Minister. As Pertinax thought the story too sensational to be used in the *Echo de Paris*, he put it into a cable which he was then sending regularly to an American news agency. Several American newspapers published the story on the eve of Northcliffe's and Steed's arrival in New York.

[1] On July 18, Mr. Hogge asked a question to which the Prime Minister thus replied : " I need hardly explain that official information is available to *The Times* through the ordinary agencies. The fullest courtesy has at all times been extended to its representatives. The fact that it has pursued a course of virulent opposition to the Government and notably to the head of the Government has not in the least influenced the Government departments . . . personally I have made no effort to induce the withdrawal of a single civility from *The Times*. . . . On Wednesday, the 13th instant, however, *The Times* published a personal attack of a peculiarly offensive and mischievous character upon the Secretary of State for Foreign Affairs, with special reference to some momentous and delicate negotiations . . . In spite of its record in recent years, *The Times* is still supposed in many circles abroad to represent both educated and official opinion in this country . . . It is therefore essential that the British Government as a whole should mark strongly its disapproval of such an attack upon the Secretary of State for Foreign Affairs at a critical moment." (Hansard, cols. 1747-1749.)

[2] For the Irish policy of *The Times* and the King's speech in Belfast on June 22, 1921, see the previous Chapter.

After Steed, in the name of Northcliffe, had dictated his statement on Saturday, July 23, to the *New York Times*, he visited the office of the newspaper to correct the reporter's manuscript before it was sent to the compositor. This done, the manuscript was initialled. In the morning's issue (Sunday, July 24) Steed was astounded to find his statement, dictated in the name of Northcliffe, published in an obscure position, while an alleged "interview," composed with benefit of double-leading and printed on the front page, was attributed to "H. Wickham Steed, the Editor of the *London Times*, who arrived with Lord Northcliffe on Saturday on the *Aquitania* and who will travel with him as far as Vancouver, B.C." He was alleged to have said that King George had played a very active part in bringing about a settlement of the Irish question and had gone to Belfast with that intention. The alleged interview continued:

It is not generally known that under the constitutional form of government the King has still a good deal of power when he chooses to use it. In this case he has done so with good effect. At the last meeting he had with Lloyd George before leaving for Ireland the King asked him "Are you going to shoot all the people in Ireland?" "No, your Majesty," the Premier replied. "Well, then," said the King, "you must come to some agreement with them. This thing cannot go on. I cannot have my people killed in this manner." When King George went to Ireland he went with the intention of making his own speech, just as his uncle, the Duke of Connaught, had done in India in the previous year.

Proceeding, the paragraph said that:

The King spoke as the head of the British Empire and not as King of England or of Ireland. "He got under the skin of the Irish people by his generosity and that is what gave them confidence in the peace overtures which they would not have felt in the Lloyd George Cabinet without his backing."

It was the King, too, Steed was alleged to have said,

who saw Smuts and got him interested in the Irish question. I know that the latter had a great deal to do with winning over the Sinn Feiners to the idea of a conference and making peace with England without separation from the Empire. He told them what he knew about the ideal Republican government and that they were just as well off with the constitutional form of management in Great Britain under their own local government. When Lloyd George and the Cabinet realized the feeling of the King and the people on the question of peace with Ireland, the invitation to de Valera to come to London

Lord Northcliffe and the Editor on the Aquitania, July 17, 1921.

followed in 48 hours. When King George sailed for Ireland the Cabinet tried to spike his efforts by making speeches in the Lords and Commons three hours afterwards which were intended to irritate the Irish people. This annoyed the English people very much and when the King returned he had the biggest reception outside of Buckingham Palace he had ever received since the war began in August, 1914.

Obviously the *New York Times* had scored over the *Herald* by putting into Steed's mouth direct statements of what the King had said to the Prime Minister. The source of parts of this material was a general conversation outside the interview that Steed had with the reporter about the King's desire for peace and his general solicitude for all his people. Steed, who had never before been to the United States, had no idea that such a conversation would be given precedence over his genuine interview dictated and initialled after reading. Nor was he aware of the " Pertinax " story published just before his arrival. But Northcliffe, of course, knew well the low standards of reporting customary in New York. Yet, during Sunday morning, when Hillier, assistant to Bullock, the New York Correspondent of *The Times*, telephoned to Northcliffe at Bullock's house for instructions how to deal with this " interview," and with the authorized statements Steed had made in Northcliffe's name, he was ordered to cable everything. Not only so, but he was ordered, without consultation with Steed, to transmit the whole as having been said by Northcliffe himself. Accordingly, the " interview " was despatched to Carmelite House in Northcliffe's name.[1] Of all this Steed knew nothing.

The Northcliffe " interview " attracted little notice in America. In England it exploded with the force of a bomb. In accordance with instructions, it was published in the *Daily Mail*, appearing in the Irish edition which was printed in Manchester. In due course it would have appeared in all the London editions but for the fact that the News Editor of the *Daily Mail* (Tom Clarke) consulted Stuart who ordered its suppression, under the power of attorney that he possessed. Caird, too, had learnt from Brumwell that *The Times* would not publish it. Freeman had at once seen that Northcliffe or Steed had been victimized and

[1] On publication, Steed at once protested to the *New York Times*, but the editor was out of town until the evening of Monday. In the meantime he authorized the *Philadelphia Public Ledger* and Reuter to deny the authenticity of the " interview." Overnight, on Sunday, he went, at Northcliffe's wish, to Washington and was busy for four days making arrangements for the Chief's projected visit to Washington. Both the proprietor of the *New York Times*, the late Adolph Ochs, and his son-in-law A. H. Sulzberger, the present proprietor, afterwards apologized to Steed for the way he had been treated in their journal. Adolph Ochs also expressed regret to Northcliffe though, as Northcliffe told Steed, Ochs was unwilling to dismiss the responsible offender, the managing editor, van Anda.

that publication would be the height of indiscretion. There followed a week of excitement, during which the office heard nothing direct, either from the Chief or from the Editor. Stuart as Managing Director was in close touch with the lawyers. Sir Charles Russell warned him that a writ of criminal libel might well be issued against *The Times*.

It was not until Friday, July 29, when Northcliffe arrived in Washington and he and Steed read the London cables, that they measured the immensity of the scandal created. For three days the British Press had reported and commented upon what was called " An Amazing Indiscretion " and " The Great Interview Mystery." Towards the end of the week, when the *New York Times*, correcting the *Daily Mail*'s statement, said that the interview was with Steed and not with Lord Northcliffe, Fleet Street's interest became even more intense. Journalists were eager to know why Monday's first edition of the *Daily Mail* could have said that the interview was by Northcliffe and why it appeared in one edition only and not at all in *The Times*. During the Friday on which the Proprietor and Editor arrived in Washington, the Prime Minister, on the motion for the adjournment of the House of Commons, said that statements had appeared in the Irish and English Press attributing words to the King of grave consequence relating to Irish policy. " It is quite impossible always to follow these [Northcliffe's] calumnious statements but here they are of a very categorical character and attribute very serious statements to the Sovereign. Moreover, they are calculated at the present moment, if believed, to prejudice seriously the chances of an Irish settlement and they have been circulated very freely, more especially in Ireland." The King had therefore authorized the Prime Minister to read the following statement on his behalf :

His Majesty the King has had his attention directed to certain statements, reporting an interview with Lord Northcliffe, appearing in the *Daily Mail* and reproduced in the *Daily Express* and some of the Irish newspapers. The statements contained in the report are a complete fabrication. No such conversations as those which are alleged took place, nor were any such remarks as those which are alleged made by His Majesty. His Majesty further desires it to be made quite clear, as the contrary is suggested in the interview, that in his speech to the Parliament of Northern Ireland he followed the invariable constitutional practice relating to Speeches from the Throne in Parliament.

" I hope that this announcement," the Prime Minister added, " may do something to sterilize the effects of the criminal

A LITTLE CONTRETEMPS.

HE STEED THROWS HIS RIDER: An Incident in the Northcliffe Hunt.

iip, and Miss Royden and her friends have at | where, I expect, the honeysuckle is as plenti

toon drawn by the late Sir F. Carruthers Gould printed in the *Westminster*
ette of August 4, 1921.

malignity which, for personal ends, is endeavouring to stir up mischief between the Allies, and misunderstanding between the British Empire and the United States, and to frustrate the hopes of peace in Ireland." British officials in Washington were not slow to follow the Prime Minister's example. A reception to be given to Northcliffe by the British Ambassador, Sir Auckland Geddes, was suddenly cancelled. This created an embarrassing situation, for, on the same Friday, Northcliffe and Steed were received by President Harding. Both were received together, and both without the introduction of the British Ambassador. They remained with the President for one hour and twenty minutes, the longest private audience ever given in the White House.[1] The relations of Chief and Editor were now better than they had been for more than a year. Northcliffe's action as soon as, he read the London cables, was immediate and correct. He cabled to Lord Stamfordham on Friday, " Please convey to His Majesty with my humble duty my denial of ever having ascribed to His Majesty the words, or any such words as were stated by the Prime Minister, I gave in that interview." Lord Stamfordham replied next day, " I have communicated to the King your message received by me this morning. His Majesty is glad that it confirms the statement made on his authority by the Prime Minister in the House of Commons yesterday."[2]

Steed remained unaware that the bogus " interview " had been cabled to London in Northcliffe's name. A brief statement to a Philadelphia journal on Monday, the 25th, was not published until Saturday. In it he made it plain that since he could not have possessed any knowledge of what passed between the King and the Prime Minister he could not have quoted their conversation. As to the reporter's action, " It was not a question of violation of confidence, which would have been bad enough. I never said it at all." The feeling of Freeman, Richmond and others was wholly on the side of Steed who, it was believed, had been misrepresented and misreported. The paper's friends and the Chief's relatives were gravely perturbed. Lady Northcliffe wired that she was " greatly distressed and ill with worry. Situation here quite intolerable." Hudson implored him " to observe silence," Rothermere urged him to " dispense with the services of Steed at the earliest possible moment." Northcliffe, however, was now

[1] *The Times*, it has been seen above (p. 603), had been of service to George Harvey, the American Ambassador in London, over the constitution and location of the Disarmament Conference.

[1] Sir Edward Grigg, the Prime Minister's private secretary, told Ralph Walter that Mr. R. W. Poole, of Lewis and Lewis, had been instructed to take action against *The Times* but that the King had restrained the Prime Minister. Stamfordham saw Grigg on July 29, 1921.

completely loyal to the Editor, and assured Rothermere by an explicit telegram, and instructed his secretary to confirm by letter, that the Editor was not to be blamed. Copies of the letter went to Lady Northcliffe, Sutton, Hudson and John Walter :

Dear Lord Rothermere,

My Chief wishes me to send you the following copy of a cabled statement which has just arrived from him:

" Steed did not give interview and complained last Monday about it full stop I did not hear of it till Parliamentary discussion Friday. Am giving no interviews but cannot prevent correspondents following and writing. Campbell [Stuart] will explain how things are done here. Am not worrying and my golf excellent."

Yours very truly,
H. G. PRICE. July 31, 1921.

To Walter he later wrote himself:

My dear Walter,

I hope you will not mind my saying I think it unkind of you to send a public telegram to Steed (as you know, every telegram in this country is public) about a matter for which he was in no way to blame. Steed has my absolute confidence. As I have said to Campbell Stuart, if you read the statement he has attacked the Queen don't believe it. The editor of a paper came on to my train last night and talking over this matter said, " You seem to take interviews quite seriously in England." Here, if you don't give one, they invent one. The reporter is sent out to get something and he has got to get it.

Kind regards,
Yours sincerely,
NORTHCLIFFE.

This closed the incident. On the first stage of his world tour Northcliffe alternated between fits of bounding energy, prophetic speechifying and dull lassitude which are reflected in the pages of the book that he compiled on his return, which was published after his death,[1] and in his correspondence with Steed.

After accompanying Northcliffe to Vancouver, and studying the Japanese menace to British Columbia, Steed went to San Francisco and thence to Washington where he consulted the Navy Department upon naval prospects in the Pacific. The Editor thus reported to Northcliffe:

I had excellent talks at Washington during my second visit with the principal people we saw during our first visit, and think I have shaped really good relations. . . . At New York, the Sulgrave Institution gave me a delightful dinner, attended by about 60 of the " best

---

[1] It was edited by his brothers Cecil and St. John and appeared under the title of *My Tour Round the World*. See Appendix II, Sources, XIV.

inds," with John W. Davis[1] at their head. The speeches were
confidential, but what Davis said about you and *The Times* and
ne would have made you blush. . . . In reply I talked to them about
the Washington Conference, urged them all to give every possible
support to Harding and Hughes in what I called " your President's
sublimely dangerous initiative." I alluded discreetly to the dangers,
and said they could only be averted by real and trustful cooperation
between the English-speaking peoples—and I added that for the
purposes of the Washington Conference at least, remember that
France speaks English.[2] The idea that there could be any danger
in the Washington Conference came as a bombshell to everybody
present, except Davis, and after some discussion, they all thanked
me for having opened their eyes to an aspect of the business which
they had not before appreciated.

Having verified at Ottawa his impressions of Canadian policy
in the event of a clash between the United States and Japan,
he sailed from Quebec on September 10. On board the *Empress
of Britain* he wrote a memorandum on British policy in the
Pacific, based on observations he had made at Vancouver,
San Francisco, Washington, Ottawa and Montreal.[3] Copies
of the memorandum were sent to Lord Stamfordham, Sir William
Tyrrell and Lord Beatty. The latter returned a practical reply :

> As you say, the British attitude towards the U.S.A.-Japan situation
> will be of paramount importance, and the outcome of the Conference
> will affect profoundly the naval policy of this Country. I do not agree
> that Japan could sweep the U.S.A. off the Pacific and capture Hawaii.
> Doubtless, however, Japan could capture the Philippines, Guam and
> Yap, and make themselves masters of Eastern Asia, and the achieve-
> ment of these objectives could not be viewed with equanimity by the
> British Empire. Were we, unhappily, drawn into the conflict,
> however, we should be able to counter the capture of the Philippines,
> Yap and Guam, provided we had six weeks to get our fleet to eastern
> waters.[4]

The Editor's return to Printing House Square at the end of September was a mere interval before his journey back to Washington
in order to report the Conference; but it was an interval that was
turned to good advantage. The Irish Conference was due to hold
a further meeting in Downing Street on October 11, and Steed had
the satisfaction of being in the office when success was confidently
predictable.

Northcliffe was in China and Japan just before the Washington

---

[1] George Harvey's predecessor at the American Embassy in London.
[2] For the French attitude towards American proposals see Appendix II, Sources, XIV.
[3] The text of this memorandum is given in the Appendix II, *ibid*.
[4] Beatty to Steed, September 26, 1921.

Conference was timed to begin. Unaware of information the Editor had gathered in Canada and the United States, he sent the Editor numerous messages urging a change of policy, and ascribing the paper's ignorance on trends in Japanese policy to the misleading of the Tokyo Correspondent, like Reuter's, by Japanese. He also found the Government of Northern China was dominated by Japan, and he described the methods which were subordinating China to Japan. Even the Chinese delegates to the Conference had been appointed under Japanese pressure,[1] and thus were not representative of South China, which was politically independent of the North.

Japan [he concluded] is rapidly squeezing everybody out of China; she has the Marshall and Caroline Islands and she is spreading out towards America by the Aleutian Islands. . . . I greatly blame *The Times*—and myself, of course, chiefly. We have been supine and ignorant and duped. My mind was for so many years looking towards the war—and looking at the war when it came, that I did not pay sufficient attention to the Far East. I ought to have made this journey ten years ago. Seeing is believing.[2]

Plainly, the policy of *The Times*, pro-Japanese since 1900, was ripe for reconsideration. Fundamental Pacific strategy must needs occupy the Conference. There remained, however, abundant reason for caution. The Editor, before leaving for the United States a second time, laid down the procedure for the office during his absence :

Unless precise suggestions are sent to the contrary by me or Willmott Lewis from Washington, there should be no reference whatever in leading articles to the beneficent part which the British Delegation may play as mediator between Japan and the United States. Any idea that the British Delegation are trying to run the Conference by mediating or manoeuvring would anger the Americans, and tend to destroy the influence of our Delegation.

The fundamental consideration for us in Washington will be that if, by any chance, there should be a conflict between the United States and Japan in the Pacific, it may not be physically possible for the British Empire to remain neutral, not on account of any solidarity between English-speaking nations, but because some parts of the Empire, notably Western Canada, would take up a hostile attitude towards Japan.

The line of argument in commenting upon the position of Japan should be to suggest that Japan in her own well-considered interests should not adopt a policy that might expose her to incalculable risks. But, in all comment, there should be an undercurrent of friendliness

[1] The statement was published in *The Times* under Northcliffe's name on October 29, when the information was described as obtained from the South China Government.
[2] Northcliffe to Steed, October 29, 1921.

owards Japan, without a superfluous word of praise. We can praise
er enough if and when she has come into line.

Wherever possible, credit must be given to the United States for
resident Harding's initiative in convening the Conference; and the
uty of all Powers to assist unselfishly in making the Conference a
uccess should be emphasized. As far as Great Britain and France
re concerned, their success will come in the prevention of war in
ie Pacific, that is to say, the avoidance of the ruin of our Far Eastern
rade, and, perhaps, of a very serious strain upon the cohesion of the
mpire.

It should be remembered that the British Delegation at Washington
an do nothing unless it is trusted by the United States Government,
nd that, generally, our object should be to promote and develop
hat trust in every way possible.

If the question of War Debts arises in connection with the
onference, we should not give any countenance spontaneously to
ie idea of the cancellation of our debt by the United States. Should
ny proposals of that kind be made, they must come from America,
nd be put forward in the interests of America herself. We should
hen examine them cautiously, without enthusiasm, and support
hem only in so far as they may be part of a general scheme to ease
he economic situation of the world, and to restore international
rade.

Having written the memorandum reproduced above, the
ditor conferred with Freeman and other members of the staff.
As he reported to Northcliffe:

I have instilled into everybody, from the highest quarters down-
vards, that should there be a conflict in the Pacific, we must
tand with the U.S. from the word " go," not only because the future
f the English-speaking world will depend upon it, but because it
vill be physically impossible for the British Empire to remain neutral.
his is now understood, and it is also understood that the best, if
ot the only chance of keeping the Japs from running amok will be
o let them understand what the position will be if they pursue an
ggressive policy.[1]

The Editor's next task was to put his policy into print. In
rinting House Square opinion had so far favoured a strict
imitation of the subjects on the Washington agenda. Armaments
ouched the emotions as well as the savings of the public.
On the Pacific, " an area that vitally concerns the British Empire "
September 22), England was less sensitive. In a series of exposi-
ory articles with which he prefaced the report of the Conference,
he Editor surveyed the intricate questions that would confront
he delegates. He believed that to regard the disarmament

[1] Steed to Northcliffe, October 25, 1921.

question as separate from Far Eastern problems (in Lewis's opinion, on November 4, the prevalent view in America) would be a grave mistake.

It should be definitely understood that no reduction in armaments or military and naval expenditure can be feasible without a solution of the grave political problems which lie in the foreground—and that no past or present commitments, obligations, or desires for theoretical consistency can be allowed to stand between the civilized world and the avoidance of a fresh conflict that might render civilization itself merely a memory and a name.

Japan's special position and needs should be considered but in conjunction with the limits to which the United States and the other Pacific Powers, whose interests were identical, were prepared to go. The assassination of the Japanese Prime Minister at this time was disturbing since he had been one of the moderates. But

there is . . . reason to believe that the most enlightened and circumspect Japanese statesmen well understand that a pursuit of the aims commonly attributed to the Japanese General Staff would antagonize the British commonwealth of nations as inevitably and swiftly as the United States itself. (November 8, 1921.)

As ever, the touchstone of Japan's attitude was her policy towards China: " The most important question centres upon the future of China and the policy of Japan towards that country " (November 12). Steed kept this question constantly before the minds of readers. In his opinion the Conference would fail if it did not find an answer to the question " What is China? " (November 9, 18 and 23). " We are treading through a maze in a fog," he quoted from an American aphorist on November 9. Two articles on Japan by Harold Williams reinforced his messages. The first described the historical distribution of territory in the Pacific, stressing the domination of the United States and Japan in the north (November 9). The second discussed the problems Japan faced. Her need to expand necessarily implied a threat to China, and the chaos in the Empire gave Japan (as Russia formerly) the opportunity to use pressure.

The Conference opened dramatically with Hughes's proposal of a 10-year naval holiday on the basis of a 5-5-3 ratio for British, American, and Japanese capital ships. This met with general approval from the delegates, and produced the energetic, practical atmosphere from which the happiest results could be hoped. Steed awaited Japan's answer with keen interest. He felt justified in hoping that her friendly reception of the proposal meant that she was encouraged by the frank sincerity of the United States. On November 15 he pointed out that she need not fear that her international position would be injured by any agreement. The next day Japan's acceptance was announced, but with reservations in the form of a counter-proposal favouring herself. In the Far East Japan again showed a friendly spirit : she was willing to withdraw from Siberia if a stable government were established, she denied territorial ambitions in Manchuria, and was ready to make a bargain over Shantung. America made no declaration of Far Eastern policy beyond adherence to the tradition of the " open door " and its attendant implications. The atmosphere was, in fact, conciliatory. *The Times*, however, was preparing a change of policy. A cable from Northcliffe, relayed immediately to Steed, described the salient features of the Far Eastern situation, and the menace presented there by Japanese " exclusiveness." He concluded that only Anglo-American unity would impress Japan. The question had only been superficially discussed between Northcliffe and Steed when they were together in Washington during August. Northcliffe's cable in November was definite :

ESTABLISHMENT ANGLO-AMERICAN UNITY THEREFORE OUGHT PRIME OBJECT BRITISH POLICY FOR UPON DEGREE IT ATTAINED DEPENDS WHOLE FUTURE FAREAST PAPER SHOULD VERY STRONGLY AND QUICKLY ADVOCATE ABROGATION ANGLO JAPANESE ALLIANCE[1]

China's case, as presented at Washington, was prejudiced by the unhappy state of the country. A fresh outbreak against her weak Government coincided with the Conference. On November 18 the Peking Correspondent frankly blamed Japan. Whether or not responsibility was hers, the problem of restoring order was immediate. It was also clear that, in spite of the protest of her delegation, China was unable herself to control the situation. The office was insistent that the delegation was not representative, and that China must remain under the protection of the Pacific Powers; also Japanese influence was undesirably prevalent, for which the Anglo-Japanese Alliance was blamed. There was no longer any hesitation. *The Times* now flatly said that no improvement could be expected until the Alliance was merged in a larger Pacific agreement (November 21 and 23). On the 23rd the leading article said firmly that " the Agreement is obsolete, and obsolete treaties themselves become a menace to the peace they were formed to protect." Not only did the Alliance hamper settlement

[1] Northcliffe to Steed, November 16, 1921.

in China. War between Japan and any Pacific Power would involve the British Empire, some part of which would inevitably oppose Japan. Taken together with the long-standing American dislike of the Alliance, these reasons made abrogation imperative. A message from the Editor frankly compared the ruling class of Japan with pre-war Germany. It was the most serious contribution to the discussion that Steed had, so far, sent and deserves quotation.

During the events in Europe that marked the growth of the crisis which ended in the Great War, and during the war itself, the attention of the world was deflected from Pacific and Far Eastern questions and concentrated on European issues. Japan, however, attended to matters within her immediate sphere of interest and gradually adopted a policy which culminated in the presentation of the famous Twenty-one Demands to China.[1] It seemed at times as though the Japanese General Staff were pursuing a Pan-Asiatic policy not unlike the Pan-German policy pursued by the German General Staff before and during the war, until it brought Germany to grief. In Japan this policy of military and economic expansion did not go unchallenged. The wiser sections of Japanese opinion understood that successive encroachments on China must in the long run bring about a conflict in which the position of Japan in the world would be at stake. They advocated, therefore, a policy of reasonable economic and political evolution as against the eventually catastrophic Imperialistic designs attributed to the General Staff. (December 1, 1921.)

In the next day's paper he concluded his analysis with a warning:

The time has come to speak with the utmost frankness. The Japanese delegation insists upon the allotment to Japan of 70 per cent. of the British or American capital ship strength. In the unanimous opinion of the British and American naval authorities, this demand is not warranted. It is justified neither by the present nor the prospective strength of the Japanese Navy: therefore, Japanese insistence raises the question of the ulterior political intentions of Japan. (December 2, 1921.)

As to that policy there were four possibilities. Japan might be threatening China, using the Alliance as a lever to extract Anglo-American assent to what bargains she wanted, she might be bent on a militarist Pan-Asiatic policy, or, finally, she might intend to challenge the British Empire.

The Times duly published these messages, though Freeman naturally emphasized the regret felt at the change that British

[1] See above, Chapter X, " Northcliffe *v.* the Editor."

policy towards Japan had undergone, and laid stress on the value and strength of Anglo-American concord. By December 3 Steed could report that a four-nation treaty abrogating the Anglo-Japanese Agreement could be expected. The draft provisions were announced on the 5th, and awaited Imperial consent in Tokyo. Although the leading article described the new prospect as promising peace, Steed could not let Japan's conduct pass unrebuked.

Japan has not, indeed, suffered any loss of dignity, and still less any curtailment of her true interests at the Conference, but her spokesmen have repeatedly found themselves on the defensive, and obliged to explain and give assurances instead of leading the way with a broad self-denying policy with which the other Pacific Powers could have gladly associated themselves. (December 10, 1921.)

The Editor felt bound to urge the necessity for speed, since the economic crisis at home was leading to a growing pressure upon America to discuss European affairs, either then at Washington or at a future conference. Not everything was going smoothly. The attitude of France on the naval question was disquieting. She was highly resentful of the American refusal to ratify the Convention of June 28, 1919, which promised support to France against any new German attack. She was equally resentful of the British repudiation of her part in the Convention. Her demand for an increased ratio created in America the suspicion that she was developing into a militarist Power. On the 19th it was announced that France had yielded on the figure for capital ships, but her attitude on the submarine question was less satisfactory. The full effect of the French attitude was evident in the stiffening of Japan over Shantung (December 22) where Japanese concessions signified to Steed a wish " to retain the reality of control while sacrificing merely its appearance."

Lewis resumed the correspondence on the 30th with a message to the effect that

bluntly and briefly the situation is that upon France will now fall the blame for any development of a nature to diminish the achievement of the Conference, and that, secure in this fact, Japan may harden her heart against the adoption of that liberal policy in regard to China without which no amicable settlement of the Pacific problems is possible. It was a Japanese writer who early in the Conference said that Japan had lost a golden opportunity to assume the leadership at the adjustment of Far Eastern affairs. She has made concessions, it is true, but they have lacked any air of free and generous renunciation. How now, if following the example of France, she should hold out in Shantung and Manchuria for " safeguards " which could and would be seen to be no more than Imperialism in disguise ? In the opinion of every American with whom I have talked such a course would gravely prejudice ratification of the Quadruple Pacific Treaty by the Senate.[1]

So far its attitude towards that Treaty has been friendly but non-committal. When it comes up for discussion it will be examined in relation to the course of action which the Powers, and particularly Japan, agree upon in regard to China. It will stand or fall as the answer is No or Yes to the question whether it tends to guarantee Japan in possession of the benefits she has secured from China by threat or by force. If the answer is Yes, no amount of textual proof of the harmlessness of the Quadruple Pact will avail to set off the belief that the spirit of Imperialism is behind it, and Senators who to-day are undecided will join the ranks of those who already condemn it.

Steed, before sailing, supplemented Lewis's message with the observation that on success at Washington would depend the whole extent of any future American participation in European affairs. (December 31.)[2]

New Year hopes of an early settlement were disappointed, though the Shantung question did at last seem to be approaching conclusion. Lewis suspected that the United States delegation was holding up the Naval Limitation Treaty until Shantung was settled (January 18 and 23, 1922). Thus the success of the Conference hung on a railway. Japan had conceded much but she insisted on retaining some control. The arrangement proposed was that China should buy the line with a loan from Japan, due for repayment in five to fifteen years, and in case of non-payment the line would revert to Japan. Until payment was complete the Japanese would retain control in the form of a Japanese traffic manager or accountant, or both. (January 21.) The arrangements for the disposal of the Shantung railway had been approved by the British and American delegations. China's decision was now awaited.

On February 1 the Naval Treaty was announced. Not only was this a signal achievement for peace in itself, but, cabled Lewis the same day, " it removes—or should remove—any doubt as to the adhesion of all the Powers here present to the treaties now

---

[1] During the fight in the Senate over the Peace Treaty American resentment at the Japanese occupation of Shantung materially contributed to non-ratification.

[2] Steed's last message from Washington was written after Christmas, when he left to attend the Cannes Conference.

being drafted concerning the Chinese mainland." The combination of the Naval Treaty and the Quadruple Pact, abrogating the Anglo-Japanese Alliance, made it possible, he continued next day, for "the United States to call on the British Empire for countenance and support without fear that loyalty to an ally or distrust of a naval competitor will condition the response." The effect of this unity between the English-speaking nations was seen when the Twenty-one Demands made by Japan upon China were finally discussed. Although Japan maintained their validity, she made sufficient concessions to satisfy China (February 4 and 6, 1922). It seemed as if the Imperial teeth had been drawn. But neither Steed nor Lewis was under any illusion. Lewis thus summed up the work of the Conference on February 6. First, as to China, he said :

This mass of treaties and resolutions cannot be fully understood unless they are seen as related to one great objective—encouragement of China to seek her own liberty, her own freedom from foreign tutelage, her own unfettered sovereignty. From the outset it has been clear that no more than this could be achieved here, that China in the last resort must save herself.

Next the Correspondent noted that

Japan undoubtedly is awake to the change which the Conference has brought about. It is her military Imperialism in China and Siberia which has been chiefly in question at Washington and she is now left to consider what her relationship to the American, British, Chinese, and Russian peoples (to name only these) must eventually be if her policy is to be continued. Her concessions in Shantung, her withdrawal of the most exorbitant of the Twenty-one Demands, her acquiescence in regard to other action to be taken in China—all this means that she has seen the writing on the wall. If she has not receded as much as impatient friends of China and exasperated foreigners in the Far East would have desired it is perhaps because she believes the ink of that writing may fade. She waits to see in what spirit the Powers—and chiefly the United States and the British Empire—will carry out the engagements they have here entered into.

So far, so good : a confidential memorandum on Far Eastern policy, dated March 31 and circulated in the office at the beginning of April, laid down the line to be adopted in the immediate future, and prescribed the creation of a public opinion that would keep the Government up to the mark and compel it to deal firmly with all

Japanese delinquencies. The Editor was not willing to suppose that the Japanese had changed their plan in consequence of the Washington Conference, though they might change their tactics. The Washington Agreements would give an opportunity for greater control over Japanese action by " an association of Powers." It was an opportunity that must be used to the full. Public opinion should insist on every advantage being taken of the Washington decisions, imperfect as they were; other wise the odium Great Britain had incurred through appearing by loyalty to the Anglo-Japanese Treaty to countenance the grasping and oppressive policy of Japan would be incurred in heavier measure by all the Powers associated in the Washington Agreements. Evil results to white civilization would follow; so the Editor believed. He did not at the time follow up this line of thought.

A major intervention from Northcliffe, who had arrived at Marseilles on February 18, 1922, confused all the Editor's plans. A happy new year was not to be vouchsafed to him.

XV

AFTER NORTHCLIFFE'S WORLD TOUR

FOR the creator of the most powerful single engine of publicity ever known, and for the architect of the most spectacular political career in modern history, 1922 was a year of fate. Northcliffe and Lloyd George, parties to one of the most significant of all wartime political alliances which had become one of the bitterest peacetime antagonisms, never met after the Armistice. For the next three years they exchanged nothing but abuse. At the opening of the new year both men were buoyant. In the summer Northcliffe died and in the autumn Lloyd George went into permanent political exile. For a full year *The Times* office was the destined theatre of dramatic changes and desperate expedients unparalleled in its hundred and thirty-seven years. Among them was the threatened supersession, which all but succeeded, of the Editor by the ex-Prime Minister. The old year, it has been seen, was pregnant with anxiety for the office, above all to the Editor; compared with the new year it was a holiday.

Northcliffe, homeward bound from Penang, celebrated New Year's Day by sending a Napoleonic telegram in his most flamboyant style remembering " everyone I am fond of, all the great armies of people who work for me on the St. Lawrence in Canada, Newfoundland, Paris, Manchester, London, Gravesend and everywhere else." How proud and happy he was to know that his confidence in his staffs, and their confidence in him, had never been so great as on this New Year's Day ! Before Midsummer Day, he was to wire from Switzerland to Sutton at Carmelite House in a different key: " I shall give you all hell when I get back." The " great armies " knew the Chief had not been really well since his operation in 1919[1]; they had seen him go on the world tour in July, 1921. The ranks took it for granted, now that he had returned, that he had also recovered. They were quickly to have more than sufficient evidence that " The

---

[1] See Chapter XI, " A New Editor," above.

Chief" was so well that he would stir up "everyone I am fond of" whether at Carmelite House or at Printing House Square. Both staffs had long experience of the Chief's energy. As the world tour reached its close the more spasmodic he became. Somehow he was physically exhausted but his mental activity was quickened. He was soon to show them new aspects of his unpredictability.

Northcliffe always felt braced by a first of January. The present was no exception. The combination of a new year and his being nearer home gave him immense vitality. Landing at Colombo, the Chief was quickly on the mainland investigating, challenging, arguing with all in reach, and planning or deciding for the future. All oriental news was tainted. "Outside Washington, Paris, Berlin, Rome, Madrid, Petrograd, my news services must be combined and personally inspected every year," he wrote to Steed. At this time (January 6-13, 1922) the Editor was at Cannes for the Anglo-French Conference and Freeman was in charge of the paper.[1] While Briand outraged French opinion by allowing Lloyd George to teach him golf, and Millerand was forced to send for Poincaré, Northcliffe progressed on his journey. He was at Beirut on February 11, Port Said on the 13th. He arrived at Marseilles on the 18th. Reaching Europe by these stages he showered letters and cables upon Walter, Steed, Freeman, Lints Smith and, of course, Sutton. It was not the fortunes of the Coalition that interested him. He had forgotten Lloyd George for the moment. His own "mighty structures" interested him more. As arranged, he put up on February 19 at Cap d'Ail, near Nice, to rest after the journey. In the library he found back numbers of The Times, the Weekly Edition, the Literary Supplement and the Educational Supplement. On the table was a welcoming telegram sent from the Editor in the name of the staff expressing the hope of seeing him in London shortly. On the following day he received from Stuart the trading accounts for the second half of 1921. These were the figures that the management had interpreted as showing at least that The Times had passed a dangerous corner. The Chief saw them in a very different light. He addressed a telegram to Stuart, Steed, Lints Smith and Freeman. It gave little prospect of the Chief's return being a round of pleasure for them:

FEBRUARY 22nd. IN VIEW APPALLING GROSS FIGURES JUST RECEIVED AM RETURNING IMMEDIATELY. FIGURES ARE WORSE THAN I PREDICTED TWO YEARS AGO. ALL THOSE EXPLANATIONS AND STATISTICS WITH

[1] For the Editor's movements at this time see Chapter XVI, "The Coalition Stands," below.

WHICH IT WAS ATTEMPTED TO DOPE ME MAKE VERY
PATHETIC READING TODAY. I PREDICT POSITION WILL
GET STEADILY WORSE IF LAST TWO YEARS' FATUOUS
OPTIMISM PREVAILS. HOPE STUART UPON WHOM
RESPONSIBILITY CHIEFLY LIES WILL HAVE PLANS
READY FOR ME WITHIN SEVEN DAYS. HE SHOULD
CONSULT SUTTON AND CAIRD. BUT SUTTON VERY
BUSY. CHIEF.

The seven days having elapsed, Northcliffe duly returned to
London. He was not immediately seen in Printing House Square,
but Stuart had a series of interviews with him at Carmelite House.

The Editor, having in mind the events of the previous spring,[1]
suspected that a coup of some sort was being engineered. The
suspicion was presently seen to be well-founded. In February
Lord Rothermere, who had been campaigning against Lord Allenby
in the columns of the *Sunday Pictorial*, sent *The Times* a fierce
denunciation of Lord Allenby's policy. It was designed to
occupy a whole page advertisement in the paper, and was
diametrically opposed to the policy of *The Times*, but since it was
offered as an advertisement was not necessarily subject to
the editorial pencil. The Editor believed that the Middle East
would erroneously interpret *The Times* as having expressed an
editorial view, and not as having merely published an advertisement. In Palestine the imputation to the paper of a statement
that Allenby had been discredited would be serious. Either the
wording of the advertisement must be altered, or it could not
appear. Rothermere, told of the Editor's decision, at once
complained to his brother. Northcliffe took the matter seriously.
Had not the Editor evaded visiting Palestine at his personal
insistence?[2] Had he not already had reason to complain of
Steed's inaction following his telegraphed wish for a leading article
attacking Balfour's attitude towards Zionism? This was the
sort of independence *The Times* people always thought they could
claim with impunity, and he was not going to put up with it any
longer. The Editor was always making him look foolish. He
must act.

The Editor, the man who had travelled with him to Washington
little more than six months ago, was now to be discredited before
his own staff. Northcliffe could accomplish this with the greater
ease and effect by introducing his criticisms of the Editor into an

---

[1] Northcliffe had planned to drop *The Times* in the spring of 1921. See the previous
Chapter.

[2] The Editor, with the United States Ambassador, George Harvey, had been seriously
shaken in a motor-car accident at Cannes during a recreation hour at the Cannes
Conference, and needed time in which to recover.

announcement to the principal staff he had already decided o
wholly proper grounds to make. The Chief told his Managin
Director that the editorial troglodytes of Printing House Squai
needed a kicking, and that Stuart should read out to them a nev
" epistle " to these Laodiceans and he would write it. It woul
bear eloquent witness, etc., to their highly reinvigorated Chief
estimate of their low intelligence and working capacity. Th
message would not be flattering to the editorial people, h
prophesied; but it was not aimed at Stuart or Lints Smith, an
they should not feel offended. And the " epistle " would nc
long be delayed. In the fortnight after his arrival the Chie
raced through every department at Carmelite House, Fleetwa
House and Printing House Square. None of his editors o
intimates, except Sutton and Stuart, escaped criticism and threat
expressed in crude and fierce language. Stuart noticed tha
Northcliffe's attitude to the Editor was different from that eviden
when they were in America. When Stuart was shown th
draft of the " epistle " he was alarmed and protested that th
Chief had gone too far, that the reading to the conference of sucl
a communication from him would, in all likelihood, lead to th
immediate resignation of the Editor and his principal assistants
The Chief replied that any such resignations should be acceptec
but said he might make arrangements for communicating th
" epistle." Walter, hurriedly shown a draft of it, raisec
objections similar to Stuart's. There was somethin
behind the " epistle " he did not guess. Only Stuart knew tha
Northcliffe had decided on a change of price of *The Times*
It was a move that had been in his mind for a year or more
and had been the original motive for summoning the staff. The
demonstration against Steed, and the denigration of the editoria
staff, were afterthoughts; but, whatever Walter or Stuart thought
they were going to be combined with it. For the better
dramatization of both, the " epistle " was ordered to be read
at the usual hour of the afternoon editorial conference. The day
was March 2, and it was a Thursday. The change of price was
to be announced in that night's paper and made on the following
Monday. Nobody but Stuart knew this.

So many were summoned to the editorial conference
that the meeting was not held in the usual place but in
the Board Room. Even the reporters and the Parliamentary
gallery staff were told to be present, and all the sub-editors.
Stuart and Lints Smith had been reminded beforehand that
any strictures upon them which would be made in the
" epistle " would not be seriously meant. The Editor

ceived no warning of what was on foot when he took the chair, nd looked over the usual schedule of the day's principal Home nd Foreign news. So far as he knew, the Chief might be about speak his mind about the Coalition or the current talk of Fusion" about which he had been silent.[1] The Editor had een left without consultation on any political subject since they arted at Vancouver and Northcliffe proceeded on his world tour. . G. Price, Northcliffe's principal private secretary, came in ith Humphrey Davy, Northcliffe's second secretary, and aid he had a message to read to the conference. Price was bviously ill at ease, and read the message in a quavering voice. Readers," wrote Northcliffe, " were deserting *The Times* on ccount of editorial *gaffes*." There must be no more of them. Ie, Northcliffe, was responsible for policy; the Editor and his aff for the blunders. His kindness to them had been blame-orthy. " But I am not going to be gentle in the future as in ie past," and, turning the audience's attention to Walter as a ource of misfortune, he said that " if pressure is put upon me y the other proprietors, as seems likely to be the case, I shall istitute a root and branch inquiry into the administration of *he Times*, the expenses thereof and the personnel." The udience was restive and the one point in the Chief's " stink-omb," as they called it, of interest to them was a change to alf price for registered readers; copies over the counter would e sold at twopence on the following Monday, March 6.

The conference listened until Price had finished, when the ditor asked, " Is that all ? "; to which Price answered, That is all." The conference then proceeded and ended as sual. It was a Black Thursday for the editorial department. At a onference after the conference, the Editor prevailed over the inten-on of some of his important colleagues to resign by pointing ut that such a result could only gratify Northcliffe's ambition nd serve his purpose. The Editor would not allow himself be forced to resign, nor would he accept the resignations f others. The Editor, rather, felt inclined to ride this new storm s he had that of the previous year. He decided, however, to cure a lawyer's opinion on the degree of provocation necessary constitute unlawful dismissal. He consulted Sir Charles ussell, as Northcliffe's special legal adviser, with the assumption at Russell would inform Northcliffe. Meanwhile, it was Steed's nmediate expectation that Northcliffe would foresee his action nd forestall it, perhaps, by sending an offensive paragraph be published in *The Times*, knowing that, as Editor, Steed

[1] For " Fusion " see Chapter XVI, " The Coalition Stands," below.

would have to refuse. The prompt consequence would be one of Northcliffe's open telegrams in affectionate terms ending " Deeply sorry to part." The argument would only be over the compensation, for Steed had a document in his possession.

On Saturday, of course, there was no attendance in the editorial department. The rest of the office was busy with making the arrangements and adjustments called for by the change of price on Monday. The paper was 3d. in 1908 when Northcliffe came. In 1913 it was reduced to 2d., and in the spring of 1914 it was reduced to 1d. Rising costs, particularly of paper successively put it up to 1½d. in 1916, to 2d. in 1917 and to 3d in 1918. This had never been satisfactory to Northcliffe. As early as 1916 and often before 1919, he had startled Dawson with threats of pricing *The Times* once more at a penny and making it " a popular paper," with the advantage to the reader of a comprehensive insurance scheme. Now, in the spring of 1922, the Chief decided that it should be reduced to half price, *i.e* to 1½d., provided readers would register with their newsagents. This, according to the " stink-bomb," would be the " greatest leap in the dark in the history of Printing House Square." Nobody could deny that the post-war slump was hitting *The Times* hard. In the last 12 months the advertisement revenue had declined 9 per cent., and was still decreasing. The Chief's " stink-bomb " spoke of " those who enjoyed the handsome emoluments at Printing House Square, provided out of the proprietors' pockets," but it told the conference no facts about revenue. The " stink-bomb " had tailed off by Northcliffe's saying that his doctors wished him to be out of England in March. His eyes and throat were troubling him, but that he did not mention. His last word was that during his absence, Stuart would have his power of attorney. " I warn Sir Campbell that he has his hands full and I shall hold him to very strict account." On Sunday afternoon Stuart visited the Editor in his room. It appeared that Northcliffe was astonished by Steed's behaviour and that, in Stuart's opinion, he had wished him, and did wish him, to resign. The Editor answered that in that case he should make proposals in accordance with the letter of agreement of June, 1919.[1] Stuart said he would bear this in mind and retired to take charge of the really important business of the day: the change of price on Monday, March 6. It was, indeed, a hazardous change and was revoked after Northcliffe's death.

Before leaving London (in the company of Sutton) Northcliffe circulated a second message that gave a certain amount of praise

[1] Made in the circumstances described in Chapter XI, " A New Editor."

to the editorial staff, though he wished " people would not ask me why we do not get as good leaders as the *Morning Post*. I am asked that every day. The third leader has disappeared."[1] He added, in oblique reference to certain appointments in the Foreign and other departments of Printing House Square that Stuart was soon to announce, " Now that the task of producing the paper has been devolved there will be more time to attend to this vital matter. . . . I hope that a little more attention will be paid to the Axe in Printing House Square. I have left Sir Campbell Stuart complete control with power to direct from 10.40 a.m. but I trust that it does not mean that he will be pestered by everybody in the office. I also trust that he will be a little more firm than he has been in the past and mingle his amiability with discreet insistence." On March 7 the Editor managed to see Sir Charles Russell the solicitor, who had just met Northcliffe. Steed asked Russell what he, as Editor, should do in certain circumstances. Russell was hesitant. When he lately lunched with Northcliffe, he said, he found him so abnormal that he considered him incapable of business, and judging from his appearance, unlikely to live long. Russell advised Steed to remain as Editor and defend the interests of the staff.

Now Northcliffe's attitude towards the Editor was equivocal. He had, to all appearances, said and done nothing more to secure Steed's resignation. Before he left he sent for him and in discussing the political situation in a friendly way, without a hint of animosity, he asked the Editor what he thought should be done about the International Economic Conference due to meet at Genoa early in April. The Editor answered that as the Conference must fail it would be well not to give it much space in *The Times*, and he had decided to send Hubert Walter from Paris as Special Correspondent, with Vernon Bartlett from Rome as his assistant, but should certainly not go himself. Northcliffe agreed, and they parted on the best of terms.

Walter, Steed, Stuart and the office generally were now able to look forward to a period of relative calm though of uncertain length. Walter and all whose judgment counted in the office believed that in spite of Northcliffe's vagaries he was far more likely than they to be right on the fundamental principles and practices of the trade, and on the questions of price, circulation and revenue from sales and advertising. On the other hand, the Chief had no interest in what his colleagues thought about anything. His plans were made without their knowledge,

[1] *I.e.*, The " light " leader, now known as the fourth leader, imitated from the *Morning Post*, and resisted by the office.

and would be carried out with or without support. Only Stuart knew his mind, or was given his confidence. The hesitating and uninformed office inevitably gave way; the returned Northcliffe became more than ever Chief, and his Managing Director, Stuart, more than ever powerful. On every side the Editor detected signs of intended change, involving his own position. He suspected that while travelling Northcliffe had decided first upon a radical alteration of the relation of the editorial and managerial departments that would entail a sacrifice of power and prestige by the Editor. The Editor knew Northcliffe better than anyone in the office, save the Managing Director. But this superior knowledge, even with the support of Freeman and others, gave him little confidence that, in opposition to Northcliffe, he could maintain the editorial position against proprietorial and directorial pressure. The Editor's independence and responsibility, in the historic Printing House Square sense, might be brought permanently to an end.

Meanwhile, Walter meditated on his personal and family situation and discussed it with his uncles, Ralph and Hubert. All knew it, on several grounds, to be critical. Unless increased circulation, secured at the half-price concession to registered readers, brought in higher advertisement revenue the paper must daily lose heavily. From Monday, March 6, the circulation at 1½d. went from an average of 110,818 in March to 165,441 in April, and the loss was £1,000 a week. The figure must rise in proportion as the price remained low, the circulation increased, and the advertisement revenue remained stable. That would be a very serious matter, and probably jeopardize the whole fabric of Printing House Square. Could that be Northcliffe's design? It might well be that he was about to force Walter out of the business. The family felt acutely anxious, but agreed that they could do nothing but wait for Northcliffe's next move. All he had done when departing for France was to say that the day would come in the spring when the final crisis would develop and he would return. This was a repetition of the situation as it was in March, 1914. The newspaper trade, like any other, has to adjust itself to rising costs. Northcliffe had " saved " *The Times* in 1914; now, eight years after, he had to repeat his triumph. Certainly Northcliffe in 1922, any more than in 1914, could neither abide nor afford failure. There was just the chance that under the pressure of continual weekly loss on *The Times*, he might offer Walter his shares in accordance with the agreement made in 1913. That was possible. What was far more probable was that Northcliffe would do nothing of the kind, but rather

ower the price of *The Times* once more to a penny and turn it
nto a " popular " paper. That was the sort of journalism in
vhich he could not fail, though *The Times* would cease to be
The Times. Then it would be Walter who would be driven to sell
.hares. To sell now, however, besides effecting a complete break
>f the family with *The Times*, must discourage the office more
.han any other action that could be taken. That was as far as
'ohn Walter could then see. If Walter went, who was the one
>ulwark against Northcliffe, others would go. This was certain.
Freeman and one or two others had long known how anti-
Walter Northcliffe really was. The " stink-bomb " convinced
.hem that he was anti-Steed. This was new. It was obvious,
1ow, that Northcliffe was awaiting a pretext to force him,
1s he had forced Dawson, to resign, or, if he would not oblige,
:o instruct Stuart to dismiss him. The Editor could only survive,
1nd the tradition of impersonal, independent, and responsible
:ditorship with him, if he could count upon the support of Walter.

At this time Walter had no reason to suspect that Northcliffe
was thinking of dismissing Steed, nor at any other time. On the
:ontrary, he had come to regard the relationship between
Northcliffe and Steed as a firm and enduring alliance, based upon
1 natural affinity of temperament and outlook and reinforced by
1 strong personal sympathy and mutual admiration. As a natural
:onsequence of this close and, as he thought, exclusive friendship,
Walter found himself relegated to the unaccustomed and uncon-
genial role of odd man out. There is no reason to think that he
held this as a grievance against Steed, who was scarcely a free agent
in the matter. His disagreement with the Editor was over policy,
or rather over the tone and manner of its expression in the paper.
Northcliffe knew this, as he knew everything else. For other
reasons Stuart recommended Steed's dismissal.

Stuart had always accepted, and sympathized with, Northcliffe's
desire as Chief Proprietor to be master in Printing House Square.
He was perfectly willing and completely able to advance the Chief's
plans and had no objection, if required, to being " Managing
Editor " as well as Managing Director. Since 1919, the Editor
apart, Stuart already had the most influential position in the
hierarchy. The further promotion that the Chief had in view
could only be secured at the expense of the Editor. The new
Editor in 1922 was in the identical position of the old Editor who
resigned in 1919. That was the situation after the first week of
March, 1922. How long it would last nobody knew. Northcliffe
was fully aware of the balance of power in Printing House Square.

He knew that the eclipse of Steed must attach Walter more closely to himself, and to that extent obstruct any outside plan to change the control. It was a fact, probably known to Northcliffe, that Ralph Walter and Hubert Walter were already speculating, as before in 1908, upon the names of various respectable and monied men who might be willing to rescue *The Times* from Northcliffe. It looked as if the 1908 situation was repeating itself. Once more the quarrels of *The Times* and its personalities were to provide a legal case, suitably complex and satisfactorily protractable. Northcliffe was not supposed to know of these inquiries, but his reference to the reliability of his ferrets and his spies was never an empty boast, and it is probable that he knew of most of Walter's moves. Northcliffe had many of the most able solicitors in his service; whispering about Printing House Square has always been a pastime in Fleet Street (and still is). Northcliffe was aware of the readiness of Sir John Ellerman to enter into a new controlling syndicate, if one could be created. John Walter, too, suspected there might be others besides Ellerman who were anxious to assume the control. The strongest candidate, certainly, though John Walter and others did not then know it, was Rothermere whose manoeuvres in 1921 were almost successful. He had lately boasted to his political mentor, Lovat Fraser, that he would have *The Times* before the end of 1922. Fraser thought that he wished to advance the political career of his son, Esmond Harmsworth, elected for Thanet in 1921 as the " first anti-Waste " M.P. Then there was Beaverbrook. He certainly knew much of what was going on. He was a very close friend of Rothermere. Northcliffe, in a statement made to irritate his financial brother, said that the Canadian was a man of his own sort. " My friend Beaverbrook is a worker, his newspapers and the fine position they are gaining was not due to Millions but to Mind. He works as hard as I do." In addition, there would be others, unknown, who would be keenly interested if it became known that Northcliffe, under doctor's orders, or family pressure, decided to reduce his responsibilities. Then it would be seen whether if Northcliffe's interference and extravagance ceased *The Times* would again pay as a business. Good judges believed it would.

Northcliffe had himself now absolutely given up the idea, whatever others imagined, of abandoning *The Times*, selling his shares, or abating his control. He no more wanted Steed to be independent than he wanted to share control with Walter. The Walter-Northcliffe agreement of 1913 stood, and during its continuance Walter was engaged to support Northcliffe. That was the governing factor. It gave him an option to purchase

Northcliffe's shares if he wanted to sell, or if he died. Northcliffe showed no signs of doing either. Walter could not alter the agreement ; he must accept the situation and could only change it for the worse, *i.e.*, by himself selling to Northcliffe. Northcliffe would like that more than anything else in the world, provided he dictated the figure, for then he would be undisputed master of Printing House Square and realize an ambition cherished even before 1908. It was an ambition for which he had been working consistently, as Stuart knew; his own appointment crystallized it. Northcliffe's attitude towards the Editor was not really new. It had been in his mind when he dismissed Steed's predecessor. After his change of mind over selling the paper in 1921, and during his tour, he had thought it all out. He decided to be absolute master in Printing House Square before he died. That was the essential article in the entirely new editorial plan. It had matured some time between late 1921 and early 1922. A wholly new constitution for Printing House Square would place him in a far prouder position than before. Northcliffe would be, in his own person, the greatest single journalist the world had ever known and Steed would have a position outside the office; a high position as political adviser to the Napoleon of Fleet Street, while he, Northcliffe himself, would edit the paper through Brumwell, the Acting Editor, or " Associate " Editor, as he would shortly describe him. About this he had, so far, said nothing to anybody, at least in Printing House Square.

In the meantime he must first have Steed out of the way attending international conferences, discredit the editorial department by constant criticism, and thus, finally, tire Steed of departmental work; secondly he must exalt Stuart as Managing Editor as well as Managing Director. On March 18 Northcliffe wired Stuart suggesting that Steed should go to the Ambassadors' Conference due to open in Paris on April 3, and visit him in the interval. On the 19th, the Editor wrote assuring " My dear Chief " that he did not " feel at all happy at leaving, but would do as suggested." He told Sutton that it was his " settled judgement that the difficulty of combining the functions of Editor with those of travelling correspondent is great, and renders the maintenance of any consistent editorial policy almost impossible." This was precisely what Northcliffe wanted. Now, by reading a mass of his own and his competitors' newspapers, the French and foreign journals, telegrams arriving daily from his managers, letters and memoranda of all kinds, he enabled himself to instruct Printing House Square on Far Eastern policy, to criticize the line on Japan,

animadvert on the Jewish, Greek and Turkish policy, argue abou
the effect of Genoa on Anglo-French relations. By the end o
the month he had tired out every responsible member of Printing
House Square.

On March 27 *The Times* was reduced to 1½d. withou
exception. On March 31, the Editor, willing or not, lef
for Pau in company of Sir William Beach Thomas whom
Northcliffe intended to send on a journey round the world fo:
The Times and the *Daily Mail*. When they arrived at Pau
Northcliffe sent Beach Thomas back to London. Steed went fo:
a walk and a drive with Northcliffe in the afternoon, and wa:
struck by the incoherence of his talk and the sensitivity of hi
nerves. The slightest noise startled him as though it had beer
a pistol shot. On one point he was insistent and consistent
unless Steed went to the Genoa Conference he would go ther
himself and show up Lloyd George's intrigues. Steed was convinced that he would go—and that, if he went, a disaster woulc
follow. Against his will, Steed promised to go, and returnec
to London to make what arrangements he could.[1] Early in Apri
he went back to Paris on his way to Genoa, and as, by that time
Northcliffe had come up to Fontainebleau, he lunched with him,
St. John Harmsworth and Hildebrand Harmsworth. It was jus
over three weeks since Charles Russell had warned the Editor tha
Northcliffe was abnormal. By this time the Editor had othe:
reasons to conclude that Russell had not exaggerated.

After Fontainebleau, Northcliffe went to Pau. His mind wa:
racing at an ever-increasing speed, and the pressure he put upor
his " great armies " (the Napoleonic term was repeated) was correspondingly intense. It was not only the editorial staff tha:
were worn down by the constant streams of telegrams. They
all arrived from Pau, but not only from Northcliffe. Lints
Smith and others of the managerial staff had been summonec
there in connexion with the change of price. They sent, as they
were ordered, messages on every aspect of the price-battle
On the 26th a new wire to Stuart said that the Chief had hearc
that the *Morning Post* had lowered its price—" a fight betweer
the three papers will result in victory of the best. The *Telegraph*
in many ways superior to us, must be compared minutely. Whc
gets small advertisements will be one of the deciding factors
Last week's papers excellent but many things done badly.'
According to him, " D's return was worth one column daily.
Chauffeur case mishandled; should have been on home page

[1] For Steed's original dispositions about Genoa see above, Chapter XVI, " The
Coalition Stands." He arrived at Genoa on April 8 and returned to the editoria
chair on June 20.

University kissing case badly done; have told Lints Smith to dismiss legal man. Lints Smith tired and too gentle. Leaders still too long. Coming great fight biggest in history of paper." More telegrams came to Lints Smith on his return and to Akerman, his assistant: " Do you both understand that if we do not get classified we shall be beaten ? Every classified advertisement is news which none of you, Stuart, Lints Smith, Akerman, Robbins and Brumwell seem to understand." (April 1.) Those named well understood, as the whole trade did, that the obtaining of a constant supply of situations vacant and wanted, of houses and flats to let, and notices for the agony column and the births, marriages and deaths, was the most difficult of all the tasks of the industry. They were doing their best, but this was nothing like enough. Caustic criticism of almost everybody in the office and almost every feature of the paper came unceasingly. NO, NO, NO, a telegram ran, THE ARTICLES MUST BEGIN ON A MONDAY. STRICT JEWS DO NOT READ NEWSPAPERS ON A SATURDAY. LUCKY DOGS. The fight of *The Times* with the *Morning Post* and the *Daily Telegraph* was just what his soul craved. It recalled to him the days in 1896 when he was preparing to stagger Fleet Street with his halfpenny *Daily Mail*; it reminded him of the great and subtle struggle in 1914 with the *Daily Telegraph* and the *Morning Post*, when he had suddenly and cunningly reduced the price of *The Times* from twopence to a penny.

When on March 6, 1922, he had reduced it from threepence to three-halfpence to registered customers he employed a device by means of which he could reduce the price of *The Times* without violating his " gentleman's agreement " with Lord Burnham : that either of them would give the other notice of any change in the prices of *The Times* or the *Daily Telegraph*. Northcliffe solved this problem—to his own satisfaction—by writing a note to Burnham announcing the change on the afternoon or the evening of the day before the change came into effect. It was sharp practice. The *Daily Telegraph* was then price twopence. When instead of being half price to registered readers *The Times* was priced at 1½d. to all, whether registered or not, " The reduction in price," an announcement said, " will not involve any variation in the quality of the News Services of *The Times*. On the contrary, as a result of Lord Northcliffe's world tour, many new correspondents have been appointed in places in which hitherto no journal had been represented." As the days passed Northcliffe argued over telephone and telegraph the merits of an extension of the free travel insurance scheme initiated for the

readers of *The Times*. So the office was harried. They must al
work. He, himself, was not going to remain idle in Pau any
longer than he could help.

The moment the weather changed he would be on their backs
let that be understood by the Black Friars. Changing his mind
suddenly on April 1, after sending off a mass of telegrams
he entrained at Pau to Orleans, and reached there his waiting
Rolls-Royce in which he went to Fontainebleau, a place his
Napoleonic soul loved. He went on to Paris at midday or
the 6th and caught the boat train to Victoria. He went straight
to see his mother, as he always did when he had a serious
doubt on his mind. In the packet of papers sent up to him at
Totteridge he saw for the first time *The Times Diary and Index
of the War*, and at once looked for his name. It had but one
reference, and he did not feel complimented. A tart telegram
was immediately sent off to Stuart about this unhappy publication
THE CHIEF WOULD LIKE TO KNOW THE NAME OF
THE AUTHOR OF THIS BOOK SO THAT HE CAN
COMMUNE WITH HIM. THE CHIEF IS PROFOUNDLY
UNGRATEFUL TO HIM. As good as his promise, he was not
in gentle mood. That became clear to his secretary at Dover
when he sent a private telegram to Sutton and Stuart, in which
he told them that a happier office than Printing House Square
" thinks that I am miles away in the south of France. They [at
Carmelite House] little guess that the earthquake is so near."

In public he showed amiability. On April 10, the *Daily Telegraph*
reduced its price to 1½d. in order, as it stated, to satisfy the demand
for a cheap as well as a good newspaper. Northcliffe, who
owed Burnham an apology for not giving him the covenanted
notice well before March 6 of a change of price in *The Times*,
gave instructions that a leading article from Printing House Square
should congratulate their colleagues of Peterborough Court.[1]
Northcliffe was, in fact, greatly disturbed by the *Telegraph*'s
price reduction, and he decided to meditate.

The " earthquake " did not erupt in Carmelite Street until
April 17. An avalanche of criticism then fell upon Caird,

[1] The colleagues appreciated the compliment. " The praise of *The Times* is an envied
possession on all occasions, but never more than when it is given professionally, as from
one journal to another. It is the most famous, as it is one of the oldest of the great
English newspapers, and preserves and renews in age the freshness and vigour of youth.
The Times has half a century more of fame and honour to its credit than the
Daily Telegraph. It won the distinction of being the most independent newspaper in
England, and indeed in Europe, more than a century ago, through the courage and ability
of the second John Walter, whose powerful traditions, carried on in unbroken line by
Barnes and John Delane, have been maintained by the genius of its present chief
proprietor, Viscount Northcliffe. The *Daily Telegraph* is glad to front the future in the
company of *The Times* with friendly rivalry for the maintenance of the dignity and the best
interests of English journalism."

Stuart, Akerman and Tom Clarke. It covered threats of disagreeable new plans. As an ultimatum, in order to show Carmelite House how to do their job, he threatened to write an article. This last menace matured quickly. On April 18 " Watch Japan " appeared in *The Times* and the *Daily Mail*. By his orders the article and argument were cabled to all parts of the world that there was no real Japan, since all the Japanese were held down by a few militarists planning to conquer the whole of China. On the day of publication he gave a luncheon at his house to Jack Dempsey, the heavy-weight boxing champion. It was not the fresh apple and dry toast that he was observed to take but his appearance that alarmed his colleagues at Carmelite House. Hitherto they had interpreted the Chief's behaviour as exaggerated, but not uncharacteristic. Now it was different. How different, or why, was not known. The alarm turned into consternation when the Chief appointed one of the commissionaires at Carmelite House to supervise what he denounced as the " coarse, abominable and offensive " advertisements that the advertising staff of the *Daily Mail*, under one of its most respected heads, had taken so much trouble to get. It was decided that there was something wrong with the Chief.

One or two persons in privileged positions for observation had arrived at this conclusion some weeks earlier. It has been seen that when Steed saw Northcliffe *en route* for Genoa he came to the conclusion that Russell's opinion, expressed on March 7, was not baseless. Northcliffe was " abnormal." The Editor had noticed that the Chief was developing a squint. Somebody else had since observed a thickening of the neck. Steed drew the conclusion that Northcliffe's symptoms could only be explained by a disease that, at times, influenced the brain. In Paris on the way home, on April 6, Steed talked seriously to Hubert Walter, the Paris Correspondent. He was a director of The Times Publishing Company and a proper person to be informed of the situation and its dangers. Steed said that Northcliffe was " going mad " and urged the necessity of bringing John Walter back from Morocco at the earliest possible moment. Hubert Walter was impressed, but when he met Ralph the two brothers decided not to follow Steed's advice. When John Walter did return at the end of May, he acquiesced in the view that Steed's account was exaggerated. That was not so improbable; for Northcliffe, however unwell, and whether or not his malady affected his brain at any time, was well enough to command long lucid intervals. For instance, on May 3 the Chief attended at Carmelite House a farewell luncheon to W. J. Evans, the retiring

Editor of the *Evening News* who had been so largely responsible for
that paper's immense prosperity. The Chief was in fine form and
joked about his age. " What! I am only about two years junior to
Evans," he told the party. " I shan't stay on when my powers
begin to go. One can't keep at it always. Of course I have had
the advantage that I have conserved my energy . . . but I'm
getting on." He was, in fact, within three months of his 57th
birthday. The mood quickly passed, and on May 11 he made
an excellent and effective speech to the Empire Press Union.
Most people who had thought him " abnormal " believed they
were mistaken. He had only been up to his tricks. The Chief
continued to amuse himself by talking about his " approaching
retirement," yet he let it be known that the day upon which he
would turn over the business " to you young fellows " would not
come for three or four years. Meanwhile, he would again go
abroad. Stuart had advised him against remaining in England
while W. R. Hearst was in the neighbourhood. He accepted
this advice but would not leave until the last minute, since being
on the scene in London stimulated him so much. Yet there was
still nothing that Northcliffe saw that could please him.
" Carmelite House is out of control "; his instructions were again
not being obeyed. Things were done that he himself would not
have tolerated. Of all things in the world, the Newspaper
Proprietors Association had decided to reduce the wages of
compositors. Northcliffe would rather leave and break up the
Association than put up with this sort of thing. He protested
to Riddell and Burnham that " Capitalists have come into Fleet
Street who have made fortunes in other industries with no
experience of newspapers at all. It is unreasonable that they
should take part in dictating the wages of printers who have been
associated with newspapers all their lives." He meant what he
said. On May 3, 1922, *The Times* left the Association.

Northcliffe was now at the highest pitch of exaltation. He
must correct, by his own example, the poverty of the features
of the *Daily Mail* and the obtuseness of its Editor and Manager.
A series of articles, written in the crisp, didactic style he then
favoured—every paragraph a telegram—was entitled " Newspapers and their Millionaires." These were printed in the
Daily Mail early in May. They gave offence, perhaps rather
more than he intended, to almost everybody on and off
his staffs. His colleague, W. G. Fish, who was deputed
by the *Daily Mail* to attend the meetings of the Newspaper
Proprietors Association, was named; he was described
as " young and indiscreet." The whole of Fleet Street and

Carmelite Street having thus been set by the ears, the Chief departed to the Continent. One of Northcliffe's reasons for going abroad was to plan; he could plan better in comfort in France where he would not be followed about by the men of Fleet Street and of the "Servants' Hall," *i.e.*, the Press Club. He did not like these people looking at him and watching him about, when both he and they knew he was not up to the mark. He was thinking, too, of *The Times*. That place, too, was "out of control" and once more he must act.

It has been seen how Northcliffe had insisted on Steed's going to Genoa to report the Conference and threatened, otherwise, to go himself. The Barthou *démenti* gave him the pretext he had long desired.[1] At last Stuart was telegraphed the instruction: ARRANGE FOR STEED'S RESIGNATION. Between May 17 and 19 Lints Smith—sent by Stuart to Paris, where Steed was taking soundings, with instructions to "arrange" this "resignation"—had hours of fruitless discussion with Steed regarding the conditions of an agreed settlement. The Editor stood his ground while Stuart saw nothing "abnormal" in dismissing him. On the contrary, as he had understood Northcliffe's mind since he came to Printing House Square, Stuart had foreseen the possibility of this disagreement. Nor did Stuart feel in the least anxious about Northcliffe's health. It had never been robust, anyway. There was no reason why, with frequent holidays, he should not continue to direct his properties. That was the basis of Stuart's position: to act as Northcliffe's *alter ego*. Rather Stuart was more concerned, at that time, about his own health.[2] In the meantime the sale of the paper at the new price was increasing. Northcliffe's return to London took place at a happy moment. He was exhilarated by the rise of the average circulation to 178,465. All talk about his health being bad died down. Walter, seeing him so active, considered him to have quite as good a life risk as his own. They met at Carlton Gardens on Wednesday, May 24, the day before Northcliffe was to return to the Continent. Northcliffe was full of confidence and answered Walter's scepticism by offering to buy his shares. Walter said he would think it over. Northcliffe said that if he was willing to sell Sutton could deal with the matter while he was away. Walter noticed at this talk nothing unusual in Northcliffe's manner or appearance. The truth was that at this time Northcliffe's health, physical

[1] For the Barthou incident see Chapter XVI, "The Coalition Stands," below.

[2] Stuart was, in fact, laid up in the last week of May. He then went to Canada to recuperate and did not return until August 7. See Chapter XVII, "The End of the Northcliffe Regime."

and other, varied. One day he was wilful, venomous and erratic, the next day cool, kindly and consistent. At will he could be one or the other. To Walter, Northcliffe was only slightly more erratic than he had ever been; he might be arbitrary, but then he had been arbitrary in 1908. Certainly the appointment on May 9 of Harold Williams as Foreign Editor the side-tracking of Freeman and the appointment of Brumwel in his place, were arbitrary enough. The changes had been made by Northcliffe and Stuart without consultation with anybody; not even with the Editor. Walter was entitled to think that these appointments were the beginning of a series of radical changes to take effect in the ensuing years. There was no sign of Northcliffe's retirement from any cause. While abroad Walter had come to see that the vague and clumsy arrangement he had made with Northcliffe in 1913 was never going to work. Walter felt that his position was personally undignified to the point of impossibility, and would become publicly so in a year or two.

Arthur Walter's death in 1910 had entailed long family discussion[1]. His successor, the fourth John Walter, was discontented with the same honorific sinecure and wanted to regain a more active position in the Proprietary. The settlement arrived at in 1913 seemed to secure that position for him by giving him an option to purchase at Northcliffe's death, or earlier, all Northcliffe's shares in return for Walter's consistent support. Yet he had no real jurisdiction over the property, and no hope of it until Northcliffe's death. Northcliffe was not yet 57 and might live for another ten or twenty years. For fourteen years Walter had hoped that, by the exercise of patience, he might be able to regain control of the family property. Now that he had been out of the country for six weeks he could judge more clearly. He now made up his mind that he could not go on. The facts were simple: there was no room for himself and Northcliffe in Printing House Square; no room in Printing House Square for Northcliffe plus anybody else. When on that afternoon of March 16, 1908, Moberly Bell had counted out 320 £1,000 bank notes in the presence of the Judge, *The Times*, everybody thought, came under the merely nominal control of X. That nominal control had now become a reality in every sense of the word, for Northcliffe brought with him, as he would say, not merely his money but his mind. The old question of control had been settled so far as to remove the obstruction caused by the small

---

[1] See Vol. III, Chapter XIX, " The Sale of the Walters' Printing Business," and Chapter XXIV, " End of the Old Gang," for these discussions.

proprietors; though, in accordance with their one reasonable
demand, the property was transferred to the ownership of a legal
company that limited their liability. The settlement also provided for the continuity of the association of the Walter family
with *The Times*. The appointment of Arthur Walter as Chairman
was a voluntary acceptance of the value, in Northcliffe's estimate,
of the respect in which the family of the founder was held. The
control was held by Northcliffe as part of an understanding with
Sir John Ellerman, who in 1908 saw *The Times* to be nothing
more than an opportunity of making a cash profit. Indeed, as
long as Northcliffe was there and had his agreement, made in
1913 with Walter, *The Times* could not be to Ellerman anything
more than a source of cash. Hence Ellerman was more than
willing to back anybody whose record proved him, as Northcliffe's
had, to be a big moneymaker; and he was prepared, up to a point,
to wait for his profit. But Northcliffe was not fond of him, or
of the prospect of his ever having political power over *The Times*.
All Ellerman could do was to ask for his money back.
Northcliffe, therefore, had nothing to lose and everything to gain
when, in 1908, he decided to offer to Arthur Walter the
Chairmanship of The Times Publishing Company with succession
to his son. The capital in 1908 was £750,000. At this figure
the capital remained until October, 1920, when it was increased
to £1,000,000 for reasons that related to increased costs. In 1920
Lord Rothermere, it has been seen, insisted to Northcliffe that
the price of white newsprint used by *The Times* was about to rise
and persuaded him to buy all available stocks of it.[1] In the event,
the price of this paper, far from rising, dropped appreciably,
but not until Northcliffe had spent £100,000. The loss was so
great that in combination with other factors, it decided Northcliffe
upon making a new issue of capital. As usual his motives were
mixed. A large new issue could not but embarrass John Walter,
and challenge his relative position *vis-à-vis* himself and Ellerman.
Northcliffe had to offer Walter the opportunity to buy his due
proportion, but hoped he would fail to lay his hands on the
money. The issue was one of 250,000 Ordinary shares of which
215,000 were issued. To Northcliffe's surprise and regret
John Walter subscribed for 75,700 at par. He found some
difficulty in so doing and was glad soon afterwards to sell 10,700
to Ellerman at 22s. 6d.

This was the position in May, 1923, when Northcliffe's ingenuity
in inventing every means to irritate, fatigue and affront Walter
succeeded in convincing the latter that he had had enough.

[1] See Chapter XII, " The Editor under Pressure," above.

It would be better, Walter thought, for the ultimate credit of the family name, if not immediately for that of the paper, were he to cease to carry either the honours of a nominal Chairmanship o the genuine responsibility of a large, but not controlling, block of shares. After painful reflection John Walter resolved tha Northcliffe being Northcliffe, with as good a life as anybody's he now had no alternative but to sever connexions with him. A he could not buy Northcliffe out he had better go out himself by selling his shares at the best price. Northcliffe had foreseen and planned for this settlement. It was to be a supreme coup; to obtain now what he had so long wanted : undisputed and absolute mastery, proprietorial and editorial, of this proud, mysterious unique newspaper. He had never really expected John Walter to sell, but he had taken every step ever since 1908, to bring him to do so—on terms favourable to himself. It had taken all his subtlety and patience over fourteen years to force Walter out. By skilfu arrangement and planned extravagance he had depressed the Ordinary shares. He had seen to it that the Company had only twice paid a dividend on its Ordinary share capital. The settle ment with John Walter was in sight.

What was the condition of the editorial department? At the end of May a state of crisis existed, the extreme acuteness of which was probably unknown to anybody but Steed and Stuart They had not come to terms, and Lints Smith failed to persuade the Editor not to edit. The Editor rejected a post in Paris as a general European Correspondent on Blowitzian lines. He would either be Editor or be dismissed. At this point Northcliffe decided that he neither wanted Steed as Editor nor desired to dispense with his services. Doubtless he decided, also, to try some other method of forcing Steed out of the editorial chair while keeping him in the service of some of his newspapers. Thus, Northcliffe, who had gone off on an expedition into Germany (where he convinced General Sir Alexander Godley, the British Commander at Cologne, of his abnormality) telegraphed instructions that Steed was to return to the office and resume work as Editor immediately. Steed had survived one more crisis of the 1921 sort; but there was a crisis of another order to be faced.

If in May, 1922, the cash situation was not easy, in June it was difficult. The advertising and circulation figures were responsible. The revenue from the first had declined while the increased circulation at the lower price had resulted in a loss. The June, 1920—June, 1921 advertisement revenue was

£792,216. For the year June, 1921—June, 1922 the figure was £703,497. Since the reduction of price the loss from March 6 to May 15 aggregated £46,000. The Manager's opinion was that *The Times* was heading for the rocks. Any seller of shares would judge it better not to wait. On May 29 Walter saw Sutton and told him that as serious differences between himself and Northcliffe were continually arising, he could no longer cooperate with him in the conduct of the paper, and had decided to part with his interest in *The Times* newspaper and to offer his shares to Northcliffe. The seriousness of this step becomes obvious when it is remembered that, in accordance with the agreement come to in 1912 and signed in 1913, "In the event of Ld. N.'s death J. W. is to have the first option on Lord N.'s Ordinary shares."[1] By selling now Walter would destroy the basis of the option. On Wednesday, June 7, Northcliffe paid for the shares at the par rate. The sale ended the Walter connexion with *The Times* that had begun in 1785. There could be no doubt in Walter's mind that this would be the effect of the sale, for Sutton, in all fairness, drew his attention to it, and asked him, in Northcliffe's name, to remain as Chairman of The Times Publishing Company, Ltd. This Walter at first refused and later said he would consider it. But at the time of transfer he was against further collaboration. The agreement of January 1, 1913, was thus endorsed on June 15:

I the within named John Walter acknowledge that the within named Viscount Northcliffe has purchased from me the whole of my 215,000 ordinary shares in the within named Times Publishing Co., Ltd. and that it was one of the considerations for the said purchase that the within agreement should be cancelled and that all rights reserved to me thereunder should be surrendered. I accordingly agree to the cancellation of the said Agreement and the surrender of all my rights thereunder.[2]

Walter had sold his shares and in doing so, had necessarily sacrified his option. It was a catastrophic act.

Given John Walter's indifference to gossip regarding Northcliffe's mental state, it was a natural thing for him to do after his three years in Spain, and return to association with a Northcliffe freed from every restraint. Walter had all the provocation to risk a pitched battle with him, but only another Northcliffe could do this and hope for success. And Walter would not try to cast out Beelzebub by Beelzebub. He was incapable of it. He was not a newspaper man

---

[1] From the pencil note in Northcliffe's autograph given to Walter and used as the basis of the agreement drawn up by Soames, Edwards & Jones, and signed on January 1, 1913.
[2] See also Chapter XVII, " End of the Northcliffe Régime."

in any sense; certainly not in Northcliffe's; and, if he did not sell, and Northcliffe did go and leave Walter with a free hand, there was no guarantee that *The Times*, or the family, would be the better for it. What could Walter do in the meantime? He would leave, and then wait. By selling his shares he would at least make it clear that it was not he who was dismissing valued members of the staff in order to have his dividend. Walter, therefore, would sell, leave and wait.

But waiting was not in Northcliffe's style; changing his mind was. He had second thoughts about the effect upon the public of Walter's withdrawal. After all, it might not assist his campaign against Lloyd George. There might be other inconveniences. On June 10 Northcliffe wired thus:

URGENT SATURDAY SHALL BE VERY SORRY IF YOU DON'T ACCEPT CHAIRMANSHIP FULLSTOP DIDN'T LIKE YOUR LETTER SAYING WE DISAGREED FULLSTOP AS MATTER OF FACT CONSIDERING ALL WE HAVE BEEN DEALING WITH WHO ARE GOING WE HAVE NOT GOT ON SO BADLY ESPECIALLY CONSIDERING WE WERE SUD-DENLY THROWN TOGETHER FULLSTOP SHALL BE HONOURED IF YOU WILL ACCEPT CHAIRMANSHIP AND HOLD IT FOR REST OF YOUR LIFE AND YOUR LITTLE SON AFTER YOU FULLSTOP BUT I MUST KNOW THIS WEEK AS ONE OF MY BROTHERS WANTS IT FULLSTOP

NORTHCLIFFE

This was a sudden " grasshopper " change of position on his part. The reference to Walter and his son is a reversion to the suggestion made by Sutton on May 29, when Walter had not taken him seriously. The fact was that he wanted neither Walter nor " one of my brothers." What he really desired was such a renewal of health that he could himself personally direct and manage all the departments. This he knew he could not expect and had reconciled himself to the maintenance of the old Chairman or the appointment of a new one. The urgency of the matter arose from the fact that Rothermere, having in mind his son Esmond, had asked Northcliffe for the appointment, and Northcliffe, whatever he may have said to his brother in the past, had now decided that he did not want his relative in that position. Whether he really wanted to bring back Walter, or was in a fit state to resolve such a question, was to be revealed quickly.

John Walter conferred with Ralph. Ralph, consistently opposed to his nephew's selling his shares, now had his chance. He

THE FLEETWAY HOUSE,
FARRINGDON STREET, E.C.

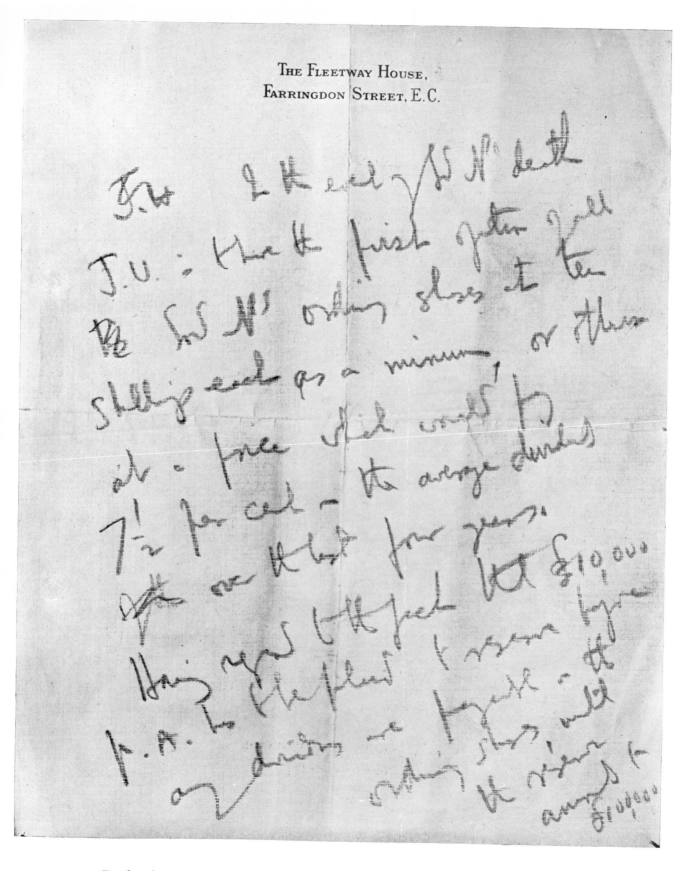

Draft of the option to John Walter in Northcliffe's holograph (end of 1912).

ersuaded his nephew to revive the question of the option. This as certainly an important question to put since it was only easonable to suppose that Northcliffe, having secured the Walter hares, would recast his Will. Late on Sunday night, June 11, Valter wired the following telegram:

OUR TELEGRAM RECEIVED ON RETURN FROM OUNTRY LATE TONIGHT FULLSTOP YES I ACCEPT ENEROUS OFFER OF CHAIRMANSHIP PROVIDED IT ARRIES WITH IT OPTION ON YOUR CONTROLLING NTEREST AT PRICE ARRANGED IN OUR AGREEMENT OF ANUARY FIRST NINETEEN THIRTEEN   JOHN WALTER

The telegram, addressed to the Hotel Christol at Boulogne, as delivered after Northcliffe had suddenly decided to leave or Paris. In reply to a telephoned message from his secretary, Valter wrote confirming his telegram and adding that

I agree with you that it is most desirable in the interests of the aper that the [family] tradition should remain unbroken; but aving parted with my rights as a proprietor, because I found that 1 fact I was not exercising my duties as a director, I cannot see how should be justified in retaining the office of Chairman. But I do eel that the plan [regarding my option] I have suggested, while aving you (with your now larger holding of ordinary shares) an bsolutely free hand would seem to counterbalance the anomaly of he situation. I see no other way.

Meanwhile the formalities regarding the transfer were being ompleted and the family were busy discussing the impending uture. But while the Walters were considering their position Northcliffe was visited with one of his surprise "intuitions." Valter or not, he would bring back his old friend Steed, against vhom, and himself, people had been conspiring. The telegram to tuart instructing him to arrange for Steed's resignation was ent in the middle of May. Since then numerous meetings with ints Smith over terms had ended in disagreement. Lints imith talked to Stuart, and Steed consulted his lawyers. The aper was being conducted by Freeman and Brumwell. On Thursday, June 8, Price, Northcliffe's principal secretary, elephoned to the Editor from Boulogne. Steed was at ome when Price rang up. He read him the following ressage: "If Steed is agreeable I should be glad to see im in Paris on Sunday evening at 8 o'clock at the Hotel Plaza-Athénée." Price added that he personally would be very lad if the Editor came because he thought the visit would vercome numerous difficulties, especially as he knew the Chief's

645

affection for the Editor to be unabated. The Editor, who ha
looked forward to resuming his work in the office on Sunda
night, June 11, now changed his plan and prepared to cross th
Channel during the week-end. On Friday night he was startle
to receive from Northcliffe a wire, sent from Boulogne at 9 p.m.

HAVE PURCHASED WALTER'S ENTIRE INTEREST
THUS SACKING TWO OF YOUR CHIEF ENEMIES
LINTS SMITH AND WALTER. AM VERY PLEASEI
YOU ARE COMING.

It was a message that Steed could not credit. He was amaze
when Walter, on being asked on Saturday if he had sold, replie
that he had. The position of the office, Steed thought, had bee
very gravely weakened. His interview, due to take place in Pari
on Sunday, was unlikely to be agreeable in any respect. But befor
giving a statement of the conditions which brought about the en
of the fourteen-year-old régime at Printing House Square it i
necessary to turn back to the relations of *The Times* with th
Coalition Government, the consequences of Northcliffe's insis
tence upon the importance of the Genoa Conference, and th
question of the future of Lloyd George and the Coalition.

XVI

THE COALITION STANDS

FROM the first day of the year 1922 the prospects of a Happy New Year for His Majesty's Government seemed faint. Nevertheless, in spite of the heavy and consistent attacks of *The Times* and reverses in the constituencies, the Government were destined to recover prestige and be stronger in June than in January. That Northcliffe should now be returning was not propitious, yet their main anxiety when the year was still young arose from within, as is the nature of Coalitions. Before Christmas the Prime Minister and Birkenhead were convinced that there was only one way to deal with the Die-hard Conservative element within its bosom, and the disunion within the two major parties: a prompt appeal to the country. Beaverbrook recommended that course; McCurdy, the Chief Liberal Whip, was in favour, while Chamberlain would decide when he had the report of the Conservative principal agent. Churchill was opposed, though he agreed with Lloyd George and Birkenhead that the right " Die-hards " and the left " Wee Frees " could be outflanked if the two " National " wings were combined into a new party with a new name under the Prime Minister's leadership. Thus Lloyd George would find himself at the head of a party and not merely possessed of a personal following. With a scheme of this sort in mind, with or without a prompt appeal to the country, the Prime Minister departed for Cannes to meet Briand.

The opinion of *The Times* was that a General Election would be " profoundly unpopular in the country." (January 10, 1922.) Within a week the Prime Minister was back from Cannes. The meeting had not been a success, but it had been agreed to hold an international economic conference at Genoa in the spring. *The Times* said on January 12 that Britain had sought to barter the guarantee of French security, contingently given by the Treaty of Versailles, against French concessions that would gravely weaken the position of France towards the Rhineland.

It was notorious that the Entente was not "cordiale." With Franco-British disagreement at Cannes was linked the dispute between the Nationalist Turks and the Greeks in Asia Minor, which threatened to become critical. Also the question of some measure of recognition to be given to Russia lay unresolved between Britain and France. It was hoped at an international economic conference in Genoa to deal with international financial obligations and thus open the channels of trade and, so far as Britain was concerned, help reduce unemployment. The fall of Briand, reported in the paper of January 13, and the succession of Poincaré did not seem propitious. In the opinion of *The Times* Briand had tried to do too much too quickly.

On his return the Prime Minister faced the question whether he should go to the country or not, and if so, when. Guest, the Conservative Coalition Chief Whip, was optimistic as to the result of promptly putting what he called the idea of a "Fusion" Party before the country. He confidentially imparted to the Prime Minister his opinion that the time offered the supreme opportunity for the formation of the Central Party, and the establishment of the great triumvirate consisting of Lloyd George himself, Birkenhead and Chamberlain. This would, he thought, depend upon Birkenhead's willingness to put his position in the Tory Party to the test. Certain recent developments would appear very conveniently to have played into his hands: Younger had joined the Diehard movement; Chamberlain was discredited for lacking initiative and leadership; while Bonar Law had stepped aside rather too definitely to assure himself of continued public interest. Guest's personal knowledge of the House of Commons and of the Coalition-Tory movement made him confident, he told the Prime Minister, that at least one-half of the Tory Members would listen to a Fusionist appeal against Labour made by Birkenhead. To Guest's mind, the position that February resembled that which Lloyd George had boldly, and successfully, tackled in late 1916. It was for Birkenhead to take the same steps as had then been taken by Carson. Chamberlain however, reported that the Party agents objected to the risk of an election. On January 16 Lloyd George said publicly that there would be no February election. Yet the "Die-hard" element continued to press the demand. Thus the *Morning Post* wrote:

Now or never must the Conservative Party break its fetters renounce the unholy alliance of the Coalition, and emerge as an independent unit. As matters stand the Conservative Party is nothing but an agency for carrying into execution either a Liberal policy of series of policies, which, in whatever they consist, are certainly not in accordance with Conservative principles. (Feb. 6, 1922.)

On February 7 when Parliament reassembled, gossip ranged as usual over personalities and policies. It was agreed that the " Die-hard " case seemed to be winning increased support in the constituences. On February 13 the " Die-hard " ministers saw Chamberlain and asked him to make an end of what they described as an " unnatural " union. As on previous occasions the Conservative leader refused. The Prime Minister himself had a case he wished to have considered. He still wanted an election.

On February 20 a Labour candidate beat a Coalition Liberal at Camberwell. It was a Labour gain and let loose a lot more anti-Coalition talk. But Ministers were too busy preparing for Genoa to be able to stump the country in their own defence. The Conference was announced in *The Times* of February 23. The crux, it was understood, was the recognition of Russia. A " Conference " before the Conference was arranged. On February 25 Poincaré and Lloyd George met at Boulogne. At this time the Prime Minister felt extremely uncertain of his authority and on February 27 wrote to Chamberlain saying that under existing conditions he thought he could render no useful service. He mentioned the uncertainties and delays arising out of political changes on the Continent, and emphasized the necessity of firmness in the lead that Britain ought to be giving to the world. If Britain were to lapse into a succession of changes Europe would lose " the advantage of having one great country in its counsels which possessed a stable Government." He was, he said, so impressed with the importance of securing a stable Government " that I urge you to agree to my freedom so that you may be in a position to form a homogeneous Government." Nevertheless, Chamberlain, on advice, sought to overcome the Prime Minister's objections, and finally succeeded. Camberwell had spoken: a powerful Conservative motive for continuing the Coalition was fear of Labour.

However, there was no doubt that the Coalition was failing to coalesce. On March 2 *The Times* Parliamentary Correspondent said that Lloyd George had asked Chamberlain to enforce a measure of discipline upon the Conservative Party. On the same day a leading article dealt with the embarrassment which the " Cabin Boy " (as Birkenhead called Younger) had caused the Captain and the owners. Next day the headlines referred to the " Tottering Coalition." Also on the 3rd Chamberlain spoke at Oxford to the effect that the Party leaders were unanimous that the national interests, " yes, and I may add, although I do not put it before the national interests, even the interests of our own Party . . . would be injured by the Prime Minister's resignation."

A defence of the Coalition, the Party of the future, and an attack on " Socialism " were the main themes of a speech by Churchill at Loughborough next day. " Both the great historic parties in the country are united against the rapidly growing Socialist, or semi-Socialist, Party, whose doctrines and principles are as harmful to the principles of Liberalism as they are pernicious to the general interests of the Empire." What the speaker desired was " unity and Coalition." He looked forward to the day when " out of Coalition there shall arise a strong united permanent national party." In the meantime the Coalition was " a very good Government, though I say. it as shouldn't. (Laughter.) I go farther, and say it is the best Government I have ever seen, and I have a fairly long experience. (A voice— ' Dead as a doornail.') Mind you don't tread on that nail." (Loud laughter.) Churchill, proceeding, claimed, as regards foreign policy, that the Coalition's policy of stability and peace had given it great influence in the world.

When we have two statesmen of such eminence and experience as the Prime Minister and Sir Arthur Balfour working together in cooperation, in fullest intimacy and confidence, what right have irresponsible newspapers, which have to obey the instructions they receive from the individual who happens to be the proprietor—what right have they to pour contempt and obloquy upon an Administration which is so representative of the councils of the world ? (Cheers.)

As for the " Socialists," they, the speaker said, were unfit to govern. It was a confident speech, but *The Times* remained unimpressed with the prospects of a united permanent national party. " How is that possible when Ministers fail to achieve unity in the limited circle of the Cabinet." Mr. Churchill was again hankering after " his previous Centre party " only a few hours after Sir L. Worthington-Evans had made his proud boast of the inherent strength of the Conservatives. " The men are there," he said, " and a Government could be formed every bit as well qualified by character, experience and fitness as any Government formed in this country." Thus members of the Coalition Cabinet spoke with different voices. It was clear, *The Times* concluded, that in the view of Chamberlain and Worthington-Evans " the future is with the historic Conservative Party." And to that Party, Coalition and the current jargon of " Fusion " were becoming increasingly odious (March 6). As to " Fusion " the Parliamentary Correspondent said on March 7 that it meant the formation of a Centre Party, which certain members of the Government, including the Prime Minister and Churchill, would like to see established. Although there was a strong body of Unionists who would resist such a proposal and remain independent of a Government formed on such a foundation, the idea of " Fusion " was being canvassed. It was done cautiously and tentatively, but, the Correspondent felt, " more may be heard of it."

But the " Die-hard " sentiment rallied after an indiscretion that ended in the dismissal of Montagu from the India Office. When on March 9 the Coalition Liberal Minister confirmed his " resignation," the House of Commons gave him the biggest cheer of the session. The circumstances were judged by *The Times* to be " without precedent in our recent political history." (March 10.) A message from the Viceroy (Reading) had been published with the sanction of the Secretary of State, but no other Minister was informed, no consultation between Ministers had taken place, and no Cabinet decision was made upon what amounted to a pronouncement of policy. Inspired by Muslim opinion, it sought in advance of a conference to lay the basis of peace between the parties who were the subject of the message, *i.e.*, the Turks and the Greeks. The cheer was interpreted by *The Times* as a reproof to Montagu's act of defiance of Cabinet authority. It was acknowledged that India was excited (Gandhi was arrested on March 10) but the principle of Cabinet responsibility was none the less important. The dismissal of Montagu was regarded as a contribution to the simplifying of the muddle, and the Coalition was once more criticized for its lack of coalescence. That trouble in India should be added to the crisis in the Near East was awkward enough. On the same March 10, too, the United States claimed payment for the expenses of her occupation forces of £48,200,000—to rank before reparation payments. *The Times* said the claim was " a surprise for which nobody on this side of the Atlantic was prepared." (March 14.) The British claim was for £25m. The situation became difficult for the Government when first Lord Derby and then the Duke of Devonshire declined Montagu's place. " The Coalition is dying before our eyes," then wrote *The Times*.[1]

At this point the Prime Minister asked Beaverbrook to express an opinion about his personal position. He was asked because the Prime Minister was wont to show the same respect for the judgement of the Press Lords, as being in contact with popular feeling and having the capacity to interpret it, that Chamberlain gave to the Party managers. This was Beaverbrook's reply:

[1] For the circumstances in India in which Montagu published his statement, see below, Chapter XXII, " Imperialism ; a New Phase."

Private and Confidential.

Vineyard, Hurlingham Road, Fulham, S.W.6.

March 13, 1922.

My dear Prime Minister,

You were good enough to ask me to send to you during your holiday my thoughts about the general political situation and your own relation to it in the future. I feel sure that what you mean by this is that I should write you a perfectly candid statement of my views as though I were writing to an equal, and that you will not misinterpret my frankness as showing any lack of deference to your high position.

My opinion has been for some time past that the continuance of the Coalition, and of your headship of it in the form of 1918, has become impossible.

You have before you two alternatives: (1) To become the absolute head of a " Fusion Party," leaving out Die-hards and Wee Frees on each side. (2) To move definitely to the Left with your own supporters and to secure in time a Liberal re-union, of which you must ultimately possess the leadership.

Until about a fortnight ago, I think that my inclination would have been to advise the movement to the Left. In many ways, it is much the best plan. It would mean the rehabilitation of the Liberal Party as a potent force in the national life and an opposition ready to take office in rotation with the Conservatives. I am tempted towards it myself because I think I should have found myself in sympathy with the policies which a Liberal Party would undertake under your leadership. A re-united Party of this character could not be " high and dry " as its pre-war predecessors.

Unfortunately it appears to me that very serious obstacles to this course have arisen recently. Winston evidently does not mean to go in such a direction if he can help it. His tendency is all to the Right and his principles becoming more Tory. I am sure he would not fancy being shut up in a coop with you even for a short time. And such feelings may be natural. But if he remains behind, several other Liberal members of the Government would do the same.

It follows that Austen Chamberlain, or whoever was your successor if you left the present Coalition, would simply be at the head of a new Coalition, differing from yours in being more Tory and less Liberal—much on the lines of the Coalition of Salisbury and Joseph Chamberlain in the 80's and 90's. Your own Liberal following would be sensibly diminished and divided and, in consequence, the prospect of re-fusion with the Wee Frees greatly postponed and perhaps actually endangered. All kinds of practical difficulties I need not elaborate would also crop up.

(2) I therefore return to the " Fusion Party " as the best alternative to-day. Here time is the essence of the contract. Two years ago I believe the task would have been comparatively easy. But the whole tendency recently has been adverse. In this matter I have no definite knowledge but I believe that Bonar Law is far more likely to find himself in agreement with you than is Austen Chamberlain, who will reflect the pressure of some of his official followers. It is obvious that the whole proceeding means an intense wrench and supersession of a separate Conservative leader.

None the less, I believe it to be the best plan. But if it is to be done, it has got to be done immediately. If your mind moves in this direction, you ought to forfeit your holiday and come back almost immediately to set the negotiation on foot.

On reflecting on what I have written, I do not find it very illuminating. But I am sure that what you desire from me is a statement of the facts as I conceive them, so that you may exercise your talents upon them. I confess that I cannot see an absolutely clear and certain way out of present difficulties; but I should be the last to deny that it is very probable that you will be more happily inspired than I am and see your way brilliantly and successfully through.

I hope you will come home soon for another reason, it is because we miss so much your presence in the place of the Mighty.

Yours ever,

MAX.[1]

On reflection, Beaverbrook thought over this question of one of the principal personalities favouring " Fusion "; who presented a problem. By way of addendum, Beaverbrook in the intervening two days gave the Prime Minister his opinion about the Secretary of State for the Colonies:

Private and confidential.

Vineyard, Hurlingham Road, Fulham, S.W.6.

March 15, 1922.

My dear Prime Minister,

I intended to add a postscript to my letter—not altering its tenor in any way but developing one particular line of argument—that relating to Winston. He is counting absolutely at the present moment on the formation of a new Coalition in which Austen Chamberlain would occupy the position of Lord Salisbury and he would possess the relative influence of Joseph Chamberlain on Conservative Governments. Or, to put it otherwise, he would be to Chamberlain as Premier what Chamberlain has been to you.

[1] From the copy supplied by Lord Beaverbrook and printed by his permission.

The Conservative rank and file may not see this at all. The Die-hards would have to be included in the negotiations for a new Coalition Government, because they might be able to turn such a Government out on a critical division. In addition there would be a strong view held by older members with claims that, in the event of a reshuffle, the offices should go entirely to Conservatives. I would not pronounce absolutely on this point, for Winston's recent attitude has undoubtedly conciliated some of the Die-hards, and many of the men who might not forget the change of sides in 1903. None the less if an agitation against the inclusion of the Liberals began in the Tory ranks, it would spread very far.

On the other hand, there would be considerable influences brought to bear to keep Winston in the new combination. Certain members whose seats are shaky and depend on Coalition Liberal votes would be in favour of it. The Lord Chancellor would certainly urge the policy of inclusion and would find a ready listener in Chamberlain.

I put the probability of Conservative opposition to Winston's retention of office to him the other day. He was obviously immensely surprised and had not thought of it. However he soon persuaded himself that the danger was negligible. I did not agree if, as I have just said, a campaign was started against him. It appears to me very doubtful whether the Tories would be ready to kill the King merely to put a lesser Prince in his place, even if under their suzerainty.

Yours ever,

MAX.

P.S.   This letter was intended as a postscript and now I must add a postscript to a postscript.

Let us suppose for the sake of argument that Chamberlain undertakes to form a new Government. He is at once confronted with a Die-hard demand for some declaration on the Irish Boundary question and finds the demand inadmissible. In that case he must find outside support.

MAX.[1]

While the Prime Minister was digesting Beaverbrook's advice he had ample reason to feel the intensity of " Die-hard " Conservative antagonism first towards himself, as a dominant personality, and secondly to the fact of any Liberal Leader functioning as head of a Coalition predominantly Conservative. Conservatives of more mature judgement continued to agree with Chamberlain that if the Party threw over Lloyd George

[1] From the copy supplied by Lord Beaverbrook and printed by his permission.

hile he, as Beaverbrook said he might, " moved to the Left " ith his own supporters, either he would effect the reunion of e Liberal Party, or go over to the Labour Party, the bulk of hich would rally to his leadership.

Accordingly, Chamberlain had plenty of support for his policy continuing the Coalition. He urged upon Lloyd George, when ord Derby's refusal to accept the India Office was announced, at the Prime Minister should take the earliest opportunity of finitely declaring his resolution to continue at the head of the oalition. Chamberlain himself, as a leader of one of the parties hose fortunes were inseparably bound up with his own at that me, was absolutely firm on the need to face the country boldly.

Throughout March *The Times* had led the bill page with ticles, as a rule by Gordon Robbins, the Parliamentary Corres- ondent, headed " The Tottering Coalition," " The Sinking oalition," " The Patched-up Coalition," " Disolution or Fusion," The Moribund Coalition," until Monday, March 20, when under he heading " Crisis " it was prophesied that if the Prime Minister ad to decide " whether to resign or to make a last bid for power," is decision " however reluctant, will be for resignation." Next ay, *The Times* announced that the Prime Minister, with obert Horne and McCurdy at his elbow, had decided: he ould demand a vote of confidence. In view of the Genoa onference which had been on the horizon since Cannes, the ecision was of international importance. Genoa was to be the at of an economic Conference; and there must be considered, as loyd George had promised at Cannes, the question of British, rench and Belgian claims upon Russia. One of the com- lications was the attitude of the Colonial Secretary, Churchill. e was no more willing now than formerly to consider the cognition of Russia. The Prime Minister had complicated he situation by receiving a correspondent of the *Daily Chronicle* his house at Criccieth. These interviews when published presented him as an appeaser (the word was used at this time) f Russia, who was to be invited to Genoa. The reporter went far as to say that " Mr. Lloyd George will part from his dearest olitical friend rather than abandon this great fundamental sue of politics." This statement was viewed by Chamberlain, irkenhead and others as a challenge that Churchill would recog- ize as being addressed to himself. Chamberlain believed that he Prime Minister's " policy of appeasement " [*i.e.*, towards ussia] was clearly right. As he said to a reporter, " I do not ink that any of us will differ from it. Some may be more, and some less, sanguine as to the outcome of the Genoa Conference but we shall all agree in wishing success to the Prime Minister' efforts."

Simultaneously, the situation in the Near East gave rise to increased anxiety. The pressure of Kemal, the Turkish Nationalist leader since 1919, became heavier, and the troubles of the Coalition worsened when Lloyd George refused Chamberlain' suggestion of Baldwin for the India Office, and Lord Peel was appointed. That Derby and Devonshire should have refused was taken as a pointer to the forthcoming demise of the Coalition In the country the Coalition, besides losing the by-election at Camberwell, lost in Cornwall, Leicester and South Wales. The situation was such as to justify the Prime Minister's asking himself whether he ought to go to Genoa without due backing On March 21 Chamberlain before the House of Commons raised the question whether the Government in this matter possessed the confidence of the House or not. " The whole House will recognize that it will be impossible to ask the Prime Minister to go to Genoa if there is any doubt about the authority which he possesses." The debate was fixed for Monday, April 3 Lloyd George's mind was now made up. If he did not get a solid vote he would resign. The challenge could not be avoided In the meantime, while still at Criccieth recruiting his health he received expressions of opinion from his colleagues. They were not too optimistic.

It was now believed in influential Coalition quarters that differences with Churchill over Russia had to be resolved, but that if a solution agreeable to Churchill were found, Birkenhead would accept it automatically. Thus, by the last week of March it was a matter of keeping the Coalition above water by keeping Churchill and Birkenhead in it. As at Cannes, the root question was whether Russia was prepared to fulfil her obligations, as agreed, and give solid guarantees of good faith. While the Prime Minister was determined to do business with Russia and was willing to grant recognition, Printing House Square was on the side of Churchill and gave his view powerful support.

A leading article in *The Times* of March 23 tabulated references in the Prime Minister's past speeches to the brutality and horror of Bolshevist rule, and the " sense of disgust " he felt at the prospect of dealing with those " assassins " the Bolshevist leaders. Recognition, Lloyd George had said, would never be possible for a *régime* of starvation, bloodshed, confusion, ruin and terror

1920 he said he shrank from being suspected of being a party
to any recognition of that Government. In 1921 he professed to
see a " change," and was ready to negotiate a trading agreement.
The Times proceeded to denounce Lenin and Trotsky, Tchitcherin,
Krassin and Litvinoff, as agents of a " Government of assassins
and robbers," whom it was now proposed to bring within the
comity of civilized peoples." French opinion, the paper
prophesied, would be outraged by any recognition that was
unaccompanied by most stringent guarantees, including a period
of probation. The article could not fail to impress the Die-hards,
and Churchill. Plainly the Prime Minister was in a fix. His
talents were fully equal to the task if only he could be given the
unanimous support of his Cabinet, and the substantial backing
from the House of Commons.

The circumstances in which the Prime Minister was now placed
are clearly set out in a letter from Grigg.

> 10, Downing Street.
> March 23, 1922.

My dear Prime Minister,

I have just heard that you mean to demand a free hand at Genoa
from the Cabinet and to resign if you do not get it. It is the most
splendid news I have heard since the Armistice.

As things were, the prospects at Genoa were depressing me greatly.

(1) The new demand of the Reparations Commission really puts
the lid on any policy of reconstruction in Europe until the
reparations question is dealt with. It seems to me we must come
clean out for a five years' settlement of reparations or prepare for
real chaos in Germany. I believe in limiting the annual German cash
payments to something like fifty millions sterling—or perhaps the
somewhat larger Cannes figure is practicable—and pledging that for the
service of a large foreign loan out of which Germany can pay off
the Army of Occupation charges, make a further direct payment
on the devastation account to France, and stabilize her currency
by foreign purchase of marks. But whatever the plan, *some long-
range plan at once*. Our people will suffer terribly if we fail in
deference to France to tackle this question now.

(2) I have written you a separate note on the Conference of Experts.
You will see what France is at. Her attitude regarding juridical
recognition of Russia will, I fear, make it impossible for the Soviet
representatives to come to terms of any sort. She will carry her
satellites and many neutrals with her, leaving us the hopeless position
of having come out as the patrons of Germany and Russia without
any practical advantage to compensate.

It seems to me most essential that the issue of recognition shoul
be raised before Genoa, not at the Conference.

(3) This is all the more so since France is certainly playing for
division in British opinion, even in the ranks of the Cabinet. Th
leader in today's *Times*, with its laborious research into your speeches
did not get there by accident. Steed is in Paris drawing his usua
inspiration from the pure waters of the Quai d'Orsay, while man·
people are working up *The Times* and other papers on the recognitio·
issue here.[1]

The " Die-hards " see a prospect at last of getting some rea
Parliamentary leaders, and they will not fail to press the recognitio·
question in the debate.

Here, then, the lists are set for a real issue—peace, appeasement
reconstruction on the one hand; on the other, the old doctrines o·
intervention, ascendancy and vengeance. It raises the fundamenta·
question before the Coalition—whether its colours are to be liberal—
your colours, in fact—or reactionary, under leaders whose ambition·
in that direction are now painfully manifest. I do not see how yo·
could resign on a greater issue. You would win on it before the yea·
was out.

Also, as I believe, you would bring America into Europe on th·
wave of peace enthusiasm which you could create. You could do
it without even mentioning America. The people there would follow
your fortunes on that issue breathlessly, and would see Europe wit·
new eyes in the light of the gun-flashes from the great artillery whic·
you would bring to bear on the old reactionary camps.

I write like a Liberal, you will say. I am one on this issue, an·
two-thirds of the Unionist party will prove so too when they are
brought up against it. But you must bring them up with a round
turn, not allow them to feel they can dictate. At present the
" Die-Hards " are watching you, as the old reactionaries in Europe
watched Napoleon in 1814, fighting the most brilliant campaign of his
whole history from a soldier's standpoint but exhausting himself and
his army when both needed breathing-space for a fresh start. How
different would have been his history in 1815 if he had not over-fough·
the campaign of 1814, winning brilliant battles for an inadequate
result.

I had a great talk a night or two ago with Hilton Young, whom·
I always feel to be a kindred spirit—and, apart from that, certainly·
the best mind of his age in politics. He has since written me the
letter which I enclose. It summarizes our common views—except

---

[1] Downing Street believed that Poincaré was from the start opposed to Genoa.

ıat I would have the title of the Grand Army the "*National*," ıstead of the " Constitutional," Union of Conservatives and Liberals. It is awful to have written all this, but I had to write.

Yours ever,

E. W. M. GRIGG.[1]

Plainly, in view of Birkenhead's and Churchill's stand regarding Russia, the Coalition was ill-fitted to face the " Die-hards." On aturday, March 25, Carson spoke out uncompromisingly:

You may talk of Chamberlains, and Hornes, and Churchills, and Birkenheads, and all the rest of them, but believe me, the Government s the Government of Lloyd George. I do not blame Lloyd George; wish I could do it. But remember, patriot, worker, statesman, lriver, as he was during the war, he is still Lloyd George, and in my ıelief at the present moment, I do not know whether consciously ›r unconsciously, Lloyd George has the old mission that he always ıad in his heart, that is to destroy the Conservative and Unionist ▪arties.

On the same day Churchill, speaking at Northampton, was ·eported as having said " it would be a great disaster if the Con- ıervative Party were broken up " and laid stress on the importance ›f a united stand by Liberals and Conservatives against the Bolshevist and Communist menace. *The Times* was quick to ›oint out that the Genoa policy, as it had been forecast by ınspired publicists, was incompatible with Churchill's speech at Northampton. He had now publicly disclosed their disagreement. Genoa, as the paper understood it, was the opposite of Northampton. The paper emphasized the lesson of Chertsey, ∧here the Conservative candidate who was elected had been ınpledged to the Coalition. If the health of the Coalition was ıot improving, Lloyd George's was. He was getting back to ıis old form; to the delight of his friends. " The discomfiture ›f the Harmsworth Press," wrote Lord Lee, " is almost comic; :hey were so sure they had you this time, and *now*—well, I hope :hey have grounds for apprehension as to what you may say ıbout them. I think it is high time that Northcliffe had another ⅃ose and I hope you will add a little for my sake ! "[2]

The little good news that the paper reported in that week :ame from Paris where, after protracted negotiations between Curzon and the French and Italian Ministers, Poincaré and

[1] Printed by the kind permission of Lord Altrincham.

[2] Lord Lee of Fareham at the Admiralty to the Prime Minister, March 26, 1922. Printed with the permission of Lady Lee.

Schanzer, agreement on the Near East was reached on March 27
The Times was delighted at this " excellent example of how
diplomacy should be conducted. In regard to the extremel
difficult and involved situation in Turkey, they have achieved .
decision that must be regarded as statesmanlike." This wa
much better than the results obtained in unprepared conferences
where delegates given incompetent advice, and having in view
the ulterior motives of domestic politics, engaged themselves in
an effort to deal with economic, strategical and ethnic realities
" They have not made peace in the Near East, but they have laid
a basis for peace . . . they have reaffirmed the unity of the Allies
which is the most effective instrument for re-establishing peac
in the Near East. We gladly admit that this has been done with
a thoroughness which we had hardly dared to anticipate, in view
of the grave errors on the part both of France and of Grea
Britain. . . ." The agreement provided that Turkey should recove
full sovereignty in Asia Minor, including Smyrna, ove
Constantinople and over a considerable part of Thrace which
was to be demilitarized on both sides of the frontier. Th
freedom of the Straits was to be assured and guaranteed by ar
Inter-Allied Commission under a Turkish President, and by the
presence of Allied troops at Gallipoli. The demands of the
Indian Moslems were in essential aspects satisfied except, for
strategical reasons, that Adrianople was placed under Turkish
rule. But a compromise was effected (March 28). This, at
least, was auspicious for Genoa.

The Prime Minister had returned from Criccieth on March 27
It was understood in Printing House Square that he planned to
give full immediate official recognition to Russia, and that or
Monday night (27th) he proposed this to his colleagues of the
Cabinet. Chamberlain dissented and Churchill said he would
resign if the proposal were acted upon. A compromise was
reached. This was reported in *The Times* of March 29, when the
paper argued in two leading articles the case against going to
Genoa and recognizing Russia. The motion of confidence read
as follows: " That this House approves the resolutions passed by
the Supreme Council at Cannes on a basis of the Genoa
Conference and will support H.M. Government in endeavouring
to give effect to them." This limited and innocuous motion
was thought to be as much as could be expected. The credit of
the Government was strengthened on March 30 when the Irish
Peace Conference came to agreement.[1]

[1] For *The Times* and Ireland, see Chapter XIII, " The Problem of Ireland."

On Monday, April 3, the day of the debate on the vote of confidence, *The Times* reminded readers that the motion was of the utmost gravity to the Empire and to Europe." The leading article warned the House of Commons that narrow as the sense was of the words the Prime Minister's interpretation might be broad, and Mr. Lloyd George, " is not always wise in the choice of his methods." In the debate the Prime Minister was not at his best, but the majority for the Government was 78; " inevitable " said *The Times*. The paper reported, but made no reference to the Prime Minister's remarks about the criticisms of the opposition Press. Judging, he said, by the criticism of the " grotesque conglomerate " who were in opposition, he could only imagine that their new Government " would have its principles enunciated and expounded by the *Morning Post*, the *Daily Herald*, the *Westminster Gazette*, the *Daily Mail*, and *Comic Cuts*. (Loud laughter.) I do not mention *The Times*, because that is only a tasteless rehash of the *Daily Mail*." (Laughter.)[1]

On Tuesday, April 4, the paper announced that when the Genoa delegation left on Friday the Prime Minister would be accompanied by Curzon, Horne and Evans. Curzon, however, was indisposed, and went later. *The Times* was displeased that the Delegation comprised no fewer than 92 persons. The opening meeting was arranged for April 9. A multitude of official, semi-official, and Dominion delegations and representatives also proceeded to Genoa. Eminent publicists, J. L. Garvin among them, were known to be taking up their quarters in the hotels. *The Times* announced on April 6 that " South Africa will be represented at the Conference by Sir Edgar Walton, the High Commissioner, the Hon. R. H. Brand and Sir Henry Strakosch." The paper itself had thought fit to make less striking arrangements. The Editor believed that the objects defined at the Cannes Conference had yet to be adequately studied; that there were obstacles to the realization of the Cannes policy of developing trade with Russia; and that a hurried Conference, with Poincaré in power, would compromise relations with France. He hoped the Conference would do more good than harm, but expected little and hence thought the paper adequately represented by the Rome Correspondent, Vernon Bartlett. Before leaving London for Pau, where he had been advised to rest, Northcliffe agreed with these decisions. At Pau he changed his mind, and sent for the Editor. The com-

[1] Thus the Prime Minister obliged Lord Lee's wish to see Northcliffe given " another dose." (See the previous page.)

position of the national and Dominion delegations was impressive
and in the circumstances described in the previous chapter h
insisted that the chance of the occasion becoming significan
justified full representation of *The Times*, and pressed the Edito
to go, saying that otherwise he would go himself. In view o
Northcliffe's state of health, which alarmed the Editor, he con
sented to go; and with great reluctance hurried back to make th
necessary arrangements.[1]

By this time the Editor was inclined to think the Conferenc
might do mischief to the Entente, which he was convinced mus
long remain as a corner stone of any permanent reconstructio
of the fabric of Europe. The unexpected change of plan made i
necessary to act quickly, and accommodation was scarce in a
overcrowded provincial city. Through the good offices of th
Marquis Visconti Venosta, of the Italian delegation, and th
Italian Foreign Office, the Editor was accommodated at th
Hotel Savoia, where he found a number of the French expert
and delegates. It was quickly alleged (and repeated) that th
Editor had deliberately chosen to go to the Savoia in order to b
close to the French.[2] In his attitude to the Entente the Edito
was doing no more than maintaining the position that *The Time*
had occupied since 1901-1902, and confirming the thesis whicl
Lavino, his predecessor at Vienna, had acted upon when he wen
to Paris in 1902 as the paper's Correspondent in succession t
Blowitz.[3] The Entente was altogether an essential factor in th
paper's understanding of Continental politics. Steed did not invent
though he reinforced, this outlook. By coincidence the Edito
arrived at the Hotel Savoia on the anniversary of the signatur
of the Entente. On April 8, 1922, he was certain that the Entent
was not merely as desirable but as necessary as it had been in 1901
In 1922 the situation was that Anglo-French agreement turne
on the Russian question. As it seemed to *The Times*, th
immediate result of a rupture in Anglo-French relations woul
be a Franco-German *rapprochement*, for which the German
were working. Industrially and commercially, France an
Germany scarcely competed. The same could not be said o
England and Germany. France, if affronted by Britain, migh
make concessions to Germany, and leave Britain in associatio

---

[1] For Steed's visit to Pau and the circumstances which forced him to go to Genoa,
see the previous Chapter.

[2] *Cf.* W. P. and Zelda K. Coates, *A History of Anglo-Soviet Relations* (London, 1945
p. 82): " *The Times* . . . sent its special Correspondent to Genoa, no less a person tha
its editor, Mr. Wickham Steed, who perhaps with the object of emphasizing the journal'
support of the French attitude, took up his residence at the same hotel as the Frencl
Delegation."

[3] See Vol. III, Chapter XIII, " The Anglo-French Entente and German Pressure."

with Bolshevist Russia, whose interest in the promotion of European stability was not obvious to Printing House Square.

Northcliffe was no less convinced of the importance of preserving the Entente. He had, it has been seen, decided that Genoa would be a test of statesmanship. Having procured the attendance of the Editor, he constantly sent him complimentary and, as he thought, inspiring telegrams which, however, did not fail to report successes scored by others, as for instance on April 16:

GARVIN TELEGRAPHS *OBSERVER* CONFERENCE WILL MARK BEGINNING NEW REUNION EUROPE, OR END ENTENTE, WHICH WOULD BE ENDED NOT BY ANY DECISIVE STROKE BY LLOYD GEORGE, BUT BY VOTE ELECTIONS WHICH BOUND TAKE PLACE NEXT SIX MONTHS. THIS REAL ISSUE FOR FRENCH STATES-MANSHIP. THIS IS WORTH WATCHING.[1]

Important news reached *The Times* in April concerning Russia and Germany. It arrived on the afternoon of the 17th. The world suddenly learnt that the two Powers had signed an agreement at Rapallo. *The Times* of April 19 assumed that the Allies had been " duped." It was undeniably a surprise, and the situation was not eased by the Russian explanation that the negotiations with Germany had been proceeding since January. The leading article accused Germany: " she has gone behind their [the Allies] back to deal privily . . . with Russia." The Allied protest to Rathenau[2] encouraged rumours of the immediate collapse of the Conference; and Steed criticized so severely the insolence of the Russians that it was taken for granted in P.H.S. that the delegations would return at once. Meanwhile the " unholy alliance " was correctly recognized in the office to be a greater danger to France than to any other Allied Power. A Russian and German association was a manifest peril to all Europe, and yet it was obvious to everybody in the office that no pains would be spared by certain people at either end to connect the wire between Berlin and Moscow. " That would have been attempted had Germany been the victors; it was still more certain to be attempted when she came vanquished out of the struggle." Readers were reminded that the German General Staff had facilitated the return to Russia of Lenin and Trotsky. Once

---

[1] This telegram was sent through Harold Williams who sent an identical telegram to J. Ward Price, Special Correspondent of the *Daily Mail* at Genoa.

[2] Appointed Foreign Minister at the end of January, 1922.

more the lesson was that the Allies must stand closer together than they had done in the recent past. (April 20.)

On April 20 the Prime Minister received a group of Press representatives to whom he made a speech in which he expressed himself " as confident as ever that this Conference will be a success, and that it will end in the pacification of Europe and in the formulation of schemes which will restore a very broken and devastated Continent." His optimism, *The Times* thought, was misplaced. The British seemed not to have taken the measure of the Bolshevists. " Our amateur diplomatists in the playground of European conferences have hitherto had little experience of the ways of hardened conspirators." (April 21, 1922.)

On April 24, Poincaré made a long, carefully phrased, and very emphatic statement of his Government's policy. He prophesied that the Pan-Germans were on the look-out for an occasion to foment trouble sooner or later in the marches of the East, and to retake by force the Polish regions taken from Germany as a necessary preliminary to the reduction of French strength. The Russo-German Treaty, he said, set the seal upon a *rapprochement* which might become tomorrow a direct menace to Poland and an indirect menace to France. While French opinion would have understood the immediate abandonment of Genoa, the Allies were indulgent. But, the French Premier warned, " We will remain at Genoa only on condition that there is no concession to Germany or to Soviet Russia." The Russo-German Treaty (concluded Poincaré) put before the Allies one of the most formidable problems they had had before them since the Armistice. The speech meant that France was not minded to give up any rights conferred by the Versailles Treaty. The leading article commended a declaration of Lloyd George, made the same day, that the Conference would be a failure unless it brought France and Britain " into the closest relationship." *The Times* was happy to have the Prime Minister's authority for its own view that " there can be no reconstruction in Europe, and there can be no assured peace in Europe, without the cordial and active support of our French Allies." Meanwhile the experts were considering the Russian financial proposals, and the pasture of the Allied countries concerned. To many it seemed as if every Russian concession was surrounded with a morass of qualifications which, if acceded to, would nullify the principle. The atmosphere of the Conference was now charged with anxiety. On examination Poincaré's speech was found uncooperative, also the publicity given to it. Nor was the comment in certain English newspapers

n the Russo-German Treaty appreciated by the Prime Minister.
)n April 25, Grigg took the opportunity of his customary
tatement to the British and American journalists to rebut
ertain allegations and deny certain rumours. The Russian
fficial spokesman had informed the Press that entire cancellation
f war debts was intended. There were so many mis-statements
1at the Prime Minister could not pursue them. He desired
1e journalists to publish on his behalf an appeal to the British
ublic " not to believe any statements about the Genoa
Conference that are made in *The Times* or in the *Daily Mail*."
Ie would deal with them in Parliament. Printing House
quare ignored the implication that its reports were untrustworthy,
nd repeated its conviction that the beginning and end of a
ound European policy was a close and definite understanding
etween France and Britain. The existing understanding was
oon to be put to the test.

The Prime Minister, in the effort to reduce British unemploy-
1ent by accommodating Russia, and opening up that market to
3ritish goods, was disposed to be firm with the Continental
ations. On May 3, *The Times* announced that, to the Prime
Minister's secretariat, Belgium stood in the front rank of
' wreckers " of the Conference. She had formulated on May 2
er reservations to the Allied Memorandum. The Russian
roposals with regard to the private property of non-Russians
ere unsatisfactory. On the 5th, Steed said that Belgium had
 done something more than refuse to sign a document ;
he has broken a spell." Some animosity was manifested
t the heralded return to Genoa of M. Barthou who had journeyed
o Paris in order to confer with Poincaré. On Friday, May 5,
: was announced that the Prime Minister was seeing Barthou
n Saturday.[1] It was believed that he might have an important
uty to discharge, for on May 5 the Prime Minister had informed
1e chief Polish delegate, Skirmunt, that if the Conference
id not reach full European agreement Great Britain would
evert to a policy of isolation. Skirmunt communicated this to
teed. On that day (May 5) also, the official British Press
pokesman declared to A. de Gobart, a Belgian representing the
3russels *Soir* and Paris *Intransigeant*, that:

One of the two English officials entrusted with the relations with
1e Press, Mr. Noble Hall, has just said to me textually: " Mr. Lloyd

---

[1] It quickly became evident to the principals of delegations that Barthou's interview
ith Lloyd George would not necessarily be pleasant. This was obvious, also, to Steed.
e was personally as well as professionally interested in the forthcoming confrontation.

George is determined to make France choose between Belgia
friendship and the friendship of Great Britain. If France remain
on the side of Belgium and if Belgium, by her obstinacy, causes th
negotiations with the Russians to fail, there will no longer be an
question of the Blackett scheme [relating to the suspension of inter
Allied war debts], and everybody will have to pay their war debts
With us it is one thing or the other."

The Prime Minister waited all the morning of Saturday, May (
for Barthou, who had felt bound not only to converse first with
the French delegation, and then to see Jaspar, the Belgian delegate
but to see also Schanzer, the Italian Foreign Minister. Henc
Barthou did not see Lloyd George until the evening of Saturday
What passed became the subject of international controversy
and involved Steed.

It is necessary to examine the matter in some detail. Th
Barthou-Lloyd George interview took place late on Saturday
The first semi-official account of it was given to Havas, and th
gist of it appeared in the Paris *Excelsior* on Sunday, May 7:

Mr. Lloyd George for his part might exercise a preponderatin
influence upon the outcome, but he seems tired and discouraged by th
difficulties accumulated on the path of the Conference, and he prefer
to let events take their course without attempting any longer t
direct them.

The dream, doubtless too ambitious and premature, that h
cherished, the dream of attaching his name to the reconstruction c
Europe amid the general reconciliation of European states and by th
raising up of Russia, is perhaps on the eve of collapse, and it is n
without bitterness that the great statesman can think of th
disillusionment which a notable part of British opinion may con
sequently feel.

" That France," he declared in a sad voice, " placed in the positio
of having to choose between Belgium and England, should hav
turned towards Belgium is certainly her right, but this chivalrou
attitude is not perhaps devoid of some ingratitude towards a grea
and loyal ally whose services to the common cause were so heavy
and, doubtless, in future this situation might cause England to b
less exclusive in the choice of her friendships."

It was in the light of information to this effect that Steed sen
his Sunday message to London, for insertion in Monday's paper
He described the interview between Barthou and Schanze
regarding the alleged attempt of the Anglo-Dutch petroleun

nterests to secure a practical monopoly of the world's oil
upplies by making surreptitious agreements with Russia. The
Correspondent proceeded to _ say that Barthou's immediate
nterview with Lloyd George would probably be unpleasant.
All Steed knew at the moment he sent his message was that,
fter the interview, Barthou was due to make a statement to
British journalists, which Steed had deputed his assistant to
ecure. Bartlett in due course brought Steed a full written
eport of Barthou's words. They seemed to be too general in
haracter to justify any comment or interpretation that might
e of interest.

This decision, as it later appeared, was crucial, at least to
he Editor's career. At home his articles had already aroused
ympathy for the Prime Minister among the many members
f the British public who disliked seeing their representative,
vhile absent on national business, subjected to the hostile
riticism of a fellow Briton. In such conditions it was essential
hat the Editor, acting in the capacity of Special Correspondent,
hould not offer the slightest room for the suggestion that he
vas partial in his presentation of facts or relation of events. The
eeling at the time in non-Party as well as Party circles was that at
Genoa *The Times* had badly overplayed its hand. France was far
rom popular and the strenuous support given to her claims
by Steed created in many quarters a tide of indignation against
he paper and the " Northcliffe Press." Friends of the Prime
Minister could assure him that his policy of standing up to France
had brought him a new access of popularity. From a strengthened
position, therefore, Lloyd George prepared to deal a heavy blow
t Printing House Square and Carmelite House. It was in the
highest degree unfortunate for *The Times* and the Editor that an
ccident should play into the hands of the Prime Minister.

It would have been better prudence for the Editor, if the worse
ournalism, had he chosen to send the colourless account which
vas all that his assistant, in common with the rest of his
olleagues, had managed to secure. Such, however, had never
been Steed's methods. It was not his accurate reporting of
he open transactions of a conference that had impressed
Moberly Bell, Mackenzie Wallace, Valentine Chirol and, finally
Northcliffe. Steed's reputation in Printing House Square had
been high ever since October 24, 1896, when, alone of foreign
orrespondents, he had penetrated Bismarck's authorship of the
rticle on Russo-German relations in the *Hamburger Nachrichten*

and enabled *The Times* alone to publish the fact that it was th
Iron Chancellor himself who had revealed that his ow
" Reinsurance " Treaty had been signed behind the back o
Germany's partners in the Triple Alliance.[1]

Such a speciality necessarily carries dangers with it. Steed'
correspondence had been free from the " canards " that soo
ruin the reputation of lesser men who practise the art of hig
personal journalism of the international order. Criticism of hi
point of view, and of the personal form in which it was expressed
had not been lacking in the office. Steed had from the first bee
a man of conviction, instinctive and intellectual, whose belief
moved him to action. Early in his term in Rome, Moberly Bel
had found it necessary to warn him not to take sides: " You
duty is to be an impartial observer. I do not say you are
partisan, but I fear that if you are not careful to guard agains
such a thing, you might in time come to have a leaning that way.'
Bell's warning was not superfluous. The Correspondent had
" in time " come to have a very strong " leaning that way.'
Before Genoa, before Cannes, before the war, he had taken par
—he had taken part with France. To him this was the same
thing as to take part against the enemies of Britain. He had
been too often correct to be " impartial " before he was appointed
Editor, or to change when he came into the chair. At the Pari
Peace Conference he had shown a distinct " leaning." As Editor
he continued to work as the born believer he was in individualism
nationalism and patriotism, as the English instinctively under
stand these attributes. At Genoa he took part against the
rampant internationalism, equally that of the Vatican, as he had
in the past, and that of the Kremlin. He attacked the incipient
isolationism of Downing Street as vigorously as he had criticized
the Hapsburg monarchy's rule over its multi-national dominions.
For the same reason, and with a view to the future of Anglo-
American relations, he had taken part against English misrule
in Ireland.

It was as a partisan of Anglo-French cooperation that he
listened at Genoa on the night of May 7 to certain informants
he knew from past experience to be reliable. They told Steed
what had passed at the Lloyd George-Barthou interview on
Saturday, and also gave him an account of what Lloyd George
had on Sunday morning told Philippe Millet, the foreign editor
of *Le Petit Parisien*. The accounts of these two interviews

[1] See Vol. III, Chapter X, " Hostile Europe."

convinced Steed that the gravity of the matter made it necessary to supplement the message already sent to Printing House Square. Accordingly another message was telephoned by Steed. It appeared under large headlines.

WRECKING
THE ENTENTE

PREMIER'S THREAT
TO FRANCE

STORMY INTERVIEW

THE OIL FIGHT

A critical phase has again arisen at Genoa. M. Barthou, on his return from Paris, informed Mr. Lloyd George that France could sign the concerted document to the Bolshevists only if it was brought in accordance with the Belgian view. Mr. Lloyd George replied severely, saying in substance that the Entente between Great Britain and France was at an end.

Dispatches on the oil issue will be found on page 9.

(By Wickham Steed)

GENOA, MAY 7.

The Correspondent himself thus commented on the interview:

LATER.—I find that I seriously under-estimated the facts when, in my earlier message, I suggested that yesterday's interview between Mr. Lloyd George and M. Barthou was not entirely harmonious. According to reliable information, the British Prime Minister spoke severely. Whatever allowances may be made for his disappointment at the failure of the Conference hitherto to give him the results for which he professed to hope, the fact remains that his language yesterday was in accord with the most extreme interpretations of his policy that his partisans have advanced.

In substance he told M. Barthou that the *entente* between Great Britain and France was at an end. Great Britain considered herself henceforth free to seek and cultivate other friendships. His advisers had long been urging him to make an agreement with Germany, even at the cost of abandoning British claims to reparations. France had made her choice between British friendship and Belgian friendship. She had opted for Belgium, although the help she had received from Belgium was not comparable to the help she had received from Great Britain. The British Government felt very deeply the conduct of France.

Henceforth France might stand alone with Belgium, and see what advantage that would bring her. He (Mr. Lloyd George) knew that what had happened was not M. Barthou's fault. M. Barthou had done his best to be conciliatory, but he had had no freedom of action. British opinion was hostile to France, and his (Mr. Lloyd George's) advisers, especially Lord Birkenhead, the Lord Chancellor of England, had been constantly advising him to break with France. Letters from all parts of the country gave him the same advice. In fact, he, the Prime Minister, was almost the only friend France had in England. But now he must look in another direction.

M. Barthou seems to have been overwhelmed by the Prime Minister's vehemence and to have essayed a soft answer in the hope that it might turn away Mr. Lloyd George's wrath.

After sending his message, Steed met Camerlynck, the official interpreter who was present at the Lloyd George-Barthou interview. At two points he corrected Steed's impression of what had passed. First, Lloyd George had not spoken " violently " but severely. Steed instantly telephoned the correct word to the office, and the emendation was duly made. Steed had reason to be pleased with the day's good fortune.

Steed was less fortunate later in the evening. Much too late for correction, he learnt that the account given by his informants was a conflation of the Lloyd George-Barthou interview and the Lloyd George-Millet interview. It was to the latter that Lloyd George made his remarks about Birkenhead, and not to Barthou; and Steed found that he had transmitted as part of the substance of the Barthou interview the reference to Birkenhead actually made to Millet. This gave the Prime Minister an opportunity he was triumphantly to embrace. He immediately elegraphed to Chamberlain instructing him to deny in the House of Commons the accuracy of the dispatch in *The Times*, nd at a meeting of the British and American Press, denounced he paragraphs in question as " just the ravings of a person who s insane with desire to wreck the Conference. He is not esponsible . . . I cannot conceive that anything said during hat conversation (with Barthou) could be so interpreted. There s nothing which remotely indicates anything of the kind which as been reported to me. There is not a word of truth in it. The French delegation is outraged by it." Steed's first action vas to telegraph to Northcliffe. His message marked " ON NO ACCOUNT TO BE PUBLISHED " identified his informants and their ources.[1]

The office, while Steed was absent, was in the charge of Campbell Stuart, who, naturally, was impressed by the strength of language n which the accuracy of the dispatch was denied in the House of Commons on the same day (May 8). Chamberlain, answering a question, said in strict accordance with the Prime Minister's wire: " I have seen the report published by *The Times* this morning, a summary of which appears to have reached the Prime Minister. . . . He has asked me to say that the account in *The Times* is a deliberate and malicious invention (cheers), and to contradict it at once. The Lord Chancellor, who is also mentioned in *The Times* report, has already repudiated it."

Notwithstanding these and other denials it was, of course, well known to the principals of delegations and to distinguished journalists, and from a variety of sources, that the Anglo-French Entente had for some time been markedly less than cordial,[2] and that the report of the interview in *The Times* was substantially correct. It was known, also, that immediately after the interview Barthou had telegraphed to Poincaré reporting that the British Prime Minister had " employed language of exceptional gravity."

On Monday, also, Steed met Barthou who said that he had

[1] In the meantime there appeared on Monday morning the leading article by Harold Williams in *The Times*, double-leaded, emphasizing the import of the " amazing " news which the paper's Correspondent had telephoned.

[2] Garvin had said this in the *Observer*. *Cf.* the *Observer* of April 30. Garvin's article on the text " Reconciliation or Ruin," said that " Either there will be the beginning of a new Europe or there will be an end of the Entente." Poincaré is denounced as the " Kaiser of the Peace." On May 7, Garvin said that Lloyd George was fighting in the open, and Poincaré in ambush. See also the *Manchester Guardian* of May 8. " If the Genoa Conference goes on it can only do so in a form which recognizes that European relations are no longer based on the Entente."

been requested by Sir William Hankey and Sir Edward Grigg on behalf of the Prime Minister to deny the accuracy of phrases in the report as printed in *The Times*. Barthou at first refused, but afterwards agreed, under strong pressure, to authorize a qualified denial, since it could not be gainsaid that the message at certain points was inexact. The French delegate confirmed the accuracy of the statement that the Prime Minister had said approximately: " France has made her choice between British friendship and Belgian friendship. She has sided with Belgium against us though the services rendered to France by Belgium during the war were not comparable with the help she received from Great Britain." Barthou added: " We do not admit that we have taken sides against England." He was asked to write a letter addressed to Lloyd George for publication. Meanwhile, Ward Price of the *Daily Mail* had obtained from Barthou a declaration, personally corrected before it was telegraphed, in which Lloyd George was said to have alluded to " a parting of the ways." The same journalist on May 9 acquired an account of Lloyd George's interview with Millet, which the latter was disinclined to publish since he had volunteered to Grigg not to let it out in the form of an interview. He had no hesitation, however, in affirming in *Le Petit Parisien* on Tuesday (May 9) that whether one wished it or not, the Genoa Conference, in the opinion of those best qualified to judge, had created a " crise des alliances." The principal cause, in Millet's considered opinion, was the British Prime Minister, and he advised Frenchmen calmly to await events.

Meanwhile Barthou's letter to Lloyd George was circulated by Reuter. Although the French delegate had stated to a meeting of representatives of the French Press that he had no intention of issuing any denial, the terms of the letter in fact written went so much further than had been expected that it was believed that, in acknowledgement of a new understanding, Barthou had agreed to provide a letter stating that at the interview the Prime Minister had not said a word that could be interpreted as an intention to loosen the bonds of friendship that united the two countries, and that he viewed the future of this necessary union with complete confidence.

On the same Tuesday morning, first thing, Steed received from Campbell Stuart a telegram reporting the issue through Reuter of Barthou's contradiction, and asking for a message for publication in next morning's issue of *The Times* giving evidence corroborating the impugned statements. Steed later met Barthou by chance. After an exchange of greetings, the chief

French delegate said, " You understand I was obliged to issue
a *démenti*. Lloyd George had heard of the statement I had made
last evening to the Correspondent of the *Daily Mail* and regarded
it as confirmation of your message. Therefore he asked me to
write him a statement that some of the phrases mentioned in
your message were not uttered by him in the course of Saturday's
conversation. As those precise phrases were not uttered I was
obliged to comply with his wish." " But," said Steed, " Your
letter goes further than that. It states that Lloyd George did not
say a word that could be interpreted as having the intention of
breaking Anglo-French friendship. Did not Lloyd George say
to you on Saturday, ' France has made her choice between
British friendship and Belgian friendship. She has sided with
Belgium against us, though the services rendered France by
Belgium during the war are not comparable with the help she
received from Britain.'? " Barthou's reply was " Yes; that is
true; Lloyd George said that. But we do not admit that we have
taken sides against England."

Proceeding, Barthou enlarged upon the difficulties of his
position. To have refused to issue a denial would certainly have
offended the Prime Minister, and possibly aroused resentment in
France, who wished to maintain the Entente. In the face of this
statement the Correspondent managed to maintain his usual
phlegm. After leaving Barthou and returning to his hotel Steed
found a message from Northcliffe sent through the Correspondent
of the *Evening News*:

URGENT BOTT CASA DELLA STAMPA GENOVA

PLEASE CONVEY THESE MESSAGES TO STEED AND
[WARD] PRICE BEGIN HEARTY CONGRATULATIONS YOU
HAVE SAVED THE ENTENTE HE DARENT GO BACK ON IT
NOW SIGNED CHIEF.

This telegram was sent from London on the 9th at 8 a.m. and
received in Genoa on the 9th at 11.15 a.m. Steed, therefore,
reasonably believed that Northcliffe had understood the
telegram he had sent on Monday immediately after Lloyd
George had denounced him in Genoa, and Chamberlain had
pilloried the paper in the House. Steed's telegram must be
quoted:

HENGILPRI [H. G. Price, Northcliffe's Secretary] LONDRA

MAY 8

FOR CHIEF ON NO ACCOUNT TO BE PUBLISHED STOP
MY INFORMANTS WERE GERAUD ECHO DE PARIS
AND DELACRETELLE JOURNAL DEBATS WHO JOINTLY

RECEIVED INFORMATION FROM COLRAT MEMBER FRENCH DELEGATION MASSIGLI SECRETARY DELE-GATION WHO PRESENT AT INTERVIEW STOP AFTERWARDS OBTAINED CONFIRMATION CHIEF STATEMENTS FROM CAMERLYNCK OFFICIAL INTERPRETER WHO ALSO PRESENT INTERVIEW STOP SUBSEQUENTLY LEARNED TOO LATE FOR CORRECTION THAT STATEMENT ABOUT BIRKENHEAD BEEN MADE PHILLIPE MILLET PETIT PARISIEN NOT TO BARTHOU THOUGH MY INFORMANTS HAD ORIGINALLY MIXED THEM TOGETHER STOP STRONG BRITISH PRESSURE BEEN PUT BARTHOU ISSUE DENIAL BUT OTHER MEMBERS DELEGATION OBJECT STOP PONCET SECRETARY ADJOINT FRENCH DELEGATION CALLED TODAY READ MY MESSAGE OF SUNDAY NIGHT ASSURES ME IT JUSTIFIED BY GENERAL SENSE OF MINUTES INTERVIEW.

In reponse to Stuart's request, Steed sent more than one telegram embodying the declaration of the head of an important delegation directly corroborating the substance of the message in question; which Stuart, however, decided not to publish. He suppressed also the publication in the *Daily Mail* of Ward Price's telegram. It is not known whether this was done at Northcliffe's direct instructions.[1]

The combination of denials by the Prime Minister, Chamberlain and Barthou placed Printing House Square in a situation that was as uncomfortable as it was unfamiliar. On May 10 *The Times* contained no leading article on Genoa. On the 11th the paper backed up its Special Correspondent by reprinting from the *Echo de Paris* an article by " Pertinax " which described the operative phrase in Barthou's *démenti* as " entirely incredible," and proceeded to state that the British Prime Minister had indeed made use of words of " exceptional gravity " in the course of the interview. Meanwhile Steed was continuing to send dispatches. They were accorded less prominent positions. The Anglo-French crisis was over and Steed had played his part in influencing its settlement. But his position in the office was not what it had been. The intentions of Northcliffe were known perhaps only to

---

[1] For Ward Price's telegram see Appendix II, Sources, XVI. See also the telegram addressed to Steed on May 9, 9.52 a.m. CHIEF'S TELEGRAM TO YOU AND PRICE WRITTEN IN IGNORANCE BARTHOU'S DENIAL HE THINKS YOU HAVE BEEN DUPED AGAIN NONE-THE-LESS HE BELIEVES GOOD WILL RESULT. PLEASE REPLY MY TELEGRAM SENT YOU FROM LONDON 2.15 THIS MORNING. STUART. The word " duped " here refers to the New York interview described above in Chapter XIV. It was Northcliffe's custom to lay upon his colleagues the blame for any personal dereliction.

Stuart. Others guessed at them. Northcliffe had sent the Editor more than one peremptory telegram; that was known. Those who had some knowledge of the Chief's habit expected some action to be taken, and when the office learnt that Sir Charles Russell reported that the Prime Minister contemplated entering an action against *The Times* for libel, it was taken for granted that the Editor would choose to resign. Stuart sent Lints Smith to see Steed in Paris and press him to take this course.

Steed, however, stood his ground, proposing to accept the action if it were entered, and cross-examine the Prime Minister. The prosecution was not entered, and the question of resignation was not pressed. But the incident, as a whole, seriously weakened Steed's position in the only place important to him, *i.e.*, in the office. The judgement of John Walter and Campbell Stuart was that the Editor had lowered the standard of accuracy that *The Times* had patiently built up. The incident had certainly afforded a pretext to critics to say that the consistent and vigorous criticism that Steed had launched against the Prime Minister in the leading columns of the paper was biased. There were many who urged that Steed had compromised the reputation of *The Times* for impartiality. Finally, whether or not Steed had risked the paper's reputation for accuracy or impartiality, the Prime Minister had been placed in a position that enabled him to complain, as politicians always did when faced with consistent and vigorous criticism, that Printing House Square was carrying on a personal vendetta. Unwillingly the Editor had, it was said, strengthened the very Coalition he was at such pains to destroy. The effect upon the weekly Press was far from fleeting. The *Spectator* described the " Genoa Recriminations " as a " National Humiliation," and the Editor of that influential weekly expressed his " disgust and indignation " with " the Prime Minister, Lord Northcliffe and his Chief Organ," etc. " *The Times* cannot possibly be excused for making the situation at Genoa, bad before, infinitely worse by its methods of criticism and disclosure." As for Lloyd George, he had handled the Conference with astonishing " levity and irritable recklessness." This did not justify *The Times*.[1] *The Nation* printed an account of " the most explicit and the most mischievous report " that *The Times* had published, adding that the truth " we imagine " was that " Mr. George did speak gravely and plainly " but not in a menacing fashion . . . " The French hug the delusions that Lord Northcliffe and Mr. Steed are typical English politicians."[2]

[1] *Spectator*, May 13, 1922.
[2] *The Nation*, May 13, 1922.

The article in the *Observer* welcoming the Prime Minister on his return from Genoa was pitched in another key. Lloyd George was rewarded with an ovation in the writer's best style. " Genoa,' he said, " was a battle for the soul of the world." There was a complementary excommunication of the Prime Minister's critics " Men like Lord Northcliffe, with their preaching of a three-fold lunacy of hatred and suspicion, will never be happy, it seems, until they drive Germany, Russia and Japan into one another's arms with ultimate consequences over all Asia destructive of every sane hope and aim." Garvin warned his readers not to listen to any of the " hundred gramophones " of one man who was " full of personal kinks and political hallucinations."

This call from Garvin's trumpet brought the Prime Minister an enthusiastic welcome from members of the Coalition. On May 26 a splendid company, under the Chairmanship of Lord Long, and including Lords Lee, Derby, Birkenhead and Balfour, and twenty other peers, honoured the man who, in the Chairman's words, had been " pursued by calumny and abuse of an unparalleled character," and even attacked " from the comfort of the editorial chair and the safe seclusion of the editor's private room." It certainly looked as if the energy with which *The Times*, under Steed, had pursued Lloyd George had lifted him higher than ever in the esteem of public opinion. According to Birkenhead, Lloyd George's prestige and influence were " incomparable." Indeed, whatever *The Times* said to the contrary, the health of the Lloyd George Coalition appeared better in June than in January.

It was impossible to say the same of Northcliffe's condition, or of Steed's editorship. The Editor had known for weeks that Northcliffe's critical condition was not only of the physical order. He knew that his tenure of the editorial chair was subject to a moment's notice. He knew on June 9 of Walter's sale of shares and surrender of the option. He had been summoned to Paris to meet Northcliffe on June 11.[1]

In order to get a good night's rest Steed went independently to Paris on Saturday. Northcliffe left the Boulogne hotel (the same to which he had summoned Moberly Bell in 1908) by an early train the same day, made a scene on the platform of the Maritime station, cursed his secretary, told the stationmaster that there had been an attempt to assassinate him, harangued all the officials and, on the journey, insulted the conductor of

---

[1] In the circumstances described at the end of Chapter XV.

he train. The train arrived at Paris in the afternoon and
Northcliffe was accommodated in a suite on the fifth floor of
he Plaza-Athénée. Within twenty-four hours Steed was to see
or himself how well-founded, or otherwise, were the fears that
e had entertained since Northcliffe's return, scarcely four months
before, from his world tour.

XVII

END OF THE NORTHCLIFFE REGIME

WHEN Steed called at the hotel on Sunday evening, June 11
1922, he found waiting in the lobby P. A. Goudie, for man
years Editor of the Paris *Daily Mail*. He said he had just beer
designated Manager of *The Times* in succession to Lints Smith
Addressing Steed, Goudie said, " Be prepared for a shock. Th
Chief is not himself," to which Steed replied, " Does that surpris
you? " " Not altogether. I have seen it coming on for a lon;
time," Goudie replied. Steed was taken by the manager of th
hotel to Northcliffe's apartment on the fifth floor. He found hir
in bed, scantily dressed, obviously excited. For a moment, wher
the lights were turned up, his left eye showed a diagonal squint
His lower lip bore a dark scar as if he had been burned. Seizin;
Steed's hand he said how keenly he had felt the separatior
from him, and rehearsed in a gabbling voice the circumstance:
of his poisoning by the Germans, and the attempted assassinatior
by his secretary at Boulogne. The change in the editorshir
was a dastardly attempt to separate him from Steed, he said
It had failed. Nevertheless, if Steed wished to leave there woulc
be no haggling about terms. He, Northcliffe, was to be Editoi
of *The Times*, Brumwell his acting Editor, and Steed woulc
travel with him as his Personal Political Adviser.

In an interval made possible by Northcliffe's valet, Steec
was able to rejoin Goudie and other members of the *Daily Mai.*
staff. From the manager of the hotel they learned of Northcliffe';
plan to leave Paris early next morning for Evian-les-Bains in
a special carriage made available by the Chairman of the P.L.M.
Meanwhile, upstairs, Northcliffe had seen the shadow of his
dressing-gown hanging on the door and mistaken it for an intruder.
When Steed returned to the apartment he found Northcliffe
continuing to wave at the shadow a Colt pistol (the valet found
that its seven chambers were loaded) with his finger constantly
on the trigger. Clutching a book of piety with his left hand,
and the pistol with his right, he now insisted that Steed should

ccompany him to Evian where he would meet Lady Northcliffe, Sir Robert Hudson and Sir Frederick Treves. Steed's efforts o persuade Northcliffe not to leave Paris but to arrange for Lady Northcliffe to come to the hotel were futile. He was absolutely determined to go to Evian. After four hours at Northcliffe's bedside, Steed withdrew to consult Goudie. It was decided to summon a doctor at 6 a.m. in the hope that, at the last minute, he might dissuade Northcliffe. Steed returned to the Plaza-Athénée at 5 a.m. to find the barber at work on Northcliffe's hair. An hour later his Rolls-Royce arrived at the door of the hotel ready to catch the 8 o'clock train from the Gare de Lyon. The doctor summoned by Goudie duly arrived. He was refused admittance but upon request waited in an ante-room and agreed to travel in the train as far as Bellegarde, the French-Swiss frontier town. Steed went back to his own hotel, telegraphed to Sutton asking him to come to Evian, and went to the Gare de Lyon where he waited. Northcliffe arrived on the arm of his valet, with two minutes to spare. The party consisted of Steed, Goudie, Warden (Editor of the Paris *Daily Mail*), a telephonist, a shorthand writer and Brown, the valet. During the journey Northcliffe wrote a number of highly libellous telegrams which Steed destroyed, talked incessantly, astonished everyone with alternate rambling and uncanny lucidity of his speech. At various stages of the journey he insulted and threatened the waiters in the train for their clumsiness, and cursed his companions. Goudie and Warden, and their clerks, were told to go on to Geneva.

At Bellegarde Sir Robert Hudson, aware of Northcliffe's condition, was on the platform with a motor car ready for the 50-mile drive to Evian. In the car Northcliffe continued to talk incessantly, urging and bullying the chauffeur to drive ever faster and faster over the narrow and winding road. Speeding between 45 and 50 miles an hour the car drew up towards 8.30 at the Hotel Royal, Evian-les-Bains. The Manager, the porters and the page boys of the hotel, arrayed in honour of the expected nobleman, were insulted and driven off into the portico. At last he was got to rest and installed by Lady Northcliffe in an apartment on the second floor. He flatly refused to see Sir Frederick Treves. A strong injection of morphia relaxed him for a time, but he soon resumed his habit of talking incessantly until 1 a.m. on Tuesday morning. By this hour he had talked almost without a break since 5 a.m. on Monday, when the barber had come to the Hotel Plaza-Athénée to cut his hair.

During the evening of Monday, June 12, Hudson, Treves and Steed consulted. From Lausanne Treves summoned a brilliant French nerve specialist, holding British medical degrees, who arrived later with a trained nurse and a male attendant. He certified Northcliffe as insane. They all passed the night close to the patient's room. As the night progressed an increasingly serious view of the case was taken by Treves, and Hudson wired home for Dr. Seymour Price. A serious view was also being taken in London. During Tuesday, as the result of telegrams that Northcliffe got his valet to dispatch, action was taken at Printing House Square and at Carmelite House. It was not what the Chief intended. Steed had given strict instructions to Harold Snoad, Northcliffe's secretary, to send no telegram without referring it to him; but as the Chief sent Snoad to the Post Office with a few harmless telegrams which Steed had passed, Steed feared that Northcliffe would bribe a waiter or a nurse to send some other telegrams without his knowledge. Hence, as soon as Snoad returned, Steed then (June 13) telegraphed to *The Times*

FROM WICKHAM STEED, HOTEL ROYAL, EVIAN-LES-BAINS. DISREGARD ENTIRELY UNPUBLISH ANYTHING RECEIVED DIRECTLY OR INDIRECTLY FROM HERE UNLESS SIGNED AT BEGINNING AND AT END BY GEORGE SUTTON OR BY ME. WARN DAILY MAIL. WICKHAM STEED, HOTEL ROYAL, EVIAN-LES-BAINS.

Snoad was sent back to the Post Office with his telegram. He had hardly gone when Northcliffe sent for Steed, cursed Snoad for being so long away, and asked him to write for him perfectly sane telegrams to his mother and sister. Then he said to Steed : "Now I want to send another telegram. Somebody in London is playing me tricks, so I want it to go in your name, like this :

LINTS SMITH, TIMES, LONDON, FROM WICKHAM STEED, HOTEL ROYAL, EVIAN-LES-BAINS. YOU ARE A RASCAL AND A THIEF. I WILL HAVE THE LAW ON YOU. IF YOU DON'T LEAVE THE OFFICE IMMEDIATELY I WILL COME WITH THE POLICE TO TURN YOU OUT. ACKNOWLEDGE RECEIPT TO ME HERE. WICKHAM STEED, HOTEL ROYAL, EVIAN-LES-BAINS.

When Steed, astonished that Northcliffe should have read his mind, had written out this telegram Northcliffe asked him to take it, with the others, to the Post Office and send them off himself, which Steed promised. When Snoad returned, Steed

epeated the order to send nothing without his knowledge, and
hen went to the Post Office, counted the words in the
elegram to Lints Smith, and sent another telegram of a
ifferent kind using the same number of words. He was
areful to take a receipt for it and the two other telegrams.
)n his return Northcliffe sent for Steed. " Have you sent
hose wires ? " he asked. When Steed said " Yes," he was
sked for the receipts. When handed them, Northcliffe looked
.ard at the receipt for the telegram to Lints Smith. " Quite right,"
e exclaimed, " forty-nine words ! " This was the exact number
f words, without signature, in Steed's substituted telegram.

At three o'clock Sutton arrived at Bellegarde on his way to
Evian. As the Chief did not know that Steed had sent for him,
nd Sutton had announced his journey by wire, the Chief was
urious that he should have come. He wrote him an insulting
ote for Pine, the chauffeur, to deliver to Sutton at Bellegarde,
vhich he handed to Steed who at once tore it up. When
utton arrived at the hotel, in spite of Northcliffe's (intercepted)
nessage, he was severely scolded, and dismissed from the room.
'here was no train until the evening. As Sutton announced that
nembers of the family would be arriving in the morning, the
xhausted Editor decided to return with Sutton that night. It
vas a decision unwelcome to Northcliffe, who had planned a
our they would take together in Switzerland when he should be
little better. Steed's reply was that he needed some more
lothes and linen and must go back to London to get some.
'hat Northcliffe's attitude, at that moment, was friendly is clear
rom his answer : " Get them in Paris and come back here
mmediately." It was quite different in the evening when Steed
vent to take his leave. He began his attack on Steed by flattering
im. He then tried, and nearly succeeded in the effort, to break
teed's nerve by belabouring him and his family with every kind
f indecent insult. With great strength of mind Steed cut him
hort by saying : " These are not things that I can listen to.
ioodbye." As events were to fall out, this was the last that the
.ditor saw of Northcliffe.

Meanwhile there was infinite consternation at Printing House
quare and Carmelite House. At midnight on June 12
Iubert Walter called on Ralph and informed him that he had
eard indirectly from Paris that Northcliffe was insane and there
as a queer story about a revolver. At last it seemed pretty
lear to both Hubert and Ralph Walter that Steed had not been
) far wrong on the point of insanity, and that the sale must not

go through. Ralph and Hubert Walter breakfasted together (
Tuesday, the 13th, and went all over the ground again. The sam
morning John Walter telephoned his bankers, telling them not
hand over the share certificates without further instructions. F
had now decided that he would not deliver until he ha
received an answer to his telegram and letter linking tl
option to the Chairmanship. The confusion was great. Tl
registration of the transfer of John Walter's shares was held u
and Sutton was prevented from forwarding the arrangement l
an urgent need to consult Northcliffe. In the meantime, tl
signed transfer lay in the custody of his Solicitor. Nothir
would arise until Sutton returned. On the other problem: wh
to do if Northcliffe were really insane, the best brains in tl
office proceeded to confer. Freeman, in addition to having firs
class editorial ability, was a practical man of business. He was
most able and loyal Deputy Editor to Dawson; and Steed, wh
as Freeman knew, had always backed him and defended hi
against Northcliffe. The Deputy Editor had with him the Edit
of the *Literary Supplement*. The latter suggested that in the eve
of Northcliffe's death some suitable person should purchase tl
property and control the paper. More than that, he had, on tl
advice of a friend, sought out Sir Guy Granet of Lee, Higgins(
& Co., the Boston and New York bankers, who acted in behalf
a man he had known at New College, Oxford. He had not spoke
definitely to Granet nor could he do so since the man from Ne
College would need to have at least the outline of some plan (
other; and nobody could yet say what the constitution (
The Times would be when Northcliffe died, or was certified, or f
some other reason ceased to control it.

The legal status of the option after Walter had sold his holdir
was also unknown, but this essential point appears to have bee
the occasion of brief mention only. When questioned abo
" the New College man " the Editor of the *Literary Suppleme*
replied that the man was John Astor, the younger son
William Waldorf Astor, the present peer. Walter decided that r
step could be taken until the crucial question of Northcliff(
state of mind was definitely settled. There was still no pro
that Northcliffe's mind was unhinged or his health beyond repa
This, too, was Sutton's opinion.

There were strong elements of hearsay and hesitation in tl
decision. The arrangements made by The Times Publishir
Company in the latter part of 1922 would have been different
Walter, when he sought to recover his option, had gone to Pa

HUBERT WALTER

) see Northcliffe, and, incidentally, make up his mind on the
uestion of his health. As it was, the only information on the
ubject came to him indirectly from Steed, who had been thought
) be an alarmist. But Walter did decide to question Steed as
)on as he should return from Northcliffe's company.

The leave-taking at Evian on Tuesday evening by no means
ut an end to the Editor's professional association and
nxious personal connexion with Northcliffe. On Wednesday
norning Steed and Sutton arrived in Paris and met Lints Smith
vith whom they went on to London, after Steed had used his
nfluence with the French Government to save Northcliffe from
ction by the local authorities of Savoy against a person certified,
s Northcliffe had then been. The Editor's instructions to
.ondon had already been acted upon. The directors of the
)aily Mail had met and decided that nothing was to be published
)ver the name of Northcliffe unless by the written authority of
George Sutton. A statement about Northcliffe's health was
)ublished in the *Daily Mail* on Wednesday, June 14. On the
ame day it became known that Caird and Fish, two of
Northcliffe's co-directors of Associated Newspapers Limited
which owned the *Daily Mail*, the *Evening News* and other journals)
nad taken out a writ for libel against the Chief. On the same day,
fohn Walter agreed that Ralph Walter should consult Grigg,
ell him the whole story of the sale, and the circumstances
)f its confirmation, and ask him to decide whether Walter
should inform the Prime Minister or Balfour, or both.
That great changes must occur in the management and editorial
departments was inevitable even if the doctors' optimistic
report were to be justified. Meanwhile, it was necessary to
prepare motions to be put to the meeting of the directors of
The Times Publishing Company Limited. The Articles of
Association provided for seven days' notice of a board meeting.
Advised by counsel, Walter instructed Soames to deliver the
delayed transfer to Northcliffe's personal solicitor, William
Graham, during the morning of June 15. The Company
formalities then went forward and Ralph went to confer with
Grigg.

The Prime Minister's Political Secretary, Grigg, was a convinced
Liberal Imperialist. Naturally he was anxious to see *The Times*
come into the right hands. Besides being in a position of influence
he was familiar with the organization of the office as he had
come to Printing House Square in 1903 to work in the

Imperial Department.[1] More recently, he had fough
a full war in Flanders and France as Staff Major o
the Guards Division, and when the war was ove
he had accompanied the Prince of Wales, as military
secretary, on his tours to Canada, Australasia and the
West Indies. In 1921 he went to Downing Street to help with the
Imperial Conference, and became Private Secretary to the Prime
Minister.[2] He was fitted in every way to advise *The Times*. Like
Ralph Walter and Hubert Walter, he was a New College man, and
was on excellent terms with both of them. Also he was intimate
with Milner and Geoffrey Dawson. At this critical point
nobody was better informed than Grigg. He thought that
possibly Walter had not been well advised, urged recourse to
Poole and maintained that nobody else was of any use. He
reminded Ralph that Poole was also the solicitor to Lloyd George.
Grigg might have added that Poole also acted from time to time
as the solicitor to Northcliffe and Rothermere. Poole being
away, Grigg himself promised to have a discreet word with the
Prime Minister. Poole, in fact, returned on the night of
June 16th and the first serious Walter-Poole-Grigg conversations
then took place. Poole was evidently very interested. He first
cautioned the Walters that only that morning he had been retained to deal with the writs served against Northcliffe by Andrew
Caird and Walter Fish.[3] But these actions, he prophesied,
would not mature, and he agreed to consider the matter as a
whole, *i.e.*, the sale of Walter's shares, the status of the transfer
and of the option, and the possibility and nature of a syndicate to
acquire the Northcliffe holdings.[4]

Meanwhile at Evian, on Wednesday morning, Northcliffe was
abusive of everybody. It was agreed that he should be taken
home as soon as Dr. Price arrived. It was in the evening of
Thursday, June 15, that Steed reached Victoria and went home
to rest. From Evian on Saturday night, the 17th, Northcliffe,
accompanied by Lady Northcliffe, Leicester Harmsworth
(Rothermere had not gone to Evian), Robert Hudson, Dr. Price
and two nurses set off on the journey to his home at No. 1, Carlton
Gardens, where it had been decided he was to rest and receive
treatment. The Chief's friends in London were not unhopeful.
Dr. Price telegraphed his report to Sutton on Saturday:

[1] For Grigg's services to *The Times* see Chapter I, " The New Imperialism."

[2] J. T. Davies, Sir William Sutherland and Miss Stevenson were his Private Secretaries.

[3] See previous page.

[4] The preceding paragraphs are based on notes made at the time by John Walter and
Ralph Walter, now filed with P.H.S. Papers.

CONDITION AT PRESENT GRAVE BUT ENTIRELY
RECOVERABLE I THINK. SENSE OF PROPORTION NIL.
WILL TAKE MANY MONTHS.

On the night of Sunday, June 18, the Chief, better in some
respects and with little appetite for rest, arrived at Victoria.
The Editor, having no desire for a repetition of Tuesday evening's
experience, did not go to the station to welcome him. He left the
office in good time to avoid any contact with him, and took care
not to return after dinner.

Hardly had the Editor got home from the office when an
awed Brumwell telephoned to say that Northcliffe had already
been asking for him and seemed very excited. Five minutes
later Northcliffe rang Steed at home. He began by cursing
him for having broken faith with him; he had not gone back to
Evian, nor had he awaited him in Paris; he had not even gone
to Victoria to meet him. Steed was no longer Editor.
Northcliffe would send the police to turn him out of the office
if he ever dared go back to Printing House Square. Steed's
answer was that there was one thing and one thing only
Northcliffe had to do and that was to keep quiet and get well;
and that " Until you get well I will continue to look after things
at the office." Northcliffe answered : " I'll forgive you this
time, but never do it again." This was not the only telephone
call he made in the next few hours. He possessed, what few
or none seemed to know, four separate telephone lines from his
bedroom at Carlton Gardens. He now used them one after the
other to tell members of the staff of *The Times* and the *Daily Mail*
that they were sacked. His threats to come down to Printing
House Square and have them turned out by the police convinced
Lints Smith that it was necessary to have the office guarded by
police with instructions to stop Northcliffe himself and turn
him back should he attempt to get into the office. On Monday,
June 19, three of his telephone lines were cut, but he continued
to use the fourth. Nobody in the office now believed that his
health could be sufficiently restored to enable him to resume
any measure of the effective control of Printing House Square
that he had exercised for fourteen years and three months.
What was to happen ? And who was to take charge at
Printing House Square?

John Walter, with or without shares, with or without option,
was not powerless. He was still Chairman. The medical report
that Northcliffe's health was " entirely recoverable " but that it

" will take many months," was made on the 17th when Walter received notice of a meeting of the Directors called for Monday afternoon the 19th, for the passing of the transfer.

On Monday morning Walter went to see Steed. This was the first time the Chairman and the Editor had met since the first week of April. It has been seen that John Walter had heard second or third hand of Northcliffe's state of health. It was on March 7[1] that Charles Russell had warned Steed that Northcliffe was abnormal, and on April 6 that Steed said to Hubert Walter, " Northcliffe is going mad."[2] At ten o'clock that Monday, June 19, Steed had spoken on the telephone to Andrew Caird, who said that on Saturday he had heard from Rothermere that the news was reassuring and that with prolonged rest and quiet there was good hope of recover. This was the substance of the doctors' report to Robert Hudson and Sutton. What now was Walter to think? The Editor said he could tell him. Walter then listened to an eye-witness's account of what had happened since the previous Sunday, June 11. At this recital Walter asked the Editor if, at the Board, he would move a resolution to defer passing the transfer. Steed said he had not liked the idea of such a sale and therefore would oppose the Board's passing the transfer, difficult as it was to prove Northcliffe's present insanity. But when the directors assembled at five o'clock in John Walter's room, the secretary, with Soames, the solicitor, said that as the seven days' notice had not been given the meeting was invalid and that the meeting must be postponed from Monday until Tuesday week next, June 27.

On the night of Monday the 19th Steed and Brumwell brought out the paper. During the evening Northcliffe, using his fourth and only instrument, telephoned every conceivable kind of message to Printing House Square and to Carmelite House.[3] After 3.50 p.m. on June 20 Northcliffe's medical advisers cut off his last telephone. The directors of *The Times* were at last convinced that Steed had not exaggerated Northcliffe's condition. It was realized that Northcliffe was not merely unwell; he might quickly die. There were endless complications in view. Northcliffe

---

[1] See Chapter XV, " After Northcliffe's World Tour," above, p. 629.

[2] *Ibid.*, p. 637.

[3] Many of which were directed against the Editor, e.g., " Do you know that Mr. Steed's private telephone is still connected. Will you have it cut off at once. Do it yourself. Send this telegram to Steed: ' Your private telephone is cut off to-day.' Sign it *Times*. If Mr. Steed insists upon coming into the office have him turned out by the Police. He is not allowed in. I have been very nice to him; but he has turned against me." (From the shorthand notes of G. Beer, P.H.S. Papers.)

was back in Carlton Gardens, yet the governing instrument was the so far unrevoked Power of Attorney he had given to Sutton, Graham and Stuart. It was, they knew, very inclusive and gave them power to sell and purchase shares, draw on the bank, deal with property and engage staff. It was, and this they did not know, irrevocable from July 15, 1921, for twelve months and continued in force thereafter until revoked.

Meanwhile, Grigg was not inactive. On the evening of the 16th he had an hour's discussion with the Prime Minister about *The Times*. Lloyd George was deeply impressed. The news was most important. It was, indeed, necessary to re-establish the property, and the proper way to do this was to maintain John Walter as the Chief Proprietor; there should be no attempt to make the paper pay big dividends, perhaps not so much as 5 per cent. Of course, capital would be necessary. This, the Prime Minister said, he would undertake to find. As to policy, he could be definite. *The Times* should be mildly Liberal Imperialist in tone, independent in home issues, and in foreign relations give reasonable support to the Government. The governing aim should be the pacification of Europe. In reporting the conversation to John and Ralph Walter, Grigg added that he had reason to think that Lloyd George would like to resign, after the settlement of the Irish crisis, and might himself be ready to edit *The Times*.

There is no evidence that, at this time, the Prime Minister snatched at the chance of becoming Steed's successor in the control of the instrument that had done so much to injure him. On the other hand he could not be blind to the value of the leading journal to the causes he and others had at heart. Those who believed in his capacity and in his social programme had excellent reasons for wishing him to lead in the period of reconstruction as he had led in the war. His colleagues, Balfour, Birkenhead and Chamberlain, were backed by very strong Conservative support. After Genoa and the tussle with Steed the Prime Minister's position seemed stronger. It could be made more so with the acquisition of *The Times*. The paper was the means with which to win the great post-war campaign, not necessarily for Lloyd George as the leader of one of the historic parties, but, perhaps, of a Centre " Fusionist " party, or new Coalition, or of a social force.[1] With what degree of seriousness the Prime Minister

---

[1] For the Coalition and the scheme for its continuance in a different form see Chapter VI, " The Coalition Stands "; for the collapse of these schemes, see next Chapter, The Coalition Dissolves."

in the early summer listened to such a scheme is not known. I may well be that he neither encouraged nor refused the suggestion that he should consider the editorship. In the late summer the Prime Minister's interest in such a future for himself seems to have increased. On June 16 Grigg was persuaded that the Prime Minister was interested in the destiny of *The Times* and would help in finding the money for a syndicate that would maintain the position of John Walter. Walter naturally felt a real sense of relief and pleasure that there was at last in view a prospect of settling *The Times*. The projected settlement was not destined to progress swiftly. A week passed and all that became known to John Walter was that the Prime Minister had seen Rothermere on June 20.

On the 23rd, a friend of David Davies asked for an appointment to see John Walter. Davies,[1] who had commanded the 14th battalion of the Royal Welch Fusiliers at home and in France, was recalled in 1916 and appointed Parliamentary Secretary to Lloyd George. He was in earnest regarding *The Times*, which he saw as an instrument for peace. If the Prime Minister were willing to accept his suggestion Davies thought *The Times* could make a mighty contribution to "the general uplifting of the nations." He did not expect the paper to make money, but if it were to do so the income might be allocated to philanthropic objects. He felt he could carry his sisters with him in this enterprise and wished first to talk it over with Walter. Walter did not know the details of Davies's plan, and did not wish to see him without consultation with Poole, who advised against the meeting. Poole's reason was not given and is not revealed in the correspondence. In all probability he had engaged himself in some degree to Rothermere, from whom he thought, perhaps, better terms for the Prime Minister and Walter could be secured. As things turned out it was unfortunate, from Walter's point of view, that he and Davies did not meet. The Davies scheme did not, however, lapse; but its progress was made slowly and in circumstances that were bound to prejudice its chances. While Davies had obviously talked to Grigg, who was prepared to assist him, he had evidently neglected or failed to attach the support of Poole.[2]

Next day, the Prime Minister told Grigg that he had seen Rothermere and had talked to him about the possibility of the

[1] He was created a Baron in 1932.
[2] For the details of the Davies scheme, see below, September 21.

ale of *The Times*, and had decided to instruct Poole, in
his capacity as solicitor to Lloyd George, to examine the
legal position. On the same day, June 24, Ralph Walter
lunched with Dawson, who, not knowing and not being told
what was afoot, expressed his disappointment that John Walter
had sold his shares, and urged that he should in future consult
Poole. Dawson, very naturally, was thinking of clearing his way,
in certain eventualities, to exercise an influence on *The Times*,
not necessarily as Editor. He was already a director of public
companies and might be happy, Conservative though he was, on
certain terms to take a seat on the board of a pro-Lloyd George
and Liberal Imperialist newspaper. This being reported to
Poole, Dawson was asked to go and see him. Later, Poole saw
the Prime Minister, told him how the transfer stood and generally
reported on the situation.

The date of the valid board meeting of The Times Publishing
Company called to pass the date of the valid transfer of Walter's
shares was June 27. That meeting decided to secure legal opinion
before sanctioning the transfer. The legal question was put
to the Company's solicitors, Messrs. Soames, Edwards and Jones.
They replied on July 3, enclosing the opinion of Maugham, K.C.,
that as the Power of Attorney gave Sutton ample power to effect
the transaction " as fully and effectually as Lord Northcliffe
himself," there was no justification for delaying the registration of
the transfer. On the point of insanity, counsel said that a contract
made by a person of unsound mind was not voidable if the other
party to the contract believed at the time he made the contract
that the person he was dealing with was of sound mind. At
the relevant time Walter was demonstrably of that opinion.

This opinion of counsel crystallized a very awkward situation.
At the board meeting on July 3 Hubert Walter reluctantly proposed, and Brumwell seconded, and it was unanimously agreed
to pass the transfer for registration. Steed, too, was present and
agreed. Nobody could raise objection to counsel's statement
that both Sutton and John Walter believed that Northcliffe was
sane at the date of the latter's agreement to sell. After this
collapse of their hopes, John, Ralph and Hubert Walter conferred.
It was decided that John Walter, as a last resource, should write
to Poole, in these terms:

                                        July 3, 1922.
On May 29 [1922] I decided for reasons which had been accumulating
for some months past to offer my ordinary shares in *The Times* to
Lord Northcliffe and to resign the chairmanship of the Company.

Matters had in fact reached a point where I could neither work with Lord Northcliffe nor continue to allow it to be thought that I approved or accepted responsibility for his acts. The decision was a hard one to take. It entailed the severance of the family connection with *The Times* which had continued unbroken for five generations, and which there was good reason to hope might continue indefinitely. It entailed the surrender of an object for which I had been working in the face of constant annoyance for a good many years, namely, the eventual recovery of the control of the Paper in virtue of my agreement with Lord Northcliffe of January 1, 1913. But hard as the decision was there seemed on May 29 to be no alternative and I acted accordingly.

At that very moment, had I but known it, the reasons which impelled me to take that step were being removed. Had I waited a few days longer I should have known what we all know now, that in consequence of the calamity which had overtaken Lord Northcliffe it was of the utmost importance that I should hold on to my own shares and to the agreement of 1913 which reserved me the refusal of Lord Northcliffe's at a fair price. Now, what I should like you to do, is first to devise some means whereby I can recover the shares and the option that I have surrendered, or, if that is impossible, their equivalent as near as may be; and, secondly, to consider how I can find the necessary capital to enable me to exercise the option in question, bearing in mind that those who supply it should be qualified both by character and position to assist both now and in the future in maintaining the high traditions of the Paper as a national institution.

In conference with Walter on the same day, Poole admitted that the Prime Minister had not yet disclosed the names of his friends who had undertaken or would undertake to provide the money for *The Times*. This was true, but the Prime Minister had said that a quarter of a million was ready, and more if necessary. It was agreed that the names would certainly need to be suitable. Poole then submitted that Dawson should return, have a seat on the board " and virtually run it." This looked as if in Poole's mind either the new board would give the Editor his orders, or the Editor would sit on the board with John Walter and others and conduct *The Times* through an " acting Editor." Such an arrangement was reminiscent of the Northcliffe and Rothermere methods, and Ralph Walter, as a traditionalist, was against it. He was all for Dawson as Editor as long as Lloyd George did not want the job, but he was a stickler for the old system of the Proprietor appointing the Editor, and leaving him to edit. The conversations with Grigg about Lloyd George were inevitably secret from everybody, including the office. Steed, for all his knowledge of the Northcliffe side, knew nothing more of John Walter's plans than the mere fact of his talk with Dawson

For obvious reasons, Walter needed to keep secret the means by which he hoped, with the assistance of Poole, to regain his shares and his option.

On July 4 the Prime Minister again saw Rothermere and, later, Poole. The Northcliffe family was against any sale now, Rothermere said. He, in particular, had decided to wait. There should be no sale of any kind without Poole's being informed before anybody else. That was agreed by Rothermere. There was no risk of any sale to Beaverbrook.[1] Rothermere's position was deliberately equivocal. He continued to urge upon Poole that he was too old to take over the reconstruction of the property and said he had told the Prime Minister this. However, if he changed his mind and decided to do his best to get *The Times*, he was at least certain that in the event of his success the policy of the paper would be to support Lloyd George and the Coalition. He gave the Prime Minister a clear outline of what his own political position as Chief Proprietor would be. He thought, given appropriate conditions, that Lloyd George would win the next election. *The Times* might be of great assistance. Certainly its opposition, if continued, might be gravely damaging. If Lloyd George lost, or chose beforehand to retire from active politics, there would be a place for him at Printing House Square in association, as he vaguely planned things, with Rothermere's son and heir, Esmond. The idea attracted the Prime Minister and he encouraged Rothermere to talk to him about it. The Prime Minister did not communicate Rothermere's statement to Grigg and hence it did not reach Ralph or John Walter. It was known only to the Prime Minister himself, and probably to Poole, that it was Rothermere's plan to provide the Prime Minister with the editorship, if and when he should resign his office. Again, it is not known with what degree of serious intention the Prime Minister, in July, encouraged Rothermere to consider him as the future Editor. On the other hand it is certain that Lloyd George, unsure of his immediate political future, was considering a variety of plans and, according to his wont, discussing them with his confidential secretaries to not one of whom, however intimate his talk, did he frankly or fully declare his intentions or reveal his plans. A factor in the situation was that the Prime Minister had respect for Rothermere's power of prophecy regarding electoral futures

---

[1] Beaverbrook was in constant and intimate touch with Rothermere. Although everybody believed, with J. L. Garvin, that Beaverbrook in a personal capacity was a competitor, or would be, he had decided otherwise; nevertheless he was in close touch with Lloyd George and some of his friends who aspired to secure control of the paper.

and was, for this reason alone, prepared to listen to him. At the same time Lloyd George approved the plan proposed and supported by Walter, Grigg and Dawson.

The significant advantage was that the Prime Minister bound himself to revert to the " traditional " constitution of *The Times* by giving the Walter family the position it held before the control came into the hands of Northcliffe. This was satisfactory. What the family envisaged as the " tradition " was the hereditary connexion and jurisdiction over the property which originated with John Walter I's occupation of Printing House Square in 1784, and the foundation of *The Times* in 1785. Thus, their primary interest lay in the maintenance of the family connexion with Printing House Square, rather than in the securing of any amount of money that might be made out of the sale of such connexion. What a family needed to sustain its future was a business connexion, and that was what Walter's first duty, as head of the family, amounted to. An extra £50,000 or more gained by the sale of such a connexion would only be lost or wasted by the next generation, or the next but one. Nobody could guarantee the intelligence of a succession of eldest sons; their social position and income might be made secure. In the Lloyd George scheme a competent colleague, a man of business acceptable to the Chief Proprietor, would again manage the concern and recruit the staff, while John Walter would live at Bear Wood and come to Printing House Square to deal with important matters of policy, including the appointment of the Editor and the Manager. This had been the traditional relationship since 1817; this was the relationship that had been broken in 1908 and that John Walter and Ralph Walter were striving to restore in 1922. It had all been written down over and over again during the struggles with the small proprietors that began in 1893, with the first Sibley *v.* Walter case.[1] Bound up with the relationship of the Walters and Printing House Square as a publishing organization was another tradition that needed to be accepted though it had not been written down.

This tradition concerned what was published, *i.e.*, *The Times* newspaper, the *Weekly Edition*, the *Literary Supplement* and the rest. As the editorial tradition of *The Times* had never been called in question by Mrs. Sibley it had never been necessary to commit its definition to paper. In 1907, when Arthur and Godfrey Walter were negotiating with Pearson, it had been agreed

---

[1] See Vol. III, Chapter XIV, " *The Times* in Adversity and Litigation."

hat " subject to the absolute control of the board " the appoint-
nent of the principal members of the staff be vested in the two
Chief Proprietors. The clause specified the " principal members."
They were the Editor, Assistant Editor, Foreign Editor, City
Editor; the chief leader-writers and Correspondents in the
capitals and political and commercial centres of the world. It was
not considered necessary to introduce any safeguard, implicit or
explicit, designed to protect the political principle, habit, doctrine
or practice of editorship to which experience over a century might
have given something more than the mere force of custom. The
reasons why this safeguard was overlooked are plain. First,
here was no precedent for it; secondly, the Editor was not a
party to the agreement of 1908, and was not being consulted in
1922. There was no requirement to consult Buckle, Dawson
or Steed; their business was to edit, not to capitalize the property.
In the constitution of Printing House Square custom was the only
factor that required *The Times* to be as independent politically, as
Printing House Square was financially.[1] And custom was
he basis of the right claimed by Walter and Pearson in 1908
to appoint the Editor and the "principal members of the staff."
In the 1922 conversation with Poole, the independence of the
Editor of *The Times*, as it had been established by the second
Walter in 1817, and maintained by the third in 1841, and
he fourth Walter in 1894, was not discussed, confirmed or
re-stated. It was not necessary, Walter thought, to do more in
1922 than had been done in 1908.

It was the Chief Proprietor's responsibility to decide,
according to his conscientious estimate of the national interest,
the paper's policy towards party; and to choose an Editor
willing to and capable of pursuing it. Thus John Walter III,
for instance, chose Buckle as the successor of Delane. But as
the Chief Proprietor recognized that the property must suffer
from too frequent changes of Editor he made provision for
continuity by adopting a pragmatic attitude, as John Walter II
did to the Whigs in 1834; and this was the attitude of John
Walter IV towards politics in 1922. In full consistency with
the past the present Walter, struggling to regain control of the
property in 1922, disregarded the changes which might, or might
not, subsequently take place in the editorial appointments and in
the political allegiance of the newspaper. The primary essential in
July, in the light of the information at his disposal, was to settle

---

[1] Pearson, however, thought himself entitled to approach J. A. Spender who,
distinguished Liberal publicist as he was, had never edited a newspaper that was independent either politically or financially. There is no reason to believe that he consulted
Arthur Walter regarding this project. See Vol. III, p. 561.

the ownership and to keep Beaverbrook out of the control Rothermere was not yet, apparently, a competitor. He was putting it about in July that he did not want *The Times* for himself Walter was also among those who did not then know that Rothermere was in earnest about getting *The Times* into his hands

In all the circumstances it was perfectly reasonable for John Walter first to approve a scheme which would include himself as Chairman, and secondly Lloyd George as Editor if the arrangement were to appear workable. The reports of Grigg and Poole indicated that the scheme was practical. The restoration of Walter as effective Chairman was in itself a sufficient guarantee of editorial independence. A clause similar to that of the Walter-Pearson agreement would doubtless have to be drafted and the principal appointments would, under the sanction of the board, be reserved to John Walter and another, representing the financial interest Grigg now, at the end of July, viewed as suitable David Davies who had unsuccessfully sought an interview with John Walter on June 23.

The worsening of Northcliffe's health at the end of July coincided with a loosening of the ties which bound the Coalition together; other schemes, with the Prime Minister in control of the policy rather than as Editor, were discussed. It is still impossible to say whether Lloyd George positively desired to occupy the editorial chair, but it is certain that he was the pivot of at least two other schemes besides Grigg's and Rothermere's, all of which depended upon the Prime Minister's willingness to direct the policy of the paper; all four schemes were known to the Prime Minister; all were independent, and all secret from each other. Unknown to John Walter, to Grigg and to Dawson, the Prime Minister had, by a date that has not been ascertained, reached a complete understanding on the point of editorial authority with Rothermere, who had agreed to appoint Lloyd George as Editor of *The Times* with control of policy independent of his own control of finance. It is out of the question to believe that the Prime Minister would have agreed to settle with Walter on any less advantageous terms. Rothermere, moreover, had the money with which to purchase the control, and he had the skill to make the property pay. Rothermere was a business man and meant business, *i.e.*, he meant to acquire control of *The Times*. This then, was certain early in August, though it was unknown to the Walter side. Thus the Prime Minister was discussing simultaneously and separately both the Grigg-Walter and the Rothermere schemes. So far, so good—for Lloyd George there was an obstacle, however, to the Prime Minister's ambition to control *The Times*. Neither the Prime Minister nor Poole knew that Rothermere, in view of the strength of Conservative opposition in the constituencies to the continuance of the Coalition, was discussing then, and later, *The Times* and its future, with Bonar Law.[1]

It has not been discovered whether Poole's inclinations then lay in the direction of Rothermere or of Walter, but the latter under-stood that Poole could not answer the question about the option, put to him on July 3, by return of post.[2] The situation was, of, course, delicate in the extreme. From the moment of cutting the wire of the last telephone at Carlton Gardens, the Chief was known to all his staffs to have no authority. The vacuum thus created inevitably led to a struggle for power. What the future would be for *The Times* none could tell. Others besides Walter were taking up their positions. On Monday, July 10, Rothermere did act. He sent for Brumwell and warned him to be discreet. He then appointed him " associate-editor "—a description entirely new to the office, and not sounding well in the ears of the old-fashioned. This done, without Steed's knowledge and against his known wish, Rothermere told Brumwell to have a leader written opposing the threatened inquiry into Lloyd George's distribution of honours. Returning to the office, the " associate-editor " duly instructed a leader-writer to write in the sense directed by Rothermere. Unexpectedly the Editor returned after dinner. When he read the proofs of all the leading articles including that on the bestowal of honours, he re-wrote it, retaining only an innocuous opening. The incident did nothing to tranquillize the agitated office.

Steed was more determined than ever to stand his ground. He was exceptionally well informed about Northcliffe and was the only channel of knowledge the office had. At no time did he deprive his colleagues of important knowledge, though he seems to have found no opportunity of coming to an under-standing with John Walter. He had early knowledge of Northcliffe's health, the Power of Attorney given to Sutton, Graham and Stuart, and had been aware of Northcliffe's intention to get rid of the Walters, though not of the means. He knew most of what was impending but was unaware of any plans John Walter had. The member of the family to whom he had always

[1] This paragraph is based on information for which *The Times* is indebted to Lord Beaverbrook. See Chapter XIX, " Rothermere *v.* Walter."

[2] But that Poole acted solidly for Walter in the first week of October is certain. See Chapter XIX, " Rothermere *v.* Walter."

talked freely was Hubert Walter, whom he told on July 11 that he knew that John Walter, in view of certain contingencies, had recently seen Geoffrey Dawson hoping he might have in mind a probable purchaser. Steed also told Hubert Walter about Rothermere's action in the matter of the leading article on the distribution of honours and said that Rothermere was determined to get him dismissed and a new Editor recruited immediately.

In the meantime, the many legal requirements obstructed the realization of any plan, and while matters dragged on, Northcliffe's health was no longer reported as " recoverable." By the first of August the informed were fearful that he could hardly last another week. His strength, nevertheless, was not negligible. For the past fortnight, Steed then told the staff, Northcliffe had been " an animated log " but he was capable of great will power. Ten grains of morphia had no effect on him and 20 acted merely as a tonic. It seemed impossible that he could live beyond August 8 or 15. He had made the Will of which he had several times spoken. According to the Articles of Association, Northcliffe could not bequeath his shares in The Times Publishing Company Limited outside his family; and if he was too jealous of Rothermere to leave them to him, he might order a sale and thus provide for the heavy death duties. As shares sold in parcels would fetch a smaller price than the whole carrying control, Northcliffe would surely wish his executors to find one purchaser. On August 1 Freeman, in the light of the information that the office had, urged Hubert Walter to remind John Walter that he must have ready, at the right time, the necessary money. The " right time " might be any moment. Hubert Walter expressed the hope, without going into detail, that the family had already made progress with a scheme. But John Walter, on August 3, had heard nothing further from Grigg or Poole. It was urgently necessary to discover exactly what the situation was, to know precisely what had passed between Poole and Lloyd George, and to know clearly what was in the mind of the Prime Minister.

On August 4, by way of hastening the Walter-Lloyd George scheme, Ralph Walter went to No. 10, Downing Street, and told Grigg that Northcliffe was unlikely to live another week and that as it was thought that the whole of his shares would be sold *en bloc*, it was necessary to find out at once precisely what the Prime Minister intended; and, if there were a serious hitch, to proceed with another proposal. Grigg agreed to see the Prime Minister at the earliest possible moment. At this point Ralph Walter viewed himself as in a difficult and unfortunate position.

He had pressed Poole upon John Walter at the suggestion of Grigg, backed by Dawson; he had approved the Lloyd George scheme that Poole and Grigg had proposed, and now after several weeks no progress had been made. That was bad. John Walter had disclosed all his plans and figures; Poole had not only done nothing but had not even disclosed the plans and figures of the other side. That was worse. Poole had not even managed to see the text of Northcliffe's Power of Attorney; or, if so, had said nothing. It looked as if Poole, so warmly recommended by Grigg and Dawson, was at work on some entirely different scheme arranged, conceivably, with the Prime Minister.

Meanwhile, John Walter, at Bear Wood, felt disinclined to come to town. Ralph Walter, therefore, went to Bear Wood on August 6 and reported to his nephew the recent conversation with Grigg, and they talked for hours. Of the huge amount of consultation, discussion and talk in which the Walters had already participated at breakfast, lunch and dinner, only a fraction is chronicled in these pages. John Walter argued that there was happily no immediate risk of a sale to any person without his being previously informed by Poole, according to promise. Things were not so urgent as Freeman and Hubert Walter made out. The law did nothing in a hurry. The lawyers were interested in fees, not in speed. A Committee or Receiver might be appointed immediately if Northcliffe's family asked for it, but this was unlikely so long as there was the remotest chance of Northcliffe's recovery, and even if one were appointed the legal people would succeed in delaying any sale, and possibly even the question of sale, for at least five or six weeks. The Master in Lunacy would have to be consulted and would take time to consider, etc., etc., before he could arrive at his decision. It would not necessarily mean any sale at all. It might well be made in the interest of Northcliffe's heirs, of whom Lady Northcliffe would probably be the most important. This was John Walter's main argument.

Also, Poole, he said, had given it as his opinion that two or three months were likely to elapse before any question of sale arose; and if once Walter approached people with a view to raising capital for the purchase of Northcliffe's shares it would get about that the paper was for sale and that would damage it; besides which, the activity of competitors would be stimulated, and the price raised. Therefore Walter would lie low and make no move at present. As to the Prime Minister, Poole, in whom

Ralph had lost faith, had said that he had given up none of his interest in the future of *The Times*. That was all. Ralph Walter left Bear Wood feeling very discouraged.

On the morning of the 8th Grigg played golf with the Prime Minister. He told Lloyd George that Northcliffe might not last through the night, and that in all probability *The Times* would be sold, and perhaps the *Daily Mail*. All this might happen quickly. The Prime Minister said that his policy with regard to *The Times* was unchanged; it should go back to John Walter. He did not say with whom Walter should work as a partner. Further conversation was inconclusive as Lloyd George emphasized the view that Walter could do no more, as things were, now that the transfer had been registered, and the effort now to cancel his transfer to Northcliffe might not succeed. Nothing practical could be done until the legal position was known. It was necessary to wait until the Will was proved. That was all the Prime Minister said after Grigg's warning that Northcliffe might not last the night. In reporting this conversation to Ralph Walter, Grigg, without saying whether it was known to Lloyd George, mentioned that Rothermere was talking of Northcliffe's holding being sold and realizing one million pounds. And Grigg added that he could think of nobody who would put up such a sum without the prospect of some return. Beaverbrook, he said, was certainly not the sort of man to do that. So it was a million pounds, perhaps, that Walter had to find if he hoped to regain control. Grigg thought a million was not an impossible sum to secure if only there was time. But Northcliffe might die that night. This was not encouraging to one about to set out to raise a million pounds from men of business, with or without the unimpeachable backing of the Prime Minister. Poole had more than once said that business was business and *The Times* was a business, to be bought or sold as a business. It seemed as if the Northcliffe executors would view it in that light. Rothermere and Sutton were sufficiently aware of the importance of money and of " the best price." Time, such as there was of it, they had.

After August 8, the day of the golf match between the Prime Minister and Grigg, the question of time rendered the position more and more critical. On the Walter side nobody appeared able to move swiftly. On August 7, however, Stuart, Managing Director of *The Times* and Managing Editor of the *Daily Mail*, returned from Canada. He was at Carmelite House on the morning of the 7th, and at Printing House Square later, busy picking up the threads, and planning a course of action. On the 10th Northcliffe's doctors saw it as certain that the end could not long be delayed. Conviction, as it had now become, quickened the activity of all those who wished to step into Northcliffe's position at Printing House Square. Any scheme, of any kind, in whomsoever's interest, now needed to be put into shape with the greatest speed. And by the 10th there were still no names from Grigg of any of the Prime Minister's monied supporters. John Walter could only hope that neither Rothermere nor Beaverbrook was seriously planning to get control of *The Times*.

The climax came on the morning of August 14, when the following notice was issued:

VISCOUNT NORTHCLIFFE DIED AT TWELVE MINUTES PAST TEN THIS MORNING. THE END WAS PERFECTLY PEACEFUL.

P. SEYMOUR-PRICE
HERBERT FRENCH

The Chief was fifty-seven years and one month old when he died from ulcerative endocarditis.

The creator of *Answers* (1888), *Comic Cuts* (1890), *Sunday Companion* (1894), *Home Chat* (1895), the *Daily Mail* (1896), and the *Daily Mirror* (1903), the restorer of the *Evening News*, and the saviour of *The Times*, was unquestionably the greatest popular journalist of his time. To begin with, his technical capacities ranged widely. He had performed all the work of the editorial, advertising or layout man, and knew the uses and costs of copy, type, ink, paper and binding. He was a publisher of weeklies for boys and girls, monthlies for men and women, educational, recreational and patriotic magazines, histories and popular encyclopaedias. A biography of the complete man, the innovating publisher, omniscient journalist and courageous patriot, would require volumes. Because it has not been attempted the full measure of his genius has not been taken. The relevant chapters of this volume illustrate the ruthlessness and cunning of his policies, and illustrate his failings and shortcomings in greater degree than any other account, so far published, of this extraordinary man. But, as he was never a saint, he was not always the opposite. His faults were as conspicuous as his virtues. His moral courage made him one of the most remarkable public figures at a period when great men were not as scarce as they have since become. As a journalist his deep respect for the public weal and healthy public opinion made him supreme in his time as it had Barnes and Delane in their day. Like them, he was a journalist in the old and true sense of the word. He was what they would have recognized : a conductor of opinion. At his best, he was as great as Barnes, because he was himself an original character and writer. Like him, he was execrated; like him, he at times led, and at other times goaded, public opinion. Harmsworth, like Barnes, knew that " John Bull, whose understanding is rather sluggish, requires a strong stimulus." He knew, like Barnes, that " to get him to move you have to fire ten-pounders at his densely compacted intellect before you can make it comprehend your meaning." Like Delane, Harmsworth knew the importance to " John Bull " of worldliness, of society, and of snobbery. As Harmsworth, he knew the popular taste ; as Northcliffe he never lost his sympathy for the middle class. One of his last remarks was that he would like again to be " Mr. Harmsworth." Like Barnes and Delane he had the job he wanted. He worked hard because he loved the newspapers he made, and was made for. It was because he was made for them that he was so original, creative, active, versatile and curious. He was no imitator of other men or their publications, except, at the very outset, of George Newnes and his *Tit-Bits*. He was then twenty-three. After *Answers*, he thought for himself and acted for himself. He was a creator. As a newspaper proprietor and organizer he was as creative as John Walter III, always to him " Walter the Great." But he far surpassed " Walter the Great," as he did every other proprietor, in his enveloping affection for the craft. He gave his whole heart and soul, all his life to the writing, printing and publishing of encyclopaedias, books, magazines and newspapers, which he loved more than all the rest of Fleet Street combined. That Northcliffe's feeling for newspapers was a true love is proved by the fact that he did not make them his by, or for, mere money.

Alfred Charles William Viscount Northcliffe knew that he could have won " success " at far less effort and at almost no risk if he had adopted for the *Daily Mail*, the *Evening News*, or the *Weekly Dispatch*, the formula of the nineteenth-century Sunday scandal sheet. Crime and pornography were, are, and will remain the easiest way to the largest circulation in the world. That would not mean success to him. Also he could have adopted the latest New York methods of news-selecting, sensationalizing and display. He never allowed that sort of thing in the *Daily Mail* or the *Evening News*. From the first, Harmsworth had too much honesty, too much self-respect, too great an esteem for journalism and too much concern for his staff to choose either of these short ways to fortune. A proprietor's capacity to write will always set limits to the policy of stealing other men's ideas as a means of making money. Northcliffe was not an illiterate proprietor. He began as a writer, always liked writing, and was writing within six weeks of his death. Nobody who could write as well as Northcliffe, at his best, did for the *Daily Mail* would lose his affection for the writer and his craft. He ranked him, and the compositor who served him, high above the capitalist who came from outside Fleet Street to amass money by enslaving writers and compositors. Alfred Harmsworth was a journalist at the age of sixteen, a proprietor at twenty-two, a baronet at thirty-eight, a baron at forty, and a viscount at fifty. The supreme popular journalist was a failure in everything else.

Northcliffe was a failure in his private life, a greater failure in his public life. Success at his trade came too early. Well before fifty he was far too fond of his own way, and far too certain of getting it at Carmelite House and Fleetway House to be able to tolerate the compromises and delays of politics, or to have a chance of succeeding in a Ministry. He was wise enough to decline the Air job. The British War Mission was an unqualified success because it was soon over. Had it been a long job he would have tired of it, as he tired of everything except his and other people's newspapers.[1] He knew their history and knew how and why they had been from the beginning, even until his own youth, insolvent sheets bolstered up by politicians and their agents. In his young days it was accepted that no good newspaper could possibly be made to pay. It took Northcliffe to make politicians respect newspapers as a discipline for those apt to forget pledges, evade decisions, or conceal facts. In 1904 to advocate in the *Daily Mail* such an unpopular measure as conscription was to take a risk from which Ministers flinched. His campaigns against Haldane, Kitchener, Asquith and Lloyd George were paralleled only by Barnes's philippics against Brougham and Althorp, and Delane's attacks on Crimean inefficiency. The man had no lack of moral courage. He did nothing for money, though his native ability attracted millions and gave him the power to bestow fortunes on all his principal colleagues. The history of his popular newspapers, when written, will form the fittest monument to him and his genius. He needs to be appreciated as the journalistic pioneer of motor travel, air travel, daylight saving

---

[1] His health permitted him little part in the conduct of the Crewe House Department of Enemy Propaganda, as has been seen in an earlier Chapter.

and the numbering and registration of motor cars, not to mention such diversions as gardening competitions, "Ideal Home" exhibitions and many more. The *Daily Mail*, the *Evening News*, the *Weekly Dispatch*, which he vitalized, and the *Daily Mirror*, which he founded and made over to Rothermere, were his greatest achievements, and every detail of their making and their progress stimulated their creator to fresh creations.

The Times was not his creation but he re-created it. Yet he neither understood it nor felt at home in it. He came to it too late. He had long admired and coveted its influence, and wished to possess it for himself as the crown of his career. He struggled and conspired to secure over Printing House Square the absolute control he enjoyed at Carmelite House and Fleetway House; and if his health had not failed success would have been his by the end of 1922. In that case *The Times* would have been edited and written by a different staff, and a new "saviour" of its historic quality might have been called for.

The Times had exercised a unique influence in journalism before he was born. When, as a humble baron, calling himself "Mr. X," he came to Printing House Square at the age of forty-three, he could not aspire to surpass the achievements of Walter II, Barnes and Delane. The task was to get the old "barnacle-covered whale off the rocks and safely into deep water." In 1908 he could count humility among his virtues; but when, four years later, the "Old Gang" of Buckle, Bell and Chirol went, and the young John Walter was subjugated, Northcliffe thought he would be master in their house. The new people would call him "Chief," a title which the "Old Gang" had refused him. His humility evaporated. The men appointed by Northcliffe must be young and able, strong to carry out his orders; different in every way from the "weaklings" that Bell had allowed, or taught, to obstruct him and his plan. That plan was manifest in 1912 when Dawson was placed in the chair of Barnes, Delane, Chenery and Buckle. But the new Editor was no less aware than his predecessors that the quality of *The Times* could only be guaranteed by men whose ability earned them the responsibility of organizing it. Such men were not induced to enter the office by the mere suggestion of a salary, or to remain in it by the prospect of an increase. This was what Northcliffe did not understand; this was why he failed to make the best of his opportunity at Printing House Square. He did not learn the lesson that in the office of *The Times* personal power, whether of the Proprietor or the Editor, must be limited.

The quality that gave the paper its distinction was not conferred by one man; it was the contribution of a society. To understand this it was necessary to have been a member of it, which he never was. Those who had this advantage stood firm against him.

When Nicholson was succeeded by Howard Corbett and Lints Smith, the desire for a degree of power in Printing House Square equal to that he enjoyed at Carmelite House took greater hold of Northcliffe. From 1912 nothing could dissuade him from trying to use *The Times* as an agency for the promotion of his own personal influence and personal importance. His first " brainstorms," then occasional and slight in their incidence, brought with them a marked degree of megalomania. As early as 1910 there had been whisperings that the Chief was not always in his right mind. Now more than ever he had to be right in everything and found it necessary to blame his errors on his colleagues, and take the credit for their successes. Northcliffe's increasing control over Printing House Square did nothing to arrest a tendency manifest since 1912 to regard himself as the " Napoleon of the Press," the " Demon of Fleet Street." He liked to sign his letters as " Lord Vigour and Venom," alternatively as " your obdurate, affectionate Chief." It was a conception so utterly at variance with all the traditions of the office that a quarrel with the " Old Gang " could not be avoided. But Northcliffe, who worked and worried Bell to death, dismissed Buckle and the " Old Gang," did not stop there. Seven years later he drove out the Editor of his own appointment, and all but drove out his second Editor within two years. He achieved absolute power in 1922 when he forced Walter to sell his holding to him. Yet even at the beginning of 1922 resistance to him in Printing House Square was not broken.

For fourteen years after the death of Arthur Walter the defence of the paper's historic quality was conducted, first by Bell and Buckle and Chirol; then by Dawson, together with Freeman, Chisholm, and Shadwell, to mention only those members of the staff who served under the old regime and are no longer living. John Walter at all times did his best to protect it. Their actions were reported by spies in the office chosen by the Chief for their capacity to render a slavish obedience to their ennobled employer. Northcliffe had plumbed the depths of the English petty bourgeois appetite for titles. It was not that he was a snob; far from it. He was quite straightforward about distinctions. Leading members of his staff must have titles. In a country like this and at their time

of life a baronetcy or a knighthood might be of business advantage
to their employer. It amused him to employ knights and baronets;
it did not amuse him that all three of the Editors of *The Times* he
had known should refuse handles to their names. As for himself,
he was merely mercenary: " When I want a peerage I will buy one,
like an honest man."[1] It would help him to get people to
genuflect to him and he required such men in all his staffs.
The Times was no exception. After 1912, he had inside the office
help that enabled him to keep the proud Square in a permanent
condition of nervous disheartenment. Arbitrary changes in the
staff, threats and prophecies of more to come never ceased. When
war came, it was hoped the direction, if not the nature, of
Northcliffe's impulses would change. Only a respite was granted.

Northcliffe's disappointment in 1919 made him still more
" northoleonic " and omniscient. He never forgave the Prime
Minister's insults of 1919 and 1920 and spent himself prodigally
in the attempt to make himself more powerful than before,
certainly than the Prime Minister. The determination to destroy
Lloyd George took him captive. There was plenty of room for
criticism in the minds of moderate men, and widespread doubt
in many quarters, about the methods of the peacemakers and the
degree of liberality that ought to be extended to the defeated
apostles of unrestricted terrorism. The " Napoleon of Fleet
Street " gave anything but moderate expression to these criticisms.
The campaign against Lloyd George, Curzon, and the Coalition
had no parallel in all journalism since Barnes's attacks on the
Lath-and-Plaster Cabinet, and Althorp's and Brougham's
answering " War on *The Times* " in 1834. Most men disliked
these specimens of belated early Victorian hard hitting, and many
readers of *The Times* protested. At a moment when every
additional reader was important, subscriptions were cancelled
all over the country. The heads of appropriate departments in
the office knew that they would be asking for instant dismissal,
conveyed by a scalding telegram, if they reported to the critic
of Haldane, Kitchener, Asquith and Lloyd George their own
disquiet at the loss of sales.

Northcliffe's anti-Lloyd Georgism had the powerful support
of the Editor who had, it has been seen,[2] his own reasons for
being in opposition. It was equally Northcliffe's and Steed's
view that the circumstances and interest of the country, not to

[1] In fact he did pay for his peerage.
[2] See Chapter VIII, " Peace Making."

mention those of the Continent, did not permit of mere milk-and-water criticism of the Prime Minister. Albeit from different motives, both pursued the aim of breaking up the Coalition with the same relentless purpose as the winning of the war. In Northcliffe's eyes the forces that helped to put Lloyd George in would now put him out. Northcliffe was engaged in the exercise of the personal power that he had come to love during the preceding ten years, and he loved it most when, as in 1921 and 1922, he made up his mind that the Prime Minister was distrusted to such a degree at home and abroad that to force his resignation was a patriotic requirement. The circulation of *The Times* was secondary to a personal vindication identified with a patriotic purpose. It mattered not who gave up the paper; for, provided you are right, unpopularity pays. It was one of his permanent convictions that since most politicians fear to take risks with their reputation few rise to the position of statesmen.

There his philosophy stopped. It was not merely that Northcliffe's love of personal power made him incapable of a statesmanlike attitude towards Printing House Square. The man who envied none of his Majesty's Ministers was jealous of the mere gentlemen at Printing House Square who kept him at arm's length. Because they, the anonymous recalcitrants in the Proud Square, were strong, the struggle between his personal sensationalism and their impersonal journalism was protracted over a long period. Yet it was a struggle in which he must ultimately win. His power would prevail. After fourteen years' effort to secure obedience he prevailed upon the acting Editor on the night to insert over a dispatch from Genoa the line " By Wickham Steed." The Editor suddenly ceased to be anonymous. The convention of a hundred and thirty-seven years had come to an end. Northcliffe had won. The proud, detached spirit of the aloof society of scholars in Printing House Square had at last been broken. He had beaten them first by continually keeping the Editor out of the office. Then he had sent his deputy on holiday; and, while he was absent, he had instructed Stuart to deliver the final blow : to replace Freeman by Brumwell as the Editor's deputy and his own personal agent. Brumwell was given the position that Dawson and Steed had so long fought to preserve for Freeman.

It had been a set-back to the independent party when Saunders and Braham left simultaneously, and a man from the lobby of the House of Commons was news editor

without reference to the Editor.[1] That was ten years earlier;
it was a portent. The appointment of Brumwell was no vagary
to be related to Northcliffe's illness. It was high strategy.
Were the Editor to be defeated in the struggle to appoint his own
deputy, his whole position would be lost. In May, 1922, it
was lost. Had Northcliffe not been ill at the time, he would
certainly have strengthened his position by other appointments.
Stuart and Brumwell would have had instructions to promote
those known as favourable to the centralizing tendency.
Steed had unwittingly contributed to this tendency when he
accepted responsibility for the political control of the *Daily Mail*,
the *Evening News* and the *Weekly Dispatch*. It was the only
alternative Steed saw to the system by which Northcliffe started
his own policies in the *Daily Mail* and gradually forced them on
Buckle and Dawson, but it necessarily contributed to the system
of centralization. Stuart, as Managing Director of *The Times*
and the *Daily Mail*, was its greatest example.

This tendency, it should be emphasized, became an essential
factor in Northcliffe's conceptions from 1919. As far as Printing
House Square was concerned, it was no mere aspect of struggle for
power between a new and an old set of habits; it was not a collision
between efficiency and its opposite. He was aware from experience
that he could not understand the higher qualities of the high-priced
journal, but he knew he could invent, manage and make profitable
a penny popular form of *The Times*, and this involved the paper's
conversion from the impersonal to the personal. Then there
would be no problem. His solution would, of course mean a
change of habit, method and outlook at Printing House Square,
and bring with it an increase in his own power, and that of his
Managing Director and Advising Editor. He would preside over
Steed and Stuart. The former would be his Editorial Adviser
and he, the Napoleon-Northcliffe, would be the Editor-in-
Chief of *The Times*. In 1921 it was all thought out. In 1922 it
was all ready.

After May, 1922, the resisting elements in the editorial
department were gravely weakened. None of them knew any
department other than their own, not one of them was prepared
with a scheme by which the paper at a high price could be made
to pay, though Freeman was right in thinking that Northcliffe's
extravagance was most to blame. John Walter knew how the

---

[1] At the time Steed was abroad. The new man was a Scot, capable and industrious
but with no knowledge of foreign countries, languages or affairs. Northcliffe advanced
Scotsmen whom he viewed as hungry men who would, in consequence, do his bidding.

GEORGE MURRAY BRUMWELL

paper had been running down for forty years, and how Bell had told his father as long ago as 1890 that *The Times* could not possibly pay. The resistants began to lose heart, and talk of leaving. Others saw their way towards a compromise.

If Northcliffe recovered, even though partially, he would undoubtedly increase his personal pressure upon the paper. If he died, his Will (John Walter had sold his shares and with them his option) would in all probability mean the transfer of his interest to the member of his family most suitable in all the circumstances, one with the necessary means, enterprise and knowledge of the trade : Rothermere, who continued to say he did not want it. To him they preferred the living Northcliffe, with all his known personal faults and accumulated transgressions against the office. The gentlemen scholars of Printing House Square stood aloof from him and desired him to let them alone; even so, most of them felt even in June and July an affection for this strange, suspicious and so often generous genius. Because he knew the entire trade better than anybody in or out of the office, they were proud when they earned his praise. They knew that he and he alone had transformed the early Victorian survival into a contemporary newspaper with a prospect of a commercial future not less impressive than its past. If in 1922 he could only prejudice its future character, he had given it a present. They did not oppose him out of sheer wanton desire to obstruct. They admired him, if not all the methods by which his success and power had been achieved. All that Freeman, Richmond and the rest who opposed him wanted was that he should curb his extravagances, and leave the Editor free to edit the paper in accordance with its tradition and character. Northcliffe's illness, too, impressed the dissidents. All rallied to him, prepared to forget and forgive the past.

When he died the whole office mourned him. Steed, who had borne more anxiety on behalf of the paper than any member of the staff had ever been called upon to endure since Bell had been worried into an early grave, gladly complied with Northcliffe's dying request for " A full page and a leader by the best available writer on the *night*." *The Times* was proud to print all the messages of condolence from the King and Queen, Queen Alexandra, Princess Victoria, the Duke of Connaught, Princess Christian, President Harding, the President of the French Republic (Millerand), the Viceroy of India, Lord Reading, the ex-King of Portugal (Dom Manoel), the Prime Ministers of Canada, Newfoundland, Western Australia, South Australia,

Victoria and a vast number of diplomats, statesmen, publicists, inventors, etc., who recognized in him a unique figure, one whose courage, ability, enterprise and probity made him a great patriot and the world's greatest newspaper proprietor. At a meeting of the directors of The Times Publishing Company Limited, held at Printing House Square, John Walter, as Chairman said :

We meet to-day under the shadow of a great calamity, a calamity that has long been expected, but which nevertheless has come upon us at last as a sudden and a stunning blow.

Lord Northcliffe was more to us than the Chief Proprietor of *The Times*, much more than our colleague on this board. He has been for many years the master who has refashioned directly or indirectly every detail of the paper, who has been the inspirer of every department, of every member of the staff. The whole of this place has been so permeated by his influence that it is impossible as yet to realise what life and work here will be like now that his influence is withdrawn. Without his genius, his tremendous personality, it is safe to say that the paper to-day would have been very different from what it is; and, let us not forget it, in making that series of momentous changes which only his foresight and courage could have carried through successfully, he was guided constantly by a thorough knowledge of the paper's history.

By his death *The Times* and all connected with it have suffered a loss which we cannot estimate, and to which I at any rate cannot now give adequate expression. I am sure you will not expect me to say more.

On the motion of the Chairman, seconded by Stuart, a Resolution was passed in silence recording the deep sense of loss the Directors had sustained by the death of the Chief Proprietor, and expressing their profound sympathy with Viscountess Northcliffe, Mrs. Harmsworth, senior, and other members of the family.

Two independent judgements on Northcliffe's achievement need to be quoted. The first is by Lloyd George.

When the [1918] election was impending I had the luck—bad or good—to have an unmendable break in my relations with Lord Northcliffe. They were always precarious. He wielded great power as the proprietor of the most widely read daily paper and also as the owner of the most influential journal in the kingdom. He was inclined to exercise and to demonstrate that power. When he did so most politicians bowed their heads. He was one of the outstanding figures of his generation. He was far and away the most redoubtable figure of all the Press barons of my time. He created the popular daily, and the more other journals scoffed at it and the populace derided it at every political gathering of all parties, the more popular it became. But apart from his success with the half-penny paper he also made *The Times*, which was then [1908] a rather discredited and down-at-heel pundit of the Press, once more a power in the land.

He was an unrivalled window dresser, but in spite of all that was said to the contrary by rivals and by snobs who worshipped the conventional, the goods on the shelves were none the less excellent because they were attractive and cheap. I remember his telling me at one of the few political dinner parties he ever attended—and how uneasy and unhappy he was in unfamiliar surroundings—that he had a far better organization for obtaining foreign news that mattered than the cumbrous, costly and ineffective machinery of the Foreign Office. There was too much truth in his observation. His quest of sensational news landed him once or twice—not oftener—in disastrous exposures. He was just as biased in his opinions as any other partisan paper, but the bias was his own, and not that of any party or party leader. He influenced opinion by selection of news, choice of its page, spacing, and headlines. In effect, this method was often unfair and suggestive of something which was contrary to the truth. He owed no allegiance to any party, so that every genuine party man deplored his paper. Most of them bought it and read what was in it and then damned it.[1]

The second is from Lord Beaverbrook:

He [Northcliffe] was the greatest figure who ever strode down Fleet Street. He had created the character, the type and temper of every newspaper which he owned, and there have been few changes since he left. He established his conception of journalism, not only by the direct influence which he brought to bear on that part of the Press he controlled, but indirectly by the example which he set to his competitors.[2]

The Editor wrote the leading article on Northcliffe's death. It recognized his pugnacity in matters of national and Imperial concern; his tenacity in seizing and holding on to the essentials of politics, notwithstanding reverses and disappointments; his divination, proved true time and time again, of events still unforeseen by others. Northcliffe, *The Times* said, had not left behind him any elaborate political testament. His bequest was his example in seeking steadfastly his country's welfare and in pursuing, with fearless independence, the ends he thought right. England's peril

---

[1] D. Lloyd George, *The Truth About the Peace Treaties* (London, 1938), I, pp. 265-6.

[2] Lord Beaverbrook, *Politicians and the Press* (London, 1928), I, p. 99.

he foresaw and foretold long before the war. The record of t
work and accomplishment for the State, for the Empire, for t
Allies, for the ideals of the English-speaking peoples and f
civilization itself, remained, the paper said, his bequest to those w
would do him honour. It was for them to use it, not as the hidd
talent, but so as to cause it to fructify. "Such will be the aim
this journal which during fourteen years has steadfastly kept in vio
the great objects he served. Not slavishly or by mere imitatio
not uncomprehendingly or by bald reiteration of watchwor
grown old, but in constant endeavour to preserve the best of t
spirit, it will strive to uphold the causes for which he stood,
the unsparing vindication of which he shortened his days." S
wrote Steed for the paper on "the *night*" of Northcliffe's deat
He died, it has been seen, just before 10.15 a.m., very convenient
for his morning newspapers, but the *Star* and not his ow
Evening News first told the public.

From eleven o'clock on that morning of August 14, Printin
House Square, Carmelite House, Fleetway House and the who
of Fleet Street seethed with rumours. A sedulously repeate
story about *The Times*, believed by J. L. Garvin, was that Joh
Walter had taken control and had appointed Hugh Chisholm a
the new Editor. This was obviously premature, to say the lea
for the delays of the law, as John Walter saw, obstructed ar
change of control and, until the Will was proved, all Northcliffe
properties would continue to be governed by the Power of Attorne
he had given to Sutton, Graham and Stuart.

At the funeral service in Westminster Abbey on August 1
the immense congregation, overflowing into Parliament Squar
included a representative of the Prince of Wales. Lloyd Georg
was represented by Grigg, and Winston Churchill was represente
by Mr. J. E. Stephenson. The crowds that lined the route t
the cemetery at Finchley testified to the affection in which h
was held by the public.

Out of respect for the departed Chief no changes were mad
in the "structures," of whose creation he was so proud, unt
after the funeral. This over, the board of the *Daily Mail* decide
upon a number of changes in the organization of Carmelit
House. The system was ended by which the post of Managin
Editor of the *Daily Mail* and that of Managing Director c
The Times Publishing Company were held by Stuart. Th
capital situation Stuart had to deal with on the death of Northclif
was that the shares in The Times Publishing Company Limite
were owned, principally, by the following :

	Preference	Ordinary	Total
Lord Northcliffe	20,986	505,997	526,983
Sir J. R. Ellerman	46,095	128,424	174,519
Arnholz, Sutton & Ellis ...	51,500		
John Walter	41,502	400	41,902
Mercantile Investment & General Trust	17,000		
Colonel Gordon	16,666		
General J. B. Sterling	10,000		

These were the chief owners. In addition

H. G. Price held	8,500	
and T. E. Mackenzie held ...	7,000, both on account of
Lord Northcliffe, while		
The Moorgate Trust held ...	8,000	
and the London General Investment Trust and the United Discount and Securities Co. Ltd. held	1,000, both on account of
Sir J. R. Ellerman.		

The properties in the meantime continued business as usual, though many of the persons concerned were anything but happy. At Bear Wood the interval was an exceedingly anxious one. It had been accepted on June 15 that Northcliffe was unaccountable for his actions, and on July 3 that in the opinion of Maugham, K.C., there was no legal justification for delaying on that account the passing of the transfer, or the completion of the sale of Walter's shares and surrender of the option. When the transfer was passed, Poole had been instructed to recover the shares and the option dependent upon them; but he had effected neither. There had never been any chance of his, or anybody else's, persuading Sutton of all men to go back on the deal he had made with Walter on June 7. Everything, as far as Walter was concerned, hinged on Northcliffe's Will. That of June 13, 1919, had originally contained the option in accordance with the Walter-Northcliffe agreement of January, 1913. But it was next-to-certain that the clause was either deleted by codicil or omitted from a later Will made after Walter's sale of his holding had destroyed its basis.

Outside the Walter family and the Northcliffe family it was quite natural that those interested in the newspaper for political reasons should, immediately on Northcliffe's death, speculate on the means for acquiring control. This was what John Walter feared would happen. Not only had he lost his option, but outsiders with political influence and somebody's cash would intervene. Northcliffe died on the morning of August 14 Within a couple of days Birkenhead (Lord Chancellor in the Coalition Government) ignorant of the preliminary discussions with Poole, Grigg, and Rothermere, impressed upon the Prime Minister the immense desirability of Northcliffe's holding being acquired by a syndicate led by those whom they could trust with the direction of its political tendency Birkenhead, believing that secrecy as well as speed was essential to success, forthwith went on holiday with his friend Sir Warden Chilcott, Member for Walton. While away, he addressed the following note, as

From THE LORD CHANCELLOR to THE PRIME MINISTER

August 19, 192

I have little doubt but that all the money required for the purchase which I recently discussed with you and which are so important in our mutual interest can be obtained from an unimpeachable source (*not* H.[1]). What remains is to discover whether there is a willing *and complete* seller. When are you coming South ?

F.E.[2]

The note was delivered by Chilcott's servant, garbled in a thick cloak of obscurity, with a covering letter informing the Prime Minister that Riddell was shortly meeting " F.E." to discuss the matter, as " *no time* should be wasted, for reasons which no doubt are apparent to you."

Lloyd George was better informed. He thus replied to " F.E."

Criccieth,

August 20, 192

Thanks.—but nothing can happen until N.'s Will is proved. Then we must get busy. It will take at least a fortnight from his death I assume that then the Executors will be in a position to sell but a depends upon the Will. I think I shall be in a position to tell you more about it in another week's time.[3] You and I are to meet at Cherkley[4] for the next weekend and we can then interchange views on this and many other topics—kindred and otherwise.

---

[1] The identity of " H " is not known; it may have been H for Harold Harmsworth *i.e.*, Rothermere.

[2] Printed by permission of Lord Birkenhead.

[3] Lloyd George was seeing Poole regularly.

[4] The residence of Lord Beaverbrook.

The entry under August 26, 1922, in the Visitors' Book
at Cherkley

The agenda for the meeting at Cherkley was not unknown o the party's host, for Beaverbrook, then in Deauville discussing Turkish affairs with the Aga Khan, thus wrote to Lloyd George:

Dear P.M.,

Now that you have joined the " Men of Property " where Winston s a pillar of the Temple, I want very much to entertain you at Cherkley on August 26. The only poor man that will be tolerated s F.E.—and he has a right to move in the company of the rich or reasons which I won't give.

I have been very ill for days. At one moment I thought that I might at last get ahead of Lord Northcliffe. It all came from drinking first and swimming afterwards—instead of the other way about.

Don't answer this letter. Let Davis [J. T. Davies] send me a telegram here to say that you will come on the 26th.

The French are fine cooks.

Yours ever,

MAX.

More correspondence flowed, but nothing practical came of " F.E.'s " scheme. The Prime Minister was right. The Will did need to be proved before business could be done.

In the week after the Cherkley meeting, *i.e.*, on August 31, *The Times* reported that on the previous day the Registrar at Somerset House had made an order, with the consent of he parties concerned, for the appointment of Sutton as Administrator *pendente lite* of the Northcliffe Estate. The Administrator had to consider several testamentary documents. The first Will was dated 1919 and had two codicils. Either might invalidate the option contained in the Will itself, and there was the later Will made in 1922, which almost certainly did so. Another point the Administrator had to bear in mind was that speed was necessary. Between August 30 and September 8 he had to make a preliminary payment to the Inland Revenue Commissioners on account of Estate Duty. To do this Sutton had to borrow £850,000 from Coutts & Co. The Commissioners were pressing for complete settlement within six months and Sutton estimated that he would have to find another £1,800,000 on the basis of a 40 per cent. tax on the Estate. Thus affairs progressed more rapidly than the Walter side were prepared for. The litigation, according to rumour, might begin at once as the result of a plurality of Wills. Even so, John Walter knew better

713

than to take it for granted that if the 1919 Will, with the option
the basis for which had disappeared on June 15, 1922, were
contested, it would be held valid.   For two weeks from August 3
Walter was a prey to doubt and anxiety.   The whole future
connexion of the family with the paper, and his own personal
position, were at stake.   The terms of his association with
syndicate would depend upon the goodwill that the option
carried with it, and it was manifest that he had lost it when
the transfer of his shares went through.   The only hope could
be that some obscure legal consideration might rest on its revival
and acceptance.

This was indeed a faint hope.   That the 1919 Will contained
clause giving Walter the option was morally certain.   It had been
agreed in 1913 and nothing had occurred before 1919 to invalidate
it ; but, as Sutton had frankly told Walter on June 15, 1922
the date of the delayed transfer, a Memorandum was signed, and
was in the Administrator's hands, to the effect that Walter had
surrendered all rights reserved to him under the 1913 agreement
The text of the memorandum admitted no doubt:

I the within named John Walter acknowledge that the within
named Viscount Northcliffe has purchased from me the whole of m
215,000 ordinary shares in the within named Times Publishing Co
Ltd., and that it was one of the considerations for the said purchase
that the within agreement should be cancelled and that all right
reserved to me thereunder should be surrendered.

I accordingly agree to the cancellation of the said Agreement and
the surrender of all my rights thereunder.

DATED this 15th day of June, 1922.

SIGNED SEALED and DELIVERED BY⎫
the above named John Walter in the presence ⎬ J. WALTER (L.S
of :   ⎭

J. Charles Soames,
      Lennox House,
         Norfolk Street,
            Strand, W.C.2,
               Solicitor.

This was clear warrant for the redrafting of the relevant clause
in the Will.   Nor was there the slightest reason to suppose that
the cancellation of Walter's option on June 15, 1922, had been
overlooked by Northcliffe, Sutton or his lawyers.   Significantl
Walter's telegram and letter accepting Northcliffe's offer of th

Chairmanship of the Company provided his option clause were restored had not been answered. This was enough to prove that Northcliffe's mind was made up against the option. Any hope lay in the possibility that Northcliffe had not carried into writing his intention of suppressing the option clause. But Northcliffe, ill as he was, did not suffer from lack of legal or financial advisers. These, then, were the facts present to Walter's mind at this time. But these facts were not known to the world at large. Hence there were surprises for the politicians and others on Monday, September 4, when Sutton, as Administrator of the Estate, with Montague Ellis as his solicitor, began the work of complying with the Will dated March 22, 1919. That it should be this Will was the first surprise. To Lady Northcliffe it was a disappointment. To John Walter, it was quite the reverse, for it was found to direct that as soon as possible after death, and before attempting to dispose of them otherwise, his executors were

to offer to John Walter of Printing House Square in the City of London by letter all the shares of whatsoever description in the Times Publishing Co., Ltd. standing in my name or in the name or names of any nominee or nominees for me at my death at the best price obtainable.

The option was to remain open for three months and Walter was to complete the purchase in six months. If only this Will should stand Walter had a firm chance to regain control of the property.

Furthermore, in the codicil of June 13, 1919, Northcliffe settled his other properties and, in doing so, added an instruction intended to bind his executors as to the future of *The Times* if Walter did not exercise his option :

Judging by my experience at the time when *The Times* newspaper was for sale and by the fact that I have declined one and a quarter million pounds for the shares of the Associated Newspapers Co. Ltd., there will undoubtedly be persons and syndicates who will desire to obtain control of these newspapers and the vast Newfoundland concern, which embraces an area exceeding 3,000 square miles, to whom it might not be desirable for patriotic reasons to sell the same.[1]

I therefore direct my executors to let the final choice of a purchaser of the said shares rest with my brother, Viscount Rothermere, if living, with whom I have discussed the matter and who will not dispose of these interests to any person who is not British born, nor to any company not wholly or at least preponderatingly of British

[1] Northcliffe is referring to the efforts of Miss Brodie-Hall and the Wiener Bankverein to secure *The Times* in 1908. *Cf.* Vol. III, pp. 454-455 and Chapter XVI, " *The Times* for Sale."

birth, and if, unfortunately, Viscount Rothermere should die before the shares are sold, I direct my executors to follow a like course. But I suggest that the sale take place as rapidly as possible, having regard to all the surrounding circumstances.

This was the position as the 1919 Will and codicil left *The Times*. There was no other testamentary disposition touching the paper. What then was the status of the option ? Was it invalidated by the last, the 1922 Will ? That Will was found to vary from that of 1919 in many details, and in the important respect that it increased the extent and value of the legacies to Lady Northcliffe; but it made no new disposition regarding *The Times*, refrained from explicitly cancelling the Walter option and, in fact, left the paper unmentioned. Clearly this Will was intended to be an entirely new Will. It was phrased as if the 1919 Will had never been made. It was dated April 27, 1922, *i.e.*, four weeks before the interview with Walter during which he offered to buy his holding. Now while Northcliffe had the right to make a new Will on April 27, he could not then dispose of the option; and he had not, in fact, done so. Evidently, therefore, when making his new Will he had determined to open the question of purchasing the shares and the option with Walter, and did both as soon as possible, *i.e.*, on May 24 ; and completion took place, as stated above, on June 15. Hence the second Will left *The Times* and the option unmentioned. But, what was all-important, no codicil covering the situation as it had changed on June 15 had been made subsequently. The documents that bore on the option consisted of the Will of 1919 that agreed the option, and Walter's signature to the transfer of June 15, 1922, which surrendered it. Thus Sutton's application for leave to execute the 1919 Will (and nothing else, since there was no codicil) gave Walter back his option.

Against Sutton (and the option) was the April 27, 1922 Will, and the stand Lady Northcliffe took upon it. The situation became awkward for all concerned when Lady Northcliffe, with legal advice, decided to contest the Administrator's decision to apply for leave to execute the Will of 1919. Such an action, if successful, must have the effect of destroying Walter's option. Rumours of Lady Northcliffe's suit against Sutton soon reached John Walter. He had everything to gain by Sutton's decision, nothing to gain from any litigation except time; and the time, he felt, would be of little use without the option. It happened, however, that the legacies and dispositions under both Wills were such as to engender a compromise; nobody wanted litigation.

But several interests, outside the families concerned, still wanted *The Times*. Birkenhead had not, so far, succeeded in promoting a syndicate capable of talking business. The Prime Minister's future, however, was so important that others showed their eagerness to see him made responsible for the policy of the paper. Soon after September 4 the Prime Minister discussed a new scheme involving a capitalist so rich as to be in a position to be of practical service to him: Sir John Ellerman. He was already the owner of 12,424 (against Northcliffe's 505,997) Ordinary shares. Lloyd George's advisor in this scheme was Sir Howard Frank,[1] who was in close touch with Ellerman. Frank was the auctioneer who had built a business, Knight, Frank and Rutley, out of his recognition, new in the estate business at the time, of the advantages of newspaper advertising on a very large scale. On September 8, Frank thus reported his findings to the Prime Minister. They were disappointing.

8th Sept., 1922

My dear Prime Minister,

I saw J. E[llerman]. to-night. He says he is creditably informed that one million has been offered for *Northcliffe's interest*, and he led me to believe this was by Cowdray.

He seems to think *he* would in all probability *be* able to purchase for one million and fifty thousand pounds. He states that the time has come when he must say he will either buy himself, or not stand in the way of a sale to others. He is disposed to put in £600,000 including his present interest, and £50,000 working capital if the remaining £650,000 is found for him to buy with. This means he would retain 40% and those who found the balance something over 50% as there are still a few small shareholders, who would be negligible as far as control is concerned. He would require to limit the dividends on the £650,000 to 10%, as he says he believes in the end he could make *The Times* pay, and if he succeeds to the extent of over 10% he considers he is entitled to anything beyond. I do not think this matters, as they will in my opinion be lucky if they ever see 10%.

He would be rid of the present Editor, but would retain C. Stuart. Walters [*sic*] might be tolerated for the sake of the name so long as he could not interfere.

This means that J. E. would run *The Times*, and I do *not* think he will put up the money unless he does.

J. E., however, with C. Stuart and Walters [*sic*], is not so bad, and the alternative might be far worse. He says it is his intention to run it upon absolutely impartial lines in the interests of the nation.

---

[1] Sir Howard Frank was land valuation adviser to the Ministry of Munitions from 1916 and later became Director-General of Lands.

The last four words, however, can be variously construed, and if this arrangement matures you are putting your head into the lion's mouth; not an enviable position if acute divergence of views arises.

If the matter is to proceed upon these lines he wants a banker's guarantee for £650,000 on *Monday* or Tuesday. Can this be given?

He also told me Rothermere had purchased N.'s interest in the *Mail*.

Inverforth, who knows nothing of to-day's interview with E. suggested this morning he might see E. on Monday, but I will not arrange this unless you wish. I have no copy of this letter which I suggest is destroyed.

I shall be at Walton tomorrow, at the light house Sunday and in town Monday.

Yours sincerely,

HOWARD FRANK.

Please excuse a hurriedly written and perhaps a little abrupt letter, but I have to go out. H. F.[1]

Plainly, Frank's warning was worth attention, though Lloyd George was not the man to put his head into any lion's mouth. A disconcerting point in Frank's letter was Ellerman's report that " One million " had been contemplated as the price of Northcliffe's interest. Evidently the vague " quarter of a million " that Lloyd George four months earlier had mentioned to Grigg as being available for John Walter needed supplementing. Ellerman's " creditable " adviser was wrong about Cowdray, but in other respects Frank was well informed, since he was aware " the time has come when he must say he will either buy himself, or not stand in the way of a sale to others." This was accurate. Frank also knew that it was necessary, in view of the revelation by Montague Ellis of the existence in the proved Will of the option, to take Walter into account. Most important of all was the revelation that a really large sum of money was required, option or no option. Somebody as rich as Ellerman or Rothermere was required.

Among those to whom the prospect of acquiring control of *The Times* appealed was David Davies[2] who, it has been seen, had tried to see Walter in June. Unknown to Frank, Grigg, Birkenhead, Beaverbrook, Rothermere, Walter, Ellerman or Stuart, David Davies had been at work on a scheme that brought in the Prime Minister. It is not known whether Davies was aware, beforehand, of the conditions its author might like to

[1] Printed by permission of the executors.
[2] Later Lord Davies.

impose. His scheme was more definite than any others and represented a formidable challenge to competitors. Davies was possessed of means, and had access to any further money that might be required. He had, moreover, a clear idea of the purposes he wished *The Times* to serve. Not all of them may have been palatable to the Prime Minister or some of his advisers. A contemporary memorandum of the Davies conditions survives.[1]

Sept. 21, 1922

D.D.'s Proposal

Suggested Heads of Agreement re *The Times*

1. That the total purchase price to be paid for the property does not exceed £900,000.

Of this total amount of £900,000, £400,000 to be found by X's[2] other friends, and £500,000 by the D[3] interest.

2. If the property can be secured at a lesser amount the total sum required must be found in the above proportion, e.g., if the property costs £800,000 X's interest finds £350,000 and the D interest £450,000.

3. That X undertakes to become Managing Director and Editor of *The Times* within six months of his relinquishing his position as Minister of the Crown.

4. That during the period which elapses between the acquisition of the property and the date of assuming the Editorship, arrangements for editing the paper are to be made by the Board of Directors.

5. That X be willing to enter into a Contract with the Board of Directors to place his services entirely at the disposal of the Company for a period of three or five years, and that during that period he is prepared to sever his connection with the House of Commons. This arrangement to be subject to three months' notice on either side.

6. That the Board be empowered to modify this arrangement by arrangement with the Editor in any way they think fit should in their opinion the necessity for doing so arise.

7. That the main lines of policy of the paper should be agreed upon beforehand, and incorporated in a document, and that subject to the provisions enumerated in this document the policy and direction of the paper should be entirely in the hands of the Editor and Managing Director.

8. That all matters relating to the administrative and business arrangements of the paper shall be controlled by the Board of Directors.

[1] Communicated by Dr. Thomas Jones.
[2] X—Lloyd George.
[3] D—Davies.

9. That the Board of Directors shall consist of five persons, two nominated by the D interest, and three by other shareholders. The first Chairman to be nominated by the D interest.

A peculiarity of this scheme is that Lloyd George should not only be Editor but Managing Director of *The Times*. Such a head as No. 3, even in a tentative project, could hardly have been included without some authority from the Prime Minister; moreover, head No. 7 gives Lloyd George complete and absolute control of the " policy and direction of the paper." It will be noticed that the project is dated September 21. It bears obvious marks of having been in preparation for several weeks, and the drafting probably began before September 4, the date of Ellis's revelation of the option and the date of Lady Northcliffe's claim that the second Will be proved.

The Davies scheme did not, as head No. 1 stood, offer quite the sum required and it was, in fact, too late by a week to stand a chance. It has been seen that after September 4 Sutton exerted himself to avoid litigation over the Wills. He had to reconcile the beneficiaries of the 1919 Will and those of the 1922 Will. If he failed litigation would result. To avoid this, Sutton strove to secure an agreement. This was the most anxious moment of all for Walter, who now knew the 1919 Will contained the option clause and that the 1922 Will disregarded it. If Lady Northcliffe and Sutton came to an agreement to accept the 1919 Will, on certain conditions, would the Court of Probate allow the option clause in spite of the surrender ? and would Lady Northcliffe object ? These were the crucial decisions for John Walter. Lady Northcliffe could and might object to the option clause. She could open the way for the straightforward and direct purchase of her husband's shares by Rothermere. By not opposing Walter's option she could give him a chance of redeeming the family connexion and, even if he failed, the entry of Walter into competition with Rothermere would tend to raise the figure of the " best price " from which Lady Northcliffe would benefit. In fact it would be good business for her to allow the option. Walter's mind was suddenly set at rest when Stuart said that he had authority to say that the option written into the 1919 Will would not be contested by Lady Northcliffe. Next Ellis sent Walter an official copy of the option.

Walter had overcome the first and greatest obstacle to his regaining a decisive voice in the affairs of *The Times*. From this moment, no scheme, as Davies's scheme attempted, could afford to ignore him. It must pay any promoter of Lloyd George's interest to combine with the representative of the founding family, who now possessed an option undisputed by Lady Northcliffe to purchase the deceased's shares " at the best price." John Walter, remembering that the Duke of Devonshire had been willing to back his father's scheme of reorganization after the failure of Pearson's scheme in 1908, called upon him and gave the Duke a full account of the situation so far as it had developed. The Duke expressed his willingness to support his scheme to the extent of £50,000 if required. Walter explained that there was a chance that John Astor might under-write the whole purchase. The Duke expressed approval.

On September 14, John and Ralph Walter saw Poole. A syndicate was discussed, including perhaps, the Duke of Devonshire and John Astor (suggested by John Walter), Lord Inverforth and Lord Pirrie (friends of Lloyd George's, suggested by Poole). There was no explicit mention of Lloyd George's desire to be Editor, and John Walter thought that as Lord Inverforth and Lord Pirrie were connected with the *Daily Chronicle* they could hardly be considered suitable members of the projected new board. This was tantamount to a rejection of all the schemes of Lloyd George's friends, though it did not necessarily put an end to the talk of associating Lloyd George himself, out of office, with the editorial policy. What did necessarily follow was that a move should be made towards Astor. Walter instructed Stuart to this effect. Whether the end of the Northcliffe regime would also mean the end of the Harmsworth family connexion with the paper was now about to be settled; whether the end of the Coalition Government was at hand and whether it would mean the end of Lloyd George's term would also now be seen.

XVIII

THE COALITION DISSOLVES

THE prospects of the Coalition in the late summer of 1922 were anything but bright. Circumstances had changed since May when Lloyd George returned from Genoa. *The Times* was partly responsible for the change for the worse. For eight weeks after June 14, when Northcliffe was first officially admitted to be in the hands of the doctors, the Editor was at least free from immediate professional and political anxieties. He had no knowledge of John Walter's conversations in July and August with Grigg, or of any plan to purchase Northcliffe's shares and to use the control of the paper in the interest of Lloyd George. The death of Northcliffe on August 14, however, coincided with new rumours of dissension within the bosom of the Coalition, and of trouble abroad. The Editor now faced very serious difficulties, both personal and political. Nevertheless, the death of the Chief Proprietor incidentally gave Steed an opportunity to dispel the view often expressed that the criticisms of Lloyd George and the Coalition in *The Times* had been wholly inspired by Northcliffe. Steed had never, in fact, espoused Northcliffe's personal animosities but had acted on what he, rightly or wrongly, held to be the principles of sound administration.

Throughout the period from June to October, during which the ownership of *The Times* was being competed for by Lloyd George, Rothermere and others, the political attitude of the paper remained constant, with the Editor in effective control following a simple policy. He thought the country needed a strong Conservative Party and a strong Liberal Party. He had by no means abandoned his conviction, expressed to Northcliffe in 1919, that the ensuing years must raise acute questions of labour policy and that an increase in the strength of the Parliamentary Labour Party would follow. But this would not be seen, he thought, in the immediate future. At the present time the Labour Party did not have the necessary strength, and hence the alternative to the Conservative Party was the Liberal Party; either of these would be an alternative to Coalition. The practical point reached in politics was that the existing Coalition, rightly established in answer to the necessities of war, had been rendered unnecessary by the signing of peace, and unwholesome by its actual leader's disregard of principle. In any case, Steed was persuaded that a Coalition was an expedient. The current tone of the paper towards the Government, though critical, was moderate. That the Entente had not after all been ruptured was in the Editor's eyes a main justification of the paper's recent action. But as the Coalition had emerged with credit, the immediate need was to look to the future. The road to recovery after Cannes and Genoa lay through Washington.

The Washington Conference had seemed to indicate that the United States would gradually change her mood of 1920. She had refused to attend the Conferences at Genoa and The Hague. The failure of the former Conference had been prophesied, and American non-participation was thus justified : in fact, American policy towards Russia should be a guide to Europe. But to bring America back to Europe was not going to be easy. French unpopularity in the Capitol was such that the paper's loyalty to the Entente was less easy to maintain; and, as *The Times* was fain to hope that America would return to the international fold since otherwise no permanent peace could be looked for, the tone of the leading articles was influenced by the old principle of *Anglo-Saxonia contra mundum*. The basis for this tone, however, was not that " blood is thicker than water." It was Page's dictum that " the same human coin rings true to each of us, the same rings false "[1] that was used. The theme now was that the superficial similarities had in the past caused misunderstanding; fundamentally, Britain and America were very different nations but they did pursue the same ideals. The immediate fact, however, was that America's return to isolation left the Allies with the problem of German reparations and inter-Allied debts, and the United States Government had made clear the fact that it had no intention of cancellation. In the opinion of Printing House Square and the City Office it would be a first-class mistake to continue to believe that America would or should follow a policy of cancellation. In the previous year, after Chamberlain had announced that Great Britain had proposed cancellation and the United States had refused, *The Times* expressed its belief in an early funding of the British debt to the United States. " We are a nation of shop-keepers, and our commercial interest as well as our commercial honour forbids us to discredit our paper." This strict view was taken on February 8, 1921. Keen criticism of the Government began in the early

[1] June 7, 1913, at a Pilgrims' banquet. Walter Hines Page was American Ambassador in London, 1913-1918.

summer of 1922 when it became known that a French mission was going to Washington without due indication of British intentions. All that was known of British policy was the " regrettable " declaration of the Prime Minister made on May 31. Lloyd George argued that unless United States pressure were relaxed Great Britain could not relieve her own debtors and the effect would be to drive Europe to bankruptcy. *The Times* argued that if Europe were to set her house in order America could be expected to help. The paper did its best by constructive and critical comment to educate opinion on both sides of the Atlantic. The subject appealed to Steed, who had not abandoned an early interest in finance and economics.

A series of articles published in July discussing a possible settlement of the war debts question attracted attention. The articles were meant, in the first place, to persuade Sir Robert Horne, Chancellor of the Exchequer, to push for an early funding of the British war debt to the United States (£1,000,000,000 in gold on five days' call) so that Britain might be freed to deal with her European debtors. After writing the articles the Editor instructed Courtney John Frederick Mill[1] (who had been appointed City Editor in succession to Hugh Chisholm, in February, 1920) to show proofs to Montagu Norman, Revelstoke, Henry Bell (of Lloyds Bank), McKenna (of the Midland Bank) and others, and to ask their opinion of the course proposed. He was to add that unless cogent arguments were pressed against, publication would proceed.

The City men approved. After the publication of the second article Horne offered his thanks to the Editor for the " splendid help you are giving me. I am having a stiff fight in the Cabinet, and your articles are the very thing I want." The Editor answered that they were intended to " ginger " him up; upon which he said he had no need of " gingering," though other members of the Cabinet were " pig-headed." A day or two later Montagu Norman telephoned to the Editor that Balfour (then Foreign Secretary) was writing a note to Britain's European debtors. Balfour, Norman insisted " is saying indirectly to the United States, ' We will pay you if we must but you will be cads if you ask us to do so '. You will understand what the effect of that is likely to be in America." Upon this, the Editor telephoned William Tyrrell at the Foreign Office saying that he had bad news. " So have I," he answered, " Come to see me." The Editor went at once to Tyrrell who showed him a corrected,

[1] Mill joined *The Times* in 1908 and died on December 10, 1938.

printed draft of the Balfour Note. It justified all that Montagu Norman had said. When the Editor asked Tyrrell what could be done, he advised the sounding of the City, and perhaps getting leaders of the banks to protest to Downing Street. The Editor accepted Tyrrell's suggestion; the protest was made but met with no success. The Editor thereupon sought the counsel of the American Ambassador. Steed came, he said, to see George Harvey, journalist, not George Harvey, Ambassador. He wanted George Harvey, journalist, to tell him how he could best act. Steed explained the danger of such a note as Balfour was preparing, and the consequences of the failure to organize a City protest. The Ambassador, who was already aware of Balfour's intention, said that George Harvey, Ambassador, could hardly have listened to the Editor, but George Harvey, journalist, could say that Bonar Law was the one man who could put his foot down and prevent the Balfour Note being sent. Otherwise, said the Ambassador, there might be no hope of a decent settlement of the British debt to America. The Editor immediately went to Bonar Law, whom he found sceptical. The Conservative leader said he thought the Editor was misinformed. When Steed assured Bonar Law that he had seen the draft note in print, Bonar Law answered that drafts could be altered, and that in any event, he " as a politician " did not feel he could intervene. Bonar Law confessed later that he had been in error.

Throughout July and August *The Times* was full of articles, letters and dispatches regarding the debt. On August 1, the paper reported the dispatch of what was called " Lord Balfour's Note," and reproduced the text. The leading article did not appear until the next day. The hope was expressed that the paper's " estimate of the influence of the Balfour Note upon America may prove to be wholly erroneous." On August 3 a leading article insisted that the Note made this country " the prisoner of what may well be the least-informed sections of opinion in the U.S." That was the net result of the ill-inspired and well-written Note. The Government were strongly criticized for having bound their own hands in advance and having forced those of their Allies. The Note had been sent in spite of the warning of *The Times* and all who understood America. If an arrangement for funding the British debt in America had been made before discussion of European finance, this country would have been her own master; now American resentment was roused because Britain had thrust responsibility for European difficulties on her, and France was encouraged to press more rigorously on Germany. Hope of settlement was destroyed by the failure, bluntly described on August 14 as such, of the London Conference.

The office, for the reasons arising out of Northcliffe's death on the 14th, was distracted. At the same time there was only bad news to put into the paper. The country itself was in no cheerful mood. On August 21 *The Times* recorded the national unemployment figures—1,333,700. On August 23 the paper announced that Michael Collins, with Arthur Griffith, the most powerful of the pro-Treaty leaders in the Irish Free State, had been ambushed and killed. Abroad, the Middle East conflict which had begun six months earlier was now a source of deep anxiety. On September 8 the paper announced the approach of the Turkish Nationalists under Kemal to Smyrna. The city was occupied by the Greeks who were in Anatolia by the Treaty of Sèvres, signed by the Constantinople Government on August 10, 1920. The Treaty had been immediately repudiated by the Nationalists. They believed they could expel the Greeks by force and that they could divide and defy the Western Powers. During the first week of September, "informed circles" in London were frankly alarmed. It was not forgotten that the signatures to the Treaty cloaked serious rivalries between Britain, France and Italy. Britain's position was particularly delicate; and, in a leading article of September 9, *The Times* emphasized the need for " calm and circumspection on the part of the two European Great Powers who are also great Mahomedan Powers." The main interests of Britain and France were the same, "however much their secondary interests may differ, or may seem to differ." The paper never deviated from the line that to weaken the Entente involved danger. The cordiality of the Entente must be maintained. The office was convinced that the Turks would not resist the " common will " of the three Allied signatories, and that without the " common will " the Turks might challenge the Sévres Treaty, with devastating effects upon the Versailles, Trianon and St. Germain settlements. The fundamental interest was the pacification, stabilization and reconstruction of Europe. Britain's policy was unworkable failing close alliance with France, and the Coalition's policy of ignoring her vital interests was blamed. That French political life was not free from elements that were ready to embarrass Britain was admitted. Events in the Near East might play into the hands of every kind of trouble-maker.

On September 11 the paper announced that the Turks had seized Smyrna, and, within the week, it reported the destruction of the city by fire, and the massacre of a large section of the Greek population, involving a total of 120,000 victims. Thus the Greeks were made to pay for their success at Versailles.[1] The Turks now turned their eyes towards Constantinople.

The British Government had already decided that the control of the deep sea separating Asia and Europe was a cardinal British interest, and any attempt by Kemal to occupy the Gallipoli Peninsula and Constantinople should be resisted. While League intervention was being studied, General Harington, Allied C.-in-C. at Constantinople of a mixed French, Italian and British force, was not only urging the necessity of Allied military unity, but also doing his best to convince the Kemalists that it was an accomplished fact. At the same time, he was telling the War Office that he could not alone hold Constantinople " at all costs." Twenty-four hours later Harington warned the War Office that French promises had not yet been fulfilled, but he remained of the opinion that provided Allied unity were made plain Kemal would not attack Constantinople. Rumbold, the British Ambassador, agreed, but he, too, placed no reliance on the French. That all was not well in Anglo-French relations was keenly felt in Printing House Square.

The French Cabinet met on Thursday, September 14, while the British Cabinet was due to meet on the afternoon of Friday, September 15. In the office it was hoped that the Cabinet would have before it unambiguous statements of the attitude that the French and Italian Governments intended to take towards Kemal. Difficulties were increasing all round. The Russian Government had sent a Note maintaining that no settlement of the Near East conflict would be complete without Russian representatives, and it was accepted in the office that Russia was dissatisfied with the Treaty of Sèvres and critical of Britain's support of Greece. The Russians, in fact, soon made no secret of their partiality for the Turks. *The Times* (September 15) warned the country of the gravity of the situation by asking whether England and France had yet " awakened to the fact that they stand face to face with the most serious crisis which has confronted them since 1914 ? " The leader-writer was Flanagan (who wrote on the crisis of July and August, 1914). He had been writing regularly since August 28 and was to continue

---

[1] In May, 1919, when Wilson resisted the Italian claim for Fiume, Venizelos obtained for the Greeks a mandate to occupy Smyrna for the ostensible purpose of protecting the city's Greek population. It was suspected at the time that the real object was to forestall an Italian occupation. There had been much pillage, arson, and slaughter when the Greeks arrived.

writing on the international crisis until October 5. He was relieved on September 6, 23, 24 and 30 by the Editor, who also wrote a daily news summary of the crisis for the bill page. By the 14th when the French Cabinet met, the country still showed itself uninterested in the crisis, though there were protests against the reported arson, pillage and massacre. There was little serious concern until the 15th, when the paper printed a prediction from its Correspondent in the Near East, dated the previous day, that Kemal would demand the evacuation of the Straits by the Entente, also an early evacuation of Constantinople.

It was believed by most of the Asquithian Liberals and by many of the Conservatives that the Prime Minister was incorrigibly anti-Turk, and that he was embarrassed by his Foreign Secretary who was regarded as no less anti-Greek. In fact, the Prime Minister at this time was endeavouring to be impartial, but he was not prepared to allow the resettlement of Europe to be upset by the Turks. What Lloyd George wanted at this time was to get it realized that from the moment Greece threw over Venizelos and placed its destinies in the hands of Constantine a pro-Greek policy in Anatolia was out of the question, and he claimed to be a supporter of Curzon's policy as to European Turkey. The Foreign Secretary, however, thought that the Prime Minister was himself seeing Greek emissaries and had encouraged Venizelos to visit England.

It was known in the office that the relations between the Prime Minister and the Foreign Secretary were cool. Obviously, the Cabinet on the 15th would be a critical meeting. *The Times* did not give the names of the Ministers who attended, but it observed that Curzon, the Foreign Secretary, was absent. A semi-official communiqué, published in *The Times* after the " protracted " meeting, read :

We understand that there is complete agreement between the British, French and Italian Generals with regard to the maintenance of the neutrality of the whole of the demilitarized zone under the Treaty of Sèvres and that a joint ultimatum is to be sent by the three Governments to Mustapha Kemal on the subject. This step is to be taken pending a more permanent arrangement, which the British Government agrees shall be the subject of a conference. The Allied Powers are preparing to send reinforcements to the neutral zone in case there should be any imminence of an attack by the Kemalist forces, and the Fleets are being instructed that no Turkish troops are to be allowed to cross from the Asiatic Coast to Europe. Neither are the Fleets to permit transport for the purpose of transferring a Turkish Army to Europe. (September 16, 1922.)

Thus it had been authoritatively decided to resist aggression upon Europe by the Turks, and Harington, the C.-in-C. at Constantinople, was instructed accordingly. He was to " make exertions " to prevent Kemal turning the Allies out of Constantinople; and he was to secure " firmly " the Gallipoli Peninsula in order to maintain the freedom of the Straits. By -telegram, the Prime Minister informed the Governors-General of Canada, Australia, New Zealand, and South Africa, and the Officer administering the Government of Newfoundland, that the British Government had received notification that the French Government and the Italian Government would act similarly. These Powers, with Greece, Rumania and Serbia, whose participation was foreseen, had all been informed of Britain's " intention to make exertions." The British Government, at least, meant business; so it seemed. Reasonably, therefore, Saturday's leading article described the situation as amounting to a " grave emergency," which demanded firmness and coherence in British statesmanship and the closest understanding with France. So far, the leader was a restatement of the thesis laid down earlier in the week, i.e., that the crisis was twofold : the risk of war with Turkey involved the risk of a break with France. This meant the probability of an isolated Britain being saddled with unlimited Near East responsibilities as well as with disorder in Moslem lands.

But the leader of September 16 did more than re-emphasize the implications of this thesis. The Correspondent in the Near East had telegraphed from Constantinople on the 14th a message which the writer of the leader (the Editor) described as " important." Rauf Bey, the Kemalist Prime Minister, had promised in a recent speech that, just as the Nationalists would celebrate the recapture of Smyrna, they would soon be celebrating the retaking of Constantinople and Adrianople. That was the Correspondent's first item of news. He proceeded to estimate the immediate risks.

In face of this and similar warnings, the British Government appears to have decided to send one battalion for the present to Turkey. It does not appear to be realized in London that the time for speeches and attempts at bargaining is already past. If we mean to defend genuinely British interests such as the freedom of the Straits, we must be prepared to take the necessary military precautions. The mere dispatch of ships to Turkish waters by itself is useless, except to cover evacuation.

Even assuming that France supports us, as she may up to a point, we cannot expect her to bear the brunt of the defence of the Straits and the neutral zones, and the longer British statesmen wait, Micawber-like, for something to turn up to their advantage, while they omit to take the defensive steps which the situation demands, the more they will indispose our Allies, whose interests, like our own, demand an early settlement of the Near Eastern troubles, the more they will encourage the extremists in Angora and Moscow, the more they will jeopardize our ludicrously insufficient forces and our very great interests in Turkey.

Clearly the Correspondent was satisfied that the forces available and promised were insufficient to carry out the stated policy of defending the Straits. He believed that hesitation in London was responsible for tepid French and Italian cooperation, and that the time for speeches and diplomatic action was past. It was time for action, if the Government meant what it said.

It was not overlooked in the office that the Correspondent was in close touch with Rumbold and Harington. The paper therefore supported the Correspondent's demand for the taking of "the necessary military precautions." And "if at the twelfth hour, the British Government show wisdom, coupled with energy and firmness," said *The Times*, abating under the pressure of events its hostility to the Government, "they may receive a greater measure of public support than that to which the demerits of their past policy would entitle them. . . . National interests may require that they should receive some degree of public countenance until the more immediate danger is past." (September 16, 1922.)

The Times, in the face of national crisis, was preparing to lay aside its objections to the Government of the day in order to press a national policy upon them. That the degree of danger was real enough, and could be measured, was obvious. The famous German General, Liman von Sanders, was busy pointing out that the recent victories of the Turks were arousing the enthusiasm of the whole Moslem world. The French and Italians, the General claimed, "would endanger their entire position in the Near East were they to oppose the Turkish standpoint and to adopt that of the British Prime Minister." Calcutta equally with Stamboul, he said, was decked with flags. The leading article admitted that the General's statement was "not entirely fantastic," that the danger was genuine "and it needs to be calmly faced. . . . The first necessity is the cultivation of a close understanding with France." Thus *The Times* was for appropriate action provided French cooperation was assured.

During the Saturday (September 16) on which this leading article and the Near East Correspondent's message were published, Ministers met at Downing Street. In the evening, and too late for most of the Sunday newspapers, a statement of Ministerial policy was circulated to the Press.[1] The British Government, it said, recognizing the seriousness of the position, wished a Conference to be held " as speedily as possible." But such a Conference, as Kemal had been informed, could not be held while there was any question of his attacking the neutral zones by which Constantinople, the Bosporus and the Dardanelles were protected. Secondly, the Government held it " futile and dangerous in view of the excited mood and extravagant claims of the Kemalists, to trust simply to diplomatic action " and ' adequate force must be available to guard the freedom of the Straits." This had been the burden of the " important " message from Constantinople published in that morning's issue of *The Times*. But the office believed the wording of the Government's statement exceeded its intentions and its plans. Nobody in Printing House Square could see how Britain, unsupported, could make war in the Near East. Hence, the paper's comment, printed on Monday, the 18th, expressed doubt whether the Government meant what it said. " They have laid down their policy. They have proclaimed it in emphatic and sonorous phrase to the Turks, to their Allies, and to the world. Are they resolved enough and honest enough to adhere to it, whatever it may bring ? If they are not, the sooner they don the white sheet and read their recantation the better." (September 18, 1922.) The " emphatic and sonorous " phrasing of the statement pointed, in the opinion of the office, to Churchill as the draftsman responsible, and with him in a position of influence, some immediate development was looked for.

On the Monday morning when this comment appeared, a meeting of Ministers was convened at Downing Street. There were present, besides the Prime Minister, Birkenhead, Chamberlain, Curzon, Churchill, Worthington-Evans, Arthur Lee and Robert Horne. They considered the situation, in consultation with the Service Chiefs. In reporting this meeting in *The Times* of Tuesday, the Editor (who wrote the news summary) added a reference to Saturday's statement. According to the Editor, " Ministers recognized, though they do not publicly admit, that the publication of the semi-official statement issued on Saturday evening was a serious blunder. The

[1] It did not appear in the *Observer*, but the *Weekly Dispatch* secured it in time for Sunday's issue.

suggestion now appears to be made that its issue was due to a secretarial mistake "—a reference to the large personal " secretariat " of the Prime Minister that had so often been criticized in the House of Commons and in *The Times*. The Editor added one sentence that may have given slight pleasure to the penman responsible for the " sonorous phrasing ": " It is not suggested, however, that the document was drawn up by secretaries."

The foreign page reported remonstrations from Paris at the enunciation of an apparently bellicose policy without previous consultation with France. It was announced, however, that Curzon was that day going to Paris to seek agreement. " His disposition towards the French standpoint is taken to be more conciliatory and statesmanlike than that of some of his colleagues." The leading article gave Curzon the blessing, cordial, full and most uncustomary, of *The Times*. " We trust he will be received in France as the representative of the saner tendencies of British policy in foreign affairs."

Meanwhile Downing Street was not pleased at the reference to a " secretarial " misjudgement, and later in the day circulated a denial of the suggestion that the policy statement published on Saturday lacked authority in any degree. When *The Times* printed the communiqué on Wednesday, the 20th, the paper added that the denial was " taken as evidence that the Cabinet are not yet fully alive to the extreme delicacy of the position in which they have placed the country." Saturday's Downing Street statement, it was now said, was a declaration of policy that " represented the decisions of the Cabinet on the previous day, and was issued with the approval of all the Ministers present in London, in order that public opinion throughout the Empire should be left in no doubt regarding the aims and intentions of the British Government on a critical question of Imperial policy, on which the support of the Dominions has been invited by telegraph." As to the last-mentioned aspect of affairs, the statement proceeded to say that " The Cabinet is well satisfied with the support accorded to it, not only in this country, but in the Dominions."

In the office it was believed by Monday, the 18th, that the policy statement issued on Saturday in the previous week represented principally the views of the Prime Minister, Birkenhead, Churchill and Chamberlain. During that week-end it had become known that at no stage in the drafting of Saturday's statement had the Foreign Office been consulted, or even been informed. Indeed the Editor learned that Curzon first saw the statement in the box of papers he received on Sunday. The explanation, as the office knew, was that the Prime Minister and the Secretary for the Colonies, Churchill, regarded the Foreign Office as pro-Turk. Hence, the Prime Minister held aloof from Curzon and relied rather upon Churchill and the " secretariat." Among the unlooked-for effects of Saturday's statement, and the mode of its promulgation, was a change in the attitude of *The Times* towards the Foreign Secretary. It was a notably sharp turn, for Curzon not many months previously had severed relations between *The Times* and the Foreign Office.[1] Ever since the crisis reached the point of gravity, *The Times* had recognized the necessity of supporting the Government in so far as Ministers enacted a national policy. But the paper could hardly maintain this attitude in the face of open Ministerial disunion. The Editor now thought that the Prime Minister's disregard of his Foreign Secretary must create confusion in the Allied and neutral Chancelleries, above all in the French Foreign Office. The French were right, he believed, to say that the Saturday statement was not only comprehensive but threatening. Certainly, it opened with a call to a peace conference to be held " as speedily as possible," but, as certainly, it ended with a call to the Dominions to support Britain with contingents. The objections that the French, from their point of view, saw in British policy were rendered all the more weighty by Saturday's statement that appeared to drag them into a situation which was unexpected, dangerous and intolerable. Poincaré was not the man to accept at British hands such a situation without protest.

The office was depressed at the probable upshot of Curzon's interview. Poincaré was not only French Prime Minister, but Minister of Foreign Affairs. Curzon's task was to associate him with Great Britain and Italy in calling a halt to the impending Turkish advance upon Chanak and Constantinople. Curzon deserved every support. Lloyd George planned to send, in support of Curzon, Birkenhead who was being encouraged to hope for the succession to the Foreign Office. A protest by the Foreign Secretary and an awkward wrangle preceded a last-minute decision that Curzon alone should go and conduct the talks with Poincaré and Sforza. By huge exertions, he succeeded

---

[1] Curzon had been very ill with phlebitis in May and June. He recovered in July but, in a letter to his wife, written at this period, reports: " This morning I was thrown back by reading the two vile paras. in *The Times* and the *Daily Mail*, a part of their ceaseless vendetta against me . . . I am, indeed, ill treated, for the Northcliffe people will not spare me even in my illness and seem intent on getting me out alive or dead." Curzon to Lady Curzon, July, 1922, Ronaldshay, III, 291.)

in getting France and Italy to agree to address a joint invitation to the Turks to attend a Conference at Venice.

The Times was delighted with the Foreign Secretary's success. The Entente had been saved, and saved by him. This accomplished, the paper felt that the crisis had passed and that it could justifiably return to the congenial task of opposing the Government. Severe criticism was meted out. The response from the Dominions did not justify Ministerial hopes, or, indeed, statements regarding " contingents." The previous Tuesday's communiqué, issued by the Secretariat as a rider to the communiqué of the previous Saturday, professed that the Government was " well satisfied with the support accorded to it not only in this country, but in the Dominions." The information regarding the attitude of Australia and Canada in the possession of the office did not justify Ministers being " well satisfied."[1] Australia would undertake not to refuse to send troops in case of war; South Africa hesitated, and Canada was faint-hearted. The office had reason to believe that the " support accorded " did not, in fact, justify the statement of the Government. All the Dominions were indignant at the publication in the British Press of an appeal to them before they had been consulted and when they remained dependent upon newspapers for the information that would enable them to measure the crisis. They did not relish the tone of the telegram sent by the Secretary of State to the Colonies.

Meanwhile, Saturday's statement was being digested in this country. Its publication had coincided with talk that the unpopularity of the Coalition in the Conservative constituencies was now increasing at such a rate that the existing administration would have to be remodelled, or at least reshuffled. The Prime Minister's health, it was also being said, was such that his place should soon be taken by Chamberlain. Party leaders like Sir George Younger were in favour of a continuation of the Coalition under a Conservative leader, while Members of Parliament, and candidates to the number of eighty, were pledged to vote against any Coalition. The country was clearly against war and

---

[1] The source of the paper's information on the Australian Prime Minister's reply is unknown. There is abundant evidence in the Lloyd George Papers that the Dominion considered that it ought not to be " stampeded " when " no information suggesting that the Empire was likely to be involved in hostility and no telegram bearing upon recent developments in the Near East have come to hand." Hence the Colonial Secretary's telegram " came as a bolt from the blue," etc. The Governor-General of Canada (Byng) vigorously protested against the appearance in the Press of British Government statements including Canada before the Dominion had been consulted or informed. In 1928, Mackenzie King, as Prime Minister, took credit for having averted a European war over Chanak. *Cf.* Chapter XXI, " Dawson's Second Innings."

suspicious that the Coalition was drifting into perilous waters. Even if the crisis passed an election would destroy the Government. This was what was being said by the critics and prophets in the lobbies and was known therefore to the Parliamentary Correspondents of the newspapers, including *The Times*. The Press as a whole was convinced that the Government had got itself into an impossible position. It had assumed a warlike posture when it did not possess the moral authority with which to impress either the country, the Dominions, the Allies, or the Turks.

On the 21st Grey wrote a letter to the Editor. The former Foreign Secretary's words were blunt. " On Saturday, our Government announced to the world a whole scheme of action, apparently without consultation with France. This was a terrible mistake. The reply of France has been the withdrawal of the French forces from Chanak. . . . If what the Government contemplates is separate action in the Near East, we may be heading for disaster." *The Times*, on the same day, took a more hopeful view. The Editor's summary on the bill page said that:

Though secrecy is maintained upon the precise course of the Paris conversations, there is reason to believe that the French Government showed increasing appreciation of Lord Curzon's standpoint during the day, and that the decision to summon a Peace Conference without more ado was reached largely in deference to his representations. . . . The British Government had not received up to last night any detailed information as to the progress of the negotiations in Paris. (September 21, 1922.)

The communiqué issued in Paris recorded agreement as to the advisability of summoning as soon as possible a conference to which Turkey, Greece, Yugo-Slavia, and Rumania would be invited, and " at which the conditions of the future peace will be laid down." Meanwhile, official circles in London were insisting that the Government would maintain the freedom of the Straits and the neutrality of the Asiatic shores commanding them. The Paris Correspondent confirmed that the proposal of a conference came from the British Foreign Minister and by next day the situation was believed to be much easier. The leading article did not now refrain from criticizing the Government. The policy statements (*i.e.*, of Saturday, September 16, and Tuesday, the 19th) which had already been described as " permeated with self-complacency," were again both denounced. The Government's attitude towards the Dominions was inexplicable. " It is difficult to understand why they are keeping back the Prime Minister's dispatch to Mr. Hughes, the Prime Minister of

Australia." Objection was also taken to the Government's habit of secrecy at such a time. "It is difficult to understand why the members of the General Council of the Trades Union Congress which waited upon the Prime Minister yesterday should be privileged to hear a statement from him on the Near Eastern situation while it is withheld from the general public." Responding to these complaints, the Prime Minister, at short notice, summoned a meeting of journalists for Saturday. A report of Lloyd George's speech occupied two columns in the paper of Monday, the 25th. In the presence of Austen Chamberlain, Horne and Churchill the Prime Minister insisted that the Government's purpose was peace; "Peace is our object. ... We want the League of Nations to guarantee the freedom of the Straits in the interest of all nations."

Two days earlier, in a letter to *The Times*, Lord Salisbury (acknowledged leader of the Conservative "Die-hards") backed Grey's demand for common action with France. The situation was now again serious, for by this time Mustapha Kemal had concentrated his troops against Chanak, and the retention of Constantinople was rendered precarious. There could be no Peace Conference under these conditions. And it was doubt about the constitution of the Conference that moved the Turks towards Chanak and Constantinople. In London four or five meetings of Ministers were held in forty-eight hours, with naval and military advisers in attendance. On September 29 *The Times* described the situation as "grave." With the leading article there was printed a letter to the Editor from Ramsay MacDonald pointing out that every by-election showed "how incapable the present Parliament is to represent public opinion, and an election should precede any Government action which will settle our future as a world State." A decidedly serious decision was taken during the day. The British Government sent Harington new instructions amounting to an ultimatum that might lead to immediate hostilities.

On September 30 *The Times* printed a demand for the summoning of Parliament, signed by Conservative members, and a sharp letter from Walter Long saying that Ministers would be better employed in their offices than on the floor of the House. A tense feeling prevailed. But peace was saved by the C.-in-C. at Constantinople. Harington, who had opened negotiations in the name of the Allies with Kemal before the new instructions reached him (as *The Times* announced on September 30), considered himself justified in disregarding the new instructions and in continuing his earlier negotiations. By great skill he persuaded Kemal to accept the invitation of a fully representative Peace Conference. Hopes rose. But there were the usual delays.

The promise of a pacific solution won by Harington was jeopardized when, on the morning of October 6, the British Cabinet, in view of the position taken up by the French representatives at the Mudania Conference, decided that France should stand shoulder to shoulder with Great Britain in resisting any further Turkish advance, and that if she did not unequivocally agree the British garrison would evacuate Constantinople. *The Times* learnt this serious news from Bonar Law, who had been informed of what had passed at the Cabinet meeting of the 6th. In a telephone message to the Editor the Conservative leader proposed to visit him, but the Editor offered to call at Bonar Law's house on his way to the office. Bonar Law told him that there " was almost a split in the Cabinet over the Chanak crisis." There were some members of the Government who were not averse, he said, to a breach with France. Admittedly, Poincaré was " extremely difficult " but " Curzon thinks a last effort ought to be made to get France to stand with us at Chanak against the Turks. He has gone to Paris by the 2 o'clock train and may meet Poincaré to-night." He then said that he had written a letter to the Editor in which he reviewed the antecedents of the crisis, and its present dangers, not only in the Near East, but also its repercussion upon the Moslem feeling in the Arab States and in India. The letter, said Bonar Law, expressed the view that the burden of taking necessary action should not fall upon the British Empire alone. The prevention of war and possible massacres in Constantinople and the Balkans was not, he thought, a special British interest. Rather it was an interest of humanity. Nor was the securing of the freedom of the Straits a special British interest; rather, the interest of the world. " The course of action for our Government seems to me clear. We cannot alone act as the policemen of the world. The financial and social condition of this country makes that impossible." Hence, he argued, Britain should plainly remind France " that the position in Constantinople and the Straits is as essential a part of the Peace settlement as the arrangement with Germany." This admission and agreement would prepare the way for Britain to meet France (and Italy) in a united front.

In conjunction with Grey's and Salisbury's letters, Bonar Law told the Editor that the immediate publication of his letter would perhaps assist Curzon in his difficult task with Poincaré. When certain changes in its text had been made the Editor agreed to publish it. He offered first to take it to the Foreign Office and ask Tyrrell to have it telegraphed, or telephoned, to Curzon that he might know the backing he was next day to get from Bonar Law and *The Times*. Secondly, the Editor offered to leave a copy of the letter with the French Ambassador, and ask him to telegraph, or telephone, it to Poincaré so that, before meeting Curzon, Poincaré would know the extent to which Curzon was supported. Finally, the Editor suggested giving the letter to the Correspondent of the *Petit Parisien* with instructions to telephone it to Philippe Millet, and to ask him to inform " Pertinax." Thus, when, according to custom, they saw Poincaré at eight o'clock, Curzon could be given further support.[1] The letter to the Editor duly appeared in *The Times* of October 7, while Curzon in the face of great difficulty succeeded in negotiating an agreement with Poincaré.

The Chanak crisis had implied a grave danger to the existence of the Conservative Party. It was possible, the Conservative leader believed, that, had a minor war with Turkey been undertaken, a general election would have followed. In such an event, the pattern of November, 1918, might well have been repeated: *i.e.*, the wave of a " khaki " vote might have borne the Lloyd George Coalition to a renewed lease of power. This the successful negotiations in Paris had for the moment averted. But the situation remained gravely dangerous to the future of the Conservative Party.

Such was the immediate domestic political possibility; rather probability, as Bonar Law saw it. It amounted to a remodelling of the " Fusion " Party, or " National " Party, or " Centre " Party that had been discussed since January, 1921, *i.e.*, a new type of Coalition. This 1922 " Middle " Party would also be constituted under Lloyd George, but have Birkenhead, Churchill and Chamberlain in the principal positions. Bonar Law said that such a " Middle " Party would in fact continue the Coalition; also it would destroy the Conservative as well as the Liberal Party. He

---

[1] Millet (*Petit Parisien*) and " Pertinax " (*Echo de Paris*) were both inclined to adopt the British point of view in regard to the Kemalist danger, and to the attitude taken up towards it by the French representatives at Mudania under the inspiration of Franklin-Bouillon. " Pertinax," in particular, was outspoken in his criticisms of Poincaré's current policy. The support of two such influential journalists was of the greatest value while Millet's organ, the *Petit Parisien*, had the largest circulation of any French newspaper. The *Journal des Débats*, which had a considerable circulation among the educated classes, the *Éclair*, *Ère Nouvelle*, and *Gaulois* (a society paper) all adopted the same attitude. Gauvain of the *Journal des Débats* was a warm and able advocate of the British point of view, and constantly pointed out to his readers that the friendship of Britain was worth a great deal more than that of the Kemalists.

End of Bonar Law's Letter to the Editor of *The Times* published on
October 7, 1922.

From the original in Bonar Law's holograph, with pencil corrections
by H. Wickham Steed.

himself felt he could not oppose the Government on what must seem to the country to be a patriotic issue, but he had drafted a letter informing the Conservative committee in his Glasgow constituency that he must decline to stand at the next General Election, and announcing his withdrawal from public life. It was true that the state of Bonar Law's health was a complete justification of his action. Many prominent Conservatives shared Bonar Law's view that a continuation of the Coalition must spell disaster to the Party. Of these, Amery and Chamberlain remained, after discussion, in favour of a National Government. This followed from their desire to find a compromise that would not necessitate the resignation of Lloyd George. At some point later in the party discussions, Amery and Baldwin joined in opposition to Churchill, Birkenhead and Chamberlain.

Meanwhile, an armistice in Asia Minor, signed on October 11, relieved international tension, and permitted statesmen to concentrate on the party issue. The paper for October 12, announced that the fate of the Coalition still hung in the balance. A rate of 35 per cent. was accepted in the London insurance market for the payment of a total loss should there be a General Election before the end of the year. In other words the odds against that contingency were equivalent to about two to one. A mission to Washington in connexion with a British Foundry Delegation was postponed " for domestic political reasons." *The Times* headed its first leading article " From Crisis to Crisis." The leader laid down that " It is no longer a question whether this Government should hold office indefinitely, but whether its disruption or its overthrow should be consummated in the immediate future or towards the end of the year." (October 12, 1922.) On the day these words were published, Rothermere announced to Sutton, the Administrator of the Estate, his readiness to bid for the shares of the late Lord Northcliffe.

XIX

ROTHERMERE *v.* WALTER

THE dissensions within the Coalition, and the virtual certainty of its dissolution during either the autumn of 1922 or the spring of 1923, had a stimulating effect upon all the schemes that were maturing after Northcliffe's death for the acquisition of his controlling shares in *The Times*. The sponsors of all these schemes were well aware that every consideration, political, personal and commercial, made speed and secrecy essential to success. It has been seen that John Walter's indirect and indefinite negotiations with Lloyd George through Poole had lost much time. When Campbell Stuart, on his return from Canada, had been instructed and empowered to get to work he knew he had little time to waste. His first object was to secure the money for the purchase of the control; secondly, he was to get the best cash equivalent for John Walter's option in any new partnership. The capital sum required was now known to be much larger than had been supposed. In June, 1922, the Prime Minister's friends, with the exception of Rothermere (and probably Beaverbrook, who was intimate with him), had underestimated both the sum of money required and the difficulty of raising it.[1] The banker's guarantee of £650,000 asked for by Ellerman, representing half the total investment, was not ready on the 11th or the 12th of September; and there was no sign of it. David Davies asked for £500,000, and this was not yet in sight. These figures related to experts' valuations that rightly ignored political considerations. The political crisis gave the whole affair a partly uncommercial character. So far, politics had been given consideration only when the need for additional cash support arose. It was natural for the Prime Minister's circle to be actuated by the motive of reversing the inimical policy of *The Times*, and it was natural for them and their experts to suppose that his monied friends would join in the risk. The figures drawn up by these experts were business figures, not necessarily the " best price " mentioned in the will, forthcoming if a purchaser were found who was interested in something

[1] For the abortive schemes in which Beaverbrook, Birkenhead, Howard Frank, David Davies and others were interested, see Chapter XVII, *ante*.

eyond business. By August and September the political crisis
ad extended. Events might well bring forward a purchaser who
/ould bid higher than a business figure for the political control.

Stuart, therefore, was given no easy task when he left the
oard of The Times Publishing Company on September 14,
922. He knew that John Walter was good for £100,000, and
hat the Duke of Devonshire could be relied upon for another
50,000. Poole was unable at that stage to commit Lloyd
George to anything. In that respect he started level with
Ellerman and Davies. All three needed support that could only
ome from outside the Downing Street circle, although all three
/ere ready to associate themselves in varying degrees and
ntimacy with the Prime Minister. There remained John Astor.
t was not known how far Astor was prepared to go. The sum
o be found depended upon an unknown factor. Poole had
evealed nothing of what he knew (if he knew anything) of
Rothermere's plans; and neither the Lloyd George nor the
Walter side knew that Rothermere was talking matters over with
Bonar Law.

This was the situation as Stuart set out in search of a million
ounds. He went straight to the office of Lee, Higginson & Co.,
ne of the banking houses responsible for the Astor Estate, and
aw Sir Guy Granet. There followed many long talks. Within
week Stuart had progress to report. Granet visited Stuart
n the Managing Director's room at Printing House Square, to
ay that he was in favour of his client, John Astor, associating
imself with the business under discussion. It had been known
ince June, when mention had first been made of " a man from
New College," that Astor might be helpful, but nobody had been
ble to say, precisely, to what extent he would help. And,
learly, with regard to a property involving a large sum, Astor
/ould necessarily take advice. It was of capital importance,
herefore, that after Stuart's talks, Granet should come on
eptember 22 to say that he was not merely in favour of a scheme
y which his client, John Astor, would associate himself with
he Times, but in favour of his underwriting the whole of the
um required to enable John Walter to exercise his option to
urchase it. This meant, in effect, that provided the details
/ere satisfactory, Lee, Higginson & Co. would make that
ecommendation to their client.

Simultaneously, Buckle had been talking to the Duke of
Devonshire, and had then communicated the facts to Walter.
hey discussed the scheme, or what there was of it. Walter was

741

discouraging. He thought it fair to tell Buckle that he ha‹
seen the Duke and that Stuart with his sanction, was alread
at work on another scheme and had made a certain amoun
of progress. By coincidence, Granet was in the office talkin
to Stuart at the time of Buckle's visit. Immediately afte
Granet's departure Stuart came to Walter's room, whereupo
Buckle withdrew to allow Walter and Stuart to converse. Late
Buckle and Stuart met and on September 23 Buckle agai
saw the Duke. The essence of his scheme was to safeguar
the position of the Editor and his function as it had bee
exercised since the time of the second Walter. But Buck
failed to make his scheme go.

In any case, the prospect of a renewed term for Steed woul
not please everybody. It was more than likely that the ne\
Proprietors, whoever they might be, would want to appoin
an Editor of their own choice. The editorial situation did no
necessarily hinge on personal considerations, although inevitabl
personalities entered into it. Steed was forced by Dawson'
experience and his own to resist encroachment of manageria
upon editorial authority. This had been the essence of Steed'
conflict in April, 1921. He was not likely to abandon th
position now, and Stuart, who had entered the office with th
ambition, nourished by Northcliffe, of making himself head o
the office, was equally determined not to yield. Hence, at
later conference with John Walter on the same day, Septembe
23, Stuart argued that it would be well if Steed were dismisse
at once.[1] It was decided that, as Steed had a document of som
sort, Sutton's opinion as to Steed's dismissal should be secure‹
As Stuart continued to insist that, in the circumstances, Steed'
connexion with *The Times* was harming it, he thought there wa
reason to believe that Sutton (who knew Northcliffe's mind
would concur. All were agreed until, to Stuart's surprise
Ralph Walter with John's agreement went further and said tha
it might give satisfaction if it were known that Dawson wa
returning. But the property had yet to be recovered by, o
for, Walter. It was merely decided, that day, that Stuar
should seek Ellerman's and Sutton's agreement to Steed'
dismissal. Any written document, undertaking, or contrac

---

[1] At the Board Meeting on November 17, 1922, with John Walter presiding, Stee
and Stuart clashed. The Editor said he could not recognize certain appointments sin‹
he had not been consulted. He claimed the right, as Editor, to exercise discretion as t
the choice of his assistants or associates and told the Board that he had already proteste
to Sutton against one of the Managing Director's appointments.

such as it might be, was not with the Company but between Northcliffe and Steed. But Sutton, when Stuart saw him on September 25, declined to support a change of Editor until he had seen Sir Charles Russell, and the matter dropped for the time being. Stuart, however, was giving the Astor-Walter scheme his whole time and energy and was more rapid in his moves than all the rest, including the Prime Minister's friends. Asked late on the night of the 25th exactly what his ideas were, Stuart expounded. They were simple, he said. Astor, whom he had seen, would underwrite the whole, with Walter and Astor holding the majority of the shares and having joint control. Astor was willing ; that he could assure them. If and when they disagreed there must be some Board of " Governors " or " Trustees," as suggested by Ralph Walter, to whom appeal could be made. This was sound enough, the two Walters thought. Stuart, after all, had the right ideas. More than that, he had secured the money. Thus the two Walters and Stuart found themselves in accord on the main points. A lunch was arranged by Stuart to take place at his house.

The company assembled at No. 1, Hyde Park Gardens, on the following day, September 26. There were present John Walter, John Astor, Campbell Stuart, Ralph Walter and Robert Grant, jnr., of Lee, Higginsons. Towards the end of lunch, Stuart made a short speech to the effect that the company had better now talk business. Grant then said that John Astor was prepared to put up " about a million pounds to purchase *The Times*" outright,[1] and that Astor would wish only to retain the complete business control, leaving editorial control to be shared equally with John Walter who, it was hoped, would accept, for life, the chairmanship of a then undefined Corporation. Walter replied that he agreed that Astor should underwrite all the shares and these could be held by himself, in Astor's behalf, pending the formation of a Chartered Corporation or something of the kind. He himself would take 100,000 £1 shares, in the Company or Corporation to be formed, at par on the basis of a capitalization of one million pounds.

As to control, John Walter held that it would be quite satisfactory if Astor and he should jointly, and equally, control editorial policy ; but that in the unlikely event of disagreement either or both should be able to consult a Board of " Referees " or " Governors " who would purchase qualifying shares. Walter

[1] " Outright," *i.e.*, to provide the equivalent of the " best price " necessary to acquire control.

pointed out the great difficulty that had always been found in delimiting the functions of the Editor and those of the management, and instanced the difficulties which had arisen between Bell and Buckle. Proceeding, Walter asked that the business control should be shared equally with the editorial control as between John Astor and himself, with permission to appeal to the " Governors." It ought not to be possible for the public to feel that, in spite of all that had been said, *The Times* had once more passed into the absolute control of one man. The constitution was very important. If Walter or Astor were to die and were to leave his shares to any heirs who were clearly unfitted to hold them, " somebody," *i.e.*, the " Referees," " Governors " or " Trustees," ought to have power to find some suitable and willing person to hold the shares. Walter's points regarding the relations of the Editor and Manager were discussed and agreed to. An equal share in the business control Walter did not insist upon. As to the Board of " Governors," nobody at the lunch cared to foresee that the shares might be unattractive as an investment and the services of the " Governors," therefore, made difficult to find or retain. The atmosphere of the lunch being so buoyant, Astor suggested that Stuart and Grant should confer and draw up some sort of document embodying the agreed ideas. It could be signed next day, perhaps, as Astor was going to Scotland that night. It was necessary for him to go well out of town since the knowledge that he might be behind Walter must encourage a competitor, Rothermere for example, to make a high bid. It was arranged that he would leave his Power of Attorney with Grant, and that Grant would rely upon Stuart to manage the affair in the name of Walter, and in his name only. All that Sutton, Rothermere and the Court were to know was that Walter was bidding alone. That was the end of a successful meeting.

But on reflection during the next morning, the 27th, the Walters thought that the meeting had been somewhat rushed. They were certainly over-tired with the endless meetings they had attended and neither they, nor Astor, nor Grant, seemed to have been given the time in which to think out these important matters in any detail. They had not really discussed the important matter of the business control. Too much had been settled too quickly, and John Walter must tell Stuart so. Stuart, however was still active. In his opinion what had been settled was too little and not quickly at all. He was spending no time on second thoughts but was anxious to get much more done, that he might speedily have the paper. He had been busy already that ver

RALPH WALTER

DIRECTOR OF THE TIMES PUBLISHING COMPANY 1922-1937

From a photograph

morning while John and Ralph Walter were thinking of the risks of doing things too hastily. Well before midday of the 27th he had satisfied Grant that *The Times* was a sound financial proposition, though he may have failed to convey any clear idea of the peculiar character of the journal. As financial adviser to Astor, Grant wished to give his client the correct advice ; Astor, for his part, was concerned to do the right thing in the right way. He had been, and was still, content to leave all the financial details to Grant, whose ideas were clear : " about a million pounds " was a lot of money to provide, and must carry financial control. Stuart understood this and assured him that the Walters would not misread the situation.

However rushed the lunch on the 26th had been, much had been accomplished, and on further reflection John Walter concluded that he had a great deal to be thankful for and to hope for. He knew too much about Printing House Square and the lawsuits that had embittered his father's lifetime and a good deal of his own ever to expect any arrangement about it to be ideal. The heads of the draft agreement would be the real test ; something to live and work with. John Walter envisaged an agreement between men who were already substantially united in the desire to restore *The Times* to its old position. Ralph Walter seized the opportunity to act as the creator, the draughtsman and the architect of a perfect constitution that would for all time enthrone the head of the family that had founded Printing House Square and created the paper, its prestige and its prosperity.

In the afternoon of the 27th Ralph Walter went to 80, Lombard Street, for an earnest talk with Robert Grant. After the principal points of the proposed new constitution had been recited, Grant expressed the view that they must next consider what each side was contributing. Astor was contributing the power to underwrite on a scale of " about a million pounds " : Walter his option and his good will. Ralph Walter contended that John Walter's option had a real market value, and so had his goodwill. He had lost £200,000 over the Northcliffe connexion. He thought it would be recognized that Walter's interest on his shares should be guaranteed until such time as general dividends should be declared. Grant agreed that this might be done. This was undoubtedly generous. They talked of Astor's business control, and Grant explained its necessity from a banker's point of view. Ralph Walter desired to be told precisely what " business control " meant and illustrated the difficulty of definition by emphasizing the lesson of experience that editorial was always distinct from, and sometimes opposed to, business control. The discussion then took a direction that few business men could be expected to follow. Grant, a New England banker, was quite unable to elevate *The Times*, as Ralph Walter seemed to invite him to do, to the level of sacred scripture. The discussion was tedious.

The next session occurred later in the same day at John Walter's house in Bryanston Square. The two Walters, Grant and Stuart met and it at once became clear that the situation was not an easy one. While John Walter was strongly in favour of one man buying the control he was equally opposed to one man, whosoever he was, exercising it. Apart from this, John Walter was prepared to consider an agreement drawn up in very general terms. Grant, however, could not justify such a large investment on the part of any client of his unless that client had the financial control. Ralph Walter stood out for precision and fullness in the drafting of the agreement. It seemed a deadlock. Walter could not get the paper without Astor any more than Astor could get it without Walter. At the rate Astor and Walter were negotiating between themselves, thought Stuart, neither would get it. He was for agreement to proceed and would stand no procrastination. There were others in the field. Rothermere was unlikely to delay, and neither must they. Nobody knew what Beaverbrook was up to. There was no time to lose. The draft must be completed that night. Nevertheless, the deadlock continued. In the middle of it all, John Walter was summoned to the telephone to answer a request for an urgent appointment next day, if possible. It came from a very insistent correspondent. He returned to find that, in Ralph's view, the prospect of losing *The Times* altogether seemed less of a disaster than the initialling of an Astor-Walter agreement that had not been fully thought over and verbally perfected. Ralph Walter was prepared to discuss the matter on the morrow, and the day after, and for ever, if need were. At last Stuart succeeded in persuading both sides to revert to his earlier suggestion that, while Walter and Astor should, together, hold the majority of the shares, since there was the possibility of disagreement between them, as well as the likelihood of disagreement between the Board of Governors, John Walter might nominate a representative to be associated with the management. To this everybody agreed.

The heads of an agreement were then drafted in the form of a letter addressed by Walter to Astor, and sent to Grant:

September 27th, 1922.

Dear Major Astor,

I think we are agreed that if possible the whole of the late Lord Northcliffe's holding in *The Times* shall be bought by me, you advancing the money for the purpose up to say in the neighbourhood of one million pounds, in order to secure the control of the existing Company.

In view of the national character and importance of *The Times*, we agree that we should then seek reconstruction under a special Charter. To this end it is agreed that you shall finance my acquisition of the rest of the shares of the Company as necessary and as opportunity offers. The shares acquired as above shall be held in trust by me for you. I agree to buy from you one hundred thousand pounds worth of Preference Shares as soon as they are available. There shall then be formed a Corporation divided into say one million pound shares.

My feeling is that in consideration of the option contained in Lord Northcliffe's Will of March 2nd, 1919, and of the other advantages I may have and of the Goodwill which I am able to contribute to the arrangement, I should be allotted one hundred thousand shares in the Company to be formed, for which I am prepared to pay one hundred thousand pounds, such shares to be in the form of five per cent. Preferred Ordinary shares, to rank for dividend with the ordinary shares whenever a dividend is declared above that amount. You have kindly suggested, and I agree, that I should be appointed Chairman for life, and I should be glad if you would be Vice-Chairman.

It is proposed that the whole of the shares shall be allotted in the first instance among say ten Governors, including ourselves, who shall be mutually agreeable to us both, and each of whom shall hold at least five thousand shares in his own right, and that no new Governors shall be appointed without the consent of the existing Governors, that is to say, that should any Governor come to part with his shares, they shall be transferred to a new Governor only with the consent of the majority.

It is further agreed that the control in Editorial matters shall be vested equally in ourselves, with appeal to the Board of Governors, but the business and financial control shall rest with the majority of the shares. It is understood that you will hold the majority, although you agree to my being represented in the management.

These arrangements shall come into force as soon as we shall have acquired the control of the present Company and during the interval the control in all matters shall be vested equally in ourselves.

I am,

Yours very truly,
JOHN WALTER.

Grant acknowledged receipt on September 28 and, when accepting, " on Major Astor's behalf," the terms of Walter's letter, he enclosed a copy of his power of attorney, " irrevocable for one calendar month from the date hereof," which was September 26, 1922. Thus at last the money to the amount of " about a million pounds," was appropriated for the purchase. As to the purchase itself, the Walter side had to reckon with risks. It was a fact that Lady Northcliffe would not contest the clause, if it remained, relating to Walter's option. That fact justified Astor's appropriation and Walter's association with him. But it had yet to be discovered whether Northcliffe had carried the effect of his purchase of the Walter holding to its logical conclusion by cancelling the option. It was not known whether Rothermere could do about Walter's option, if it remained in the Will, what Lady Northcliffe had decided to do. It was, on the other hand, certain that Rothermere's resources were such as to permit him to safeguard his family's interests by running up the price to a figure impossible, perhaps, to Astor unless he chose to upset his other investments.

Rothermere's plans were well laid. He knew better than any man what *The Times* was worth, and what could be done with it. Unknown, of course, to the Walter side, Rothermere with his unique experience of newspaper management and knowledge of finance had satisfied himself that, conducted without extravagance, *The Times* would average a yearly profit of a quarter of a million. Secondly, he wished to establish his son, Esmond, as the effective Chairman of The Times Publishing Company with authority over the management that would be complete, save that the son would respect his father's financial recommendations. In the third place, Rothermere intended to separate *The Times* from the *Daily Mail*, and avoid Northcliffe's centralizing process involving a single editorial control of the Printing House Square and Carmelite House publications. In Rothermere's plan *The Times* would once more be an independent newspaper, one that the world would at once respect ; and, he even thought John Walter in a short time might respect it.

748

Rothermere's mind was fully made up. Of this, the telephone conversation with the insistent caller that John Walter had conducted at Bryanston Square during the discussion with Grant and Stuart was proof. The urgent request for an interview came from Sir Andrew Caird, whom Walter told he would see. Walter next informed Stuart, who immediately saw Ellerman. Stuart then learnt that Rothermere had offered to join with Ellerman to buy *The Times* ; and that Rothermere must have his answer by September 29. That was the day Walter was to meet Caird. When they met, Caird explained that the impending issue of the Daily Mail Trust led Rothermere to think that it might be well if Walter chose to be associated with him in the purchase of Northcliffe's shares in The Times Publishing Company. The suggestion had originated with Caird and was approved, as Rothermere did not want *The Times* to fall into the hands of Beaverbrook who, it was thought, was anxious to secure control of it. Also there were others, known to Rothermere, who wanted control but could not be relied upon to keep the paper up to the high level it had then reached, as both Walter and Rothermere would wish. Caird added that, by joining forces with Rothermere, Walter could secure this result upon terms extremely advantageous to himself. The unique resources and acknowledged newspaper success of Rothermere, with his great commercial ability and experience, offered a greater guarantee for the future prosperity of *The Times* than any other possible contribution that had been heard of, *e.g.*, the Rhodes Trust. To be exact, Caird said, Rothermere, with Ellerman retaining his present holding, might subscribe the sum of perhaps £800,000 necessary to buy *The Times*, and Walter would be Vice-Chairman of the Company, a position more satisfactory to himself in all respects than he had occupied hitherto. This, said Caird, was Rothermere's final offer to John Walter, and it would not be repeated. Walter's answer was brief : he was at work on another scheme. He did not say that this scheme had been completed, but ended the interview by civilly thanking Caird for his and Rothermere's suggestion. Caird regarded the subject as closed for the moment and retired to consult Rothermere.

Meanwhile Stuart had been to see if he could detach Ellerman, the owner of some 128,000 shares, from Rothermere and get him on Astor's and Walter's side. On being appealed to, Ellerman said he would do nothing until October 3, the day that Caird, it now appeared, would again desire to see Walter. At this, the second Caird-Walter interview, Walter expressed the hope that

" whatever happened " *The Times* would be independent of other newspapers. " You never liked the connexion with Carmelite House ? " asked Caird who, evidently, did not know of Rothermere's plan to separate the direction of *The Times* from that of the *Daily Mail.* " On the contrary," replied Walter, " I consider that the friendly relations which existed between Carmelite House and Printing House Square have been beneficial, even if in some cases the relationship has been too intimate." Caird acknowledged that the use by both journals of the same foreign correspondents might be an instance of what Walter found objectionable in practice. On the broad question, Caird reminded Walter that he had so much to gain from Rothermere's offer that, in all prudence, he should give it serious consideration. To this suggestion Walter replied once more by politely asking Caird to thank Rothermere and to say that, for reasons he had given, he still felt morally bound to proceed with his own scheme.

Simultaneously Stuart, who held a key position as a negotiator had been approached by Lloyd George's friends, by Sir Basil Zaharoff, and by Lord Rothermere, among others, but Stuart was no less determined that the property should revert to the old family in association with a partner John Walter judged suitable. Rothermere's detachment from political preferences, in the personal sense, became definite at or about the beginning of October. He saw Lloyd George often ; that was normal. Also he saw Bonar Law ; that was less normal. No note survives to throw light on the estimate of the future held by Rothermere at the end of September. It seems likely, however, that he leant rather to Bonar Law but was unwilling to commit himself. That Poole, as Walter's solicitor as well as Lloyd George's, could rely, at the beginning of October, upon the latter's willingness to back Walter is certain. At some time between September 30 and October 3 Poole informed Lloyd George that Walter had secured the financial backing that seemed sufficient. The Prime Minister then said he would like to see Campbell Stuart, and in due course they met at lunch. The scheme was discussed and the Prime Minister expressed himself as, in the words of Astor's adviser, " quite satisfied with the prospect of you and the Walters acquiring the property and will help in any way he can, although that will probably not be much."[1] At this time Lloyd George had every reason to welcome the opportunity of making direct contact with *The Times* and offering to help the Astor and Walter scheme.

[1] Robert Grant, Jr. to John Astor, October 4, 1922. (Astor Papers.)

That scheme was quickly taking shape. Having seen the Prime Minister between September 30 and October 3, Stuart had seen Lady Northcliffe, and next made an endeavour to bring Ellerman to Walter's side ; or, what was almost the same thing, to pursuade him to sell him his holding. This Stuart succeeded in doing. On Astor's behalf he paid Ellerman £160,530 on October 7 and another £30,000 on October 10 for his shares. Thus ended Ellerman's connexion with *The Times*. The terms of this transaction should be noted. Ellerman, it has been seen, had bought 10,700 shares from John Walter on June 15, 1922 ; he paid 22s. 6d. for them, while Northcliffe bought Walter's 214,900 shares on June 15 for 20s. Stuart secured Ellerman's 128,424 shares at 25s. in October. If these figures are compared with those realized at the sale in Court of the controlling shares held by Northcliffe's estate, it will be appreciated that Stuart's purchase of Ellerman's shares at 25s. was a financial master-stroke. He had much more to do. Early in the second week of October, *i.e.*, a few days after his successful deal with Ellerman, Stuart secured information that Rothermere was about to notify the Administrator that he wanted to make a bid for *The Times* that he thought would be larger than would be made by anyone else. The decisive moment was approaching. Such a bid from such a quarter would be the final test of strength. It was now a simple matter. There was nothing to be expected from Birkenhead, Howard Frank, David Davies, or any other political friends of the Prime Minister. It was Rothermere only who was challenging Walter, but, intimate as he was with Lloyd George, he was not moved, it has been seen, by political so much as by family and financial considerations, though the political moves that took place simultaneously greatly interested him.

On the night of the 10th there was a meeting of Conservative Cabinet Ministers at which the Chief Whip, Sir Leslie Wilson, was also present. On October 13 Chamberlain defended Lloyd George in a speech at Birmingham, and urged the expediency of preserving the Coalition " in a new form if necessary." Next day Lloyd George spoke at Manchester, on similar lines. Neither speech was considered satisfactory by *The Times*; and party objection gathered so much force that Chamberlain was compelled to face the Unionist members of Parliament and such Conservative Peers as were Ministers. He was then Chancellor of the Exchequer and Conservative Leader of the House. He had been in Asquith's First Coalition Cabinet (1915-1916) ; and in Lloyd George's Coalition Cabinet he had been one of the

Ministers without Portfolio since 1918. He was in a very strong position and possessed great authority in the Party. But Amery, Baldwin and others were now resolved that the Coalition should not go on. They were supported by Curzon and Leslie Wilson, who, as Chief Whip, wielded much influence. Bonar Law's views were known, but the state of his health made it appear unlikely that he would attend. A principal supporter of Lloyd George and Chamberlain was Balfour. The most energetic opponent was Baldwin.

How Rothermere stood was very doubtful to everybody. That he would be active in planning to possess and reorganize *The Times* was obvious to all, but his political intentions were unknown to Printing House Square.[1] What mattered to the Walter side was that no prospective political changes would abate his ambition to keep the control of *The Times* in the family, or reduce his capacity to pay. Rothermere could plank the money down with his own cheque, which nobody else, he was sure, could do ; Walter alone certainly could not do it. Rothermere now acted. The text of his official letter to Sutton was firm ; it was business-like ; it was anti-Walter :

October 12, 1922.

To Sir George Sutton :

With reference to the shares held by you as Administrator of the Estate of the late Lord Northcliffe in The Times Publishing Company, I beg to inform you that I am prepared forthwith to bid for these shares and I am of the opinion that the sum I am prepared to bid is probably higher than would be offered by any other possible purchaser.

You will readily understand, however, that I am not prepared to make any bid merely for the purpose of its being used to fix a price upon which to offer them to the Walter family. The bid I am prepared to make would have to be either rejected or accepted within a short space of time, say a week.

As financial conditions are constantly changing I cannot say that I am prepared to remain a bidder for long—therefore the matter would appear to be urgent and I should be much obliged if you would bring the whole question before the Judge.

ROTHERMERE.

The case was, in fact, due to come forward in four days ; and Rothermere was serving notice upon Walter that he would not only bid against him, but complete within seven days. Rothermere knew the figures at which the shares had changed

[1] Or, there is reason to believe, to Lloyd George and Bonar Law at this point.

hands, and may (though this is doubtful) have known the price Ellerman had received from Stuart a week or two previously. Rothermere had clearly stated his readiness to put down a sum " probably higher than would be offered by any other possible purchaser," but he had been careful not to fix his figure. He was explicit on the main point : his figure when named was not " merely for the purpose of its user to fix a price upon which to offer the property to the Walter family." He was quite safe, he thought, in bidding a large sum and imposing a narrow time-limit. In the short interval of a week, or little more, Walter could hardly organize a syndicate prepared " forthwith " to pay a sum equal to Rothermere's high figure, whatever it should prove to be. He had reason to feel confident that *The Times* would be a Rothermere property in a very short time ; within four days to be precise. As neither the letter to the Administrator nor the probable sum to be offered by Rothermere was known to the Walter side, there was every reason for Rothermere to feel the ground firm under his feet.

This was more than could be said of the politicians. Excitement was mounting in anticipation of the meeting called for Thursday the 19th at the Carlton Club. On the afternoon of Sunday the 15th Lloyd George returned to London from Manchester, where he had spoken, saw Churchill, and dined with him and Birkenhead. At Manchester the Prime Minister had said that " if there is to be a change of Government no man would welcome it more than I. Office is a great shackle." Whether Lloyd George was destined to remain " shackled " or freed to occupy an independent platform was soon to be settled. So, too, was the question whether he might be elevated to a certain editorial chair. Whether *The Times* was destined to remain attached to the Harmsworth family or restored to effective connexion with Walter would also be settled by the 19th or thereabouts.

The Government and *The Times* were both approaching their respective points of crisis with equal rapidity. The fate of the paper might be determined first, for on Monday, October 16, there were summoned before Sir Henry Duke (Judge in Chambers), Messrs. Poole, Tomlin and Luxmoore, representing Walter ; and Maugham, representing Sutton. The summonses were duly obeyed. John Walter and Campbell Stuart were in Court, but there was, very deliberately, no representative of John Astor who had prudently gone off to Scotland. Maugham produced an affidavit containing the assurance of a bid. The Administrator had refrained from naming the bidder, the bidder had abstained from naming the price. What Walter knew from his talk with Caird, and from what Stuart had picked up, was that the bidder could hardly be other than Rothermere, though he, like his brother in similar circumstances, had gone to Paris while the sale was determined. The omission to state a figure was quite in order, for when Tomlin put Walter's case, he too did not name a figure. Walter believed that Rothermere had £800,000 in mind. Caird had said something to that effect, and the day before the funeral of Northcliffe, Stuart had met Rothermere, who then mentioned the same figure as his maximum. But in Court the Judge was given no figures, and to enable the parties to define their respective bids Duke adjourned the hearing until Thursday afternoon, the 19th.

This was the day of the meeting of the Conservative Party leaders. Rothermere was known to be returning from Paris on the night of October 17. On October 18, Grant, John Walter and Ralph Walter conferred about Rothermere's probable price. It was feared that it might be awkwardly high. After being referred to, Astor expressed his unwillingness to lose *The Times.* As to tactics, Grant was as opposed as ever to giving Counsel any figure. It was clearly going to be a very close finish, and Rothermere's price would reflect the political tension and the expectations aroused by the meeting due for Thursday the 19th at the Carlton Club. Unknown to everybody except possibly Beaverbrook, on the night of Monday the 16th the Editor saw Bonar Law and tried to persuade him to go to the meeting and back Baldwin. He hesitated, first on account of his health (which was worse than most people realized) and secondly because he believed that if he were to take part in overthrowing the Government, he could not refuse if sent for and asked to form an Administration ; and if he were to do all this, and dissolve Parliament, he did not believe he could possibly get a working majority. The Editor stated his views and emphasized them in a subsequent letter :

PRIVATE AND PERSONAL.

1 a.m., 17th October, 1922.
Dear Mr. Bonar Law,

Since our brief conversation to-night, information has reached me which strongly confirms my conviction that unless you decide to lead the opposition at Thursday's meeting of the Unionist Members of the House of Commons, there will be no hope of maintaining the cohesion of the Party. You best know the course you ought to pursue ; but looking at the situation as an outsider with some knowledge of national and foreign affairs, it seems to me that the maintenance of a strong Unionist Party is a pre-eminent national and Imperial interest. You have it, I believe, in your power to defend this interest and also to set such an example to the Liberal Party that it too would feel impelled by instinct of self-preservation to close its ranks and thus to restore something like stability to the political life of the country. I need hardly say that whatever influence *The Times* possesses will be used in this sense. As long as I direct its policy, it will support men and parties that work for national and Imperial ends.

Forgive me for thus intervening in a matter which I know is the subject of your most anxious thought, but the moment is very critical, not only in the fortunes of the Unionist Party, but in those of the nation.

Believe me, dear Mr. Bonar Law,

Very sincerely yours,

H. WICKHAM STEED.

The moment was apparently critical. But although Baldwin was the most active, he was by no means the most impressive proponent of the resumption of what *The Times* described as a " homogeneous Party Government." He may have been working hard to destroy the Coalition, but he had only recently become President of the Board of Trade, and it was not certain that he, Curzon and Amery could muster the necessary support for a motion to withdraw from the Coalition. Balfour and Chamberlain were the leading figures in the Party and their stature in the eyes of the country gave them authority in the Party. It was unlikely that Baldwin and his friends could bring off their coup. What was certain was that if Bonar Law made up his mind to join Baldwin the result would not be in doubt. But Bonar Law's health was against his coming to the meeting. Also, he had been Lloyd George's chief colleague and joint founder with him of the Coalition at the end of 1916, and was still loath to destroy the Government from which he had only resigned, for reasons of health, in March. Moreover, he still doubted if the Conservatives, when they went to the country, would come back with a working majority. With the Editor he discussed the question on the nights of October 17 and 18. With Younger, the Chairman of the Conservative Party, he had gone through the records of every constituency. They had, he told the Editor, both concluded that a majority larger than 25 could not be hoped for. The Editor prophesied a majority of 75, though he was unable to offer any other evidence for his optimism than an acute sense of smell. He urged Bonar Law to go to Thursday's

755

meeting. Bonar Law said nothing. However, the Editor left the house on the evening of October 18 with the feeling that he would be justified in saying in the following day's issue of *The Times* that Bonar Law would attend the meeting.

Just after *The Times* went to press that night Bonar Law telephoned to the office to ask if there was anything new. The Editor told him that the only important news was the announcement that *The Times* would publish in the morning, to the effect that Bonar Law would attend the Carlton Club meeting and oppose the Government. " But I have not yet decided to go," answered Bonar Law. The Editor again pressed him to attend, and by upsetting the Coalition give the country a chance of returning to straightforward party government. Were he to do this, the Editor promised the backing of *The Times*. It was a question only of healthy party government, and the Editor said he would say the same if Asquith were in Bonar Law's position. The Editor was supported by his close colleagues, who also believed that the Coalition had outlived its usefulness and that the country needed a strong Conservative and a strong Liberal Party. He thought from the tone of Bonar Law's final remarks that he was likely to attend, and retained the note to that effect in the commentary on the crisis for the first column of the bill page. He had regularly written these notes since the beginning of September.

On the morning of the Thursday, October 19, fateful for the Government and for *The Times*, the late editions of the paper reported the figures of a by-election at Newport, Mon. In 1918 the result of the contest between the Coalition Liberal (14,080), Labour (10,234), Independent (647), was a majority for the Co. Lib. of 3,846. The new election was fought by a free Conservative (13,515), a Labour (11,425), and a Liberal (8,841) candidate who had Coalition support, giving a Cons. majority of 2,090. The victor's agent said that he had secured many votes from a Labour district. The reason was that " the working classes have never understood the Coalition arrangement. They looked upon it, rightly or wrongly, as a ' wangle ' and as an attempt to ally capitalist forces against the workers." His candidate, the agent said, stood for old-fashioned clear-cut party lines which was what the country wanted. This, too, was what Baldwin, Amery, and *The Times* wanted. And this was what they read in *The Times* before going to the Carlton Club in time to arrive at eleven o'clock. They also read the paper's comment : " The country will see in it a most complete condemnation of the Coalition Government as such and a vindication of those Conservatives throughout the country who have been so determined to preserve their individuality in previous by-election contests."

The report of the meeting at the Carlton Club on the 19th occupied a whole page of *The Times* of the next day. The chief speakers were Baldwin, who came first, Balfour, and Bonar Law. The latter was greeted with the greatest volume of cheers. This was significant. Certainly, the effect of Baldwin's speech was damaging to the Coalition. He prophesied that continued Conservative association with it would inevitably result in the Party's destruction, as had already happened to the Liberals. But it was Bonar Law's participation and reinforcement that made Baldwin's case irresistible. Balfour's speech in defence of the Coalition failed. By a majority of 187 to 87 the party resolved to withdraw immediately. Lloyd George resigned. That was inevitable. The surprise was that he took with him Chamberlain, Balfour, and Birkenhead.[1] By lunch-time the verdict was known in the clubs ; the Government was out.

It was after lunch that the fate of *The Times* came up for decision. All were in Court, before Duke, that afternoon. Maugham for Sutton was present with Rothermere's firm offer, in contract form, for a stated figure. This figure must have been fixed the previous day, when Rothermere realized that the cracks in the Coalition were now past mending and that the Prime Minister might resign in a matter of days or even hours. It had even been reported to the Walter side that Rothermere had already been to Bonar Law. He had, this report alleged, offered him the support of his newspapers, including *The Times*, which he was about to purchase, if Bonar Law would advance him in rank and give his son a position in the Ministry. This story was not believed and it was not true. The fact was, rather, that Rothermere had refused to offer the support of his newspapers, though he had been urged to do so by his son, who had expectations of a position from Bonar Law. The new Prime Minister, personally, was in a dubious position. He had announced his retirement from politics but it was his presence at the Carlton Club meeting that had sealed the fate of Lloyd George. Yet he felt able to take office only for a short time.

[1] Beside Birkenhead and Balfour, Robert Horne (Chancellor of the Exchequer), Worthington-Evans (War), Lee (Admiralty), also sided with Lloyd George and Chamberlain, and signed a statement of reasons.

While the Court was taking its seats, the Prime Minister-elect sent for the Editor, discussed with him the formation of the new Cabinet, and mentioned his inability, on account of health, to continue in office for more than a period that must be so short that he believed it only fair to inform his colleagues of it. The Editor endeavoured to dissuade the Prime Minister-elect from so doing, and on his return to the office wrote to him to that effect :

PERSONAL & CONFIDENTIAL

19th October, 1922.

Dear Mr. Bonar Law,

On thinking over our conversation this evening, the objections to an avowed and concerted time-limit to your leadership of the Unionist Party and to your tenure of the Premiership seem to me very serious indeed. Were it announced that you have agreed to act only for a year, there would inevitably be some decrease of enthusiasm in the immediate future and a considerable increase of uncertainty as to the position a year hence. There would also inevitably be movements within the Party in favour of this or that prospective candidate for the succession—and of Elishas there would be no lack. Therefore I, who am to some extent in touch with political and public opinion, would beg you earnestly to consider whether the present insistence upon a time limit would really diminish the burden of the offices which I trust you will soon hold.

The great need of the moment seems to me to be for swiftness and decision in action, so that those who might be glad to perpetuate uncertainty shall have no time to diminish the start you have given to your Party.

Please forgive me for " butting in " but the matter is too important for reticence.

With kind regards,

Very sincerely yours,

WICKHAM STEED.

Bonar Law, no doubt, had already prepared Rothermere among others for an administration that would need to be reconstructed at an early date. In the circumstances Rothermere's decision not to promise support was reasonable. It was a decision, however, that did not affect his intention to possess himself of *The Times*. Walter and Stuart were correct in holding that Rothermere was confident of his power to secure *The Times*. Rothermere had already secured the *Daily Mail* and was preparing an issue of Daily Mail Trust Debentures by which the purchase was to be financed. Rothermere's business adviser, F. A. Szarvasy, who was in charge of the issue, met Grant early on the 19th before the case came on and, in conversation about the finance of the *Daily Mail,* pointed out to him that an additional £900,000 debentures had been reserved for the acquisition of an additional property " ; and Grant, when asked if he could guess at the " additional property," answered " *The Times.*" Szarvasy nodded. Hence when Walter, his Counsel and friends took their seats in Court they appreciated the fact that Rothermere was completely confident of success. Neither he nor anybody knew of Walter's contract with Astor. Curiously, Steed's anti-Coalition and pro-Bonar Law policy now played into Rothermere's hands. All Rothermere had to do in October was to assure the Conservative leader that *The Times,* under him, would not necessarily reverse the policy laid down by Steed. Although the Walter-Astor side did not believe that Rothermere had been to Bonar Law, they had in fact met.[1] Their conversation was never noted, but could not have been unfriendly, although Rothermere would not guarantee his support.[2] His interest in politics was, however, in no way lessened, but he preferred, before committing himself and the newspapers he already controlled, to await the result not only of the Party meeting but of the Court.

These were among the reasons why, in the afternoon when Rothermere's figure was called for, his Counsel was instructed to name a figure far higher than anything considered by the Walter-Astor side when the hearing began. They were nervous enough when Counsel indulged themselves with a discussion on the option, and debated whether there was still reasonable doubt as to its validity, &c., and its duration, &c., since the Will had not yet been proved, &c. At a certain point in the argument Maugham rose to say that it had occurred to Sir George Sutton and his advisers

that a fair *via media* to all parties would be this, that Mr. Walter, although the Will has not yet been proved, should have his right of

---

[1] Walter did not know that the Editor had business with the Conservative leader on the evening of the 19th. He had had to wait some minutes. When Bonar Law was free he apologized for keeping the Editor waiting, and excused himself on the ground that Rothermere had been with him. The Bonar Law Papers contain evidence that on October 19, 1922, Rothermere had urged Bonar Law to attend the Carlton Club meeting and encouraged him to expect effective support from Conservatives. Rothermere himself, however, adopted a waiting attitude.

[2] Bonar Law had sent for Esmond Harmsworth and offered him, in writing, the position of Parliamentary Secretary to the Board of Education. Harmsworth had to refuse when he failed to persuade his father to give Bonar Law the support of the *Daily Mail.* Harmsworth disliked the idea of being embarrassed like his uncle, Cecil Harmsworth, then Under-Secretary for Foreign Affairs during the period of Northcliffe's attacks on the Coalition.

pre-emption recognized, but with a variation, namely, that instead of having three months in which to make up his mind, he should make up his mind in a very short period.

Of course, if it is asked why he should do that, the answer is, because it is not certain that he has any rights at all. If there is to be any dealing with this interest at all, it is a case where, it seems to me, both sides may very well be advised to make something in the nature of a concession to the other. If, by reason of any opposition, the thing should not go through, it may be that Mr. Walter will lose all his rights. That is, to some extent, a matter of gamble, of which I know nothing.

What I was going to propose was this : if Lord Rothermere exchanges with the administrator, subject to your Lordship thinking that it is a proper course, a contract conditional to the sanction of your Lordship of the contract for the purchase of the whole of the shares at the price in question—there is no objection to my stating the figure ?

Here Counsel paused, and, there being no interruption, completed his observations with a sentence that astounded the Court : " The figure suggested is £1,350,000, payable, according to the terms of the document before me, as to £500,000 within fourteen days of the Order approving this agreement, and the balance at certain other dates."

It was a stupendous sum, far greater than had been estimated in the Birkenhead, Ellerman, Frank or Davies schemes. Moreover, the head of the firm of W. B. Peat and Co., Chartered Accountants, whose advice, given under affidavit, Sutton had taken before accepting the Rothermere figure, had stated in his affidavit that the business, as such, did not justify such a figure. But it had been offered. Hence, said the accountant Peat, " I am, therefore, of opinion that it would be unwise of the Executors of the late Viscount Northcliffe to risk the loss of the offer of Lord Rothermere." Peat proceeded to say that he was well aware that there were " peculiar political circumstances at the moment which may influence a buyer in acquiring *The Times* newspaper, and also in inducing him to give a fancy price for it," and, he reminded his client, in June Northcliffe had purchased the 214,900 ordinary shares from Walter at the price of £1. In expert opinion, therefore, Rothermere's was not a commercial price ; it was a " fancy " price. It was, to all appearances, not only a " fancy " but a final price, and so it struck everybody in Court. Rothermere's position in October, 1922, was that of Pearson in February,

GEORGE AUGUSTUS SUTTON

1908: "Pearson intends to outbid everyone and obtain the paper". But the history of *The Times* was to repeat itself even more closely.[1]

By chance Stuart had found himself at the first week-end of October with friends, one of whom conducted a telephone conversation in a voice of such stridency that the company overheard the figures and the particulars. Everybody heard the conversation, but only Stuart understood their reference. He immediately warned Robert Grant, Astor's financial adviser, that the increased amount that would be required destroyed all their provisional estimates. Obviously, the Lloyd George crisis had made all the difference. Grant was quite unable to relate the value of the opportunity created by the coincidence of a political crisis in Downing Street with the day's proceedings at the Royal Courts of Justice and to translate that opportunity, such as it was, into financial terms. What was clear to him was that the extra money had to be found quickly, and while Walter and Stuart were engaged with the Courts, Grant was active with the banks, for he had little time even with the day's grace that Stuart had so conveniently given. All listened to the proceedings in Court, as the factor of time came into the transaction. This was Rothermere's triumphant gesture : while he increased the price, he had at the same time lessened the time available to his competitor. Only by a miracle could Walter find this huge sum in the small interval Rothermere had devised. Rothermere not only had the money at call ; he could that day produce half a million. When Tomlin, for Walter, asked if he might know the dates of payment annexed to the Rothermere offer, he listened to an absolutely unexpected statement :

Mr. Maugham : Your Lordship will not mind my telling Mr. Tomlin ?

The Judge : State anything you think right.

Mr. Maugham : There are some dates for the payment of the balance, and the last date suggested, I think, is February 15, 1923. Subject to that it is payable, after the first instalment of half a million, in instalments.

The Judge : £1,350,000 payable half a million down and the balance within the next four months : that is what it comes to.

Mr. Maugham : That is the substance of it, my Lord.

[1] For the nearly successful effort of Cyril Arthur Pearson to purchase the control of *The Times* in 1908 and his defeat by Moberly Bell and Northcliffe, see Vol. III, Chapters XVI and XVII, " *The Times* for Sale," etc.

It was a staggering statement to earlier participants in the business, such as Poole ; but, of course, after the events of the morning at the Carlton Club, Poole and his friends had other things to consider. Walter was less agitated, thanks to Campbell Stuart, but he still did not know the extent to which the time factor and the high figure affected Astor.

Walter's Counsel asked for time. Walter (with Astor still unnamed) had to decide whether to exercise the option within the short period suggested, at the " best price " now so unexpectedly high ; insist upon having his option for three months and thereby open a new legal discussion with a chance of a decision that would lose him the option ; or refuse to come forward at all. That was how Walter now stood. As for Rothermere, he knew or thought he knew, that John Walter lacked the means with which to compete. He had no suspicion that John Astor was with him, though he had doubtless learned of Birkenhead's, Ellerman's, Davies' and other projects, all of which were vain since none of them could produce the sum equal to his own, offered in the form of a contract, in the time he had himself set, and all with the agreement of the Administrator. Rothermere, quite reasonably, believed that Walter's offer, too, would fall short of his " best price." Even if he could raise his figure there remained the vital point of time. Apart from the amount of the purchase price, impossibly high as he believed he had raised it, Rothermere knew that Walter could not ask for an extension of time without reopening the whole question of the option.

The upshot was that the Administrator, with the sanction of the Judge, could conclude a contract with Walter, or failing him, Rothermere, for the sum named. In other words, no third party could intervene even with a higher offer. At first it was not clear whether the existing figure could be revised by the bidder if he desired. But when Harman said that " On behalf of Lord Rothermere, who has made this offer, I should like to say that he would like another chance of bidding," the Judge replied : " I cannot conduct either a negotiation or an auction," and he proceeded to ask whether counsel considered it " judicious " to provoke Tomlin (for Walter) at the moment. The argument was pressed by Clauson (for Lady Northcliffe), who said that " if Lord Rothermere were prepared to offer, let me say, another quarter of a million, I should feel great difficulty, in the interests of my client, in agreeing with the suggestion that the price at which Mr. Walter was asking your Lordship to sell to him, was the best price obtainable, which is the price at which he had the option." He added, a moment later, that " events are happening every day in the political world which affect the value of these shares very materially." After further argument, the Judge again declined any suggestions that could result in negotiation or dealing. The price offered by Rothermere in his contract with Sutton, dated October 19, must be accepted as the " best price " within the meaning of the Will that gave Walter the option. That was the ruling. Rothermere's actual figure must be accepted or rejected by Walter ; and if he rejected it the Judge must immediately on rejection sanction the Rothermere-Sutton contract. Putting the matter beyond doubt, the Judge said to the assembly of Counsel, " You at the Bar are able to advise your clients to negotiate. I cannot." Duke did recognize, nevertheless, that any figure needed consideration, and assented to Tomlin's request for an adjournment. But he could not permit more than a few days. The Court would adjourn from that day, Thursday, to the following Monday. Walter had a week-end in which to decide.

To Walter and Astor's advisers, the one satisfactory feature in the day's proceedings was that the other side, having conceded the option on terms, the Judge would not consider the intervention of a third party. The bidding was limited to Walter and Rothermere : one or the other was due to pay a vast and unrevisable sum of money within four months. Astor to date had already paid out nearly £200,000 to Ellerman. Rothermere's offer for the Northcliffe shares only was £1,350,000. The two sums amounted to more than half as much again as Astor had promised to provide. There was no doubt about it, Rothermere had set a pretty problem. John Walter's arrangement with Astor entitled him to offer " about a million," and Astor had gone no farther than to express an unwillingness to lose *The Times*. Stuart's knowledge, accidentally acquired in advance, of Rothermere's intention to offer such a high figure had given Walter the relief of a valuable interval for negotiations over and above the Judge's adjournment ; and Grant had, later, agreed with Stuart to make what arrangements he could in the short time available. Everything, therefore, now depended upon Astor's decision. He had to be consulted, for Grant had to lay

hands not on "about a million," but on what would amount,
with the Ellerman purchase, to more than a million and a half.

This extra half-million or more that Rothermere's offer called
for appeared to Grant to make all the difference between buying
The Times as a business and buying it as something else, say a
sort of "trust." From any banker's point of view, a startling
change of values was involved. The last two transactions had
been (1) the transfer of Walter's shares to Northcliffe which
went through on June 15 at 20s. and (2) Ellerman's to Stuart on
October 7 and October 10 at 25s. Rothermere's offer amounted
to 52s. 6d. each for the ordinary shares. It was a figure that
Rothermere could be certain in his own mind no business man,
no banker, no investor would for a moment think of equalling.
In other words, Walter with Astor, on October 19-21, had to
face buying back for a premium of 32s. 6d. the shares Walter
himself had sold in June for 20s. This premium amounted to
£335,781. On this basis it was difficult for a banker to assess
the value of Walter's option. But that was a matter that could
be left. What had to be done at once was to settle the question
whether Astor would go forward at Rothermere's figure ; or
whether he would refuse, in which case Walter must, with all
the risks that delay would entail, apply to the Judge for leave
to keep the option open for three months while he found
alternative support. What Astor, who was still discreetly in
Scotland, would say to the proposition in the form it had now
assumed needed to be ascertained by Grant with all speed.
As Astor's adviser, he had to explain the situation to him. That
would be easy. If Astor were willing to challenge Rothermere's
figure, Grant would have to be in the position to assure his
client that he knew where to find the odd half-million pounds
required. This could not be easy. Yet, by cabling about
mortgaging and the like, Grant managed to satisfy himself that
he could, if instructed, lay his hands on that sum. The
explanation being made, Astor made his decision and instructed
Grant to proceed with Walter and get *The Times* on Rothermere's
"best terms."

At 4 p.m. on Monday, October 23, before Duke, the Judge in
Chambers, the Administrator, in virtue of the Will with the
option, made an offer in writing of all Northcliffe's shares to
John Walter at Rothermere's price. The letter was given to the
Judge who handed it to Walter and assured Tomlin, Walter's
counsel, that *The Times* would be his client's if he complied

with the terms of the Administrator's draft. Sutton's draft recognized the option for a week only, and thus concluded :

Unless this offer is accepted by you by notice received by me or my solicitor on or before 6 o'clock p.m. on the 30th day of October, 1922, it is to lapse.

This offer is made and kept open for the period aforesaid in consideration of your agreeing that if you fail to exercise the option under the offer and the sale to Lord Rothermere under the Conditional Contract is completed the offer shall be taken in satisfaction of any option which you may otherwise have in respect of the shares in question under any of the testamentary dispositions of Lord Northcliffe.

With Astor's decision behind him, Walter said he had no difficulty in accepting Sutton's limitation to the option; whereupon, the terms being agreed, Sutton signed his letter in Court.

This was the decisive moment ; Walter was in the position of Moberly Bell in 1908. He too had a secret backer, with himself, able to meet the competing price. But it was now the turn of the lawyers to delay its climax. Time was spent upon discussion of the proper form and correct phraseology to be followed and used in the execution and drafting of the contracts, contingent and other. At last, this talk was cut short by Tomlin, who rose to say, " I think I can simplify it. I have just had authority to say that Mr. Walter will exercise his option. He will exercise it by writing here and now, if you please, a statement that he is exercising the option. That being so, I think the only Order that is required is that your Lordship shall sanction the sale to him upon the terms embodied in the offer, and that is all. That is an absolute contract made now to-day." The Judge agreed that this seemed to be the case. Tomlin then rose to contend that Walter's addition to his written acceptance of the words " And I hereby exercise the option " brought into existence " an absolute final contract between the Administrators and Mr. Walter, and everything else falls to the ground." If this were so and the Judge were to agree, and would say so, the decisive moment had arrived. The Judge did agree, and said," I approve the contract now made between the Administrators and Mr. Walter." All that remained was the signing of the official certificate. Immediately, *The Times* came under the authority of John Astor, whose name was still secret, and John Walter. There was no delay, no need to extend the option for the week in accordance with Sutton's letter. The paper had changed hands.

The price was huge. Walter's bill was £100,000. Astor's final and total bill, as discharged by the following April, was £1,580,000, thus made up :

1922				£	s.	d.
Oct. 7	Paid Sir John Ellerman	..	..	160,530	0	0
Oct. 10	Do.	..	..	30,000	0	0
				190,530	0	0

			£	s.	d.			
Nov. 3	Paid Northcliffe Exors.		500,000	0	0			
Dec. 19	Do.		499,952	0	0			
Feb. 15	Do.		350,000	0	0			
						1,349,952	0	0
Nov. 28	Paid Sir Campbell Stuart	..		..		12,500	0	0
	Paid Barclays Bank :							
Nov. 28	Interest on Loan		397	5	3			
Dec. 22	Do.		62	9	4			
						459	14	7
1923								
April 20	Paid Lewis & Lewis ..	..		..		151	13	3
	Stamp Duty on transfer of shares to the Holding Company (paid)			..		15,405	11	0
	Registration Fees of Holding Company (paid)	..		..		107	15	0
	Additional Capital Duty on Increase of Capital of the Holding Company to be paid—say			..		6,000	0	0
	Various costs and disbursements (details not yet available)—say	..				4,893	6	2
						£1,580,000	0	0

Grant paid the first half-million to Sutton within ten days of the sale, and the rest in accordance with the dates set out in Rothermere's letter.

The Times had changed hands on October 23, 1922, on the day of the announcement that Bonar Law had formally accepted from the King the task of forming a Government. Within twenty-four hours the crisis over *The Times* was a memory and its reconstruction was a task.

XX

THE NEW PROPRIETORSHIP

THE last week of October, 1922, found the country governed by a new Administration and *The Times* owned by a new Proprietorship. After October 19, the Editor happily looked forward to the conduct of the nation's affairs according to consistent principle. Nor was there reason to question the general lines of the new Administration's policy abroad. Under Curzon British foreign policy would rest upon an Anglo-French understanding. Bonar Law knew he could rely upon the Editor to give him the general support of *The Times*. There was coming into view, however, an aspect of the change in proprietorship that was soon to affect the position of the Editor. On October 24, the day after the purchase of *The Times* by Walter and Astor, two incidents made the day a memorable one for him. In the afternoon the Foreign Secretary asked the Editor to call on him. Their discussion ranged over the question as to whether or not Britain would be in a position to go to the Turkish Peace Conference on the basis of a far-reaching agreement with France. Curzon sought the Editor's views as to the best means of securing complete agreement with France, and expressed the hope that as *The Times* had played a by no means unimportant part in averting a rupture with Poincaré over the Chanak crisis, the paper would again give its support to the same policy. Curzon asked the Editor to see Tyrrell with a view to ascertaining the precise contemporary attitude of the French authorities. The Editor promised that the paper would do what it could for Curzon's policy with which he cordially agreed.

The second incident arose from a decision arrived at regarding the editorship. Astor, for his part, had been considering the best means of stabilizing the property and strengthening a staff long harassed by every sort of threat and kind of pressure. The best advice that he could secure regarding the editorial side of the problem was unanimously in favour of returning to the impersonal, anonymous principle established by the Walter family, and followed by John Walter III, Arthur Walter and Buckle.

John Walter was, of course, most strongly in favour of discontinuing the methods that Northcliffe had employed in his later period. Astor had been for some years a Director of *The Observer*, then edited by Garvin, who himself had broken with Northcliffe. Hence, Astor's knowledge, such as it was, of newspapers, encouraged him, too, to favour a break with Northcliffe's methods. In this frame of mind, on October 23 he consulted R. H. Brand, who strongly recommended the policy of wholly dissociating *The Times* from the Northcliffian ambience. He was in favour of making changes in the editorial and managerial departments, and urged the return of Geoffrey Dawson to the post he had vacated under Northcliffe's pressure in 1919. It was desirable, Brand thought, to act quickly. He sent by hand on the morning of Tuesday the 24th a note to Astor telling him that:

G.D. and I will be at All Souls together at Oxford this week-end. You might consider if, as I say, you (and Walter) settle on him, whether you could get him straight down to Dover [where Astor was standing as a Conservative candidate] first, or whether I could speak to him, or what.[1]

At dinner at Carlton House Terrace that Tuesday evening Astor, Walter, Granet, Brand, Grant and Stuart considered the successor to Steed, J. L. Garvin, J. A. Spender, and other names were mentioned. Walter's view was that, in all the circumstances, Dawson was the better name and, this being accepted, Brand was given the task of sounding him at the week-end. John Walter was empowered to give Steed notice to go.

Next, John Walter and Stuart, with Poole attending, discussed the means of arranging for the change of Editor. When Steed returned from the Foreign Office on October 24 he found awaiting him a note from John Walter, whom he straightway visited. Steed had always hoped that the property would pass into the hands of a sound, independent, public-spirited group, no one of whom would hold the controlling share, at whose head Walter would stand as a kind of constitutional monarch. Such an arrangement, Steed had thought, would correspond with the traditions of Printing House Square, of the family, and of the wishes of representative friends of the paper. He was now first informed that an arrangement of precisely this character had been made and, secondly, that it involved a change of Editor. Walter's contemporary memorandum needs to be reproduced:

[1] R. H. Brand to J. J. Astor, October 24, 1922 (Astor Papers).

ROBERT HENRY, LORD BRAND
DIRECTOR OF THE TIMES PUBLISHING COMPANY 1925-
From a photograph

October 24, 1922

The day following the sale I had a talk with Astor who was now jointly and equally with myself responsible for all decisions affecting the Paper, and as a result of that conversation had to inform Steed with very great regret that the change in the proprietorship would entail a change in the Editorship.

Greatly as I regretted it, I felt compelled to tell him this myself at the earliest possible moment as we were old friends and colleagues on the Paper of over 20 years standing and because I knew perhaps better than anyone the great services he had rendered the Paper and the difficulties he had had to contend with.

Moreover, I hoped that in a friendly talk with him as between old friends I might come with him to some arrangement whereby the Paper might retain his services in some other capacity than that of Editor, for although his position in the journalistic world was great enough to assure him of an independent and brilliant career apart from *The Times*, should he wish to make one, I thought it would be a pity from his point of view no less than from ours that he should sever his connexion with the Paper at the very moment when our troubles seemed to be over and a fair prospect was opening out.

I wished therefore to make him the following suggestion: that we should give him a year's salary and thereafter a retaining fee of £1,000 a year, paying him extra for any work he might do for us, while allowing him opportunity to write for any papers which were not competitive with *The Times*.

He was obviously very much taken aback by what I had said but listened without interruption and when I had done [he] asked whether he might enquire why it was thought necessary to decide on a change of Editor.   I said that Astor and I wished to keep the policy of the Paper in our own hands, that he, Steed, had impressed his own personality so strongly on the Paper's policy and had impregnated it so thoroughly with his own views that the risk of disagreement with him on some important question, at any moment, was greater than we were willing to incur, and that a change could be made more easily and appropriately now than later.[1]

He asked whether it was proposed to turn the Paper definitely into a Conservative organ, I said no.   The Paper would remain entirely independent of Party.   He asked whether he was to take this as definite notice to leave.   I said yes.

He then dwelt at some length on his services to the Paper, the hard work he had done, how he had spent himself in its service and recited his relations with Northcliffe, alluding to Northcliffe's confidence in

---

[1] From June 19 to date, and thence to November 30, Steed enjoyed complete and absolute control of the paper and had personally pledged the paper's support to Bonar Law in the imminent election.

him and to the agreement Northcliffe had given him in 1919. Finally he asked when he was expected to leave. I said as soon as possible, immediately if he could make it convenient to do so.

He asked who would carry on. I said Freeman until a new Editor was appointed. He said it would be undesirable for the Paper that he should leave at once as he had all the strings in his hands with reference to the approaching General Election, to the change of Government and to the strained relations with France on the Near Eastern question. That he was engaged in consultation with Curzon on the latter points and engaged in assisting the F.O. at a very critical juncture.

I said that I saw the importance of this consideration and that we naturally wished to consult his interests as well as those of the Paper in the matter. He said he could give me no definite answer on the spot but must consult his solicitor and would come back in a couple of days and let me know his decision.

While Steed was considering his personal position, the new Cabinet was announced in *The Times*. It was welcomed, though " among the, perhaps, inevitable defects " was the high proportion of members of the upper House. Salisbury was Lord President of the Council and Deputy Leader in the House of Lords, Curzon was at the Foreign Office and Leader in the House of Lords, Peel at the India Office, Derby at the War Office, Devonshire at the Colonial Office. Other interesting appointments were Baldwin as Chancellor of the Exchequer, Amery as First Lord of the Admiralty, Wood at the Education Office. " The reception should be favourable " and should ensure to the Prime Minister the good will of all who looked for " an efficient and business-like Government in charge of national affairs." Preparations went forward for a General Election.

In the issue that announced the names of Bonar Law's new administration, October 25, *The Times* thus informed the public of its own new proprietors:

THE TIMES
NEW PROPRIETORS

It is announced that the shares in The Times Publishing Company owned by the late Lord Northcliffe, as well as those owned by Sir John Ellerman, have been acquired by Mr. John Walter, and that Major the Hon. John Jacob Astor is associated with Mr. Walter in their acquisition.

It is the intention and object of Mr. Walter and Major Astor to maintain the highest traditions of *The Times* and to ensure its continuance as a national institution conducted solely in the best interests of the nation and the Empire.

That day, October 25, Walter telephoned to the Editor, asking him to call and see him on his way to the Foreign Office. Steed duly came, and on the subject of Steed's allusion the night before to his agreement with Northcliffe, Walter said he had not liked to mention the matter before. It seemed to him extremely disappointing and even incredible that an old member of the staff such as Steed, in the position he occupied, could make such an agreement without informing Walter of it at the time. Steed thereupon went into the history of the agreement. He narrated the circumstances, said that he had never wanted it and that it was forced upon him by Northcliffe. Walter urged that any such agreement was against all the traditions of the paper and that it seemed to be aimed entirely at himself. It was clearly not designed to bind Northcliffe who, *ex hypothesi*, was to be dead within a few weeks of its signature, but to bind his successor, who in all probability was to be Walter, as Northcliffe and Steed must then have known. The Editor replied that Northcliffe was only concerned for his, Steed's, future, and although he had expected that Walter would gain control on Northcliffe's death he thought that he might either have to borrow the wherewithal to buy the shares, or that he might be subjected to pressure from strangers unfavourably inclined to Steed. These were the conditions in which Northcliffe designed that agreement for his protection. Walter said that he hardly felt complimented, and that it was curious, to say the least, that both Northcliffe and Steed should have kept it from him for two years, and that he should only have learnt of it accidentally. Neither Walter nor Steed enjoyed the interview. Obviously, the lawyers were to be brought in before Steed could be got out of the editorial chair.

Meanwhile, on October 27, Bonar Law's manifesto was published. In the opinion of *The Times* it was a " straightforward " Conservative document. The new Prime Minister had come forward with a policy of " tranquillity and stability, both at home and abroad, so that free scope should be given to the initiative and enterprise of our citizens." A large part of the work of the Cabinet secretariat was to be transferred to the Foreign Office. Frank and full cooperation with France was promised. Maintenance of good understanding with the United States was to be striven for. There were to be close and continuous consultations with the Dominions and India. Trade was to be developed within the Empire and an Imperial economic conference to consider methods was to be summoned. The paper's leading article commended the emphasis upon free scope for private enterprise and initiative. Also, " The new

Prime Minister could not have begun his election address more satisfactorily than by announcing his determination to put an end to the Cabinet secretariat in its present form and to hand over to responsible Departments of State the functions which it has improperly undertaken " (October 27, 1922).

The Editor, under notice of dismissal, rejoiced in the access to power of a party with traditional respect for British institutions and the departments of State. In particular the reduction of power of the Cabinet Secretariat gave him satisfaction. In practice it had become a Prime Ministerial Department, and had ever been an object of aversion in Printing House Square. It had conducted important national and international affairs " apart from, and even in subversion of, well-tried constitutional practices and safeguards." This would now cease. The country had learned a lesson. The time had gone by when foreign affairs could be regarded as of small concern. The paper took for granted a Conservative victory. Its first job would be the re-establishment of peace. Proper support should be given to the League, and notice should be taken of the Empire. *The Times* which had urged on the late Government the immediate desirability of calling " an economic conference of the Empire," hoped that the new Government would act as soon as possible after the election. The dates had been fixed. Nomination day was November 4, the election on November 15, and the new Parliament would assemble on November 20.

It was now to be seen whether the Government would, in fact, get anything like the electoral backing that *The Times* was prepared to give and was giving. Journalists and historians of journalism would now see how close was the paper's relation to public opinion. Younger's estimate of a very narrow victory, say 25, was still seriously regarded in party and newspaper circles. The Conservatives had not held office since the resignation of Balfour in December, 1905. The majority that the office judged as probable was that of 75 which the Editor gave to a doubting Bonar Law on October 17. *The Times*, so far, had reason to be pleased. The eminence, size and composition of the Conservative group that sided with Lloyd George was an unwelcome surprise but, broadly, the paper's hopes, expectations and predictions were at least within the bounds of possibility. The Editor had special cause for satisfaction. He had disagreed with much of the policy of Lloyd George, even before the end of the war. In particular he had objected to the war aims of Lloyd George ; the latter had been

772

slow to recognize the inevitability of the collapse of the Hapsburg monarchy, and the desirability of preparing the way for the liberation of the subject races. Steed had come independently to the same conclusion as Asquith : Lloyd George's unique gifts did not include amongst them the capacity to arouse trust. In addition the nature of the Coalition was such as to encourage ambiguity, vacillation and prevarication. Thus Lloyd George had pursued a wrong course in Ireland. Towards France he had long been lukewarm, and finally at Genoa inimical. He had been ineffective and dangerous over Chanak. As to American relations, the authority he gave to the Balfour Note first humiliated and then burdened Britain. After the election of 1918 Lloyd George had attempted, in conditions of national reconstruction, to stand at the head, not of a party, but of a following. It was a position that no man could assume without being driven to the adoption of every kind of device. He was compelled to make expediency equivalent to principle. Anything could be expected from one in that position, and Steed had been glad to support all those who would bring it to an end. He had himself " thundered," as has been seen, against the ex-Prime Minister. In doing so he had, as John Walter told him, " impressed his own personality so strongly on the Paper's policy, and had impregnated it so thoroughly with his own views." It was this, as well as his connexion with Northcliffe's policies, that decided the new Proprietors, with the support, on other grounds, of Campbell Stuart, to give Steed notice to leave. Astor, independently, had been given similar advice. There was no chance of the decision being reversed, though the new Proprietors had no fault to find with the policy Steed had followed since Genoa. He had been largely responsible for making it effective, but, apart from personal considerations, the new Proprietors, like the new Administration, wished for " tranquillity." They had determined to return as quickly and as completely as possible to the old ways that existed before the Northcliffe regime.

Rapid steps were being taken to follow up the change of Proprietorship and the notice of dismissal to Steed by the appointment of his successor, in the terms of the resolution, arrived at on October 24. On the 30th Brand reported to Astor : " I have sounded G.D. He is going to think the matter over. . . . There is the problem of the Editor's relations to the Managing Director [Campbell Stuart], which post did not exist in his time. However I put it to him as a matter of duty. He will think over it carefully and will talk to me again in a day or two. I hope ultimately he will take the job. . . . Meanwhile I understand Steed is remaining at *The Times* for the present. I think myself that this is all to the good." On the 31st Dawson reported to Milner that the new Proprietors had invited him to resume the editorship and " We had a long talk, and he walked back to Manchester Square."[1] A few days later " Arthur Lawley looked in to see me [Milner], rather uneasy about the prospect of G. Dawson's returning to *The Times*. I told him my own view that *if*, but only *if*, the conditions of the appointment were entirely satisfactory, G.D. ought to accept."[2]

Steed's position was not comfortable during the period October 24-November 5. Meetings took place between Sutton, Stuart and a tribe of solicitors: Poole and Ellis (for Walter and the Northcliffe estate, respectively), and Withers (for Steed). Stuart refused to raise Walter's terms and Withers refused to come down in his. The Northcliffe-Steed agreement was to stand. Withers also said that Steed had given him instructions to consult eminent counsel and mentioned Sir John Simon. Stuart then wished to join the Northcliffe estate in a single settlement to preclude legal proceedings. *The Times*, it was suggested, should pay the paper's liability (*i.e.*, the sum Walter offered) and the estate should pay a lump sum by way of satisfying Steed's further claim against Northcliffe. After much argument this arrangement was accepted by both sides as the basis of a settlement. It did not, by itself, satisfy Steed. He had not resigned and had no intention of doing so. He would accept his dismissal as due in some measure to Walter's desire to symbolize the break with the Northcliffe regime. He also interpreted it as a success for the policy that Stuart had pursued ever since his appointment by Northcliffe as Managing Director, of subordinating the Editor to the management.

This was an aspect of the affair that had not escaped the attention of the new Proprietors. On November 5, at Hever Castle, Astor and Walter found themselves in complete agreement as to the kind of editorial settlement they wished to perpetuate. The Chief Proprietors would select the type of man in whom they felt confidence. In this instance they wanted an Editor who would instinctively prefer reversion to the old impersonal style familiar in Buckle's day. The Editor, when appointed by Astor and Walter, was to have freedom to exercise a judgement that was independent in the fullest sense of the word. He

[1] Milner's Diary, October 31, 1922.
[2] *Ibid.*, November 3, 1922.

vould consult the Proprietors but would not be exposed to interference from the Board, or the Manager, or Managing Director. The Board should consist of nominees, in a certain proportion, of Astor and Walter, who were not members of the staff. They would attend to money affairs. The names were Major J. J. Astor, John Walter, Robert Grant, Ralph Walter, John Pybus, R. H. Brand, Sir Guy Granet. While the Editor should be present at Board meetings he should be responsible only to the Chief Proprietors who alone were to have the right to select him. That was the Hever decision.

It was hoped that Dawson would accept the editorship upon these terms. Grant reported that Dawson had said that he must first ask Milner's agreement to his leaving the Rhodes Trust. During November 6 and 7 Dawson and Steed conferred. On November 8 Walter and Dawson surveyed the theory of the editorship of *The Times*, especially the Editor's relationship with the Proprietors, and the Management. On November 16 Brand had a talk with Dawson. " The main point he insists on is that it is essential from his point of view that it should be clear to the staff and the world that, apart from the purely business end, *The Times* is being run by the Editor and by no one else."[1] As Brand had reported to Astor on October 30, " there is the problem of the Editor's relations to the Managing Director." Moreover, Dawson now, " and no one else," reflected the view expressed by Milner on November 3 that " if, but only *if*, the conditions of the appointment were entirely satisfactory, G.D. ought to accept." Yet the phrase " and no one else " did not necessarily exclude only the Managing Director. Dawson had experienced no interference from him for, as he recognized, " the post did not exist in my time "; his troubles had been caused by the attempt on the part of Northcliffe as Chief Proprietor, whose activity made it " clear to the staff and the world that *The Times* was being run " by him. It could hardly be doubted, therefore, that what Milner described as conditions that were " entirely satisfactory " were designed to confirm the powers of the Chief Proprietors over *The Times* as to " the purely business end," but would also mean that the policy of the newspaper was not to be the subject of discussion by the Board of The Times Publishing Company, Limited. That had been agreed at Hever on November 5.

The discussion continued. It was impossible to set dates until Steed's dismissal had been accomplished, and this would

[1] Brand to Grant, November 16, 1922. (Astor Papers).

take a few days. On the 20th Stuart talked to Dawson about th
terms upon which he would accept the editorship. Meditatio
on this interview convinced Dawson that it was necessary t
write out what he believed to be a fair statement of his position
Dawson set them forth in a memorandum that was rather longe
than he had thought of when he promised Walter something i
writing. He circulated a copy to Astor and at the same time gave
copy to the Managing Director, Stuart. He then learnt directl
from him how extensive his powers had been until recently
especially over the editorial departments. Stuart told Dawso
that he had been in the habit of spending three-quarters o
his time on that side of the business. The Managing Directo
of *The Times* had been the main avenue of communicatio
between Lord Northcliffe and the staff as a whole. It has bee
seen that from 1917 he held a place in Lord Northcliffe's esteer
second only to Sutton. The connexions Stuart formed at Crew
House had given him an insight into policy and introduction
to political personages. During Steed's absences at Cannes
Genoa, Spa and Washington his authority increased, inevitabl
at the expense of the Editor, as has been seen.

In conversation with Walter, Dawson made it clear tha
while he had no right to dictate to the Board the policy t
be pursued regarding the commercial departments of Printin
House Square, he could not consider returning unless his authorit
over the editorial departments and the editorial pages, once give
him, was exclusive, complete and final, until the Proprietors dis
missed him. In effect this meant, immediately, that eithe
Stuart or Dawson had to give way. Stuart had played suc
an important role in establishing the new Proprietorshi
that he could hardly be disregarded. A complication aros
out of Stuart's resignation on August 17, 1922, of his positio
of Managing Editor of the *Daily Mail*. He could not we
assume managerial, as distinct from directorial, responsibilit
even for the commercial departments of Printing Hous
Square, without disturbing the arrangements that he had himse
made with W. Lints Smith by which the day-to-day managemen
should be left in Lints Smith's hands. It was an arrangemen
that was perfectly suitable in Northcliffe's time and was we
calculated to serve the policy by which Stuart should become
under Northcliffe, the Managing Director and Managing Editor c
The Times as he already was of the *Daily Mail*. Stuart, i
his talk with Dawson, judged that since it was the desir
of the new Proprietors to make a fresh start, free fron
the associations of the past fifteen years, his own position a

an associate of Northcliffe was, or would be, difficult. Stuart suggested therefore that, if Dawson should decide to return, he, Stuart, should as from the end of the year cease to be the Managing Director and join the Board with no more executive power than any other member. Such a solution, Stuart thought, would allow the new Editor the free hand he desired. Dawson agreed. This would mean that if the arrangement was accepted by Astor and Walter, Stuart would become a life Director of The Times Publishing Company, Limited, to take effect from January 1, 1923, while W. Lints Smith would become sole Manager.

The way was thus made clear for Dawson to set down in writing a statement of the position of Editor, making clear beyond any dispute the essentials of editorial responsibility and independence as he wished them to be under the new Proprietorship. It was the first time that this part of the tradition of the office had been committed to writing. In 1907, it has been seen, the abortive Walter-Pearson agreement regulated the powers of the signatories, giving them both, jointly, jurisdiction over the principal appointments. In 1908 a similar agreement gave Northcliffe and Walter the same authority, with the consequences that have been chronicled in the preceding volume. The basic question at issue between John Walter and C. A. Pearson, and between Arthur Walter and Northcliffe, was identical. In both situations the Walter of the day needed a partner, and irrespective of the share capital they each represented, he demanded equality of power over the editorial departments. In 1922 the Editor himself was in effect and for the first time consulted about the drafting of the Articles of Association that governed the editorship. By definition, the Articles regulated the relations of the Chief Proprietor (Astor) and the co-Chief Proprietor (Walter) but now, for the first time, they went beyond this and sanctioned a statement of the rights of the Editor.

Partly as the result of his earlier experience of Northcliffe and partly by his talks with Steed, who recommended his successor to make his position " bomb-proof," the statement Dawson had drawn up amounted to a working constitution that would regulate the future relations between the Chief Proprietors and the Editor, and between the managerial department and the Editor. The Editor frankly recognized that no arrangement, in practice, would remove the overlap between the editorial and managerial departments. It was necessary, therefore, to claim on the Editor's behalf an equal voice with the Manager, left by the resignation of Stuart in sole charge of matters which, though financial in nature, and therefore rightly managerial, affected the public presentation and estimation of *The Times*; it was necessary, too, that both Editor and Manager should fully discuss such matters before the Proprietors made their decision. For the future, the Editor was not a person employed to state the views of the newspaper, with a responsibility limited to what in transatlantic organization is known as the " editorial " page. His jurisdiction was to extend absolutely to everything presented in the news columns of the newspaper, and relatively to the advertisement columns; it extended to the *Weekly Edition*, in like manner, and to the other Supplements issued in connexion or association with the parent newspaper. This was to be the understanding henceforth.

In Dawson's opinion no contract between the Proprietors and the Editor was necessary, or even desirable, since the Editor could only conduct his side of the newspaper if he held the confidence of the Proprietors. It was possible, notwithstanding, to lay down a few administrative principles that might conduce to smooth working. It was necessary, in the first place, that the Editor should choose directly or indirectly, and take responsibility for, his assistants and correspondents. Dawson and his friends naturally took it for granted that the Proprietors were keenly interested in their property as a property, and were in a financial and commercial position to ensure the independence of Printing House Square from the risk of outside political influence.[1] In future, therefore, the role of the Chief Proprietors would be to guarantee the security and independence of the Editor, who was to have sole control of the policy and staff of *The Times* and all other publications issued from Printing House Square. The Chief Proprietors and their agent, the Manager, would concern themselves solely with the financial and commercial aspects of the property, thus leaving the Editor a " free hand " to conduct the paper as he thought fit so long as the Chief Proprietors had confidence in him. These were the conditions of the appointment that Milner regarded as " entirely satisfactory," the acceptance of which would alone justify his releasing Dawson from the Rhodes Trust. The memorandum, it cannot be doubted, was a joint production of Milner and Dawson. They were determined that " apart from the purely business end " it must be understood that " *The Times* is being run by the Editor and no one else," and the memorandum made this demand quite clear. It was dated November 18, 1922.

---

[1] It was because Arthur Walter relied upon his manager, Moberly Bell, to ensure the commercial independence of *The Times* that Buckle's editorship was obliged to submit to what Barnes and Dawson would have regarded and been able to reject as managerial aggression.

MEMORANDUM

I am anxious that there should be no sort of misunderstanding about my conception of the duties and responsibilities of the Editor and of his relations both with the Proprietors and with the Manager of *The Times*. None of them, as I recognize, can be defined precisely. The conduct of a newspaper differs from every other business in the world inasmuch as it has two quite distinct objects which are ultimately both dependent on one another, yet are in constant opposition. They can only be achieved by the closest cooperation and by daily compromises. All that is possible (and most necessary) is that there should be complete agreement from the outset as to the constitutional method of working.

These two objects, of course, are (1) to reflect and guide public opinion by producing a good newspaper and (2) to make money by producing a profitable newspaper.

Each purpose for obvious reasons depends on the other, and it is equally obvious that, in detail, the activities of Editor and of the Manager, who are respectively responsible for carrying them out, must often clash. The example of this is the question of the relative space to be devoted to news and to advertisements and of the character of the advertisements. A less frequent example is such a question as arose when it was decided to reduce the breadth and to increase the columns of *The Times*. I regard these as primarily questions for the management, but the Editor should certainly have a voice in their discussion. He must in any case have final authority (which I do not think has ever been disputed) to strike out any advertisement whatever which in his opinion is mischievous—such, for instance, as the political manifesto masquerading as an advertisement, with which we were confronted on the eve of the war. These are examples of comparatively small and simple problems, about which there is not likely in practice to be much difficulty; but the general question of the amount of expenditure required, e.g., to make the foreign correspondence worthy of a good newspaper, as compared with the immediate financial return required, is one in which the Editor's views should carry equal weight with the Manager's in its decision by the Proprietors.

I should say here that there is, of course, no question about the right of the Proprietors of any newspaper to do what they choose with their own property. They are the ultimate arbiters and Court of Appeal. But it is necessary that their intentions should be known in advance by those to whom the conduct of their property is entrusted. Every Editor worth his salt must have a " free hand " to conduct his side of the paper as he thinks best so long as he is in charge of it. The power of the Proprietors is exercised properly by the appointment and dismissal of the Editor, not by interfering with his work or doing it themselves. I have never, myself, been able to see that any " contract " with an Editor over a period of years can be devised except on conditions which will involve either his writing " to order " when he differs from the Proprietors, or their complete abdication. All that is possible in practice is that Editor and Proprietors should have confidence in one another, and a clear undertaking to work in the constitutional manner suggested in this Memorandum.

The editorial side of the paper, for which the Editor is primarily responsible, means, of course, everything printed in it, except the advertisements. It should hardly be necessary to emphasise this but for the new and most misleading practice of describing the leading articles, notes, etc., as the " editorial page ". In my opinion the first business of the Editor of *The Times* at the present moment is not so much the expression of the paper's views as (a) the restoration of the reputation of its news columns for absolute accuracy and impartiality, and (b) the re-establishment of such a system of editorial control as will prevent, e.g., what happened the other day, when two successive leading articles dealt with pronouncements which some other hand had taken out of the paper altogether. In any case the Editor must be responsible just as much for the presentation of news, letters, pictures and the " captions ", etc., as for the opinions expressed by the paper. Incidently he must be responsible for the various supplements published by *The Times* and for its *Weekly Edition*. The greater part of the work of supervision is necessarily delegated to others, but the ultimate responsibility must be clearly understood.

This leads naturally to the question of the editorial staff, which again means all those engaged in producing the editorial side of the paper as defined above. No Editor can do his work properly if his assistants or correspondents are liable to be appointed except by his own choice or with his full approval.[1] Innumerable difficulties have arisen in the past from this form of interference, which can be represented as quite compatible with what is called " a free hand in policy." Here again is a case in which there must clearly be the closest cooperation between Editor and Manager. It is the business of the latter, subject always to the Proprietors or their Board, to say what the paper can afford in staff and salaries and to make the formal appointments in the name of the Company; but, with this limitation, the Editor must be ultimately responsible (however much he may delegate the choice of their subordinates to heads of departments) for the selection of his assistants at home and abroad, and for the allocation of their duties.[2] In the light of past experience it is perhaps necessary to add that the Proprietors should act only through the Editor and the Manager in their respective spheres—in other words, there must be no risk of either being confronted with " instructions " given to some member of his staff without his knowledge. One of the most fertile sources of misunderstanding and confusion has been the disregard of this elementary principle of administration.

I have referred hitherto to " the Manager " as the head of the business side of the organization. This was the title by which he was

[1] This was the point upon which Steed and Stuart had clashed at the Board Meeting of November 17, 1922. See the previous Chapter.

[2] Dawson did not demand the right to change existing arrangements. He was, as the future proved, thinking of the practical arrangements and wished only that no changes be introduced without his knowledge and approval.

WILLIAM LINTS SMITH

ASSOCIATE MANAGER AND MANAGER OF *THE TIMES* 1915-1937

From a photograph

known throughout my editorship; but all that I have written applies equally to the position of " Managing Director ", which did not exist in my time. The point is important because a " Managing Director " is *ex hypothesi* a member of the Board, while the Editor is not necessarily a member. Personally I think it arguable that the Board should include no salaried administrative officer at all, whether on the managerial or on the editorial side. It would in that case be detached altogether from administration, and the necessary liaison would be maintained by the presence (as a matter of right) of Manager and Editor at all Board Meetings, and by formal communications from the Secretary. If, however, the Board were to include the Manager or Managing Director, but not the Editor, then the latter would tend inevitably to become the subordinate of the former, who would in effect be the embodiment of the Proprietors in daily attendance at the office. This, of course, is an alternative method of organization—a salaried Managing Director acting as the spokesman of the Board or of the Proprietors, with an Editor and a Manager (the former no doubt free from interference in the expression of the views of the paper) at the head of the other side of the work under his general direction as representative of the Proprietors. I do not myself think it is a good method, and personally I would not take a hand in it in any capacity. I regard the complete equality of status, in their respective spheres, of the Manager or Managing Director on the one hand and of the Editor on the other hand, as a fundamental condition.

It was not taken for granted by Dawson and his friends that the Chief Proprietors would accept these conditions, for they knew they went beyond the implications of the talks at Hever on the 5th. On November 21 Milner noted in his diary that " Dawson's rejoining *The Times* still hangs in the balance." The memorandum, " entirely satisfactory " as it might be to Milner and Dawson, embodied a set of demands that, if accepted, would place Dawson in the position of an autocrat over the whole of the editorial content of the paper, its " presentation of news, letters, pictures and the ' captions '," as well as over " the opinions expressed by the paper " and over all the Supplements. Steed, it has been seen, had exercised a similar editorial power in the months between the illness of Northcliffe in June and the present time, but he had made no appointments or dismissals of staff, and had Campbell Stuart as a colleague in the capacity of Managing Director—a position, and not merely its present incumbent, that the Memorandum would render superfluous. Moreover, when Walter dismissed Steed on October 24 he answered his question why it was thought necessary to decide on a change of Editor, by telling him that " Astor and I wished to keep the policy of the paper in our own hands, that he, Steed, had impressed his own personality so strongly on the Paper's policy and had impregnated it so thoroughly with his own views that the risk of disagreement with him on some important question, at any moment, was greater than we were willing to incur." But this statement was not to be understood literally. Walter was a Conservative, and Astor was actually the Conservative Candidate for Dover and was busy nursing the constituency. It did not greatly affect Walter, therefore, that, according to his Memorandum, Dawson " must have a ' free hand ' to conduct his side of the paper as he thinks best so long as he is in charge of it." The important fact was that Dawson's personality made him exceptionally sympathetic to Walter. What mattered to Walter most was the attitude and tone—the behaviour in fact—of the paper. These were of far greater concern to him than questions of Government policy; these he was content to leave to those *ex officio* called upon to deal with them, namely, the Prime Minister and, say, the Editor of *The Times*. It was natural for Walter at the break-up of the Coalition to welcome the advent of a Conservative Government, though Steed may have appeared to him to have been hasty in offering Bonar Law a blank cheque at the start.

The Conservatives, it was thought, might easily lose the election through divisions in the Party: Austen Chamberlain and Balfour were men of great power in the country. Steed had assured the incredulous Prime Minister that he would be returned with a clear majority of 75. The result was completely uncertain throughout the campaign. Meanwhile, the Lloyd George party predicted a resounding victory for the Coalition. Bonar Law's electioneering slogan was " Tranquillity." It was a policy that suited Walter, Astor, and Dawson; the question whether it suited the electorate would not be known until the middle of the month. On the 17th *The Times* announced the result of the election. Steed's prediction was borne out : Bonar Law was returned with a clear majority of 77. Astor had won Dover.

The time had now come; it was necessary to decide upon the Editor and his " free hand." Within 24 hours Dawson sent his Memorandum to Astor and Walter. No immediate acceptance or answer was vouchsafed. First Steed's position needed to be cleared up. This was done on November 22, when the lawyers arranged an agreed settlement. Steed was thus able to notify the Secretary of the Company that " acceptable arrangements " having been made, " his withdrawal " from the service of *The Times* at the end of the month had been agreed. There was still some delay before Dawson was answered. On November 24

Milner's diary records that " Geoffrey Dawson came. *The Times* affair is not yet quite settled." It was not until the 29th that Astor informed Dawson that he and John Walter had considered his letter " very carefully." They had come to the conclusion that " it fairly represents the traditional constitution of *The Times* as far as it is possible to define it, and that it conveys a true idea of the lines upon which we intend that the paper shall be conducted in the future."[1] Thus the Milner-Dawson conditions were accepted. Dawson was desired to resume the editorship forthwith, or at least to take charge even if he could not regularly attend the office. Walter was prepared to arrange that Brumwell should act as Deputy Editor during the interregnum. Steed's *ultima editio* of *The Times*, containing his last leading article (it was a topical piece on the Tutankhamen tomb) was the issue of December 1, 1922. He handed over a healthy paper to his successor. The circulation in the period of Northcliffe's illness rose, at the $1\frac{1}{2}$d. price, in April to 165,441 (compared with the previous year's 112,191). By July, 179,218 was the figure, when there was the usual summer drop. In October, with the help of the General Election, the sales rose again. At Steed's departure the average sale reached 184,166, the highest figure *The Times* had known since 1914 when its price was lowered to one penny.

The dismissed Editor had been in uninterrupted control from June 19 until November 30. It was a period of national upset with a General Election, of international tension with a crisis in the Middle East. Above all it coincided with the death of a Chief Proprietor and the attendant personal and professional anxieties. It was a matter of 23 weeks, *i.e.*, 142 issues of *The Times*. In addition to editing the paper, the dismissed Editor wrote leading articles on Home and Foreign affairs, War Debts, Reparations, Unemployment, Ireland and the Dominions, the Election and finally the new Cabinet. In all Steed wrote 86 leaders, an average of nearly four a week for 23 weeks. Never before in the history of *The Times* had one man written so many articles in so short a time. Steed had joined *The Times* as a junior foreign correspondent in 1896 at the age of 25 and was dismissed from the highest position on the paper at the age of 51.

The change in the editorship was an inevitable corollary to the change of Proprietorship, and the intention of Walter and Astor to disengage *The Times* from the name of Northcliffe; it also corresponded with the mood prevailing in political circles,

[1] Astor to Dawson, November 29, 1922. (Astor Papers copy).

not only of the Conservative Party. Chanak created a widespread feeling against precipitate and adventurous action. The Conservative Party chose Baldwin instead of Lloyd George; the same mood now in the ascendant at Printing House Square preferred Dawson to Steed and Lints Smith to Campbell Stuart. The new Proprietors of *The Times* and the electorate both chose " steadiness." A country tired of sensation and the " first-class brains of F. E. Smith and others " was bent upon " tranquillity " and going slow. The new Proprietors wished for less " militancy " in *The Times*, and shared the prevailing distrust of powerful personalities and " brains." They were happy to leave policy to the Editor of their appointment. If Astor's and Walter's belief that Dawson's Memorandum represented the " traditional constitution of *The Times* " cannot be confirmed, it did convey " a true idea of the lines upon which we intend that the paper shall be conducted in the future." The full implication of the Memorandum, which by Astor's and Walter's letter of November 29 had the force of an agreement, could not, in the nature of things, appear quickly. An agreement made in a national mood of " tranquillity " and distrust of " brains " might or might not be workable if the country found itself facing difficulties. Time would tell. The Chief Proprietors were no more able in 1922 than any other men of affairs to foresee what the next five years would bring. In the meantime, they had plenty of reconstruction work to do in Printing House Square. Walter was the best judge of the " traditional " and " constitutional " relations between the Proprietors and the Editor, and between the Editor and the Manager. Walter's acquaintance with Dawson, although never intimate, had been long enough—32 years—to preclude any misgivings as to the use he might make of his " free hand." True, the Editor's " free hand " had always been understood to imply agreement with the views of the Chief Proprietors, or at all events avoidance of conflct with them. This was a natural and indeed an inevitable limitation, and Walter had no reason to suspect that Dawson was asking for any freer hand than his predecessors had enjoyed. Walter, in fact, thought he had every reason to be pleased at the way things were shaping. Astor was equally satisfied that he would get on well with Dawson.

Having settled to re-appoint Dawson, the new Proprietors turned their attention to the legal constitution of the Company. It has been seen that on September 27, 1922, Astor and Walter agreed that " in view of the national importance of *The Times* " the partners should seek the reconstruction of the Company under a " special Charter." It was agreed that the whole of the shares represented by Astor's and Walter's investment should be allotted to so many " Referees "—or " Governors "—who would purchase them. This would prevent *The Times* again being, or becoming, a function of absolute private property or an instrument of personal ambition. It was as important to preserve, as it had been to regain, the paper's " historic " independence. A conception, of a somewhat naive and romantic order, lay behind this aspiration, and the innumerable legal consultations to which, like all preceding attempts at reform in Printing House Square, it led. The basis of the new attempt to safeguard *The Times* from a repetition of the excesses of personal influence with which Northcliffe's name was, at this time, most conspicuously associated, was a respect for the age, as well as the quality, of the paper.

The Times was regarded as unique. It is true that in 1922 the *Morning Post* was its senior by thirteen years, yet Printing House Square was convinced that it had become the most historic newspaper; an institution in fact. Ownership, either in whole or in part, by the same founding family who had conducted the editing, printing and publication on the same site for nearly 140 years, was certainly unparalleled in the London newspaper trade. The new co-Chief Proprietor, with the new directors, felt from the beginning that they had connected themselves with a property so hallowed by time that it had become rather more than an old-established family business undergoing reconstruction. Respect for the antiquity of the place was freely accorded; and, indeed, somewhat exaggerated, in accord with a tendency that Northcliffe had checked but not eradicated. After his death the conception of *The Times* as a precious inheritance from a past, thought of as remote, gained in vigour. Such a conception was already noticeable early in the decade after 1884, when the paper celebrated the completion of its first century by the commemorative striking of a portrait medal of the three Walters. The hundred years, to the Victorians a vast space of time, had even then transformed the original commercial speculation into an honoured family possession. John Walter III as Chief Proprietor felt himself in a position of trust answerable to his conscience and his country. Buckle as Editor did not ask himself what he should say in its leading columns, but rather " what shall *The Times* say ? " In the '80s the individualism of Barnes and Delane had yielded place to a proprietoral-editorial collectivity. *The Times* of John Walter III and Buckle, unlike the " bloody old *Times* " of John Walter II and Barnes, had become a respected national institution, representative of interests and tastes of a confident and complacent governing class. The Parnell case made no difference to the feeling in the office that *The Times* was uniquely deserving of the respect of all right-minded Englishmen.

It was natural, therefore, for Walter III at the age of 75 to consider ways and means of securing continuity of character of such a unique newspaper. His steps to organize some form of charter or guarantee were nullified. A generation, almost, had passed after he had first found it necessary to warn his sons, John and Arthur, to " be on the watch lest any attempt be made by any of your co-proprietors to interfere with you in the management of the concern." He had then said that he " strongly " recommended them to apply for the Court of Chancery's permission to sell the paper " rather than submit to any interference." Previous pages of this history have recorded that the will of John Walter I entailed the splitting of shares into fractions, and fractions of fractions. The owners of these had, since 1838 and 1842 at least, obstructed the hereditary Chief Proprietor. They are found doing so in 1867, in 1885, and again in 1893. The culminating manifestation occurred in 1908 when, as has been seen, it was the dissidents and not the Chief Proprietor who effected the sale of the paper and set in train the circumstances that brought it into the hands of Moberly Bell and Northcliffe.

Thus, for more than two generations, *i.e.*, from 1838 to 1908, the rights of the hereditary Chief Proprietors, John Walter II, John Walter III and Arthur Walter had never been unchallenged. The small proprietors attacked the hereditary, as they said usurped, powers of the Chief Proprietors. No attempt to modify the character of *The Times* had been intended. But that might be the next demand. Hence the Chief Proprietors cannot be accused of mere selfishness when they resisted the claims of the small proprietors. The Walters were well aware that any combined effort on the part of the proprietors of small fractions to make the Chief Proprietors responsible to them for policy, would ruin the character of the paper. The fifth Walter (John Walter IV, Chairman of the Company 1910-1923, co-Chief Proprietor 1923 at the present day) knew as well as his predecessors the mischief of divided counsels. It was the main reason why, like his father, he gave Northcliffe a free hand. There could not be two masters in P.H.S. and the Walters and Northcliffe agreed in 1908 that the maintenance of the paper's historic character was paramount. For the Northcliffe of those days *The Times* was such a national monument that he would feel bound, he said, in due time to " leave it to the British Museum,"[1] as he told Esher. This was not just a fairy tale. A month later Northcliffe discussed with St. Loe Strachey the possibility of making arrangements whereby *The Times* should become "a permanent national institution." Strachey's suggestion was that *The Times* should be vested by Northcliffe's will in a body of independent Trustees, who should appoint the Editor and Manager, and generally control the paper. The Trustees he suggested were:

The Lord Chancellor, or Lord Chief Justice, or Master of the Rolls.
The Speaker of the House of Commons.
The Archbishop of Canterbury.
The Vice-Chancellors of Oxford and Cambridge.
And the Editor and Manager for the time being.

Strachey proceeded to say that the Editor should be irremovable, as judges are irremovable.[2]

But this, destined as it was to be the model of the scheme that was adopted in 1924, was not practicable in 1908. There was no point in selecting Vice-Chancellors, Archbishops, and Judges to supervise and maintain the character of a journal whose future financial stability was as impredictable as that of *The Times* in 1908. There did not exist in 1908 the basis for any such scheme. The paper had first to be made solvent. In the meantime Northcliffe, from the point of view of members of the staff sympathetic to the " Old Gang," became more autocratic. In 1910, on the death of Arthur Walter, John Walter IV sought a way of limiting the absolutist interpretation Northcliffe was then placing upon the " free hand " given him. He made a suggestion, natural now that he was a minority shareholder, that " the shareholders should now agree that a permanent authority should be nominated, to whom the shareholders representing not less than one-quarter of the shares, should always have the right to appeal on grave matters touching the welfare of the paper." Walter then put forward as possible members of such " permanent authority " the Speaker of the House of Commons, the Governor of the Bank of England, or the Chairman of the Trustees of the British Museum. The idea was not acceptable to Northcliffe. It was often said by him, and

---

[1] *Cf.* Northcliffe to Esher, July 9, 1908: "I propose, if I am spared, to leave in my will an endowment and a suggestion for its [*The Times's*] direction by such a committee as that of the British Museum, to preserve it [*The Times*], perhaps for some generations." See Vol. III, Chapter XXI, " Reform in the Office."

[2] *Cf.* St. Loe Strachey to Northcliffe, August 10, 1908, quoted in *The Spectator*, September 22, 1922.

of him, that he was disinterested in mere money. In fact he manifested to John Walter a shrewdness about money hardly less keen than that of his brother Harold's. Northcliffe was no more likely to forget that it was money that had bought control of *The Times* than John Walter would forget that *The Times* was made not by money but by certain qualities in the people who conducted it.

In 1913 when Walter rearranged his holdings and yielded the 150,000 7 per cent. Preference Shares which Northcliffe had handed over to his father in 1908, and the accrued, but unpaid, interest on them in exchange for Ordinary Shares, he secured what he most desired, *i.e.*, the option to purchase Northcliffe's shares. By this sacrifice Walter assured himself of a chance in the future of maintaining the paper's character, or restoring it if lost. It would not have interested Walter to be a Chief Proprietor of any newspaper other than *The Times*, or of *The Times* having a character other than that it had borne in his father's and grandfather's time. It was absolutely consistent and necessary, therefore, for Walter to make the maximum use of his option when, after ten years' struggle against Northcliffe's tyranny and vagary, it had been the means of his regaining influence in Printing House Square. He had complete trust in Astor and it was logical for both to come to an agreement in October, 1922, to limit transfers of the shares representing the controlling interest, to approved persons only. The clause is, in fact, a restatement of Walter's 1910 memorandum to Northcliffe. The proposal first made in 1922 was that the whole block of shares purchased with Walter's option and Astor's money should be broken up and allotted to ten persons chosen by Walter and Astor, to be called " Referees," " Governors " or " Trustees " or some other convenient title; no new functionaries of the kind were to be appointed without the consent of the existing nominees.[1] The point of this was that a Governor should only be allowed to transfer his shares if he had the consent of the majority to the personality of the transferee. It was part of this scheme that John Walter should be Chairman of the Board of Governors and John Astor Chairman of The Times Publishing Company. Thus responsibility for the character of the paper would be shared between Walter and Astor, while responsibility for the property would be Astor's. It would, incidentally, amount to a definition of the functions of the two " Chief Proprietors," as they were described.

[1] See Chapter XIX, " Rothermere *v.* Walter," p. 744.

While Astor was quite agreeable to this scheme, or any other that would secure the same objects, the lawyers discovered objections. The discussions occupied months, and it was not until January, 1923, that the legal men agreed that the most practicable scheme for the realization of Walter's object was a Holding Company, or a Voting Trust, to be formed to acquire the controlling shares. While Astor would be Chairman of the Board of The Times Publishing Company, Limited, Walter and he, as controllers of the voting power, were to be known as the " Chief Proprietors," and together controlled The Times Holding Company, Limited; Walter was to be co-Chief Proprietor for life. Further, the Holding Company was appointed to supervise transfers of the controlling shares. In doing so, Astor and Walter were " to give due weight to the hereditary principle." The question of the control of *The Times* in all matters of editorial policy was settled by vesting it solely and equally in the Chief Proprietors, by whom the Editor should be appointed, and to whom alone he should be responsible. In its essentials the draft of January 3, 1923, satisfied the intentions of Walter and Astor, and they accepted it. On detailed scrutiny by some of the lawyers the text was found to be faulty. By exchanging questionnaires and writing memoranda and counter memoranda, they succeeded in delaying signature until June, 1924. The matter was then confidently thought to be satisfactorily settled.

On July 15, 1924, Astor presided over a gathering of Trustees at Carlton House Terrace. The company, in addition to Astor and Walter, consisted of :

The Editor (Dawson).
The Manager (Lints Smith).
Robert H. Brand.
The Lord Chief Justice (Hewart).
The President of the Royal Society (Sherrington).
The President of the Institute of Chartered Accountants (Mellors).

The Warden of All Souls (Pember), and the Governor of the Bank of England (Norman) were invited but were unable to attend. Walter informed the company that upon the purchase of the control by Astor and himself, they found themselves agreed as to their policy :

Our primary object being to restore *The Times* to its old traditions, one of our first steps in this direction was to induce Mr. Geoffrey Dawson to resume his position as Editor, with a free hand, at the same time giving our Manager, Mr. Lints Smith, full responsibility for his department, with results which exceeded our most sanguine expectations. Your presence here to-night sets the final seal on a bargain which admittedly involved a great risk, but which has already, I am convinced, justified itself in the public view.

Walter's remarks were supported by the President of the Royal Society and the President of the Institute of Chartered Accountants. So far, so good; but when the Lord Chief Justice joined his colleagues in appreciating the compliment paid them by Printing House Square he proceeded to raise the question whether, after all, it was legally possible to create a permanent Trust of the kind contemplated. Discussion of this point occupied the rest of the night. It concluded in orthodox terms by a resolution to seek counsel's opinion. In due time Clauson, K.C., was asked, and upon his recommendation some verbal changes were made in the draft. When the Lord Chief Justice saw the new phrasing he was pleased to say that it appeared to him as being almost watertight, though not quite. A new recourse to counsel was narrowly averted, and the new constitution of *The Times* was at last settled. On August 7, *The Times* made the following announcement :

In accordance with a plan which has long been under discussion, a Committee has been established for the special purpose of safeguarding future transfers of the controlling shares in *The Times*. These shares, it should be explained, are those of The Times Holding Company, Limited, and are all held by Major the Honourable John Astor, M.P., and by Mr. John Walter, who together constitute the Chief Proprietors of *The Times*. The Committee has no other responsibilities so far as *The Times* is concerned. It is not in any sense identified either with the management or with the editorial policy. The sole object underlying its appointment is to ensure, so far as is humanly possible, that the ownership of *The Times* shall never be regarded as a mere matter of commerce to be transferred without regard to any other circumstance to the highest bidder, or fall, so far as can be foreseen, into unworthy hands.

With this object in view it has been thought desirable that the members of the Committee should act *ex officio*, that they should be precluded by their position from active party politics, and that they should represent various elements—*e.g.*, judicial, academic, scientific and financial—in the national life. The following therefore have been invited, and have consented to serve :

> The Lord Chief Justice of England,
> The Warden of All Souls College, Oxford,
> The President of the Royal Society,
> The President of the Institute of Chartered Accountants,
> The Governor of the Bank of England.

They cannot, of course, bind their successors; but in the event of any one or more of the future holders of their offices declining to act, or being incapable of acting, provision has been made for the appointment of members to the Committee in substitution for them.

The Committee is constituted under the Articles of Association of The Times Holding Company, Limited, and the following extract from the Articles to be adopted for this purpose defines the principles which are laid down for its guidance in the event of any projected sale of the Ordinary (that is the controlling) shares:

" In coming to their decision whether any proposed transferee is a proper person to hold Ordinary shares of the Company, the Committee shall have an absolute discretion and may give or withhold their approval on any ground whatever which they may think fit and proper, and without their being bound to give any reason therefor, it being the intention and an instruction to the Committee that inasmuch as the Company holds the absolute voting control in The Times Publishing Company Limited, which owns *The Times* newspaper, the Committee, in coming to their decision, shall have regard to the importance of (*a*) maintaining the best traditions and political independence of *The Times* newspaper, and national rather than personal interests, and (*b*) eliminating as far as reasonably possible questions of personal ambition or personal profit."

Thus was settled the constitution that still governs the paper. The creation of the Committee of Trustees was made possible in the first instance by the faith of Astor and Walter in the " best traditions " and " political independence " of *The Times*. It was made practicable by the new momentum that Northcliffe's genius gave the old newspaper. The vitality and prodigality of his ideas and the energy and perseverance behind them laid the material basis for Astor's and Walter's constitutional guarantees. There remained outstanding one act of rationalization that Northcliffe had not accomplished. The site of Printing House Square belonged to several members of the Walter family; it comprised a number of leaseholds and freeholds and the conditions of its lease to The Times Publishing Company were practically inconvenient. The building was completed (out of his own resources) by John Walter III in 1874 and was the first of its kind in London,[1] but a half-century had rendered it antiquated and overcrowded. As the instinct of Astor was for rebuilding, it soon became necessary to face the question whether to erect a new building at the expense of The Times Publishing Company and, if that were answered in the affirmative, the further

---

[1] See Vol. II, pp. 493-4.

question whether it would not be better if the Company purchased the freehold of the site. The preliminaries were long drawn out, and when both questions were answered in the affirmative, valuations were slow in being made and slower still in being agreed. Legal delays, the bane of the house for generations, protracted the negotiations; and it was seven years or more before The Times Publishing Company, Limited acquired the site, the ownership and the control of Printing House Square.[1] During this period, losses by death and retirement, with replacement by new recruits, impaired the continuity of editorial thinking which, on foreign affairs at least, had been a feature of the office for well over a generation. Some of the decisions made by the Editor rendered the breach permanent for the duration of his editorship, and, towards the end of it, entailed consequences of some public, even international, significance. As events turned out, foreign affairs became of paramount concern in Dawson's second innings under the new Proprietors, and foreign affairs were not his chief interest.

_____

[1] Surveys were made and plans drawn for a new building, of which a portion only had been completed before 1939.

XXI

DAWSON'S SECOND INNINGS

THE important change made in *The Times* promptly upon Dawson's return in the New Year, 1923, had been discussed in the previous autumn: the relation of the price of the paper to rising costs of newsprint, etc. The reduction of the price, one of Northcliffe's last acts, had duly resulted in a gain of circulation but in loss of money, as not only newsprint but labour costs were mounting. The first step towards balancing accounts was to make arrangements to drop the free insurance scheme that cost £500 a week. As notice was required by the insurance company it was not until June 4, 1923, that the scheme was abandoned and the price of *The Times* raised from 1½d. to 2d. The net daily sale, then 187,323, fell steadily until December, when it began to rise. Already in the summer of 1923, however, the paper was in a healthier condition financially than it had been for months; also, the wholly unfamiliar calm created by the new régime gave the staff the opportunity they had long desired to put forth their best efforts in the service of the paper. The Editor, to whom the new Proprietors had given the power to choose his own assistants, decided to maintain George Freeman, Murray Brumwell and Harold Williams in the key posts at which he found them. Freeman had been his own deputy in 1918 and later Steed's, while his retention of Brumwell and Williams, as Night Editor and Foreign Editor respectively, lightened the burden that had been greatly increased by the suppression at the Editor's own insistence of the office of Managing Director. Thus the risk inherent in the recruiting of new men was removed, and a large measure of continuity in the editorial department assured.

Dawson's second term began placidly. He had every reason to rejoice at the change of system from proprietorial interference to passive approval. *The Times*, after nearly fifteen dynamic years, wanted a year or two of steadiness; in his own words, "even of stodginess." The practice of startling the public, he thought, had been carried so far that the opposite

793

policy was essential. The public now required soothing, and Dawson espoused what he called a policy of " giving fair play to the Government," without necessarily following them at every point. This became a permanent principle of his editorship as long as a Conservative or National Government was in power. As he had been happy to support the 1916 Coalition so he was ready to champion the 1923 Government, to an extent that would have exposed him to the charge of lack of independence had Northcliffe been the judge. This attitude was the more inevitable since he was a Conservative of the Right with a loyalty to party greater than had been felt by Buckle or any of his predecessors. The political situation into which Dawson came in 1923 exactly suited one who was less interested in the policy than in the biology of Government. To him the art of politics lay rather in finding and fitting the man to the required job than in the excogitation and formulation of measures in advance. Hence to the Editor journalism was less a means of deciding what things to do than of selecting the men to do them. Dawson's re-entry into the office, therefore, could mean no departure from the line then being followed by *The Times*; for, as has been seen, Steed had freely espoused the cause of Bonar Law whom he saw as the only practical and desirable alternative to Lloyd George. For three months from January 1, 1923, when Dawson resumed the control, *The Times*, except in respect of tone, was consistent with Steed's issues of the preceding three months.

Notable differences in the standpoints of Steed and Dawson, however, soon became manifest. First, the latter was no less an Imperialist and Unionist in 1923 than in 1913. As such he was far more interested in Commonwealth harmony than in Continental friction. It had never been his habit to match his close connexions with Empire statesmen with similar friendships with European statesmen, or even journalists; nor had he at any time made the direct acquaintance of personalities in American politics. He had no foreign languages, no knowledge of economics, and no interest in Reparation questions. Hence, the letter that Bonar Law wrote to *The Times* on French policy and the Chanak crisis which precipitated the fall of the Coalition was much to Dawson's mind: " We shall have no alternative but to imitate the Government of the United States and to restrict our attention to the safeguarding of the more immediate interests of the British Empire." Dawson's immediate predecessor would not have viewed the security and prosperity of the Empire in dissociation from European conditions. While Steed was quick to recognize the difficulties that Poincaré made for Bonar Law, he habitually resisted discords in Anglo

GEOFFREY DAWSON

EDITOR OF *THE TIMES* 1912-1919 and 1922-1941

From a photograph

French relations however uneasy these might become, or breaches in the Treaty, imperfect though that instrument obviously was. To encourage Germany at the expense of France would be bad business for Britain, for Anglo-French solidarity was a primary requirement of British foreign policy even under the League. It followed that the Versailles Treaty, notwithstanding admitted faults, was for him part of the law of Europe, not to be departed from except by agreement, above all with France and Britain. It has been seen that this had been Steed's position in 1922 at Genoa, as against Lloyd George.

If Dawson, too, became antagonistic to Lloyd George after 1922, it was for a different reason. A leader he wrote by way of reply to a letter from the ex-Prime Minister (printed in *The Times* of June 15, 1923) said that his electoral mandate to go to Versailles had been extracted by a " disastrous and wholly unnecessary campaign " which was a " blot on his great career," for he had made himself the champion of those who sponsored the campaign " to squeeze the Germans until the pips squeaked." Dawson knew from his own experience as Editor during the autumn of 1918 that the Prime Minister was then in favour of a " moderate " peace; yet it was in vain in 1923 that Lloyd George pointed out that in 1919 *The Times* had attacked him for letting the Germans off.[1] In January, 1923, Dawson's position towards Germany was no different from Milner's in October, 1918. Both, then and since, belonged to the " moderate " peace group. Thus Dawson's attitude to foreign policy and to the Treaty differed from his predecessor's. First he desired, as an Imperialist, to avoid Continental commitments; secondly, he believed that the provisions of the Treaty affecting Germany created risks ; thirdly, he was persuaded that the collective security of the Commonwealth, plus that of the League of Nations, would balance British disarmament, which was economically desirable and otherwise necessary. Finally he believed in Treaty revision.

This whole programme of strengthening Commonwealth relations, limiting Continental commitments, and encouraging European pacification by sponsoring revision would have been practicable if only Reparations did not awkwardly stand in the way, and drive Dawson to rely upon German promises. This led to a tolerance of the weakening of the French connexion, to the extent that France did not accept the British thesis that Germany could be trusted to pay, voluntarily, a specified sum that

[1] For *The Times* and the peace of 1919, see Chapter VIII, " Peace Making," *supra.* For the paper's (Dawson writing) unreserved admiration and championship of Lloyd George see above, Chapter X, " Northcliffe *v.* the Editor." See also Appendix II, Sources, VIII.

Germany would accept as practically related to her economy as stated by herself. Although the general tendency of Dawson's mind was to disengage Britain from European responsibilities, there was, however, no sharp change in the paper's attitude towards external affairs. The foreign department continued to be directed by Harold Williams, one of the collaborators of the *New Europe*, who had been brought by Steed to Printing House Square in 1921. They had much in common, above all an interest in the Slavs; and Williams, like Steed, equally disliked Prussianism and Bolshevism. As an intimate of the Russian Liberals and Constitutional Democrats, Williams was well-equipped in the knowledge of the past and present languages, the literatures and the politics of Russia, Poland, the Balkans and the Succession States. He supported Steed's foreign policy with marked energy, particularly when the Bolsheviks were invited to Genoa, and his objection to Lloyd George's policy quickened when the Russo-German Treaty was announced from Rapallo. He was a fluent writer on the problems of the post-war settlements of the Middle East and Far East. Williams, having so quickly justified Steed's choice, was appointed to the permanent staff; and on May 11, 1922, he was promoted to the position of Director of the Foreign Department.

Ten days after Dawson's return to the editorial chair the French and the Belgians, after a German default on Reparations, occupied the Ruhr. A week later *The Times* reported that a certain Adolf Hitler, described as leader of the National Socialist Workers' Party, had addressed a " huge " demonstration in one of the largest buildings in Munich. The agitator said that the National Socialists were organizing and recruiting an army of revenge which would restore Germany to her former greatness. A serious attack by Storm Troops on the Allied War Commission's office followed the speech. Such incidents led *The Times*, by the pen of Williams, to emphasize the principle that " we should do nothing to lend colour to the supposition that we are weakening in our insistence on Germany's fulfilment of her obligations." The situation was recognized to be insecure, and *The Times*, in view of discussions which had spread to Canada, argued that " So long as the centre of the international friction lies in Europe, London will always be overtaken by the final rush of events before Ottawa." On the well-worn theme of an Imperial Foreign Policy Dawson was outspoken: " An instant decision will have to be made. It might well be impossible for the British Government to consult its own Parliament before it advised the King to declare war. It might well be impossible with all the will in the world, to wait for the judgements of the Dominion Parliaments." This was said by way of comment upon Borden's doctrine of equality of nationhood and Bruce's demand for a common empire foreign defence policy. The problems implied were not new and were destined to remain urgent throughout Dawson's second innings and to exercise a dominating influence upon his attitude towards Germany, Treaty revision and the policy known as " appeasement " later. This had been initiated as a kind of " movement " in Britain and America already.[1]

Soon after the Peace Conference unemployment at home and the need for settling the conditions of trade abroad made Reparations and War Debts urgent. Bonar Law's resignation (on genuine grounds of ill-health) and the succession of Baldwin made reconsideration opportune. *The Times*, having applauded the Debt Settlement that Baldwin brought back from Washington, was beginning to see in the recovery of Germany, Britain's best customer before the war, the restoration of British trade, the cure for British unemployment, and the means of funding the American Debt. Therefore pacification of Europe must follow the American settlement. It appeared that the German case for revision of the Treaty was difficult to answer; at least by a nation of shopkeepers. On a business basis the Versailles Treaty must be ranked as bad to the extent that it demanded more than Germany could afford to pay; it was impracticable if, for technical currency reasons, she could not transfer such huge sums of money. Both charges were now widely accepted. Four years before, in Paris, similar criticisms had been heard and listened to by a circle that included Smuts, and the resulting mixture of statistical dialectics and malicious wit was published by John Maynard Keynes before the end of 1919. *The Economic Consequences of the Peace* disillusioned the " practical " men of affairs. The book also went far to destroy American acceptance of the Treaty and the Covenant. Above all, Keynes's economic analysis completely dispelled British belief in the necessity, justice and feasibility of Reparations, as demanded by the Treaty. The book, when reviewed in *The Times* of January 5, 1920, was given three columns which forcibly stated the paper's position at that time. Keynes's work was then described as providing " comfort for Germany," written by one with a bias throughout " akin to that of a conscientious objector." The " clever " young don (he was 36) who wrote

[1] See Chapter I, " The New Imperialism," and Chapter XXII, " Imperialism; A New Phase." The words " policy of appeasement " were not unfamiliar to the Coalition Government. *Cf*. Austen Chamberlain writing to Lloyd George, March 25, 1922: " Your policy of appeasement is clearly right." The policy towards Russia was under review at the time.

this book had placed the Allies on the " same moral level as Germany in regard to the war "; his book displayed towards European facts a striking " ingenuousness." The review, while rejecting Keynes's criticisms of the economic provisions of the Treaty, set against them the political and moral errors of the Conference. The reviewer (Steed) reminded the reader that revision, described as " this necessary work," would fail if approached " in a spirit of forgetfulness of German guilt, of undifferentiated anxiety to help Germany to escape the consequences of her felony." In a final paragraph the reviewer said that if the war had demonstrated one fact above all others, it was that the economists, bankers and financial experts who preached the impossibility of war because " it would not pay " talked " parlous nonsense." It remained that Germany went to war in 1914 because she had made it pay in 1871 and believed she could make it pay again; and she all but succeeded. Keynes's argument that German enterprise and organization should be put in the position to " set in train in every Russian village the impulses of ordinary economic motive " was particularly obnoxious and was firmly rejected. Germany should not thus be allowed to renew the struggle. The book was dismissed as a piece of pro-German pacifism and a disservice to the Allies, for which their enemies would be grateful. The positive points made by the review were that revision was, or would become, necessary and that the process should take place through the League of Nations. In 1922 Keynes published a sequel, *A Revision of the Treaty*, which reinforced the contentions of the earlier book. By the late summer of 1923 the attitude of *The Times* was radically different from that of 1920. Within three or four years after the Treaty was signed, these two books had completely changed the climate of opinion and it was felt, after four years' experience, that the American defection left the League too weak to guarantee any peace that it organized. Mussolini's occupation of Corfu on September 14, and threat to leave Geneva if he was interfered with, did nothing to dispel this fear.

Meanwhile the number of British unemployed rose, and the total spent in relief since the end of the war rose to some £400 millions. Many Conservatives, including Dawson, saw the remedy in a protective tariff. This idea the Dominion Prime Ministers, gathered at the London Economic Conference held in August, encouraged. On October 16 Baldwin told Dawson of his belief in protection, and in the development of the Empire and its markets. The Editor told him that the risk of upsetting the Government was too great, and he wrote a leader to that effect for *The Times* of October 21. However, Baldwin, speaking at Plymouth on October 25, endorsed the suggestion of a tariff. At once Liberalism and Labour manifested dissent; Churchill rejoined the Liberal party; Parliament was dissolved in November ; Protection was heavily defeated at the polls on December 6. Lloyd George and Asquith joined hands and did well, except that Churchill was defeated, by totalling 159. The figures were Conservatives 258, Labour 191 and Independents 7. Thus Conservatives, though the largest Party, were in a minority of 99 against the combined Opposition. The solution was another type of Coalition. Asquith refused a Liberal-Conservative combination, and thereby lost for the Liberals the opportunity (which turned out to be their last) for that Party to constitute an alternative Government. Asquith next decided to associate Liberals with the Labour vote of " No Confidence," and the Government was defeated by 328 to 256. Thus came into power the first Labour Government. Reinforced by converts from Liberalism it was constituted on January 22, 1924, by Ramsay MacDonald as Prime Minister and Foreign Secretary.

At this time there were not lacking in the Foreign Office and out of it people who looked askance at the prospect of a France, our Channel and Atlantic neighbour, strengthened by a permanent hold upon the Ruhr, or a Rhineland republic independent in name only. Such observers would much prefer to hand the occupied provinces back to Germany. A substantial section of British public opinion in 1924 was, indeed, pro-German in spite of the recently signed Russo-German Treaty. That Treaty was felt to be an affront in Geneva, but by this time British public opinion was more or less bored by the League, and *The Times* began to take less interest in its discussions. It was not realized that British disarmament after the Russo-German Treaty would inevitably be interpreted as proving disinterest ; and as inevitably acting as an incentive to international re-grouping in the pre-1914 style. The Labour Government was naturally unwilling to criticize Russia. On February 1 Britain took the step of recognizing the Soviet Government, a measure that had been promised in the election manifestos of both the Labour and Liberal Parties, and consistently fought by Williams in the leading columns of *The Times*. The way was thus prepared for the Anglo-Soviet Conference which opened on April 14, 1924. A general commercial Treaty was signed on August 8. British business interests objected in a statement published in September, and a run of ill-luck soon made difficulties for the Government. The law was set in motion against a Leninist weekly, the editor of which had urged soldiers, who had received no orders of the kind, to abstain from firing upon fellow-countrymen on strike. But the Director of Public Prosecutions, who had taken steps preliminary to an action, later withdrew. In the ensuing debate on November 4 the Government was defeated.

At the election the Conservatives were returned with 412 seats against 151 Labour, 40 Liberal and 12 others. To the great satisfaction of *The Times* Baldwin was firmly reinstated. The issues to be faced were vital. They affected home and foreign policy, economics and debts, industry and unemployment; all related to disarmament which it was the business of the League to compass. This was manifest during the Labour régime. MacDonald had already declared his readiness to agree to the Geneva Protocol that imposed on member States the obligation to act against an aggressor defined as a State that refused arbitration. This new Protocol was regarded by MacDonald as a great advance on the Draft of Mutual Assistance previously discussed and rejected by public opinion in Great Britain as inconsistent with the spirit of the League. It was then believed that mutual assistance or defensive alliances arranged within the League would part Europe into hostile groups, destroy the Covenant, and thus prepare the way for war. It followed that the best way to make France feel secure was not to enter into an Anglo-French pact but to urge the policy of moderate and conciliatory action towards Germany. The arguments against the Entente, and later against military conversations, were again heard. Britain and the Empire, *The Times* said, could not afford an undefined commitment made in the interest of the security of a European Power; to make such a commitment serve, an element of secrecy would be involved. The immediate result of such commitment and secret understanding would be that France, Poland and Czechoslovakia would be encouraged in the conviction, which British opinion now held to be dangerous, that the way to preserve peace was to keep Germany down by force. The Baldwin Government, while respecting the force of these arguments, was unable to agree that the 1924 Protocol was a real improvement on the 1922 Draft Treaty. There followed discussion in the Cabinet and the enunciation by Austen Chamberlain of the doctrine, as then accepted at home, by which foreign affairs were to be regulated.[1]

[1] See below, Chapter XXII, " Imperialism; A New Phase."

A constructive proposal was soon forthcoming from an unexpected source. " The German Government has made proposals that amount to a voluntary—as opposed to a compulsory—acceptance of some of the most important clauses of the Treaty of Versailles." Williams put his greatest energies behind Chamberlain's Locarno policy. Though he was, himself, not prepared to bury the past the evolution of a new attitude towards Germany was now rapid. Not " Security " but " World Opinion," it was believed, would now enter into the regulation of international relations. " This is an event in the history of Europe. British and French diplomacy should grasp this occasion with both hands. For British diplomacy, at any rate, it is an exceptional opportunity to get out of the rut of perpetual hesitation and negation." (March 13, 1925.) The British Government set to work on an alternative to the rejected Protocol which, said Amery speaking as Colonial Secretary, " would have committed this country and the British Empire to military intervention in every conceivable conflict which might have occurred anywhere, without giving it in return any protection at all adequate in corresponding security." In conversation with the French Premier on February 26, 1925, Williams learnt that in Herriot's opinion—and he said he was extremely pacifist—the country of which he had charge must feel secure, which was not the case. He was convinced that Germany was growing stronger every day with loans that had benefited her industrialists. The nationalists were becoming stronger and the democrats weaker ; there was an evident desire for revenge. Moreover, Herriot said, the plan was that Austria should be united to Germany, and that " in a short time." He answered Williams's negative by saying yes, it would be so in two years, perhaps. He proceeded to say how important it was for all the Allies to engage in a pact, and he replied affirmatively when asked if France would include Germany in the pact. Williams then asked an important question: What about the Eastern frontiers of Germany? He added that Britain could make no commitments in that direction and that while Germany would agree to a Western pact, she would remain free in the East. Herriot astonished Williams by saying that he did believe it possible to make an arrangement with Germany about Eastern frontiers. The talk then, and after, went on pacts and protocols. These were aspirations.

The death of Milner on May 13 gave the Editor the opportunity to commemorate the achievement of the great Imperialist, and he wrote again on Dominions and Colonies on July 1. The topic came as readily to Dawson's pen as Locarno did to Williams's.

On September 26, 1925, *The Times* announced the German acceptance of an invitation to meet British, French, Belgian and Italian Ministers at Locarno. Chamberlain, therefore, met not only Benesh, Briand and others, but Stresemann also, and after much discussion agreed upon a Treaty of Mutual Guarantee that included Great Britain, France, Italy, Belgium and Germany, and envisaged the reception of Germany as a member of the League. Great optimism prevailed on October 16 when the draft was initialled. The attitude of the Dominions, however, disposed the office to remain hesitant, though ready to congratulate the Foreign Secretary.[1]

There was a change of attitude observable in Germany during the stages preliminary to the Conference, and the prospect of her inclusion in the League. The change was welcome, but the consequent optimism was soon shocked. The step Germany now took was known in advance to certain of the Locarno Powers, but it was wholly unexpected by the public, and it is not clear when precisely the office became aware of it. In December, 1925, *The Times* said that the Russians and the Germans were conversing, but it was not until April 14, 1926, that the paper was able to announce, on the basis of " several excellent sources," the pending signature of a new Russo-German Treaty. The *Berliner Tageblatt* immediately printed a firm denial that signature was imminent; though admitting it had now itself learnt that conversations had been continuing for a year. When *The Times* called it a new " reinsurance " Treaty, the Berlin paper said the term was misleading, for any Treaty to which the talks might lead would be in harmony with the League Covenant and Locarno. *The Times* was not pleased. Having championed Germany's admission to the League in the name of " fair play," the paper regretted the step and the proffered explanation. " It must be repeated that formally, so far as can be seen at present, the signatories of the Locarno Treaty can raise no objection to this step." The paper was glad to be able to say at least this. " But the fact that such a Treaty can be negotiated is a sharp reminder that events in Europe are not taking the course they were expected to take earlier in the year." The office now understood that Locarno had not really registered a change of purpose where it was most needed, and recognized that it was exceedingly awkward that such a Treaty should have been made by a new League member with a Government opposed to the League.

A quick response came from Czechoslovakia. Benesh, with the support of France, addressed a questionnaire to the

[1] See Chapter XXII, " Imperialism; A New Phase."

Locarno Powers. It appeared in public and in *The Times* before it had been received by the Berlin Embassy for transmission to the German Government, which promptly interpreted Benesh's action as an unwarrantable breach of diplomatic decorum and an interference with Germany's right to negotiate in her own way with whomsoever she pleased. *The Times* did not feel reassured when Stresemann spoke strongly against the maintenance of an occupation army of 82,000 as illogical and inconsistent with the Anglo-French policy of peace by security, and that it must be Germany's first task to regain sovereignty over German soil, and all other tasks must give way before that. In the same speech Stresemann defended his Government and the new Treaty. " We did not inform *The Times*, but when the negotiations appeared to be nearing a conclusion we informed the Powers with whom we negotiated the Pact of Locarno, and openly and loyally told them what our intentions were. It was from these diplomatic discussions that the news reached the British Press."[1] When the Treaty was signed in Berlin on April 24, 1926, it was officially described merely as an extension of Rapallo to cover the new situation created by Locarno and the German entry into the League. The only consoling factor that *The Times* could see in all this was that, apparently, the initiative came from the Russian side. The situation as a whole was now made most difficult. What had happened was that the Eastern situation had been changed by the Franco-Polish and the Polish-Rumanian Pacts of 1921, and Germany and Russia had adapted themselves to it. The result would be certain: the re-establishment of the group system. Europe was drifting into hostile camps. *The Times* continued to regret the proof that events gave of the accuracy of its forecast, and in August, on the occasion of the signature of a commercial treaty between Hungary and Czechoslovakia, the paper said that when " regional understandings " were recommended after the collapse of the Protocol, something rather different was intended. " The Locarno Treaty fulfilled expectations. Are the treaties [Germany-Russia; Germany-Austria; Russia-Turkey; Turkey-Bulgaria] which have followed it filled by the same spirit? " (August 28, 1926.)

[1] The paper's original source was the pacifist Junker, Helmuth von Gerlach, who recommended the Berlin Correspondent to read his " Peace-Paper." The Correspondent there picked up hints of the German-Russian negotiations. He mentioned the subject to the British Ambassador (D'Abernon) and was left in no doubt that talks were in progress. He duly reported his findings to Williams, who later asked the Correspondent to make the announcement " From Our Own Correspondent." As this rubric above such an item was likely, in the judgement of the Correspondent, to secure his expulsion, the announcement appeared in *The Times* without date line on April 14. The publication forced the German Foreign Office to give out the text of the Treaty. This was done next day at a specially summoned Press conference, at which Horstmann, one of the higher officials, took the Correspondent aside and told him that they had intended to keep it secret and were disappointed that *The Times* had secured news of it.

The disappointment felt was greater than the paper expressed. Locarno was a contribution to European pacification that the Foreign Secretary had taken largely on his own responsibility, without the positive cooperation of the Dominions. This was an aspect of the situation that the Editor touched upon in a leading article published in October just before the Imperial Conference of 1926. When their Report was available, the Editor congratulated the delegates on having faced the questions that beset the relations of the Empire with foreign Powers : " Are we a single unit for purposes of diplomacy ? Or half-a-dozen separate units ? In what guise do we take part in International Conferences ? How far can one nation commit its partners to the obligations which it has undertaken for itself ? " Yet, after all the laborious drafting of the experts, the " practical result " will be " precisely what we all please to make it." The " governing consideration " remained: neither Great Britain nor the Dominions could be committed to acceptance of a series of obligations except with the definite assent of their own Governments. This was agreed, as it had been agreed earlier. *The Times* thought the Conference wise not to attempt to lay down a Constitution for the British Empire. What the Conference had done was to provide " an agreed and authoritative picture of the Empire as it is." (November 22, 1926.) The Editor consistently opposed all attempts on the part of " legal pedants " to demand close definition of " dominion status," or the " right of secession," and resisted all manifestations of nationalism that might weaken the British Empire, which, in his mind, was an actual League; a League in being, with long-standing common interests, commercial and other, that could gain nothing from any attempt at codification. The Editor equally opposed all efforts to bind Britain, or the Empire, to an enforceable guarantee of all *de facto* arrangements on the Continent of Europe. Thus he was positive on the Imperial side and negative on the Continental side.

Manifestations of nationalism were by no means limited to certain parts of the British Empire. They were increasing in all parts of the old German Empire at a rate that alarmed the French. The office had taken note but, while viewing them as significant, thought them curable if the right steps were taken forthwith. *The Times* thus expressed itself after a League agreement about German disarmament:

The time has now come when the task of checking dangerous developments of German militarism must be left to other forces—to a German public opinion enlightened and reassured by a freer and closer intercourse with neighbouring nations, to a developing sense of vital common interests among the European peoples, and to the growth of international economic organization . . . [these are] the only forces that can effectively restrain the will to war in Germany or in any other civilized country. And it is this will to war that is the root of the matter. (December 13, 1926.)

Reliance upon an " enlightened German public opinion " did not impress the French then, or later. But in *The Times* reference to " World opinion " grew in frequency and significance. The steps from the " Locarno spirit " to " World opinion " and to " enlightened German public opinion " reflected the increasing value that the office was prepared to set upon the " moral " factor in Continental relations. It was a factor that was destined to be given increasing weight in Printing House Square as it dealt with France and Germany, and later with Czechoslovakia, when the Germans evoked the principle of " self-determination " to justify their attacks on the Treaty.

The English, however, had sudden cause to reduce their liabilities in the West. China had been gripped by a new nationalist, anti-foreign and anti-British movement. It led in 1925 to a severe boycott against British goods, and the Government published a statement on December 28, 1926, which was succeeded by serious anti-British rioting at Hankow on January 3, 1927. A force of Royal Marines was dispatched on the 26th, and an infantry detachment a few days later. The Government believed that the Chinese were relying upon the promise of Russian diplomatic assistance; and on January 24, 1927, the Foreign Minister of the Canton Government boldly asserted that there could be no peace between Chinese Nationalism and British Imperialism. The Chinese demand was for complete independence. In 1923 Sun Yat-sen had met Joffe, the Russian agent in Shanghai, and been promised assistance against foreign imperialism. Next Borodin began organizing the Chinese (Kuomintang) Army; also when Sun died, in March, 1925, Madame Sun became a Communist. But a year later Chiang Kai-Shek coalesced with the right wing of Kuomintang and seized power, with a policy that laid stress rather upon Nationalism than upon " Communism," and general strikes against Britain and British business firms were promptly ordered.

The Far East dispute naturally drew attention to the importance of the Navy to a great commercial country, and British opinion was less than well prepared for the call for naval disarmament simultaneously made by the American President. On February 10, 1927, Coolidge, in a note to Great Britain, France, Japan and Italy, revived the proposal for a limitation of cruisers, destroyers and submarines, as to which agreement had not been reached in 1922. The suggestion found no favour with France and Italy, who argued that naval disarmament was a part of general disarmament and could not be given separate treatment. British opinion, too, was adverse to the American plan which was understood to adopt the 5 : 5 : 3 ratio for Britain, America and Japan, with suitable ratios for the other powers. London did not see that the moment was as " opportune," as Washington claimed, for re-opening the naval question. The country's Far East obligations alone might strain the Admiralty's resources in the very class of vessel involved in the discussion. But the debt to America and unemployment at home, as hitherto, were linked to Government spending, principally on armament. Comment, therefore, was not hasty. The uncertainty of the world situation was such that, even a year before, the paper admitted that " Disarmament is not a subject that profoundly moves European opinion " (April 24, 1926), and now there was real reluctance to participate in the Conference due to take place at Geneva in June, when Britain, America and Japan were to assemble. The expectation was that there would arise from it at least a Three-Power Pact that would complete the work of the Washington Conference of 1922. In 1921, *The Times* acknowledged, there had been a risk, if not a probability, that confused developments in the Pacific might lead in time to some kind of naval conflict in which America, Japan and Great Britain might be involved. But in the context of 1927 things were so different that " certainly the need of the United States for a large navy requires more detailed elucidation than has yet been given." . . . So much so, *The Times* added, that " An explanation of the American case for a large navy would, indeed, throw great light on some of the newest problems of international security." Japan's suggestion of a security pact between the three Powers was interesting and might be a " more effective guarantee of peace than any laborious computation of naval ratios." But, concluded the paper, that would raise a new issue in United States policy.

That it was not the intention of Washington to enter into a joint security pact but to limit naval ratios in terms of classes of ship, and that to the advantage and satisfaction of American pride, was quickly made manifest. On June 26 Willmott Lewis cabled from Washington the following unwelcome and emphatic message:

It is felt strongly in responsible quarters here that a good purpose will be served by the publication abroad of the following authoritative statement: " The United States cannot and will not accept anything short of parity with Great Britain in all classes of ships.". . . The sharing of the commanding position which Great Britain has held for more than a century sets, as it were, the seal upon an American engagement to accept responsibility as a world Power. (June 27, 1927.)

This blatant demand represented, of course, the culmination and realization of the ambition of the " Big Navy " group that had been active in Washington since 1914; it was a reaffirmation of the decision taken in Washington in 1916 during the " Freedom of the Seas " controversy; it was the logical conclusion of the arguments put forward by Admiral Benson at Paris in 1919.[1] The Americans, of course, were far less interested in " responsibility " than in " parity," but few in the office, as it was constituted in 1927, cared to express their remembrance of what had happened in 1916 or 1919, and *The Times* chose to comment on Lewis's message in deliberately puzzled terms: " It is not quite intelligible here why the United States, secure beyond her oceans, requires immense battleships and a number of cruisers at least equal to our own. No doubt her authorities know." . . . Anyhow, there was no intention in Britain to enter into an " absurd naval competition with the United States." As a practical measure of reduction Great Britain had proposed smaller " big " ships; while the United States was setting a high standard of size. (June 29, 1927.) The Conference was bound to fail if it began with a large self-sufficing country's refusal to admit of a small country's special need; particularly of a small country with a large trade, importing nearly all its own food and requiring a large number of small cruisers for police work; and having on hand a dispute in the Far East.

The Conference did end in failure on August 4, 1927, and attention was again centred upon Europe. Early in 1928 *The Times* rejoiced in what it called the " middle-of-the-road " policy of Marx and Stresemann. The paper was favourable to everything that helped trade and supported the League but was unwilling to increase British liabilities for existing Continental arrangements, and remained sceptical of the value of *ententes*, eastern and western, within the League. Meanwhile the American demand for naval parity rankled. It was hoped that despite appearances nothing would come of these American proposals.

[1] As described above in Chapter IX, " The Problem of America "; see also Chapter XIV, " The Naval Treaty," above.

When, in the new year, news came of a new international projec
to " outlaw " war, *The Times* gave it a tepid welcome. In Januar
the paper thus commented upon the U.S. Government's invitatio
to France to adhere to the new Pact:

It may be extraordinary, it is perhaps not unnatural, that, in spite o
this array of treaties, pacts, covenants and declarations, a certai
nervousness or uncertainty still persists in Europe, that conviction i
not even yet firmly established that war may not at some time brea
out somewhere. This state of mind should not be entirely unintelligibl
in the United States, where Mr. Kellogg makes suggestions for th
universal rejection of war as an instrument of policy, while his colleagu
of the Navy Department sends down to Congress a Bill providing for
" very substantial sea armament " in accordance with the President'
conception of the needs of national defence. (January 6, 1928.)

The fact was that *The Times* had been forced to the conclusion that
until the League's strength was adequate in the east and the west
Britain must herself possess a force capable of defending th
Empire. In other words the office, by 1928, was reluctantly of th
opinion that " collective security " was not yet a reality. At th
same time, it became certain that, contrary to the hopes of Printin
House Square, success was about to reward the efforts of th
group in American politics and industry that had long bee
pressing Washington for increased naval appropriations. Th
Secretary for the Navy's " Big Navy " programme, introduce
on January 11, reached a formidable figure, although it wa
destined to be reduced by domestic repugnance to spending
The Times wrote sharply:

At the time of the Armistice the British Empire had a navy whic
outnumbered the combined fleets of the United States, France, Ital
and Japan. Without making bargains with other nations we scrappe
the half of it. Then came the Washington Conference, and the Britis
representative agreed at once to further great reductions. Ship afte
ship that had cost millions of pounds (and that had saved the countr
at Jutland) was broken up or sent to the bottom of the sea. There is n
need to belaud unduly the British action; it was regarded at the tim
and is still regarded, as a policy of economy and common sense natura
in the inauguration of an era of peace. But it should not be forgotten o
belittled. (January 21, 1928.)

Towards the end of the month, after the failure at Genev
already reported, Coolidge, as Lewis telegraphed on January 2
was " profoundly disturbed and greatly annoyed." He believe
that Winston Churchill and others in the Cabinet had deliberatel

decided upon a "challenge" to the United States, and had broken off the Conference accordingly. The leading article said that, in fact, the harm was done by Lord Robert Cecil's action :

The Big Navy group at Washington have found in it just the political weapon which they wanted. . . . There can be no doubt that this [Cecil's] criticism of our Government's attitude on that occasion has greatly influenced American opinion in favour of the programme for a very substantial sea armament, and has strengthened the anti-British tendencies of its advocates. (January 30, 1928.)

The moral was that it was " of the greatest importance for the immediate future of the world that political contact between the British Empire and the United States should be full, frequent, and easy . . . the methods for promoting political intercourse cannot be invented in a day." The paper added in reversal of its previously expressed opinion the statement that " The Dominions can help, particularly Canada." (January 30, 1928.) Almost simultaneously, *The Times* found it necessary to admit that " His Majesty's Government in Great Britain is in far closer relationship, so far as effective organization goes, with Berlin or with Washington than with Ottawa." (February 1, 1928.) It was evident enough, League or no League, that neither Britain nor Europe could regain prosperity without American and Canadian assistance; also that both these transatlantic countries could only remain prosperous with a healthy Europe. Hence Britain finally agreed on July 19, 1928, to the Pact of Paris, by which war as an instrument of government policy was " renounced." It was later adhered to by 15 Western nations and was ultimately signed by Coolidge and Kellogg on January 17, 1929, and by Soviet Russia, Poland, Esthonia and Rumania on February 9. The Pact known as the Pact of Paris, or Kellogg Pact, came into force on July 24, 1929.

These events coincided with the completion of a number of important changes in the editorial department at Printing House Square that had been begun in the spring of 1927. In April the Editor negotiated for the return from the *Observer* of Robert M. Barrington-Ward, M.C., D.S.O., who had been Editorial Secretary, and Home and Foreign sub-editor from 1913 until 1914 when he enlisted. Barrington-Ward rejoined on October 10 with the understanding that he would be the paper's principal leader-writer on home affairs and miscellaneous domestic topics. By coincidence, at the time Barrington-Ward reappeared in the office Gordon Robbins resigned in order to accept a responsible and lucrative appointment in the large and prosperous general publishing business directed and controlled by Sir Ernest Benn. The consequent vacancy enabled the Editor to give Barrington-Ward the position of Assistant Editor. Thus the man who had been engaged as a principal leader-writer taken from a weekly newspaper was forthwith given a responsible administrative position in succession to a man of marked experience in daily journalism Barrington-Ward's earlier period of service had been so slight that he was virtually a stranger to daily newspaper work when he rejoined in October, 1927. He promptly proved his capacity to stand the test equally as leader-writer and administrator. It was no small achievement for a newcomer to go so far in so short a time to repair the loss that the paper sustained by the resignation of Robbins. Barrington-Ward, however, had come with the primary purpose of writing on home affairs. He was from the first an eager, prompt and versatile writer able to tackle party topics, incidental events, ceremonial occasions and all manner of day-to-day comment. As a man of principle he was able to convey conviction to the high degree that he felt it, and was much at home in work that involved the enunciation of doctrine. Dawson took pride in the selection of this recruit and was quick to make use of his colleague's peculiarly swift power of analysis, telling construction of phrase and capacity to provide, at short notice, leaders of pith and point, obviously the work of a writer with an ambition to have his work read and remembered.

The personal relation between the two men was close, though their domestic and political attitudes were not identical, for while both were convinced Conservatives, Barrington-Ward had a radical streak which his chief lacked. As to foreign policy, they found that they saw " eye to eye " on Germany and on Continental affairs. After Barrington-Ward had been in the office a year Dominion subjects became the Editor's main preoccupation except during 1928 when, as a stalwart supporter of the religion preferred by the English governing class, he championed the new text of the *Book of Common Prayer* in a large number of leading articles. The Editor was a close friend of the leading proponents of the revised *Book*, and he was greatly disappointed when an Erastian Commons rejected it on doctrinal grounds by 266 to 220 It was a result that Barrington-Ward privately approved. In his opinion—he seldom missed Sunday Church—the Christian religion was far too precious an inheritance, and much too important a moral element in English life to be compromised by association with the magic and superstition of sacramentalism to the extent it was manifested in the 1928 *Book*. An interpretation of Christianity freed from the miraculous would render it valid for our time, since it would emancipate the modern mind from outworn dogma and enable a clear view to be taken of its true and unique content: the moral teaching of a human Christ. Thus would the intelligent section of the community be reconciled to the established Church as one of the monarchical institutions of the country, and enable it to play a greater part in the reconstruction of a country in need, among other social cohesives, of ethical inspiration. Emphasis upon ethics was rooted in Barrington-Ward's character. It forbade him to consider national or international action in terms of material power separated from a higher principle than itself. For him politics was not to be dissociated from ethics; but both, rather, seen and respected as two aspects of the same human activity. Barrington-Ward possessed a full share of that purposefulness that distinguishes the Puritan, and to him journalism was less a profession than a vocation, literally a " calling," and therefore a means of doing, or getting done, something of which the righteous-minded community felt the need. The tendency, already noted, to recognize after the war the emergence of an independent factor variously described as " a standard of honour," " the rule of ethics," " enlightened World opinion," " international morality," found in Barrington-Ward a fervent apostle. After his return *The Times* urged more insistently than before the significance of the ethical factor, above all in its relation to the Treaty of Versailles as affecting Germany.

Thus, when on October 10, 1927, the Editor welcomed Barrington-Ward, and knew he had strengthened the office by the attachment of a zestful and versatile man, it immediately became clear that the new writer, engaged to deal with home topics, entertained convictions about Continental affairs.[1] He was quick to discuss international relations with Harold Williams from whom, too, he was not afraid to differ even on the two basic questions: Russia and Germany. Barrington-Ward judged Williams to be too fixed in opposition to the Bolsheviks— forgivably, he admitted, in view of his personal experiences. As to Germany, he found Williams, even after Locarno, too unyielding. At this time Barrington-Ward was already in frequent conversation with Bernstorff, Dieckhoff and Dufour of the German Embassy in London, and found it convenient to maintain the association. He had at this time solid convictions about the viability of the chief Succession States, Poland and Czechoslovakia, and had already made up his mind, after talks with Benesh, that the minority question had not been settled. Barrington-Ward liked Williams, although his views were different from his own, and it is

[1] B.-W. had written regularly on these subjects for the *Observer*.

regrettable that the latter's health began to fail within a year of Barrington-Ward's arrival in the office.

Williams fell ill early in June, 1928. Flanagan, too, broke down at the same time. Casey had one of his colds but " Barrington-Ward," Dawson noted, " has been a tower of strength, a good administrator, full of initiative, and finding time to help me with two or three excellent and important leaders."[1] The office was still short of men in the late autumn. In November Williams returned, apparently well. On the 5th he wrote a leader, and next day collapsed. He died a fortnight later, and to *The Times*, said the obituary, " his loss is irreparable." It entailed upon the Editor the necessity of providing a head for the Foreign Department, obviously one of the most important of all editorial positions. It had been occupied in turn by men who generally took rank, in the view of the office, and of the world, next to the Editor; on occasion circumstances made the Foreign Editor even more important than the Editor himself.

The post had been originated in 1890 soon after Moberly Bell took in hand the task of re-planning the foreign side of the paper. Arthur Walter and Moberly Bell decided that *The Times* needed a " specialist " in foreign diplomacy, and found him in Donald Mackenzie Wallace, who became in 1891 " Foreign Assistant Editor," and later " Director of the Foreign Department." As such he directed the Department until the end of 1898 when his assistant, Valentine Chirol, was appointed in his place with the same title. He conducted the Department for fourteen years, until his resignation in the circumstances described in Volume III. At this time Northcliffe authorized the renaming of the old " Colonial Department " and the creation of the Imperial and Foreign News Department. He also proposed to mark off a European Department under Steed, who was about to leave Vienna. Northcliffe did not then proceed with the creation of the European Department, and the war postponed further action. Steed, when ultimately appointed, was called " Foreign Editor," but the title that Stuart gave his successor, Harold Williams, was that of Wallace and Chirol. Williams accepted the title, but was indifferent to its use, and was equally satisfied with the title of " Foreign Editor," or none at all.

In the earlier period the Manager had organized intelligence from foreign agencies and correspondence, as William Delane had organized the " Extraordinary Express " from India with the

---

[1] Dawson, Notes on the Staff, August, 1928; in view of his cumbrous surname, B.-W.'s initials only, as used in all office conversation, are given in the rest of this book.

HAROLD WILLIAMS

assistance of Thomas Waghorn in 1838. The practice of *The Times*, even in Delane's time, was to recruit the Foreign staff through the Chief Proprietor and his agent the Manager. Thus Moberly Bell appointed Wallace with the support of Arthur Walter, and against the inclination of Buckle. It was only when it appeared that Wallace could also write leading articles that Buckle became reconciled to the arrangement. Bell also recruited Chirol in 1892 and, with Wallace's approval, appointed him to succeed in 1899. It was Bell, too, who recruited Steed (on the introduction of Chirol) and appointed him to the Foreign staff in 1896. The Editor's approval of these appointments was implicitly assumed rather than explicitly secured. The practice continued throughout Bell's tenure of the managerial office, and it was upon his advice that Northcliffe agreed to put Steed in charge of Europe, again with the assumed concurrence of Buckle. In this instance the Editor remonstrated, unavailingly however, when the appointment was actually made by Bell's successor, Nicholson. The old practice was continued by Campbell Stuart who appointed Harold Williams in 1922 without notice to Steed, whose agreement he rightly assumed, since Steed had brought Williams into the office.

A complete reversal of policy, therefore, was implied when the new Proprietorship of *The Times* accepted Dawson's definition of the Editor's and the Manager's respective positions. The Editor disinterested himself completely in the salaries and conditions of work of his colleagues and left these entirely to the Manager. For this reason only was the latter bound to concern himself with the functions of the Assistant Editor, leader-writers, sub-editors and other members of the department. In other respects the Manager was henceforth a housekeeper responsible for the charges for advertising, the sale of the paper and its Supplements, the process of printing and the costs of production, and the staffs responsible for these departments, while the Proprietors remained a court of appeal. *The Times*, an institution before Northcliffe came, was a trusteeship now that he had gone. The new Proprietors transferred to the Editor of their choice all the power over policy exercised by the late " Chief." The Editor not merely possessed power to a degree unknown to his predecessors but to an extent impossible for himself, even by delegation, to exercise; and, so far from recognizing the necessity to surrender power, he was temperamentally inclined to take more of it. He concerned himself with the financial health of the paper, its profits, the presentation of the paper to the public and the circulation, as well as the means by which it was promoted. The

Editor was accustomed, for his own guidance, to make regular notes and memoranda on all these topics. The work, doubtless, came easily to the former Estates Bursar of All Souls College, Oxford, and the ex-Director of the Consolidated Goldfields of South Africa, and the late Secretary to the Rhodes Trust ; other sides of the editorial burden, such as recruiting, which came less easily, were followed up with less enthusiasm. In 1929, as in 1923, he viewed the constitution of Printing House Square as an office consisting of one sole Editor and one sole Manager. It was true that the news trade had become accustomed to extensions of the titles " Editor " and " Manager," and that *The Times* office itself was now familiar with an " Art Editor " who looked after the picture page that Northcliffe and Stuart had introduced; also there was an " Advertisement Manager " who attracted revenue from that source; and heads of departments were commonly addressed by titles that would not have been admitted before Northcliffe's time. These, Dawson thought, were vernacularisms and meant nothing. It was otherwise with the title of " Director of the Foreign Department," which reached back nearly forty years.

Stuart's rearrangement of the News Department had been adversely criticized by Dawson during the conversations preliminary to his return but, when appointed, he had not seen fit to alter them. Among these was a reorganization of the duties of the men responsible for sorting, reading and recording news that was telegraphed or telephoned from home and abroad direct by the paper's Correspondents, or indirectly by agencies. Dawson agreed in 1923 that a department responsible for all oversea news, whether from the Continent, Dominions or elsewhere, was necessary. Thus was the " Imperial and Foreign News Department," with a staff of its own, made permanent. But there was an important distinction. Whereas in the past the Manager and, more recently, the Managing Director, had been responsible for the organization of the news services, the constitution accepted in 1923 gave this responsibility to the Editor or his delegate. This, therefore, was the situation from 1923 until the end of 1928, when Harold Williams died. In the circumstances in which he found himself the Editor was slow to make up his mind about a successor. At the time of Williams's death the Editor was about to leave for India to study the constitutional issues that were coming to the forefront of Dominion politics.[1] A division of the foreign work between three leader-writers was adopted as a temporary measure. While Dawson was away both Brumwell

[1] See Chapter XXII, " Imperialism; A New Phase," *post.*

and Barrington-Ward reported that the substitutes were doing well at their tasks.

On his return in the spring, the Editor said he would cast round for a new Wallace, Chirol or Steed, as the office contained nobody capable of being promoted to the post. Wallace knew India as well as he knew Russia and Europe. Chirol knew China and Japan as well as India and Europe; he also had some knowledge of the United States. Steed's knowledge extended to all European countries with the exception of Russia, and to the United States. Williams possessed an exceptionally wide knowledge of Europe and Russia, and a special knowledge of the Pacific. The available leader-writers, competent as they were, could not be compared with any of these. The makeshift arrangement which Brumwell and B.-W. reported to Dawson as working satisfactorily at the time was one by which the leaders on foreign affairs were undertaken by those who knew the countries by experience, and had maintained contact with the political personalities in the respective capitals. Thus, one writer suitably equipped became responsible for leaders on the East, *i.e.*, from the Balkans to India; a second specialized in Western Europe and the League; a third supplemented both. A fourth wrote on Dominion affairs and Anglo-American relations, and a fifth assisted with African and Colonial problems. In the autumn of 1928 W. F. Casey, formerly of the Paris and Washington offices and until now chief Foreign sub-editor, was promoted to the foreign leader-writing staff. A welcome reinforcement was D. D. Braham, who returned after 16 years in Australia. In his earlier period he had written on foreign affairs, but now specialized in economics and currency questions. He was the one new source of strength that the office could report at this period; and the Editor had yet to find a man of mature judgement, versed in foreign affairs, eastern and western, able and willing to write leading articles at short notice, and capable of instructing leader-writers and revising their articles. Dawson decided, in the summer of 1929, that he would make permanent the temporary arrangement that had operated since the previous winter. It was a decision of vital importance, involving the suppression of the problem of Foreign Editor, and entailing important consequences to the foreign policy of the paper. It was the most important decision of Dawson's second innings and most deliberately reached.

To abolish the office and title of Foreign Editor or the equivalent was the logical decision for him. The editorial staff of a newspaper, he believed, could not be organized in a rigid hierarchy.

The positions in it needed to be elastic since in reality they depended upon individual capacities and interests; and these were liable to change. Thus he made a principle of improvisation, the essential point in journalism being that men should write on subjects that they had made their own, while the essential point in editing was that all policy, selection and appointment of writers and correspondents, like all power over the acceptance or otherwise of their contributions, should remain in the hands of the Editor. He rejected the idea that foreign policy by its nature required that a man be set aside to give his whole time to the study of its complexities, and preferred to rely upon his personal intuitions.

The Editor's chief colleagues took a different view of the needs of the office and of the newspaper. The Assistant Editors, Brumwell and B.-W., both firmly urged the necessity of filling the position. The Editor does not appear to have opened his mind to his colleagues any farther than to emphasize the difficulty of finding the right type of man for the job. There is no sign, however, that he made serious enquiry in any direction. The subject was raised more than once by the Assistant Editors, but until the time of his retirement in 1941, Dawson chose to take responsibility for the foreign, as for other sides, of the paper. The Editor considered himself able efficiently to formulate policy, occasionally write, instruct and correct leader-writers, secure special contributions, circulate among political and other groups, make visits abroad, assure himself of adequate holidays and recreation, and simultaneously be responsible " just as much for the presentation of news, letters and pictures, and the ' captions ' etc., as for the opinions expressed by the paper "; also to be " ultimately responsible for the selection of his assistants at home and abroad, and for the allocation of their duties "; and on top of all this to supervise, shunt, promote and recruit his staff. No such burden had been borne by Barnes, Delane, Buckle, Dawson in his early period, or even Steed ; or by any former Editor of *The Times*.

While Dawson thus widened the range of his editorial authority he was, at the same time, adding to his moral authority over writers by himself writing very frequently and always admirably. After the first year of his second term he had worked himself back into his stride as a daily journalist and had since borne the brunt of writing the more important leading articles that pronounced upon home and Dominion affairs. For this task Dawson was from the first exceptionally well informed, and wrote confidently and convincingly. He was never equally competent in foreign affairs. On the contrary, he had no natural interest in Continental tensions and, as has been seen, knew none of the leading personalities, had never read recent European political history and knew no foreign language. On the German question he had slight knowledge, though his convictions were solid. They amounted in 1929 to what they had been since 1923. He saw no reason to believe that the Allies had been economically defeated by the obstructive tactics of Germany; rather he was one of the many who thought that the pacification of Europe and the restoration of British industry might already have been accomplished but for the recalcitrance of the French and their unwise treatment of the Germans. Dawson seldom wrote on such topics, however, and was glad to leave them to Williams. From 1929, apart from employing leader-writers upon the topicalities of Franco-German and League affairs, the Editor grew accustomed to rely for his important " policy " leaders, foreign and also home, upon B.-W. This represented a notable change in office habits. The office was changing in other important respects.

The year 1929 marked notable losses from the staff. Chirol, who had corresponded on foreign affairs since 1892, died on October 22, 1929. His last contributions appeared posthumously. Flanagan, who had been writing leading articles since 1886, died on November 16, 1929. His last piece of writing was a leader on the powers of Ministers which appeared on November 1. Flanagan had, like Chirol, Saunders and Steed, lived and worked through the whole of the period from 1900 to 1914 which saw the re-orientation of British foreign policy under Lansdowne and Grey. Flanagan had himself written most of the leading articles on foreign policy during the development of the grouping of the powers, and was responsible, under Steed, for the " crisis " leaders of 1914. He had done less writing of this kind during Williams's tenure of the Foreign editorship and it was unfortunate that they both died within the same twelve-month. The double loss caused more than a regrettable gap in the staff: it had as its consequence a serious breach in the continuity of the thought of Printing House Square, above all on the German question. The attitude of the paper towards Germany, like the attitude of the country, had changed significantly since Locarno. The rejection of the Protocol had inevitably led Britain to help the pacification of Europe by redressing grievances in conference, particularly those of Germany. It was a policy that came naturally to the Editor and he had no hesitation in personally championing it. The difference in the policy of *The Times* towards Germany in the years from 1908 to 1914, and in the years from 1928 to 1939, is simply stated: in the former period the paper habitually led public opinion, in the latter it habitually followed it. There were two reasons for this. First, as has been seen, Dawson had from the beginning of his second term favoured " steadiness," or even " stodginess "; the practice of " startling the public," as familiarized by Northcliffe and Steed was abandoned. Secondly, as will be seen in the next chapter, the public, having been soothed by a period of " steadiness " in the leading articles of *The Times*, allowed itself to be led by utopians of various sorts, until the paper itself became utopian, faithfully reflecting the views of a Government which, as the most ruthless realist knew, was in touch with the trend in the constituencies. That trend was pro-German; and not only in the constituencies.

The voice of public opinion was so clear that the Editor might well argue that there was no need for a Foreign Editor. Dawson took the decision to abolish the position of Foreign Editor in July, 1929. An event in the first week of that month pointed the direction that *The Times* would take during the next ten years towards Anglo-German relations. On the 5th there was celebrated in Oxford the 25th anniversary of the establishment of the Rhodes scholarship system. The gathering included about 200 Rhodes Scholars from the Commonwealth, the United States and Germany. The Chairman, the senior Trustee, was Baldwin, at the time the leader of the Conservative Party that had been defeated by Labour in the preceding May. He said that " for some time "[1] the Trustees had been considering the renewal of the German Scholarships established by Rhodes. "Almost ten years have now passed since the Peace Treaty was signed, and the Trustees believe that the removal of misunderstandings and the promotion of friendship between German- and English-speaking peoples by educational means is even more important than it was when Mr. Rhodes added that codicil to his will."[2] Baldwin was followed by the Prince of Wales who, as a Magdalen man, testified to the pleasure " he had that evening of shaking hands with a Magdalen man who is a German Rhodes Scholar whom I have not

[1] Probably since the beginning of the year, for the Rhodes Trust Act amending the provisions of Rhodes's will and giving the Trustees further powers received the Royal Assent on May 10, 1929. The extension of the powers of the Trustees which enabled them to renew the German scholarships was thus provided for.

[2] The original codicil was dated January, 1901: " I note the German Emperor has made instruction in English compulsory in German schools. I leave five yearly scholarships at Oxford of £250 per annum to students of German birth, the scholars to be nominated by the German Emperor for the time being. Each scholarship to continue for three years so that each year after the first three, there will be fifteen scholars. The object is that an understanding between the three Great Powers [Britain and the Commonwealth, the United States and Germany] will render war impossible and educational relations make the strongest tie. C. J. RHODES." See the *Will and Codicils of the Rt. Hon. Cecil John Rhodes, etc.*, Oxford, 1929, p. 15.

seen since 1914." Among those present were the Trustees who, beside Baldwin, were L. S. Amery, Otto Beit, H. A. L. Fisher, Lord Hailsham, E. R. Peacock and Geoffrey Dawson. The Secretary to the Trustees, in succession to Dawson, was Philip Kerr, later Lord Lothian. A few days after the report of this function there appeared in *The Times* a leading article written by the Editor commenting upon it:

In so far as there was any conscious incursion into international affairs it was in the announcement made by Mr. Baldwin, the presiding Trustee, that a fresh start was to be made in allotting Rhodes Scholarships to Germans, some of whom, dating from pre-War days, were present to hear it. Of that wise decision it is sufficient here to say that the unanimous approval with which it has been greeted, by these assembled representatives of every quarter of the English-speaking world, is its sufficient justification. (July 9, 1929.)

The proceedings at Oxford were prominently reported in the German Press. The *Vossische Zeitung* was happy to see " Another War chapter closed," and *Germania* recognized the event as a symptom of the re-awakening of international solidarity and of Anglo-German friendship.

To the conception of the relation between the two countries that underlay the renewal of the German Rhodes Scholarships *The Times* was destined to remain faithful for ten years. The act had met with an approval that was " unanimous." It had even been sponsored by an ex-Prime Minister and by the Prince of Wales, both speaking on the same platform in the optimism generated by the agreement on the total evacuation of the Rhineland, and the prospects of a Five-Power Naval Conference. The latter half of the year was, in fact, relatively peaceful. Stresemann's death on October 3 was greatly regretted, as also the fall of Briand later in the month. The collapse of the New York Stock Exchange on October 28 was alarming, but the important political news of the month was the Viceroy of India's pronouncement on Dominion Status on the 31st.[1] The appointment on November 4 of the Macmillan Committee on Finance and Industry was followed ten days later by a decision to slow down work on the Singapore base. On December 18 the Government succeeded with their Bill for Unemployment Insurance providing, at the cost of £12½ million, for increased allowances and the extension of the transitional period. The year ended gloomily.

---

[1] See Chapter XXII, " Imperialism ; A New Phase," *post*.

The New Year opened with news of importance. On January 21, 1930, the London Naval Conference prepared the way for the announcement on April 22 of the Three-Power Treaty between the United Kingdom, United States and Japan. By this time the effects of the financial crisis in America were being felt all over Europe, and for the March quarter the number of registered unemployed in Britain rose to 1,677,473, which was the highest for eight years. The same thing happened in Germany. The political situation of that country was recognized to have been greatly aggravated by the sudden death of Stresemann in the previous October. On June 29, 1930, the evacuation of the Rhineland was completed in accordance with the Hague Conference decision. This, however, was not enough to strengthen the Brüning Government. It was unable to with-stand the concerted opposition of the Social Democrats, the Communists and the Hitler-Hugenberg Nationalist coalition. When the election for the new Reichstag was held on September 14, 1930, the voting was sensational. The total number of votes cast, 31 million in 1928, rose to 35 million in 1930. The Social Democrats lost half a million; the Communists gained a quarter of a million; the outstanding and menacing feature was the increase of the Hitler vote from 800,000 to $6\frac{1}{2}$ million and the gain of 107 seats. The Weimar Republic was in a state of collapse when on November 14 the Imperial Conference closed with a postponement of the Empire Trade issue to a new Conference to be held at Ottawa.[1]

The office looked forward to the first great Disarmament Conference fixed for February 2, 1932. To the accompaniment of an outbreak at Shanghai, the Conference listened to Germany's demand for equal treatment. As a disarmed country, she demanded armaments to the standard adopted, whether great or small. Germany sought to emancipate herself from the Versailles ban by a device that had proved successful six years before. In 1919 she had been forbidden all air activity and all manu-facture of aeroplanes. In 1922, when the ban was partially lifted, she sought to circumvent the manufacturing and designing restrictions then imposed by the Council of Ambassadors. It was part of the understanding reached on April 14, 1922, that the Allies, as long as occupation lasted, were to enjoy the same facilities that were granted to the German air industry. The Germans were thus able legally to limit the Allies to the extent the Allies limited them. The reaction of the airlines was naturally

---

[1] See Chapter XXII, " Imperialism; A New Phase."

unfavourable, and commercial arguments finally secured the Paris Air Agreement of May 22, 1926, which removed all restrictions on German aircraft. Thus German civil aircraft building and training took place in thorough measure under the direction of Captain Ernst Brandenburg, who had led the heavy London daylight raid of 40 Gothas on June 13, 1917. Already in 1931, the German Air Force existed with training grounds in Russia.[1] The important German armament event of the time, however, was the launching on May 19, 1931, of the *Deutschland*. Her design had been a matter of some controversy since she was on the stocks. When she was launched in the spring of 1931 she was found, in the judgement of *The Times* Naval Correspondent, to be " the most formidable ship in existence." On the day before the launching the Naval Correspondent said that

she is fast enough to decline action with any existing capital ships, most of which have a maximum speed of 23 knots, but she is also strong enough to destroy any existing cruiser, the armaments in which class are limited by the Washington and London Treaties to 8-in. or 6-in. guns. (May 18, 1931.)

Foreign Press representatives had great difficulties in obtaining information, or in being present at the function. Thus, at this time, while Germany was strengthening herself, Britain and the other " victorious " countries were allowing their armaments to become obsolescent in the name of peace and economy. There was no comment, for the moment, in the leading columns of *The Times*, on the German naval achievement. The Hoover plan of a moratorium on inter-governmental debts, to which Britain agreed on June 22, was speedily acted upon. *The Times* published a leading article which appealed to Germany not to proceed with her naval programme:

If Germany has any mind to contribute to the consolidation of Europe she has the opportunity now. Help has been given to her without conditions. Can she not show her appreciation by a small voluntary act of renunciation, such as an undertaking not to continue, during the period of the Hoover moratorium, the construction of the *Ersatz-Lothringen* [the second " pocket battleship"][2]? (July 9, 1931.)

On the benign assumption that Germany was interested in obeying the territorial and other articles of the Treaty, and was conducting a policy of complete fulfilment, the writer proceeded to say, in words fully in accord with the vague idealism generated in Britain by the League, and the League Union, but chosen with a

[1] C. G. Grey, *Luftwaffe*, p. 59.
[2] Later renamed *Admiral Scheer*.

degree of naivety remarkable for Printing House Square even in
1931: " The psychological value of such an undertaking would
be much greater than any possible value which the ship will have
when built." He proceeded to say, what was undoubtedly true,
that

compared with those of other countries of equal importance the German
Navy, limited by the terms of the Peace Treaty, is extremely weak; and
unfortunately the chief consequence of building up to the Treaty
limits seems likely to be the further construction of rather more
powerful vessels in other fleets.

The fact, as stated by the Naval Correspondent on May 18, was that
the Treaty of London which limited British building expired in
1936. By that time Germany would have a squadron of fast
11-in. battleships in the water. Germany would not then be so
" extremely weak." The leader-writer thus struggled to find
some ground for optimism:

It has indeed been one of the few happy signs of decreasing mistrust
between France and Germany that the estimates for a ship to outclass
the " pocket battleship " were drastically reduced by the French
Chamber in a recent vote. But the motives for reducing the appropriation were mixed; and the fact remains that there is a definite danger of
naval competition between France and Germany if the construction of
the Treaty ships continues.

There was, indeed, " danger." France had the gold as well
as the will, and her decision to reduce her vote for ships was
a device to give Germany an opportunity of reducing her rate
and speed of building. The French reason for hoping that
Germany might do this was not " psychological." The Paris
Correspondent reported that the French attitude was
" hardening." France was not to be taken as being willing to
abandon her demands already formulated. She objected to the
" pocket battleship " programme and to the projected Austro-
German Customs Union. By an unkind coincidence the British
Navy paid its first visit since the war to Kiel, where, by another
coincidence, there was a German officer ready to assure the
English that he felt at home with them, as kinsmen.

Eight weeks after the launching of the *Deutschland*, the German
financial crisis became acute; banks closed; the rate of interest
was raised from 7 to 10 per cent., and even to 15 per cent. At
home, gold losses now reached a critical point, and on August 8
the Bank of England issued a strong appeal to the Prime Minister

for economy. Meanwhile Britain was given another opportunity to manifest her admiration for German technical ability. On August 19, 1931, the *Graf Zeppelin* made a successful flight over London and descended at Hanworth. Dr. Eckener, her pilot, was ceremoniously met by the Under-Secretary of State for Air, E. S. Montagu, who presented him with a gold box, inscribed. A leading article celebrated this " hopeful omen for the future," and when the airship left for her return flight, Dr. Eckener was handed a number of copies of *The Times* " with the compliments of the Proprietors."[1] Plans involving a proposed 10 per cent. cut in the unemployment dole led to a split in the Cabinet, and on August 24 the resignation of the Ministry was announced. The formation of a National Government followed and the Bank succeeded on August 28 in borrowing from France and the U.S.A. On September 15 there were further withdrawals of gold from the Bank, and on September 21 the Bank abandoned the gold standard. On September 29 the League Assembly adopted a resolution for one year's armaments truce as from November 1. While the financial crisis was worsening in Britain and Germany, the British National Government, divided as it was between Socialists and anti-Socialists, sought a solution to its internal troubles by going to the country. A General Election was welcomed by *The Times*. The paper thus defined the issue:

This General Election is being fought primarily to secure a definite and unqualified result—namely, the resounding repudiation of Socialist irresponsibility. . . . This election will be the supreme test of democracy in two respects. It will test the common sense of the electorate in returning a House of Commons which will save the country beyond a peradventure from the Socialist policy of insolvency. It will test the sincerity and the ability of that House of Commons itself to justify the peculiar degree of trust which it will have demanded from the electorate by pursuing with unprejudiced determination any and every method of restoring our national solvency. (October 9, 1931.)

That the importance of the election was recognized in the country was demonstrated by the volume of correspondence received by the Editor during the month. Confidence in the response of the electorate was justified. A " crushing victory " had been secured by the National Government. The following day *The Times* considered the results :

The power of the British people to grasp economic truths—and their courage in facing unpalatable truths—is the first unquestionable fact which emerges from this election. But it is equally beyond question

[1] Report in *The Times*, August 20, 1931.

that this power would not have been revealed to so magnificent an extent if the election had been fought on party lines. The second and even more important conclusion, therefore, is that this victory is a National victory and not a party victory, and that conclusion is proved by every subsidiary circumstance. . . . The verdict of the electorate is therefore as deliberate as it is decisive. These enormous majorities do not mean that people have voted blindly anti-Labour or anti-free trade or anti- any of the minor issues of politics. They mean, broadly speaking, that the nation has passed judgement on leaders who got into difficulties; who admitted the difficulties, and then (all but a courageous handful) ran away from them; and who finally strove to escape judgement by fighting the election on the crudest cries of class and party. (October 29, 1931.)

The composition of the Cabinet was the important question next day:

That there must be reconstruction on a large scale goes without saying. The Cabinet of Ten was an appropriate body for dealing with the immediate crisis of the Budget; but there are strong practical objections to keeping it at that figure permanently. Public administration in these days has become so complex, delegation to Cabinet committees so frequent and so necessary, the case for securing a broad backing for Cabinet decisions so important that the efficiency to be derived from small numbers is probably more apparent than real.

After expressing regret that Snowden was leaving the Exchequer, the Editor referred in his leader to the guesses of the gossips as to his successor, and noted the curious omission of Baldwin's name, " the best choice of all if he would take it." He continued:

One further point is worth emphasis in this process of reconstructing the Government. The broad purpose which is commonly described as the restoration of the balance of trade will require for its achievement during the next few months an unusual number of conferences with the Dominions and with foreign countries; there will be occasion for innumerable special inquiries outside the regular routine of administration; the Indian Round Table requires incessant statesmanship already; commissions of the most vital character will call for chairmen of Cabinet calibre. . . . The new Government would be far better equipped for its gigantic task if two at least of its most competent members were to be held in reserve, without even a sinecure portfolio for the duties of a " flying squad." (October 30, 1931.)

Names put forward were Sir John Simon and Sir Robert Horne and when *The Times* gave the constitution of the new Cabinet on November 6, 1931, Simon was assigned to the Foreign Office. On this appointment the paper observed that " a great lawyer of brilliant practical attainments will be in charge of our relations with foreign countries during a period in which negotiations with those countries must be of the very highest intricacy and importance." The Cabinet as a whole was approved in Printing House Square. Baldwin, who was Dawson's " best choice of all " for the Exchequer, was in as Lord President, and Neville Chamberlain was Chancellor of the Exchequer. Churchill was excluded. The Editor's judgement was thus summarized:

The only question which arises out of the list is whether the Cabinet is likely to prove harmonious enough to give an early and definite interpretation to the policy of the " free hand " and strong enough to translate that interpretation into effective action. The answer is, in the first place, that the list is the Prime Minister's own choice, that he has chosen only men who have made a considerable sacrifice of party interests in the past, who are broadly agreed upon the nature of the tasks to be accomplished, and who have all agreed to approach them with minds unbiased by the past. So far as the seeds of future disunion can be eliminated, the Prime Minister has clearly done his best to eliminate them. (November 6, 1931.)

Dawson was personally delighted at the return to high office of his colleague on the Rhodes Trust, Baldwin, in whose ability, common sense and integrity, if not his industry, he reposed complete faith. Events in both continents emphasized the vital and urgent importance of economic rehabilitation. The year 1932 opened inauspiciously, first with an announcement by Bulgaria of her impending default on external obligations. This was followed by an Austrian default. The March election for the German presidency registered another step forward by the Nazis. Hindenburg received 18 million votes, but Hitler received as many as 11 million. The point of difference was that Brüning had supported Hindenburg because he expected him to favour his Government as he had done before; and Hitler, while not objecting in principle to the old President, disliked, on grounds of party tactics, his being nominated by Brüning and the Social Democrats. The election was hardly over before the Brüning Government's policy, which included cuts in the German unemployment dole, failed. Thereupon Hindenburg called upon von Papen who was thought to be assured of the support of Hitler. Papen's first act was to dissolve the Reichstag. The general election, which ensued in July, gave the Nazis 230 seats, the Social Democrats 133 and the Communists 89. The portent was clear, Hitler had won many new recruits. As in previous months not a few Nationalist demonstrations had disturbed the peace during the spring of 1932. The first of April witnessed an event that lifted the pride of the jingo type of German to a new high level of patriotic emotion. April 1 was a great German naval occasion. It has been seen that the *Deutschland* was launched in 1931. She was now commissioned and Bismarck's birthday was selected as the appropriate anniversary. Moreover, on the same day a second ship of the same type was launched and a third was announced to be on the stocks. At the function at Kiel, Admiral Raeder, who had been Chief of the Admiralty since 1928, spoke. He referred to Scapa Flow where " our magnificent fleet preferred a willing death to ignominious surrender," and evoked the spirit of Jutland which was " a symbol of the nation's future." The new battleship was then named by the daughter of Admiral Scheer, upon whose grave a wreath dedicated to " The Victor of Jutland " was presently laid. The event was reported in *The Times* (April 3, 1933) but not commented upon. The design of the *Deutschland* became of public interest. Her main features were already known to naval architects and strategists. It was later confirmed that to be within the limit of 10,000 tons set by the Treaty, armour had given way to speed and guns so that she might be too fast to be overtaken, and too powerful to be tackled by any other cruiser. She was the first to save weight on rivets by adopting electric welding, and the first large battleship to be motor-driven. The *Deutschland* type, the so-called pocket battleship, was designed with Britain in view as the probable enemy, and the fact made obvious by Admiral Raeder. The point, however, was not taken up by *The Times*, although the *Deutschland* was, as the Naval Correspondent had said in 1931, " the most formidable ship in existence."[1]

It was not known, or at least not believed, in the office that Germany was also secretly evading the stipulations of the Treaty ; that whatever the political, economic or social changes that Germany had undergone since her defeat, she was steadily increasing her air, military and naval strength beyond the limits set by Versailles. The Editor's attention was distracted by the moral nausea felt by everybody outside Germany at recent attacks, surpassing all previous brutalities, upon the Jews, with which the exultant Nazis celebrated their victory at the elections. They did not, however, have a clear majority, and Hindenburg did not see fit to make Hitler Chancellor. The lack of a clear majority

[1] In 1939 the *Deutschland* (1933), *Admiral Scheer* (1934), and *Admiral Graf Spee* (1936), were already reported as responsible for numerous sinkings of British ships. The *Graf Spee* was engaged in the River Plate action and took refuge in Montevideo. On December 17 she left neutral waters and blew herself up. (See *The Times*, December 18, 1939). The *Scheer* was sunk at Kiel by the R.A.F. on April 9, 1945 (see *The Times*, April 12, 1945). The *Deutschland* (Lützow) was also sunk by the R.A.F. (*The Times*, April 21, 1945.)

gave Papen the pretext for dissolving the Reichstag, and thereby preventing a Nazi–Centre combination with a majority. Papen next declared a state of emergency; announced Germany's withdrawal from the Disarmament Conference; decided upon an economic policy based upon reduction of wages, and created special courts for political offences and threatened the death penalty for acts of political violence. On November 3, 1932, Berlin was surprised by a sudden transport strike against a wage cut of two pfennigs an hour. The strike became a demonstration against the Social Democratic Municipality by a coalition of Nazis under orders from Hitler, with Communists under orders from the Comintern. In the clashes with the police, the Hitlerists and the Stalinists fought side by side. Hitler had now completely puzzled the German wage-earners and it looked as if Stalin must win them since Papen's policy of wage-cutting automatically gave the Communists the leadership of the wage-earning class. The Nazis could not afford to stand aside. They had to compete, all the more so as the country was facing an election, its fifth since the beginning of the year. The Berlin Correspondent reported that there was a general expectation that the Nazis would lose seats, and return with about 200. On the 7th, the results showed that the Nazis had lost two million votes and 35 seats. In seats, the result read: Nazis 195, Social Democrats 121, Communists 100. After this, their first serious setback, the Nazis naturally went farther to the Left, against the Socialists, and therefore necessarily with the Communists, as in the Berlin strike, which continued in conditions of semi-civil war. It did look as if the Nazis had finally conferred the leadership of the working class upon the Communists. This was the upshot of Papen's policy, and the inference of the election figures.

The decline of Hitler was marked. The Communists had gained at their expense and at that of the Social Democrats. For the first time too, as an election manoeuvre, the Communist Party had thundered against Versailles and against Poland. The new Reichstag was due to meet not later than in four weeks' time. Hitler proclaimed on November 7 that the middle-class parties revived by Papen were " driving the masses to Bolshevism." The Times published an expository leader on November 8. " On the whole," the paper concluded, " there seems little reason to expect any immediate change in the outward semblance of German political life. President Hindenberg does not favour quick changes." Meanwhile " political life " continued in deadlock. On November 17, Papen's resignation was announced in the middle of discussions on Herriot's disarmament proposals. The aged President saw Hitler on more than one occasion and offered him the chance of acting as the leader of the largest party in any democratically ruled country, and of trying to form a Government from his own and other parties. Hitler's position, therefore, was that he had to enter a coalition and give up his idea of a Nazi State, or continue to demand his unshared power in conditions that the last election demonstrated to be growing daily more disadvantageous for him. On the day after the result, Hitler had said that his attitude was one of " ruthless opposition to all overt and covert enemies of the renascence of the German people. No compromise, no negotiations with these elements! . . . Negotiations are not to be thought of until the present régime and the parties supporting it are annihilated." (Reported by the Munich Correspondent, November 8, 1932.) On November 24, the Berlin Correspondent telegraphed that Hitler had refused the Chancellorship on Hindenburg's terms, and reported that General von Schleicher was a possibility. The Correspondent added, with great perception, that " with regard to the suspicions which have been entertained abroad since the General's utterances of last summer, it might be as well that he should come right into the open with full responsibility for German policy, especially if that were the only way in which orderly conditions would be preserved within Germany during the winter. It might then be realized that German foreign and military policy is the same, whoever is Chancellor, Foreign Minister or Defence Minister." (November 28, 1932.) The salient point in the reconstruction of Germany's power had been appreciated by her people. They had seen immediately in 1919 how reparations could be turned to their profit. By 1922 they had redesigned their factories; by 1932 the Versailles provisions upon war munitions could not then be imposed without crippling her peace manufactures; and without encouraging Germany's peace manufactures, Germany's creditors could not hope to be paid even a percentage of the Reparations they demanded. Thus Germany was able to compel the victors to finance the munition and manufacture account of the defeated, and create their own ruin.

This was not understood in Britain. In France, by 1932, knowledge that the Germans had outwitted them was current. In the autumn, the Paris Correspondent reported that the French suspected that the intentions of Germany were to disturb the peace by an aggressive action at no distant date. The French argument was that further disarmament " to the point of equality " was inadmissible unless all nations showed an equal desire for peace and an equal respect for the rights of their neighbours

Until these equalities had been established, " equality of rights "
as demanded by Germany should not be conceded. Peace
could only be assured by the superiority of those who desired it.
By " peace " France understood the preservation of the existing
order, and it was believed by an increasing number of Frenchmen
in the autumn of 1932 that Germany was imbued with the will to
change that order, and by force. This was true, though the
office was unwilling to admit it. The French thesis was that a
respect for the Treaty at the time was the only way in which a
disturbed Europe could then and there achieve stability, at least
until a new concert of Europe could decide upon the next step.
Britain, though aware of the popularity in Germany of resistance
to the Allies, was unaware of the risks of making concessions to
German pressure. Schleicher felt, as well as knew, that any
Chancellor must revive the defeated country's power to check-
mate the conquerors.

The Socialist General tried to enter into relations with the
Left Nazis, the Social Democrats and the Christian Trade Unions;
while Hitler continued to denounce the Social Democrats
as the chief enemy of the working class; the Communists,
under the orders of the Comintern, joined in the same cry.
Though *The Times* felt that the appointment of Schleicher might
have been justifiable, the choice of a soldier was unfortunate from
the international standpoint. A leading article uneasily recalled
that in the past the same General had made public his belief
that Germany would " in any case " reorganize the Reichswehr,
and would no longer tolerate the " degrading " provisions of
the Treaty of Versailles. However, comfort was drawn from
Schleicher's known sympathy with democratic procedure and his
interest in the trade union movement and the welfare of manual
workers. " He certainly appears to be the most representative
personage in German public life at the moment; and there are
obvious advantages in having him in a responsible position."
The paper proceeded to say that

> The trouble with militarism in Germany before the War was that
> it was irresponsible to Parliamentary or public opinion and yet
> ensconced behind a political facade. General Schleicher has shown
> that he is by no means unresponsive to popular opinion; and, if a
> General is to combine with a Field-Marshal as the directing power
> in Germany, it is at least desirable that he should be the Minister
> answerable to public opinion at home and abroad for the policy
> of his country. (December 3, 1932.)

It was a settled belief of Printing House Square that there
existed a public opinion " at home " [*i.e.*, in Germany]

to which the Chancellor was "answerable"; and, equally, that there then existed a public opinion "abroad" [*i.e.*, in the world] which effectively exerted a degree of moral authority or some "psychological influence" over him. It was a belief that existed in Britain; it was not a belief that existed in France, or in Germany herself. Germany knew then, as Prussia had known three generations earlier, that her foreign policy could be made effective only by strength. There was no doubt in the mind of Admiral Raeder that "modifications of the Peace Treaty" would not be granted except to a Germany strong enough to render the Treaty expensive and difficult to vindicate. How far this process of regaining freedom "to dispose of its own armed strength" had gone, was largely ignored in Britain and in *The Times*, although the Paris Correspondent pointed out that in France it was believed that "equality in effectives has almost been achieved and that something more than equality is in sight." (December 10, 1932.) French opinion was not given much attention in the office. Ever since Chanak, suspicions of French policy and fears of what it might lead to had deepened. While it was recognized that the reduction of our commitments on the Continent was a real British interest, and a strong Imperial desirability, it was not perceived that in the current state of Europe the mere suggestion of a lessening British interest in the Continent would compel France to assume greater responsibilities, and permit Germany to adopt stronger measures. Dawson and B.-W., in common with many British politicians, were less alarmed at the growth of Germany's power than at the firmness of France's intention to remain in the Rhineland. By marking such indications as could be found of German respect for "enlightened world opinion," and for the process of peaceful revision, *The Times* endeavoured to create an atmosphere favourable to the negotiation of an agreed settlement. It would be necessary, therefore, in the New Year, to continue this policy, to show sympathy with Germany's grievances and to emphasize her qualities of neighbourliness. The effect of Baldwin's and Chamberlain's policy, and of Dawson's and B.-W.'s leaders, was to lead the British people to believe in a Germany that never existed. Neither the Prime Minister nor the Editor understood that patterns of foreign policy tend to repeat themselves. They were unable to believe that Germany's combination of a living military tradition with an existing sense of defeat alone created dangers in the European situation, and that concessions of any kind made on account of German pressure would aggravate them. The Berlin Correspondent had more than once conveyed the warning that in foreign policy Germany was single-minded

nd that she was determined to regain her complete freedom to
se her armed strength as seemed best to herself, and to obtain,
hereby, whatever modifications of the Treaty were in her view
ecessary. This was a view that German politicians of any sort
ad no interest in broadcasting. The new German Chancellor
uickly reassured international opinion. On December 16 he
ave out what *The Times* called " a most carefully balanced
tatement," which, it was expected, would do much towards
llaying the mistrust aroused by his appointment.

The Chancellor and his Foreign Minister, Baron von Neurath,
re at least both men with whom it should be easy to negotiate. They
re apparently masters of the situation at home, and they are frank
nd conciliatory in their definition of foreign policy. (December 17.)

On December 31 *The Times* announced that the nameplate of
he German light cruiser *Emden*[1] was to be returned to Germany
y the Government of Australia " as a token of goodwill."
[he gesture must have delighted Germany if not France. It
qually delighted Printing House Square. The position of the
ditor, and of his chief Assistant, was clear and definite: to
natch von Neurath and other Germans in being " conciliatory
n their definition of foreign policy," and to encourage
he Chancellor, or any successor he might have, to be
' answerable to public opinion at home and abroad for the
olicy of his country," as the paper said on December 3. The
rchitects and sponsors of this policy were by no means alone.
hat the country as a whole supported them cannot be denied.
n the light of available information and recent memory it is
bvious enough that the course of Anglo-German relations would
ever run smoothly if Britain should seek to negotiate with a
jermany that did not exist. No German Government had ever
een able to conceive of itself as settling an issue of foreign policy
1 terms of her " public opinion," in the English sense of the
vord. This had been overlooked in Printing House Square.
he degree of optimism shown by *The Times* in Dawson's second
nnings towards Germany would have appeared singular to
'lanagan, Saunders, Chirol and Steed. The paper's historic sense
f responsibility, combined with the old standards of knowledge,
agacity, and critical capacity, were reserved for issues that lay
ar from Europe, though close to Printing House Square. The
ditor's highest capacities found their fittest exercise in the field
f Empire. Dawson made a notable contribution to the solution
f problems, especially in India, which had been postponed from
'ersailles and were, in 1933, strictly comparable for their urgency
nd dimension with Continental complications.

[1] Destroyed by the Australian light cruiser, *Sydney*, on November 9, 1914.

XXII

IMPERIALISM; A NEW PHASE

THE great Imperial problems relating to foreign policy tha
lay behind the acute international tension prevailing in the
years immediately preceding the war of 1914-1918 were b
no means wholly solved at the Peace Conference. Moreover
as has been seen, the foreign policy of the Coalition exposed
itself in 1922 to criticism from Australia and Canada keene
than had ever before been experienced. The relation of Britai
to the Dominions had not greatly developed since 1912.[1] Muc
criticism was heard in 1913 from those who saw the Entent
taking the place of Empire partnership; and, in Dawson'
second innings, from those who were interested in the question
of "Dominion foreign policy" and a "related Dominio
strategy" that were continually under discussion. These wer
subjects with which the Editor of *The Times* would necessaril
concern himself; even if, unlike Dawson, he had no specifi
training, or particular interest in them. The need for an Empir
expanding in a jealous world to look to its defences, and th
recognition that Empire defence necessarily presupposes Empir
unity, were axiomatic to Dawson. No single point of Britis
policy, he thought, was of more urgency or of greater importanc
than the consolidation of Imperial sentiment and Dominio
power; and neither of these had, in his second innings at P.H.S.
advanced in the degree for which he had hoped and worked
even before he first came to the office. The main South Africa
problems had, it seemed, been dealt with. There remained
those of Anglo-Canadian trade, and difficulties arising fron
increased Canadian nationalism, and the rise of Imperialis
isolationism. But Canada's Dominion status, at least, had lon
been settled, and one of the worst of the problems with tha
settlement.

Over and above all Dominion questions there was another
so huge as to involve the political fate of a portion of the globe
so large as to be the equivalent of a sub-continent. India wa
not a self-governing Dominion. Britain's interest in India wa

[1] *I.e.*, the period described in Chapter I, " The New Imperialism," which surveys th
ideas of P.H.S. on the Empire as they were expressed in the period 1887-1913.

a prime factor in foreign policy. In Wallace's and Chirol's time the menace to India came from Russia, and the Viceroy had been allowed to formulate a " regional " foreign policy which included the regulation of affairs in Afghanistan, Arabia, Nepal, Tibet and other contiguous areas. In Curzon's vice-royalty the Persian Gulf lay rather in Delhi's direct than in London's indirect sphere. The problems involved in the transfer of any appreciable measure of self-government had long been the preoccupation of the best brains in P.H.S. Mackenzie Wallace and Chirol both envisaged the proper study of foreign policy as one whole, not to be adequately understood if separated, even if Continental, Middle Eastern and Far Eastern relations were given independent consideration. Both realized that Eastern Mediterranean, Asian and European politics had been basically altered by the laying down of the Trans-Siberian Railway and the Baghdad Railway. It was one of Dawson's conspicuous merits that he did not limit his interests to South Africa and Canada, but extended them to every actual and potential Dominion. He could point to abundant precedent in the office and, indeed, he owed his appointment very largely to the body of Imperial doctrine whose origin reached back to Moberly Bell and Amery.

Northcliffe's banishment of Chirol six months before he appointed Dawson deprived *The Times* of the head of its Imperial and Foreign Department and robbed it of a zealous student of Indian affairs with a reputation in this field as high outside Printing House Square as within it. As events were to prove, *The Times* could no more do without the wisdom of his long experience of India than Chirol could live without some form of personal contact with the paper. Though he was one of the most competent observers alive of the European political stage, the East was always nearest his heart, and it was India, which he first visited in 1883, that captured his real interest throughout the latter years of his service to the paper. To such a trust-worthy adviser Buckle was content to leave the shaping of policy on Indian affairs. Chirol was a staunch supporter of the British Raj ; but was convinced, with the certainty of one who had relentlessly probed every aspect of the problem, that the sovereign Power must proceed steadily and gradually along the path of increasing the share of Indians in the government of their country. While seeing this as inevitable, he was by no means willing that extensive powers should be hastily conceded. He reverenced the solemn responsibility Great Britain had assumed for the landless and illiterate peasants who were unable to speak for themselves. Simultaneously he had no doubt that those Indians in a position to rule were mostly quite unprepared for the heavy burdens which ordered government entailed. The peroration in Lovat Fraser's four-column article on " Britain's Future in India," written three years before Dawson's elevation might have been Chirol's own :

To hold what we have, to make concessions slowly and cautiously, to rule justly and fearlessly, to continue our thankless endeavours to advance the well-being of India without praise and without gratitude, and never to do anything to impair the stability of our rule—these things must suffice. (June 28, 1909.)

In this evolutionary process two significant stages had already occurred since Chirol's association with the paper began. Parliament's right to administer through the Secretary of State and the Government of India was still unchallenged. But Dufferin's Indian Councils Act of 1892 had considerably extended the field over which the Provincial Legislative Councils were permitted to express opinion, and had conceded some slight advance towards the principle of election—" recommendation " it was called—to some of the " non-official " seats on the Councils. Seventeen years later, when Chirol was acknowledged one of England's best informed observers of Indian affairs, the principle of election to the " non-official " seats on both the Governor-General's and the Provincial Councils had been established by the Indian Councils Act of 1909, commonly known, after the Secretary of State in Asquith's Government and the Viceroy of India, as the Morley-Minto Reforms. Between December, 1908, and May, 1909, *The Times* published seventeen leading articles on India and twenty-five special articles from Correspondents stationed there. So high was Chirol's reputation that Morley frequently consulted him on particular aspects of his reforming schemes, and when Chirol received the accolade in 1912 it was generally accepted to be a mark of recognition for services at this time.

Criticism of the Morley-Minto Reforms was offered in plentiful detail from Printing House Square. The nomination of Sinha, a Bengali lawyer, as first Indian representative to sit on the Viceroy's Council,[1] was an alarming event. " For the first time since the foundations were laid of our Empire in India, the supreme authority will shortly pass from exclusively British hands," opened the leading article of March 24, 1909. It went on to say that " The attitude of Hindu opinion does not tend to

[1] He resigned next year, to return to the Bar, and was succeeded by a Moslem, Ali Imam.

dispel the misgivings occasioned by Lord Morley's abrupt breach with the traditions of the past "; for " to the whole Mohamedan body it must be repugnant." While the Liberal Cabinet and its Conservative critics alike denied that Parliamentary government was being aimed at in India, Fraser's survey already quoted urged that the reformers, in the conviction of nearly every experienced administrator, were going too fast. They were not likely to bring permanent or even prolonged peace. Only Gokhale, the Moderate, among all native leaders, understood what was meant by the colonial self-government for which they were calling. The others sought not representative government but personal authority. What was to be done about the native States ? Self-government was a cry of the Brahmins ; it was not even in the interest of Moslems, who lacked intelligent leadership. Anarchists might be expected to continue their campaigns.

The reforms recently instituted in India have left almost entirely unaffected those essential conditions which chiefly concern us. So far as there is any menace, direct or indirect, to the continuance of British rule in India, the reforms have not abated that menace in any material degree. On the contrary, it would not be difficult to demonstrate that their ultimate and inevitable effect must be to accentuate it. We are face to face with the antagonism, open or veiled, of a very large proportion of the Indian peoples. Our rule is disliked, not because it is bad, but because it is alien ; and if we were a race of administrative archangels the situation would be very much the same. Our difficulties in the future are likely to arise in a great measure because we are reluctant to recognize this tangible fact. We want to be loved for our good works ; yet it is not our works, but our presence that is chiefly resented. (June 28, 1909.)

The best type of English adviser on Indian affairs was handicapped by a suspicion that some of his countrymen were not disinterested, others were unimaginative, and that Indians who were politically alert realized as much. Fraser's special article thus proceeded :

Many of our difficulties are due to the fact that we have never made up our minds as to our purpose there . . . Reflecting Civil Servants have said to me : " What are we here for ? If I only knew that, I should know how to order my life and my duty." The civilian nowadays is perplexed and puzzled. He sees the conflict of the rival ideas—the one that we are in India for the good of the people, and the other that we are there primarily for our own good.

British observers in 1909 found ample ground for misgiving in outbreaks of murder and violence which extreme Brahmin Nationalists had been sponsoring spasmodically since the turn of the century, and which had now, in the words of a leading article on August 23, " for the first time since the Mutiny " brought the Government of India " face to face with a political agitation, more or less openly hostile to the maintenance of British rule." Had there been no other acts of violence—and these were but two of the most sensational in the protracted story of anarchy and bloodshed—the quiet purpose of the young Hindu and self-styled patriot,[1] Madar Lal Dhingra, convicted for the murder of Sir Curzon Wyllie at the Imperial Institute in London on July 1, and the attempt with bombs on the life of the Viceroy, Minto, at Ahmedabad on November 13, would have sufficed to convince Chirol that the extremists' quarrel with the rulers of India arose from bitter resentment at their very presence in the country. This militant unrest was seen by *The Times* as part of the great nationalist impulse sweeping like a wind across the Asiatic continent. One gust had carried Japan, newly risen to the rank of a first-class Power, to military and naval victory against Russia. In India it was fanned by quickened aspirations for political freedom resulting from a study of English Liberal writers. " Not only have we established the reign of law there," asserted *The Times*, " but we have indoctrinated thousands of the most intelligent of our Indian fellow-subjects with the learning and the theories of the West." Bengal had been restive since its partition in 1905, one area being predominantly Hindu and one mainly Moslem in population. Whereas *The Times* would vindicate partition as fairer to the Moslem minority and conducive to better administration, intractable Bengalis saw only the old game of *Divide et impera*. Moslem discontent, for which the paper was always watching and with which it frequently sympathized, could also be regarded as a symptom of Asiatic nationalism quite as much as of religious scruple, and Moslem loyalty to the ruling Power was often emphasized.

The year 1910 ended with a session of the Indian National Congress at Bombay which *The Times* Correspondent there regarded as the nadir of the movement for which it stood. Denunciation of the reforms was not accompanied by any constructive amendments. With one grievance the paper sympathized :

No Imperial question more urgently demands careful and

---

[1] The Maharajah of Kashmir wrote to *The Times* on behalf of the Hindus abhorring such a false conception of patriotism.

statesmanlike consideration than this question of the position of our Indian fellow-subjects in the Dominions . . . but in this matter the Government of India can do nothing without the help of the Imperial Government, and the latter in turn can do nothing without the help of our self-governing Colonies. (January 3, 1910.)

The point was amplified in No. 33 of Chirol's special articles, September 10, 1910, and a leader the same day on " The position of Indians in the Empire." Only the most vigorous constitutional action could avert catastrophe. Chirol gained something of a personal triumph when Minto announced plans early in 1910 to restrict the activities of Hindu anarchists and particularly to suppress seditious journals—a measure *The Times* had championed in articles on " writings which are intended to breed murderers." The connexion between crime, journalism, and opinion was thus traced :

> The most deplorable feature of the Nasik case,[1] as of all the other crimes which have stained the fair name of India during the last year or two, is the reluctance of the Indian public to help the authorities in their investigations. When an official is assassinated, the vernacular Press calls upon heaven to witness its deep and unctuous indignation. Public meetings are convened, at which the leaders of the Indian communities express their abhorrence of such dastardly acts. But these protestations are never followed by any active attempt to join hands with the Government in hunting down the organizers of the crime. (March 30, 1910.)

Later that year, during his last visit to India before retiring (he was later to revisit the country on behalf of the paper), Chirol made his own weighty contribution to the understanding of the whole Indian problem. Scholarly, exhaustive, judicial, the thirty-seven articles on " Indian Unrest " which he turned out in only two months, the first appearing on July 16, were later republished in book form, Morley accepting the dedication. They were also to involve an ultimately unsuccessful libel action lasting from 1915 to 1919 with B. G. Tilak, the Brahman whom Chirol designated[2] " the father of Indian unrest." The articles all went to show that unrest was ages old and was in origin not only political but also social and religious. It was for Great Britain to break down the " unnatural alliance " between reactionary Brahmanism and Liberal education, while encouraging the best elements in the philosophies of East and West. In a

[1] A. M. T. Jackson, Collector of Nasik, was shot dead on December 21, 1909.

[2] In his sixth article, July 25. See Appendix II, Sources, XXII.

strong and impartial Executive, determined to let no wave of violence sweep it from the path of justice, and regarding as its first duty " to hold the scales even between the different communities over which they rule and to keep faith with each and all, so that their word shall be above even the possibility of suspicion," (October 7, 1909) lay for Chirol the guarantee of the welfare of Indian peoples. As a corrective to this general picture of disaffection, the Empire Day Supplement for 1910 noted " sincere and general grief at the death of the late King-Emperor." A cool head and the forces on the spot, it said, could overcome every ill so long as the Empire was at peace.

At the end of 1910 Morley and Minto were succeeded respectively by Crewe and Hardinge of Penshurst. On November 12 *The Times* first saw the possibility of the King-Emperor George V holding a Coronation Durbar at Delhi, and when this was confirmed the paper spoke of an " Imperial necessity." Throughout 1911 preparations for this ceremony overshadowed all other Indian news. Sombre enough was the background : neither reform nor repression had any effect in checking the tale of conspiracy, dacoity, and outrage with firearm and bomb ; there was nearly a disaster when the monsoon failed to break throughout July in parts of the north and centre ; rulers died in Hyderabad, Cooch Behar, Nepal. Heart-searching by the sovereign Power was reflected in *The Times*. Fourteen pages were devoted to India in the 1911 Empire Day Supplement; and, if a patronizing note was still audible, even more distinct was the sense of responsibility.

Asia . . . is neither changeless or asleep. Her peoples are quickening into a new life, and her resources in all the factors which go to build up wealth are still almost unused. Her time is coming soon, and on British policy before all others must depend the manner of its coming and its effect upon the West. We are the guardians of a great tradition, but the conditions are changing and with them the forms of guardianship must also change. As we associate the Indian peoples more closely with the mechanism of our rule, so must we give more and more consideration to their sentiments and views in the policy of rule. Their growing desire for industrial development, and with it a measure of fiscal autonomy sufficient to its needs, will test as nothing else can test the morality of our power. The touchstone of the Empire is there.

Before Their Majesties sailed on November 11 the paper was full of topics like ceremonial dress for the Durbar, Indian places of interest, customs and curiosities, while Curzon started a correspondence on archaeology. December, with its climax in the incomparable ceremony of the 12th, was a month of brilliant pageantry and much more ; never before had a Western monarch landed in India, and the welcome from millions of his subjects was inspiring. In its description *The Times* rose to a great occasion. It eschewed sensational news, attributing to accident a mysterious fire at one of the Durbar camps and a premature explosion of fireworks at Delhi. In this exciting atmosphere 1911 went out with the announcement of administrative changes which the paper applauded. Delhi became the capital instead of Calcutta ;[1] Bengal was raised to the rank of a Presidency ; Bihar, Chota Nagpur, and Orissa were merged into a Lieutenant-Governorship ; and a Chief Commissioner was nominated for Assam. Chirol's period came to an end with India looking forward to at least a lull in internal strife. But like many other Viceroys, Hardinge was the victim of attempted assassination when making his state entry into Delhi on December 23, 1912. He had, moreover, entered upon a term in which the first World War was destined to break out, a fatality that he had, by his own observation, suspected to be inevitable if Germany were to continue her policy of pressure. Accordingly Hardinge's intention as he told Steed, was to preserve the loyalty of India to the British cause in the forthcoming struggle, whenever it should occur.[2] When Dawson was appointed Editor, he was slow to declare himself, and it was not until the summer of 1914 that attention was switched from Ireland to India when Crewe, as Secretary of State, presented his ill-fated Council of India Bill. Morley's surreptitious attempts in recent years to undermine the effectiveness of the Secretary of State's Advisory Council, thereby removing the most immediate restraint upon the Minister's freedom of action, had not escaped comment in Printing House Square. The new Bill's replacement of discussion in council by individual consultation was, both to the Editor and to the forthright but erratic Lovat Fraser who had become chief adviser on Indian affairs, the Liberals' culminating push to wrest effective control of the peninsula from the Government of India and invest it in Whitehall. Fraser had little enough regard for the competence of the Indian authority whose indecisive handling of disturbances in Bengal had repeatedly led *The Times* to chide for inaction ; but with J. S. Mill he believed that

[1] Curzon strongly condemned this change in the British Parliament on February 21, '12.

[2] For Hardinge's knowledge of German policy from 1908, see Vol. III, Chapter **XX,** "Domestic and Foreign Discords," p. 610.

The Executive Government of India is, and must be, seated in India itself. The principal function of the Home Government is not to direct the details of administration, but to scrutinize and revise the past acts of the Indian Governments; to lay down principles and issue general instructions for their future guidance and to give or refuse sanction to great political measures which are referred home for approval. (See leading article of June 29, 1914.)

The Times saw the measure striking at the very principle of preventing the seizure of power by the autocrats on which British rule had rested. If passed, it would free the Secretary of State to rule India on his own responsibility from Whitehall. "It transforms Lord Crewe into a Great Mogul in a frock coat," gibed the leading article on June 29 entitled "The Attempt to Destroy the Council of India." On July 7 the Lords rejected the Bill. Fraser's stand did more than cloak a sincere disdain for government by cable. It reflected a sympathy, if anything warmer than Chirol's own, with India's legitimate desire for a greater share in the management of her own concerns. How far Fraser's view of the constitutional situation was coloured by India's loyal response at the outbreak of the First Great War[1] is difficult to judge, but he was soon looking ahead to the clamour for "further modifications in the control exercised from this country upon Indian affairs" (September 27, 1915) which he felt the war was bound to let loose. What form those modifications should take, he was uncertain. In any event, major changes in the midst of the greatest war the Empire had ever waged were unthinkable. Even the proposal to create an Executive Council for the United Provinces led to a Government defeat in the Lords on March 16, 1915, and a sharp rebuff from *The Times*. Hardinge, coming to the support of the Government, was said to deliver "what really amounts to an attack upon Parliament." (March 29.) The problem, as the calendar moved into 1916 and early visions of rapid victory faded, was to put the damper on hopes prematurely raised of startling constitutional advance. When Hardinge returned to England in April his rule was enthusiastically appraised by *The Times* despite the avowal that it had been associated with no major reform save in education. Calm was the desideratum. There were already signs that some sort of conspiratorial *rapprochement* between the All-India Moslem League and the predominantly Hindu National Congress was afoot, though Moslems were seriously divided as to whether provincial autonomy would benefit them or not. I

[1] "The Indian Empire has overwhelmed the British nation by the completeness and the unanimity of its enthusiastic aid." (September 10, 1914.)

Madras, Mrs. Annie Besant—" that obstreperous old harridan," as Dawson called her when writing on October 18, 1917, to Lord Chelmsford (the Viceroy who had succeeded Hardinge)—was active. She was leading her Home Rule for India League in the cry for complete self-government; and this " mischievous movement " was being seconded in London by George Lansbury. Extremist politicians of both the leading religions were shrewdly doing their best to use Great Britain's trials as a lever for prizing out further concessions. Such tactics could only damage India's claim to wider freedom when the war was won. " Lightly to raise extravagant hopes and encourage unrealizable demands," wrote Fraser on June 19, 1916, echoing the Viceroy's Budget speech, " can only tend to delay and will not accelerate political progress." Besides, Fraser was still not convinced that the Government of India could keep its house in order. How was he to shake the complacency of that body without affronting the loyal masses ? Sir Stanley Reed in Bombay and his corps of correspondents in various parts of the sub-continent, though they provided adequate coverage of day-to-day matters, only occasionally speculated on the turn of events.

The answer was afforded in part by one of Fraser's many London acquaintances " in the know." An Indian War Loan, it appeared, was to be raised early in 1917. Here was the opportunity he had been seeking. Fraser had watched with somewhat jaundiced eye the expenditure of Sir William Meyer, Finance Member of the Viceroy's Executive Council, on public works—' thrusting drain pipes upon unwilling villagers, and constructing new schools, precisely as though the war were a distant upheaval on the planet Saturn "—while the rest of the Empire was steadily tightening its belt. Now a good monsoon in 1916 had ensured a rich harvest. Orders for war equipment had given a fillip to Indian industry such as it had never known in peace-time. Why had not the Indian Government shown willingness earlier to share the financial burdens of the war ? Peremptorily Fraser wrote on December 22, 1916 :

Whatever sacrifices India may have made as a result of the war, she has made no conspicuous financial sacrifice. The people of this country are paying for India's services, and for the war material she is supplying, and Mr. M. de P. Webb,[1] an acknowledged authority, has estimated that by next March Great Britain will have pledged herself to reimburse India to the extent of £50,000,000. This is an unequal sharing of war burdens.

[1] *The Times* Correspondent at Karachi.

Fraser did not then know that the Viceroy, with the support of Meyer, had already offered to take over the interest charges of some portion of the home war debt. Nor had he realized how delicately balanced were Indian fortunes a year before. Chelmsford wrote bitterly to Dawson:

I . . . arrived in India on April 5. On April 28 Kut fell. A storm of obloquy had already burst on the Government of India and our task was not made any lighter by the fact that it was generally regarded that we could do no right. In my speech on September 5 to my Legislative Council I pointed out what India had done both on the military and medical side and I think it must have been obvious to anyone reading between the lines of my speech that in April, 1916, we were down on bedrock. From April to October we were busy in refitting. There was an augmentation of 20 per cent. on the cavalry and of 40 per cent. on the infantry while the number of recruits enlisted was greater than the entire strength of the Indian Army as it existed on August 1, 1914. . . . In England you can see for yourselves what is being done. Here were are far off and we necessarily have to work in the dark because until we have our measures completed and approved by the Departments at home it is impossible to reveal what we are doing.[1]

In India things began to take a more ominous turn. Hindus and Moslems had come out openly at Lucknow in December, 1916, in an unnatural alliance for constitutional advance. Mrs. Besant's adherents were capturing the National Congress, drawing more moderate members in their train.[2] Even more significantly, extremist politicians were openly restraining volunteers for the Indian defence force and advocating " passive resistance " to Government orders. Two factors alone gave any cause for optimism. One was that Indian troops were standing firmly by the Empire, giving daily proof of loyalty to the Crown. Then came the Political Testament of the Hindu Moderate leader in Congress, Gokhale, who died in 1915. It was acclaimed in both England and India when made public by the Aga Khan in August, 1917, as providing a reasoned basis for discussion on relations between the two countries. Chelmsford meanwhile, somewhat naively convinced that voluble elements could be won over by promises of gradual progress towards responsible government within the Empire, had begged for an unequivocal declaration of policy from E. S. Montagu, who took over the Secretaryship of State from Austen Chamberlain in July, 1917. Fraser

[1] Chelmsford to Dawson, February 23, 1917.

[2] She was chosen President of the Congress at the end of 1917 and was accorded a scornful leading article on January 2, 1918.

had written off the Government of India as incapable of keeping trouble-makers in check by vigorous methods. While he saw no virtue in capitulation to the extremists' demands, he believed it necessary to forestall the effects of their propaganda, and so accepted the expediency of a clear statement of British intentions. This must imply no sudden, ill-thought-out surrender of responsibility. A gradual increase of the self-governing function was all very well as long-term policy; but good order inside India and security from external aggression would need to control the rate of advance.

On August 20, 1917, Montagu made in the House of Commons this famous pronouncement:

The policy of His Majesty's Government, with which the Government of India are in complete accord, is that of the increasing association of Indians in every branch of the administration, and the gradual development of self-governing institutions with a view to the progressive realization of responsible government in India as an integral part of the British Empire.

He added that he was proceeding to India for private talks with the Viceroy; and that " progressive realization " must occupy several stages. Dawson and Fraser seized the significance of this new approach. For the first time since the momentous days of 1858, British aims in India were clearly defined. Responsible self-government within the Empire was the end officially laid down. Fraser was gratified to find not only a constructive forecast designed to allay the suspicions of the noisy, but also a warning to them that the goal was distant. *The Times* restated its " objection on general principles to the visit of any Secretary of State to India." If there was any risk of a contest for control between a Minister and a Viceroy, it unhesitatingly affirmed " the paramount position of the King-Emperor's representative." Autocracy in Delhi was preferable to autocracy in Whitehall. Above all, the paper saw its duty as to the British public, " the final arbiters in this grave problem," who would " shape their judgment by the spirit in which the Government's announcement is received in India." (August 21, 1917.)

Fraser would have preferred the pronouncement to be accompanied by a direct warning and, if necessary, stringent measures against anti-British agitators. Two days after Montagu spoke, a message from the Bombay Correspondent began: " At the last session of the Indian National Congress and of the Moslem League, the Moderate party disappeared." Clamour was met instead by Chelmsford, at Simla, on September 5, with an appeal for restraint and moderation. Quickly, to Fraser's great personal satisfaction, one voice, possibly the most compelling in British India at that time, was raised in round condemnation of the high priests of passive resistance to British rule. On September 13, in the Viceroy's Council itself, Sir Michael O'Dwyer, Lieutenant-Governor of the Punjab, soundly rated all those Indian politicians who were covertly or in the open preaching opposition to Government orders, and particularly arguing against joining the defence forces. Chelmsford saw all his patient efforts at conciliation nullified in one afternoon. Sir Michael was of course compelled to express regret for "disturbing the spirit of harmony," but *The Times* in a leader on November 6 was "glad to observe that he did not withdraw his criticisms" and ventured the opinion that instead of reproving him the Government of India should have reprobated the tendencies O'Dwyer condemned.

In taking O'Dwyer's part, *The Times* was not merely advocating the paper's traditionally "strong" policy towards subversive elements. Fraser (for the pen was his) also, consciously or unconsciously, perpetuated the paper's accustomed support for the direct representative of British rule in closest touch with the people towards whom that rule was directed. Chelmsford's main concern had been lest he should be thought guilty of expressing conflicting viewpoints. It was impossible for him as Viceroy, he wrote to Dawson, to sit down under what appeared to be a flagrant disregard of his request.

It was brought home to me that the impression was rife that I was speaking with two voices—one preaching conciliation and the other, through O'Dwyer, giving my real views. I could not remain under such an imputation, and to my mind I had to make it clear that I had no part or lot in O'Dwyer's utterance. It was no doubt a good fighting speech full of sting and unpalatable truths, and there are times when speeches of that kind are wanted and do good. But coming when it did, the results were deplorable. My appeal for moderation and good will had had, I think I may say, a great effect. The O'Dwyer incident undid my work in a minute and started a bitter controversy on racial lines which is still going on.[1]

Nevertheless Whitehall prolonged O'Dwyer's tenure of office for a year. Both Dawson and Fraser regarded the Viceroy's assessment—rightly as events were to prove—as more than a

[1] Chelmsford to Dawson, November 17, 1917.

little optimistic. The former's reply, while explaining the paper's general attitude, made it plain that championship of O'Dwyer was no routine expression, but a deliberate judgment in the light of available facts.

Please remember, if you are ever disposed to resent our distant comment, that the traditional policy of *The Times* is to stand by the representatives of British rule, and that successive Viceroys have often been helped by our support of them as against the Home Government. Occasionally it happens that a provincial governor gets the benefit of this policy if he happens to come into conflict with the Government of India. Though it was before my time, I am told, for instance, that we supported Bampfylde Fuller against Minto and I believe that we also backed Northcote when Curzon tried to deprive the Governor of Bombay of the right of corresponding direct with the Secretary of State. I only mention these things to show you that the comments of *The Times* on Indian questions are not made at haphazard, though I am sure you realize this.[1]

Dawson added that the paper proposed to offer no further comment on the vexed subject of constitutional reform until Montagu returned from India to place his and the Viceroy's proposals before Parliament.

Between Montagu's homecoming and the issue of his Report in 1918, Chirol wrote a series of four articles describing the " tense expectancy " in India. Dawson also entrusted him with the leading article which appeared with the Report on July 6. Hard things had been said about Montagu before, but now " No more able State Paper has been submitted in our time to the people of this country in regard to Indian affairs." Noting the loyalty with which India had rallied to the Imperial cause in war, *The Times* was ready as never before to visualize a closer association between Britain and the sub-continent. Its traditional argument was not shaken, for " the Report clearly shows and states emphatically that, whilst self-government must henceforth be the goal of British policy in India, it can only be reached by gradual and experimental stages "—inevitably, in a land where " democracy is in most respects thoroughly foreign." As to the important changes, " long overdue," in provincial administration :

Within that sphere the principle of specific devolution is to be applied by the transfer of certain limited powers of government and administration to Indian " Ministers," associated with, but

[1] Dawson to Chelmsford, January 28, 1918.

distinct from, the Governor-in-Council, and responsible for the exercise of those powers to the Legislative Council, in which there is to be an Indian majority elected on the broadest franchise possible under existing conditions. The machinery by which these changes are to be effected is ingenious and, perhaps unavoidably, very complicated, and there are many points wisely reserved for further inquiries on the spot, such as the nature of the franchise and the extent of the transferred powers in the different provinces.

Chirol, from an Olympian height, then declaimed :

The Report offers a bold scheme of constructive statesmanship which requires very close study. . . . Its ultimate success or failure will depend on the Indians themselves. . . . If, rejecting once and for all the dangerous counsels of impatient visionaries and bitter fanatics, they respond wholeheartedly to this generous appeal, the trust placed in them will be justified, and India will be carried a long stage forward along the road on which we are pledged to set her feet. (July 6, 1918.)

The news columns quoted Montagu's three chief formulas : for local bodies, as much popular control and independence from other authority as possible ; for provinces, some responsibility now, to be complete as soon as conditions permitted, in legislation, administration, and finance ; the Government of India to remain answerable to Parliament, but the Indian Legislative Council to be made bigger and broader. Crucial proposals were : complete separation of revenues between Central and Provincial Governments ; provinces to be ruled by Governors and Councils with both Indian and European members ; franchise to continue on a communal basis (this was deprecated in principle but desirable for the safeguarding of minorities). At the centre the Viceroy's Legislative Council was to be replaced by a Council of State and an Indian Legislative Assembly, each with some nominated and some elected members. Here was the genesis of what came to be called " dyarchy "—according to *The Times* " a repellent word attributed to Sir William Meyer." By reconstruction of the Provincial Executives, a group of " transferred " subjects was given to Indian Ministers directly elected, on whose advice the Governor would normally act ; while other subjects were " reserved " to the Governor. Altogether the Montagu and Chelmsford document was loudly acclaimed as a permanent contribution to political science. It satisfied alike in structure and in conception. The remark, " Our reason is the faith that is in us," seemed like a pervasive motto. Sinha, in London as delegate to the Imperial Conference, "unhesitatingly" believed that the Report laid the foundations of an Indian Constitution "which will contribute to the solidarity and unity of the Empire in like degree as the genius of Campbell-Bannerman achieved in the case of South Africa." (July 8.) *The Times* now deemed it wise to put the brake on over-optimism and appealed in a leader on July 31 for searching discussion in detail. The Report, in fact, had united in hostility ultra-Conservative Englishmen like Lord Sydenham with Indians who rejected all but what the Viceroy called "cataclysmic changes." The same day brought a dispatch from Simla, where Mr. Justice Rowlatt's Committee on sedition had unanimously linked revolutionaries in Bengal with German plots.

Thus 1919 was the most momentous year in India for a generation. That year saw placed on the Statute Book the Government of India Act with all its implication of "dyarchy." Gandhi, "an emotional but sincere agitator," with his preaching of non-violent resistance came into the news. Fierce agitation over the passing of the Rowlatt Acts against sedition culminated in tragedy at Amritsar. The new ruler of Afghanistan, Amanullah, attacked frontier tribes at several points in the summer; "the Afghan war cost £14,000,000 and the young Ameer is toying with Bolshevism," explained *The Times*. Moslems were worried by the Allies' delay in coming to terms with Turkey. There was widespread war-weariness, accentuated by the great influenza epidemic which had affected nearly three-sevenths of the population and carried off six millions. Costs of the necessaries of life were rising steeply. Happier auguries were the acceptance of India as an original member of the League of Nations; promotion of Sinha to the Under-Secretaryship of State and his creation as the first Indian peer; and on Christmas Eve the Royal Assent to the new Act was accompanied by a proclamation of political amnesty to the fullest extent compatible with public safety, and a statement that the Prince of Wales would go out next year to open the Chamber of Princes.

All these developments were followed with intense interest at Printing House Square. Even before the war ended, Sir Stanley Reed at Bombay had been requested to stir up his satellite correspondents and put together a weekly bulletin of general news running to 500-700 words; which was difficult, he pleaded, because of censorship. There was one other impediment, which provoked the paper to a leader:

Because Government business chokes the cables, Press messages are often delayed for several days. The consequence is that the Nile might change its course, or India might be riven asunder by earthquakes, and no one in Great Britain outside Government Departments would have the smallest knowledge of what had happened for a week or more. The contemptuous theory of the Government, which will have to be transformed by pressure from without, is that the public have no right to know. On no other theory can their present behaviour be explained. The case regarding Egypt is now notorious, and still continues.[1] The case of the Delhi riots is even more conspicuous.[2] Mr. Montagu, or his deputies, knew all about them the day after they occurred. He and they kept the knowledge to themselves. . . . The position of the Government appears to be that kingdoms may fall, satraps expire, or cities rise in troubled alarm, but until some private member rises in the House and asks a question they propose to keep their information up their sleeve. Mr. Bonar Law once said that to get information out of the Government was like drawing teeth. Hostilities have ceased, and the teeth must be drawn. (April 10, 1919.)

Of the Crewe Committee set up to examine relations between the Secretary of State and the Government of India, the paper said : " Simla and Whitehall have too long worked in separate watertight compartments, and have never rightly understood each other." (January 31, 1919.) The Secretary's Council needed " rejuvenation, but not extinction." When the Committee reported, *The Times* made a similar protest to the one made in 1914 against attempts to hamstring Council. Its personnel, thought the paper, should be selected by the Cabinet. In March came this cautionary remark, often repeated :

It has become clear that the plan of the " dyarchy " has very few sincere champions,[3] but it continues to hold the field because nobody has been able to suggest a really acceptable alternative. It may be a clumsy expedient, but should be supported unless a better method can be formulated. (March 6, 1919.)

Next day Montagu spoke at a banquet to Sinha and was thus criticized in a leading article by Fraser :

By far the most important announcement of policy in Mr. Montagu's speech was his intimation, as we read it, that the

[1] On the arrest of Zaghlul Pasha and other Nationalist leaders in March there had been riots in Cairo with fatal casualties.

[2] Six persons were killed by troops firing on a mob at Delhi on March 30, and *The Times* was unable to print the news until April 8. See below.

[3] Chirol was one of these and had a letter published on June 9 to " break one more lance in defence of the one feature in the scheme to which you appear to take the chief exception."

principle of communal representation is to be extended. The Mahomedans and the Sikhs are already promised such representation, and we conclude that the non-Brahmin communities in certain areas will now receive it also. We do not understand Mr. Montagu's dislike of the principle of communal representation, which is specially suited for Indian conditions. (March 10, 1919.)

All that the Montagu-Chelmsford Reforms needed was time and willingness to work them. They received neither. Riots at Delhi were ostensibly a mark of public disapproval of the Rowlatt Acts, but *The Times* did not believe opposition to the Acts themselves was really deep-seated. They were only permissive in scope, allowing the Government of India to retain some of the special powers it had been granted for dealing with crime and its prevention during the war. Politicians of repute, said a leading article, were using the Acts as an expedient to evoke excitement with a view to rapid constitutional change.

Mr. Gandhi has been nurtured on the doctrines of Tolstoy, and is about as practical as his mentor. Tolstoy thought that the best way to get good government was to abolish all governments. Mr. Gandhi does not go quite so far, but acts as though he believed this subversive principle. Entirely well-meaning himself, he becomes an unconscious foe to peace and order because he is in touch with far more subtle associates. Mr. Gandhi conceived a violent hostility to the Rowlatt Acts, and started a movement of passive resistance against them. (April 9, 1919.)

On April 15 Gandhi was called " a misguided and excitable person, who is used by others as a stalking horse," and there was joined the remark about Sarojini Naidu, the bilingual poetess who was ultimately to govern the United Provinces, that " Neither of these persons is in any real sense dangerous."

Then came news of trouble at Ahmedabad, Lahore, and above all Amritsar. The Viceroy spoke of " open rebellion." Though the gravity of these outbreaks was recognized by the paper, it fell, owing to the paucity of the censored news, into understatement of the loss of native lives. Months passed before the Hunter Committee elicited from General Dyer, who commanded in the Punjab, that on April 13, having prohibited public meetings at Amritsar, he opened fire without warning on a crowd estimated by him at 6,000, discharging 1,650 rounds which killed 379 persons and wounded some 1,200; that he would not have flinched from further slaughter had there been space to bring up a machine-gun; that he made no attempt to succour the wounded; and that he could have dispersed the assembly without a shot, only his deliberate purpose was " to strike terror into the whole of the Punjab." *The Times*, seeking an explanation of the " open rebellion," reiterated that the Rowlatt Acts were only a pretext. Nor was the Montagu-Chelmsford Report to blame, even though that document contained " a great deal of dreamy and even dangerous nonsense "; for " Whatever may occur now in India, spacious reforms continue to be imperatively required. Rebellion may check their introduction, but the need remains." The question, now that Steed occupied the Editor's chair, was whether Bolshevism was at the bottom of it. The Helsingfors Correspondent had seen a letter from the Bolshevik diplomatic representative at Stockholm to the Extraordinary Commission at Petrograd proving that agents were in British India who would start a rebellion in the spring.[1] Fraser finished a leader with the warning that here was a real attempt to throw off British rule altogether, and it behoved the British public to give no Indian a hearing without scrutinizing his past record. He asked that O'Dwyer should stay at his post in the Punjab. He was in a calmer mood when the apparent new union between Hindu rebel and Moslem malcontent was shown to be dissolving.

Reed, returning to Bombay from leave at the end of 1919, summed up the position in a letter to *The Times*. It was more excited and bitter than he had known for twenty-five years; friends in the Punjab said that that province was more envenomed and anti-British than since the Mutiny. " No settlement with Turkey that is humanly possible can produce other than further dissatisfaction. The Moslems are making common cause with the extreme Hindus and the atmosphere is ripe for an explosion." Prophetically, Reed ventured to say that the extremists would not boycott the Reforms, and so abandon their prospect of power, but would seek entry to the Councils for the sole purpose of wrecking them from within. Also in December there came to the office the first disclosures of the Amritsar incident. In supporting the official censure and dismissal of Dyer which followed the findings of the Hunter Committee, *The Times* was aware that it spoke for only a handful of Anglo-Indians, not all the House of Commons, and, as it turned out, for a minority in the Lords. The paper was undeterred. Chirol later forecast that the verdict of history would be to endorse this repudiation of Dyer's action and doctrine.[2] Reed, who had dissociated

[1] Dispatch of the Helsingfors Correspondent, February 19, published March 20, 1919.

[2] *Fifty Years in a Changing World* (1927), p. 258.

his newspaper *The Times of India* from the sympathy Dyer claimed and extracted in that country wrote to the Foreign Department on December 17, 1920 :

We know some of the undercurrents in the Lords. The Indian does not. He only sees that Montagu was bitterly attacked for protesting against the doctrine of preventive massacre; that the House of Lords has justified the doctrine of preventive massacre; that Anglo-Indians in England and in India have subscribed over twenty thousand pounds for the benefit of the soldier who massacred as large a proportion of an unarmed crowd as he could and admitted that he would have killed more if he had had the means. If notwithstanding he is asked to repose supreme faith in Parliament, he turns to the columns of *The Times*, which on these occasions rose to the heights of its great traditions.

These " heights " were a refusal to recede from certain postulates : that common humanity had been outraged by firing without warning and after the mob had begun to disperse; and that the whole doctrine of terrorizing a province must be abandoned by any aspirant to rule. On this issue Steed was inflexible. During the Parliamentary debates of 1920 the paper found it necessary to " remind our readers of a great principle of government which we believe to have been monstrously perverted at Amritsar." (July 8, 1920.) Persistency of the General's advocates was deemed a grave error, sides being taken most strongly in reporting the speeches. The Government defeat in the Lords, of no consequence in England, was expected to bear bitter fruit in India. At the same time, Indians must try to forgive, accepting the British assurance that wrongdoers were disowned. " We wish to hear no more of swords of honour, on the one hand, or of martyrs' memorials on the other."

Gandhi, now hailed as a Mahatma, never rose to greater influence than at this period. Neither Chirol nor Fraser made question of his integrity. Reed wrote to the Office on March 27, 1920 :

Opinions naturally differ with regard to a man who is a fanatic and is on many points quite hopelessly impracticable. He is however a very close friend of mine and I am convinced he is a man of transparent sincerity. I know the Viceroy shares this view.

But none could fail to observe that the " saintly turbulence " which the Mahatma had " elevated to a fine art " was apt to outrun his own professions of non-violence and result in sanguinary excesses among those of inferior spirituality. For this reason late in 1920 *The Times* first introduced a note of acerbity into its references to Gandhi, which hitherto had been exemplary for their tolerance. It was still a year before the rioting in Bombay on the occasion of the Prince of Wales's visit called forth the following outright condemnation :

Mr. Gandhi is doing exactly what he has done several times before. Periodically he stirs up some section of the ignorant masses to tumult, finds he cannot control them, expresses regret, and after an interval of quiescence behaves in the same way again. Perhaps too much stress has been laid in the past upon the loftiness and the purity of his motives. In practice he is revealed as a mischievous crank with a talent for fomenting disorder. He now says he has come to the conclusion that " mass civil disobedience " cannot be started at present. He will be judged by his future actions, and if he is really contrite he can best prove his sincerity by withdrawing from public life. (November 22, 1921.)

With not only the prestige of the Government of India at its lowest, but lack of faith in the sense of justice at Westminster, Gandhi had the rare opportunity, as well as the exceptional skill, to canalize all hostility to Great Britain. Gandhi's boycott included not only constitutional machinery but all the more tangible products of Western civilization, from schools to railways and imported cloth. He achieved what in ordinary times would have seemed a miracle by bringing together both wings of religious discontent. *The Times* could never have been charged with bias against expressions of the Moslem standpoint, and frequently encouraged double-column contributions from the Aga Khan ; but it still maintained that seventy million Indians could not be allowed to dictate Imperial policy in the East. Such agitators as Shaukat Ali and his brother were deemed frank rebels, without the idealism usually attributed to Gandhi. Lloyd George's declaration of January 5, 1918, that British war aims did not include depriving Turkey of lands in Thrace, was unfortunate, so far as it embarrassed the future acts of the Government. Moslem grievances must fester, thought *The Times*, through the dallying over treaty-making with the Turks. The sole crumb of comfort Reed could offer Printing House Square was that its consistent attitude to Indian affairs satisfied all but extremist agitators and Die-hards. Always quick to react against any proposal for transferring to Whitehall more control in Indian matters, the paper attacked Lord Esher's Committee on

Army Reform in India for reducing the Viceroy, "who is by statute the head of the Army in India, to a nonentity. They wipe the Government of India off the slate altogether. They convert the Commander-in-Chief into a gramophone." (October 2, 1920.)

At the worst moment in Anglo-Indian relations since the Mutiny, Chirol once again went out to study the situation. His articles bore the general title "India Old and New," and significantly opened, on December 23, 1920, with a study of Gandhi's teaching, under the heading "Saint and Firebrand." The Mahatma was beyond argument, since his conscience told him he was right. To the Western mind he might appear a madman; in the East "a touch of madness is apt to be taken for an additional sign of inspiration from the gods." Chirol came to the conclusion that fervour for Home Rule and a comprehensive boycott was dying down, but he would not underrate the strength of "Gandhiism," and his sixth article, on February 7, 1921, recorded an hour's talk with the Mahatma. Gandhi maintained that his followers could have swept the board at the elections, but was not deliberate abstention by the vast majority of the electorate a more imposing demonstration of their will to self-rule? India had recovered her soul through the fiery ordeal undergone by Hindus and Moslems, in the Punjab and over the Caliphate question, and must go on by her "soul-force" to attain to the ancient wisdom of the Vedas. Gandhi, challenged for the destructiveness of his methods, breaking up the legal and educational system and those administrative services on which peaceful life depended, replied: "I destroy nothing that I cannot replace." Chirol's nineteen articles were not all controversial or even political. He described industry, systems of worship, the structure of caste, and by perfect timing dealt with the history of Delhi and antecedents of the Princes just when the new Indian Chambers were inaugurated. But he finished in the Punjab, with a penultimate article echoing the Duke of Connaught's remark about "the shadow of Amritsar." Chirol's conclusion (May 25) was that the new popular Assemblies did really exist and represent all sections of opinion except self-exiling extremists, and that Indians were finding real power passing to them even more than appeared on the face of the Government of India Act. There were grievous dangers: non-cooperation making a twofold appeal, to the ignorant and simple through Gandhi's own saintliness, to the passionate and grasping through Gandhi's far from saintly followers; a huge rise in costs, slump in trade, disastrous currency[1] laws from Whitehall, a crushing military expenditure; the Caliphate agitation; behind all, "for the first time since the Mutiny a great wave of racial hatred." The hope for Great Britain was to push ahead with "equal partnership in rights and duties."

But the unhappy incidence of riot and massacre altered the process of shaping and inaugurating the Montagu-Chelmsford Reforms. The Duke of Connaught on February 9, 1921, when opening the new Indian Legislature, said: "Since I landed I have felt around me bitterness and estrangement between those who have been and should be friends. The shadow of Amritsar has lengthened over the fair face of India."

Peace was not signed with Afghanistan until November 22, 1921, and warfare with tribesmen on the North-West Frontier, especially the Waziris, was endemic. *The Times* resolutely opposed an expansionist policy in those mountainous border-lands, Waziristan and the Mohmand country, Chitral and Tirah, Swat and Bajaur and Dir. Precisely as in Mesopotamia, difficulties of operating and the enormous expenditure on garrisons were the objections. While it was useless to talk of "going back to the Indus" since it had been bridged at Attock, the paper wanted some reversion to Curzon's scheme put forward a score of years earlier, when militia regiments raised from among the tribesmen under British officers were made responsible for defending their own zones, while British troops defended Imperial territory. Even Chelmsford's idea of occupying a small quadrilateral in Waziristan, whence good roads should radiate through the region, was viewed with misgiving. There might be danger of Bolshevik influence filtering through the frontiers if the tribesmen were, or were made, suspicious that Great Britain was aggressive.

When Chelmsford returned from his Viceroyalty to England on April 19, 1921, *The Times* accorded him a qualified eulogy. He had gone out at a time of almost unparalleled difficulty, to find war-weariness, crippling prices, a depleted Civil Service, restless frontiers, and threatening Afghans. He had set in motion large new representative institutions, while engaged in border warfare on a scale "that made all previous expeditions in India seem like small punitive raids," and while Anglo-Indians were cynical about the Reforms, Indian Moderates urging quicker progress, extremists boycotting the scheme altogether, and a militant Moslem faction sounding discord. There was a

---

[1] The rupee came down in 1920 from about 2s. 8d. to 1s. 4d.

fault : often he had seemed a spectator rather than a man of action ; yet no Viceroy had a prouder record of actual achievement.

Chelmsford's successor was Reading, who had consulted Steed more than once before accepting the Viceroyalty, and when he was firmly seated, the Prince of Wales began his delayed tour. Sir Harry Perry Robinson went with him as special writer for *The Times*. An Indian Number was brought out on November 17, 1921, the date of disembarkation at Bombay. The Prince's tour was a magnificent success, and though the non-cooperators put forth their best efforts, only at Allahabad and to some extent at Ajmer could they induce the population to stay away from the route. Another visitor to India whom many of high degree wanted to meet was Northcliffe. In January, 1922, while on the world tour that ended with a fatal illness, he seized upon the anger of Moslems as the most explosive ingredient in the whole mixture, and the paper was easily able to relate this diagnosis to its general attack on the Coalition over policy in the Near East. " I am shocked," said Northcliffe, " at the change in demeanour and acts towards Whites by both Hindus and Mahomedans, and especially Mahomedans, who were formerly most friendly." He had talked to over a hundred from every class and sect who all showed " sullen silence or outspoken hostility." They demanded that the Sultan should be confirmed as Head of Islam and Warden of the Holy Places ; that Adrianople and the whole of Asia Minor should be restored to Turkey ; that the Armenians be invited to migrate to the Gulf of Alexandretta, or made independent, with protection by a British Residency. A leading article in that strain on January 25 was virtually addressed to Lloyd George's Government. Meanwhile it had become clear that the amity between Moslem and Hindu was fictitious.

It was now three years since the war ended and two since the Government of India Act was passed. With the task of interpreting a most confused pattern, Printing House Square had been satisfied to uphold standards and lead opinion rather than to make history. Against the chaos of boycott was set evidence that Legislative Councils were working. Political crisis was reserved for 1922. Two dramatic events occurred on consecutive days. On March 9 Montagu resigned[1] and on March 10 Gandhi was arrested. This was pure coincidence, for Montagu resigned on a technical point and the date of

---

[1] In the circumstances described above, Chapter XVI, " The Coalition Stands."

Gandhi's arrest had long been fixed. Nevertheless, the two events were instinctively and naturally connected in the Indian's " untutored mind."

The Times had pressed for both. By February it was plain that Reading, who had talked and corresponded much with Gandhi, would insist on sterner measures to uphold the law. Fraser believed the Mahatma's aim was either martyrdom, or to compel Reading to adopt repressive action ; this would result in widespread civil disobedience. Fraser's leader was significant :

Mr. Montagu made the remarkable admission that a few days ago the Government of India issued orders for Mr. Gandhi's arrest, but they have refrained from taking action because Mr. Gandhi has issued " orders " restraining his followers. In our view the Government of India have acted with unpardonable weakness, for they should have promptly carried out their original intention. . . . . The disposition on the part of the authorities to allow Mr. Gandhi to foment strife and disorder in India without let or hindrance has been a grievous mistake. It would have been far better to have dealt vigorously with him when he began to preach his subversive doctrines three years ago. (February 15, 1922.)

If Reading failed to act now, Indians would be convinced that he was afraid. Montagu was acquiescing in " the partial abdication at Delhi." It was useless to arrest " thousands of duped coolies " and ignore the real revolutionaries. Bolshevik machinations were no doubt active, yet the British Government was offering to meet Bolshevik agents in conference at Genoa, " a step which will be seriously misunderstood in India." Montagu was wise in urging a closure of the Greco-Turkish War. Britain intended to rule, and was not to be harried out of India.

We shall stay in India, and shall take a predominant part in the framing of Indian policy, because to yield up our control now would be to leave India a prey to unimaginable horror and confusion. Indians will enjoy a great and increasing share in the task of administration, but British rule will continue, British lives will be protected, British interests, which are identical with those of India, will be vigorously conserved. (February 15, 1922.)

Montagu had been generally supported because of his sincerity, but he had impaired the confidence and prestige of the Indian Civil Service and thereby weakened the authority of Delhi

The proximate cause of Montagu's resignation was that he published without consulting his colleagues in the Cabinet a message from the Government of India specifying modifications it recommended in the Treaty of Sèvres with Turkey. On the principle of Cabinet responsibility this resignation was correct and necessary. But the Indian proposals were almost exactly those noted by Northcliffe as inexorable Moslem demands : the Holy Places, Constantinople, Turkish Thrace and Smyrna, to be restored to the Sultan. *The Times* feared that Indians would conclude that Montagu had been dismissed because of sympathy with Moslem aspirations. Efforts must therefore be redoubled to persuade them otherwise. In this connexion the paper found a feasible explanation of the " Gandhi muddle " ; perhaps the Government of India desired to give proof of its solicitude for Islam by having its telegram published in both India and England before arresting " a dangerous firebrand whose propaganda had enlisted much Moslem as well as Hindu support." Montagu himself averred that he had been sacrificed to conciliate Die-hards in the Coalition, and Perry Robinson[1] wrote to P.H.S. from Delhi on March 11 that this was generally believed. On March 14, at Bombay, he found it " difficult to find a single believer in Mr. Montagu among Englishmen," though equally hard to find anyone demanding Reading's retirement. All Indians, however, looked on the ex-Minister as their friend and his removal as a catastrophe. His fall, due to his championship of reform, would prolong the " disbelief encouraged by agitators of every class in British intentions and good faith." Later in the year Reed, privately giving the reasons why nobody trusted the Government or Parliament, put Montagu's fall first.[2] It was immediately obvious to *The Times* that Moderates would be alarmed and the schism between constitutionalists and extremists might be healed.

The effect of Gandhi's arrest—he was sentenced to six years' simple imprisonment but served only two because of ill-health— might be in either direction. Perry Robinson saw it as the start of a trial of strength, but Printing House Square assured Reading that if he grasped the nettle he would find it was nothing worse. Bombay, Calcutta, Madras, all received the news with calm as it had been so long expected. Through March, events moved rapidly, but Lord Derby and the Duke of

---

[1] Sir Harry Perry Robinson had joined *The Times* in 1910 as a Special Correspondent, and was responsible for many Special Numbers. He was knighted in 1920 and received the K.B.E. See Chapter VI *ante*, for his services as a War Correspondent in France during the 1914-1918 War.

[2] Reed to Foreign Department, July 13, 1922.

Devonshire declined the India Office before Lord Peel accepted ; the Prince embarked at Karachi ; the Budget presented by the Government of India was accepted by the Legislative Assembly only after proposals to double the salt tax and to raise import duties on cotton goods had been abandoned. This month was the climax. During the remainder of 1922 discontent lessened, and India relapsed into a sullen acquiescence with occasional outbursts.

The Reforms were intended to have ten years' trial, and at the halfway mark only a handful of irreconcilables were any longer pressing for speedy revolution. By 1924, it was true, the Swarajist Party of Home Rulers had gone into the Provincial Councils with the declared intention of wrecking them, but only in the Central Provinces and Bengal did they command a majority, thus driving the Governors to special expedients. Gandhi had been released ; in England a Labour Ministry was in shaky power ; and the Muddiman Committee had been set up by the Government of India, on a resolution from Motilal Nehru in the Delhi Assembly, to inquire into the working of the 1919 Act. None of this implied that authority in either country favoured what Chelmsford would have called " cataclysmic changes." Few dissented from the view consistently held by *The Times*: ten years was an exiguous part of a nation's life. All the Reforms needed for a fair trial was good will and collaboration, but the combination of Swarajists and Indipendents in the Delhi Assembly was warned that obstructive tactics were not the way to get there. Ramsay MacDonald as Premier was commended for declaring that no British party was to be " cowed by threats of force or policies designed to bring government to a standstill." He was then rebuked for claiming that the condition of India had improved during his term of office ; told that the attitude of his administration was that of " a nerveless and helpless spectator," and his Secretary of State, Lord Olivier, had given Indians and British alike the impression that he was toying with a grave problem. In private correspondence Dawson's strictures on the Labour Government went further.

The Editor had not himself studied conditions on the spot, bu in the autumn of 1923 sent a Special Correspondent to India, who, though new to India, was much travelled and deeply read in the Orient. He was equipped with introductions to variou administrators who wrote frequently to the Editor ; one of these was Sir Basil Blackett, Finance Member of the Viceroy's Council and another was Sir Harcourt Butler, who in spare moments of governing Burma sent home a stream of pungent comment on personalities and politics on the mainland. Butler thus chaffed Dawson on August 23 : " I hope Mr. * * * is more cheerful in outlook than your previous correspondent, old Chirol, and that he plays bridge more quietly!" The Correspondent's first article, on December 11, was an appreciation of the work of Sir George Lloyd, who had just laid down the Governorship of Bombay. The Correspondent collected a mass of material and impressions, and his return was eagerly awaited in the office, where hardly anybody remained who had ever seen India.[1] One of Graves's conclusions was that more concessions could be afforded by the rulers if only both leading religions in India would apply the brake to their hotheads. Gandhi, former preacher of unity between Hindu and Moslem, was clearly the key figure, and *The Times* was gratified to note that on his release in February, 1924, he repudiated civil disobedience. Graves described him as : " In essentials no conservative Hindu political leader is more reactionary." But Gandhi was not the force now he had been in 1920 and was to become in 1930. His leadership in non-cooperation was being eclipsed by that of a Bengali Swarajist, C. R. Das.

When malcontents resolved to suspend their boycott in favour of " wrecking the Councils from within," the prospects seemed more dangerous than the direct frontal attack of Gandhi's boycott and the Moslem Caliphate agitation. As *The Times* pointed out to Das, it was easy thus to boast that the Montagu-Chelmsford Reforms were unworkable. Nobody ever imagined dyarchy would work in the teeth of determined opposition. " One of the two pillars on which it was reared has been wilfully destroyed." At the 1926 elections the Swarajists held the position in Bengal and won Madras. The point was that Congress since 1921 had set out to alter the system by " legitimate and peaceful means," but the word " constitutional " had been quietly dropped. And so, while Reformers inflicted defeat after defeat on the Government in Central and Provincial Legislatures alike, and " Dyarchy Must Go " and " People's Victory Again " were headlines in local newspapers, Printing House Square and its special writers remained unmoved, except to good-tempered denunciation. The paper never relaxed its interest in the problem.

Taken as a whole the range of the Indian problem covered by *The Times* was immense. No aspect of it was neglected.

1 Dawson to Butler, January 16, 1924.

Blackett, for instance, directed Dawson's attention to the relations between the Central Government and the Provinces, and the acute complications often arrived at in finance could be more sympathetically examined on his advice. One Indian grievance, perhaps unfairly pressed, was that the " transferred " or " nation-building " departments of expenditure, like education, health, and industrial development, were starved to provide for the " reserved " departments of national finance. Stringency indeed was at all times a factor making against the success of the 1919 Act, and this clash of interests was a main cause of the Provincial Legislatures coming to regard themselves as in permanent opposition to the Government of India. Blackett's series of Budgets, beginning to show a surplus from 1925, received patient explanation in *The Times*. When the Lee Commission made its Report on the Indian Services, however, the Finance Member's warning that this implied a descent to " the Avernus of provincial autonomy " did not persuade the paper to object to the Report, which it regarded as the most significant State Paper on India since 1919. Broadly, the Lee Report envisaged the Indian Civil Service being half staffed by natives after 15 years and the Indian Police Service so after 25 years ; while other All-India Services were to be removed from the control of the Secretary of State to that of the Provincial Governments, which meant virtually the end of European recruitment for them. When the Delhi Assembly threw out the Report by 68 votes to 46 in September, 1924, Blackett defended it for bringing overdue relief to ill-paid services. Academic as this debate was, seeing that the Secretary of State could implement the Report, *The Times* was disappointed to find such a majority for rejection on the sole ground that European recruitment ought to cease immediately. Failing early improvement in service conditions it feared that there would be an exodus of all who could resign and a deterioration in the morale of those who remained. Whatever Swarajists might say, the British Civil Service was the one safeguard of the Montagu-Chelmsford Reforms, and they were indispensable to the programme of fitting India for self-government.

Entangled with the political and economic story of the 1920s was the religious issue. If in other matters the temperature had dropped towards 1925-26, the cleavage between Hindu and Moslem was still profound and bloodstained. The basis of it was more than religious ; in places it was racial. *The Times* devoted a leader to the problem in 1924 on January 3 and September 2, and in 1926 on February 22, June 19 and August 21,

ut could do little more than record its regret at communal
disorder. Observing that there was a trend in Moslem opinion
owards favouring a Federal rather than a unitary future for
India, it was careful to find space for the Moslem plea that the
next instalment of reforms must not seek to undermine the basis
of communal representation in electoral matters, since only thus
could minorities be safeguarded.

Nevertheless in both countries there was conscious acceptance
of the idea of Indian nationhood. Civil and military services
were being made over to native administration; India debated
at Imperial Conferences; she belonged to the League of
Nations; the so-called Fiscal Convention, outcome of the Act
of 1919, permitted the country to frame her own trading and
tariff policy. Like Montagu *The Times* never shirked the ultimate
intention of granting self-government. The paper frequently
interpreted the Indian attitude to other countries. After 1923,
when turmoils on the Frontier died down, less suspicion was
expressed about Bolsheviks, though a "Red conspiracy" un-
earthed in Bengal after an outbreak of anarchism in October,
1924, worried the paper. Meanwhile, from watching events in
Egypt and Ireland, India gleaned clues to her future status in
the Commonwealth. The changes in Turkey, where Mustapha
Kemal swept away the Sultanate, persuaded Moslems to abate
their ultramontane postulates. When Reading ended his term
as Viceroy he learned from *The Times* that he had done well.
He was criticized in detail and regarded as fortunate in some of
his allies, like the Turks, the weather, and the altered tactics
of opponents. Yet, after all, he was handing on to his successor
an India less disturbed than the one he inherited.

The lull with which the change of Viceroy coincided was
welcome, naturally, to the office. Dawson faced, soon after
his own resumption of the Editorship in 1923, decisions on
Imperial doctrine, and in 1924 and 1925 gave constant attention
to questions of Dominion status, responsibility for foreign
policy, and relations with the League of Nations. On February
13, 1925, *The Times* printed the new Foreign Secretary's answer
to a question by Colonel Wedgwood. Austen Chamberlain
gave what amounted to a declaration of Empire policy:
announced that the Geneva Protocol was under consideration
by the Dominions, and concluded that the Government required
time for its consideration. *The Times* in a leading article stated
roundly that "They [the Dominion Parliaments] will not
abdicate their independent judgment to the Council of the

League on the issue of Peace or War." Borden had, in fact, already made a guarded statement of rejection on January 30, 1925. On March 13 *The Times* reported the speech which Chamberlain as Foreign Secretary made to the League Council. He submitted the new Protocol to detailed analysis, discussed the definition of " aggressor " and the viability of " sanctions." Then he concluded by saying that while " in ordinary cases " the mere threat of " sanctions " would suffice " it is easy to imagine extreme cases about which we dare not speak with the same assurance ; and it is precisely the possibility of these extreme cases, remote though that possibility may be, which fosters international suspicion, makes governments hesitate to disarm, and keeps the world on edge." This said, the Foreign Secretary proceeded : " His Majesty's Government do not share these alarms, but they recognize their serious effect, and believe them to be the main obstacles to the complete recovery of our shaken civilization from the disasters of war." But the suggestions of the Protocol were not obviously sufficient, they did not really " stiffen " the Covenant. The " extreme cases," to which he had alluded, were judged by the Government to affect certain nations, or groups of nations, rather than others. Hence the Government concluded that " the best way of dealing with the situation is, with the cooperation of the League, to supplement the Covenant by making special arrangements." These should be " purely defensive in character ; they should be framed 'in the spirit of the Covenant'." The speaker added that the Governments of the Dominion of Canada, the Commonwealths of Australia, New Zealand, the Union of South Africa and India were also unable to accept the Protocol.[1] In the opinion of *The Times*, Chamberlain's speech was " admirable . . . definite and final."

The hesitations then felt in the office arose in the main from the attitude of Canada, but the paper found it necessary in November once more to express its concern about the general Dominions' attitude to foreign policy.

Each Dominion is free to take its decision in its own time, realizing that, unlike the Protocol, the new Treaty implies no liabilities to impose economic sanctions on distant recalcitrant countries in all parts of the world . . . the process of naval blockade, implied in the Protocol, might have involved in practice every sort of complication

---

[1] Correspondence with the Dominions on the Protocol was published in Cmd. 2,458, July 17, 1925 ; reproduced in *The Times* next day.

with the United States, who is not a member of the League. (November 18, 1925.)

It was while this debate was proceeding that the Editor's mind, for the first time became seriously engrossed by the Indian prospects. He had been interested in the Peninsula, as in all Imperial problems, in a general way ; but a coincidence of political events and new appointments gave the Indian question an urgent and personal point. In consequence *The Times* recognized an opportunity and rose to it in a manner worthy of the best traditions. Through the decade which began with the Montagu-Chelmsford Reforms and closed with the Round Table Conference, a fairly regular curve in the political temperature is discernible. The lowest mark is reached about the time it was announced that Reading would be succeeded in 1926 by Edward Wood (created Lord Irwin and the future Lord Halifax). The appointment of one of his closest friends as Viceroy gave Dawson an unparalleled opportunity of studying the problem at first hand. Lord Irwin kept a far more personal correspondence with Dawson than with the men who had earlier acted as advisers to Printing House Square. Irwin was of course forearmed for trouble because he knew that revision of the Constitution was due to come up during his term of office. Not long after settling in at Simla he defined his attitude.

I have no doubt that the atmosphere as between Indians and British is much calmer than it was, and this I have no doubt is due in great part to Reading and also to the natural reaction from the high tension that previously obtained. I am always racking my brain as to how to get out of this futile and vicious circle by which we say no advance without co-operation, and they say no co-operation without advance. I cannot help feeling that it is a question much more psychological than political. One of the extreme Swaraj people said to me the other day that if only they could trust us it wouldn't matter to them whether they waited five or fifty years. How then to make them believe that we mean what we say ?[1]

Calmer though feeling was as between Indians and British, Irwin's landing had coincided with the worst Hindu-Moslem broil of the period, in Calcutta. At a dinner given to him by the Chelmsford Club on July 17 he took the chance of making a spiritual appeal. This speech impressed all hearers and was thus estimated by *The Times* :

[1] Irwin to Dawson, May 18, 1926.

Lord Irwin went straight to the real point. In India the religious interest is the deepest of all. There the search for some "fraction of the mystery" that surrounds our life is intense . . . . To this profound instinct Lord Irwin earnestly appealed. There are men in India, both Hindus and Moslems, who can understand the force of such a direct and sincere appeal to their deepest convictions. (July 20, 1926.)

The effect of earnest and eloquent words may have soon died; there were more bloody affrays; another appeal had to be addressed on the same level a year later. That effort was made and Printing House Square did its best to mobilize opinion at home behind the man who chose to arm himself with frank Christian principles.

Indian intelligence opened brightly in the year 1927. Sir Samuel Hoare, Secretary of State for Air, delivered to the Viceroy a message he had received twelve days earlier from the King. An epoch had been marked by Imperial Airways in the development of communications. The great Council House in New Delhi was inaugurated with "stately ceremonial which combined simplicity and grandeur." Simultaneously a Committee appointed by the Government of India to inquire into land reclamation at Bombay Back Bay reported that the scheme had broken down. A minor sensation that year was the publication of Katherine Mayo's "Mother India." Taken to task for not printing some letters of protest from Indians about this book, which received no specially conspicuous or laudatory notice in The Times, Dawson pointed out to the Viceroy and Sir Harcourt Butler that he "rode off on the regular, and very necessary rule of The Times that we do not admit controversial correspondence about any writing but our own." He was inclined to think afterwards that "it would have been better to let the Indians have their say because after all the book has developed into something of a public controversy." He went on to Irwin: "I hope you will let it be known that there was no question either of underrating the importance of the Protest, or of giving only one side of the case." All other events were overwhelmed by Parliament appointing a Statutory Commission to examine the working of the Reforms. Historically famous as the Simon Commission, this body was to lead directly to the Round Table Conference of 1930.

Dawson first went into print about the Commission on November 1, 1927, five days before the names of its members were announced. From the start he had no doubt what type of body it should be. A group of experts in Indian administration would have no hope of agreeing; a handful of " infinitely wise investigators, detached altogether from current contro- versies," would be unable to impose its recommendations upon practical men. Accordingly, " it should in effect be a travelling Committee of the Imperial Parliament, representative of all parties and therefore of all possible Governments." If its members would regard themselves as *rapporteurs* and not as judges, fears that Indians were to be denied a proper share in the inquiry would be groundless. The Editor wrote the same day to Irwin :

Incidentally I have succeeded by purely Socratic methods in discovering the whole *personnel* of the Commission, and here I am bound to say that I am just a little shocked. On the whole, I am inclined to think that the Chairman may be very good indeed, but he has a terribly weak team behind him. I feel very strongly that every party should have given of its best, not of its second, or third best : but of course they all rate the importance of a General Election far higher than that of the whole future of India. . . . I suppose the best that can be said of those who have actually consented is that they may be tame and harmless. It really is a one man show.[1]

The Viceroy's private expressions were equally tepid. There had been a leakage of names through Indian channels, which prompted *The Times* to state that no Minister or public servant had divulged the information it had possessed for some days. Birkenhead, the Secretary of State, found this incident " regrettable " but not " calamitous." Dawson came out again on the 9th to establish the soundness of Parliamentary inquiry and to find no harm in the choice of " men in the second flight " so long as there was a Chairman whose " intellectual predominance gives it a definitely Liberal character." Simon told his constituents in Spen Valley on November 10 :

The Commission does not go to India with any idea of imposing Western ideas or constitutional forms from without ; we go to listen, to learn, and faithfully to report our conclusions as to actual conditions and varying proposals from within.

But India did not appear likely to utter anything to be listened to. Boycott on a large scale broke out again. Sir Tej Sapru,

[1] Dawson to Irwin, November 1, 1927. His estimate was not flattering to the Labour representatives, one of whom was Major C. R. Attlee.

a Hindu Liberal, called the Commission an " affront to India's national self-respect." Jinnah led one branch of the Moslem League to denounce any Commission that contained no native investigators. Congress again under Gandhi's influence declared for unqualified independence as the goal and worked out a scheme for mass demonstrations of disapproval. All susceptibility behind such " indignant rhetoric " was incomprehensible to *The Times*. Although there was no precedent for a country collaborating with the Imperial Parliament in shaping its constitution, the Indian Councils and Legislature were free to devise what methods they pleased of working with the Commission and even discussing its Report. Here was an issue above party at Westminster; could not Indian leaders come together and see it through? It followed that such groups of Hindus and Moslems as repudiated the boycott were commended. The Delhi Correspondent on January 9, 1928, traced reasonably how affairs in India had led naturally to a campaign against cooperation. It seemed to him mainly a counter for bargaining.

While all this was proceeding and everything combined to delay the elevation of India, unitary or federal, to the status of a Dominion, the essential problem, *i.e.*, of security, was keenly debated. The conception, not to mention the drafting of an Imperial foreign policy was still a question. Recent Imperial Conferences had succeeded so far only in achieving unanimity; but, as before the war, they had failed to settle the basic questions of policy and defence. A sense of Imperial political independence had outstripped realization of Dominion naval interdependence and of the need for an Imperial foreign policy. The upshot was discussed in an important leader on January 12, 1928, written on the occasion of Amery's visit to Canada. Foreign policy, the article said

impinges with increasing frequency on Imperial policy, and the functions of the Foreign Office and the Dominions Office tend at a score of points to overlap. The last Imperial Conference did a great deal to clarify this changing situation and to bring into relief the inherent and continuing unity, amid thronging world problems, of the free association of the British peoples.

Amery's visit coincided with a notable development in Canadian diplomatic machinery. " At this very moment the Canadian Government announces an exchange of Ministers between Ottawa and Paris. These developments need cause no surprise, though they may raise some interesting problems of international law." The paper, in motherly style, warned the young Dominion against danger ahead :

No necessity rests upon her [Canada] to emphasize her standing by making superfluous diplomatic appointments which, while enlarging a Diplomatic Corps at Ottawa, might have little more than a decorative effect. That risk the Canadian Government will no doubt avoid ; she is not alone in the world as are some European States far smaller than herself, and she has at her disposal for dealing with an immense range of foreign interests the highly trained diplomatic service of the Empire. Yet it must be repeated that there is nothing in the world, except her own sense of expediency and of the bearing of Imperial interests, to prevent Canada, or any other Dominion, from sending diplomatic representatives to any country she may please. Certainly no one in this country will cavil. (January 12, 1928.)

As ever in daily journalism all thinking upon such problems was discontinuous and conducted only within the incidences of events. In the next month, the " peg " for articles on contemporary Imperialism once more lay in India. On February 3 the Royal Commissioners, led by Simon, landed at Bombay, their arrival heralded by a fanfare from the Viceroy as he opened a new session of the Legislature. Under the title, " India at the Cross Roads," *The Times* estimated the prospect :

Is India politically ripe for an extension of self-government ? Does this declaration of a boycott, based upon a patent misunderstanding, really represent the degree of political judgment that now prevails in India ? If that were so the Commissioners need hardly go beyond Bombay. The Viceroy thinks otherwise. (February 3, 1928.)

Unperturbed by a *hartal* and a flutter of black flags, Simon calmly announced his method of procedure. He wanted a Joint Free Conference of seven British and seven Indians.[1] This seemed to *The Times* over generous. It even prejudged the main question of the inquiry—whether India had in fact arrived at political maturity ; it almost implied that the period of probation was over. Anyway it failed, as leaders in the Central Assembly could only " reiterate the dreary formula " that they would not join in. Simon did not believe that the boycott would

[1] The proposal appeared in the form of an open letter to the Viceroy from Simon, dated February 6. Its appearance was carefully stage-managed, though a premature reference in the *Daily Telegraph* enabled the Congress to blunt the effect by an immediate manifesto. (Simon to Dawson, February 9, 1928.)

continue indefinitely. On February 18 a resolution on boycott passed the Assembly by six votes, but next week the Council of State resolved to cooperate. Neither event deflected Printing House Square from its doctrine that the Indian Legislature was not equal in status with the British. The Commission would go on working, amid welcome from large sections of the community; and in the end it would be for Westminster to decide what changes could be made in the Constitution of India. In fact the Commission were received with abundant respect at Calcutta, in the Punjab, Madras, and Burma. At the end of March the paper could speak of " ' reconnaissance in force ' from which its members are returning in a mood of cautious confidence." They were due for another visit in the next cold weather. Meanwhile Sir Harcourt Butler's Committee examined relations between Indian States (which covered nearly a third of the country) and the Government; this matter was " not one which can be played with or continually postponed." The Linlithgow Report on Indian Agriculture was pronounced " a document which no statesman, no administrator and no student of Indian rural economics can afford to neglect."

At their second sailing, prospects seemed to look brighter for Simon and his colleagues. Eight Provincial Councils out of nine now preferred cooperation to boycott, while three Indians from the Council of State had been nominated to join a body representing the Central Legislature for conference with Simon. This, thought *The Times*, surely killed any reproach that native views were being disregarded. Yet a fresh thundercloud was mounting. Motilal Nehru, now leading the Swarajist Party, had produced a scheme for the immediate introduction of Dominion status. His Report was endorsed ostensibly by an all-party conference at Lucknow. But no Moslems from Bengal were present; the Sikh signatory was removed from his post by his co-religionists; the Christians were not satisfied about protection of minorities. On the supreme point of abolishing communal elections the Hindus really carried no one with them, and a Moslem manifesto denouncing such a suggestion was signed even by members of the Congress Party. The office was satisfied to find that the Crown was not being repudiated, but *The Times* leader of September 8, 1928, could scarcely bestow serious attention upon so wild and superficial a project as " to open the floodgates of illiterate democracy and communal passion and to leap without any lifebelt but the Governor-General's veto into the surging waters." The Aga Khan pointed out in the correspondence columns of *The Times* fatal defects in the scheme, but his own suggestions, more Federal than unitary, were criticized as vague. The paper sympathized with the idea of rearranging provinces better to follow the divisions between faiths. On the first day of the New Year the All-India Moslem Conference declared for a Federal system.

Meanwhile, Dawson's personal concern became deeper than ever. The volume of his correspondence with regard to India grew after he made his first tour of that country in the early months of 1929. He naturally stayed with the Viceroy, and had an opportunity of studying the situation at first hand. His impressions inclined him to agree with Simon, who wrote that he was "now confident that we can carry the thing through in India, barring accidents, to the end without a hitch. Our real difficulty, which nothing can get over, is the intractable nature of the subject we are called upon to deal with. I sometimes feel as though I had been asked to spend two years over a gigantic crossword puzzle, with the tip whispered into my private ear that the puzzle has *no* solution."[1] It was more than ever necessary, however, that a solution should be found without delay. Among other things, Soviet propaganda in Afghanistan was giving the War Office cause for uneasiness. At his return the Editor saw the Prime Minister but found him unwilling to act before concrete proposals were put forward by the Commission and the Viceroy. By way of preparing opinion at home Dawson at once planned a special Indian Number to be brought out just before the publication of the Simon Report, which he expected early in 1930. He appointed Franklin Peterson, who had undertaken similar missions in Egypt and elsewhere, to be responsible for this number. Against the leisureliness of contributors, and the even worse reluctance of advertisers, Peterson made headway towards the end of 1929, and found time to send home budgets of news and observations. He liked to deal dramatically with events yet kept his sense of proportion. This extract from a letter of October 24 is typical :

Here, then, is my tip. A hysteric outburst at Lahore on January 1[2]; proclamation of a Republic; processions in streets outside with Nehru junior garlanded as the liberator of India; clash with the police; broken heads; shortlived strikes in Bombay and Calcutta; sections of railway line pulled up; a bit of rough stuff in outlying districts and probably a little shooting-up—then "as you were" and everyone settles down to wait for the report.

[1] Simon to Dawson, January 12, 1929.

[2] On that day the Indian National Congress would end its meeting there and Gandhi's " civil disobedience " was due to begin.

Through this testing year *The Times* was unquestionably closer in the confidence of the Viceroy and more stalwart in his support and that of the Home Government—even when it became Labour after polling on May 30—than any other newspaper. " All your contributions have been quite admirable," Irwin told Dawson on December 3, " and no words can say how grateful I am to you for having assisted people to retain or regain their sanity." The Editor was gratified to receive the following :

Private.   India Office,
                                                    Whitehall.
                                          11th November, 1929.
Dear Geoffrey Dawson,

Now that the storm seems almost to be over, I must just write and tell you [how] deeply grateful I am for all the help you have given. I don't mean this as personal thanks, because I know that you have done what you have done for India's and Irwin's sake ; but I should like to tell you on my own behalf, and I am sure Irwin would join with me, how very much easier our task has been made by the sane and helpful line you have taken when most people seem to have been losing their heads.

Yours sincerely,
WEDGWOOD BENN.

In Dawson's opinion Benn had done well. Olivier in the Labour Government of 1924 had inspired no enthusiasm ; Birkenhead had stirred the Editor to intermittent feud ; and when Baldwin asked whether, in the event of his Government being returned, Lord Peel should continue at the India Office, " I told him that I was quite clear that the new Secretary of State should be in the House of Commons."[1]

In spite of the plain warning given by the Viceroy in a speech made at the opening of the Assembly that no civil disobedience under whatever title could be tolerated, there were fatal riots in Bombay in February, 1929. Communist leaders were arrested. Again a " Red conspiracy" jolted *The Times*; and James Maxton, of the League Against Imperialism, was called an agent in the Bolshevik " drive to the East." On April 8, bombs were thrown in the Assembly when Simon was present, and occupants of the Government benches were wounded. It seemed obvious that the Government of India must now bring in its Public Safety Bill previously lost on the casting vote of the President of Assembly. But on April 11 Patel ruled out further discussion of

[1] Dawson to Irwin, April 8, 1929.

the Bill. The Viceroy thereupon made drastic but constitutional intervention. He supplanted Patel's ruling by an ordinance. No London newspaper gave his words in full except *The Times*, whose accompanying leader proclaimed that

Sound argument, unruffled temper, and resolute determination were never more effectively combined in a speech which may well become historic. . . . The measure in dispute bears no relation whatever to constitutional progress. . . . Nor is it without importance for the future of India that the present Viceroy should have given signal proof at this moment that he is a man of rapid decision and of inflexible will. . . .

Irwin told Dawson he had originally intended to move a vote of censure on Patel, but desisted because the latter was the authorized interpreter of rules. Between challenging his ruling and pointing out its impracticability there was a distinction of constitutional importance which the Viceroy was wise to draw. In the summer Irwin's " rapid decision " was advanced to ' statesmanship of a high order." He then put off the General Election until after the Report of the Simon Commissioners and their Indian colleagues. The fate of the Nehru Report had shown how " negative and destructive " were the present party spokesmen.

The situation now was that the Commissioners had finally come home, and the Report was expected next year. Their Chairman, besides throwing himself heartily into the British election—to Dawson's annoyance, since no Conservative was standing against Simon in Spen Valley, and nobody wanted to make his Report a party issue—had given the Indians an assurance that the Commissioners were not working out the Constitution of British India but merely assembling facts for the Imperial Parliament to study. The Butler Report had considered relations between the States and the British territories. On February 13 the Chamber of Princes unanimously adopted a resolution by the Maharajah of Patiala that all such relations must proceed from the basis of some connexion with the Crown. To Dawson there was no justification for hurrying Simon. A premature Report would look like capitulation to Gandhi who had set a time limit (i.e. the end of 1929) after which civil disobedience might be declared. Irwin was due for leave and consultation with Ministers. All these events were treated together by *The Times* in a leading article, just after Irwin sailed.

Since it is probable that the recommendations of the Butler Report will be generally supported by the Simon Commission, and certain that the Commission will make recommendations as to the future relations between the States and British India, it is clearly desirable that the Indian States, whether their rulers take part or not in the proceedings of the Council of Princes, should have their place in the subsequent discussions in London. (July 1, 1929.)

Paradoxically, Irwin's leave was the crucial episode in his Indian administration. The Home Government and their Viceroy agreed on policy, and it was arranged to announce it in a statement, now historic, to be made at Delhi on October 31. *The Times* had been apprised months earlier of Irwin's intentions. These started, briefly, with the idea of a Conference between representatives of Parliament, British India, and the States ; the Simon Commissioners should send a letter to the Government of the day, some months ahead of the Report, asking for concurrence in their having broader terms of reference to review problems proper to the States. Thus the reference to a London Conference made in the leader of July 1 was based on Dawson's independent judgment. On October 30 the India Office released the correspondence between Simon and MacDonald agreeing to such a three-cornered conference. Irwin, Benn, Simon, and Baldwin found no barriers to unanimity here. But Irwin's other idea met with opposition. He wanted the British Government to declare outright that India's goal should be Dominion status and nothing less. Though he had secured no influential support in England outside the Labour Government and Printing House Square, in Delhi he spoke his now famous words :

I am authorized on behalf of His Majesty's Government to state clearly that in their judgment it is implicit in the declaration of 1917 that the natural issue of India's constitutional progress as there contemplated, is the attainment of Dominion status (November 1, 1929.)

In the heated debate at home that this declaration caused Dawson took over the pen of the Parliamentary Correspondent as well as writing more leaders. A column of quotations from Montagu to Birkenhead backed the Viceroy's words. Dawson thus set the situation in perspective : a three-cornered conference had long been mooted and was approved by all parties at Westminster ; the Viceroy was primarily speaking on procedure and only incidentally restating ultimate ends ; there was ample precedent for using the phrase " Dominion status " while details were vague; it had a good effect in India; this was not a controversial question, for the Labour Government was at one with a Conservative Viceroy. Correspondents supported this argument. What else but Dominion status could be implied by the declaration of 1917 ? demanded Sir Stanley Reed : " The passion for equality in the eyes of the world is a dominating force in India ; if it is to be for ever denied India will be driven out of the Empire." (November 6.) Lord Lytton claimed that : " Lord Irwin, thanks to the fundamental sincerity of his character and utterances, has secured a greater measure of unanimity in India than has hitherto been obtained by any statesman of our generation." (November 7.) Gradually the critics at home spent their fire. In India even technical non-cooperators like Jinnah welcomed the Viceroy's declaration. Extremists still hoped to use it as a basis for bargaining. The hotheads of course could not be pacified, and Peterson's " tip " for New Year troubles was anticipated by an ugly incident. On December 23, the anniversary of an attempt on Hardinge's life, a bomb exploded under the viceregal train as it was drawing into Delhi. That very afternoon Irwin received in conference Gandhi, Motilal Nehru, Sapru, and Jinnah.

These last two were immediately to dissociate themselves from their fellow-Indians. The National Congress at Lahore, admirably reported by Peterson before he fell ill with paratyphoid, was memorable for three resolutions drafted by the Working Party. It would have nothing to do with the Round Table Committee ; its members would withdraw from Central and Provincial Legislatures ; they would start a campaign of civil disobedience when they thought fit. Jawaharlal Nehru as President looked forward to total independence of any British connexion and to a Socialist Republic. Never since 1922 had the message and programme of Gandhi cast such a spell. 1930 was to be the year of his duel with Irwin. The Viceroy's first epistle that year to Dawson was optimistic. Events at Lahore seemed to have given a stimulus to Moderate opinion. Both Peterson and his chief felt this idea to be unfounded ; they agreed that the only Indian political body with initiative was the Congress Party. At this exciting time they must have been delighted to have ready the special Indian number of *The Times* planned nearly a year ago on the assumption that public interest in the country would reach its height in 1930. Introduced with a pardonable flourish to that effect, the Supplement appeared on February 18. It was sold out at once, and reprinted in book form. The office had abundant reason to rejoice in the good fortune that attended its effort. The whole was a worthy successor to the first Empire number conceived and produced by Moberly Bell 21 years earlier.[1]

The attention given by Dawson to contemporary Imperial matters extended beyond constitutional questions. The Editor was deeply concerned over the tariff controversy on domestic grounds, but also on account of the fact that besides acutely dividing the parties at home it would keenly interest the Dominions. The impending Dominion Conference gave Smuts' visit to Canada at the end of 1929 unusual importance. Having then said in a speech at Montreal that the preceding ten years had been spent in establishing beyond all question the national status of the Dominions, Smuts next asked : " Cannot the next ten years be given over with the same zeal to the achievement of closer cooperation and real solidarity of policy ? " Dawson's leader on this occasion repeated that there was no reason for Britain to be afraid of such developments as the establishment of Dominion diplomatic representations at foreign capitals. This and other demonstrations of nationalism he regarded as a necessary stage of evolution. He added the criticism, usual in his writing on this topic, of the lawyers who, he contended, were misapplying their time in an endeavour to give elaborate precision to the implications of Dominion status. (January 9, 1930.) He consistently followed this line to, and therefore directly against, the Statute of Westminster.[2]

There was no respite from the urgency of practical, as distinct from the legal, burden. Gandhi now began his most spectacular performance, in which ideas far more Machiavellian were assigned to him by *The Times* than was usual in the days of Chirol and Fraser. He must know, even when insisting on non-violence, that matters never ended there. Surely he was posing as a martyr to official injustice, thus to win back those Moderates who had seized Irwin's olive branch. Anyway the Mahatma marched with 82 volunteers from Ahmedabad to the coast at Dandi, and there on April 6 he collected salt within the meaning of an Act to protect excise revenue. Unluckily, as Peterson related, no police were in sight— possibly under instruction—so " the martyrs therefore went about their job unmartyred." Already the Viceroy had exposed

[1] For the first Empire Supplement see Chapter I, " The New Imperialism," *supra*.

[2] For Dawson's attitude to the Statute of Westminster, see Chapter XXI, " Dawson's Second Innings," *supra*.

his hand to Dawson. "With Gandhi there is no chance of conciliation on any possible terms," he wrote on March 10. There followed a longer statement :

So far I have no doubt whatever that our policy of not arresting Gandhi has been right. He and all his friends had expected him to be arrested before he started his march and by that means they had counted on (1) the shedding of a great lustre about his name and cause ; and (2) sparing an elderly man the disagreeable duty of walking twelve miles a day for three weeks through dust in order to get to a hot sea-side at the end. The objection of course to not arresting him is if what I may call a " Gandhi legend " should develop to the effect that he was unarrestable. But I don't think there are any signs of this at present, and therefore after very mature reflection all the wise men—Sykes, Hailey, I, Haig, David Petrie (C.I.D.) and others—all came to the conclusion that if one could possibly do it one should avoid arrest and content oneself with confiscating his salt when made.[1]

Irwin was moreover satisfied that delay over the arrest had dislocated the tactical programme of the Congress Party.[2] The Editor turned sarcastic about critics in England who could see the right moment for action more clearly than the man on the spot. To Peterson, with closer vision still, the Viceroy's patience was psychologically sound. In spite of Gandhi's " genius for combining sanctity with showmanship," the idea of his trudging 200 miles to squat on a beach digging salt was becoming ridiculous not only to Europeans but to the more reasonable Indians as well. At last the Mahatma had to be apprehended at Surat on May 5, under a regulation of 1827 concerning the preservation of tranquillity.

With the pace of events now quicker than it had been for eight years, Indian news overflowed the columns, while comment was held back for the expected constitutional events, the Simon Report and the Round Table Conference.[3] Gandhi's arrest was one of a series of events : mob violence broke out in the chief cities ; at Sholapur policemen were murdered ; there was a rising at Peshawar, where the Chief Commissioner broke down and Irwin made a hurried inspection. Peterson, who thought this a tactical error, was by the end of May profoundly pessimistic about the Frontier. He forecast tribal war, and

[1] Irwin to Dawson, April 7, 1930.

[2] Irwin to Benn, May 8, 1930.

[3] Peterson discovered the date of the latter 24 hours ahead of the official announcement.

within a week an Afridi force descended on Peshawar and was engaged by British troops. Other reports of the first importance developed by chance, with no relation to the Irwin-Gandhi duel. An earthquake destroyed the ancient Burmese capital of Pegu on the very day of Gandhi's arrest. Amy Johnson on her Australian flight touched down at Karachi on the sixth day out, a record. " Kanchenjunga has beaten us," began a dispatch from *The Times* Special Correspondent with Frank Smythe's climbing party.

At last, the Simon Report was made public. It appeared in two instalments, reprinted as special *Supplements* on June 10 and 24 and was a " best seller " among Government publications. To *The Times* its unanimity was the outstanding point. A conclusion to be drawn from the Report was that progress had gone further towards self-government in the Provinces than at the Centre. Full provincial autonomy was now suggested, bringing to an end those " transferred " and " reserved " subjects of the Act of 1919. A Federal Assembly should replace the Central Legislative Assembly, while the Central Government should be free from divided responsibility. Defence was to remain a matter for the Viceroy. Burma was to be separated from India. Such obvious implications that Federation was the only true way of expressing unity in a sub-continent comprising the provinces and the Princes' territories were constantly upheld by *The Times*. Neither political wing at home was pleased, while Indian criticism took the expected channels. Hindus were vexed at not finding Dominion status mentioned ; Muslims and Sikhs were worried about safeguards ; Congress held stonily aloof. Among Moderates, those at home hoped the Report would not be shelved by a conference at which only Labour Ministers were speaking for Great Britain. Since Dawson was convinced that all parties should go to the Round Table, he disagreed here even with Irwin, who thought Indian Moderates might then suspect a pact among the British to prevent discussion of the Report. MacDonald took Dawson's view, while the Viceroy at his end set matters right with a promise at Simla on July 9 that the Round Table Conference would be " free to approach its task, greatly assisted indeed, but with liberty unimpaired, by the Report of the Statutory Commission or by any other documents which will be before it." All Dawson's zeal and energy for weeks were devoted to explaining the connexion between Report and Conference. " The conviction grows that it is a great State paper of permanent value. It does not follow that the British Government should endorse its recommendations offhand " (July 2). It was also time to write up biographies and generous estimates of the delegation now being assembled, 57 representatives of British India as well as sixteen Princes. There was some force in Peterson's sporting figure, " no Indian delegation without a three-quarter line composed of Gandhi on one wing, the two Nehrus in the centre, and Malaviya or Patel on the other, can possibly be looked on as representative " ;[1] but perhaps the defect was made good by the reappearance in England of " Ranji." To help colour the background that summer, Edward Thompson tried in a series of articles to remove American misconceptions of British rule in India, and extracts were printed from Montagu's Indian diary.

Thus was reached November 12, 1930, when the King-Emperor in the House of Lords opened the Round Table Conference which was to hold three sessions. It was just over two years before the National Government shaped the measure which, as the Government of India Act, was to receive the Royal Assent on August 4, 1935. The eloquent orations of that winter gave *The Times* the opportunity of especially full reporting and scrupulous assessment. At times the English was too much for note-takers — " these Indian speeches threaten to rival Shakespeare himself as a field for textual criticism," remarked a leader on November 20. After it was all over, the Editor calculated in a report to Irwin that he had personally put together 35 leaders on the whole topic. There is an accent of fatigue in his letter :

I think that for the moment we might sing " Nunc dimittis." The Round Table was dissolved yesterday in a most agreeable atmosphere of emotion—which did not, however, I am glad to say colour the purport of Ramsay's speech. . . . The P.M. and Sankey kept up their reputation to the end. . . Reading and Philip Kerr were both very good all through, and Peel came up to the scratch very well yesterday. Sapru has stood out among the British Indians, Bikaner and Bhopal among the Princes. Sastri was not bad, but rather sentimental and querulous ; Jayakar, on the other hand, was very businesslike. Jinnah was the outstanding failure. I think that he and Chintamani are likely to cause the most trouble hereafter. They have all done a good deal to educate public opinion in England, not least about your merits as a Viceroy.[2]

1 Peterson to Dawson, September 12, 1930.

2 Dawson to Irwin, January 20, 1931.

This tribute to a Viceroy who was also a friend was no flattery. The Editor's own " merits " were none the less deserving of the thanks of statesmen. He had thought hard and worked hard on the Indian problem. Although the Viceroy was his Yorkshire neighbour, the Editor would have engaged himself with equal energy had he been a relative stranger. Dawson, even with all the complications of Europe, and the problem of Germany, could not conceive of anything of greater moment to the British Empire than a happy solution of the Indian problem. He believed the Conservatives would finally have to solve it and would be in a far stronger position for doing so if they consented now to agreements made by an all-party delegation. With unswerving purpose throughout Irwin's régime the Editor held that " Die-hards " did not express even the Conservative, let alone the British, outlook on India.

Thus Irwin's term as Viceroy was ending in a highly creditable fashion. With the succession of Lord Willingdon on April 17, 1931, and during the interim before the second session of the Round Table Conference, Dawson was content mostly to let Indian news flow into the columns with ample freedom. The Conservative revolt against Baldwin for " betrayal of the Empire," symbolized by the famous Westminster election cry : " Gandhi is watching St. George's," deserved the paper's disapproval. It was won by (Sir) Duff Cooper against the candidate whom Dawson saw as determined " to use a great Imperial problem as a pawn in the domestic party game." Both Baldwin and Dawson felicitously reminded Winston Churchill by quoting his own utterances of the highly moral and constitutional line he had once taken against reactionaries of General Dyer's day.

Then on May 2, 1931, the homecoming Viceroy was greeted as his predecessors had been with an encomium. He had become for Indians " an Englishman whose character has impressed them with a new respect for all Englishmen." As a result, his efforts towards getting the Round Table Conference started had been crowned by his conversion of the recalcitrant Congress Party " in the person of its fantastic leader " to the belief that this work was worth undertaking. Lord Irwin was safely placed " among the small band of the greater Viceroys." That The Times under Dawson had in some measure helped to put him there and assure the success of the Conference, is as certain as that Dawson's predecessor helped the Irish settlement of 1922. Together both episodes may be taken as having completely redressed the debit balance accruing from the error of the Pigott forgeries.

The General Election of 1931 brought Baldwin back as Lord President of the Council in MacDonald's second National Government.[1] Within the first month of the new Government's term Dawson found himself in opposition on a measure on which he held deep convictions : the Statute of Westminster. Dawson still believed, with W. M. Hughes, that the attempt to crystallize in a formula the relations between Britain and Australia was " an act of extreme folly." In reality the Government was powerless, for the measure had been required by the Imperial Conferences of 1926 and since, and as consistently rejected by *The Times* in leading articles from the Editor's hand. As on previous occasions he now denounced the " Statute " as a piece of mere " pedantry." There was and could be " no particular enthusiasm for it, but, on the other hand, there would be no great apprehension about it." That it only defined a situation which had been tacitly accepted since 1926 was asserted in leaders on November 11, 20, 23 and 24, 1931. The fact had to be recognized that

in Southern Ireland and in South Africa, and to a great extent in Canada, it was not regarded as satisfactory that the rights they possessed and freely exercised should be left without legal definition . . . [yet] that attitude was not appreciated either in Great Britain or in Australia and New Zealand, the two Dominions where the British tradition is strongest ; but, in order to get rid of even the shadow of a grievance on the part of any Dominion, all the Governments agreed at the Conference of 1930 to a definition of those rights as set out in the Statute of Westminster. (November 24, 1931.)

The paper's only anxiety was that any shadow of grievance should be removed before the Imperial Conference to be held at Ottawa. The Conference, to be held at the end of 1931, was felt in the office to be of paramount importance. It was later postponed, and held in July, 1932, at Ottawa, where the Editor was in attendance.[2]

He was anxious first to talk to his Correspondents and to increase their opportunities to establish good relations with the delegates, and secondly to see the Prime Minister of Canada and other friends in the Dominion. The leader in the issue of August 20 was entitled " Agreement Reached."

1 See Chapter XXI, " Dawson's Second Innings."

2 See Appendix II, Sources, XXII, for an account of the Ottawa Conference.

The Editor reflected that the value of the Conference was that it drew British Ministers together and educated everybody. He greatly regretted the secession in the autumn of the Liberal Free Trade members from the National Government.[1] On balance, however, moves towards the political cohesion of the Empire had been successful. Since the time of Amery and Bell there had been several advances. If an Imperial foreign policy had not yet become practical politics, the Statute of Westminster, "pedantic" or not, had removed regional grievances and laid the basis for future agreement on international relations. The magnitude of the British contribution of the past to India was about to be matched by the grant of a new Constitution. *The Times* had reason for pride in its policy towards the Empire and the amount of space it had given to Imperial affairs since the Indian Mutiny, Gordon's death, Jameson's raid, Montagu's reforms and the Simon Report. The India Bill was pending. Much remained to be done if the Empire were to be made strategically secure, and it was hoped that European conditions would allow the time.

The only serious cloud in Imperial relations was in the sky of South Africa. When the Prime Minister of South Africa, Hertzog, arrived in time to visit MacDonald in advance of the Imperial Conference, it was known that Hertzog and Havenga (Minister of Finance) were preoccupied with a plan to formulate the "Doctrine of the Right of Secession." *The Times* once more earnestly hoped that the Conference would not allow itself to be absorbed in discussions by lawyers of "academic constitutional doctrines." Little more had been heard of this particular piece of pedantry, and the paper followed its course of commending concrete, specific, and untheoretical measures which would stimulate world trade, forward tranquillity, revive prosperity and effect appeasement. Imperial developments increased the sense of urgency with which the Editor viewed European tension, and the progress made in Anglo-Indian affairs encouraged him to play a part in Anglo-German relations. The first step, conciliation with Germany, had been taken early in Dawson's "second innings," and the paper was confident at the end of 1932 that a return to something like pre-war prosperity would be possible if European pacification, as understood by the leaders of both parties, was followed up. He decided that *The Times* should support this programme.

---

[1] Including Lothian, whose withdrawal Dawson particularly resented. "It seems to me to be his plain duty to see the Indian problem through, for he has it all at his finger tips." (Dawson to Vincent Massey, September 27, 1932.)

XXIII

APPEASEMENT
1933—1938

THE Nationalists were naturally dissatisfied with that side of
Schleicher's policy that led to a compromise with the Social
Democrats, and by the end of January decided that Hitler
was their man. On January 30, 1933, Hindenburg called on him
to form a cabinet. Its members were announced next day in
The Times, three days after the French Government had fallen.
Daladier's new cabinet, given in the paper, lasted for nearly
nine months; Hitler's retained power for twelve years.
The turnover article on January 31 dealt with the new labour
camps set up by Hitler's predecessors, and caused some little
stir. As far back as August 24, 1931, they had been described
in a letter to the foreign news editor as " a bona fide experiment,
though the Right hopes to use it for getting conscription through
the back door." Seventeen months' progress had emphasized
this tendency. The turnover now pointed out that " The new
army is now taking faint, but open, shape in the Physical
Training Camps," and only the absence of firearms distinguished
the men in photographs of one of those camps, published with
the turnover, from soldiers on parade. The first leading article,
" Herr Hitler in Office," drew no attention to the " special "
beside it, but discussed the change of Chancellor as a normal
event in German internal politics. Comfort was extracted from
the presence of only two other Nazis in the ministry beside Hitler,
though it was noticed that one of them—Göring—" controls
the police in the capital and over more than half Germany " :
nothing was said to indicate what, indeed, the office was singularly
loath to realize, that January 30, 1933, marked the beginning of
scientific and resolute warfare to a degree that the world had never
before known. The paper's attitude to Hitler's arrival as
Chancellor was expressed a few days later. His government
was to be treated exactly like any other, on its merits and on its
performance :

No one doubts Herr Hitler's sincerity; that nearly twelve million
Germans follow him blindly says much for his personal magnetism

as well as for the volume of the discontent of which he is the spokesman.
But nothing is known so far of his capacity for solid administration
and for cooperation with allies or colleagues, which are the real tests
of a ruler; and until he proves himself to possess these qualities it is
sheer waste of time to speculate about the future of Germany.
(February 3, 1933.)

Correspondents in Germany at once made it clear to Printing
House Square that the new Government's supporters, if not their
chiefs, were behaving in a way that could hardly be called normal;
" something like revolver rule or jungle justice might well impend
unless the police are immediately enabled ruthlessly to restore
order without regard for party," reported a message printed
on the foreign page on February 7. A considered review of the
achievements of the régime, printed on June 21 in a special article,
gave a balanced assessment. It cited the concentration camps as
well as the fall in unemployment, and remarked not only the
enthusiasm that the Nazi leaders could evoke but the deliberate
distortion that lay behind their speeches. " The sort of thing that
particularly appealed to Herr Hitler's home audience was the suggestion that the 224,900 Germans who had taken their lives since
the war had been driven to suicide by the Versailles Treaty ";
whereas, the Correspondent pointed out, " for seven years after
the war there were fewer suicides in Germany than in 1913." A
few days afterwards the complaints against the Peace Treaty were
taken up in a leading article on the fourteenth anniversary of its
signature, observed in Germany as a national propagandist day of
mourning. The article set foot in the snare in which the
Nationalists, and above all the Nazis, had succeeded in entangling
their neighbours. Thus *The Times* said that " Europe in fact is
placed in the dilemma of having to refuse to force what reason
suggests should at least in part be conceded, or else of yielding to
extremism what earlier was refused to moderation." (June 28,
1933.) This was a position from which the paper did not recede
until the spring of 1939. For six years the paper saw no reason
why an action that was justified by ethics and politics before
January, 1933, should be held to be falsified by the events of the
30th of that month. A political concession made to a possible
friend was not distinguished from one made to a probable enemy,
because Britain could not imagine that Germany would ever again
be her probable enemy. The distinction was not made even when,
as became apparent after 1933, a political concession was the
equivalent of a transfer of power that was bound quickly to affect
the relations of Germany with her neighbours, France, Poland and
Czechoslovakia. The policy of making not merely as many

concessions to Nazi-Germany as to Weimar-Germany, but even more, was adopted as a basic principle of foreign policy. These concessions were to be made because they remedied injustices to Germany; they were not made to Nazis as Nazis, for B.-W.'s convictions about Germany after 1933 were what they had been in 1927, and even earlier.[1]

Withdrawal from the League of Nations was the first step in the " dynamic " diplomacy of the Nazis. Germany left Geneva on October 14. *The Times* accepted the situation philosophically, and argued the case for treaty revision. While the paper was reporting the trial of Dimitrov and van der Lubbe for the burning of the Reichstag, as was alleged against them, English politicians were distracted by a by-election in East Fulham, fought by an able Labour Party candidate principally on issues of foreign policy. The Conservative Party regarded the seat as safe, since its majority two years before had been over 14,000. The paper did not regard the result as in any way anxious for the Conservatives, and expatiated at some length both on the economic advantages which the National Government had brought to the country, and on what it regarded as the self-evident inability of the Labour Opposition to do anything like as well. *The Times* as, at this period, a Conservative newspaper, was inclined to blame the Labour Party for earlier events outside any Party's control; and it did not make the point that it could have against the Labour candidate, whose programme had emphasized continued disarmament and support for the system of collective security. The outstanding fact was that the Labour candidate won with the comfortable margin of more than 4,000 votes. *The Times*, in a first leading article on October 27, 1933, congratulated Mr. (now Lord) Wilmot on a personal triumph, and wagged a mildly reproachful finger at the Conservative Central Office. It was politically true that East Fulham exactly, though for foreign policy very inconveniently, reflected the mood of the country. *The Times* was naturally affected by the result and the expressions of opinion to which it led. The repercussions upon Anglo-German policy, though not immediate, were deep. On November 17, 1933, the Editor wrote a leader entitled " What is the British Policy? " on the situation created by Nazi aggression in the Saar and in Danzig amid talk of disarmament. A plebiscite on foreign affairs had been undertaken in Germany on November 12, and nearly 90 per cent. favoured the policy of the Nazi Government. Dawson, five days later, argued that

[1] For Barrington-Ward's ideas on Germany when he returned to *The Times* in 1927 see Chapter XXI, " Dawson's First Innings."

We are all in danger of being confused by technical detail, amendments, cross purposes, and above all by conflicting views of German intentions, which in this [disarmament] connexion are altogether irrelevant. Whether Germany is soaring on a wave of moral regeneration, or sinking (as others allege) into a trough of barbarism; whether Herr Hitler means peace, as his speeches reiterate with apparent sincerity, or whether they are merely the cloak behind which his people are cultivating the will to future war—on any of these theories the case for plain dealing with Germany remains exactly the same . . . Now, if ever, is the time for the exposition of a strong and courageous British policy. (November 17, 1933.)

The paper did not then outline policy, apart from recommending " plain dealing with Germany," but on the 23rd *The Times* said :

It becomes plainer with every successive phase of the Disarmament Conference that no substantial progress is likely to be made until the question of revision is boldly faced and settled in one sense or another.[1]

· The appeal of pacificism and revisionism was closely connected in the minds of not a few public men with the need for economic recovery. The state of some of the industrial parts of the country was pitiful. In the administrative areas round Bishop Auckland, for instance, the proportion of unemployed who had been out of.work for more than 12 months ranged from 60 to 77 per cent.

In the spirit of Barnes's and Delane's Special Commissioners, and of Shadwell's method of direct investigation of labour problems, an investigation was initiated by *The Times* into the conditions in County Durham. The idea was B.-W.'s. He interviewed a " Special Correspondent " on January 24, 1934, and suggested that he should " take on a special mission to investigate and write about the derelict areas in County Durham, about which something drastic must be done." The Correspondent produced three articles entitled " Places without a Future," which were printed on March 20, 21 and 22. The last article coincided with the debate in the House of Commons on the

---

[1] In an instructive debate in the House of Commons Mr. Mabane (Nat. Liberal), spoke approvingly of this statement of policy and added that " there can be no doubt whatever that the people of this country do not desire the Government to pursue a pro-French policy, but are definitely anxious that they should adopt a revisionist policy in Europe, and that a clear lead should be given." The member, having described the Versailles Treaty as a " dictated " peace, replied that he was quoting from *The Times*. Upon this Sir A. Chamberlain corrected him. " But it was not *The Times* that invented the phrase. I want my hon. Friend, if he will be good enough to do so, and I want other people, to go behind the phrase and ask what substance is there in it. Every treaty at the close of a war is a dictated treaty—every treaty. This is merely a bit of German propaganda, caught up by *The Times* and other newspapers, as a convenient phrase to describe a situation but it becomes misleading by repetition." (*Hansard*, December 21, 1923, Vol. 284, Col. 1533.) It was a source of complaint in parts of Printing House Square that Austen Chamberlain was pro-French.

Consolidated Fund (No. 1) Bill, and the members for Durham took the opportunity of raising the issue of the depressed areas with direct reference to the articles in *The Times*. Mr. Lawson, a Labour member for the county, opened the attack:

Some of us have almost despaired of ever getting this House to pay attention to this matter but we have suddenly found an ally in an unexpected quarter. I do not suppose that *The Times* has become an ally of Members who speak for the distressed areas because they love us, but, upholding the great traditions of a great public journal, *The Times* has had a representative investigating conditions in those areas, and he has supplied articles which are roughly accurate, and, however much we may question some of the details, certainly almost perfectly mirror the condition of things in those parts of the land.[1]

He was followed by a Liberal National member for the county, Mr. J. P. Dickie:

I commend not only to South-country Members but to Members of the Government the series of three articles which have appeared in *The Times* newspaper during the present week by a special correspondent. . . . In one striking passage in yesterday's article, pregnant with meaning, he goes direct to the root of the whole matter. Having dealt with the question at some considerable length, he sums it up in these significant words: " It is the problem of saving whole communities from desolation, and it grows more intense." That is the conclusion of a visitor, a stranger, and a completely disinterested observer, and the tragedy of it is that it is literally and absolutely true.[2]

This praise, together with some criticism of details, was echoed by others, and the Minister was obliged to respond:

It is a striking and a fortunate coincidence that during the past three days there has appeared in *The Times* newspaper a series of valuable, informative and wholly sympathetic articles. I have no doubt that they will be read by thousands who will not read the report of our discussion here to-day. I think the facts ought to be known. I am very glad that the Hon. Member raised this discussion this afternoon.[3]

Accordingly, another Labour member for the county (Mr. Batey), after quoting figures for unemployment from the articles, issued a direct challenge: " What are the Government going to do with those men? What steps do they propose to take to help them? " The Government acknowledged the pressure of public opinion by appointing a Commission. When the Supply estimates for the Ministry of Labour were debated on July 25, the Liberal member for Bishop Auckland said he thought

[1] *Hansard*, Vol. 287, Col. 1402.
[2] *Ibid.*, Vol. 287, Col. 1411.
[3] *Ibid.*, Vol. 287, Col. 1510.

the nation is indebted to *The Times* for the action it took. The articles it published have been of great value; they served the purpose of focusing public attention in a way that nothing else had done since 1928. . . . I think the Minister will agree that the writing of those articles was the chief cause of the appointment of the Commissioners who have been sent into the distressed areas.[1]

At the end of the year a special Bill for the depressed areas was brought in. Mr. Batey, referring to the *Morning Post*, which had recently followed the example of *The Times*, remarked that their articles seemed " to clinch what first led the Government to realize the serious position in the North-East of England—the articles that appeared in *The Times*." [2]

The unhappy economic and tragic unemployment situation in so many industrial centres was closely connected with the mood that prevailed towards expenditure upon armament and the acceptance of commitments abroad. An isolationist feeling dominated many constituencies. The feeling of a section of London was further tested in January, 1934, by the Editor of a suburban weekly, the *Ilford Recorder*, who printed a question-naire on Peace and the League. To the question whether Britain should go to the help of France or Germany if the one was attacked by the other (as the Locarno Treaty required) the ballot registered the following answers: Yes, 5,898; No, 18,498. The ballot impressed Lord R. Cecil, leader of the League of Nations Union, and he persuaded the Union to organize a ballot on connected questions, the most popular of which was " Do you consider that if a nation insists on attacking another, the other nations should combine to compel it to stop by (*a*) economic and non-military measures? (*b*) if necessary, military measures? " This ballot was to be organized on a national basis. The Labour and Liberal Parties at once approved and were represented on the Executive Committee of the Union. The Conservatives took no official step, though a number of Conservative M.P.s gave their support. Representative intellectuals and artistes, not all from the Left, gave their approval.[3] The view held in the office is indicated by a letter from the Editor to the Berlin Correspondent.[4]

There will be plenty of British sympathy with Hitler if he manifestly sticks to the line of helping a genuine renascence of the youth of

[1] *Hansard*, Vol. 292, Col. 1801.

[2] *Ibid.*, Vol. 295, Col. 1857.

[3] Among them, Sir Cedric Hardwicke, Dame Sybil Thorndike, Mr. St. John Ervine, Dame Laura Knight, Miss Rose Macaulay, Dr. A. D. Lindsay, Sir Arthur Salter and Mr. H. A. L. Fisher.

[4] Dawson to the Berlin Correspondent, March 1, 1934.

Germany, and particularly if in doing so he succeeds in stamping on the "old gang." It is the greatest possible mistake to suppose that average British opinion[1] has swung clean away from him during the last year.

Dawson was inclined to think that Hitler himself might not be so bad if he were delivered from the influence of some of his wicked associates.

The national paper of England, like the suburban paper of Ilford, was impressed by Germany's professions and promises. At this time the Nazis, to broad sections of British public opinion, did seem to be behaving like regular politicians. At the end of June came a crisis that was far from normal, and more important than the exuberant national grief over the *Versailler Diktat* that had been organized before. On Monday, July 2, 1934, more than half the bill page was devoted to detailed reports from the Berlin Correspondent of Hitler's murderous *coup* against Roehm, and many members of the Party, on June 30. The event was a profound shock to the West, and to the League. Correspondents reported on both the morality of the slain and the brutality of their slayers; while the leading article laid stress on Hitler's violence, it did not censure it, even by implication. One phrase might even have been taken to condone what had been done: ". . . Herr Hitler, whatever one may think of his methods, is genuinely trying to transform revolutionary fervour into moderate and constructive effort and to impose a high standard of public service on National-Socialist officials." This, plainly, would not do. The Editor, who had been in the country during the week-end, arranged on his return for another article by a different hand, which meted out strong condemnation. The Roehm scandal was soon overlaid by an adroitly managed Nazi-State *v.* Church quarrel that, like earlier pre-Nazi *v.* Jew strife, effectively distracted what British attention there might have been from evidence of German rearmament.

A speech by Baldwin made only a faint impression abroad and none at home. He said on July 30 that we ought " never to forget "

---

[1] This reference to " average British opinion " is significant. It was this " opinion " that had become the one authority on foreign policy respected by the Government and *The Times* after East Fulham. No impression was made by the Paris Correspondent's message in January, which pointed out that " By the Treaty of Versailles Germany was forbidden to possess a single military machine or to train a single military pilot. It is believed here that many so-called commercial German machines are nothing but military aeroplanes in disguise. It is also believed that an adequate supply of pilots is being rapidly trained. . . . It is now thought that there are many potential fighting or bombing machines. Expert opinion here estimates that 500 of them were ready in 1932 and not unnaturally believes that the figure has increased since then. Even so, there is much more concern about the future. From information in their possession responsible French observers are convinced that within a very short time after the outbreak of war Germany could produce more military machines than the combined output of British and French factories."

that since the day of the air arm the old frontiers were gone. "When you think of the defence of England you no longer think of the chalk cliffs of Dover, you think of the Rhine." He had little support from "public opinion." *The Times* made no reference to these words,[1] but it did concentrate upon the country's weakness in air armament:

Deficiencies have accumulated until the disparity with other countries has become so great that a serious effort is needed if this country is to possess an Air Force adequate for its own defence and for its international responsibilities. Without the additions now proposed the Government would soon be unable to meet even their Locarno commitments. The political barometer in Europe is unstable with a downward tendency. There is—so Mr. Baldwin insisted—no cause whatever for panic and no immediate risk of peace being broken; but the future is uncertain. It will take not months but years to make good the deficiencies, and the task can no longer be postponed. The steps the Government propose to take should not jeopardize peace, but rather should help to ensure it. ... For Great Britain to go on neglecting her defences can only prolong and intensify the unsettlement of Europe. (July 31, 1934.)

This was by no means a popular line to take, and *The Times* hesitated to press the argument. The tide in the constituencies was running high against Continental commitments. In November another significant by-election occurred in London. The seat was the "safe" Conservative constituency of Putney, where the majority in 1931 had been 21,146. The Conservative candidate (Samuel), invited to submit to an interrogatory by local members of the League of Nations Union, replied that as a "man of peace" he was "in favour of the League," and that as to intervention against aggressors, the "circumstances would have to be altogether exceptional to warrant any boy from Putney shedding his blood in some foreign field." The Labour Party, on their side, claimed that they were the Peace Party. A portrayal of the Flanders poppy, as the emblem of those who died that democracy might live, was used to suggest that the Government was neglecting social services in order to put money into the pockets of private armament makers. The address of the Labour Candidate (Summerskill) painted a terrifying picture of the next war, whose outbreak, it was alleged, was being "hastened by the National Government which has done more to jeopardize world peace than any Government of recent times." *The Times* strove against such "intolerable and unforgiveable allegations," and

[1] It was believed in the office that what Baldwin intended to say was that in consequence of the speed now attained by aeroplanes, the sirens in England should sound the moment the Rhine was crossed by the enemy's air squadrons.

stoutly protested in a well-argued leader that, unlike the Labour
Party (and, it must be confessed, the paper itself in later years), it
did not " claim the advantages of a collective peace system while
at the same time evading its obligations, and that no party to a
system thus invoked can risk becoming a victim who at best may
be avenged but not saved." The facts were first that the
" collective peace system is so far from being perfected,"
and secondly, that its perfection would " clearly be postponed indefinitely if Great Britain were defenceless." Hence
the Labour Party's election propaganda, which exalted
unilateral disarmament over collective security, was not
only dirty, but dangerous also. (November 28, 1934.) The
Unionist majority at Putney was reduced to 2,663. There were
other portents of loss of prestige by the National Government.
Labour had already won Wakefield, Wednesbury, Rotherham,
East Fulham, Hammersmith North, West Ham (Upton) and
Swindon from the Conservatives. The Party inevitably became
extremely anxious when such a purely Conservative middle-class
constituency as Putney showed a great turnover in votes.

The Editor instructed Northend, an experienced and reliable
reporter, to spend some weeks securing the material for an estimate
of the position of the National Government in this country.
Northend toured the West of England, the Midlands, the industrial
North and Scotland, and reported that if there were an early
appeal to the country Labour would gain from 140 to 150 seats.
The two principal reasons were that the electorate desired security
of employment, and secondly that there was widespread apprehension that the country might be involved in another war.
Northend also reported that Unionists were much concerned at
the Labour propaganda, which insinuated that they were a war
party. " A feeling has been created that the Government is not
whole-hearted in its support of peace. To refute this idea a
number of Conservative Associations have undertaken to
cooperate in the taking of the League of Nations Union Ballot."[1]
Thus, in the Market Harborough by-election the National-
Unionist candidate tackled the subject by posters, speeches and
pamphlets which argued that if any policy involved a danger of
war it was that of the Socialists. He doubled the Government
majority in a seat which the Labour organizers had assured the
Correspondent they would win. On his return Northend learnt
from Labour sources that " The Peace-or-War issue is to be kept
to the forefront in by-elections. Apart from a belief that the

[1] Northend's report to the Editor, November, 1934.

campaign has political value, there is a sincere submission that, if the question is kept before the country, the nation will become so peace-minded that no Government dare commit Britain to another war."[1]

The immediate discussions before the country concerned the Versailles Reparations, and the post-inflation Loans which, according to the best information of *The Times*, amounted to double what would have been required for Reparations. (*The Times*, September 19, 1934.)   The urgent Continental issue was the forthcoming Saar plebiscite.   It took place on January 13, 1935, when the result enabled the League to order the return of the province to Germany.   On February 1, 1935, *The Times* printed the second of two turnovers on Germany and France.   They were contributed by a close friend of Dawson's and an ardent philo-German.   He referred to an

emphatic declaration of Herr Hitler himself. . . . He has said explicitly to me, as he has also said publicly, that what Germany wants is equality, not war; that she is prepared absolutely to renounce war; that he has signed a treaty with Poland removing by far the most dangerous and bitter element of the Treaty of Versailles—the Corridor—from the region of war for ten years; that he formally and for ever accepts the incorporation of Alsace-Lorraine in France; and finally and most vital, that he will pledge Germany not to interfere in his beloved Austria by force, provided all his neighbours will do the same. . . . He will sign pacts of non-aggression with all Germany's neighbours, to prove the sincerity of his desire for peace, and in armaments he asks no more than " equality " for Germany, and will accept international inspection if everybody else accepts it too. (February 1, 1935.)

These pacific intentions of Hitler were widely accepted and the way was seen open for political discussions.   On February 3, 1935, Britain and France discussed a Western Air Pact, a new reparation figure, a new measure of general disarmament and guarantees of security for the Eastern and Southern Border States, through Germany's active membership of the League.   The German reply on February 14, issued three days after Mussolini despatched his Blackshirts to East Africa, was disappointing. Europe was fast deserting collective security, and events disposed Britain to a narrower limitation of her Continental interests. The paper backed a letter from Lord Lothian on the reasonableness of Germany's desire for equality with her western neighbours in armaments, with a leading article that included these phrases:

[1] Northend's report.

Since the Government are facing facts, let the fact also be faced that the restriction of German arms to the Versailles level has gone past retrieval . . . If it is the intention of the British Government to get Part V of the Versailles Treaty superseded by a system in which all are equal, then no purpose is served by harping upon a breach of the Treaty—a breach moreover for which it is unfair to blame Germany alone. (March 11, 1935.)[1]

This was the day on which the renewed existence of the German Air Force was first formally admitted[2] to foreign diplomats and correspondents in Berlin. The comment on the Berlin Correspondent's half-column message on this matter (March 12) was restricted to three lines: " Article 198 of the Treaty of Versailles states that ' the armed forces of Germany must not include any military or naval air forces,' " and even this was dropped from late editions. Notice, however, was taken on March 18 of the German decision to form a conscript army of 36 divisions. Though this decision drove a Panzer Regiment through Article 160 of the Peace Treaty, the leading article was cautious rather than hostile.[3] Next morning prominence was given to a letter from Sir Arnold Wilson who held that " We may to-day be nearer peace, because we are nearer justice, than for many years." Inevitably, therefore, the French announcement that they would denounce Germany's breach of the Peace Treaty at Geneva was characterized as " profoundly regrettable." (March 21, 1935.) The same leading article approved Sir John Simon's imminent visit to Berlin. Sir Austen Chamberlain and four colleagues in the House of Commons viewed the article with " regretful surprise," and said so in the first letter to the Editor published next day; to which an editorial appendix, with a touch of the disingenuous, explained that objection to French action had been taken only on

[1] Lothian visited Hitler on January 29, 1935, and also saw von Neurath, Hess, Blomberg and others. Lothian had " not the slightest doubt that this [German] attitude is perfectly sincere." As to the question whether Germany once given " equality " and made strong, she would revert, if not to war, to " power diplomacy," Lothian replied that a real agreement with Germany would do more for peace than all the new pacts of mutual assistance between mutually suspicious nations that could be signed. (*The Times*, February 1, 1935.) Lothian again visited Hitler on May 4, 1937, and also saw Göring and others. Like most of the English germanophils, Lothian was unversed in the German language. Garvin and B.-W. were exceptions.

[2] The German public only heard of the admission through messages reprinted from the foreign Press: formation flights had already made it familiar with the fact.

[3] One passage in it deserves to be quoted, in view of the frequent allegation—for which there is no evidence—that *The Times* " supported the Nazis as a buffer against Communism ": " The German plea, of course, as everyone knows is that she has a potential enemy on her eastern flank, and that it is her duty to defend not herself only but the rest of Europe from the danger of armed Bolshevism. The answer to this argument is that Soviet Russia was never less likely than she is to-day to start an armed crusade on behalf of Communist principles, and that in any case Germany is being invited to take part in a Security Pact in Eastern Europe which would pool the resources of all the signatories against an aggressor, but is showing the greatest unwillingness to have anything to do with it." (March 18, 1935.)

the grounds of time.[1] The main leading article on the same page discussed the Berlin visit, and canvassed the advantages of coming to terms with Germany before Germany became exasperated. On the lines of " Agree with thine adversary quickly," the article proceeded to say that

Memel, for instance, should not be left out of the discussions. Is Germany satisfied with the present arrangement? Or is that one of the places where she looks for an adjustment? If it is, it would be a thousand times better to work for adjustment by agreement than merely to wait until the desired change may be attempted by some other means for lack of dealing with it betimes. (March 22, 1935.)

Three days later merely formal objections were discounted. In the paper's view they should not be allowed to hold up the conclusion of a genuine settlement:

Clauses of the Treaty of Versailles which were long known to be regarded as intolerable by the vanquished country have now been openly defied. They cannot of course be regarded as legally annulled by any unilateral action, but they have in fact been rendered inoperative; and it becomes the part of statesmanship and common sense to arrange for their formal disappearance under the best conditions possible. (March 25, 1935.)

That Britain should arrange for " the formal disappearance " of any clause in the Treaty that Germany found obnoxious was acceptable in the country generally. The only important centre of dissent was the Foreign Office. The Permanent Head of the Office, Sir Robert Vansittart, held the view that such a practice, if not checked, must have very grave consequences. He stood for a policy radically opposed to that of *The Times*, and so remained until, as will be chronicled in due time, he was promoted out of the way by Neville Chamberlain. The determination of the Government to avoid at all costs a collision with Germany was clear enough to the Editor. As a close personal friend of Baldwin, he gave him every support. A contemporary memorandum summarizes the points of a talk on Cabinet changes

[1] B.-W. dined on the 21st with the Runcimans, and there had a set-to with Austen Chamberlain who was shocked at his and the paper's disapproval of France's move to arraign Germany before the League Council for her new Army Law, that provided for an army of 500,000 men, which France viewed as a violation of disarmament clauses of the Versailles Treaty. B.-W. supported the opinion that there would be a clear distinction between the violation of the dictated Versailles Treaty, and of the Locarno Pacts which were the fruit of a genuine appeasement, and were freely accepted and solemnly ratified by Germany. In B.-W.'s judgement Chamberlain was fundamentally pro-French and anti-German, and had been so ever since the days when, as a student, he sat under Treitschke in Berlin. Runciman applauded *The Times* as having let " a breath of fresh air " into Anglo-German relations. This was a view commonly held at this time and greatly encouraged Dawson and B.-W.

between Baldwin and Dawson at the beginning of May. Both agreed not to bring Churchill in. This was the situation according to the Editor:

I found S.B. alone in Downing Street on the pre-Jubilee Saturday afternoon and quite glad to unburden himself about his troubles. Tom Jones, whom I'd just met in the Athenaeum, suggested that I should have a talk with him and I called, without warning, on the chance. He opened up at once on the subject of problems in connection with the impending and long-expected reconstruction of the Government.

1. SHOULD WINSTON BE INCLUDED ?

To this, contrary to some statements that had been made, he felt no personal objection, but Winston would be a disruptive force especially since foreign relations and defence would be uppermost. Moreover there was great feeling in the party about some of his recent activities against the Government's Indian policy. I suggested that the continuance of the Indian problem, even when the Bill was through, was sufficient argument for keeping him out for the present.

2. SHOULD L.G. BE INCLUDED ?

On this problem also S.B. has a perfectly open mind. He doubts L.G.'s effective support though he admits his nuisance value in opposition. He thinks that L.G. and Winston *together* would be impossible.[1]

It was not intended, therefore, to complicate " foreign relations and defence " by such a " disruptive force " as Churchill. The stand taken by the General Staff was equally definite. B.-W. reported later in the month to the Editor that

at lunch to-day X of the War Office gave me an interesting account of the struggle which the General Staff has been having to try to keep the Foreign Office straight on Germany. The G.S. is, of course, entirely in agreement with, and extremely grateful for, the line which *The Times* has taken. They think that the F.O. are practically inviting an unwanted war in time, but all their representations are met with a brandishing of the Eyre Crowe memorandum of 1908. X tells me that this document has also been waved at him. The G.S. has for the moment given up trying to persuade Vansittart and Wigram that a few things have happened during twenty-seven years. As Wigram rather ingenuously observed " It's curious that the W.O. should be doing the work of the F.O., and *vice versa*," and indeed it is.[2]

---

[1] Dawson's note, May 4, 1935.—Baldwin was not prepared to include Herbert Samuel and when Dawson suggested Philip [Lothian], Baldwin said he was a man whom he liked " but whose judgement he distrusts."

[2] B.-W. to Dawson, May 29, 1935.

Little notice continued to be taken in the office of information as to German air rearmament then available. The country was, as ever, interested in naval construction.[1] Two signed turnover articles[2] by E. L. Woodward summarizing the conclusions of his forthcoming *Great Britain and the German Navy* prepared the public six weeks later for the Anglo-German naval discussions. *The Times* found the situation in 1935 more satisfactory than in the years up to 1914, since the initiative in naval building now lay in British and not in German hands.[3] The paper's attitude was expressed, not in the leading article of June 19 that welcomed the Anglo-German Naval Treaty on the previous day,[4] but five days earlier in an article that dealt with Ribbentrop's arrival in London to conclude the talks. "AGREEMENT IN PROSPECT" was one of the headlines above a message from Paris that set the "competent opinion" in "responsible quarters," stated to be favourable, against the view of *Le Temps* that it would be "singularly disturbing." *The Times* said:

In its broad aspects, however, there is not the slightest doubt that the agreement if it comes will be generally welcomed in this country, and it should be widely welcomed elsewhere as a contribution to pacification and stability. Although in practice it involves a tacit disregard of the Treaty of Versailles, yet, inasmuch as it will substitute a new agreement for a section of the disarmament clauses of the Treaty, it will constitute an important advance in the process of getting peace established upon the firm ground of agreements freely concluded.[5] There are parts of the Treaty of Versailles which it is best "to forget about," just as the Prince of Wales said "the other day" that "We

---

[1] Churchill, in the House of Commons earlier in the month, drew attention to German air strength: "Look at the Press which supports the Government, great newspapers like the *Daily Telegraph* and *The Times*, which are now making statements much more definite than I ventured to commit myself to six months ago. Let anyone who chooses read the statement in *The Times* to-day—a paper devoted to the cause of peace and particularly friendly to Germany, a strong supporter of the Government. It says:

German strength in first-line aircraft is assumed at present to be not less than 1,020, which is double the first-line strength of the Royal Air Force, including 171 aeroplanes of the Fleet Air Arm and 264 units oversea. The strength of the British home defence force is 500 aeroplanes.

This is a very formidable assertion, and, as far as I know, it is quite correct." (May 2, 1935 ; *Hansard*, Vol. 301, Col. 607.) These facts were not allowed to influence the policy of revisionism then paramount at Printing House Square.

[2] Published on May 9 and 10, 1935.

[3] For the *Deutschland* see Chapter XXI, " Dawson's Second Innings," above.

[4] It did not, of course, escape French attention that the day of signature was also the 120th anniversary of the battle of Waterloo.

[5] "Agreements freely concluded" is a phrase continually found in the leading articles of *The Times* from 1935 to February, 1939. Here it appears to mean an acceptance of German disregard of the Treaty without consultation with France. Later the phrase is used in connexion with agreements secured by German pressure though not by armed force.

ex-Service men) had forgotten all about the war." . . . The inclination to come to good terms with Germany again does not denote the cooling of British friendship elsewhere, but it does imply that Great Britain thinks that it is time for all European countries to settle down as good neighbours—and to live no more as past or future enemies. (June 14, 1935.)

These words stand out as the plainest statement so far printed of the standpoint of Printing House Square. The agreement would be welcome " in this country." The paper was firmly settled in its belief that Germany was as willing as other countries to " settle down as good neighbours." There was no indication in 1935 or later that the office wished to abandon the lead given by " public opinion " as registered, for example, in East Fulham, and exposed in Northend's report. The paper followed the people. It was a lead given by an electorate influenced by Liberal and Pacifist idealism, and was strong enough to impose its will upon the National Government. More remarkable, Printing House Square had no perception of the intentions that lay below the surface in Germany. Instead, an invincible disposition in the paramount quarters of the office, though not in the Berlin agency, made the paper acquiesce in German professions. Dawson and B.-W., like the country, were determined to " forget all about the war." It was a mood that created for Germany the opportunity to make one more effort to achieve world power the one way open to her: by separating Britain and France and fighting both.

It must be admitted that by the autumn of 1935 Hitler had still to show much of his hand, but he had said and done several significant things. He had taken Germany out of the League of Nations and the Disarmament Conference (October 14, 1933); he had said in March, 1934, that " German boundaries have always changed. They will continue to change until all German peoples are united in one "; he had instigated the murders of June 30, 1934, and abolished the restrictions on Germany's armed forces imposed by the Treaty of Versailles (March 9, March 16 and June 18, 1935). Yet over and over again he had laid it down that Germany accepted the treaties made by his predecessors, particularly those of Locarno,[1] and had made some new ones, such as the pact of non-aggression with Poland signed on January 26, 1934. It was still possible for well-wishers to Germany to hold two views about the import of Hitler. At the time Printing House Square believed that Italy, as a Mediterranean Power, was of comparable and sometimes of greater weight. The Conference at Stresa

[1] See his speeches of January 30, 1934, or May 21, 1935, or the renewal on May 5, 1933, of the non-aggression pact between Germany and Russia.

in April, 1935, and the Italian assault on Abyssinia took up much editorial attention.[1] There were other international events of significance. From May 13-15 Laval was in Moscow; on the 16th a Czech-Soviet Pact was announced. Four days later there was a Sudeten gain of 45 seats in the Czech election and on the 25th the Germans sent a note on the Franco-Soviet Pact. At home there was a change in the National Government. On June 7, 1935, Baldwin succeeded MacDonald as Prime Minister, and Hoare succeeded Simon as Foreign Secretary. The Anglo-German naval agreement was signed on the 18th; a French protest followed. International relations became worse. Eden, as Minister for League Affairs, was in Rome during June 24-26. Three-Power talks at Paris on Abyssinia broke down.

Simultaneously the Peace Ballot organized by the League of Nations Union was about to publish its results. The "poll" had the enthusiastic support of the *Manchester Guardian*, the *News Chronicle*, the *Daily Herald* and the *Star*; while *The Times*, the *Daily Telegraph* and the *Morning Post* gave virtually no support. Meanwhile the Union's volunteers were intensely active. It became plain that the effort altogether was of a kind that the country had never before experienced. The Union's half-million scrupulous volunteers collected eleven million votes. By immense majorities voters declared themselves ready to restrain an aggressor by economic action; but it was a smaller number that expressed willingness to follow this up, "if it should prove essential, by military measures."[2] The result had a marked effect upon sections of opinion far wider than the Union's own. It was announced in the summer of 1935, a few weeks before the League appointed its Committee on Abyssinia on September 6. The Committee reported on September 23 when Abyssinia accepted; and, as foreseen, Italy rejected the findings of the League. The office was antagonized. On September 19, 1935, B.-W. thus answered a correspondent's suggestion that it was hypocritical to complain of an attack on Abyssinia, so near the Suez Canal, and to say nothing of the Manchurian or Chaco campaigns: "I feel certain that it is a very simple feeling about right and wrong that

[1] On May 2, 1935, the Editor wrote to Lord Snowden that "the view on foreign policy taken by *The Times* has a great deal of support throughout the country; but, as you clearly realize, it is very much resented in Official quarters, which have been in my opinion absurdly touchy about it. Different people tell me nearly every day that they have been warned by the Foreign Office to look to *The Times* no longer for the British point of view." (Dawson Papers, copy.)

[2] The affirmative answers to the question whether other nations should continue to stop a nation attacking another, if necessary by military measures, was 6,784,368; those ready to stop it by economic and non-military measures, was 10,027,668. See Adelaide Livingstone, *The Peace Ballot, the Official History, etc., and Conclusion of Viscount Cecil* (London, June, 1935.)

has got the British shirt out. If the man in the street is hypocritical, at least he doesn't know it."

The Times actively upheld the Conservative interest in the
General Election of November. But hardly had the Party
Press congratulated itself on a resounding victory when news
arrived from Paris of the arrangement to which Pierre Laval and
Sir Samuel Hoare proposed to secure an agreement with Mussolini.
It was not appreciated in Britain that France had lost faith in
the League's collective security and lost hope in Britain's willingness to balance the loss by a guarantee. Nor was it foreseen
that in view of these considerations and of Germany's
open rearmament and demands for revision, France must see
herself as bound to solve all outstanding problems that divided
her from Italy. Dawson was strongly anti-Italian, or anti-
Mussolini, all through the autumn and winter of 1935. Believing
as he did, that Germany meant to " settle down " as a good
European neighbour, he saw no need to keep Italy out of her orbit.
The Editor felt both the political world and the general public to
be on his side, and a series of positive leading articles made it
clear that the Government must find a policy more consistent with
the aspirations of the electorate.[1] The strongest of a series of
strong articles came from his own pen. It derided the plan for
giving Abyssinia a severely restricted connexion with the coast in
its title, " A Corridor for Camels."

The Paris proposals, with or without reservations and undertakings,
were dead for all practical purposes from the moment that their general
tenor was known. There had never been the slightest doubt that
British public opinion would recommend them for approval by the
League as a fair and reasonable basis of negotiation . . . Great Britain
can, and should take careful stock of any proposal, however improbable,
which is calculated to bring the belligerents together. What she
cannot do is to endorse an unjust peace. (December 16, 1935.)

The office was proud of the part which the paper played in an
unusual outburst of public feeling on foreign policy; though, as
the leading columns of *The Times* admitted, the public mind was so
firmly made up that on this subject it needed no guidance. The
incident is an important example of the paper's growing dependence upon " public opinion," the " feeling of the country," and
the " average view." On December 18 Hoare resigned.[2] On
that day the Editor informed a member of the staff on leave of
absence that the paper's attitude

[1] See the first leading articles for December 11, 13, 14, 16, 18, 19, 20 and 21, 1935.
[2] Later it was announced that Eden was to replace Hoare as Foreign Secretary.

is not a popular line with the Government, though I believe that most of them agree with it in their hearts. I am going to see Sam Hoare this afternoon on his sickbed. I confess that I shall feel slightly sorry for him if he is made the victim of the public indignation, for I believe that the real culprits are his colleagues in London, who have acquiesced in the slipshod manner in which the Cabinet conducts its business. Still, there is a case for a scapegoat and for some conspicuous gesture to the world that this country has not completely reversed its policy.

As you know, I have never been an enthusiast for pressing " Sanctions " (an odious word) beyond the point to which unanimity would carry them. I should quite understand and sympathize with the Government if they told us that they could get no real agreement about an embargo on Oil. I have always thought that unanimity mattered more than any particular form of economic pressure, and I cannot believe that it is much fun conducting a war of aggression with the moral indignation of the world ranged on the other side. But all this seems to me to quite irrevelant to the suggestion that we should ourselves endorse an unjust peace.

Nor am I impressed in the slightest degree by all the stories that are being put about to the effect that the French could not really help us in the event of a sudden attack, that the Italian bombers can outrange us, that the British sailors in the Mediterranean (as the French papers say) are determined to be home for their Christmas dinner, etc., etc., etc. The heads of the Services seem quite prepared to give a good account of themselves if they are attacked, and the probability of attack seems to me to be no greater than it was at any time since the war began.[1]

The year 1935 was critical. Whether, as many believe, a firm warning given to Mussolini at Stresa, or later, of firm intervention, would have halted him, or not, no such warning or intervention was made while it had any hope of success. His Abyssinian adventure, once allowed, was bound to break the League, and set the gates wide open for Hitler. *The Times* warned Mussolini that, isolated as he would find himself, he would be subject to Hitler.

Foreign affairs were inevitably thrown into the background by the death of King George V on January 20, 1936. King Edward VIII was proclaimed on January 23. In February the Italians were winning victories in Abyssinia, while the League and Britain discussed sanctions, which Dawson resolutely opposed. In the first days of March a British White Paper on Rearmament was issued. Four days later a signal event occurred in the West. On March 7, 1936, while the Editor was already in the country for

[1] Dawson to a member of the staff, December 18, 1935.

the week-end, the German Army was moving into the demilitarized Rhineland. The locum tenens in Berlin thus appreciated the position in a letter to the Editor:

Germany is working steadily and unremittingly towards a peace *which she can accept*—an agreed Peace, instead of the Versailles Peace. If we keep that in mind I don't think we need have any war scares. Germany *is* making herself fit to fight—I've no doubt of that. I've equally no doubt that she is not ready and does not want to fight now.

Obviously, in the opinion of one of the Editor's advisers (and a leader-writer), Germany in 1936 was entitled to strive for what she would accept as an " agreed " peace and, if Britain was prepared to accept the German terms, there was no need for " any war scares." The paper had the advantage on this occasion of a Sunday on which to collect its thoughts—a day that was badly needed, for Friday night's paper had been edited by Casey while both Dawson and B.-W. were away. Returning on Sunday, the two last named together prepared the long leading article for Monday, March 9, which dealt with the German re-occupation of the forbidden Rhineland. It included several strongly worded phrases of reproof, but any intimidating effect that there may have been intended to convey to Berlin was destroyed by the sentences among which they found themselves in print. If the aspirations expressed were consistent with those of the leader of June 14, 1935, they prove that this consistency had led the office far out of contact with the reality of the German leaders' jealousy of British power. The March 9, 1936, article concluded by remarking the obvious fact that " the old structure of European peace, one-sided and unbalanced, is nearly in ruins," and, as a final word, judged that " it is the moment, not to despair, but to rebuild." Familiar as the office was with the Treaty of Locarno[1] (it was referred to in the course of the leader), no mention was made of what must be one of the first points that strikes the eye of the present-day reader; that the violation of the demilitarized zone provided Belgium, France, Italy and the British Empire with a *casus belli* against Germany. There was no hint at the risk of war, and two letters written on the previous day[2] in exact agreement with the leading article's closing sentences were prominently printed. Another letter supporting the paper was published later in the week. Its content was put thus by the locum tenens at Berlin in a note to the Editor of March 12, 1936.[3]

[1] Cmd. 2525 (Accounts and Papers, 1924-5, XVI): *The Times*, October 20, 1925.
[2] .i.e Sunday.
[3] Dawson Papers.

I am delighted to see the idea of maintaining the bulk of the Locarno Treaties intact emerging from Sir John Fischer Williams' letter in the paper this morning. I've felt from the start that the ultimate solution might be the maintenance of the Treaty minus its Rhineland clauses—there is very high support for that solution here [Berlin].

The locum tenens, however, had second thoughts about the, one supposes, German diplomats[1] who held out to him such "high support" for the removal of the obligation that happened then to stand in their immediate way. He put them in strong terms into a private letter to the Editor late on March 14, 1936:

The people at the head of this show are pure gamblers and do not care two buttons for the League of Nations, which was thrown in by Ribbentrop as a sop to British public opinion. Moreover they are extremely formidable, and I do not believe for one moment that their ambitions will be satisfied by the settlement which may come out of the present negotiations.

One gets indication after indication that they are out for practically the whole programme of Deutschland Deutschland Über Alles, Über Alles in der Welt! which is sung at every pol. meeting. That expresses their mentality perfectly truthfully. It may, it is true, be interpreted in two ways; but the most disconcerting thing of all is their utter refusal to admit that any legal or moral objection can stand in their way *if once they have made up their minds that national interests* demand some new gain. . . . Germans are already starting propaganding their good faith to me, but from innumerable consultations and observations, I am convinced that to them the power of Germany is a holy law which overrides everything else.

That the Germans, whether under Social Democratic, Nationalist (Hugenberg) or Nazi (Hitler) leadership, would ever have admitted legal or moral impediments to an action of State was, evidently, strange to a well-bred English leader-writer of the 1930's. Flanagan would have interpreted the move of March 7 differently. He would have expected, from the date the Treaty was signed, the revival of the principle that the power of Germany must be the supreme law of her being and her policy. It was an estimate of Germany that had not prevailed in the office since Steed's dismissal. Even so, the event of March 7 shocked Dawson slightly. Replying two days after receiving his colleague's letter from Berlin, Dawson said, " I should be very sorry myself to place any confidence in the present régime in Germany." He did not define the sense in which he used

---

[1] Unless the phrase underlined in his letter to Dawson on the twelfth referred only to the British Ambassador in Berlin, whom he mentioned in his article.

he word "confidence," but proceeded to say that their occupation of the demilitarized zone was a "characteristically stupid blunder, as a great many Germans seem to have realized." That it was less a "stupid blunder" than a gigantic personal success, won over his Generals, had not yet become manifest in London, and a reluctance to abandon belief in German professions was confessed: "At the same time I think it sheer folly to refuse to get the utmost out of the professions which accompanied it, whether they are sincere or not." Rather might it have been argued that it was a blunder to imagine that "sincerity" could at any time arise in connexion with German professions and protestations made about power and military policy. This was better understood across the Channel. There, insistence upon French rights was foreseen. In Britain such French action was judged, if it should occur, as against French as well as British interests. Should the French insist, B.-W. wrote," they will convince everyone here that their real desire is not to be safe but to give Germany the poke in the eye which she may be said to have earned. That is the trouble of not knowing when to clinch a bargain." However, B.-W. continued, to a member of the foreign leader-writing staff, 'we must peg away without illusions about France and about Germany. It is hard to escape when we are, as the Prayer Book says, 'tied and bound by the chains of our sins' stretching all the way back to the General Election of 1918."[1] This was the high doctrine by which the policy of the paper towards Germany was henceforth to be regulated. The Editor, his chief Assistant and their friends had "all forgotten about the war." All they remembered was the Peace Treaty.

It was out of the question for B.-W. to see the new Rhineland situation in terms of power; that would be to contradict at once his own conscience and the voice of public opinion. He was by no means alone. From the first, there was in Downing Street a tendency to hope that France did not, in fact, mean to recommend or to take action. Eden, however, criticized B.-W.'s idea of a complete British guarantee for the French and Belgian frontier to compensate and reassure the French, as not meeting the need of some moral re-establishment of confidence in treaties now shattered by Germany. B.-W. was disappointed to learn that his idea was approved by Vansittart for anti-German reasons, but he put it forward in his leader of the 11th. At this time B.-W. was working prodigiously. He had a leader in six consecutive issues of the paper;

[1] Barrington-Ward to a member of the staff, March 24, 1936.

five firsts and one second, and five written on the night of printing besides making notes of all kinds[1] in advance of paying a visit to Germany. He departed for Hamburg on May 29, and was met by Erich Warburg whose father, with Ballin, had built up the Hamburg-Amerika Line. He was a member, with B.-W.'s close friend Count Albrecht Bernstorff, of a numerous anti-Nazi group. B.-W. later met Schacht (" a cool old humbug, but very able "), von Dürckheim (Ribbentrop's assistant), Frank (" a real bouncing Nazi "), Hess (" unaggressive, conscientious, quiet ") B.-W. was back in the office on June 8 and was soon at work The position of *The Times*, four months after Hitler's re-occupation of the Rhineland, was thus set forth by him in a leading article It once more evoked " British opinion ":

British opinion accepts as an axiom the existing friendship with France . . . There is nothing anti-French, or anti-German in it . . What British opinion is not prepared to accept is the leadership of France over the whole field of foreign politics, or to admit responsibility for all the liabilities which she has been accumulating since the war in the shape of alliances on the farther side of Germany And, as for Germany, British opinion is determined, in spite of many setbacks, to come to close grips with Herr Hitler's Peace Offer [of May, 1936] as representing the best immediate hope of the stabilization of Western Europe. It may prove to be a vain hope. Certainly German methods of the last few years (or indeed of the last few days), have not been calculated to foster it. (July 6, 1936.)

The paper did not regard the Franco-Soviet Pact as a helpful diplomatic achievement, for it was " the uppermost conviction of British opinion that there can be neither peace in Europe nor a League of Nations worth the name without German cooperation in bringing them about." *The Times* tacitly admitted the fact, if not the right, of German dealings with Russia. In addition, it was now necessary that the country should " not for a moment abate the resolute restoration of British armaments to an effective level." This, it needs to be emphasized for the credit of *The Times*, was more than a mere concession to " British opinion," for it cannot be contended that at this time there was any popular demand for guns. Everyone, however, was said to be in agreement that " British foreign policy must have the backing of far

---

[1] On the appointment of Inskip, after a long delay, as Minister for the Coordination of Defence, B.-W. made a note of a saying that was current and, in his opinion, rightly attributed to Churchill: " Baldwin had to find a man of inferior ability to himself and this Herculean task must require time for its accomplishment."

greater strength to enforce." Finally, "A clear understanding with Germany would not solve all the problems of the world, but it would be a strong foundation on which to build, and British opinion means to try it out." In the meantime the paper remained confident that it was only common sense to take German assurances into serious account.

A couple of months later B.-W. put clearly the position to *The Times* in a letter to Churchill, to whom he wrote that " we should certainly be against premature abandonment of the hope, supported by many authoritative pronouncements on the German side, that Germany is prepared to reach a general understanding and settlement with the British Empire." He proceeded to say that the contention he put forward might, since Churchill had invited an opinion, " help to guard an appeal for Franco-British collaboration against the risk of misunderstanding and controversy."[1] The continued absence from the staff of a Foreign Editor made it unlikely that the office would be brought to see that the contemporary German demand for an " understanding " with Britain meant what it did in the time of Holstein—an understanding on terms favourable to German ascendancy in Central Europe, the Balkans and the Near East. Until this " understanding " was secured by Hitler, and Britain neutralized as a Continental factor, surprise was, and would remain, an essential element in German foreign policy; and that whether Hitler or any other Nationalist leader was Chancellor. It was not seen in Printing House Square in 1936 as it had been thirty years earlier, under the Foreign Editorship of Chirol, that any " understanding " that Germany chose to enter into with the British Empire would involve England's dropping all " understanding " with France, as well as any prospect of an " understanding " with Russia. The issue in 1936 was whether Britain was willing to allow Germany to choose a foreign policy for herself. So far, Germany had shown her hand by leaving the League, and Britain had indicated her policy by refusing to support France over the march into the Rhineland. Britain, thus, made a step towards Germany which encouraged her to concentrate upon a foreign policy of separating Britain from France, and France from Russia. *The Times* gave further impetus to this policy by welcoming every sign of German readiness " to reach a general understanding and settlement with the British Empire." The expressions of admiration for Britain and he British Empire coming from across the Rhine inevitably

---

[1] Barrington-Ward to Winston Churchill, September 23, 1936.

awakened echoes in the Imperialist circles, including those like Baldwin, Dawson and Lothian, who were closely attached to the memory of Rhodes.[1] There is no evidence that Downing Street, or Printing House Square, still less British public opinion, understood that the principle of continuity in foreign policy was respected at least as much in the Wilhelmstrasse as in Whitehall, and that professions of respect for the British Empire expressed in 1936, would in time mean about the same as those of 1901: to "kick Britain into friendship" with Germany, and into isolation from France, Russia and the United States.[2] Those in 1936 sitting in the seats of Steed and Chirol entertained a wholly different estimate of Germany's professions.

Continuity in both the direction and doctrine of the Foreign Department at Printing House Square had been broken by the Editor's decision, in the circumstances described in a previous chapter, to suppress the position of Foreign Editor. Those in authority over the subject of foreign affairs, the Editor and his Assistant Editor (Barrington-Ward), were in no sense specialists on the subject; in any event, they were unable to spare more than a portion, relatively small, of their time to its study. It was impossible for anyone in B.-W.'s position to read sufficiently and mark well enough the course of diplomacy as revealed in the published documents, and thus lay the basis for a judgement that would be truly independent.[3] By the spring of 1936 he had

[1] The object of Rhodes's scholarship benefaction in 1901 was to ensure "that an understanding between the three Great Powers (Britain and the British Empire, the United States and Germany) will render war impossible, and make educational relations the strongest tie." See above, Chapter XXI, "Dawson's Second Innings."

[2] For *The Times* (especially Bell and Saunders) and the negotiations between Lansdowne, Metternich, Hatzfeldt and Holstein, see Vol. III, Chapter XII, "The End of British Isolation," pp. 321-374.

[3] But it needs to be acknowledged that during the years after 1920 when the German Foreign Office was bringing out its collection of documents (concluded in 1924 with Vol. XVII) Barrington-Ward read them. He presented his set to the Library of Balliol College. Unfortunately he (and not only he) overlooked the passages in *Die grosse Politik*, XVII, p. 101, quoted in the *History of "The Times"* (Vol. III pp. 324-332). In discussing with Chirol the possibility of a general Anglo-German understanding in November, 1901, Holstein submitted beforehand to Bülow that he should do so with "an appearance of unconcern." Bülow agreed and told Holstein that it was necessary not to "betray any disquiet, nor impatience, nor haste, but must make hope glitter on the horizon. This hope, after all, offers the surest guarantee against a capitulation of the English to Russia." Among the leading English pro-Germans was Garvin whose view of Germany had been influenced by B.-W. in the days when he was Garvin's Assistant Editor. B.-W. had himself been greatly impressed by Brüning. A curious fact about Garvin was that in spite of his thorough study of the documents in *Die grosse Politik* and elsewhere, and the illumination this reading undoubtedly gave him to see through Bülow's tricks (e.g. of unsuccessfully trying Zukunftsperspektiven upon Chirol) he did not perceive Hitler's revival of them, e.g., of successfully making "hope glitter o the horizon" of Lothian, Garvin, B.-W. and Dawson. Germany in 1935 was repeating her policy of 1908: to strengthen herself as rapidly as planning could make possible an use her diplomacy to assure Britain that Germany was her friend. The Kaiser's letter t Lord Tweedmouth in 1908 was as clumsy an instance of the trick as Göring's invitation t Halifax in 1936 was a subtle one.

become almost solely responsible for the treatment of Anglo-German relations. The Editor and he relied for their knowledge of the Continent less upon his Correspondents than upon certain personal sources, and thus the foreign policy pursued by *The Times* after the crucial year of 1936 became increasingly indebted, in the first place upon the Editor's ministerial friends, Baldwin, Chamberlain and Halifax, secondly upon " the best and the bulk of British opinion " and the " British public opinion " upon which Ministers themselves were dependent, and thirdly upon Commonwealth sentiment. It was an unusual course for *The Times* ; it was followed undeviatingly until 1939.[1]

Acting as Foreign Editor and Editor, Dawson imposed upon himself an impossible burden. He found it difficult to hold a course of his own through a sea of foreign telegrams. In the autumn of 1936 there was much besides Germany, Japan, or even Spain that would fail to catch the eye of an Editor not in any case attracted to foreign countries, and it is in no way surprising that the issue on which his attention concentrated seemed of British constitutional and Imperial importance. It would have been so but for the consummate skill of Baldwin. The royal Abdication question preoccupied the minds of the Government in London throughout the last three months of 1936, and the paper's influence on the December crisis is not undeserving of mention. The interested reader will find an account of it in Appendix I. The Abdication was of social importance but, as accomplished by Baldwin's adroitness, of no political significance, though he may have bequeathed a quasi-constitutional question to historians. Inevitably the crisis occupied the Editor's time to the exclusion of everything else. Dawson conducted the discussion with supreme skill and vigour. King George VI was proclaimed on December 12, 1936.

The New Year, 1937, opened uncomfortably. *The Times* was not less set than in the previous year upon its search for the basis of a " comprehensive settlement " with Germany, but the infor-

[1] See, for example, the leading article (Dawson writing) of October 28, 1937. An expression typical of the period occurs in the following paragraph: " The truth is that British public opinion is probably far ahead of the Government in its conviction that a clear understanding with Germany would have consequences more profound and more conducive to a stable peace than any other single object of our foreign policy. There is little sympathy here with the view, which has sometimes seemed to prevail on the Continent, that the proper way to treat Germany is to ring her about with vigilant allied States, sometimes masquerading as the League of Nations. . . . She has broken those limits here and there already—broken them by methods which are creditable neither to herself nor to the rest of the world—and every article of statesmanship suggests that a halt should be called to a process which must otherwise lead inevitably to war and to the downfall of civilization in the West. Let us at least be clear at what point a stand should be made, and let us make a supreme effort, so far as Great Britain is concerned, to do what is possible for appeasement before that point is reached." The paper did not succeed in being " clear " as to " the point " at which the stand should be made until it was too late.

mation to hand was not encouraging.[1] A speech by Eden on January 19 appealed to Germany to cooperate in the establishment of peace. On the 30th, the fourth anniversary of his party's taking power, Hitler replied in a non-commital speech. Meanwhile the Spanish Civil War was going badly for the Government. On February 8 Malaga was captured by the insurgents.[2] On February 16 came the British announcement of a defence appropriation of £1,500 million to be spent in the next five years, the money for which was found largely by a third increase in Income Tax. The National Defence Contribution was introduced. The Coronation of King George VI and Queen Elizabeth was solemnized on May 12, 1937. On May 28, the National Government was reconstructed, with Neville Chamberlain as Prime Minister in the place of Stanley Baldwin. The Editor, as a close personal friend of the new Prime Minister, had probably been made aware beforehand of his views about Europe. The two men were in substantial agreement from the first. Dawson had occasion that month to express his personal standpoint to the experienced Geneva Correspondent (formerly " Our Own " at Berlin and Paris) who went to Berlin as locum tenens. The Editor, in writing to him thus declared himself :

.... I am and always have been, most anxious that we shall " explore every avenue " in the search for a reasonable understanding with

[1] In the first week of the New Year B.-W. received the following from his friend Count Albrecht Bernstorff (Counsellor of the German Embassy in London, 1923-1933 and no Nazi), written from Switzerland :

January 5th, 1937

My dear B.-W.,

Just a line of thanks for your good wishes which I most heartily reciprocate and of a greeting from here where I can write freely. I have spent ten days here recovering from Germany which is getting into worse conditions day by day. The—quite superfluous—Spanish adventure is *not* popular with the people, as far as they are allowed to know anything about it. It is the first time that the fanatic little man at Germany's helm carries on a policy not backed by popular opinion or in itself due to German necessities—May God deliver us of these crazy dictators ! Life in Germany is almost intolerable, the people in power think of nothing else but war war, war, and of bullying the rest of the world into conceding them everything And every statement, every argument brought forward, is merely a lie or an excuse for carrying out a mad policy of ruthlessness.

I hope to go abroad again some time this year, if war does not render it impossible—I have completely lost every hope of Germany becoming a normal and peaceful country again for many, many years. And I cannot help seeing in Hitler the only real menace to peace in Europe—as long as he personally is not ousted from his present position there is no hope of peace. So I am *very* depressed as you can imagine.

It was very nice to have you both at Stintenberg last Spring. And the Golden Auriol [B.-W., a keen naturalist and bird-watcher, had amused his fellow-guests by his delight at seeing and hearing a Golden Oriole] will return, even if Germany remains a noisy armed camp of unfortunate people driven by a madman !

With all good wishes for a peaceful 1937.

Yours as ever, ALBRECHT B.

Bernstorff was later arrested and kept imprisoned in the sinister Nazi police station in the Lehrter quarter of Berlin until the day before the Russians arrived, when he was taken out and murdered. See the Memoir by Elly Countess Reventlow-Altenhof.

[2] See Appendix II, Sources, XXIII. *The Times* was completely disinterested in the Spanish Civil War and its possible results, but it more than maintained its reputation for the securing of news of the struggle. The policy of the paper might have been different if Dawson had not put off the appointment of a Military Correspondent, vacant since the departure of Repington in 1917, until after the German invasion of Austria. See below, p. 924.

Germany. So you will have my blessing in anything that you can do to further this end. By all means, go from Geneva to get a statement from the Chancellor if you think it will be of any service. The more personal contact there is between the two nations the better.

But let me add that in my opinion the worst possible way to an understanding is to clamour for the retrocession out of hand of all the former German colonies. I do not believe that this is what Germany really needs most, and in any case I should regard it as no more than an item for reasonable discussion as part of a comprehensive settlement. I shall have no objection myself to such a gesture as would make it plain to the world that Germany was not regarded as unfit by nature to hold the mandate for an African colony. After all we have given up one mandate already and are likely to give up much of another; and so have the French. Claude Russell, of all people, made what seemed to some to be a very sensible suggestion on this point in The Times a few months ago.

Yes, I have seen Philip Lothian and heard what he had to say. He may write something about it for The Times when the Coronation is over. One of his points is that, even in small things, the Germans have a feeling that we never hold out a hand of friendship or sympathy from this country. But for my own part, I lose no opportunity, when I see it, of trying to mitigate this sort of grievance, which is mainly psychological—witness (only within the last week) a leader of sympathy with the loss of the Hindenburg [airship] and a welcome to Blomberg as representative at the Coronation.[1]

A fortnight later, writing to the same correspondent,[2] he dwelt with naive astonishment on a particularly violent outburst of Times-hating in Berlin:

But it would really interest me to know precisely what it is in The Times that has produced this antagonism in Germany. I did my utmost, night after night, to keep out of the paper anything that might hurt their susceptibilities. I can really think of nothing that has been printed now for many months past which they could possibly take exception to as unfair comment. No doubt they were annoyed by Steer's first story of the bombing of Guernica,[3] but its essential accuracy has never been disputed, and there has not been any attempt here to rub it in or to harp upon it. I should be more grateful than I can say for any explanation and guidance, for I have always been

[1] Dawson to the Special Correspondent, May 11, 1937.
[2] Dawson to the same, May 23, 1937.
[3] For this story see The Times for April 28, 1937. It was given the turnover column of the leading page. George Lowther Steer was already, before his thirtieth birthday, one of the paper's most successful war correspondents. A South African by birth and a scholar of Winchester and New College, he entered the paper's service in 1935 to report the Abyssinian campaign from the victim's side, and was moved to Spain soon after the Italians expelled him from Addis Ababa in May 1936. His Tree of Gernika described his experiences with the Basques with a vigour its readers will not easily forget. He was killed on active service in the South-East Asia Command in 1944, at the age of 35.

convinced that the peace of the world depends more than anything else on our getting into reasonable relations with Germany.

The word " always " in the last sentence need not be taken to mean " all my life," or even in " all my editorship," but that this had been his conviction at least since 1919 is probable. The Editor undoubtedly felt that, having gained an unprecedented degree of control and responsibility at Printing House Square, he would see that *The Times* ran no risk, even indirectly, of contributing to another collision like that of 1914. This hope for relations, " reasonable " in the British sense, strongly and ably supported as it was by B.-W. after 1928, that provided the basis of the Continental policy of *The Times* was now becoming highly dangerous. *The Times* Correspondents in Europe felt bothered by the practice of excluding anything that the Germans might choose to regard as " unfair " from both the leader- and the news-columns of the paper. It looked to them as though Correspondents' messages were being " trimmed " to fit a policy. In fact, messages were cut or omitted from time to time in accordance with what was accepted by the Editor as the requirements of diplomacy.[1] *The Times* Special Correspondent in Berlin arrived simultaneously with the new British Ambassador, Sir Nevile Henderson. The two were already acquainted and discussed the German question for two hours. The Ambassador left upon the Correspondent the impression (which he recorded privately at the time) that before he arrived he had been pressed in high ministerial circles at home to accept a ready-made picture of his sphere of action.[2] The Editor's care to admit nothing to the paper that could ruffle the sensitivities of the German Government was given the only interpretation possible in Berlin: it was a sign that Printing House Square could at last be treated appropriately in the German sense.

On August 9 a brief note on the bill page recorded that three German newspaper correspondents were to be asked to leave the United Kingdom. Later that day Dr. Woermann, the German Chargé d'Affaires, called at the Foreign Office to protest, and in retaliation asked that *The Times* should be informed that its principal Berlin Correspondent was unsatisfactory to the German Government, and that his " journalistic work does not meet with their approval." A short leading article next day pointed out that

[1] There were rare precedents for action of this kind in Chirol's period (see Volume III, p. 414, for his " cutting " of Harris's pro-German telegrams from Tangier in 1911).

[2] *Cf.* Henderson, *Failure of a Mission*, (London, 1939) : He was brought from Buenos Aires, presumably because of his pro-German views and saw Baldwin and Chamberlain, then Prime Minister designate, in March, 1937. " I agreed that I should do my utmost to work with Hitler and the Nazi Party as the existing Government in Germany." (p. 56.)

" Ajax defying the ' Thunderer ' "

From the original in Printing House Square of the cartoon drawn by
the late Sir Bernard Partridge for *Punch* and published on August 18,
1937.   By permission of the Proprietors of *Punch*.

a more usual course for a government whose nationals were expelled, as were the three Germans in question, for engaging in unsuitable activities on foreign soil, would be to apologise: in any case there could be no question of the replacement of the Correspondent by one more amenable. On the three following days the Correspondent reported a sudden and violent German newspaper campaign, of which the *Boersenzeitung* was perhaps the most outrageous exponent, directed not only at his own person but at all foreign Correspondents in Germany whose views on the régime were not entirely conformist. *The Times* Correspondent had the satisfaction of seeing in the paper for August 13 a turnover article of his own on Göring's organization of the German steel industry for armament production. The article was distinguished by the fairness and accuracy that had marked all his work, but it was not the sort of article that the Germans wished to see in *The Times* or any other British newspaper, and was unlikely to be forgiven. On the morning of August 19 a polite but insistent policeman served him with an order of expulsion.[1]

The incident proves that the Nazis feared the impact of the Correspondent's news dispatches more than they valued the Editor's doctrinal articles. As Dawson wrote to a member of the public, " *The Times* has stood rather conspicuously for an attitude towards their country which is by no means universal in England. . The notion that there can be no dealings with Fascism or with National Socialism (or, for the matter of that, with Bolshevism) has found no countenance in its columns." This was so. The Editor, however, had not realized the effect of the Correspondent's dispatches upon non-Nazi Germans, for whom *The Times* was the favourite newspaper. The assistant in the Berlin Office was substituted for his expelled chief, but to mark its disapproval of the German action, the office printed his dispatches under the legend " From Our Correspondent." The policy of *The Times* was not altered by this affront. Jupiter Tonans did not loose a thunderbolt. In ministerial circles British preparations were being made for personal contact with Hitler.

On November 19[2] Halifax discussed with him the case for a Four-Power (Britain, Germany, France, Italy) understanding. Halifax admitted former mistakes; but said it was not now necessarily thought that the *status quo* must be maintained

---

[1] He left Berlin on August 21, 1937. On arrival in England his health broke down and he did not again write for the paper.

[2] Exactly a fortnight after the meeting, now known to have taken place secretly in Berlin, at which Hitler announced to the Army, Navy and Air Chiefs, his plan to subjugate Czechoslovakia and Austria.

under all circumstances. Hitler talked about colonies as being the only difference between Germany and Britain. Halifax urged Hitler to seek through the League a solution of outstanding questions (Danzig, Austria and Czechoslovakia). England herself was interested only to see that any changes should be effected by peaceful evolutions. Colonial questions, Halifax said, were undoubtedly difficult. Hitler voiced his objections to British newspapers and to influences in the Foreign Office that were adverse to Germany.[1] An announcement made on the last day of 1937 gave Dawson and B.-W. much satisfaction. The Editor and his Assistant both thought the Permanent Head of the Foreign Office responsible for a highly inconvenient, and improperly strong, anti-German line. Shortly after the visit of Halifax (then Lord President of the Council) to Hitler and Göring, the Permanent Head of the Foreign Office was promoted out of the way of the Prime Minister's policy.

The change was not objected to by *The Times*. " I cannot quite see [Sir Robert] Vansittart being set apart to consider whether the Prime Minister should continue his present policy towards Germany or not," wrote B.-W. to Dawson.[2] It was known that Hitler disliked Vansittart as an obstacle to closer Anglo-German relations and as, in his opinion, responsible for " malignant " criticism in the British Press. *The Times* felt encouraged to take a more definite course. Apart from the general objection to regional pacts, as such, and the particular objection to the Soviet-Czech and Soviet-French pacts, *The Times* was still prepared to face the implications of the position that the Editor had taken up long since. The recovery of Europe, geographically and industrially, depended more than ever before upon a solution of the German problem, and that problem could be solved only by negotiation; agreement was impossible with

[1] *Cf.* the Führer's statement to Halifax: " The fateful thing was the *rôle* of the Press. It alone was responsible for nine-tenths of the tension." The German minute proceeds to record Halifax as having said that he agreed with what the Führer had said about the dangers of the Press. He also was of the opinion that the Anglo-German negotiations should be carefully prepared. Chamberlain had told him that he would willingly take upon himself the risk of Lord Halifax's visit to Germany being misrepresented in the Press, provided this visit accomplished one step in the right direction. (Ministry of Foreign Affairs of the U.S.S.R. *Documents and Materials relating to the eve of the second World War* (Moscow, 1948, Vol. I, pp. 43-4), for the record of a conversation between the Führer and Reichskanzler and Lord Halifax in the presence of the Reichsminister of Foreign Affairs, in Obersalzberg, November 19, 1937.) On March 3, 1938, Henderson told Hitler that Halifax had that day arranged a Press conference of responsible newspaper editors, and had a talk also with the President of the Newspaper Proprietors' Association and leading officials of the B.B.C., in the course of which he had again emphasized their responsibility in the maintenance of peace; more than this could not be done. (*Ibid.*, p. 60.)

[2] B.-W. to Geoffrey Dawson, January 2, 1938.

Russia. Dawson and B.-W., like Chamberlain and Halifax, were ready to concede changes in the *status quo* of Central Europe provided they were effected by agreement and not force. There is no evidence that the Editor or his Assistant looked at the problem in ideological terms. On the contrary, they appear to have looked at it strictly in terms of peace and stability for the sake of better British trade, and of some ill-defined measure of isolation for the sake of better Commonwealth relations. Far from having any ideological preferences, the office was desirous of preventing such leagues. Nobody in Printing House Square took sides over Spain. The paper's one " idea " was to maintain Democracy as a middle term between Communism and Fascism. All *The Times* wanted Russia to do was to drop Comintern interference, and Germany to " settle down." The way to get Germany to settle down was to be reasonably conciliatory. Fortunately, in the opinion of *The Times*, this was the policy of the Prime Minister and the Foreign Secretary.

It was never easy to conciliate Russia. On January 11, 1938, the Kremlin informed the British Ambassador in Moscow of a decision to apply the principle of " parity " to all consular offices, and that no State would be permitted more consular offices than were maintained in that State. The Russian Government interpreted the principle as requiring the closing of the British Consulate in Leningrad. *The Times* said there was every reason to suppose that this request was made on political grounds, and held it to be extremely discourteous.[1] There were more important reasons why the office did not feel encouraged to accept Russia as a reliable supporter of the policy of European pacification. The paper had not been given the opportunity of appointing a Correspondent in Leningrad or Moscow since Wilton had come back to England to report in September, 1917. Approaches to the paper had been made through Russian diplomats in London and through the British Embassy in Moscow, but from none did *The Times* secure the assurance that any Correspondent it sent would be free to say what he wanted, without enjoying a privileged position compared with the journalists of other papers or nations.[2] Hence the principal source of Russian news in *The Times* remained the Riga Correspondent, R. O. G. Urch, who became among English left-wing

[1] *Cf.* W.P. & Zelda K. Coates, *A History of Anglo-Soviet Relations*, with a Preface by D. Lloyd George (London, 1945). The Authors believe that the request was due to the Russian Government's decision to convert Leningrad into a naval base. (p.584.)

[2] Eventually, relaxation of the Russian censorship made it possible to send a Correspondent to attend in Moscow during the abortive negotiations in the summer of 1939 for an Anglo-Soviet pact. He was able to visit Leningrad or Odessa from Moscow as often as he wished; but could achieve no contact with any other source of political news than a spokesman of the Narkomindel who was sometimes accompanied (Dilke to the office May 16, 1939) by a silent watchman from the secret police.

intellectuals a byword for biased and inaccurate reporting. It was never noticed that the " lie factory " he was accused of running based its messages exclusively on the Soviet Press. This was the only means of knowledge. Seldom, if ever, did a Correspondent in Moscow succeed in getting any news that was not published to the world by the Russian Press and wireless services, and he was never able to say from Moscow what he thought about such news without risking expulsion. Urch, at Riga, beyond the reach of the Russian machine, could and did say exactly what he thought about what passed through his hands. He spoke with some authority, for he had lived in Russia for a decade, spoke the language fluently, and had watched both revolutions in 1917 on the spot. He subscribed to *Pravda* and *Izvestia*, which reached him on the day of publication, and to numerous Russian provincial and politico-hortatory journals, which he read thoroughly and understandingly. His views may have been coloured to some extent by his imprisonment for two months by zealous Bolshevik xenophobes in the early days of the new régime, but for any acerbity in his messages the Russians have only their own police system to blame. His best defence is the fact that the prodigious reorganization of Russia during the war of 1941-5 was inspired not by Communist theory but by the older and surer motive of nationalist patriotism. It was hardly appreciated, however, in Printing House Square, that the Russian Government was responding in 1938 to the nationalist and patriotic impulses that had little connexion with Sovietism, Communism, Leninism or any other abstraction. The prevailing rumours of internal troubles did not encourage Britain to place any reliance upon Russian ability to play an effective part in any councils directed towards the stabilization and pacification of Europe. It was suspected, rather, that Russia herself might be the theatre of some new political upheaval. The stable country in Europe was Germany, it was thought.

Suddenly, on February 4, 1938, it was announced that a purge had taken place in the German High Command. Next day *The Times* discussed this reshuffle (of which the rise of Ribbentrop and Keitel to replace Neurath and Blomberg were the main features) in a leading article that was colourless, as B.-W. was away. Simultaneously, Papen was brought back to Berlin from the German Embassy at Vienna. Eight days later Hitler summoned Schuschnigg, the Austrian Chancellor, to a meeting at Berchtesgaden, the concrete result of which was an imposed reconstruction of the Austrian Cabinet and the appointment as Minister for Internal Security of Seyss-Inquart, a Sudeten trusted by the Nazis. These changes were announced on February 16. The Austrian crisis

SHIVER SISTERS BALLET, 1938.   *(Copyright in All Countries.)*

Reproduced by permission of the Proprietors of the *Evening Standard*

was a surprise that caught this country at a disadvantage. Britain was acutely divided as to the action that should be undertaken by the League Powers. The degree of uncertainty, in a nation whose foreign policy had been so long marked by continuity, was unusual. It presented an unexpected difficulty for a newspaper that by habit sought to lead educated public opinion towards generally accepted aims. In February, 1938, it was impossible to say that any aims were generally accepted. The Cabinet itself was divided. Chamberlain, who had succeeded Baldwin in May, 1937, was ready to do his utmost to attain reconciliation with the German and Italian leaders. It was known that others besides Eden and Cranborne were unhappy. The Editor and his chief Assistant believed that Allied impolicy in the past was to blame for the humiliation brought upon Austria ; also that there was nothing now that Britain could do about it except possibly ask pardon. The editorial doctrine had been evolved with care and logic and was shared by millions of Englishmen; some who held it then stand by it to this day. It must be admitted that Dawson's acquaintance with European personalities and problems was all too slight; that he had no personal interest in them, and that they did not attract from him, as Editor, the degree of attention which, in the circumstances, they should have done. On the other hand he was energetically supported by B.-W., who took more interest in the news from the Continent and, moreover, had French, German and Italian.

More important, B.-W.'s views about Germany derived from the moral decision he felt forced to make as to the Versailles Treaty. In principle, B.-W. accepted the German thesis that the Treaty was unjust, and he had believed ever since Versailles that the Anschluss was inevitable and should have been conceded to Brüning. Having come to this conclusion before Hitler was ever heard of, he could see no reason in conscience for refusing justice to Germany after Hitler was in power; especially as he thought that power was largely created by Germany's possession of a just grievance, and Goebbels' adroit exploitation of it. The leading article of February 17, 1938, is a characteristic expression of B.-W.'s attitude. That "a very great mass of people" held views on foreign policy opposed to those of the paper was known. The leading article of February 17 brought a protest from R. H. Brand ("Brand is always negative" was Dawson's only remark). But B.-W. was convinced that the present situation was one not for Eden but for somebody without his commitments from the past. He favoured Halifax, who was thought no less enlightened and more progressive.

On Sunday, the 20th, B.-W. switched on the wireless for Hitler's fifth anniversary address to the Reichstag, on which he had undertaken to write. Hitler spoke for three hours, less five minutes. Having written his leader, B.-W. learnt the news that Eden had disagreed with the rest of the Cabinet, and had resigned. This was regrettable, he thought, on grounds public rather than personal ; for Eden, he felt, had really no heart for the direct talks with the Dictators which B.-W. thought urgent, and the absence of which restricted diplomacy to a policy of gambling on their collapse or waiting for a new war. In this frame of mind he wrote a second leader, a short one, on Eden's resignation. The policy of *The Times* now became more explicit. It had not been adopted in a mood of hesitation and would not be dropped in the face of criticism. " Having talked with all the people principally concerned, and listened to their speeches in the House of Commons, I have come quite definitely to the conclusion that Anthony [Eden] was wrong to go when he did." So wrote B.-W. in a private note. His policy was firmly set. The appointment of the new Foreign Secretary implicitly gave it weighty support. *The Times*, nevertheless, was not unmindful of the position on defence which still needed attention. The view of Printing House Square was thus restated in February:

Our own programme of rearmament cannot be relaxed for a moment so long as Europe is liable to sudden spasms when opportunity provides an opening for a stroke of policy. It is not a time for provocative speaking and writing and least of all for empty threats. But it is emphatically a time when the British Government must be perfectly clear in their own mind about the requirements and limits of their own contribution to a settlement in Europe, and about the point at which they are bound to take a stand against pressure. (February 21, 1938.)[1]

Eden's successor as Foreign Secretary, Halifax, was a tried and intimate friend of Dawson's, an old member of the circle of Imperialist Conservatives in which Dawson had moved for a generation,[2] and a Yorkshire neighbour. Contact between the paper and Foreign Office became as close in the next two years as it had ever been, even when Delane sat in Printing House Square and Clarendon on the south side of Downing Street. It was maintained at this personal level by a daily visit to senior officials from the Diplomatic Correspondent or his deputy. A prospect

[1] On March 2, 1938, the Government announced an expenditure of £343m. on defence.

[2] In December, 1916, while he was still Edward Wood, F. S. Oliver pressed him on Carson and Milner as a candidate in a class by himself for office under the War Cabinet—(Milner Papers, private letters 1914-1918, Vol. V., Oliver to Milner, December 10, 1916).

was opening of those " active negotiations " in which *The Times* believed and had long desired to see initiated. On February 21 Italy accepted Britain's plan for Spain. This was encouraging.

The truth is that where force has been used since the war, it can be too often extenuated, if not excused, by the failure and even the refusal of Governments to find among themselves the more rational means of adjustment. (February 22, 1938.)

Eden had resigned because he disagreed with the Prime Minister's policy towards Italy after Mussolini's approach to Britain on February 10. The Italian Dictator had not been slow to seize the point that Schuschnigg's weakness would be followed up by increased pressure from Hitler; there would result an over-powering Germany in association with an Italy utterly dependent, because completely isolated. Chamberlain saw in Italy's need an opportunity to strengthen British relations and he was moved, not least by the heaviness of current armament taxation, to try his best to reach some sort of agreement with Germany and Italy. Eden believed that an Italo-British understanding was greatly to be desired, but had no trust in Mussolini or faith in any undertaking he might give. For proof Eden could point to, among other instances, Mussolini's intervention in Spain, where he had sent reinforcements in violation of the Gentleman's Agreement.

Chamberlain's policy suited Printing House Square far better. The prospect and possibility of what the paper called " more rational means of adjustment " than war, reached by a conference before the war instead of after it, had been an axiom of policy in Printing House Square for more than ten years. On March 10 Dawson and B.-W. attended Ribbentrop's farewell reception at the German Embassy, though the Nazi was not in their view other than the most patent mountebank. It was the day that Schuschnigg announced for Sunday next a plebiscite in Austria as a means of stopping Hitler. But the Führer marched into Austria on the 11th in the middle not only of a crisis in Paris, but of a purge in Moscow. Blum formed a caretaker Government between the 10th and 13th while Bukharin, Jagoda, Rykov and 18 other members of Lenin's Politbureau left in Russia were being tried for their lives by Stalin. On March 13, the day before Hitler arrived in Munich, Mussolini, helpless, might well acquiesce in the destruction of Austria.

The Times, which for ten years had believed the Anschluss acceptable because inevitable, thought Germany's action was monstrous.   B.-W. wrote a leader for March 14 on Chamberlain's speech about the situation, and his announcement that the Government would speed up armament.   Hitler was now in Vienna. *The Times* now agreed in favour of giving A.R.P priority among the new armament measures.   To the suggestion that Britain should give a pledge to Czechoslovakia, Barrington-Ward demurred.   He repeated to a friend on March 14 what he had said many times since 1919, that with 7½ million Czechs governing 3¼ million Germans and 2 million Hungarians there must eventually be trouble; he was convinced that " the country [Britain] will never fight to keep Germans and Hungarians under Czech domination."   He did not even believe that Britain could do anything for the Czechs if she wanted to.   The paper's immediate reaction to the German invasion of Austria was stern by comparison with some earlier expressions— that of December 1, 1937, for instance, in which a troubled conscience in the office had confessed that " The record of lost opportunities since the war is truly appalling, and a share of the responsibility for it lies heavily upon Britain and France." Where now was the " chance to rebuild " in the sense of the leading article of March 9, 1936?

Three days after the first news of the Austrian invasion was published, a leading article described the new obstacle set in the path of " active negotiation ":

The employment of violent means, under any conditions, to secure an end, even a legitimate end, is bound to move the British Government and people to instinctive resentment and condemnation.   It denies and thwarts the essential aims of British policy by adding to the divisions and dangers of the Continent a new store of ill-will, suspicion, and alarm.   It makes a heavy drain upon confidence, which is the capital of peace, and it undermines negotiations which, in words that Mr. Eden used of earlier talks, are themselves aimed at " repairing the damaged structure of European security."   That is the true crux of the German action.   (March 15, 1938.)

The correspondence column on the leader page illustrated the sharp division of public opinion.   On March 14 the first letter was from Lothian, who now advocated discussion with Germany " on equal terms " (backed by conscription in this country) and the second was from L. S. Amery, who demanded " an end of all discussions for a settlement with Germany."   Dispatches from the staff Correspondents also advanced counsels that conflicted in some degree with one another. On March 16 the paper published a vivid account by the Vienna Correspondent of the difficulties

of transit over the Austro-Swiss frontier, where Nazi youths in
remote villages were thumbing already printed lists of suspects
lest the latter should escape abroad. On the same day he wrote
to the Editor from Zürich about the machinery of invasion:

> In my wildest nightmares I had not foreseen anything so perfectly
> organised, so brutal, so ruthless, so strong. When this machine goes
> into action, it will blight everything it encounters like a swarm of
> locusts. The destruction and loss of life will make the World War
> look like the Boer War. . . . From what I have seen of England in my
> last visits we have no chance of withstanding this gigantic machine
> when it is turned against us, and the vital thing to remember is that
> the ultimate object is precisely the destruction of England. This is
> a thing which nobody can understand, apparently, who has not lived
> with the Germans. Their real hatred is for England.[1]

Simultaneously a Correspondent was at Prague, seeing Benesh,
who insisted that as " agreement means surrender " there must
be a firm stand. Two days later the Correspondent gave the
Editor[2] an account of the interview, saying incidentally :

> I am convinced that Nazi Germany has a long-term programme
> which she is determined to carry out—however peaceful her declarations
> are between bursts of action—and that she means both to break up
> this country [Czechoslovakia] and to challenge the British Empire.
> She is exalted: the only question, therefore, for us, as I see it, is this—at
> what point are we going to cry " halt "? . . . The [Sudeten
> Germans] are certainly one of the best treated minorities in Europe,
> now.

France had renewed her assurances to Czechoslovakia on the
14th. On March 23 Barrington-Ward met Jan Masaryk at
dinner with Vincent Massey, and the conversation led him to the
reflection that the Czechs would have served Europe better if they
had placated their minorities sooner. He does not seem to have
shared the alarm that Masaryk, as much a European as a
Czech, felt. Masaryk made the point that he and his country
had never asked Britain for support. No mention was made of
the Czech-Soviet pact, valid for five years from May, 1935, which
The Times had then, and since, strongly disliked. It had been an
essential part of B.-W.'s scheme of neutralizing Czechoslovakia
that her French and Russian alliances would be got rid of. It
was not believed in London that with Germany in power in

[1] The Vienna Correspondent to Dawson, March 16, 1938.
[2] To Dawson from Prague, March 18, 1938.

Vienna, France could be of effective help to Czechoslovakia or that the upheaval in Russia left her, at this time, able to assist.

This was the situation in which stood France and Russia, the allies of Czechoslovakia. When *The Times* stigmatized Hitler's invasion as " an undisguised exhibition of arbitrary force " the moral was that no country, " least of all our own," could afford to be bullied into false security while such methods prevailed. All doubt about the " colossal and most deplorable size " of the new estimates for Defence was gone. " There will also be fresh support for the movement for a more rapid, effective, and even compulsory organization of the people of these islands for civilian service of the type demanded by modern dangers, particularly that of a panic caused by air-raids." (March 14.) The leader emphasized the lesson that the more complete the precautions, the smaller the chances of war. The Government should see first and foremost to their armaments, that was clearly what matters most. " They will seek peace and friendship with other nations by every tolerable means. They will continue to pursue conversations where they can with any reasonable hope of success." The leader ended inconsistently with the statement that the Government would not " depart from the view which has been common to most thoughtful Englishmen, that she [Austria] was destined sooner or later to find herself in close association with the German Reich." There would, the paper said, have been no British protest if this process had developed naturally through growing confidence and mutual good-will. " What is so deeply resented here—and throughout the civilized world —is that it was thought necessary, for the sake of a Dictator's prestige, to reverse the whole process by applying to it the physical strength of the bully." The Editor, in fact, never had any real objection to the German absorption of Austria. The essence of the paper's resentment lay in Germany's " applying the physical strength of the bully." This remained the basis of Dawson's and B.-W.'s protest. As they had been convinced since the time of Brüning that the accomplishment of the Anschluss was inevitable, all they now disliked was the way it had been brought about. That was not " justifiable."

[1] Compare *Documents on British Foreign Policy*, third series, I, No. 148, enclosure; Firebrace to Chilston, April 18, 1938; " A minimum of 65 per cent. of all officers of the rank of divisional commander and above have been lost to the army. The percentage of military commissars who have gone is even higher, there being less than 20 per cent. remaining. Nearly all the more efficient higher commanders have disappeared, including all who had the benefit of higher training in Germany. The places of the liquidated officers have usually been taken by men of inferior merit, in many cases promoted for party faithfulness more than for military efficiency, and in others by the rapid advancement of quite junior officers, captains having been advanced directly to the rank of divisional commander. It may, therefore, well be doubted whether there are now available men who are capable of commanding armies in the event of war."

As to any counter-measures, *The Times* could not agree with the Labour Opposition that a policy of cooperation with Russia after the great purge of old Bolsheviks was realistic. To expect useful help in time from France was an illusion; the French Government had fallen on March 10 and was not reconstructed until March 13 when the Germans were already in Austria. America was still in isolation; Japan was distant and inimical; Italy had not been brought to Britain's side, and the degree of reliance to be placed on Mussolini's plighted word would need to be proved by time, now that he had surrendered to Hitler. The policy of *The Times*, therefore, would hardly change: to press for negotiations with the Dictators, whatever the past; and there must be direct talks, for Germany would never return to the League while Russia was a member.

To any British pledge to Czechoslovakia, Barrington-Ward remained opposed. B.-W.'s idea was to create an internationally guaranteed neutralization of Czechoslovakia which, in return, would give up its Soviet and French alliances and grant federal status to its minorities. He put this to the Editor. Dawson took it on March 21 to Chamberlain, who "thought it not impossible." An internationally guaranteed protocol that would neutralize Czechoslovakia, and turn her into a federal or cantonal Republic on Swiss lines, inevitably raised the question of the security of France; and this B.-W. left out of account. There was, rather, a tacit unwillingness to give France any specific guarantee ; still less would British cooperation with France and Russia in restraint of Germany be urged. This was a marked departure from the precedents set by *The Times* in 1905 and 1914. The paper at that period and in Wickham Steed's time had regarded an Anglo-French-Russian alignment of policy as inescapable for Britain, and the Anglo-French Entente an essential after 1919. In B.-W.'s time the paper inclined to support Germany rather than France; and, after the Anschluss, to compromise with Italy. On April 16, 1938, an Italo-British agreement was signed in Rome. It provided for the Mediterranean and Africa, and allowed for British recognition of the Italian conquest of Abyssinia.

Representatives of the French Government came to London on April 28. Daladier's position was that war could be avoided if Britain and France announced to Germany and Italy their determination to maintain respect for the rights of independent nations. At the same time Britain and France should assure Germany that, while accepting the principle that Czechoslovakia should make all reasonable concessions to her minorities, they would resist the dismemberment of that country. This involved a risk, as Chamberlain thought, which Britain was not in a position to undertake. It then became obvious to the world that Britain would undertake no commitment towards Czechoslovakia, and in less than a month came reports of German troop movements on the Czechoslovakian frontier.[1] A municipal election created the propaganda milieu in which incidents were probable, and on May 21 two Sudeten Germans were fatally shot by a frontier guard. Daladier's Government forthwith announced its readiness, in case of aggression, to fulfil its obligations, while Britain went so far as to say that her disinterest could not be taken for granted. On May 25 B.-W. discussed German policy with Baron von Studnitz, the Correspondent in London of the German Press. The " news " of German troop movements along the Czech border was false, Studnitz said. He asked why Britain should give France assurances which must encourage her to interfere with Germany and Central Europe, and why Britain was now building an air fleet " against Germany." When B.-W. asked whether Germany would accept a federal and neutral Czechoslovakia which had shed her French and Russian treaties, and whether Germany would guarantee its integrity, Studnitz affirmed that Hitler would accept it. The attempt to persuade him in this course was worth making.[2]

At the beginning of the summer leading articles displayed a frankly pro-German tone. On June 2, 1938, the paper published, as the first letter of the day, a denial by the Dean of St. Paul's that the Sudeten Germans' " separation from Czechoslovakia would weaken that country and disturb the balance of power. I do not see [Dr. Matthews went on] how this could be urged with any show of reason, because it is difficult to think that the inclusion of several million people who are opposed to the State of which they are nominal members can be anything but a source of weakness." Next morning The Times surveyed the problem in a long and, in part, an optimistic leader. " The rigid application of the principle of self-determination everywhere," argued its author, " is obviously impracticable; but for

---

[1] It is now known from the documents printed at the Nuremberg Trial that a draft Nazi directive dated May 20, 1938, prescribed that " The Propaganda War must . . . intimidate Czechoslovakia by threats and reduce her power of resistance," and that on May 28 Hitler promulgated his " unalterable decision to smash Czechoslovakia by military action in the near future " (in accordance with his statement to the military chiefs on September 5, 1937).

[2] The French Ambassador in Berlin, M. François-Poncet, did suggest a plan of putting to Hitler an Anglo-French-German guarantee of Czechoslovakian neutrality. On June 9, 1938, Halifax disallowed any plan which would require Great Britain to " guarantee Czechoslovakia."

ιε rectification of an injustice left by the Treaty of Versailles
ιε Sudeten Germans have an undoubted case." The writer
roceeded to review the historical, geographical, and strategic
rguments in favour of keeping the minority, admittedly well
eated, as it was, and thus concluded:

For all these reasons it is easily intelligible that the Czech Government
ιight not willingly agree to a plebiscite likely to result in a demand
ɔr the transfer of the Sudetens and the loss of their territory for the
.epublic. Nevertheless, if they could see their way to it, and to granting
similar choice to the other minorities, Hungarian and Polish, the
ιlers of Czechoslovakia might in the long run be the gainers in having
homogeneous and contented people, still more numerous than the
opulations of Belgium or Holland, and twice as numerous as those of
›enmark or Switzerland. If it was an injustice that these minorities
ιould have been included in the new Republic, that injustice would
e removed; and the neighbouring States which take a racial interest
ι their kinsmen would have to look after them themselves and would
›se any sort of claim to interfere in the affairs of Czechoslovakia.
would be a drastic remedy for the present unrest, but something
rastic may be needed. (June 3, 1938.)

Next morning's paper contained a letter from the Bishop of
outhwell (signed by himself and other eminent churchmen)
ʹhich deplored the possibility that religious freedom in the
udetenland might vanish, and another from Steed who accused
ιe Dean of St. Paul's of over-simplification; but neither of
ιese letters appeared on the leading-article page. John Walter,
ιking a cure at Droitwich, was moved to write to the Editor
ι the following terms:

June 4, 1938.

Ίy dear Dawson,

You sitting at the centre of events will I am sure not resent my
ffering the following criticism, although you may not agree with it.
I feel that our leader on Czechoslovakia yesterday must have come
s a shock to many readers of The Times, advocating as it did the
ιuse of the Wolf against the Lamb, on the ground of Justice. No
onder there is rejoicing in Berlin.
In contemplating the dismemberment of Czechoslovakia as a measure
f justice to the Sudeten Germans our leader writer made no allusion
› the flood of injustice and cruelty that would certainly overwhelm
ιe minorities thus handed over to the tender mercies of Messrs.
itler, Goering, and Goebbels. He seems to have forgotten all too
›on the rape of Austria and its miserable consequences. This very
ιaterial consideration is well brought out this morning in the letters
ʹ the Bishop of Southwell and Wickham Steed, which appear to me

921

to reflect the feeling of this country more truly than the letter of the Dean of St. Paul's two days ago or the cold blooded conclusion of our leader.

Yours ever,

J. W[ALTER].

To this straightforward appraisal of the difficulties that seemed to him necessarily to follow from the paper's policy, the Editor returned an evasive reply:[1]

My dear Walter,

Of course I do not resent criticism. I am really rather surprised that there has been no more of it. At the time of writing it amounts to only one letter and that not intended for publication. I should be delighted to publish a good one.

But personally I think the leader was right. My own impression is that neither Hitler nor Henlein wants a revision of frontiers. The former would probably prefer to keep the Sudeten Germans as a lever and a nuisance outside his borders, and the latter would of course disappear altogether if he were swallowed up in the Reich. What seems to me to be useful is to hold firmly to the principle of settlement by negotiation and not by force. We must somehow get away from the idea that we are merely concerned to maintain the *status quo*. I believe that this Czechoslovakian problem will be solved, and I am inclined to think that it will be solved without a revision of frontiers, but that this is more likely to happen if we leave the free choice to the people themselves. However I would like to talk to you about all this when you return.

Yours ever,

G.D.

The consequences that were bound to follow from the argumen advocated had certainly been considered carefully by the Edito and by B.-W. They were both rightly alarmed at the prospec of having to fight another European war on an issu little understood by Britain and less by the Commonwealth neither believed that Britain could fight without allies; neithe believed the Dominions were ready to share responsibility fc a war over Czechoslovakia; neither believed that, if the wa were fought and won, Czechoslovakia would be re-establishe with the inclusion of the same minorities. On every occasio when the problem was reconsidered, Dawson and B.-W. came t the same conclusion: the Treaty had established Czechoslovak

[1] Dawson to Walter, June 6, 1938.

922

and the Treaty had appealed to the principles of nationality and
" self-determination." Neither could see how in the name of
" self-determination " the Sudeten areas could be retained by
Czechoslovakia against their will. Still less could they see how
or why Great Britain could or should go to war once " self-
determination " had been invoked. Finally, their conviction that
Germany was right and Versailles wrong made it impossible for
them to refuse her justice if sought " by negotiation and not by
force." Accordingly, Walter's remonstrance had no effect on
their policy.

The diplomatic reaction to the article of June 3 was swift, brief
and definite. On the morning of June 4 the Foreign Secretary
telegraphed to Prague:[1]

I fear that yesterday's leading article in *The Times* may be misin-
terpreted by the Czechoslovak Government as representing a change
of policy on the part of His Majesty's Government and the abandonment of their efforts to bring about an agreed settlement between
the Czechoslovak Government and Herr Henlein on the basis of
regional self-administration within the framework of the Czechoslovak
State. You may let it be known, as you think fit, that this is not the
case and that the article in no way represents the view of His Majesty's
Government.

It is unlikely that the Foreign Secretary would have been moved
to send a message in which he dissociated himself so firmly from
the paper's policy without saying or writing some further comment
to his friend the Editor: but no evidence of communication
survives. It is evident from the file of the paper that in a difference
of opinion between Chamberlain and Halifax, Dawson properly
supported Chamberlain as Prime Minister; and it is conceivable,
but improbable, that Dawson published the leading article of
June 3 on a hint derived from conversations with the Prime
Minister. Sir Horace Wilson, confidential servant of three
Prime Ministers in succession, might have provided a channel for
this purpose, but in fact there is no evidence that he did so then
or at any other time. Dawson and Neville Chamberlain moved
in more or less the same circle socially, and saw each other often
on informal occasions at the houses of friends they had in common.

On June 10 *The Times* announced the Government's purchase
of 400 aeroplanes from the U.S.A. Seven days later B.-W.
discussed Czechoslovakia with von Scherpenberg (Schacht's
son-in-law); the latter assured B.-W. that Hitler was more

---

[1] Woodward & Butler, *Documents on British Foreign Policy*, third series, I, 444;
No. 374, sent at 11.30 a.m., repeated to Paris and Berlin.

concerned to break Czechoslovakia's Russian and French alliances than to incorporate the Czechs in the Reich. The disappearance of the alliances would, incidentally, give the Germans more latitude " for dealing with Prague over the minorities," for as B.-W. was still certain, there was still hope of an understanding between Britain and Germany. But, he insisted, Germany must refrain from action which would precipitate war; if she were to go slowly she would get all she wanted in any case. The solution of the Sudeten problem by some " federal " means had by now become an article of Barrington Ward's faith. He did all he could to push the idea forward, and repeated it to Rheinbaben on the afternoon of the 17th and to Albrecht Bernstorff at dinner. Next month he had a talk with von Dirksen, who left him with the impression that the Germans were ready for a peaceful settlement with the Czechs if they got enough of their way by that means. For his own part B.-W. continued to believe, as he had done since March, that a cantonal Czechoslovakia was viable and therefore a possibility, and that the release of the $3\frac{1}{4}$ million Germans from the authority of $7\frac{1}{2}$ million Czechs was desirable in the interests of all concerned. There were, of course, strategic considerations that needed to be borne in mind at home. It could not be denied that Germany was fast gaining in strength. The Editor had been in no hurry to appoint a Military Correspondent in succession to Repington who, the reader has observed, left *The Times* in 1917 for the *Morning Post*, after a dispute. Steed, naturally, in the conditions of collective security, had not appointed anybody to fill the post, and Dawson did not consider the problem until late in his second term. The coming to power of the Nazis made it easy for B.-W. to persuade the Editor to revive the position.

The new Correspondent's main interest, when first appointed, was the Spanish war and its effects on the Mediterranean situation. The Military Correspondent held firm convictions on these aspects of Empire security, but the clouds that began early in 1938 to threaten the skies of Central Europe made urgent an assessment of the strategic requirements as seen from the British side of the Channel. Fortunately, the Correspondent enjoyed close relations with the new Secretary for War, Hore-Belisha, who was appointed in the summer of 1937. The Correspondent also received the confidence of Inskip (Minister for the Co-ordination of Defence) and was peculiarly well fitted to study the situation. He discussed it with B.-W. in May, 1938. The fruit of this discussion was published in the form of a leader-page article. The headings, " The Field Force Question | Warnings from 1914-1918 | How to Help France," accurately indicated its scope. The article was published on June 17, 1938. While holding firm to the conviction that the security of Britain was linked with that of France, whose overthrow was a risk " we cannot afford to run," the paper expressed doubts about the practicability of a German attack against the French frontier. Hence, the Correspondent supported the Secretary for War's last statement presenting the Army Estimates. Hore-Belisha had admitted then (March 10) *i.e.,* twelve months or so after the reoccupation of the Rhine, that the dispatch of a field force to the Continent was relegated to the background, while the idea of repeating the mass effort of 1914-1918 was altogether excluded. The Correspondent backed the Secretary's policy with reasons. Oddly, in a Military Correspondent's article, these included the cost of preparedness in terms of money. " Until war comes any marked increase in the Army's present scale, in addition to fulfilling the prior needs of the other Services, is regarded as imposing too great a burden on the national finance, and even in war could not be carried nearly as far as in 1914-1918 without detracting from our strength in more essential spheres." The case for minimum expenditure of man-power was forcibly put. " In exerting ourselves in war to pursue the aims of our policy we ought never to forget the need of preserving what will be needed to maintain them after the war." The article, in fact, illustrated and commended novel conceptions of policy, war, victory and peace. The maintenance of British aims of policy required " the conservation not only of physical, industrial, and financial strength, but of spiritual strength." The Correspondent then proceeded to the statement that " No victory would be worth while if, in the process of winning it, the distinctive spirit of our people were extinguished and only the husk remained." The argument of the article as a whole was that of the Secretary of War: the role of the Army was defensive in the common use of the term. As to technique, mechanization was demanded. If French psychology and French needs demanded a land contribution from Britain, they could be met, the Correspondent suggested, by " a couple of handy-sized mechanized divisions, which could be formed from the present cumbrous mobile division supplemented by the rest of the mechanized cavalry regiments." But, he insisted, " we should be wise to insist on its being taken as an emergency insurance rather than as an indefinite land commitment." (June 17, 1938.)

The policy was put forward without respect to collective security; it was economical as to men and money, and isolationist

as to Continental policy. As neither pro-French, nor pro-
German, nor pro-Czech, nor anti-Russian, the policy was agreeable to feeling at home and in the Dominions. It was read less
comfortably by the French and the Czechs than by the Germans.
That it faithfully reflected the public opinion of Britain, to which
The Times deferred, cannot be doubted. The intention at home
was to avoid commitments, either military or political, on the
Continent, above all in Eastern or Central Europe. The tendency
was to limit responsibilities, and to avoid saying what Britain
would, or would not do, while encouraging no Power to take
it for granted that aggression would not be resisted. This had
been the standpoint from which The Times viewed Continental
affairs before the Germans reoccupied the Rhine in the spring of
1936. It was no different now that Czechoslovakia was an
object of German pressure. It will be seen that the articles on
Czechoslovakia which later startled the public were not sudden
improvisations but re-statements of the paper's considered and
consistent advocacy of a line and a position that had long been
implicit. It was no mere piece of pro-Germanism as was later
claimed by critics of Printing House Square. The context proves
that the Editor and the Assistant Editor had long felt uneasy at
the delay in giving the Sudeten Germans what had been accorded
to other peoples, and were very sensitive to the right of self
determination in defence of which, it was alleged, the war of
1914-18 had been fought.

It will be appreciated that the 1938 crisis mounted at a time of
year when holidays are taken most seriously by Englishmen
Dawson and B.-W. were in the country from August 8. The
latter returned on August 21, and edited until September 3, when
he went to the country and left the paper in the hands of Charles
Brodribb, who had conducted it from August 9 to August 2.
B.-W., then in charge, saw Halifax at the Foreign Office on
August 25, the day after a meeting of the Inner Cabinet
(Chamberlain, Halifax, Hoare, Simon). He found Halifax more
impressed than formerly by reports that Germany had decided to
settle the Czechoslovakian question soon, and by force. B.-W.
answered in the negative Halifax's question whether the Government should go beyond the Prime Minister's careful statement of
March 24 and make a precise guarantee. They agreed that
Great Britain must let Germany see that Britain was not complacent, and that this should be done without encouraging
Czechoslovakia to be intransigent, or embarrassing Runciman,
the British intermediary, in Prague. As for Britain, B.-W.
reflected that if war did come over Czechoslovakia and were won

CHARLES WILLIAM BRODRIBB

that country would not be reconstituted as it was. But war was unlikely.[1] B.-W. then wrote a leader on the situation. It was designed to convince Germany that Britain was anti-war, *i.e.*, anti-aggression (even to the extent of being ready to fight) but not pro-Czech.

The attitude of Germany was now recognized in official circles to be dangerous, and on the 27th Simon, in a speech at Lanark, quoted Chamberlain's statement of March 24, that if war broke out it would be quite impossible to say where it would end and what Governments would become involved, and added that, in the circumstances of the day, " there is nothing to add or vary in its [the statement's] contents." Thus Britain assured Germany, Czechoslovakia and France (and Runciman at Prague) that her disinterestedness could not be taken for granted.[2] For the issue of August 29, 1938, B.-W. wrote a leading article commenting on Simon's speech. *The Times* saw that " the attitude of the British Government towards the issues upon which the attention of the world is now concentrated in Prague follows naturally from the general line of British policy." Allusion was made to the Prime Minister's speech of March 24, and its substance re-affirmed. " It is British policy to contribute, if possible, to the control of events before events take charge of us." The task was difficult. " Those who are most fully aware that success is unattainable without real sacrifices from the Czechoslovak Government—though the process of concession cannot be wholly one-sided—are, or should be, the first to grant the patience which is indispensable to a solution." The reference to " patience " was to the organized anger of a Press campaign in Germany which in the preceding week had caused a marked increase of tension in Czechoslovakia. The solution attempted by Runciman would be permanent. That was the hope of *The Times*. " Approval of his undertaking demands reason and restraint for its accomplishment." This being so, " More and not less is to be expected from the Czechs in the way of sacrifice when it is clear that more is to be gained by it. Nor, on the part of the Czechs, can it avail to offer less than the least which will restore political security to a State threatened by the discontents of its

[1] As B.-W. wrote to the Editor on August 25, 1938, " I continue to doubt, as I think you will, whether Hitler will really be ready to take all the risks implicit in forcible action but there can be no harm, at all events, in doing what can be done to discourage any such inclination provided we are not at the same time encouraging the Czechs to offer less than they ought. He [Halifax] told me they were continuing the Franco-British pressure on the Czech Government." Coming out of Halifax's office B.-W. met Cambon (Chargé d'Affaires at the time) who said that his Government was much more disturbed than public utterances allowed it to appear.

[2] The Government made its meaning quite clear to Germany by recalling Henderson on August 28 from Berlin, for specific instructions. He returned to Berlin on August 31.

minorities. Without granting the substantial autonomy which they demand, a composite country, ringed by nations with a direct racial interest in the welfare of these important fractions of its population, lives dangerously indeed." The concessions from the Czechoslovakian Government were, "like the situation demanding them," hardly precedented. (August 29, 1938.)

For Wednesday, August 31, B.-W. wrote on the Conference of Ministers which lasted for two hours and three-quarters on Tuesday, August 30. Only four members of the Cabinet were absent, and Sir Nevile Henderson was called in. The reason for the meeting was a sudden turn for the worse in Prague due to an "unaccountably vigorous chorus of alarm, indignation and hostility" in the German Press. There was also an increased reluctance on the part of the Sudeten leaders to entertain or even discuss proposals for a negotiated settlement, adequate or inadequate. The paper said that "Britain can see no case for a breach of relations between Berlin and Prague, or for an appeal to strong measures." The negotiations had hardly as yet really been begun. "Much will now turn upon the answer to the latest Czech offer which Herr Henlein is expected to give tomorrow." The writer proceeded to restate the case for strengthening Czechoslovakia by the concession of autonomy, and said emphatically that "the larger the degree of consent they can secure to the partnership of other races in a common constitution, the less conditional must its vitality be, the less dependent upon external aids and assurances": such "aids" and "assurances" were, of course, the pacts with France and Russia that Germany disliked so much. "These are nearly self-evident propositions." By way of supporting Runciman, *The Times* added that Britain had felt compelled to make it known in time that any developments which might threaten an outbreak of armed conflict or formal war itself "must be a matter of instant concern to her, if only because a recourse to hostilities would threaten to set fire to all the combustible material in Europe, and might end by involving Britain herself, however reluctantly." As for Germany, she "alone cannot make that high contribution towards European stability and progress which would come from a settlement in Prague, but it cannot be made without her." (August 31, 1938.)

The note sounded by this leader was serious. The Diplomatic Correspondent's communication published on the same day suggested, however, that Hitler's pacific professions were "trusted in London." During the morning Halifax telephoned to B.-W. to say that he took exception to the Correspondent's statement. B.-W. answered that it needed to be read in its context, and that the object was to hold Hitler to his undertakings. This had been the line taken in 1933 and in 1936: "to get the utmost out of the professions" of Germany. Thus *The Times* continued to evoke the "moral factor." Halifax agreed that British pressure must continue on Germany—and Czechoslovakia. Halifax's point was that it was important to avoid giving the impression that British doubts about Germany had vanished, or her vigilance in any way been relaxed. During the day B.-W. was led to believe that the morning's leader seemed to have had a good effect in Berlin. But by Thursday, September 1, the crisis was still unresolved, and B.-W. felt it might be impossible for him to leave on Saturday for his Scottish holiday. He had a long talk with the Editor on the telephone, and afterwards warned one of the leader-writers to return on Sunday. On Friday, as the result of another telephone talk with the Editor, he decided to go to Scotland on Saturday, leaving a long note of instructions for Brodribb. All this time B.-W. remained convinced, as earlier, that Hitler was less interested in dismembering Czechoslovakia than in breaking her alliances with France and Russia.[1]

The leader-writer on Sunday duly prepared the article for the paper of Monday, September 5, "Negotiations Continue." With Brodribb in charge, the same writer prepared a second leader, for publication in a later issue, dealing generally with the Czechoslovak problem, in the length and form appropriate to a first leader. Late in the afternoon of Tuesday the Editor returned, and found awaiting him an uncompleted draft of this second article. He read the incomplete draft, deleted a passage, ordered it to be re-written, sent the rest to the composing room, and departed to dine. When the Editor came back, rather late, and read the corrected draft in proof, he began to doubt his decision earlier in the day to print it as that night's first leader. The completed paragraph beginning "No Central Government" (which was the revised version of the long passage Dawson had rejected before dinner) had been delivered to the composing room at 11.5 p.m. It was about 11.45 p.m. when misgivings assailed Dawson. He sent a proof of the entire article to the one senior member of the editorial staff still in the office. Casey, who was a Francophil, knew that his judgement on foreign matters carried little weight, and would have preferred to pass over the request in silence.

---

[1] Since 1933 Germany had repeatedly offered Czechoslovakia a Treaty on the German-Polish model. The offer was renewed on February 16, 1938, but declined by Benesh, who wished to maintain association with France, and had, above all, no faith in Hitler's word.

Twenty minutes before the first edition was due to go to press the Editor sent for him and asked his opinion of the article. Casey said that he did not care for it as a whole, and particularly disliked the hints with which it closed. The Editor was so little influenced by Casey's point that at 12.5 he sent out to the composing room a revised version of certain passages.

For the passage in the first edition: " In that case it might be worth while for the Czechoslovak Government to consider whether " [here began a phrase which originally ran] " *a solution should not be sought on some totally different lines, which would make Czechoslovakia an entirely homogeneous State* by the secession of that fringe, etc." For the last edition the Editor altered the phrase shown here in italics thus: " whether **they should exclude altogether the project, which has found favour in some quarters, of making Czechoslovakia a more homogeneous State** " by the secession, etc. He inserted " **conceivably** " in the last line and completed it by adding the words " **of losing the Sudeten German districts of the Borderland.**" Thus the final paragraph of the leader, as corrected by the Editor for the late editions, read as follows:

No Central Government would still deserve its title if it did not reserve in its own hands Defence, Foreign Policy, and Finance. There does not appear to be any dispute about this principle in the minds of the Government or of Herr Henlein; and, if the Sudetens now ask for more than the Czech Government are apparently ready to give in their latest set of proposals, it can only be inferred that the Germans are going beyond the mere removal of disabilities and do not find themselves at ease within the Czechoslovak Republic. In that case it might be worth while for the Czechoslovak Government to consider whether† they should exclude altogether the project, which has found favour in some quarters, of making Czechoslovakia a more homogeneous State† by the secession of that fringe of alien populations who are contiguous to the nation with which they are united by race. In any case the wishes of the population concerned would seem to be a decisively important element in any solution that can hope to be regarded as permanent, and the advantages to Czechoslovakia of becoming a homogeneous State might †conceivably† outweigh the obvious disadvantages† of losing the Sudeten German districts of the borderland†. (September 7, 1938.)

The suggestion in this paragraph was universally regarded as important and as inspired by a high official source. The decision to publish the article on the night was taken by the Editor without resort to the opinion of a specialist inside or outside Printing House Square. It was made in the normal editorial course that followed

---

† Encloses the differences between the early and late editions of *The Times* set out and *italicized* in the previous paragraph.

Corrections to the leading article of September 7, 1938, in the holograph of the Editor.

the decision of ten years earlier not to continue the search for a
Foreign Editor of the type of Wallace, Chirol, Steed or Williams,
but to place the conduct of foreign affairs, even when a situation
of extreme delicacy was reached, in the hands of the Editor
unassisted by a specialist. In the event, as has been seen, this
decision had made B.-W., a general journalist, already occupied
with administration in his capacity of Assistant Editor, and with
day-to-day writing, the virtual " Foreign Editor." On the
night of September 6 he was absent. That there was in Printing
House Square no specialist with a completer understanding of
European and World politics than a Prime Minister or a Foreign
Secretary was the result of a defect in the organization of Printing
House Square that originated with Dawson's recall in 1922.

Since 1928, the Editor had, in large part, devolved the responsibility for Anglo-German policy upon B.-W. It was not B.-W.'s
fault that, in the absence of a qualified Foreign Editor, he was the
writer of all the important detailed policy leaders on Anglo-
German relations or that he was more responsible than any other
member of the staff for the rationalizing of a policy which the
Editor approved on grounds of instinct and authority. However,
at no time did he hesitate to proclaim his convictions or to stand
by them. His leading articles of July and August prove that
B.-W. was conscientiously convinced (as he was before 1927
when he returned to *The Times*) that the political doctrine
held by the framers of the Versailles Treaty to be its justification,
the principle of self-determination of nationalities, was as morally
valid in 1938 as in 1919. He also held that certain provisions
of the Treaty, when drafted, were inconsistent with this principle;
and that for this reason Germany's claim that she had been
badly treated was also valid. A much more serious defect of
the Treaty was that Germany had not been heard at Versailles,
but had been compelled to accept it under protest. B.-W.
reasoned his course to these conclusions independently of his
colleagues in Printing House Square. Dawson came to the same
conclusions by way of talks with people of a certain cast of
thought, and his close personal friendships with Baldwin,
Chamberlain and Halifax.

At no time during the period 1928-1938 did Printing House
Square seek to follow the inspirations of the Foreign Office.
The policy of Dawson and B.-W. was their own. It was consistent and deliberate, but, inevitably, when either was away, the
expression of this policy by an alternative leader-writer could

sometimes be deficient in sense of balance; and when both were away, as happened at the week-end of September 4-6, 1938, the argument might turn out to be clumsily expressed. There was, however, no material difference between the relevant passage in B.-W.'s article of June 3 which was repudiated by the Foreign Office next day[1], and that of his colleague printed on September 7. The writer of the latter was generally regarded as a dependable writer. He was not the Editor, however, and was justified in believing that as he was writing in haste his work was to have the benefit of the Editor's correction. This it received, as has been seen; but Dawson's absence at the week-end and his late return may have given him insufficient time, before or after dinner, in which to bestow on such an article the consideration and correction it needed in the actual circumstances. The Editor decided to print the article on Tuesday night without enquiring into its impact on Prague, in the circumstances of the moment. More-over, the Editor's phrase, which also ended the article, turned a relatively mild and not obviously official looking " hint " regarding new possibilities (that might be " inferred ") into a somewhat stronger and possibly official recommendation (*i.e.*, the reference to " some quarters ") in advance of German demands, that the Czechs should see the " advantages " of " losing the Sudeten German districts of the Borderland."

Barrington-Ward heard of the article on the wireless at Clashgulloch in Ayrshire. The suggestion that Czechoslovakia should cede the Sudeten and other minority areas would, as he thought previously, " disarm " in advance a Hitler intent upon breaking off the French and Russian alliances. Whether B.-W. thought the suggestion well-timed is not known; whether if he had been in charge that night he would have said the same thing in different words may only be guessed. But it is very probable; for the calculation in B.-W.'s mind went forward, not to the actual nature of the negotiations taking place in Prague, but to the probable contents of Hitler's speech due to be made at Nuremberg on September 12. That was the dominating consideration in his mind, not the feelings or the position of the Czechs. He feared that Hitler might voice a demand for something far more serious than self-determination for the Sudetens. It is just to say that the article of September 7 in respect of Prague was most untimely; that its untimeliness in any other respect altered ultimate events is untrue. The immediate reactions, however, need to be chronicled. In the first place, the leader created a genuine

---

[1] See above, pp. 921, 923; the repudiation was diplomatic and, of course, not public.

sensation.[1] The French and Czechoslovak Governments forthwith urged the British Government to dissociate itself from the
views of *The Times*. This was not incomprehensible since the
leader's reference to the cession of the minority areas as a
" project which has found favour in some quarters " was an
unhappy phrase which could reasonably be taken as pointing
either to the British Cabinet or to the Foreign Office. It has been
seen that the argument of the article of September 7 was not,
any more than that of any other, derived. It might be argued
that in times of grave international tension, " inspiration,"
to a lesser or greater degree, would do more good than
harm. It might be demanded in this specific crisis that an
article of such importance, to be published at such a juncture, in a
journal of such weight as *The Times*, should have been written and
the date of publication chosen in the light of immediate and
precise knowledge of the negotiations; and the more so since they
were being instantly conducted by a British mediator. These considerations, however relevant to a theoretical discussion about
the relations of a newspaper with the organs of Government, do
not arise in connexion with the leading article of September 7.

Jan Masaryk, Czech Minister in London, called at the Foreign
Office that Wednesday morning, and the Office issued in the
afternoon its statement that " a suggestion appearing in *The Times*
this morning to the effect that the Czechoslovak Government
might consider as an alternative to their present proposals the
secession of the fringe of alien populations in their territory
in no way represents the view of His Majesty's Government."[2]
Runciman, too, telegraphed from Prague that " leading article
in to-day's *Times* has added to our difficulties. We are dealing
with the matter here, but it would be useful to caution them against

[1] For attacks by utopian writers with access to the columns of weeklies, see *The Week*
(September 8) and *The Cambridge Review* (December 2). Both alleged in their issues of
the dates mentioned that *The Times* had been " inspired " to write as it did : the former
imputed the inspiration to the German Embassy, the latter to the British Cabinet.
The Week's suggestion was completely untrue, but was quickly taken up. The Editor's
attention was drawn to it by several people, Churchill among them, but he regarded
it as not deserving of a formal contradiction. Theodor Kordt, the German Chargé
d'Affaires, telgraphed to his Government on September 8 that " According to reliable
information *Times* article not inspired by the Foreign Office. The possibility exists,
however, that it derives from a suggestion which reached *The Times* editorial staff from
the Prime Minister's entourage." Kordt was, of course, entitled to use his judgement
and his knowledge of London to guess at the truth, but this guess was wrong. The
Editor caused *The Cambridge Review* to be informed in a letter on December 4 that
" the suspicion on which these reflections are based is devoid of any foundations whatever;
no member or supporter of the Government suggested at any time that the ' dismemberment ' of Czechoslovakia, which presumably means the cession to the Reich of the Sudeten-
German areas, should be advocated by *The Times*. The Government indeed lost no
time in emphatically dissociating itself from the suggestion which had in fact been
ventilated in *The Times* on many previous occasions—not as a course to be followed,
but as a solution which should not be excluded if all others were to fail. There was no
question whatever of ' hole and corner politics'."

[2] Woodward & Butler, *Documents*. 3s. II.271, *n*.

adventurous speculations at a time when we are hoping to make some progress. The last paragraph of article is a recommendation of an Anschluss."

Dawson lunched next day, Thursday, with the Foreign Secretary; and, returning to the office, the Editor answered critics with a leader from his own hand for the paper of September 9, 1938. *The Times* then said, "It is really grotesque that so much righteous indignation should be expended on the mere suggestion, which has frequently been made in these columns before, that a revision of boundaries should not be excluded entirely from the list of possible approaches to a settlement. It is not a solution for which any one is likely to feel enthusiasm." The leader proceeded to argue that it was not certain that the Sudetens were " really anxious " for incorporation in the Reich, or that Hitler was " anxious " to have them. The fundamental conviction of the writer, entertained since March 24 at least, was plain enough in the final three lines: " But no other way can be ruled out altogether if it offers an alternative to perpetual quarrels in which the rest of the world is bound sooner or later to become involved." Having so written for Friday's paper, and after lunching again with the Foreign Secretary, the Editor departed for his Yorkshire house. Here he met B.-W. and in the evening discussed the situation with him. He assured B.-W. that Halifax " does not dissent privately from the suggestion that any solution, even the secession of the German minorities, should be brought into free negotiation at Prague," but he admitted that the Foreign Office was in a high state of indignation.[1]

Dawson went back to Printing House Square on Sunday, while B.-W. agreed to leave on Monday, the day of Hitler's speech to his Party at Nuremberg, which he had for three weeks thought to be of critical importance. B.-W. then gave his mind to the preparation of a reasoned presentation of the " doctrine " that lay at the base of the paper's attitude while Dawson set a leader-writer to make a first comment on Hitler's speech for the paper of September 13. " The speech, in fact, though not altogether reassuring, was not violently disturbing." At the office the Editor received a letter from Astor, who was in Scotland. After

---

[1] B.-W. made a note of this conversation on the day it took place. He added that " It seems, however, that G.D. was a little rushed with this leader. It was the day on which he came back from Yorkshire. Before he and X [the leader-writer] came back I had been putting to them the idea of the Czechs letting the Germans go " (B.-W.'s note of September 9, 1938). It is difficult to reconcile the Editor's statement as to Halifax's standpoint with the Foreign Secretary's authoritative statement to the Russian Ambassador, who called at the Foreign Office on Thursday afternoon. Maisky told Halifax that, in his judgement, this article had had the worst possible effect. " I [Halifax] told him [Maisky] that I did not in any way disagree with his judgement in this matter."

ologizing for his silence due to his hands being pretty full, Dawson thus replied:

B.-W. got back to work yesterday and we have a fairly strong team at the office. There is no reason therefore, so far as I can see, why you should come South before you intended. Indeed the predictions this morning are that events will drag on for the moment and come to a head in about a fortnight's time.

But it is difficult to predict anything in these days with events changing from hour to hour. I am not myself apprehensive of a general war, though it is obviously a time of great anxiety and there is no knowing what results any "incidents" might produce. In any case it is quite clear to me that neither we nor any other democracy will be justified in going to war in order to prevent "self determination"—that blessed word invented by the late President Wilson! Curiously enough the only people in favour of such a course seem to be our Left Wing, who are clamouring for a British-French-Russian stand against the dictators. Who would have dreamed of our going to war for such a cause in the calmer atmosphere of six months ago?

In this connexion I have little doubt that the leader in *The Times* which caused so much hubbub did good rather than harm. It was not worded *quite* as I should have done if I had had rather more time to revise it; but after all it was a very mild suggestion, and one that had consistently been made before, that no avenue should be left unexplored which might lead to settlement. If I were Benes I should definitely prefer to have the Sudeten fringe *outside* my frontiers than to keep them as a perpetual nuisance inside. The strategical argument itself was always in my opinion a weak one. After all, with a great power like Germany surrounding your country on three sides, a row of fortresses in the hills cannot mean much more than the chance of holding up an invasion for a few days. It is a case of being killed on Friday instead of on a Tuesday! And now the whole strategical argument has gone with the absorption of Austria, which offers an easy line of approach.

I know there are infinite difficulties of population and trade and commerce in any readjustment of frontiers; but I cannot help thinking that it is better to face them than to contemplate the horrors of a general war which no one wants. I am surprised myself to find how many sane people take this view; and it is a little amusing to find that the papers which were describing our mild remarks as a "sinister" suggestion less than a week ago are now quite cheerfully canvassing the same suggestion themselves. In the long run I believe that *The Times* will score by having been ahead of them, and it has already cut the ground from under the demand for "self-determination" which was quite obviously coming.

No doubt the Foreign Office did not like the article; but the Secretary of State, who was lunching with me next day, did not seem at all to dissent from my views himself. He seems to me to be exerting a very steadying influence on his colleagues, though I see no sign of any

PP

935

particular division among them. I got up at a unearthly hour yesterday morning for breakfast and a talk with Tom Inskip and lunched again later in the day with Edward [Halifax] and Dorothy, who is in London waiting partly for Hitler and partly for her second grandchild. They tell me that Attlee, who has seen the Prime Minister once or twice, is perfectly sensible, and Anthony Eden, whom I met last Sunday, did not dissent from anything that the Government were doing. As for the country at large, the main division, I suppose, is between those who are for " standing up to the dictators " and declaring war (as Winston for example would like) as soon as the first German crosses the Czech frontier, and those who are trying to localize the trouble inside Czechoslovakia, which I still believe is what Hitler wants. We put some questions to him this morning to suggest that he might at least make the contribution of telling us what he *does* want.

But of course there is no telling what any dictator may do, particularly one who has a donkey like Ribbentrop at his side, and all this may be long out of date before it reaches Millden.[1]

The Editor's leader gave credit to the Prime Minister, by whose " indomitable resolution," and by the response to it in other European capitals, including Berlin, the drift to disaster had been stayed. In this mood of assured confidence, *The Times* proceeded to support Government policy. " The one solution," as the first leading article had said on September 8, " that is barred by the moral sense of the whole world is a solution based on force or (what amounts to the same thing) on the threat of force." Support of the policy of " international negotiation " with Czech " concession," on which the Prime Minister embarked with his visit to Hitler at Berchtesgaden (near Munich) on September 15, was maintained in the face of much criticism. Yet the makers of the Munich policy were convinced that they were rendering a service to Czechoslovakia and to civilization. It was not understood after 1936 that the question was not whether the West should fight for Czechoslovakia, but that the West should at least refrain from placing the Republic in a situation where she could fight neither for herself nor for the West ; it was not perceived that, after the Anschluss, Czechoslovakia, shorn of the frontiers of the Kingdom of Bohemia which had been unchanged since 1198, would be powerless. It was not seen that, with or without an international guarantee to Czechoslovakia, Germany would gain an increase of population and the release of the troops which had hitherto been set aside to deal with the 35-40 Czech divisions. On the contrary, it was firmly believed in Printing House Square that the Republic would be " stronger " for these

[1] P.S. [In the Editor's own hand—the rest of the letter, save " Private " and the signature was typed.] " It *is* already out of date in that Edward [Halifax] has told me of the P.M.'s dramatic dash to Germany tomorrow since I began the letter. That at all events i reassuring news."

losses and the reduction of risks; it was only necessary to compass an ethical solution by an agreed acceptance of German demands. The consequences to Europe would be what they would be. The rectitude of British policy must be vindicated; nor was it seen that German claims did not repose upon a sound ethical basis. A paper drawn up in the office on October 14, in answer to an indignant protest from John Walter's Czech son-in-law, thus defended the timing of the article of September 7 :

It is nonsense that our [*The Times*] article " most encouraged Germany in her unjust claims." It was because we knew perfectly well that " the union of all Germany within the Reich " is one of the fixed aims of the Nazi Party, and because we felt confident that Hitler was going to say something pretty violent about the Sudetens on the last day of the Nuremberg Conference [September 12] that we quietly and tentatively put forward the suggestion before he did. We believed the claim to be in entire accordance with the principle of self-determination on which the peace terms were supposed to be drawn up, and we considered it best to say so *before* Hitler spoke rather than after he had demanded that there should be a revision of the frontier. All the subsequent evidence shows that what Hitler was aiming at was the complete destruction of Czechoslovakia, and now the genuine Czech and Slovak (and I hope Ruthene) part of the country is being preserved. Chamberlain by saving the peace saved Czechoslovakia from annihilation. . . . Chamberlain's only mistake, in my opinion, was the tactical one, that unlike us [*The Times*] he waited until Hitler had actually demanded self-determination before he admitted that he was in favour of it.

It is clear from this document that those responsible for the paper's policy were not displeased, after much public and private criticism, either with the timing of the article of September 7, or with its contents. Whether, in fact, the article was ill-timed, depends upon the view taken by the reader of the risks to be feared from Hitler's speech due to be made within five days of the publication of the article, and of the desirability of preventing his demand for an instant and complete military subjugation of Czechoslovakia. That speech, it has been seen, had not proceeded to the extreme demands that the leader of September 7 was designed to forestall.

An article " Back to Prague " appeared on September 14, arguing that Hitler's speech, the prospect of which had made B.-W. so apprehensive, had " left the door open for negotiation." Important was the fact that he based himself " definitely "[1] upon the " familiar liberal principle " of self-determination, and " the claim, in principle, to self-determination is fundamentally just and sound. It is the only ground upon which, in

[1] Dawson thus strengthened B.-W.'s " rather more firmly than before."

this age of nationalism, Europe can hope to be at peace and secure." Whatever the follies of German propaganda, therefore " it would be weak and misguided to rule out beforehand any solution compatible with and resulting from that guiding principle for as long as the way of free and peaceful negotiation has not been violently barred." The writer admitted that there were difficulties in the application of the principle. " Herr Hitler has disclaimed bargaining and demands German rights on a platter. Is that to be the whole of the German contribution to peace in an area in which the sparks of irresponsibility, already beginning to fly, may set the world on fire ? . . . Not one word has been heard yet of constructive German participation such as would ease the way of concession and allow revision to go its full length." The Editor again went to the country on Thursday, the day of Chamberlain's visit to Berchtesgaden. On Friday B.-W. lunched with Vincent Massey, whom he found all against a world war fought with the object of keeping large dissident minorities under Czechoslovak rule.

Next day, Saturday, September 17, B.-W. called upon Hoare. The Prime Minister having returned from Berchtesgaden, had spent all day with Halifax, Simon and Hoare, and when B.-W. arrived at Downing Street at the appointed hour he discovered that the Cabinet, which had sat all the morning, was due to meet again at 3. He was asked to return at 6. Meanwhile, he again saw Massey who referred to " the timid and isolationist Canadian Government " and the " inert Mackenzie King." When at last B.-W. met Hoare, he learnt that the Prime Minister had found Hitler *exalté*, full of his duty as liberator of the Germans, etc., etc. It was useless to broach larger questions, but the Prime Minister had told the German Chancellor he was not unwilling to discuss the question of transfer of the Sudetenland to Germany. He must consult the Cabinet first, however. After discussion, the Cabinet had agreed that Czechoslovakia was disintegrating already and it was not worth a war to stop the process. Benesh could have reached a settlement earlier had he wished. Hoare told B.-W. that the Cabinet did favour detachment of certain German areas. As for the rest, Czechoslovakia might well be neutralized and guaranteed by Germany, Russia, France, Italy, Poland, etc. There should be no rushing in with a British guarantee, but it might be necessary in the end to give it. B.-W. expressed doubt about carving pieces off Czechoslovakia unless they were fitted into some larger scheme. Hoare agreed, and thought the Czechs would accept some arrangement when they knew that the French would not march. France, it was believed by the Cabinet, was

Problem rather different.] Rest of scheme also only broadly approached as yet. Idea: neutralization of rest of C.-S. with guarantees from Germany, Russia, France, Italy, Poland etc. — [*Thought police pressure wd. accept this.*] Wd. not much in with a British fleet but might be necessary to give it — in the end — I drawed essential to fit the transfer scheme into something larger. Difficult mainly to carve bits of [*& leave it at that.*] [*He fully agreed.*]

Thinks Czechs will & must accept such a solution when they know France will not march — Important to throw all responsibility on us, France shd not be able to say that we sold & passed & they could therefore do nothing — Daladier & Bonnet invited to come over forthwith. French [*in my case*] prepared to do anything — Air Force in shocking condition. Report of Air Minister to Air Clees of Chamber. Only 20 machines fit to compare with the German first line machines. Only 700 first-line aircraft, of which a large number in North Africa.

Armed with mandate from Cabinet P.M. proposes to return to Hitler — [*Hitler summoned with his-rate sycophants, Ribbentrop etc. But*] [thinks he will respond to invitation to show himself as the peace-maker. Neville & me & so likely so to influence him. Hitler's remark on his

. . "[Cabinet uncommitted to particular scheme, plebiscite &c. Bound to be anomalies. Aim at detachment of certain German areas. (*Q.*) What about the minorities, *e.g.* Hungarian? (*A.*) Thinks they wd. be satisfied with less.] Problem rather different" &c. From B.-W.'s notes of his conversation with Sir Samuel Hoare, First Lord of the Admiralty, on the evening of September 17, 1938.

unprepared for war; she had only 20 aeroplanes fit to compare with German first-line planes, and only 700 first-line aircraft, of which many were in North Africa. Hoare emphasized that it was important that France should not be enabled to throw on to Britain the responsibility for giving up Czechoslovakia, or be allowed to say that " Britain had sold the pass and that was why France could do nothing, whereas the French were, in fact, reluctant to do anything." As for the next step in British policy, Hoare said that the Prime Minister, armed with a mandate from a united Cabinet, proposed to return to Hitler who, it was thought, might respond to an invitation to show himself as the peacemaker. Later, the French were to be invited to London for discussions and to be prevented from putting responsibility on Great Britain alone. Hence, the less interference now with Hitler and Chamberlain, the better.

The French Ministers duly arrived in London on Sunday. An Anglo-French plan was settled by Chamberlain, Halifax, Daladier and Bonnet on September 18. It was based upon an application of the principle of self-determination, and recommended the acceptance of the " direct transfer to the Reich of all territories with over 50 per cent. Sudeten inhabitants." This done, a guarantee for the new Czechoslovakian frontiers would be offered. This plan was communicated on September 19 to Czechoslovakia. On the afternoon of that day B.-W. saw Hoare again. He learnt that the French (Bonnet especially) were " abject " in their anxiety that no *casus foederis* should arise over Czechoslovakia. B.-W. extracted further details of what was now called the Anglo-French plan, of which he thought well; at least that, since the plan conceded the essentials, there would be no war. On Chamberlain's speech in the Commons reporting his conference with Hitler, B.-W. wrote:

The Prime Minister has set himself to get the work of a peace conference done before the next war, and not after it. He cannot dictate the outcome of his exertions. But one thing can be said now, even if he should fail. He has striven to the last by all that one man's energy, resource, and indifference to calumny could do, to hold up and reverse that same fatalistic slither into the abyss—the phrase in another context, is Mr. Eden's—which carried agonized Europe helplessly away in late July and early August 1914. To have moved with, and not against, the tide of events, would have brought this country by now into the worst of all perils, the peril of war upon a confused issue fastened upon an unconvinced and disunited people. (September 23, 1938.)

The Prime Minister, added the writer, could have bought cheaply for himself the ephemeral adulation of those who argued clamorously for war as the only righteous relationship between democracy and dictatorship.

The Anglo-French plan was refused by the Czechoslovak Government on September 20. Immediately, Britain and France, by agreement, told Benesh that Czechoslovakia must either surrender the Sudeten territories or face war with Germany alone. Benesh complied on September 21, and Chamberlain went to Godesberg. *The Times* continued to emphasize its conviction that, at this point, there could be no peace if the Opposition's advice was followed. " The proof is that Czechoslovakia has been faced in the last weeks with the alternatives of destruction by war or of disintegration without it." Revision had now to be attempted in the worst conditions conceivable or not at all. (September 23, 1938.) Chamberlain was in Godesberg on the day this was published. The first question asked in London was whether the upshot would be war or peace. There would be others. Would Britain suffer in honour and prestige? Ought Britain to fight Germany now, or wait till she was even stronger? Would Britain have the strength in a year's time? In these uncertainties B.-W. wrote one more leader. It alluded to the Press agitation against Czechoslovakia which " may prove to represent no more than the perilous appetite of subordinates out of hand. No one will look gladly or willingly for the alternative, but no one will flinch from it. If the German Press has faithfully stated German policy, then here is an issue on which every British citizen without exception, knows where he stands." (September 24, 1938.) This was published on the Saturday that the Prime Minister returned from Godesberg.

Later in the day B.-W. secured from Massey an outline of the Godesberg proposals, and on Sunday sat down to write upon them. They were more demanding than he had expected and, for the first time, he felt genuine sympathy with the Czechs, whose Sudeten areas must, it was said, be surrendered on October 1. " This alone is a demand which is quite incapable of fulfilment "; but the official account of the meeting had yet to be received. Full information would enable the real alternatives to be put in the balance and these, when seen in turn in Prague, Paris and London, would be found to involve " not only the honour and safety of this country, but the whole structure of European life." Only then could the last choice be made. " What course is best for the Czechs themselves, what course is right for the future of peace and security in Europe can then be judged." There was no

eed of appeals for public resolution at home, or for strong
words. " Nobody could hope to persuade official Germany of the
truth about Britain if she is not already persuaded." Britain, at all
events, knew that "Germany at need would be met by a will as
tenacious as her own, and by a power of sacrifice that would
outlast every call upon it." Having thus warned the Germans, the
writer turned to domestic critics who conceded no praise to
Chamberlain's " valour and wisdom " and " single-handed "
stand for peace. The Prime Minister had not flinched before
misrepresentation at home, and had given Britain the assurance
that " if her manhood must again be summoned to the arbitra-
ment of force, it shall be by no last-minute failure of her statesmanship and in a clear cause. What one man could do to stem the
avalanche he has done." His critics could be left to the care of
time and events. " An abrupt and mysterious process of conversion and recantation has saddled some politicians and their
followers with the belief that this country ought already to be at
war to maintain the *status quo* in Central Europe for the strange
reason that the safety of democracy depends upon the permanent
coercion of recalcitrant minorities." Few shared that view. The
leader affirmed once more that all were prepared to offer " instant
resistance to Germany if her plan is the violent overthrow of the
liberties of the Czechoslovak people." The Godesberg memorandum, " ostensibly at least," concerned itself solely with the
procedure of evacuation. " It was in the last degree improbable
that the Czech Government would accept them as they stand, and
they are understood, in fact, to have given them a reasoned refusal.
But it is not Czechoslovakia alone which is now concerned. The
part which Britain has played as mediator, and her general interest
in European peace, coupled with her close relations with France,
give her substantially, if not formally, the status of a principal in
negotiation." The position of France as the ally of Czechoslovakia, and a partner in the intervention which first brought the
idea of negotiated and peaceful cession into play, was even more
definite. This being so, " there will be a general feeling " that
Britain and France should make a joint declaration. " That indeed
is the last of all concessions which should be made to the
dictatorial method. . . . The decision between peace and war
would then rest with Germany, and with Germany alone."
(September 26, 1938.)

Daladier and Bonnet left Paris for London on Sunday, while
B.-W. was writing the leader just quoted. Chamberlain undertook
that if, in pursuit of her treaty obligations, France became actively
engaged in hostilities against Germany, the United Kingdom would

feel obliged to support her; and agreed, also, to make the undertaking public, and join with it one more appeal to Hitler who was due to speak in Berlin on September 26. The speech when made, though full of abuse of Czechoslovakia and personal vilification of Benesh, did not, in the opinion of *The Times*, close the door to negotiations, though the demand for transfer of the Sudeten areas by October 1 was still, apparently, maintained There was, on the other hand, readiness to invite the British Legion to share the task of maintaining order. Also there was a guarantee for the future State of Czechoslovakia. " If the Czechs solve the problem of their other minorities in a decent manner, then the Czech nation does not interest me any more; and I, a far as I am concerned, will guarantee it." The article dealing with this speech was entrusted to a leader-writer in order to give B.-W a night off. It was much altered between editions by Dawson, who strove to extract every fraction of comfort from a speech expressed in terms so full of menace. The fact remained that Germany's terms were " definitely harsher," bullying in style, Prussian in conception, and set forth as an ultimatum which, instead of being the basis for a peaceful transaction, implied the use of military force if the demands were not met; and met by October 1. Her original requests were no sooner granted than she now began to ask for more. The demands put forward at Godesberg may have differed from those already conceded by Benesh in small particulars, but they were all-important. The speech, however, did contain the important assurance that if the Czechs solved their minorities problem " in a decent manner," the Czech nation ceased to interest Germany. As to the question of the ultimate German objective, the gravest doubts were unavoidable.

Next day the temperature was hardly lower. The " instant occupation under dictated conditions is an intolerable demand; a speedy application of the agreement already reached is by common consent desirable," and it was pointed out that the entailed loss of the fortifications would be balanced by the new security guarantee. (September 28, 1938.) The situation was serious. There was little time to lose if peace was to be gained. In Britain a state of emergency had been proclaimed, and the Fleet mobilized on the 27th. It was now known that the German Army was under orders to break Czechoslovakia's resistance to the Godesberg demands. The critical moment was at hand. As *The Times* had said on the 26th, " It is not Czechoslovakia alone which is now concerned "; Britain and France were " concerned." It was apparent that the method of " peace by negotiation " which *The Times* had sponsored since March, and the " agreed solution " it had proposed, were about to be realized. The "negotiation" and the "solution" would consist of British and French pressure upon the Czechs, and Czech acceptance of the Godesberg demands which they had already said were unacceptable. Unless the Czechs surrendered to the Anglo-French pressure they would be invaded and the whole of Europe embroiled. There was no other choice. That was certain on the 28th. On that day trenches were being dug in Regent's Park, where both the Editor and B.-W. lived.

B.-W. went to the House of Commons after lunch to hear the Prime Minister's report. The reception for Chamberlain was great from his own side and though, for a man of his age, he looked fit, he must have been at the last stage of physical exhaustion. In B.-W.'s opinion his long account of events and of his visits to Hitler came easily, quietly and lucidly. He revealed the final appeal made that morning to Hitler and the request to Mussolini for support. There was a dramatic intervention by Simon, who handed the Prime Minister a note of invitation to visit Hitler at Munich on the next day, and saying that Mussolini and Daladier were also invited. "In a second," wrote Barrington-Ward in a contemporary note, "the whole place was on its feet. A huge prolonged cheer and a tempest of waving order-papers. I heard the unusual sound of loud clapping, looked round the partition and saw the public violently applauding in the Strangers' Gallery. . . . It was electrifying." He himself felt a sense of instantaneous relief, but instantly concluded that "we aren't out of the wood yet." He returned to the office, wrote a leader before dining, and again went back to the office. This leader, entitled "On to Munich," gave unstinted praise to the Prime Minister, and contrasted his speech with Grey's of August 3, 1914. "Where Sir Edward Grey had failed, Mr. Chamberlain has, for the moment, succeeded. It may be no more than a respite. It would be reckless to build high even upon the broad-based consultation which has now been achieved." (September 29, 1938.) It was soon known that the Munich Conference had concluded in agreement, which B.-W. admitted bore heavily upon the Czechs. "Yet they had brought it upon themselves by lending themselves to the French policy of encirclement which was artificial and hopeless from the start." *The Times* was satisfied that the relief and enthusiasm which greeted the Munich agreement were justified. They were not "the thoughtless and short-sighted rejoicings of a people thankful to have escaped at any price from imminent war." The resignation of Duff Cooper gave B.-W. the opportunity of insisting once again that the Treaty of Versailles was not merely no peace but that " nineteen years of disproof rise up against it." (October 4.) The charge against the Prime Minister was forcefully rebutted. " He and his country are represented by some of his critics as having callously sacrificed a small and democratic people to the overbearing might of undemocratic Germany." This, the staple of self-righteous indignation against Chamberlain, showed emotion divorced from thought. " It is facile and false." The Four Powers were due to meet at Munich that day. The Czechs had acquiesced, the British and French pressure upon them had procured their agreement, but they were not present at Munich with Chamberlain, Daladier, Mussolini and Hitler. It was resolved that the German occupation of the Sudeten areas should take place in five stages (altogether by October 10) to a line fixed by an International Commission, including a representative of Czechoslovakia; the delimitation of plebiscite areas was to be undertaken by the Commission, and the provisonal policing of the areas supervised by an international force. Britain and France were to guarantee the new frontiers; and Germany and Italy would join this guarantee when the question of the Polish and Hungarian minorities had been settled. This was the agreement with which the Prime Minister returned on Friday, September 30.

As *The Times* had said in 1919, by creating a new Czechoslovakia " A great deal is being risked . . . and the risk must be shared evenly between the Allies and their beneficiaries." (March 25, 1919.) The principle of self-determination as laid down by the creators of the Republic, and sponsored by Wilson without the important qualifications of Lloyd George, had enabled Germany to split British and Commonwealth opinion. On Saturday, October 1, nearly twenty years after *The Times* had pointed to the risk, the paper voiced the nation's relief that it had passed without a clash.

There were dissidents. To one B.-W. replied in terms that record the convictions in which all his leading articles over the past three weeks had been rooted:

We are absolutely snowed under with letters and yours may not see the light. Is it in any case true to suggest that *The Times* has been lacking in sympathy with the Czechs and their present plight? I could give you passage after passage in refutation. Admiration for the coolness and restraint, which Benesh has so wisely shown in these last few weeks, is one thing. " Gratitude " is another. I am sorry for him but I am not grateful to him. I regard him—along with Clemenceau, Poincaré, Austen, Barthou and others—as one of the most active architects of disorder in Europe. No one battled to maintain the disastrous artificialities of the French " system " with greater diligence and ability than Benesh. No one was more adept in using the language of the League to consecrate the *status quo*.

What has now happened has happened in the worst possible way but it was perfectly inevitable. When the French and the Czechs finally procured the defeat of Brüning's request for an economic union with Austria the thing was ended. I have the notes now of my talk with Benesh in 1920 when I ventured humbly to press upon him the view that the Anschluss was less of a peril to Czechoslovakia than the denial of it. Because all these follies created and endowed Nazism in Germany, I do not see how we are now to turn round and deny the force of the truths, axioms or even platitudes on which you and I would, I think, have been agreed ten years ago. When we fight let us fight Nazism and not Germany.[1]

There were resignations from junior members of the staff, and some of the seniors were unhappy over the settlement and apprehensive of a surprise move by Hitler, baulked of his victory march into Prague.[2] B.-W. himself was not in favour of thwarting what he regarded as a natural, inevitable, and even to some extent desirable, German expansion in South-East Europe and the Balkans. The spectre of a Mittel-Europa strangling economically all the small neighbouring countries did not frighten him as it did Arnold Toynbee, with whom he corresponded in November. The policy of actively seeking peace by negotiation rather than passively relying upon rearmament remained the staple of the paper's advocacy. A leading article by B.-W. urged the necessity to pursue the work:

In 1918 Britain forfeited, in a still notorious General Election, the power to insist on such an understanding [with Germany] and forfeited at the same time the power of leadership which has only lately been regained. The wish grew rapidly with the years, and during those years Franco-British relations were never more cordial than at times when French policy seemed to veer in the direction of appeasement. Had there been a free settlement in the years after the war, the course of political evolution in Germany would have been different. The lack of it armed Herr Hitler with his most powerful argument, which he used again yesterday. . . . In the meantime the work of peace cannot be adjourned at will. It must be pursued or abandoned. The whole discussion comes down to this. Must there be resistance to demands which ought to have been granted when Germany was weak merely because she is no

---

[1] Barrington-Ward to Nigel Law, October 4, 1938.

[2] Dissension in the office was known outside. On September 22 A. J. Cummings, having referred in the *News Chronicle* to the " crude editorial nonsense " of *The Times*, proceeded to say that " The whole world takes the view that Britain has capitulated to a show of force. If the editor of *The Times* has any doubt about the British view let him make inquiries among members of his own staff." Cummings also quotes as " another priceless gem " the remark in *The Times* about terms submitted to the Czechs not making a *prima facie* appeal. (That unlucky sentence also got into " This England " in the *New Statesman and Nation* and " Janus " in the *Spectator*.)

longer weak? Those who think so, and not Mr. Chamberlain, are advocating a short-sighted policy of cynicism and fear. (November 7 1938.)

The leader faced one significant result of Munich: that Germany had made a long step towards the recovery of her former strength It remained completely outside the convictions of *The Times* that "the course of political evolution in Germany," however "different" in form, would mean no difference in policy. A no time in Dawson's second period of editorship was it though that a post-war Germany rearmed would be a pre-war Germany revived. Hence, from the autumn of 1928 there is wanting any belief, or willingness to believe, that Germany before Hitler was preparing to retake the position she had occupied before the war and that the final consequences to the West, as well as to the East might not, Germans being still Germans, be other than they were between 1900 and 1914. *The Times*, accordingly, held to the course Dawson had set at the beginning of his second innings Yet by the end of 1938 it was obvious that public opinion in Britain was reacting strongly against Germany. Hitler delivered himself more than once of bitter personal attacks on Churchill Duff Cooper and Eden. These inevitably undermined the Prime Minister. Second thoughts about Munich on the part of a large and influential section of the public made it increasingly uncertain whether Chamberlain could hold his own to the extent of being able to maintain his peace policy. But although much of this opposition was due to a change of heart in Liberal and Labour circles, no practical alternative policy had yet been formulated by them Too many of the converted were intellectuals, utopians, sentimentalists and pacifists satisfied with a programme of resistance without the means of resistance. There was much division of opinion in these circles as to the efforts made in the middle of the month to hasten British rearmament (see *The Times* of December 21). The opposition policy, so far as it appeared to Printing House Square to be capable of definition at the end of the year, was to work for an alignment of Britain, France and Russia, and thus form a "democratic front" that would obstruct German expansion, at least under the Nazi régime, at any place and at any time. Those who advocated this policy had been slow to believe that the Germans, whether led by Prussians or Nazis who combined Prussianism with Socialism, would resist the Versailles Treaty and, if allowed to succeed, would then, by the use of agitation and mythology, arm themselves and challenge those who had imposed the Treaty upon them. This section of opinion which hitherto had regarded concession to Germans as an essentia contribution to the peace of Europe, now viewed resistance to the Nazis as the supreme good.

The Times, which was confident in September and October that the Prime Minister's case was " impregnable," was equally sure that its own doctrine, for doctrine it was, remained valid. The invasion of Belgium by Germany in 1914 had raised an ethical issue, without which there would not have existed the unanimity of public feeling requisite for the waging of successful war. It was proper, therefore, that war fought on behalf of ethical principles should be made good by a peace designed for an ethical end. The Versailles peace, therefore, was justified only in so far as it was the application of ethical principle to the reordering of Europe. It was imperfect and, as experience proved, needed adjustment if peace were to be reality; and as there could be no peace in Europe without a contented Germany, it would be a political advantage as well as an ethical gain if her just grievances were remedied. Those grievances were just because they arose out of the principle of self-determination upon which the Treaty was, in principle, based. Clearly, it made no difference to the application of the ethical principle whether these just grievances were put forward by pre-Nazi, or post-Nazi Germany; and the less so since it was held proved that it was the alleged grievance over Versailles, rather than a sense of defeat, that had given the Nazis their power. After Munich, therefore, it was still held that to remedy Versailles was to remedy Germany; to remove her grievances was to settle her claims and thereby release trade, reduce armaments and open the way to general pacification. It was not perceived that Germany, whether Nazi or democratic, would not only work for the return of her provinces, her army, her navy and her air force, but ultimately turn the tables and impose a Versailles or Brest-Litovsk upon the West. Neither *The Times*, nor the revisionists led by Keynes, perceived the risks involved in the application of ethical ideals or moral factors to political realities. It was understood in theory, but not appreciated in fact, that countries who conduct their affairs on the basis of legislation after discussion are at a strategic, military and naval disadvantage in dealing with dictators. In the spring of 1936 and in the autumn of 1938 *The Times* failed to assess correctly the importance of a close understanding with France, and to recognize that the liberation of Germany from the restrictions of Versailles could be a safe policy only if conducted in agreement with France. That Britain needed France was a belief that weakened steadily after the Chanak crisis in 1922; and Britain sought to rely instead, with the eager

support of *The Times*, on a policy of revision by " negotiation "
and " agreed settlement "; in effect it amounted to a surrender to
agitation and pressure short of the use of armed force. Dawson
and B.-W. failed to see that Munich was not an agreed settlement;
that the Czechoslovak Republic had not freely negotiated; that
the conditions essential to a stable Europe were not present; that
Germany had accomplished her will against the consciences of
Britain and France; and that she had done so by the possession
of superior striking power and the will, behind the threat, to
use it—not merely against Czechoslovakia but against Britain
and France.

The principle of self-determination that underlay the Versailles
Treaty to which the Germans appealed was, in fact, vindicated
at the sole expense of Czechoslovakia. It represented no
concession by Germany. On the contrary, it was an
immense gain to that country who from 1901 to 1914
had bent her vast energy to the task of challenging the Entente.
From 1919 to 1932, and from 1933 to 1938, Germany had
organized to outwit, outbuild and outstrengthen the West.
At home, those who were convinced by the arguments for an
ethical attitude to international politics did not observe that the
Germans, whether led by Prussians or Nazis, used the ethical
attitude solely as a means of agitation. This was clear to
observers in Berlin and was reported by *The Times* Correspondent
in 1930. The *Deutschland* was a perfect symbol of the claim that
the German Navy had beaten the British, and that the German
Army had been stabbed in the back by false promises. Next,
Hitler's original proclamation as Chancellor, February 1, 1933,
had really made it plain that " the German nation entered
the fight of 1914 without the slightest feeling of guilt on its part,
and filled only with the desire to defend its Fatherland which had
been attacked." Within a week he had demanded the revision of
the Treaty of Versailles and denounced the Polish Corridor as a
" particularly great injustice imposed upon the German nation."
But in January, 1934, he signed a joint German-Polish declaration
not to resort to force in the settlement of disputes, even those over
the existing German frontiers on the East, which Germany did
not recognize. The declaration was valid for ten years. Eighteen
months later the Polish Ambassador protested against the
reintroduction of conscription within the Reich which, according
to Hitler, was mere " restoration to Germany of equal rights
which threatens nobody but guarantees Germany's security."
Poland supported France in protesting against Germany's

violation of the Treaty of Versailles. As and when Germany felt strong enough to press for territory she invoked the ethical principle. Hitler pointed to the Germans in Memel who were " persecuted, tortured and maltreated in a most barbarous way "; expressed his resentment of the " military alliance " between France and Russia, while " Germany neither intended nor wished to interfere with the internal affairs of Austria, to annex Austria, or to conclude an Anschluss." In August, 1935, Hitler stated his conviction that " Germany during the last two-and-a-half years has occupied a different position in the world from that which she had before." Next month what *The Times* called " a significant and presumably deliberately arranged, German-Italian exchange of cordialities " took place when Hitler welcomed the new Italian Ambassador, Attolico. After the establishment of the Axis Hitler said that " Germany is a Great Power of the first rank, and has a right to possess a first-class army," and that Germany would never surrender her claim to colonies. In January, 1936, he said, " Germany is so strong now that she needs no help from the League " ; and on March 17 that the German people " will not be content with the possession of opportunities which are inferior to those granted to other people."

Germany's confidence was strikingly illustrated in February, 1938, when Hitler boasted that " just as England looks after interests which cover the whole of the globe, so also will Germany to-day look after and safeguard her relatively restricted interests." Including the protection of those fellow-Germans beyond German frontiers who were unable to ensure the right to freedom, " personal, political and ideological." But Poland respected the national relations of Danzig, and Germany respected Polish rights, " thus arriving at a sincere spirit of friendly cooperation." This he repeated on September 26, 1938. He proceeded to say that his agreement with the Austrian Chancellor gave the same legal rights to citizens holding National Socialist views as were enjoyed by the other citizens of German Austria. There were other events of a more tranquil kind. Italy was withdrawing from Spain. France was recognizing Italian sovereignty in Ethiopia, and Britain was following suit. In the autumn of 1938 the Editor received a number of visitors from oversea and was convinced that war with Germany at that time would have been misunderstood and resented from end to end of the Empire. Finally a Franco-German non-aggression pact completed, as Bonnet, its French signatory said, the work of " apaisement." A pronouncement by the Prime Minister on December 13 assured the House of Commons that Britain would give France support. *The Times* echoed Chamberlain's sentiments, though holding to the belief, expressed in the leading article of November 7, 1938, that " had there been a free settlement in the years after the war the political evolution in Germany would have been different." That the mistakes of Versailles had to be paid for by the Allies, remained one of B.-W.'s deepest convictions. Thus the sense of unredeemed defeat, that lay at the root of German readiness to exhibit physical force against opposition within and without the Reich, was accompanied on the British side by an almost morbid sense of ill-used victory that led to reliance upon moral exhortation. Even the excesses of the Nazis against racial and political minorities did not destroy the conception of the Germans as a fundamentally reasonable race of men who, treated reasonably, were not unlike the English. Hence it was more than probable that a new and reasonable statement of British peace aims would meet with an encouraging response, and open the way for a general settlement of the main outstanding problems. This would be the post-Munich policy of *The Times*. The situation was difficult, but it need not become dangerous if Britain, in spite of disappointment and provocation, persevered in the policy of pacification.

There were some among the Editor's close friends who had for some time urged him with increasing anxiety to pay more attention to the range and speed of German rearmament. Appeasement, they argued, was the one sound, reasonable and moral policy but, they now said, it could succeed only if based upon an effective balance of military strength. Dawson had too much experience to doubt the truth of this; but in terms of day-to-day comment he saw that the situation was too urgent to permit of long views. The Germans had the advantage. Accordingly, the Editor remained a convinced champion of appeasement, a term willingly and freely used in the leading columns of *The Times*, while B.-W. looked for a reasonable statement of British peace aims and of its free acceptance by the Germans as its concrete achievement. At the same time there were whispers that the Editor might not remain much longer in the chair.

XXIV

A NEW WORLD WAR AND A NEW EDITOR

SINCE the advent of the new Proprietors in the autumn of 1922, important changes had taken place in Printing House Square. In the autumn of 1938 the office heard rumours, emanating in the main from Oxford, that the Editor was not unlikely some time or other to take up a change of occupation. Nothing of the kind occurred. On the other hand a change was made on the commercial side. In October, 1937, William Lints Smith retired. He was appointed Associate Manager by Northcliffe on August 4, 1914, and Manager under Campbell Stuart (when Managing Director) on December 1, 1920. In 1922, when the new Proprietors re-established the old relations between Editor and Manager, Lints Smith was appointed sole Manager, and worked in that capacity by the side of Dawson for fourteen years. During this period *The Times*, under his commercial direction and with the benefit, it is just to emphasize, of the delayed results of Northcliffe's reorganization, rose to a degree of prosperity it had not known for over half a century. Printing House Square had been extremely fortunate in having, during its immediate post-Northcliffe period, the services of a Manager with sound commercial instincts who also possessed varied editorial experience. This enabled one who was primarily responsible to the Proprietors for the commercial direction to assist the Editor in important journalistic respects. The Manager's main task was the supervision of all the costs of production of *The Times* and its subsidiary publications, the equipment of the composing and press rooms, the staffing and direction of the commercial, circulation, publicity and advertising departments and the maintenance of the fabric of Printing House Square; also the care of the paper's branch offices and agencies at home and abroad; the whole in the interests of The Times Publishing Company Limited and its subsidiaries considered as a business undertaking. The initiation of the numerous special *Supplements* to *The Times*, with few exceptions, lay with the Manager, who alone could forecast their value in terms of advertising revenue. The completeness of the understanding between the editorial and managerial departments,

in the sense required by the settlement of 1922,[1] made possib
several innovations that concerned both departments. One (
these, which Lints Smith encouraged and which won permanenc
was the typographical re-dressing of *The Times*. It was an ente
prise which involved designing an entirely new range of types, bod
light headline and bold headline, etc., for use in the paper, aggr
gating some 38 founts requiring the cutting of 7,048 punches, (
which 1,075 needed to be re-cut before approval. The plan, a
carried out, was thorough and costly. The plan applie
to all publications as well as to *The Times*—to posters, bill
noteheadings, labels and all other forms of stationery. Th
ornamental gothic lettering of *The Times*, which had been used a
the head of the paper for 140 years, was suppressed in favour (
plain roman capitals. These plans, resulting in a complet
modernization of the paper's appearance, occupied three year
and were put into effect in a single week-end. *The Times* (
October 3, 1932, was a complete typographical novelty i
journalism. Hitherto, no newspaper in London, or elsewhere i
the world, had designed all its typographical material to serve i
own peculiar requirements.

The organization of few newspapers is as complete as that c
The Times and its subsidiary publications, and for that reason fe
newspapers could hope, with equal confidence, to commissio
the necessary designs from its own draughtsmen; and circumstance
have been against other newspapers completing anything of th
kind since the war. *The Times* began its typographical revision
at a convenient moment, and risk of failure was less in an offic
which had the memory of other innovations like the unsuccessfu
logographic invention of John Walter I who founded *The Time*
in 1785 (to advertise it) and such capital successes as the firs
power press which was invented by Frederick Koenig and Andre
Bauer, and used for printing the paper of November 29, 1814
The engineers of *The Times* in 1833, Andrew Applegath an
Edward Cowper, invented the famous four-feeder press fron
which Applegath developed his nine-feeder in 1848; all of whic
were superseded by J. C. Macdonald's and Charles Calverley'
rotary press, the first to be fed by rolls of paper instead of sheets
This, the "Walter Press," was first employed in 1868, and wa
the prototype of all succeeding rotary presses. Much re-equip
ment of composing rooms and press rooms was carried out unde
Lints Smith's management. He also supervised extensiv
re-building of the mechanical department.

[1] See above, Chapter XX, "New Proprietors."

The Proprietors, the Editor, the Manager and the typographical adviser
of *The Times*, present at the printing of the first
edition of October 3, 1932

Lints Smith's successor was his assistant, Christopher Shotter Kent, formerly of the *Daily Mail* and later Financial Controller of the British War Mission colloquially known as " Crewe House." He first came to the office on January 1, 1919, and succeeded to the managerial chair on November 1, 1937.

The chief members of the editorial staff when the war broke out had changed in the years since 1923. Freeman went to edit the *Educational Supplement* which he had initiated. B.-W., it has been seen, returned in 1927, shortly before the death of Harold Williams. Gordon Robbins resigned at the same time. In 1934 George Murray Brumwell fell victim of a serious illness and B.-W. was promoted to the position of Deputy Editor. The new deputy took his elevation seriously, and although it was given him without promise of succession he nourished the ambition without which, as he said, no candidate had a right to offer himself to Printing House Square. He ardently desired one day to occupy the editorial chair. Four years after his promotion to the deputy editorship, B.-W. was in a nursing home having a cartilage removed from his knee. While there, he was pressed by Lord Reith, Director-General of the B.B.C., to let him advocate his nomination as successor to himself. Despite Reith's pressure, B.-W. decided to stay at Printing House Square. It was an important decision for *The Times*. The tide of affairs into which the world and its newspapers were being projected was to run swifter than many keen observers were able to foresee, and B.-W. was destined to take an even larger share in leader-writing than he had in the past. He reached his decision independently, and in complete ignorance of the Editor's desire, due to be expressed at Christmas (1938) only to Astor and Walter, to retire before long.

In the early months of the new year, 1939, the consequences of the Czechoslovak crisis of 1938 to British strategy as conceived by the Secretary for War slowly became known to a few. The tone of the paper, nevertheless, was cheerful in January. " Certain grievances in Europe which threatened war have now been adjusted without war, even though, thanks to the blunders of the past, the adjustment has been hasty and crude, and bears the marks of force." So said *The Times* on Monday, January 21, 1939. The optimism was not superficial and after some setbacks later in the month was due to revive. Meanwhile preparations were being made for the visit of the Prime Minister and the Foreign Secretary to the Duce in connection with the Four-Power Pact into which it was hoped to fit Germany and Italy, as the British Government had planned in 1937. But Italy's demands on France for a territorial revision of the Mediterranean littoral made acute difficulties. Chamberlain and Halifax left for Rome on the 10th and stopped in Paris, where, as the paper said, the Prime Minister " may well have informed M. Daladier that he would leave the Duce in no doubt either of the solidarity between Great Britain and France, or of the need for an improvement in the relations between Rome and Paris as a preliminary to the discussion of the territorial claims." The return of Chamberlain and Halifax from Rome was followed by a warning from Hitler on January 20 that he would not tolerate interference in matters that concerned " nobody but ourselves." The atmosphere at home now changed. In the third week of January Dawson lunched with Halifax and was given a grim forecast of Hitler's next move—which would be westward. This statement was amplified with reports that the Diplomatic Correspondent brought in from the Foreign Office. B.-W. thought it was perhaps true that, as Halifax believed, extremists were on top. In fact, Funk had supplanted Schacht, and other Nazis had been promoted. There would, Halifax also said, be a demand for colonies from Britain, which if pressed (with German mobilization behind it) would mean world war. So spoke the Foreign Secretary on January 23, 1939.

The preparations for a state of emergency upon which the Departments of State had been working before Munich, were now sufficiently advanced to permit of the publication of an official *Guide to National Service*. It was published on January 25 and was summarized in *The Times* under a double-column heading of four decks, the first of such spaciousness since the Abdication.[1] It was a symbol of the sense of urgency now felt in Printing House Square. Hitler's speech of January 30, anxiously awaited, began at 7 and ended at 9.22. B.-W. finished his leading article of a column-and-a-quarter in time for the first edition. The speech, he felt, was unexpectedly moderate; even so, it was stiff enough. The German Führer laid it down that " a nation of 80 millions will not be willing permanently to be assessed by other nations." That, after all, was a general statement and not new. The accusation that " the great German Colonial possessions have been stolen," was categorical, and *The Times* opposed to it Hitler's previous declaration that neither war nor world domination was an aim of German policy; also his stated belief in a " long period of peace." The paper said that the approach to a colonial settlement was not barred, provided it were agreed beforehand to be the means of a sure contribution to general peace.

---

[1] For the Abdication see Appendix I.

The Times

No. 46,253   LONDON, SATURDAY, OCTOBER 1, 1932   PRICE (including Postage) 4d.

DEATHS (continued)

PERSONAL

PERSONAL (continued)

EDUCATIONAL

CONNOISSEURS' GUIDE

CLUB ANNOUNCEMENTS

BIRTHS

MARRIAGES

SILVER WEDDING

DEATHS

IN MEMORIAM

ON ACTIVE SERVICE

RIDING AND SHOOTING

MOTOR-CAR HIRE SERVICE

FARM PRODUCE

HOSPITAL NURSES

LEGAL NOTICES

SCHOOLS AND TUTORS

AT MISS KERR SANDER'S SECRETARIAL COLLEGE

MISS WOOLLCOMBE'S SECRETARIAL COLLEGE

ST. JAMES'S SECRETARIAL COLLEGE

CONTINENTAL EDUCATION (STAAD, SWITZERLAND)

DIRECTORS AND PARTNERS

INVESTMENTS AND LOANS

BUSINESSES FOR SALE

SOCIETIES

KENNEL, FARM, AND AVIARY

DOGS

FARM

AVIARY

BUSINESS OFFERS

C.O.D. SHOPPING

CHEPSTOW RACE CLUB.

MOOR PARK CLUB.

THE NAVAL & MILITARY CLUB.

THE QUEEN'S CLUB.

GARDENING, &c.

INDEX
TO
CLASSIFIED ADVERTISEMENTS
INCLUDING
SCALE OF CHARGES

The style of *The Times* from February 5, 1909,
to October 1, 1932

The modern style initiated on October 3, 1932

Hitler's promise to Mussolini to stand by him was interpreted as a threat to France. This was the most objectionable, because it was the most concrete, of Hitler's threats. It meant that there was little hope at the time for the conclusion of the Four-Power Pact which Chamberlain and Halifax had striven for since 1937. It was becoming increasingly difficult for *The Times* to hold to the political line it had laid down in the previous autumn but, in the absence of an alternative policy, the task of getting the Germans to negotiate could not be given up. The military line that the paper had taken in the previous June was, however, soon re-stated in different terms. It was known that the War Office was heavily engaged in a reconsideration of the strategic position, and the Military Correspondent prepared in December two turnover articles intended for publication early in the New Year. They gave rise to so much discussion in the office that they were postponed and not printed until February 7 and 8, 1939, timed to precede the Secretary-for-War's announcement of his plans, due in March. The articles were principally devoted to the subject indicated in the title: " An Army across the Channel." The subject had been made topical by the recent statement of Bonnet, the French Foreign Minister, that in the event of war the forces of Great Britain would be at the disposal of France, just as those of France would be at the disposal of Britain. On February 6 the Prime Minister was questioned in the House, and replied that any threat to the " vital interests " of France must " evoke the immediate cooperation of this country," and that the French Minister's statement was " in complete accordance with the views of His Majesty's Government." Chamberlain's answer was described by the Paris Correspondent as having been received in Paris as " a resounding blow in the cause of peace," since the similar declarations of solidarity by the Rome-Berlin Axis were claimed to be useful to peace by clarifying the issues in the sight of the world. " Now that the attitude of the democracies is no longer in doubt those responsible for guiding public opinion in Germany and Italy will, it is hoped, no longer encourage hopes of territorial concession from a France bereft of all but the most half-hearted British support." (February 7, 1939.)

The question asked had not, of course, been foreseen when it was decided to print the two turnovers. Hence the issue of *The Times* of February 7 that reported the Prime Minister's answer that " all the forces of Great Britain would be at the disposal of France," also published the first instalment of a full-length attack on the whole principle of sending large forces to that country. The wisdom of this course had been implicitly doubted in the same Correspondent's article of June 17, 1938. The article of February 7, 1939, was explicit. " . . . The revolutionary innovation of raising a huge army for a would-be decisive participation in the mainland struggle " in the last war was a departure from " our traditional war policy "; its justification was questionable.[1] Moreover, the Correspondent proceeded, " in retrospect the consequences of the peace that was won hardly increase its value." Such a reflection, in its nature political, was evidently not inconsistent with the editorial view. It is not to be doubted that Dawson and B.-W. approved the Correspondent's contentions, without necessarily being ready to commit *The Times* to all their implications. A highly significant statement of principle had been printed in the same Correspondent's article of June 17, 1938: the art of war consisted in so exerting ourselves and using our resources as to assure the " conservation, not only of physical, industrial strength, but of spiritual strength." For, the Correspondent then (four months before Munich) said, " No victory would be worth while if, in the process of winning it, the distinctive spirit of our people were extinguished and only the husk remained." No Continental observer would fail to appreciate this and similar statements in the Military Correspondent's articles. They clearly confirmed Britain's desire to avoid political commitments on the Continent; secondly, the paper's anxiety on February 7, 1939, to abstain from sending another army in support of France even if she were attacked.

In the same first instalment of his argument, the Military Correspondent favoured " Limited " war, against " Unlimited " war of the 1914-1918 kind, which gained only the " semblance of victory " at the price of moral " victory." The Correspondent adduced the experience of the wars in China and Spain to prove that " they afford no encouragement to the idea that ' victory ' is practicable in another great war where the armies of great Powers, differing little in armament and potential scale, would be pitted against each other." The conclusion was that " The dream of victory in modern war has nothing beyond mere speculation to sustain it." For, in considering what could now be done for France, it was most desirable that Britain should ponder the fact that " by abandoning our traditional strategy in the last war we have accustomed them to expect a renewal, if another war should come, of the great land effort to which we then committed ourselves." It was the Correspondent's opinion that the 1914

[1] The Correspondent was referring, doubtless, to the " traditional " British policy of using the navy to blockade the ports, and money to finance allies on the Continent. For a clear statement of this doctrine, as accepted by *The Times* at the beginning of the century, see Chapter I, " The New Imperialism."

precedent was " hampering " to us, and that no such " renewal " was necessary for military reasons, though it might be judged advisable on " psychological " grounds. (February 7, 1939.)

While the Correspondent was not disposed to overlook the changes in the strategic balance between 1936 and 1938 resulting from the German reoccupation of the Rhineland, the Austrian Anschluss, and lastly the changes in Czechoslovakia, he contended that they " removed any justifiable excuse for war " though he admitted that they had, what he called, " a one-sided effect upon security in the military sense." (February 8, 1939.) Yet, although the French saw themselves facing heavy adverse odds, " the sum of evidence, from modern experience, shows that the attacking side requires at least a three-to-one superiority to achieve more than a local or momentary effect." If this evidence were pondered, and the mobilizable strength of the French Army considered, " it would be seen that the German Army, even with the increased forces now available, has hardly the margin of advantage necessary to overcome the barrier—and therefore that land reinforcement from us is not a necessity." This being so, the Correspondent proceeded to emphasize the importance of equipment and the need of maintaining industry. On conscription, the Correspondent held definite opinions. He did not recommend it, for

it is hard to foresee a situation where voluntary enlistment would not, in time of war, suffice to give us all the men we can effectively utilize. It would be foolish to take more men away from industry than the maximum number for which we can provide modern fighting equipment, and still more foolish to sacrifice the superior moral quality of the voluntary principle for the sake of superfluous quantity. (February 8, 1939.)

B.-W.'s leading article, " The Defence of the West " (February 8, 1939), written to accompany these articles, was less positively opposed to an expeditionary force to France " in common self-defence." The problem, he wrote, was one that needed to be studied with special attention to the two great systems of fortification which defended the French and German frontiers. The Assistant Editor and the Military Correspondent were agreed that the Maginot and Siegfried Lines were capable of holding back the respective prevailing armies; both were agreed that in 1918 Britain failed to convert victory into peace. B.-W. argued that France had been diplomatically strengthened by the " voluntary " sacrifice (in September, 1938) of an active policy of encirclement, and " there is no disposition to fear or grudge any exertions by land—the help to be given by sea and air goes without saying—

957

that might be necessary to repel a possible invasion of France."
Only, "public opinion" would require the assurance that the
strategic plan should not be governed by the "obsessions which
committed the Allies to a maldistribution of forces in the last
War." He said that conscription "would advance matters hardly
at all . . . it might also confuse the national will and delay its
execution by precipitating futile and unnecessary controversy . . .
leadership and organization are the pressing needs of to-day."
(February 8, 1939.)

The effect of these two articles, and the leader, is to be judged
from a public statement by the Prime Minister made three days
after publication. Chamberlain repeated his words of the
6th, and assured the country that the solidarity of interest by
which France and this country were united was such that any
threat to the vital interests of France from whatever quarter it
came, must evoke the immediate cooperation of this country.
It was not said that any new British expeditionary force was in
process of organization, but it was plain that the strategical
consequences of the September *coup* were being re-estimated.
Yet the basic assumptions of *The Times* remained—that the
strength not so much of German arms but of the German case
had enabled the Reich to achieve these extensions of its sovereignty
without war. It was characteristic of B.-W.'s treatment of
the subject that before and after September, 1938, he should now
once more insist that: "A purely military calculation of the
strategic balance is incomplete. It cannot include the moral
factors which are essential to a final equation." It was still, in his
belief, the moral strength of the German case that made German
arms such a factor, and made war over Czechoslovakia impossible
to such a moral people as the British.

Within a week, *The Times* gave the provisional figures of the
new Defence estimate: £1,173,000,000 in three years. (February 16.)
Later many German reactions to the British rearmament programme were reported. On February 26 Hitler denounced
"war-mongers" and "war-agitators," and warned the world
that they would not "break Germany" with their threats.
Simultaneously, Goebbels produced an article, "War in Sight,"
for the *Voelkischer Beobachter*. He gibed at the democracies
for their failure to prevent the German successes of the
past two years, "as they did not rightly estimate the power of
the authoritarian States," and the democracies were set against a
people "whose only offence was to demand the elementary needs
of existence, among which were the former German colonies."

The article ended by saying that Chamberlain's armament programme was a serious danger to " peace."

Somewhat inexplicably *The Times* found, during the first ten days of March, a basis for optimism, and found the basis firm even after March 8. On that day the Secretary for War introduced his new estimates. He began by recognizing that the question uppermost in the mind of the House was the extent to which " we should be prepared, in the event of war, to intervene with land forces on the Continent of Europe." (Cheers.) He drew attention to the Prime Minister's references on December 13 and February 11 to the " solidarity of our interest with France " as being of greater significance than any that had preceded them. On this matter he said that no commitment had been made in the talks; but " prudent minds should be prepared for any [Anglo-French] eventuality. If we are involved in war, our contribution, and the ways in which we can best make it, will not be half-hearted, nor upon any theory of limited liability." (Cheers.) (March 8, 1939.) The speech was a direct and complete repudiation of the thesis advocated in the two turnovers of February 7 and 8. *The Times* half admitted that it was the business of the Secretary for War to prepare for the future.

As to the present, there had been no move by Hitler in the West like that prophesied by the Foreign Office in January. Printing House Square felt a refreshing calm, which was reflected in the leading article in *The Times* of March 13. " If anything distinguishes this year from its predecessor it is the knowledge that Germany has completed those demands upon her neighbours which by their own professions, they were unable conscientiously to contest, and yet have failed to satisfy while the way of orderly settlement was still open." What had happened in the previous September was tragic but just. The writer once more returned to the " moral factor." What came to a head last September " was an issue in which a consistent lack of policy, shown by great Powers and small alike over a number of years, had given Germany a right to appeal to principles that, in the event, counted for infinitely more than her big battalions." Hence, it could not be said that in 1938 democracy was " betrayed " in Central Europe. War would still have been wrong if Britain had been armed to the teeth. Given the essentials of the case, neither the spectacle of Dr. Goebbels at work, nor compassion for the suffering which *The Times* admitted was being inflicted upon thousands by belated and hasty revision and by a drastic dislocation of economic and political life, could have justified war. Once more, also, British public opinion was evoked.

This was the view held, as the constituencies have shown, by a majority of the British people—and held, be it remembered, by many of those who had been ready to go farthest in the vindication of Abyssinia, and had shared most keenly in the sense of " humiliation " acknowledged by Lord Baldwin. War was not held off in September either by lack of military resources or by an unworthy reluctance on the part of the Government to take a stand for civilization. It is a misfortune that some leaders of opinion in this country should think otherwise, but it might become a tragedy if their misjudgments were shared in other countries. . . . It is not true that the rapid progress of rearmament is reshaping British aims. They remain in 1939 what they were in 1918. Now, as then, there is a readiness to confer and to cooperate with any country, under whatever Government, that is prepared to enter negotiation in the spirit of reciprocity. (March 13, 1939.)

The leader ended by saying what had been in B.-W.'s mind since the events of September: the time had surely arrived for a " broader statement of the peace aims of Britain " than had yet been attempted. It should be a " re-definition of the practical idealism, forward-looking yet realistic, which is indispensable to British policy, and can make it a rallying ground for all peoples of goodwill." So said *The Times* on March 13. That was the paper's practical suggestion to the critics of Munich.

On the day this was published, Tiso, the clerical politician who had become Slovakian Premier and leader of a separatist party, sought the help of Germany. He visited Hitler to complain of the action of the President of the Czechoslovak Republic in dismissing the Slovak Government instead of promulgating the independence of Slovakia—as Tiso (and Hitler) had demanded on March 11. The independence of Slovakia was declared on March 14, immediately after Tiso had seen Hitler. Hácha, the Czechoslovak President, was called to Berlin. He had no alternative but to surrender to Hitler's threats, for German and Hungarian troops were already moving. Chamberlain told Hitler that the partition of Czechoslovakia between Germany and Hungary was not in the spirit of Munich; but, to the satisfaction of *The Times*, he refused to make the defeat of his own hopes of Munich a reason for repentance. Yet, even at Printing House Square, what had happened had no palliation. " Possibly a plausible defence might have been made even of German action in Slovakia," but it was otherwise with the violent extinction of the Czech homelands of Bohemia and Moravia. (March 16, 1939.)

This was " Militarism in Action." The " invasion, occupation and annexation of Bohemia and Moravia, are notice to the world that German policy no longer seeks the protection of a moral case." The "moral case," or "moral factor," had been set against the threat of force by *The Times* for six years. Hitherto, in each of the three successive German *coups* (the Rhine, Austria and Czechoslovakia) " it has been difficult not to allow some extenuation for it in the Allied blunders of the past, and not to see in it some substance of justice." (March 16, 1939.) No such extenuation was possible in this case, and the paper said so. This was the first occasion on which *The Times* admitted that Germany was following a policy of threats even against non-Germanic neighbours, and of acquisition of their territories in defiance of all promises. It was no longer possible even for Printing House Square to suggest that Germany could be restrained by evoking the " moral factor." The paper's policy, followed so earnestly and consistently for years, was now collapsing. There was little point at the moment in making a " broad statement of British peace aims," though the paper would, in due time, revive the suggestion. Firm support was given to the compulsory Air-Raid Precaution Bill, now to be placed before Parliament. On the 18th *The Times* noted as " significant " the fact that Robert Hudson, Secretary for Overseas Trade, was visiting, for commercial reasons, Warsaw, Helsinki, and Stockholm ; and, also, Moscow. A full-scale Press campaign against Britain now began in Germany. *The Times* was confiscated on arrival in Berlin on March 22 and for two consecutive days.

On March 22 *The Times* announced that on the previous night the Lithuanian Government had decided to cede Memel to Germany. Next day Chamberlain addressed the House and restated British policy, and *The Times* remarked " that the German subjugation of Czechoslovakia had hoisted a danger signal for all Europe, no single Power excluded." (March 24, 1939.) The paper repeated its aspiration (see the leader of March 13) that the Prime Minister would take the opportunity to enunciate the principles which determine British opinion. Matters were becoming urgent, for signs of tension continued to multiply. The Warsaw Correspondent's long despatch sent on the 26th reported new Polish defence measures, the demonstrations of patriotic Poles carrying placards " Danzig is not Memel," and the statement made in the Polish Army's organ that " We are ready." When the Berlin Correspondent sent on the 27th his account of the German newspaper protests against alleged Polish outrages on German women and children, he added that the campaign conformed to a type familiar to readers of the controlled Press. He reported next day that the impending visit to London of Beck, the Polish Foreign Secretary, was viewed in

Berlin with the deepest suspicion. When on April 1, *The Times* reported Chamberlain's assurance to Beck that Britain would give all support to Poland if her independence were threatened, there was instant reaction in Germany.

To *The Times* the declaration in support of Poland went directly against the grain. The paper had long held out against such pacts and guarantees as inconsistent with the League; they ran contrary to Locarno; they were opposed to Imperial sentiment. These general principles had been championed since 1923. Applied to concrete instances they had resulted in the paper's resolute opposition to engagements to intervene on behalf of Czechoslovakia in 1938. *The Times*, which had always refused to consider any commitments on the Continent, above all in Eastern Europe, continued in the same habit, which remained strong after Germany had subjugated Czechoslovakia and acquired Memel. Hence, agreeably with its general principles, the paper urged on April 1 that the key-phrase in the Anglo-Polish declaration was not the " integrity " but the " independence " of Poland; as, the paper added, " Integrity might have meant an unconditional guarantee of all the existing Polish frontiers." The undertaking given to Poland was, indeed, acknowledged to be necessary, but *The Times* could not write of the pledge enthusiastically, though it stood behind its purpose. It was not foreseen that the phrase distinguishing between " independence " and " integrity " and emphasizing a preference for the former, would be interpreted as minimizing the British undertaking.

The paper was again the centre of contention: the phrase was denounced by Churchill as " sinister " and by others as " similar (the article did, in fact, come from the same pen) to that which foreshadowed the ruin of Czechoslovakia." Churchill's point was made by others, who denounced the " Printing House Square crowd."[1] *The Times* was brought into conformity with this protest against " minimization " by a leader of B.-W.'s that appeared on April 4. This rejected all " watering down." The undertaking was a " stand against aggression as such, against vicious and retrograde aims of military conquest, and in defence of

[1] Hugh Dalton's language. *Cf.* Janus in the *Spectator* of April 7, 1939; " I am not surprised that *The Times* figured so largely in the foreign affairs debate in the House of Commons on Monday [April 3]. No single factor contributed so much to the disasters of last September as *The Times* leader on the 7th of that month, suggesting that Czechoslovakia might be wise in her own interests to let the Sudeten-German areas go. And when *The Times*, in its comments last Saturday [April 1] on Mr. Chamberlain's historic declaration in the House of Commons the previous day, appeared to set itself deliberately to whittle down the effect of the declaration—suggesting, for example, that there was no undertaking to defend Poland's ' integrity '—immediate mistrust and alarm was created at Warsaw, and the suspicions aroused at Moscow are not dispelled yet, in spite of Lord Halifax's immediate repudiation of the construction *The Times* leader-writer seemed to be putting on the declaration."

the independence of sovereign national states, against predatory force." The British refusal to accept ideological differences as a basis of international division was again emphasized, and applied " no less to relations with the Soviet than to relations with Nazism or Fascism. British Ministers have made that clear, whatever the stage at which the U.S.S.R. may decide to enter the consultations. . . In the meantime there is nothing half-hearted about the British move." (April 4, 1939.)

The Editor did not read the criticisms of Churchill and Dalton with any degree of embarrassment. He had been at his desk on the night of April 1, and took full responsibility for his leader-writer's expressions. Dawson thus wrote to a favourite correspondent:

. . . Since then [March 28] much has happened—most notably the British undertaking to support Poland if her independence should be threatened. It was a good declaration, I think, and was extremely well received in a full debate in the House of Commons yesterday. Incidentally, there was a certain amount of rather silly talk to the effect that *The Times* had weakened the force of the declaration by its comments. These people do not read *The Times*. What we had actually done was to point out that the declaration was not a mere pledge to respect every inch of the territorial *status quo*, but a guarantee of independence against aggression, which is a much bigger thing. My letters this morning suggest that the wiser heads are beginning to realise this.[1]

The Times was still anxious, in B.-W.'s words, to insist that in Britain " there is no fear and no jealousy of a powerful Germany exerting all the strength which lawfully belongs to a skilful, courageous, energetic and disciplined race." Yet " the answer to a campaign for the military domination of Europe would be, cost what it might, the answer which the British people has never failed to give throughout the centuries." (April 4, 1939.) The paper, however, could no longer resist the conclusion that " for the first time " the Nazis had moved into the open with a " full programme of Prussianism." Henceforth the leading articles in *The Times* no longer sought to strengthen peace by imputing to the Germans virtues they had long obviously despised, or to make the assumption and express the conviction that, as members of the comity of nations, Germany would automatically, by the compulsion of the " moral factor," keep her promises.

[1] Dawson to Stanley Washburn, April 4, 1939.

The change in tone is not to be associated with the alteration in the status of B.-W. that occurred during this period. It has been seen that at Christmas the Editor had mentioned to the Chief Proprietors a vague wish to retire. They had not taken the suggestion as requiring any immediate action. But Dawson was serious, and during March thought over his position. At the beginning of April he wrote persuasively asking for release:

> I have always had a horror of the sort of situation which I have seen in some other offices and businesses, where a man grows older and slower without realizing it himself and his friends are too kind to point it out to him. It seems incredible to me, but it is a sobering fact that it is thirty-three years since I began to contribute to *The Times* as its South African Correspondent and twenty-seven since I was first appointed its Editor. Moreover, I am convinced that, in a large organization like that of *The Times*, there should be a steady flow of promotion if the staff is to remain contented and up to the highest standard of efficiency. It will always be difficult for Editors to suggest to their colleagues that the time for retirement comes to all of us unless they are themselves prepared to practise what they preach.

> In saying this I must not be taken as subscribing to the dangerous heresy that everyone should retire at a certain age or after a certain period of service. There are obvious differences in this matter between the various professions, between this and that branch of the same profession and between one individual and another. But the responsibility for editing *The Times* is so exacting, so continuous, and so delightful, that the temptation to cling to it too long is peculiarly insidious. Nothing would distress me more than to feel that by yielding to it I was becoming a drag on the great institution with which I have been proud to be associated for so long.

> I am clear therefore that you should regard this as the last year of my Editorship, and should settle the precise date of my retirement as suits the paper best.[1]

To this request of the Editor the Proprietors agreed in writing and let B.-W. know that he would be appointed in succession. It was an appointment that obviously promised no change in the paper's Continental policy, but events rather than doctrines were now to become paramount. From the date of announcement of the Anglo-Polish Pact a counter-move was certain to be made by the Axis Powers.[2] That it would amount to something serious might be taken for granted. Meanwhile, the trade-talks between

---

[1] Dawson to Astor, April 4, 1939.

[2] The pact was not signed until August 25, when it became a reciprocal Treaty. See below, p. 978.

Russia and Britain were developing, it was known, into political negotiations. On April 28 the Berlin Correspondent reported Hitler's first move: he had denounced the German Non-Aggression Pact with Poland, and the German Naval Pact with Britain. The denunciations were announced in the course of a speech that lasted two-and-a-half hours. He talked of his idea of peace, whose basis should be non-interference with Germany; the alternative was war. Clearly, Danzig was in his mind, and Poland. Unlike Czechoslovakia, she did not stand alone, and the leading article in *The Times* said that Poland " can in any case negotiate, not only with her arms ready in hand, but in the knowledge that her sovereignty and independence are fully guaranteed by the combined might of Great Britain and France." (May 1, 1939.) This was a very different tone from that of the leaders on Czechoslovakia in the previous September. *The Times* was now certain that the issue was nothing less than that between peace or war, over Poland and the guarantee given her by Britain and France. In Germany the issue was not less clear. The Berlin Correspondent reported on May 3 that the German Press was full of warnings concerning the dangerous path Poland was treading. The current " outbreak of Polish chauvinism and over-confidence " was the fruit of the " blank cheque given by Great Britain to Poland. *The Times* errs, it is asserted, in saying that Poland can negotiate more easily from the position of strength given by the alliance of England and France." As Printing House Square estimated the situation at this point: the possibilities were Conference, Deadlock, War.

On the 4th, the paper emphasized points of contact between the British and Russian Governments which made cooperation for the specific purpose of resisting aggression both natural and desirable. " Whatever criticisms may be heard here of Soviet methods and outlook, military aggression is an international crime against which the U.S.S.R. has set its face as resolutely as any of the Western democracies. The common declaration or agreement of the Soviet and the democratic countries could, therefore, be directed as plainly and as simply as possible to the particular purpose for which it is being negotiated—the defeat of aggression." (May 4, 1939.) The Polish Foreign Secretary, Beck, spoke to his people next day, and *The Times* found him " firm without being provocative." He had " constructive suggestions of a statesmanship which refuses to be merely negative. The Polish Government cannot see their way to handing over Danzig to the Reich, or to granting an extra territorial road and railway across Polish territory."

Diplomatic moves followed in rapid succession. The Prime Minister's statement on Anglo-Russian negotiation occasioned caustic comment, reported by the Berlin Correspondent (May 25), on " Christian England's arm-in-arm friendship with Bolshevist Russia." But indirectly, the Correspondent said, the Reich Government hoped for an improvement in their own political, as well as their commercial, relations with Soviet Russia. The Berlin Correspondent emphasized the importance for German policy of removing the risk of a war on two fronts by defeating " Einkreisung " or " Encirclement," through the medium of polite addresses to Russia. It was being said that Stalin's speech of March 10 showed his reluctance to be drawn into "Einkreisung": hence the difficulties in the path of the political negotiations with the West. It was with Poland, not with Russia, that Germany had a dispute. That was the German line at the end of May. On June 4 Hitler suddenly appeared at Kassel, and once more rebutted the war-guilt accusations of the Versailles Treaty. " Neither before nor during the war had Germany any War Aims. She had wished only to pursue a peaceful programme of internal development. The responsibility for the 1914 war lay with the ' Einkreisung ' policy of the Western Powers," and he once again repeated his version of the Versailles " Diktat." The designed effect of the speech was to raise his hearers' appetite for war and stimulate hatred of the West. Some of the misunderstanding that underlay Hitler's speech, when viewed out of context, was still thought to be genuine by *The Times*. Halifax said on June 8 that propaganda had convinced many Germans that " Great Britain's main motive is ' to hem Germany in '." And it was true, added the paper, that propaganda had largely achieved its purpose. (June 9, 1939.)

The Foreign Secretary's recent speech also touched on the question of the Baltic States, which " is understood to create the chief obstacle at the present moment to the conclusion of an Anglo-Russian agreement." The paper endorsed Halifax's statement that the " British desire was to maintain their [the Baltic States'] neutrality inviolate." On June 12 Mr. (now Sir) William Strang went to Moscow with further instructions from the Foreign Office. Simultaneously, in a two-day debate in the Lords just ended, the Foreign Secretary emphasized the conciliatory nature of British policy; while, in the words of *The Times*, " by no means whittling down the absolute determination of Great Britain to fight, if necessary, for a victim of aggression." The paper admitted that a section of public opinion was " perhaps rather more sceptical than the Government of the possibility of reaching any permanent settlement with the German and Italian dictators." This being so, the old Four-Power (Britain, France and the Axis) idea must be abandoned in favour of a Peace Front (Britain, France, Poland and Russia). Armament and conciliation were the Government's immediate aims, and this dual policy, *The Times* believed, " undoubtedly corresponds in the main with the desires of the British people." The intention to create a " Peace Front " was later explicitly championed, though in reserved phrases. The paper protested, however, that " no more tragic or disastrous error could be made by any of the totalitarian States than to imagine, because we are disposed to settle difficulties by discussion and compromise, that we are therefore (in Lord Halifax's words) less resolute, less resilient, and less vigorous than any other people."

Among the " totalitarian States " *The Times* included Japan who, at this point, was blockading the British Concession at Tientsin, and intensifying a general anti-British campaign. The paper called upon the Government to act without hesitation in the defence of British interests in the Far East. " Public opinion demands nothing less." (June 19, 1939.) A day or two later the Warsaw Correspondent said it was believed in the Polish Capital that the Russian Government had summoned their Ambassador from China for consultation, and that Lozovsky, the newly appointed Deputy Minister of Foreign Affairs in Moscow, had been placed at the head of the Far Eastern section of the Ministry, and that during the week he had engaged in long talks with the diplomatic representative of General Chiang Kai-Shek. Opinion in Warsaw inclined to the view that the appointment of Lozovsky indicated that Russia intended to pursue a more active policy in the Far East. (June 22, 1939.)

Simultaneously the paper reported the visit, the third of the series, of the British and French Ambassadors, accompanied by Mr. Strang, to Molotov, the Russian Foreign Minister, and that Mr. Strang and Mr. Roberts (of the Foreign Office) were returning to inform London on the course of the negotiations. The Tass Agency circulated this news, and added that, in the view of " circles close to the Commissariat for Foreign Affairs," the new proposals " did not show any progress compared with previous proposals." *The Times* Correspondent concluded that all that could at present be said was that " no news is good news." Another page of the same issue reported the Berlin Correspondent as saying that the German Ambassador was expected to return to Moscow within a few days. " For the moment the German-

Russian negotiations are still at the stage at which no commitment has been made on either side." Molotov had said in a recent speech that Russian political relations need not affect German-Russian trade relations. On June 24 the Special Correspondent's message from Moscow recorded that it was only assurances from Britain and France that could preserve the sovereignty of the Baltic States, but that Russia would regard the possibility of any threats to the Baltic in much the same light as Britain and France would regard a threat to the Low Countries. How the Western Allies were to meet the Russian demand for security in these Provinces without infringing Baltic sovereignty was the task confronting British and French diplomacy. Halifax saw Maisky on the evening of June 23 in an atmosphere that was felt in London to be discouraging. It was thought here that if Russia intended to take part in the " Peace Front " that was being striven for in London, she would declare that the independence of States should not be impaired by threats of force, and assist to organize common resistance to those threats.

It was obvious to all the world that by this time the negotiators were encountering difficulties. On June 30 *The Times* printed an important message from its Special Correspondent at Moscow. Zhdanov, he reported, had published in *Pravda* a statement that the British and the French did not want a real pact acceptable to the U.S.S.R., but only talks about pacts, so that by making play with the supposed intransigence of the U.S.S.R. they could " use their own public opinion to pave the way to a deal with the aggressors." As the *Pravda* article ended with a statement that the next few days would show whether this was so or not, it was believed in Printing House Square that the Kremlin expected shortly to receive further proposals. Zhdanov's article said that the negotiations had reached a deadlock after 75 days' talk,[1] while the Soviet Government had taken only 16 days to express their views. The " problem " of a triple guarantee of Latvia, Estonia and Finland, was an " artificial " stumbling block. What the British and French really wanted was a pact that would place the U.S.S.R. in the position of a hand-labourer carrying the whole burden. (June 30, 1939.) On the same day, *The Times* reported, approvingly, a speech by Halifax " . . . The immense effort which

---

[1] The Anglo-Soviet discussions opened on April 15, 1939, with a proposal that the U.S.S.R. should promise assistance to certain east European States on the lines of the Anglo-Polish pact. Russia replied on April 16 with a proposal that she, with Britain and France, should conclude a defensive pact of mutual assistance against aggression with a guarantee by the same powers for the eastern and southern European States, including all those on the frontiers of the U.S.S.R. These proposals were remitted to London, but on May 3, before the British reply was received, Russia dropped her Foreign Minister or Commissar, Litvinov, in favour of Molotov.

Great Britain is making, by alliance and by warlike preparations, for effective intervention if it should be necessary," was not directed against any nation, but against the use of force. By the beginning of July the tension over Danzig was recognized as sounding a new and high note of urgency. Halifax spoke gravely to a receptive House. *The Times* perceived that " Not since the War has a pronouncement of the kind commanded this unanimity of approval." The leader proceeded to warn peace-breakers:

Britain was ready enough to treat with scrupulous—as some thought it, overscrupulous—justice, the appeal to self-determination which carried contiguous blocks of Germans into the orbit and jurisdiction of the Reich. But it was the use of this cry which put the brand of fraud and violence still more deeply upon the subsequent disruption of Czechoslovakia and the denial of self-determination to millions of Czechs. To-day . . . Danzig is already a self-governing German territory, enjoying all the rights of expression and suppression that belong to a Nazi régime. It lacks nothing but formal incorporation in the Reich . . . there is far more than a local issue in the relations of the Free State with Poland. . . . It is clear as noonday that Herr Hitler's designs upon Danzig are not racial but strategic . . . the now familiar series of devices which Nazism may employ at Danzig can therefore deceive or impress no one, except perhaps the Germans . . . All the countries concerned know where they stand—including the German Government unless it is still beset with wishful thinking and false information. There will be no conflict unless Germany provokes it, and war is not inevitable unless Germany makes it so. (July 3, 1939.)

The Prime Minister made a statement on the same subject in the House on July 11. It was endorsed by *The Times* on July 12; Danzig was an international question. " It can be settled— and settled easily—by cooperation. It cannot be settled by domination." On the 18th the Berlin Correspondent telegraphed that Schulenberg, the German Ambassador in Moscow, was returning once more to Berlin for consultation.

Meanwhile, British feeling was fast becoming apprehensive. The public were well aware from the obvious signs of preparation that affairs were taking a turn that was anything but favourable to peace. Air-raid sirens were being tested and shelters were being dug when a domestic agitation began which involved *The Times* in controversy. On July 10 *The Times* printed at the head of a column on its leader page a letter from the veteran Liberal, J. A. Spender. He deplored an attack on the foreign policy of the Prime Minister by Sir Archibald Sinclair, leader of

the Liberal Party. All parties, said the writer, had agreed that
the next steps should be calculated to give the world a display of
British unanimity, while Sir Archibald's contribution was
apparently intended " to assail the Prime Minister in unmeasured
terms and hold him up to odium as an incompetent man of
infirm purpose." Nine prominent Liberals, led by Lady Violet
Bonham-Carter, addressed a reply which claimed that Sir
Archibald's speech justified no such interpretation, but rather
that thousands of Liberals, with men of other parties, had misgivings lest the Prime Minister were not taking appropriate
measures " in this grave and critical hour." If, wrote the nine
Liberals, Chamberlain wanted to show that national unity
existed, he should include in his Cabinet Winston Churchill and
Anthony Eden, for they had consistently advocated the policy
Chamberlain was at last taking up. On the same July 10 the
Editor privately answered Lady Violet that while he was willing to
register her dissent and that of the other signatories from
Spender's view, he had already refused to open a correspondence
involving a discussion, necessarily invidious, of Churchill's
personal merits, " and he has for that reason declined a number
of letters on the subject, most of them, as it happens, contesting
the demand for his inclusion in the Cabinet." The Liberals'
letter could, therefore, be printed only in part. At this point
the signatories sent their letter, with a statement that
The Times had refused it, to the Liberal Press, and to the
Daily Telegraph (also the news agencies) whence it was seized
upon by national and provincial papers. Finding its way back
to Printing House Square as an item of news, it was published
partially on July 12, in so far as it constituted a Liberal reply
to Spender and omitted the Churchillian peroration. Other
letters, more than half of them supporting Spender, including one
from the Countess of Oxford and Asquith, had likewise been held
back a day in fairness, though to the unconcealed indignation of
the writers. A leading article amplified the Editor's reasons for
declining the letter of the nine. Lady Violet and her friends had

proceeded in the final paragraphs to join in the now familiar clamour,
which is not always inspired by the most ingenuous motives, for the
instant inclusion of Mr. Churchill in the Cabinet. From that particular clamour The Times has steadily held aloof—not at all from
any lack of appreciation of Mr. Churchill's outstanding qualities,
but from the conviction that a newspaper agitation on the subject
was both mischievous and futile. Even his most enthusiastic champions
should have known enough of politics to realize that this was not the
way to set about it; and The Times, if it had once encouraged them,
would have felt bound in common honesty to print a number of

letters from responsible writers who took a very different view. To those of us who feel intensely that Mr. Churchill may well be needed in a Government again, and that his recent services as a detached critic of the present Government have not been negligible, such a public controversy over his personal merits is altogether deplorable. His friends have already done him infinite harm. (July 13, 1939.)

It happened that a by-election was to be held on July 13 in North Cornwall, held by Sir Francis Acland (deceased) for the Liberals by a majority of only 836 at the election of 1935. The *Manchester Guardian*, the *News Chronicle* and the *Daily Mirror* were all confident that Spender's letter and the suppression of the defence of Sinclair were parts of a plan designed by *The Times* to win for the Conservative candidate the support of Liberals by discrediting their leader, and showing their party as rent on vital issues. As it turned out, P. L. Horabin increased the Liberal majority in North Cornwall to 1,464; and the *Manchester Guardian* believed Spender's letter was of less effect than the Prime Minister's refusal to raise old-age pensions. Before this result was known, however, a wave of reprobation broke against *The Times*.

The mildest remarks, perhaps, were those of the *Daily Telegraph*. That esteemed organ of opinion accused its contemporary of abandoning the duty of giving space to letters which did not coincide with editorial opinion. On policy the *Daily Telegraph* claimed that " when people speak to-day of a reconstruction of the Cabinet they are thinking first and foremost of the inclusion of Mr. Churchill. . . . That the existence of this demand should be bottled up and ignored would, in our view, be wholly contrary to public policy." The *News Chronicle* found it to Dawson's " lasting discredit " that, having refused space for the letter of the nine Liberals when they first offered it, he did not gracefully bow when it was circulated at large, but gave only half the text and no admission that he was the original recipient. His " lamentable partiality " was more regrettable because of the by-election. The *Daily Express* asked simply: " Did Sinclair do right? Yes. Did *The Times* do wrong? Yes." The *Daily Mirror*, which had long been amusing Printing House Square with its references to " *The Times* Fifth Column " excelled itself. " From its first furtive acquiescence of [*sic*] the Hitler menace, right up to the notorious Czechoslovakian sellout, *The Times* has pursued a policy that has put heart into every reader who has the Fascist and the anti-democratic cause at heart. The latest incident . . . is well in the Himmler tradition. *The Times* is still regarded abroad as the foremost journal of considered British opinion. But it cannot be long before it is universally known that the *Daily Telegraph* has taken up the reins discarded by Dawson in his death throes of journalistic suicide." *The New Statesman and Nation* inevitably moralized: " It is a not uncommon thing for *The Times* to give prominence to a highly damaging attack on an individual whom it wishes to discredit, and then to reject his reply or to print it sometimes after a lapse of time in small print on an obscure page. Sometimes it is a cause rather than an individual it thus misrepresents. The public rarely knows of these iniquities, and *The Times* sails on with an aggravatingly sanctimonious air, damaging private reputations and national reputations all the more effectively." *Time and Tide*, too, spoke of " a mischievous piece of irresponsible censorship." The *Spectator* declared that *The Times* was losing its status abroad as an organ of British opinion, through " disingenuousness which appears to have become inveterate." It was notable that *The Times* had omitted from the Liberals' letter the passages calling for Mr. Churchill's entry into the Cabinet and for vigorous discussion and criticism of affairs. The incident did not close yet, for A. G. Gardiner, formerly editor of the *Daily News*, sent *The Times* a letter on the journalistic ethics of banning the Liberals' epistle. In turn refused, he communicated the fact to the *News Chronicle* and the *Manchester Guardian*, which accorded it publication in full. He had written to *The Times* that " At a time when the evils of dictatorship are so rampant, it is, to say the least, unfortunate that an editorial censorship of opinion should be set up in a forum so traditionally impartial as the correspondence columns of *The Times*." That paper had absolved itself on the gound that a letter from Lord Cecil had covered " A.G.G.'s " points about policy; but the *News Chronicle* observed that Lord Cecil had not referred to the journalistic question. Fortunately his arguments drew correspondents to *The Times* on to the broader plane of diplomacy, and after July 19 the controversy of Spender *versus* Sinclair and his supporters was removed from the leader page.

The situation in Europe did not, in fact, permit *The Times* to devote much space to the affair. It was true, and remained true for some weeks, that while Churchill was not, and never had been, a favourite at Printing House Square, there was less disposition than at any time since 1922 to underrate his intrinsic worth. Precisely for this reason the Editor was determined not at this time to print letters demanding his inclusion in the Cabinet in July. Such a correspondence in his favour, printed then, could not fail to bring letters in opposite sense. This would plainly be undesirable in the national interest and in that of Churchill.

The Editor was clearly right not to provoke attacks on a public man of the greatest potential value.[1] The anxieties of the time were rapidly increasing. Simultaneously with the Spender controversy over Churchill, the Berlin Press was breaking out with repeated expressions of respect for Russia. *The Times* Correspondent at Berlin said when reference was made to the negotiations at Moscow between France and Britain, the impression was conveyed that " Soviet diplomacy was making a laudable stand against the machinations of the encirclers." The favoured propaganda device of denouncing " Einkreisung " had been used as a general term of abuse since April; it was now used with particular reference to Russia's position. Towards the end of July, when the German propaganda machine was preparing to exploit the 25th anniversary of the War of 1914, the Press was filled with attacks on Britain as the " arch-encircler." Both in Berlin and in London thoughts were centred upon Moscow. On July 31 Chamberlain announced the despatch of British and French military missions to the Kremlin.

In July and August all England was drenched with pamphlets edited by Dr. Goebbels and posted at Danzig. Among the many correspondents who addressed *The Times* on the subject was a letter that the Editor chose to print on August 12. The writer complained that he had been asked to read some of the more venomous of the German attacks on Britain, and asked the purpose of such attacks which, he said, necessarily aroused anger here. " The deep and widespread admiration of the English for the German people, and indeed, for Herr Hitler, is, it seems, being destroyed of malice *prepense* by the German propagandists themselves. Why? " (August 12, 1939.) On publication John Walter wrote from Switzerland to ask the Editor whether the writer's statement was a " tribute to Hitler " or a " calculated falsehood." And, Walter proceeded, " supposing Goebbels heard the prayer [of the writer to *The Times*] and out of his great mercy stopped sending German propaganda to England," we might lose an irritant that would " awaken the English Conservative out of his fool's paradise." He emphasized to Dawson his impression, confirmed by the newspapers of Switzerland, that " the Dictators were the hammer and British Empire the anvil."[2] Walter was correct in thinking that in Europe the decisive moment was felt to be immediately at hand. In Britain there were signs of ministerial preoccupation.

[1] For Dawson's last leader, in which he extolled Churchill, see p. 981 below.

[2] Walter (from Vevey) to Dawson, August 19, 1939. The Editor's reply (August 22, 1939) was that " I did not as a matter of fact publish the letter myself on Saturday (August 19) morning. I had gone away in the vain hope of getting an unbroken week's rest. But I have looked at it again to-day and cannot help thinking that you have misread it."

On August 4 *The Times* published as its first leader a commemorative article. It was marked by notable revisions of opinions it had held since 1923. The Nazis, the paper now said, had " mesmerized " the Germans into believing that all history began with the Treaty of Versailles. Something of this kind had been said before in *The Times*; but an argument less familiar to readers, at least since 1923, was that the Treaty of Versailles " was without the slightest doubt a generous settlement compared with those settlements which, after temporary successes, the German Empire imposed upon Russia and Rumania." There may have been blemishes, " as is now freely and generally recognized "; but the " final victors of the War themselves " did genuinely wish to " establish the reign of peace and justice " among the nations. Their fault was that they had then been too optimistic. This said, *The Times* returned to the position it had defended for more than a decade, though it now held back from blaming the " final victors " for creating the German menace by their own blunders. To-day, however, " unless the catastrophe of 25 years ago is to be repeated on a vaster, more destructive, and more demoralizing scale, the peoples of all countries must set themselves to try to understand the point of view of those who were then their opponents." All countries should realize this. Britain's own view was then stated: " The one point on which this country will not and cannot compromise is the unscrupulous use of force in the settlement of international disputes." But this, it was emphasized, should not be an obstacle to peace anywhere. (August 4, 1939.)

Ten days later there came many diplomatic activities and rumours. While Hitler and Ciano were talking together at Salzburg, and the British and French military missions were conferring with Voroshilov at Moscow, important personages were meeting at Warsaw and Danzig. The rest of the month was full of intense speculation. On the 16th *The Times* said that the British and French missions to Moscow " seem to be making good progress," thus bringing nearer the inclusion of Russia on a " Peace Front." The completion of this purpose was now ardently and urgently hoped for, since it was believed that the recently reported Axis meetings meant that Germany and Italy were putting into shape their own ideas of a " settlement in Europe." *The Times* now said that " No words can add to the certainty, simple but immensely grave, that Britain, with her allies, will go to war without the smallest hesitation to frustrate a German assault upon the independence of Poland, whatever the attempt to cloak and obscure it with the details of the dispute over Danzig. The answer to force will be force, and it will be given decisively." (August 16, 1939.)

The leader proceeded to revise still further the convictions previously held by the paper. All the " best-sellers " that propagated here and in the U.S.A. the perversions of Goebbels could not " subvert the truth that international cooperation could have made the Munich settlement a charter of peace and security for the non-German provinces of Czecho-slovakia, and increased the stability of Central Europe." *The Times* no longer had the slightest trust in Germany: " Herr Hitler's subsequent response to this acid test of good faith is well known." His appeal to self-determination was false, a monstrous betrayal of Germany's plighted word. The aspect of affairs was radically different now, and the " peace powers " would deal with it. When they had perfected " the diplomatic and military instruments of defence, the moment will have come for them to formulate the principles on which they are jointly ready to found a new peace and the terms on which they for their part are prepared to negotiate a settlement." *The Times*, therefore, was now ready to face the worst; and the worst was probably at hand. " The intermediate ' war without guns ' cannot last indefinitely." In the end nations must agree or fight, and know what they fight for. Dawson and B.-W. for the first time felt that the country was unanimous. Printing House Square itself was at last undivided on the German issue and the article reflected the fullest confidence. A constructive line was taken: the next task would be " to determine in common the essence of a positive programme and to put it before the world."[1] It would represent the path of negotiation for those caring to take it. *The Times* now crisply said, " negotiation, so far as it concerns Germany in particular, can lead nowhere unless Germany abandons her present idea of what constitutes Lebensraum." The paper recognized that there could be no appeal back to

[1] Light on a practical " positive programme " as it was understood by *The Times* at this point is reflected by a letter to a correspondent: " We do not wish to interfere with the normal and legitimate expansion of German influence in Europe, but that we have always resisted military domination on the Continent, and shall, if it is again attempted, resist it again. If that is self-interest, it is also the interest of the greatest number. I do not know what other reply Germans would expect us to give to such a threat. Most of us desire above all things a settled understanding with Germany but our confidence is deeply shaken, if not shattered, when it becomes possible for German policy to switch over in twenty-four hours from self-determination to an unheralded and astonishing appeal to the precedents of the Holy Roman Empire. My complaint is that an intelligent German should be able to accept this barely credible *volte face* quite uncritically. He would only have to pay a visit to this country to discover that the simple explanation which I am suggesting is right and that British distrust of German policy and its purposes has nothing in the wide world to do with jealousy or malice. The war and the peace have taught us, if we needed to be taught, that there can be nothing normal in Europe without a strong Germany." (B.-W. to a correspondent, May 10, 1939.)

Versailles; it looked forward to a new Covenant. "It is for the peace Powers to formulate in good time the basis of a possible discussion. After the 'next war' a peace conference will have to be held. Everything is to be said for holding it before the 'next war'—but upon the condition that it is a genuine conference of peace. Until that is proved possible, the best and only practical service to peace is to man its defences in full strength."

A leader of B.-W.'s was headed "The Whole Peace Front." The article had been written before the author left for his holiday, and was meant to be kept in reserve, but Dawson, after a talk with Halifax and Cadogan on the 15th, decided to print it without delay in order to impress Mussolini, with whom, it was then believed, Hitler was angry. It would be well to take advantage of any difference between the Dictators. "The French and British military missions to Moscow seemed to be making good progress in their consultations with Soviet experts, and their work increases the assurance that there will be no long delay in the completion of the 'Peace Front' by the inclusion of Russia." The purposes of the "Peace Front" were then set forth. The first purpose was to prevent war, but the Nazi interpretation of Lebensraum must be abandoned. (August 16, 1939.)

It could no longer be doubted that to hold Hitler back was becoming daily more difficult. The fact was obvious to the public when, a day in advance of the appointed time, the Prime Minister travelled down from Scotland on August 20 to preside over a Cabinet. The paper's next first leading article, entitled "Critical Days," pointed out that the situation in this August only superficially resembled that of last September; really it was fundamentally different. It was not said that news from Moscow was discouraging to the West, but it was understood in the office that the Germans were still confident that Britain would have second thoughts about the guarantee to Poland. *The Times* thus disposed of any idea of a change of policy : "This country has given a specific pledge from which it will not and cannot recede. It had given no such pledge to Czechoslovakia." (August 21, 1939.) It is not known whether the office, at this moment, was aware of the view held in Berlin that Russia herself desired a share in the spoils of Poland, but next day's paper (August 22) reported from Berlin that Germany would sign a non-aggression pact with Russia, and that the "well-informed" in Berlin believed that the pact would remove all danger of war from Europe. Britain, it was argued, having suffered so grave a diplomatic defeat, would not care to carry out her obligations to Poland; therefore the full German demands would be granted, and hence a new order in Europe would be established. Berlin disavowed all intention of attacking England, or the Empire. If only England were now to show " common sense " an excellent understanding with the rulers of Europe would at once be possible. Meanwhile the German Press campaign against Poland continued.

There was deep gloom in the West. The Berlin Correspondent's message was reproduced in the French Press and caused a profound impression. The Paris Correspondent reported that those Frenchmen who, a month before, expressed doubts about " dying for Danzig " now realised that something more was at stake. On August 23, the day of the signature of the German-Russian Treaty by Ribbentrop and Molotov, *The Times* Special Correspondent in Moscow concluded his message by referring to the *rapprochement* as part of a " poker game " being played. " If there is one thing the contracting parties can be sure of it is that no Pact that they sign will necessarily be binding." Notwithstanding this proper scepticism, the immediate effects were unlikely to be pleasant for the West, and less likely for Poland. Parliament was called to meet on the 24th. The Government, meanwhile, informed Beck that the German-Russian Pact would in no way affect their obligation to Poland. One more effort for peace was made by Britain. While " poker " was being played in the Kremlin by the Russian Prime Minister and the German Foreign Minister, the British Ambassador was ordered to fly to Munich with a letter from the Prime Minister to the Führer. It was then known from the message of the Berlin Correspondent that Germany and Russia had already agreed to partition Poland (August 25, 1939) whereas, earlier, it had only been thought that the British and French had reached an *impasse* over Russia's demand for a safeguard of her interests in the Baltic States. However, according to *The Times* Correspondent in Moscow (who enjoyed special facilities for observation), Voroshilov had revealed that the breakdown was due to difficulties of another kind: Britain and France could only be given effective support if Russian troops went into Polish territory.

While Russia and Germany were coming closer together, intense feeling in and about Danzig had been artificially generated by the Goebbels propaganda machine. *The Times* gave much space to reports of disputes over customs inspection and incidents at the East Prussian and Polish frontier, and the announcements of August 21 left little doubt in Britain that a German attack on Poland was imminent. It was more than ever necessary to warn Germany that any idea that Britain would abandon Poland was an illusion. This, therefore, was the burden of the British Prime Minister's letter delivered to the German Führer by the British Ambassador personally, and that of leading articles in *The Times* which were written with the hope of impressing official circles in Berlin. The meeting between Hitler and Henderson took place during the same twenty-four hours in which Molotov and Ribbentrop signed the Russo-German Treaty, and when the Danzig Senate declared Förster to be the Head of the State of Danzig. The Führer replied that projected British and French measures could only be directed against Germany and that in the event of their being carried into effect, he would order immediate mobilization.

Next day the Polish Government reminded the Danzig Senate that the Constitution of the Free City made no provision for Förster's appointment, and warned the Senate against the policy of *fait accompli*. Late on August 25 it was known that Hitler had cancelled his Tannenberg speech, due to be delivered on the 27th. Instead Hitler, then in Berlin, had sent for the British and French Ambassadors, to whom he made proposals. On the same day it was announced that the Anglo-Polish Pact, that had been initialled earlier, had been signed in London as a Treaty of Alliance. On Saturday, August 26, Henderson flew to London. Various compromises were considered on the 26th, e.g., the British and French urged the Poles to offer exchange of populations. This was a scheme to which Beck was inclined to agree. On August 28 Henderson returned to Berlin, when *The Times* published a communication from the Diplomatic Correspondent which stated the British view: " It is not we who have to choose between peace and war. The decision lies in Berlin, and this country is ready no matter which side the choice falls. In the Government's view— unchanged in spite of the rising tension—there is no question in Europe that could not be solved by restraint and by negotiation, given good will and the absence of threats." The leading article of the same day quoted and italicized the message of the British National Council of Labour to the German people: " *If Poland is attacked, Germany will be at war not with Poland only but, from the first day, with Great Britain and France, who both stand firmly by their pledges.* We have no wish to destroy the German people. We have been, we still are your friends." The article laid stress on the destruction of confidence that Germany after Munich had introduced into international relations, and said that any negotiations with Germany must be conducted henceforth on equal terms; while there would be very different guarantees in future for the observance of her solemn undertakings. The point then reached was precisely stated: Britain will stand by Poland " if she decides that she must fight for her independent existence." (August 28, 1939.)

Parliament met next day and listened to grave statements by the Prime Minister and the Foreign Secretary. Hitler's reply was received during the same day. Germany was prepared to negotiate and accept the good offices of the British Government to secure the immediate despatch of an accredited Polish plenipotentiary who must, however, be in Berlin by midnight on August 30. The British Government decided not to advise the Poles in this sense, but instructed Henderson to put it to the Germans that they should adopt the normal diplomatic procedure and transmit their proposals to Warsaw through the Polish Ambassador in Berlin. Simultaneously, the British Government urged restraint upon Germany and Poland and pointed out to Hitler that it would probably not be practicable for the negotiations to be undertaken that same day. When Henderson saw Ribbentrop he was refused a copy of the German proposals—on the ground that the Polish plenipotentiary had not arrived by the stated time. During the evening the Polish Ambassador expressed his country's willingness to negotiate on equal terms, and Ribbentrop listened in silence. Before 6 o'clock on Friday, September 1, German troops crossed the Polish frontier. " Soon afterwards German aeroplanes were bombing Polish cities." *The Times* Warsaw Correspondent reported that bombs fell on the city at 9 a.m., and that during the day there were five or six supplementary raids of incendiary and explosive bombs. " One Man's Crime " was the title of the first leader on Saturday. " The power for destruction that he has chosen to use has never in history been so completely concentrated in one man's hand." On September 4 *The Times* reported that Britain and France were at war with Germany, for the second time in twenty-five years. The same issue reported that the Donaldson liner *Athenia* had been sunk 200 miles west of the Hebrides. The war was obviously to be " unrestricted," for the ship was torpedoed without warning in the fashion of the first Anglo-German War. But, wrote *The Times*, the British nation hoped that a consequence of the war would be the liberation of the German people from what the paper now described as " one of the vilest tyrannies that has disgraced modern Europe." The British nation " certainly hopes that another result will be the re-establishment of the confidence between the two countries which the perfidies of Hitler alone have made impossible." (September 5, 1939.)

The office was now faced, in addition to the necessity to organize for war, with its domestic crisis, aggravated by enlistment. When, in the spring, the Editor told his deputy, unexpectedly, of his correspondence with the Proprietors about his projected retirement, it was clear to the latter that in point of editorial assistance the office had long been understaffed. The fact was that B.-W. had himself been so busy so long upon so much that his appointment to succeed Dawson would open a gap, the bridging of which would be difficult. Any man half as cautious as B.-W. would choose to think over the fact that while Dawson had had him as his deputy he, himself, had none in sight. But while Dawson proceeded with his preparations to retire, B.-W. was pondering his staffing difficulties. Four months before Dawson was due to leave war was declared.

* * *

Whether the Government wholly abandoned appeasement after the German attack on Poland, or whether they expected that the British and French declaration of war would be followed by a German withdrawal, or even hoped that the worst would be limited war, are questions that cannot yet be answered until the documents are available to the public. To what extent, if any, *The Times* shared in the apparent hesitations of 1939-1940 must be left for discussion and judgement by a future writer.[1] For obvious reasons, the formal and critical narrative of this History of *The Times* may not be continued beyond the end of appeasement and the beginning of war.

It is possible, however, to chronicle the principal facts about the situation in P.H.S. First, the immediate effects of enlistment emphasized to B.-W. the extreme undesirability of weakening the office still further by allowing Dawson to retire at the date arranged. His representations to Astor, Walter and to Dawson duly resulted in the latter's being prayed to remain, which he agreed to do. It was not until nearly two years later that B.-W. judged that he was sufficiently well supported. The office had then been adequately reinforced and it was decided that, with a staff capable of advocating with persuasiveness and consistency B.-W.'s reconstruction policy, Dawson's plan could be carried out. It was agreed that B.-W. should succeed in the autumn.

[1] Some of the implications arising from the policy followed by the paper from 1923 to 1939 are discussed in the " Postscript " following this Chapter.

ROBERT MCGOWAN BARRINGTON-WARD

EDITOR OF *THE TIMES* 1941-1948

From a photograph

A symbolic leading article appeared on September 8, 1941. It dealt with Churchill's then leading position. " So far as any man in the world can be regarded as indispensable, Mr. Churchill has earned that much-abused title. Like no one else in sight he has the courage, the imagination, the power of leadership which are the attributes of a great War Minister. England is fortunate indeed, as she has so often been fortunate in the past, in having produced the man to fit the emergency." Giving his article a, perhaps gratuitously, speculative turn, Dawson proceeded to say that the " problem of his ultimate successor should never be far from the mind of the far-sighted leader." So Dawson, at the right time, answered (by implication) those critics who, in July, criticized *The Times* for not making the potential war-leader a focus of present debate. This, it turned out, was Dawson's last leader.

The change took effect on October 1, 1941, and *The Times* then lost the services of an Editor whose gifts, intellectual and social, marked him out for a supreme position in journalism or in any field in which he had chosen to exercise them. He shared the same elaborate education, and the same tastes, the same devotion to the cause of Unionism and the same means of acquaintance with the world of affairs as Buckle, and a high degree of continuity between the two editorships resulted. A signal difference distinguished the two. Dawson, unlike Buckle, was a born writer and controversialist, loving intimacy with a wider range of political personalities, and relished seeing in print his personal criticisms of individuals and their policies, written in the knowledge that they would be read with gusto in the circles that he frequented. Dawson delighted in and keenly enjoyed the opportunity his position opened to him of influencing the trends of politics and the careers of friends. No man was more faithful to family, village, county, school, college and university. He gave lifelong adherence to his chosen leaders, above all Milner, Baldwin, Chamberlain and Halifax. No man was more intelligently aware of the fact that men are as important as measures, or intuitively convinced that the men necessary were to be found in greatest number among a certain class. He had intimate friends, to mention but Milner and Lothian, among Liberal Imperialists, but he never forgot his loyalty to the Conservative party. He formed no friendly connexions with Labour Ministers; not even with Snowden, whose anti-French stand he could not help admiring. The intimate connexions he had were with the hereditary English governing class, the middle class gentry and their ennobled offspring. He, himself, ended as he began, a simple Squire, with all the Yorkshireman's dislike for frills and

histrionic tricks. Artificiality of manner was foreign to him.
His appearance matched his manner. Just as he disliked
ostentation, he was not conspicuous in inches. What was
physically obvious about him was a masculinity, a robustness and a
stockiness proper to one as fond as he was of the open air. He
played tennis whenever he got the chance; he was an ardent
shot and lover of horses. When Editor of the *Star* in
Johannesburg he drove every day to his office in a smart kind
of dog cart, and managed to keep up his shooting until well
over sixty. The observer would notice his finely shaped head,
but there was nothing in his manner to mark him out in any
gathering of influential men, for he did not draw attention to
himself. As the incumbent of an editorial chair of some
eminence, Dawson had no temptation to self-inflation. He
knew, as many public men knew, that his abilities would win
him distinction wherever he chose to exercise them. This was
sufficient to give him confidence. In talk, he was at all times
straightforward, colloquial, preferably blunt. There was nothing
enigmatical about him and he encouraged the same easy confidence
equally from colleagues in junior positions as from men in the high
offices of State.

In his first term as Editor he was apt to daunt leader-writers
by the minuteness of his instructions. He would deliver them
in writing, and received more than one protest, also in writing,
against the habit. Later he saw the advantage of discussing
the subject proposed with the writer of his choice; and, in his
second innings, once a man had proved his capacity, he gave
him an established right to suggest a subject and a line of criticism.
To certain writers Dawson, giving minimum instructions would
say " I shall want a short piece to-night from you on so and so."
Later in the evening, after he had arranged the letters to the
Editor for publication, he would visit the leader-writers to
see that all was going steadily ahead. On this evening peregri-
nation he was to be seen at his most characteristic, walking
slowly, his shoulders hunched and his feet falling heavily, carefully eschewing any sense of bustle or false importance. He was
full of banter and good humour, with a cheerful word for any
member of the staff whom he happened to pass in the corridor.
He never made the mistake of whispering in corners with his
writers, but rather stood in the doorway, giving encouragement
or advice, speaking loudly as if he had no secrets from his writers;
or, indeed, from anyone in the building. He was, indeed, not
given to any inhuman degree of discretion, which spiced his
always-cheerful talk and made him welcome in any gathering

of men. Thus, in his maturity as Editor, his manner was communicative and apt to get the best out of his writing staff. He had a deep respect for the craft. Every man knew beforehand that his composition when sent up would not be smitten with trifling corrections. Dawson was not the man to make petifogging suggestions that he knew would harass any writer. He always invited the frank criticisms of colleagues upon leading articles that he chose to write. He was himself a good though, he said, laborious writer. The serious sense of method and application that gained him a first class in his Honour Mods. and a first class in his Final Schools led him at need to make copious and detailed notes in advance of writing a leader. His composition seemed never to be hurried. He practised a handwriting which was aristocratic, almost Bourbon; it was distinctive, ornate, and seeming to be formed by a very supple wrist rather than by the fingers. It reflected the complete absence of hesitation and fluster that marked his approach to any problem, person or topic. His remarkable capacity to decide quickly the innumerable questions that present themselves every day, was accompanied by a strong reluctance to discuss in detail the serious questions of the time. He preferred that such problems be reserved for private study and reflection.

In conversation it was imperative that such questions be handled lightly. If anyone attempted to entrap him in discussion, or hold forth to him, he was swift in closing the interview. Those in professional contact with him were soon made conscious of particular forms of Dawsonian disapproval. Those lacking a hereditary sense of social tact were briefly dealt with. It was a serious obstacle to a man's progress in the office if he were so unfortunate as to qualify for the description of " Bore." Anyone valuing his intimacy sought not merely to avoid his personal inclusion in this damning category, but was careful to avoid pressing on the editorial notice the views of any public man who had once been thus labelled and excommunicated. Dawson was an accomplished editor though he was not, and did not pretend to be, without the prejudices proper, in his opinion, to an Englishman whose profession it was to sit in judgement upon his fellow-men. He was 67 years of age, an Honorary Fellow of Magdalen College, Oxford, and a Doctor of Civil Law *honoris causa*, of his University, when he retired.[1]

His successor was fifty years of age when he took charge of *The Times*. He had been in the office thirteen years when he assumed responsibility for drafting a war policy of his own.

[1] Geoffrey Dawson died three years later; see p. 989 below.

The new Editor was apt to say that the burden of conducting *The Times* was less heavy in war than in peace time. The national concentration upon the one main task of victory simplified the work of editing. Nevertheless, he had inherited, he would say, several of the great problems common to peace and war which had long challenged his predecessor. Questions of Dominion consultation remained unsettled, aspects of Anglo-American relations needed close attention. At home the constitution of the Cabinet and the direction of the war required constructive criticism. So far, the degree of continuity between the two editorships was high. The new Editor's attitude towards the domestic social objectives which the struggle with the enemy could be made to serve, showed that he was independent alike from his predecessor, from his party, and from Ministers.

B.-W. was not a Right Conservative but a Radical Tory, and his editorship is remarkable for the vigour and persistence with which *The Times* urged that the heroism of the forces on active service and the will of the severely tried population at home both needed the support that could only come from the firm pledge by the Government that the nation's social aspirations would be fulfilled. Apart from these considerations, Hitler's boasted " New Order " necessarily created discussion among neutrals. In Britain there were debates on " Reconstruction." B.-W. was inclined by temperament to welcome social change in advance, prepare for it, and so control it. He had early given proof of his belief in what is called the Welfare State by his recognition of the problem set by the mass unemployment in North-East England during the early nineteen-thirties. The articles he then designed and ordered forced the Government to appoint an Unemployment Commission.[1] This was a concrete demonstration of B.-W.'s ideas of journalism and editorship as a means of getting something done. He now looked forward to helping the prosecution of the war by a programme that would encourage the people at home, hearten the subjugated peoples of Europe, give even the Germans the prospect of some alternative to National Socialism. In his talk with the Proprietors, it was agreed that B.-W. should take it that it was the duty of *The Times* to prepare for great social changes after the war, and that it was the function of the paper, as at all times, to apply common sense and rational exposition without prejudice to issues as they arose, and thus gain acceptance of novel but necessary changes.

The new Editor was born on February 23, 1891, the son of

[1] See Chapter XXIII, "Appeasement, 1933-1938."

Mark James Barrington-Ward, an Oxford man, and successively assistant-master of Clifton, and Canon of Truro. While the family was growing up he was one of H.M.'s Inspectors of Schools, and expected his sons to take education with some seriousness. At Westminster a fear of laziness, inefficiency, and resulting failure to justify parental expectation, governed the behaviour of his fourth son and earnt him at the age of 17 the Captaincy of the School. R. M. Barrington-Ward, when he came up from Westminster to Balliol in 1909, came up to work; deliberate waste of time would ever deserve rebuke from a conscience kept as sensitive as his. It was not that the young man was a prig or a pot-hunter. If he succeeded it was because, being the son of his father and having a sense of judgement very early matured, he chose to apply his mind to the right thing, in the right way, at the right time. While taking his part in games, relishing talk and loving debate, he would be ready for the question paper when the time came. Added to a firm will, he had that first essential to success: an enviable memory. His progress at Oxford was rapid: Secretary and Treasurer of the Union in 1911; Librarian and President in 1912. He was an outstanding President; though he brought to it neither spectacular cleverness nor rare brilliance. What distinguished him was a sureness of judgement combined with rapidity in debate. He could convincingly deploy a mass of facts, challenge an array of figures, establish or destroy hypotheses at speed, while reserving, rather than flourishing, a keen wit and a rich humour.

Robert McGowan Barrington-Ward was " Robin " to his many intimates, and " B.-W." to his host of friends. In the schools B.-W. did well, though in his finals he surprised everybody by doing much less well than his obvious talents promised. He came down with one technical qualification, and one professional inclination; he had been responsible for *The Oxford Magazine* and, while editor, had enterprisingly secured from Ronald Knox the MS. of the now famous paper on Sherlock Holmes. He was interested in law and had already determined to go to the Bar. Towards the end of his time, a meeting with one who became a life-long friend, Edward Grigg, now Lord Altrincham, led him to consider the possibility of a future in journalism. Grigg had been in charge of the Imperial Department,[1] naturally pointed B.-W. towards Printing House Square, and offered to recommend him to Geoffrey Dawson. In his highly deliberate manner B.-W. considered, reconsidered and ultimately decided to accept, Grigg's offer. This would not be incompatible

[1] See Chapter I, " The New Imperialism."

with the completion of his studies for the Bar. With such influence behind him, so desirable a candidate was sure of a sympathetic reception, above all, in an office then notoriously prone to the selection of Oxford men for its higher posts.

B.-W. was first appointed to the staff in 1913. He served as Home and Foreign Sub-editor, 1913-14, and Secretary to the Editor from February 16, 1914. He had not drifted into journalism; he had decided upon it. He now recognized *The Times* as his vocation and was ready to work to deserve such promotion as his talents and industry might be held to justify. His first leading article, dealing with the Channel Tunnel, appeared on August 5, 1913. Twelve months later war came, and though B.-W. was the last man to feel a military vocation, he was among the first to volunteer. On August 21 he was gazetted a Second-Lieutenant of the 6th Duke of Cornwall's Light Infantry, and gave instant proof of outstanding qualities. He was promoted Captain in 1915 and Adjutant in 1916. In the following year he was promoted to the General Staff and attached to the 58th Division. In 1918 he was at G.H.Q. The principle of life that forbade him to ask of others any effort he was not himself prepared to make long kept B.-W. close to the battle-field. He was engaged in the fiercest fighting. " I shall always remember his grand qualities during the Battle of the White Château, Hooge, early in 1915," wrote one of B.-W.'s sergeants, " His coolness was remarkable. . . . He and I were two of the few who survived this grim battle." B.-W. never forgot his men and their needs, and his men reciprocated his affection and pride in him. Between the battles of Hooge and Bullecourt, where he was wounded, B.-W. was decorated with the M.C. In the following year, while serving on the General Staff, G.H.Q., he was awarded the D.S.O.

When he returned to civil life the situation at *The Times* office had materially changed. Northcliffe had superseded Dawson and in other respects had made Printing House Square unfamiliar. B.-W., whose choice of *The Times* had been so deliberate, was disappointed, but he had no mind to abandon journalism, and enthusiastically accepted Garvin's offer of a responsible post on *The Observer*. He was grateful for the opportunity to work with a journalist of supreme capacity and went to Tudor Street with the purposefulness that was native to him, though without prejudice to a possible return to Printing House Square. The experience was of lasting benefit to him though the work was less than completely satisfying to one who had tasted daily comment on daily affairs. Should the opportunity to return to *The Times* present itself, he knew that he would feel tempted to reconsider his position on the weekly. This possibility apart, he gave unstinted support to his paper and its chief. B.-W. was Assistant-Editor of *The Observer* for eight years. During this period, *i.e.*, between 1919 and 1927, he settled his mind upon matters of the first importance, in particular, as has been seen, of foreign policy. By the time he returned to Printing House Square[1] as a member of the staff that Dawson collected in his second term he was a practised performer. Printing House Square is not unused to service of quality; yet in living memory nobody worked harder and more variously then he. B.-W. did everything and did it speedily. His appetite for work entailed a hearty rejection of anything like a narrow delimitation of his position, for he was prepared to interest himself, on behalf of the Editor, not only in the circulation and advertising of *The Times*, but in every aspect of the presentation of the paper to the public. The proposal to revise completely the typography of the paper was of great interest to him. Decision and judgement are of the essence of editorial efficiency. B.-W.'s answers to questions, and his pronouncements upon events, were automatic and instantaneous. The speed at which his mind worked amazed the office and disconcerted his older colleagues. " No good asking B.-W. to discuss the point," complained one colleague, faced by what he considered a three-pipe problem, " He will give the answer before you get your penny in."

For over ten years B.-W. was engaged in the widest variety of tasks that had been known to fall to one pair of editorial hands. At no time did he oblige others to do for him what his conscience directed him to do for himself. His remarkably rapid power of thought and action permitted him to indulge an eagerness to be read, and a controversial type of mind, by the writing of leading articles. He had to be sparing with the time he gave to routine work. This was why he gave speedy answers to colleagues. Just as a man he was deliberate and cautious, so as a writer he was meditative and slow. Rapid as he was in the dispatch of business, he was never rash in the writing of leaders. Rather he was apt to be more than cautious. Respect for the ascertained facts, for the sagacious assessment of their bearing, and for the opinion of those in the position to check them, guarded him against unqualified generalization. In writing about foreign policy he particularly wished to be what he called " judgematic " and to hold steadily the balance between extremes. This attitude of mind was congenital. He was incapable either of going to extremes or of seeing only one side of an issue. As the view he decided to adopt

[1] As described in Chapter XXI, " Dawson's Second Innings," p. 811.

was conscientiously held, only a new fact or new conviction could change it. This habit gave him the reputation of being "inflexible." On the one highly controversial issue of Germany he held the same conviction for twenty years.

As early as 1919 he came to the conclusion that the peace with Germany was not "judgematic." It was a blunder because it gave the Germans a grievance, and to give the Germans a grievance was to give them a source of strength. He campaigned against Versailles in *The Observer* and in *The Times*. After talking with Benesh in 1920 he came to the conclusion that a German-Austrian Anschluss as sought by Brüning was less of a peril to Czechoslovakia than its rejection would be. B.-W. was far from wanting to reward Germany for sowing the seeds of the old war; what he wanted to do was to remove the motive and grievance that would make for a new one. He believed that the possibilities for peace were increased by the removal of European grievances, notably Germany's, and resisted the demand for a *cordon sanitaire* round Russia. He welcomed recognition of the Soviet. The war was the greatest disappointment imaginable for one who so well knew what fighting meant.

From October 1, 1941, when he assumed responsibility for *The Times*, B.-W. discharged his heavy task with the utmost conscientiousness, great ability, and with marked independence of Ministers. The responsibility for which he had worked during 14 years was his for some three years when his health showed signs of failing. He appointed as his deputy William Francis Casey, who had spent 28 years' service for the paper in Printing House Square, in Paris and in Washington, and possessed a rare range of experience. Soon after the end of the war, B.-W. went to Canada and the United States, spending freely of his energy and time in Ottawa, Montreal, New York and Washington. He did not succeed in saving his strength, and when he returned, it was obvious to his closer friends in the office that he would need very severely to ration his energy, and would not again be able to work the always inhuman hours that his theory of conscientious journalism so long imposed upon him. A fourteen-hour day had long been his practice, backed by a theory that a week-end of ardous physical exercise in the country would restore the balance. It was justified years earlier, but B.-W.'s later use of this device had meant that what he gained at the week-end he overspent before the middle of the following week. He had, therefore, run through all his capital, and in 1947 it was plain to all but himself that no rest of any length whatever would ever bring back the B.-W. of ten years ago; though, if he could be persuaded to restrict his day to that of an ordinary prudent man, he might return to the office in a state of health equal to the task of Editorship. But the task is, necessarily, a heavy one. Dawson left, tired to a degree that he did not realize, and died on November 7, 1944. The incessant interruption, the constant switching of the mind at less than a moment's notice, from one urgency to another; the innumerable decisions demanded; the multitude of people to be interviewed; the many telephone calls, exact a price that no man can afford indefinitely. B.-W.'s four years of active war service was still being paid for, and he had to his credit twenty-one years of service in Printing House Square, when the strain began to tell upon him, and it became clear to his deputy and the office as a whole that either B.-W. would stop the old routine, or the old routine would stop him. Leaving the paper in charge of his deputy, he departed for a health cruise to South Africa at Christmas, 1947, from which he never returned. R. M. Barrington-Ward, D.S.O., M.C., Hon. Fellow of Balliol College, Oxon, died at Dar-es-Salaam on February 29, 1948, at the age of 57. His term of editorship fell short of seven years, though he had long shared the hardest work with Dawson. It has been seen that his range of interests and capacity to write fitted him in the highest degree for the leading position in the office. It has been seen, also, that events forced him to give his time principally to foreign affairs and war— subjects which interested him far less than home politics and social betterment.

The future writer who, when the documents are available, sits down to assess the contribution that B.-W. made (as Editor) to his country's cause and his paper's prestige, will bear witness to his power as an architect of policy in wartime, to his capacity as the head of a team, to his industry, versatility and self-efface-ment. It will be found that the resolution and vigour of his war policy and the enlightenment and progressiveness of his peace policy more than repaired the damage made to the reputation of *The Times* by Dawson's and his own pre-war policy of appeasement. It may be, indeed it was, tragic that he was not given the time in which to continue to expound rationally and persuasively the novel and necessary social and economic changes that the effort and expense of two world wars in one generation rendered inevitable.

B.-W.'s basic political philosophy contained little that was unfamiliar to Printing House Square. Forty years earlier Shadwell had worked, not in vain, to correct any tendency to make resistance to social change a principle. But B.-W.'s interpretation of the standards, political and social, set up since 1909 was certainly broader than Dawson's. His was a younger and more contemporary mind, rooted in the deepest experiences of his generation. On his 50th birthday when he was about to succeed Dawson, B.-W. set down, for a private eye, the position in which he stood.

My life was really forfeit in 1914 and it is the merest, the least deserved of flukes that I have survived to enjoy so much of which war robbed the pick of my contemporaries. The more reason to remember the mission which August, 1914, and survival have together set men like me—namely, to strive for the creation and organization of peace, above all things, and for the liberating truths at home at whatever cost to conventional opinion. Revolution cannot do it. It is to be questioned whether revolution as such has ever achieved anything *on balance* : but evolution, active and painful evolution must. On my own humble anniversary it is well to have this old resolution sharp and clear again.[1]

His mind being thus set, B.-W.'s attitude towards the General Election of 1945 was consistent; and, in consequence, the paper found itself, after it, in the familiar position of being able freely to give general support to the Government that the country placed in power. B.-W.'s deputy shared his standpoint, and at the time of his death was by no means disposed to turn aside from B.-W.'s example in this, and other respects. The Chief Proprietors were in accord, and they appointed, as Editor of *The Times* from April, 1948, William Francis Casey, who is the present occupant of the chair.

In 1949 Christopher Shotter Kent, C.B.E., retired. He was possessed of considerable newspaper experience before he joined the British War Mission in 1917 and went to Washington. Later he served on Northcliffe's personal staff and travelled frequently to and from Paris. He joined the management of *The Times* in 1921 and in 1937 was appointed Manager in succession to Lints Smith. Kent saw the paper through the war carrying, in addition to the normal burden, the responsibility of protecting the day and night staffs during air raids. The office was bombed on the night of September 25, 1940, the story of which, and other checks to production, is on record.[2]

An important decision affecting the public was made on April 7, 1941, when the price of the paper which had been 2d. since June 4, 1923, was raised to 3d. in order that the complete service of *The Times*, as a national register of news, should continue.

[1] B.-W.'s manuscript note, dated February 23, 1941.

[2] *When the Sirens Sounded*. An account of Air Raid Precautions in Printing House Square, 1937 to 1945. (P.H.S., 1949.)

As on every occasion since John Walter III stablized the price of the paper at threepence in 1861, thereby making the decision which fixed its character, circulation (*i.e.*, sales of issues) was sacrificed. Fullness of reporting was not sacrificed, nor its quality. When Northcliffe reduced the price to one penny in 1914, the standard confirmed by John Walter III was maintained, and in spite of threats to the contrary, Northcliffe held consistently to the Walterian principle. He wrote in 1916 that:

Of one thing I am convinced—that it is our duty to maintain *The Times* as a complete record and again to increase the price, rather than reduce the size. That seems to have been the sound policy of those who have gone before us in the house of the Dominicans. We shall have to encourage the old policy of " *The Times* lent to read." I have very little doubt that the paper will soon be restored to its old price of threepence.[1]

The raising of the price to threepence in 1941 was a measure by which the Proprietors and the Manager protected the completeness and the quality of the " record." Once more circulation was sacrificed, a loss that no manager can view with favour. Kent took willingly upon himself the responsibility of making good this and other war-time losses, and thus continued the " sound policy of those who have gone before us." In succession to Kent the Chief Proprietors appointed Francis Mathew as Manager from June 30, 1949. It has been possible, by typographical devices, to maintain and even increase the volume of news and advertisements without further increase of price. It is the hope of the Chief Proprietors that by various expedients they may continue publication at the old price.

*　　　　　*　　　　　*

The paper that was first published by John Walter I from Printing House Square, on January 1, 1785, price twopence-halfpenny was, he promised, " to be of no party." It was a private, commercial and typographic production designed to inform, instruct and amuse the public. The paper succeeded by methods of its own, which this History has endeavoured to illustrate, in preserving its independence, while, on occasion, influencing the nation's affairs. Upwards of 52,000 issues have been printed on the same site, and the Chief Proprietors have their rooms in the identical house occupied by five generations of the founding family. *The Times* is the oldest London daily newspaper. Its continuity of publication was not interrupted by the General Strike of 1926, responsible as it

[1] Northcliffe to the Manager, December, 21 1916. The price had been reduced in the spring of 1914. See above, Chapter IV, " Price One Penny."

was for the suspension of the whole of the Metropolitan Press, with the exception of *The Times*.[1] The paper also enjoys continuity of ownership. In its 166th year the Chief Proprietors are Colonel John Astor and Mr. John Walter, great-great-grandson of the Founder, who are in accord in maintaining the continuity of the paper's politics : " to be of no party."

That it is still the duty of *The Times* to report news as accurately and fully as possible is axiomatic. There can be no prospect of a sound public judgement on affairs unless newspapers discharge this duty. But the mere reporting and printing of the day's news by the Press is, possibly, a less important function than it was. The effect of broadcasting has been to break the monopoly of newspapers in the reporting of events, and to lessen their social value so far as they restrict themselves to it. As broadcasting, so long as it is under efficient control, can report more quickly and vividly than the Press, it has been necessary for some newspapers to increase their social value by the provision of entertainment. For *The Times* it remains necessary rather to give more attention to comment, documentation and interpretation. As the consequence of technical developments outside the printing trade, leading articles and turnovers have become more necessary, since they serve the intellectual classes as a corrective to total dependence on broadcast news; the interpretative dispatch from a foreign capital, which in form is half-report and half-comment, is also of greater importance since it aids the reader in search of a coherent and comprehensive account of events.

It is safe to say that new forms of presentation and comment will develop in journalism—printed, wirelessed, or televised. The " highest standards of journalism " have never been fully equal to all the necessities of the time; nor are they now. The propaganda of a secular and materialist philosophy, designed to strengthen a huge but intellectually antiquated, gifted but economically backward, ingenious but under-industrialized country, will be dangerous for the technically advanced but relatively complacent democracies to the extent that the newspapers fail to realize their obligation. The German-Russian philosophy of aggression gives unaccustomed significance in the most empirical countries to the force of ideas as weapons. A contemporary " feature " apt for the new period of " ideology " has yet to be evolved by the news trade.

Resistance to the comparative criticism of ideas is characteristic of England. It leads newspapers to avoid discussion of theories

---

[1] For the emergency methods employed at Printing House Square that enabled *The Times* to appear, see *Strike Nights in Printing House Square*. (P.H.S., 1927.)

CHRISTOPHER SHOTTER KENT

MANAGER OF *THE TIMES* 1937-1949

From a photograph

of political action in order to concentrate upon concrete practical endeavour; to ignore definition of ideas in favour of debate about planning. Nevertheless, it is plain that the counter-process of ideological pressure needs itself to be dialectically urged, if it is to be effective. Without prejudice to the collection of news, which is itself susceptible of a broader interpretation than it usually receives, the discussion, exposition, and projection of ideas is necessary if British democracy is to be protected against inherent weaknesses of its own and the diplomatic triumphs of the aggressors. This cannot be doubted. The change in China, which marks the climax of one of the greatest redistributions of power the world has ever witnessed, is in large measure the consequence of the propaganda of ideas upon which unlimited dialectical labour has been lavished. This change alone renders the study of the pedigree of ideas vastly more practical than ever it was. It is not remarkable, therefore, that public opinion to-day should be in a far more healthy state than it was twenty years ago, when realistic political thinking was shirked, and peace was cheap at any price. The consequences of this change of mood are important to the practice of journalism. The present rallying of politically mature readers to *The Times* is largely due to the pressure of events. This, the most responsible of all sections of opinion, stands ready to be braced for the immediate tasks before it; including, as they may, the decision whether vague talk favouring " Western values," or the " British way of life " is sufficient, by itself, to sustain such " values " or " way."

In the making of " The Thunderer " and in the tradition established by *The Times* and tested under Northcliffe, there is implied a quality of journalism that shall develop in terms of absolute contemporary validity. The present age is pregnant with huge and sudden shifts in ideas, politics, economics and power. In our time, the survival of parliamentary democracy depends, let the value of wireless be admitted, upon a high standard of printed journalism; and, as much as anything else, upon the future ability of *The Times* to expound, evaluate, and present rationally the deeper implications of all that is significant in events, and discern in them the evolving pattern. The criticism of contemporary political organization, national and inter-national, fundamentally applied, reaches back to beliefs which the whole conspiracy of aggressive materialist propaganda works to obscure. It may well be that an analytical and dialectical element in journalism will not easily be grafted upon the tradition established in any historic office, but it is not rash to say that aggression will never again be met at Printing House Square in terms of mere " Munich." Rather, the paper will use its strength to urge the arming of the country to any extent necessary, and in every mode, including the weapon of ideas. It may be necessary, too, in the light of the lessons of the inter-war experience, for the Press to speak a little louder than has been customary since Northcliffe's time. " Newspaper writing," said Barnes, " is a thing *sui generis*, it is in literature what brandy is in beverages. John Bull, whose understanding is rather sluggish—I speak for the majority of readers—requires a strong stimulus. He . . . dozes composedly over his prejudices which his conceit calls his opinions; and you must fire ten-pounders at his densely compacted intellect before you can make it comprehend your meaning or care one farthing for your efforts."

But if changes in the outlook and accent of all those who write political comment result in a type of journalism very different in direction from those initiated by Northcliffe forty years ago, they will in Printing House Square neither reach less resolutely towards contemporary realities—nor respect less faithfully past traditions; traditions, that is to say, which are based upon the presumption that there is to-day and will be left in the future, as there existed in the past, a public with sufficient respect for itself to demand the best newspaper that can be provided. The History here concluded affords ground for belief that the vitality of the paper's tradition, established under test, will guarantee beyond its present anniversary, continuity in mechanical inventiveness, in capacity to assure modest prosperity, in timely expansion of its service of news, in honesty of exposition of views, in generous provision of space to the views of readers, in consistency of demand for political freedom, in determination of preference for the anonymous principle in writing, and in stubbornness of the maintenance of editorial independence. Without continuity of all these, *The Times* would cease to be *The Times*.

As to the spirit in which continuity will manifest itself in the future, it may be well, in an age in which man-made dogma masquerades as divine revelation, to take a passage from a leading article published a generation ago. The leader was occasioned by a speech in which political terms were so tendentiously used that *The Times* printed a statement of the principles that should infuse the mind of anyone who would claim to be a true Liberal. The definition, though written at short notice in the ordinary course of journalistic work, may stand to-day as representative of the continuity of thinking in Printing House Square:

A Liberal in our view is not a man who swears only by Cobden or Bright, Gladstone or Asquith. He does not necessarily take his economics from the Manchester school, or his idea of social ethics from Bentham, Mill, or Ricardo. He is a man who believes in individual liberty as a good in itself, though a good conditioned by the duty of public service and by a sense of individual responsibility towards the community at large. He fears no change of social or economic form, provided that the substance of freedom be preserved. He would exclude none, men or women, from their full share in public life, but would strive to secure for all equality of opportunity. He believes in combating error by truth, in the employment of persuasion rather than force, but holds that, at all costs, the right of the majority to rule within constitutional forms must be upheld. In public life he is opposed to all forms of tyranny or dictation, monarchical, bureaucratic, syndicalist, communist, or semi-presidential. He has profound faith in the genius of the British people to adapt their institutions and their economic arrangements, without utter dislocation, to the changing needs of a changing time, and he believes that this genius is not the monopoly of any class or party, but that all, including the Labour or " Socialist " Party, possess their share of it. (March, 19, 1920.)

With similar principles *The Times*, conscious of its continuity with the past and present, looks forward to the future—*Tempus fuit, est, et erit*.

[Postscript

POSTSCRIPT

IF, for the reasons given,[1] the present History of *The Times* is suspended at the outbreak of war in 1939, the policy sponsored by the paper in the preceding sixteen years merits critical examination. Such examination must take account of the character of *The Times* itself as a daily publication, of its tradition both as a national register of news and organ of national opinion, and of the outlook of the Editor whom its proprietors restored to his earlier functions after the death of Northcliffe had brought about a change of ownership. Astor, Walter, and Dawson then deliberately reverted to a definition of journalism with which, they believed, John Walter II, John Walter III, as well as Barnes and Delane, would have been in agreement. Northcliffe, while foremost in his admiration of John Walter II, Barnes and Delane, had departed signally and, as many thought, appropriately in time of war from this definition. Steed had maintained this departure in the early post-war years which were hardly a time of peace, and was—as some thought, appropriately—dismissed as an impediment to a revival of the ostensibly older definition that was more in harmony with the period of political tranquillity which the coincident changes symbolized. Still, the questions remain whether this definition was adequate to cover the conditions of 1923-1939, and whether, given similar conditions, Editors like Barnes and Delane would have clung to it.

With some aspects of the definition all, including probably Northcliffe and Steed, would have been in accord. None would have contested the fundamental fact that a daily journal such as *The Times* can be conducted only by men able to combine rapidity of judgement with the art of writing swiftly, and with willingness to accept risks ; that the essence of an Editor's task is to make sure, night by night, that his leading articles shall be found apt next morning by most if not all the readers for whom they are written ; and that an Editor and his leader-writers do not write for posterity, however fondly the Editor may hope that posterity will recognize the soundness of his judgement. The Editor and his assistants have, as a rule, to reckon with the certainties of the night, and with the probabilities of the morning. It needs no small degree of craftsmanship quickly

[1] See above, p. 980.

997

to master telegrams and other pieces of information, and to interpret them to the public. To " views " not obviously related to facts or current events they pay scant respect. Hence the tendency of Editors as different as Buckle, Dawson, and B.-W. to cold-shoulder " viewy " people, a tendency consonant with the habit of Printing House Square for at least half a century before Dawson began his second term. The broad editorial policy was to take into account the changing moods of the electorate and the changing fortunes of politicians. It was a national policy adequate to *The Times* in a period when Britain was at peace with Europe.

It was only in Northcliffe's later period, from 1914 to 1922, that the validity of this mid-Victorian definition was called in question. Northcliffe no longer felt bound to observe the principle that *The Times*, the national register of news, should also be the national instrument for the furtherance of a nationally agreed policy, and could only lose influence by theorizing in advance of public opinion. In his time the paper advocated measures, *e.g.*, conscription, irrespective of any " general measure of agreement " because such a measure was judged in advance of national agreement as necessary for national survival. A reasoned demand for the introduction of compulsory military service was made and repeated in leading articles until Parliament and the country were ready for it. Thus, the " general measure of agreement " was created ; it followed and did not precede the paper's campaign. Had Dawson who, under Northcliffe, was responsible for this campaign, been taken to task for departing from his predecessor's definition of the paper's functions, he might have invoked the older example of Barnes ; for Barnes, as was pointed out in the first volume of this History (p. 209), " fought first for the maintenance of a healthy opinion, at that time only a nascent element in politics : secondly, for leadership of the public opinion created largely by his own efforts." But the success of the conscription campaign, carried as it was into Northcliffe's other newspapers, fostered in Northcliffe a habit of embarrassing the Government and startling the public by attacks on Ministers and demands of every kind. The attacks may not have been gratuitous nor the demands always unwarranted : witness the attack on Kitchener in 1915 for preferring shrapnel to high explosive as a means of destroying barbed wire entanglements ; but they represented a type of journalism that, pushed too far, was bound to defeat its own object, and Northcliffe pushed it very far. By restoring the mid-Victorian definition, and abandoning the policy of creating

ublic opinion, *The Times* went far in the opposite direction.
he general sense of the people was to be trusted; and the
lected Government, Conservative or National, was to be given
eneral support, and the King's Ministers were always to be
iven fair play. As it turned out, the electorate was not
ensible, statesmen were not wise, and *The Times* came near to
bdicating its function of leadership. Strict adherence to the
efinition that the newspaper's purpose is to serve the day and to
oncentrate upon issues of immediate importance had over-
hadowed the realization, so far as it may be said to have
xisted even in part, of the vastness of the shifts in power that
ad occurred during and since the 1914-1918 war, and the peace
ettlement. But before looking into the extent to which
onsiderations of this order affect the definition of journalism
eld by Dawson and B.-W. it is desirable to note certain
nplications and some of the circumstances of the definition
pon which they rested their policy.

When Northcliffe died three and a half years after the signing
f the Versailles Treaty, Britain was settling down very
ncomfortably into its post-war polity. The country needed
o engage in a ruthless re-examination of her position in the
orld. She was trying to finance a rising standard of living
vithout having the means, and to cover up the poverty of the
ation's thinking with an apron of clichés, uncriticized and
nmodified, taken from the pre-1914 era, a period more remote
rom the experiences of the post-war world than many earlier
pochs. Until Britain had taken stock of these vast changes
he must inevitably have been unprepared and hence doomed
o be the servant and not the mistress of events. A chief cause
f her misfortunes was that her people were armed with little
iore than a sense of fair play to her debtors and compromise
vith her creditors. No other country had such a sense of fair
lay. For this reason it is possible to hold that every major
ecision agreed to by *The Times* between 1931 and 1939 was
ght in the insular sense, and yet to acknowledge that an
isular outlook must bring the country near to continental
isaster. It was not understood that the effects of the events of
917, 1922 and 1933 were permanent, and that something more
ian a temporary disturbance of the political order had happened,
omething not to be dealt with by the dispatch of a competent
eporter to the spot, and by the interpretation of the best leader-
riter on the night. The appropriate comment was made in
ie day-to-day sense, but the real significance of events was
iissed. *The Times* reflected clearly the common national

prejudice against anything which might be regarded as a habit of generalization. An attempt to measure the trends of contemporary history or indulge in doctrinal speculation lay outside the province of journalism, as *The Times* defined it. In the result the paper lost an opportunity of leading public opinion in serious contemplation of the changed character of politics; international and, by repercussion, national.

This is why there is no sign in the office between 1923 and 1933 of a sense that the world of 1914 had gone for ever, and that the seizure of power by the Bolsheviks in 1917, by the Fascists in 1922, and by the Nazis in 1933 combined to present a capital challenge to political thinking. But, taken together with the emergence in these countries of a revolutionary attitude towards ideas, news and information, this capital challenge rendered obsolete many of the habits of mind that underlay the paper's conception of journalism, and presented it with a challenge to its form of expression. The new Russian, Italian and German outlook was social, doctrinal and radical. The British, French and American remained individualist, optimistic, and conservative. The poverty-stricken dynamic Central Powers were able to create a mass response for a radical programme of resistance, if necessary armed, against Versailles. Theirs they alleged was a forward-looking constructive programme, buttressed by scientific planning, fully representative of twentieth-century ideas. They arraigned the rich but feeble capitalist Powers whose *laisser faire* programme was, they said, representative of obsolete nineteenth-century ideas.

This might have mattered little if the distinction between war and peace had been as absolute as the British electors wished to think and *The Times* liked to contend. But the determination of Germany to fight for her new social programme and a new distribution of power favourable to herself, was being conducted in a fashion wholly new to this generation. It was not perceived by those responsible for daily comment on the day's news that the dissatisfied Powers had no interest in what the British and French called a stable economy and a feeling of security in Europe. The terms of reference accepted habitually by journalists working in P.H.S. were eminently reasonable. It was their business to exercise their judgement and comment immediately on news sent at speed; it was not their business to cogitate at leisure and express themselves at their chosen time as historians or the political philosophers can do. Nevertheless journalists who aspire, as Dawson and B.-W. did, to influence

public opinion and public policy are not immune from the verdict
of history upon the policy they initiate or support, above all
in relation to issues of war and peace.

The views of *The Times* upon the risks of war between
1936 and 1939 were far less disapproved at the time than later.
It was afterwards that " the Printing House Square crowd," as
Dr. Hugh Dalton called it, was accused of bringing on the second
war by its benevolence towards Germany ; just as after 1918
the paper was accused, by American historians, of responsibility
for the first war by its malignance towards Germany. The
latter charge has been dealt with in the previous volume.[1] The
truth is that before 1914 the paper influenced British policy
by its independent part in building up the defensive Japanese,
French and Russian alliances ; while before 1939 British and
Commonwealth opinion were allowed to influence the paper.
The Times did not truckle to popular sentiment after the failure
to secure an Anglo-German understanding in 1901, because the
paper then recognized that Germany had decided to isolate
Britain, a truth that received little notice elsewhere. The
Liberal public opinion of the post Boer-War period firmly rejected
the warnings of Printing House Square (and Carmelite House),
but *The Times* was content to keep its course, independently
of the Government and of the electorate. The paper's confidence
was based upon conclusions to which it had been led by its
Own Correspondents whose sources of intelligence were full
and reliable ; the paper's judgement, thus correspondingly
confident and independent, enabled the paper to challenge an
inert national will.

In this way *The Times* was faithful to its own traditions and to
the definition of journalism conceived by Barnes and John
Walter II in the thirties and forties of last century, and formulated
trenchantly by Delane, with the approval of John Walter III,
in 1852. If Buckle's outlook tended to be somewhat insular, it
was supplemented by that of Moberly Bell whose first care, after
accepting the position of Assistant-Manager, had been to bring
a former foreign correspondent, Mackenzie Wallace, back to
the paper as Foreign Editor, and to find a place for Chirol.
Through Chirol and Wallace he appointed Saunders, Steed and
George Morrison of Peking whose private reports, even more
than their published dispatches, contained information of a high
significance. All these men would have subscribed to the definition
of journalism written for Delane by Robert Lowe in February,

[1] For a rebuttal see Vol. III, Appendix, Sources, pp. 800 *ff*.

1852, as a counter-blast to Lord Derby's strictures on *The Times*
for its criticism of Louis Napoleon's high-handed suppression
of French liberties :

It may suit the purposes of statesmen to veil the statue of Liberty
and to mutter some formulary of disingenuous acquiescence in foreign
wrongs, dictated by their fears rather than by their convictions ; but
we prefer to await for our justification the day when the entombed
and oppressed liberties of Europe shall once more start into life and
array themselves under the standard to which we cling. For to what
after all, are the statesmen of England to look for strength and national
power, if injuries and offences arise against us, but to the enlightened
resolution of the people of England to uphold the principles on which
our own polity and independence are founded ?

Nor would they or, indeed, Northcliffe have dissented from
Delane's further definition of a journalist's duty :

The duty of the journalist is the same as that of the historian—to seek
out truth, above all things, and to present to his readers not such things
as statecraft would wish them to know but the truth as near as he can
ascertain it.

Notwithstanding many shortcomings in its observance, the duty
of wishing the readers of *The Times* to know " the truth as near
as he can ascertain it " was an essential point in the conception
of journalism cherished in Printing House Square in its early
Victorian period. It was later practised, more resolutely, perhaps,
in comment on foreign than in home affairs, throughout the
period of Arthur Walter. It continued in force after Bell had
brought in Northcliffe and found expression from the beginning
of the war up to the sale of the paper, in consequence of
Northcliffe's death.

*   *   *

The combination of Dawson and B.-W. after 1928
synchronized with a fundamental alteration in the old system of
building up policy, above all in respect of foreign affairs. Before
the 1914-1918 war, as has been seen in the preceding volume,
Printing House Square was served by foreign Correspondents
not merely unrivalled in number and quality by any newspaper
before or since, but unequalled by any Government, home
or foreign. If this unique staff did not, as a whole, long
survive the death of its creator, Moberly Bell, there remained
Correspondents of first-class quality in the principal European
capitals, and in Washington. Secondly, under Arthur Walter's

proprietorship, the office possessed a powerful weight of logical direction and leader-writing ability in foreign affairs. This combination of direction and writing did not long survive the deaths of Chirol and of Flanagan, and the dismissal of Steed. By the death in 1928 of Harold Williams, the last Foreign Editor, the paper's intelligence, independence and leadership in foreign affairs were permanently lowered. This declension was most conspicuous and disastrous in the department of Anglo-German relations. No responsibility attaches to the correspondence, for the two resident Correspondents who successively from 1920 to 1937 represented the paper in Berlin were the equal of their predecessors, Saunders and Mackenzie. Neither nourished any bias in favour of Nazism; both recognized the dangers of German rearmament before Nazism became a force. One was expelled. The reason why *The Times* failed to provide the country with the basis for a sound judgement on the real objectives of German foreign policy is that the foreign correspondence was not made, as hitherto, the basis of the policy expressed in the leading articles. Thus a radical change had been effected in the outlook of Printing House Square between 1923 and 1928.

Some of the reasons arose out of the personality and interests of the Editor, and have been indicated. It is necessary to allow, however, that the Imperial developments of the period would have affected the judgement and decision of any Editor, whatever his interests. Indeed, to a large extent a change in the basic power of the British Cabinet had been inevitable since 1911 when the discussions of the Imperial Conference included the principle of consultation between Dominion Governments about Treaties. From 1917 it became the practice to communicate full intelligence on the progress of the war to Dominion Prime Ministers, and confidential information on foreign affairs was soon regularly communicated to them. The Imperial War Conference of 1917 agreed that India was to be fully represented at all future Imperial Conferences. Also, a special Imperial Conference was to be held after the war to consider adjustment of constitutional relations. It was then understood that any such readjustment, while completely preserving all existing powers of self-government and complete control of domestic affairs, should be based upon a full recognition of the Dominions as autonomous nations of an Imperial Commonwealth and of India as an important portion of the same; that the right of the Dominions and India to an adequate voice in foreign policy and in foreign relations should be admitted, and that a future Conference should provide some arrangements for continuous consultation on all important matters of common Imperial concern, and for any necessary concerted action, founded on consultation, that the several Governments might determine.

Manifestly, the demand for " an adequate voice in foreign policy and in foreign relations " by the Dominions was bound to create problems for the Commonwealth as a kind of Federation, for Britain as a United Kingdom, and for *The Times* as a newspaper which had become acutely sensitive to the trends of opinion in the home country and oversea. The paper was not slow to point out that while such a demand apparently went far to banish the imminence of war for the Dominions it undoubtedly increased the risk of war for Britain. The fact remained that the Versailles Treaty had been signed separately on behalf of Canada, Australia, New Zealand, South Africa, and India. Thereafter it became the regular practice for these countries to be separately represented in all international conferences whether convened by the League or not. Such conditions were bound to affect the thinking of the office, and the allotment of space. The crisis over Chanak in 1922 made Printing House Square aware that the great Dominions would never again allow Britain to presuppose their national participation in every war in which she was engaged. Henceforth particular, or general, Dominion association with the mother country's wars was not to be automatic. After 1922 the Empire Prime Ministers' demand for " an adequate voice " in foreign policy was unquestioned. The problem was discussed in 1923, and at every subsequent meeting of Dominion Prime Ministers. Had *The Times*, after 1922, stood in danger of turning a deaf ear to the " adequate voice," an incident in 1928 would have sharpened its sense of hearing. In May of that year the Prime Minister of Canada, Mackenzie King, claimed to have averted a European war by his stand over the crisis of 1922.[1]

The time and energy given by a man so susceptible as Dawson to such considerations led him to view European realities in the light of Empire issues ; he came to look upon the Continent with the detachment of a Dominion journalist. It was an outlook based on the assumption that Germany, however strong she was allowed to become, would never use her strength to reach the objectives for which she had fought from 1914 to 1918. When, as late as the spring of 1937, the Imperial

[1] See above, Chapter XVIII, " The Coalition Dissolves," p. 734, and Appendix II, Sources, XXI.

Conference laid emphasis upon peace between the nations and the " adjustment of national needs . . . by methods of cooperation, joint inquiry and conciliation," *The Times* found a perfect expression of its own conception of foreign affairs. Here was a policy agreed by Britain and the Dominions in accordance with their claim for " an adequate voice " with the Government of Great Britain in everything concerning foreign policy. Here was absolutely sound Imperial theory, to be admitted and acted upon. When during the summer of 1938 Mr. R. G. Menzies, then the Attorney-General for Australia, visited Europe, he said that he looked forward to the time when wireless telephony would make it possible for the Dominions "to speak with one voice, which will be the voice of peace." And when, after visiting Germany, Mr. Menzies left for home on August 8, 1938, he issued a statement which bore directly upon the problem. He wished, though he did not say so precisely, to see something like an Imperial Foreign Affairs Committee brought into existence in some British or Commonwealth capital. " For all I know that centre may some day be in Canberra, or Ottawa, or Pretoria. Meanwhile London remained the focusing point of the British world, and it was undoubtedly true that the Government of Great Britain recognized that ' on all large matters ' it should speak not only for Great Britain, but for British people all over the Globe." By coincidence, on the day this statement was made, the Australian Minister for External Affairs spoke at Melbourne. Mr. W. M. Hughes then said that the Australian Government could exercise no effective voice in Imperial policy unless they were fully informed of events while situations could still be moulded by appropriate policy. But, he said, the news given to the Dominions generally came after the event or when the situation had so developed that only reluctant acquiescence was possible. It was in the Dominions Office, which was " from many aspects a complete anachronism," that the delays occurred ; and, Mr. Hughes demanded, messages should come direct from the Foreign Office or the Prime Minister to the Dominion Prime Ministers.

While Mr. Menzies' statement and Mr. Hughes' speech were being digested, the Sudeten leaders were preparing to reject the Czech proposals for a solution of the minority question. The Australian Attorney-General found that in some ways the Germans did not understand the British character.

This may be our fault even more than theirs, but everybody will hope that mutual understanding will grow between two of the greatest and most virile nations in the world. It is surely a truism to say that nobody in Germany wants war, since every intelligent person, both in and out of Germany, knows full well that a major European conflict may well end in the material defeat, if not the actual moral destruction of all the combatant nations.

The principles of the totalitarian State, as Germans freely admitted to me in Berlin, are not suited to the British genius, but I do hope that we British people will not too easily accept the idea that because personal liberties have been curtailed in Germany the result is necessarily a base materialism. There is a good deal of a really spiritual quality in the willingness of young Germans to devote themselves to the service and well-being of the State.

The Times, commenting upon both Mr. Menzies' and Mr. Hughes' contributions to the discussion, found the former's references to Germany " excellent as models of views that may hope to command very wide assent throughout the Commonwealth and Empire." (August 9, 1938.)

In the first week of September the British Commonwealth Relations Conference opened at Sydney, under the Presidency of the Prime Minister, Mr. Lyons. Some eighty delegates from all parts of the Empire assembled to discuss the future of the Commonwealth on September 3, 1938. Mr. Menzies, in Melbourne, made a new statement in the full tenor of conciliation, and corresponding closely to the doctrine of Printing House Square. He urged Australians not to take sides too hastily over Czechoslovakia. *The Times* reported him as believing

that the ultimate solution of the problem must be the creation of a Federal State on the Swiss model, which could be given a guaranteed neutrality. In a mad world cool heads were more precious than the wagging tongues of partisans. Britons should uphold their reputation for judicial fair play. Germany might never have had a dictatorship if the Western Powers had shown more sympathy and understanding. If we could persuade Germany that we were prepared to give her justice we might drive out the evil spirits of suspicion and hatred.

The proceedings at Sydney were clouded over towards the end of the session, and by the 17th the European situation made it difficult for the Conference to keep to its agenda and it ended with little progress to report.

The unsolved problems of inter-Imperial relations, outlined in the public statements recorded in the preceding pages, however, continued to dominate the Editor, who knew that cleavage on foreign policy between Britain and any one of the Dominions must be disastrous to the very highest interests of the whole Commonwealth. The possibility of such a cleavage had long been manifest to him, and had convinced him that the way to a firm policy lay in the avoidance of issues calculated to arouse Dominion misunderstanding and resentment. That Stanley Baldwin and Neville Chamberlain were in absolute agreement with the Editor is not to be doubted. Mr. Menzies and Mr. Hughes confirmed their common view. The Editor was also made aware of the views of Australian and Canadian statesmen by private conversation. Numerous friends from oversea talked to him bluntly in the summer of 1938, and made it impossible for him to resist the conclusion that Britain could not carry the Commonwealth into a war to maintain the Versailles arrangements in Czechoslovakia. A subtle process of mental adjustment led him to conclude that Germany intended to abstain from force, and to adopt a policy based on her readiness to act as a good neighbour and employ only peaceful means to achieve a revision of the Versailles Treaty. These convictions about Germany were widely shared in the British Isles.

The year 1936 gave *The Times* a last opportunity to return to its pre-1914 and pre-1923 policy towards Germany. In 1935 or in 1936, but not later, *The Times* could have hoped with reason to succeed in a main effort, made in terms of the old Walterian or later Northcliffian definition of the function of journalism, with all the strength it could have mustered, to warn, inform, instruct and educate the Government, the Commons, the British public and the oversea Commonwealth. There was more than enough material in the office to serve as the basis of a positive foreign policy independent of the Commons, the constituencies and the Government. There were, however, considerations which, in the minds of Dawson and B.-W., would override any such plan. They had virtually abandoned the practice of basing a foreign policy of the paper's own upon the dispatches, published and private, of " our own " Correspondents abroad. This was the essential point of distinction between the old building of policy, and the new, that became explicit after 1928. It is hard to deny that the old system, with its clear and un-deviating line towards Germany, had been rendered anachronistic. First, there was the fact, and all the consequences that flowed from it, of the insistence in 1919 by the Dominions of separate signatures to the Treaty of Versailles ; these implied a right to free judgement. Secondly, there was the existence, with all its effects upon policy, of pacifism in Britain. No newspaper, no

Editor, could find it an easy task to reconcile firm Imperial isolation, increasing British pacifism, and revived German militarism.

Like other Editors, Dawson was bound to take into account the positive action of the Government ; he also consulted his personal preferences among Conservative statesmen. He was close to Baldwin and Chamberlain ; he was intimate with Halifax. There is no sign that he consulted statesmen, whether Conservative or not, who were known to oppose the policy of the party. But even had the Editor differed from Baldwin and Chamberlain, he would have argued that it is no use telling politicians to do what politicians had decided is utterly impossible. There is force in the argument, except to an Editor who has made his newspaper an instrument that creates conditions in which a statesman might decide otherwise.

To assist a Government of whatever complexion to find a national policy had become one of the important functions of *The Times*. This, however, is a function that was not performed, as Dawson and B.-W. endeavoured, by simply advocating half-measures on every occasion, or sitting on the fence and softening rearmament into " re-equipment " or " the thorough organization of British resources." It was essentially a positive task, and it demanded in the thirties both a sense of history strong enough to relate the circumstances of the day to those of the past, and to distinguish permanent national interests from temporary party expedients, and a broad enough view of contemporary politics to enable *The Times* to indicate in what direction history was tending.

But, it was held, so long as political man acts from a sense of his immediate interest, and not from ideological belief or metaphysical speculation, the daily newspaper that desires to influence that sense must comment accordingly, and abstain from prophetical or philosophical analysis or exposition. In consequence the paper's comments on day-to-day policy during the critical period were bound hand and foot by political expediency and personal loyalty, whereas its usefulness depended on an ability to stand aloof from contemporary politics and politicians, and note the direction in which the world was moving, and why. *The Times* should rather have performed the service, indispensable in this democracy, of defining clearly the decisions which had to be taken, and setting forth the worse as well as the better implications of policies adopted by the Government. Instead, the paper, like the country, adopted the

Government's policy with " a general measure of agreement."
It would be a mistake to suppose that the office regularly
followed ministerial suggestions, though it did so when Ministers
were pressed by public opinion in Britain and in the Dominions.
Pressure of this kind was nothing like so strong before 1914 as
since. This difference in the pre-1914 attitude of the paper
compared with that of pre-1939 had its main root in the
increased respect accorded to popular sentiment. Already
strengthened by the concessions made to Labour during the war,
democratic pressure achieved paramount influence through
Baldwin's extension of the franchise in 1928. Backed by Liberal
intellectuals and Conservative squires, the effect upon the
Government and upon *The Times* in point of foreign policy was
disastrous.

After 1936 it was too late for *The Times* to demand that Britain
and the Commonwealth should abandon their conceptions of
a Germany that had never existed, to argue against one-sided
disarmament as a contribution to " peace," or to insist upon a
clear statement of the limits of concession. Missing this last
chance, *The Times*, like Ministers, the country generally and the
Commonwealth, were all unwilling to face the hard fact that
peace is not to be had by peoples who allow their Ministers
and their newspapers to tell them that it can be had without an
industrial and financial effort only less burdensome than war
itself. But this was precisely what the British nation insisted
upon. The British Prime Minister and his party Whips, and
The Times were convinced that in the existing state of opinion
in the constituencies emphasis upon defence was impolitic.
The Times was sure that to let Labour in must make matters
worse. In sum, therefore, Printing House Square, like the
Government, was helpless in the face of an apparently
isolationist Commonwealth and a pacifist Britain. Years of
difficulties with France had increased sympathy for Germany,
and the romantic appeal of almost everything German to so
many English minds, including Dawson's and B.-W.'s, made
The Times so pro-German after 1922 that the paper could not, in
1936, even consider the necessity to modify its policy.

*   *   *

It is not exact to say that *The Times* omitted to draw attention
to defence needs. The paper did so regularly, but to little purpose.
All its leaders on rearmament were expressed in terms too general
and unemphatic to create the necessary sense of urgency. When
Chamberlain, to his lasting credit, was trying in 1935 to force

Baldwin to action, the paper gave him scant support : " The necessity of spending on defence is bound in any case to be as distasteful to the public as it is to the Government ; but if the public are once convinced of its necessity and of the desire to make it as little burdensome as possible, they will rally, as they did before, to those who have the courage to propose it." (October 4, 1935.) But the " desire to make it as little burdensome as possible " took precedence and the leaders on the subject repeat deceptive safeguarding phrases which, indeed, became typical of the time. The intention was sound enough but as conviction was wanting in the writer it was not conveyed by his articles. The tendency towards inaction in the Cabinet was inadequately resisted, and " the public " remained unconvinced of any necessity to rearm.

On the day the last quoted article appeared, Baldwin addressed a Conservative Conference at Bournemouth. He was most enthusiastically received. The Prime Minister pledged the National Government to continued support of the League of Nations as the preserver of peace in Europe, and spoke in general terms only of the need for British rearmament. *The Times* next day expressed the feeling that the Prime Minister had " never been so unchallenged a leader of his party, so he has never been as certainly the spokesman of his country." The paper approved the Prime Minister's sense of proportion ; he understood that the League existed to restrict the area of hostilities [Abyssinia] not to spread it. The paper agreed that the corollary of the failure to prevent Italian aggression must be the " re-equipment " (the word " armament " was deliberately avoided) of Britain, " so that it may play its full part in upholding League principles." The whole address was reckoned " an exhortation to steadiness at the present and to readiness in the future." The Prime Minister was left unrebuked for failing to convince the public of the necessity of organizing defence. (October 5, 1935.) A later leading article surveyed the problems arising out of inter-Service relations without giving a reminder of the urgency of the situation. The need upon which stress was laid was chiefly for good housekeeping ; to make a scientific analysis of the problems involved in defence in order to avoid unnecessary and futile expenditure.

Nearly a year later, the Prime Minister, speaking at the Lord Mayor's banquet at Guildhall, combined a characteristic condemnation of the folly of competitive armaments with an expressed determination to defend the institutions of this island ; including, as *The Times*, thinking of Hitler, added next

day, "a system in which political hysteria can find no place."
Little more was said. But in the debate on the Address that
same week the Prime Minister was driven to defend his policy
more precisely. Churchill contrasted the rapid growth of
German land and air forces and the inadequacy of British
defences. He wrought havoc with various contradictory
statements made by Baldwin during 1934 and 1935, and
dismissed the suggestion that the Government was hampered in
its defence plans by lack of public support : " The responsibility of
Ministers for public safety is absolute and requires no mandate."
The blame for delay and confusion belonged to the Prime
Minister and the Government alone : " They were decided
only to be undecided, resolved to be irresolute, adamant for
drift, solid for fluidity, all-powerful but impotent " ; the least
the House could do would be to demand a Parliamentary inquiry
into the state of our defences. The Prime Minister, in reply,
feeling himself prevented by reasons of national security from
divulging details of our defences, sought to reassure the House
by affirming that good progress was being made. A late start
was inevitable since " a democracy is always two years behind a
dictator." Proceeding, the Prime Minister warned the House
that he proposed to speak " with an appalling frankness." He
then set himself to deal with the question of a public mandate
for rearmament :

From 1933 I and my friends were all very worried about what was
happening in Europe. You will remember at that time the Disarmament Conference was sitting in Geneva, and there was probably a
stronger pacifist feeling running through this country than at any time
since the War. I am speaking of 1933 and 1934. You will remember
the election at Fulham in the autumn of 1933, when a seat which the
National Government held was lost by about 7,000 votes on no issue
but the pacifist, and that the National Government candidate, who
made a most guarded reference to the question of defence, was mobbed
for it. That was the feeling that was in the country in 1933. My
position as the leader of a great party was not altogether a comfortable
one. I asked myself what chance was there within the next year or
two of that feeling being so changed that the country would give a
mandate for rearmament. Supposing I had gone to the country and
said that Germany was rearming and that we must rearm—does
anybody think that this pacific democracy would have rallied to that
cry at that moment ? I cannot think of anything that would have made
the loss of the election from my point of view more certain.

The leading article in *The Times* on November 13 expressed
the view that the Prime Minister had not entirely satisfied the

House, mainly because he did not realize the strong desire in the Services and outside for a Ministry of Supply; nor was the Government's exposition of policy "altogether adequate," though Inskip's facts and figures were "significant." The article left unnoticed his "appalling frankness" over the Fulham by-election, and concluded by resisting a vast expansion of the Army, and its fulfilment by conscription in the event of another war, as many soldiers were contemplating. *The Times* opposed to the soldier's view that of the statesman, whose responsibility it is "to take both a wider and a longer view," to determine how far the maximum effort in one sphere can be reconciled with the needs of other spheres, to "look beyond the military victory" and to ensure that the steps taken for "this purpose" do not overstrain the fabric of the nation and damage its future. (November 13, 1936.)

The timing of this article was unfortunate. Next day Hitler repudiated the clauses of the Versailles Treaty governing inland waterways. Although the point of this was that the clauses governed the use of the Kiel Canal, *The Times* of the 16th, while denouncing the theatricality of the action, took care to show its sympathy with Germany. "The whole system was as unilateral, and therefore as indefensible, as the disarmament clauses. Unlike them, however, it was already in process of being modified to meet well-founded German objections." (November 16, 1936.) A second leading article in the same issue, however, took delayed notice of the charge that the Government had delayed rearmament for two years after Baldwin had become aware of its necessity. The leader agreed that democracies must be persuaded and cannot be dragooned, but mildly suggested that "certain preparations for expansion, at small cost and without any sort of panic-mongering" might have been put in hand. On the whole, the paper accepted the Government's optimism, and believed that a Parliamentary inquiry, as sought by Churchill, would do more harm than good since it would endanger the existing national unity. No correspondence on the subject of the debate was published, and no account given of public reaction to it. All the leading article of the 16th would concede was that Baldwin's reply to the charge of delay "has clearly been misunderstood," but that this was so "very largely because of the language which he used to express it." (November 16, 1936.)

The Editor remained personally and editorially loyal to Baldwin, whom he extolled as a Prime Minister who had "never [before] been as certainly the spokesman of his country." Dawson's first principle of policy was to back a Prime Minister with whom he was in substantial agreement and who was substantially supported by public opinion. That was Dawson's fixed conception of editorial independence and editorial responsibility, as the matter presented itself in his second innings. Neither Baldwin nor Dawson appreciated the fact that the policy of appeasement, without armament, involved the gravest risks to security. Unenlightened public opinion was sovereign master of the Government and of *The Times.*

Only Hitler's march into Austria made the paper say that " No country, least of all our own, can afford to be lulled into false security." The warning would have been given much earlier had the foreign policy been directed by men like Chirol and Saunders who were equipped with a real knowledge of Germany. There were several in the office forty years earlier who knew Germany well ; rather too well for the Germans as they themselves confessed. Such men (Steed was the last journalist and Crowe the last official) had been few in England for more than a generation. The mass of English politicians and most journalists before the turn of the century and since knew little of Germany ; and, after 1919, less. Baldwin, Chamberlain and Halifax possessed no deep knowledge of the European continent. They, like Dawson, were interested in the wider world of the Asian, Australasian and American continents. Exactly as Bülow reported from Windsor in 1899, when he accompanied the Kaiser on his visit to Queen Victoria, it could be said in 1938 that " the British politicians know little of the Continent. Many of them do not know much more of Continental circumstances than we do of conditions in Peru or Siam. They are also, according to our ideas, rather naive in their artless egotism, as well as a certain blind confidence. They find difficulty in believing in really evil intentions in others ; they are very calm, very phlegmatic, very optimistic." Bülow added that, in 1899, the general feeling in England was more favourable to Germany than the feeling in Germany was to England. This, too, was the fact in 1938. " Therefore those Englishmen who, like Chirol and Saunders, knew from personal observation the acuteness and depth of Germany's unfortunate dislike of Britain, are the most dangerous to us," Bülow had then correctly reported. And, moreover, " If the British public realized the feeling reigning just now in Germany, it would cause a great change in their view of the relationship between England and that country."[1]

[1] Bülow to Hohenlohe, November 24, 1899. See Vol. III, p. 307.

The ruling powers of Britain from 1923 to 1938 were certainly naive and blindly confident; they too had difficulty in believing in really evil intentions of others. Hitler had the advantage over Bülow that he could, as Bülow dared not, affront *The Times* by expelling the paper's Berlin Correspondent. Dawson and his friends outside the office, with no successor to Chirol, Saunders, Steed or Williams inside the office to warn them, propagated their naivety and confidence among a self-deluded public.

*   *   *

The point had been reached at which public opinion was in direct conflict with public interest. The theory, inherited from the nineteenth century, that the electorate is a body of rational beings accustomed to weigh evidence, reaching conclusions and translating them into political effect on or before election day, was out of date. A new factor introduced itself when an electorate, itself almost coterminous with the public before 1914, was suddenly and largely increased by Baldwin in 1928. It was this huge and ignorant body of opinion that was asked, by an extra-electoral ballot, questions on foreign policy which did not lie within its knowledge and could not do so unless a Prime Minister, a Foreign Secretary, or a journalist of the right dimension and quality, would undertake to educate, inform and arouse it as to the risks of its situation.

In the early nineteenth century when the opinion common among the possessors of the franchise began to be viewed as a force bound eventually to find expression in the House of Commons, and all parties were assumed to have an interest in conforming to it, it was understood, even at the time, to entail risks to the State. It was recognized by *The Times*, then, that influence upon electoral opinion entailed increased vigilance and responsibility upon editors and journalists—if they were to rise above the pocket editors of the eighteenth century. Barnes was well aware of the dangers to the responsible journalism he was striving to create when Croker could argue in 1829 that " the day is not far distant when you will (not *see* nor *hear*) but *know* that there is someone in the Cabinet entrusted with what will be thought one of the most important duties of the State, the regulation of public opinion." It was this " regulation of public opinion," that *The Times* then wished to wrest from the hands of " someone in the Cabinet " and itself exercise—discreetly but freely. Barnes's successful struggle against Croker's doctrine and plan was his greatest contribution to journalism and to England. While the Whigs and Radicals were agitating for the "freedom" of the Press, meaning relief from taxation, Barnes was concentrating upon the vital point, the "credit" of the Press, meaning freedom from indoctrination. The "regulation of public opinion" by a Government bureau, he used to say, was a thousand times more degrading to the Press than any taxation under which it might suffer. Barnes's idea of an Editor, rather, was that through his newspaper, be it the *Examiner*, or *The Times*, he should inform, instruct and encourage public opinion to act in the line of its duty and in the defence of its interest. Such a principle of editorship was bound to entail conflict with party, and with much else that Englishmen so greatly value. The accusation of disloyalty was often hurled at the "Turnabout," but the principle of preferring public interest to personal loyalty was not given up by Barnes or Delane. By 1848 Clarendon could say, "I don't care a straw what any other newspaper thinks or says. They are all regarded on the Continent as representing persons or cliques, but *The Times* is considered to be the exponent of what English public opinion is or will be and as it is thought that whatever public opinion determines with us, the Government ultimately does, an extraordinary and universal importance attaches to the views of *The Times*." [1] In the time of Clarendon "public opinion" was neither vast in extent, ignorant of the national interest nor lacking in firmness of will. Nor was *The Times* backward in correcting the tendency of public opinion to sink into complacency and torpor.

This conception of the function of *The Times* as " the exponent of what English public opinion is or will be " on foreign affairs is well stated in a letter to Granville who had reported to Reeve that Louis Napoleon was " irritated and annoyed beyond measure by the language of *The Times*." Reeve's reasoned reply, approved by Delane, included a statement of principle which is vitally important to the conception of a free Press, and above all to the type of journalism practised at Printing House Square:

The responsibility of journalists is in proportion to the liberty they enjoy. No moral obligation can be graver. But their duties are not the same, I think, as those of statesmen. To find out the true state of facts, to report them with fidelity, to apply to them strict and fixed principles of justice, humanity, and law, to inform, as far as possible, the very conscience of nations and to call down the judgement of the world on what is false, or base, or tyrannical, appear to me to be the

[1] Clarendon to Henry Reeve, June 18, 1848. See Vol. II, Chapter V, " *The Times* and Lord Aberdeen, 1841-1855," p. 92.

first duties of those who write. Those upon whom the greater part of political action devolves are necessarily governed by other rules.

The conclusion may be applied to the conditions obtaining nearly a century after Louis Napoleon.

This nation is a good deal enervated by a long peace, by easy habits of intercourse, by peace societies and false economy. To surmount the dangerous consequences of such a state, the Government will require the support of public opinion, and that can only be obtained by convincing our countrymen of the truth that we have now a dangerous and faithless neighbour. Happen what may, there is nothing so important as to sustain a tone of moral independence among the people of England, who will grudge no sacrifices if they are convinced that the principles they cherish are even indirectly threatened from abroad.[1]

To sustain " a tone of " moral vigour among the people will always remain a task. Indeed as Reeve said, " nothing is so important," and clearly, if statesmen decline it, as the desire of re-election may induce them, it necessarily becomes a task for journalists, above all when the electorate is expanded. As John Walter III put it, although journalists may aspire to be statesman-like, their responsibility is not to Governments, home or foreign, but to the instructed reader ; and hence, *The Times* said, the journalist is " daily and for ever appealing to the enlightened force of public opinion." He does this by making all he knows the property of the nation, whereas the statesman's habit (it might even be his duty, *The Times* conceded) is to keep most of what he knows to himself. But, however essential to statesmen " concealment, evasion . . . the surrender of convictions to party objects, and the systematic pursuit of expediency " may be, they are " absolutely destructive to the credit, the power, and the success of a public writer. . . ." Hence " of all journals, and of all writers, those will obtain the largest measure of public support who have told the truth most constantly and most fearlessly." (February 6, 1852.) To John Walter III and Delane the demeanour of *The Times* towards public opinion eighty years after their day would have appeared incomprehensible. They would have estimated the behaviour of both parties, and of the paper, after the by-election at East Fulham, as an abject surrender of conviction to demagogy and a contemptible pursuit of expediency. A Conservative majority of 14,521 was converted into a Labour pacifist majority of 4,480.[2]

---

[1] Reeve to Granville, January 17, 1852. See Volume II, Chapter VIII, " Journalism Defined," p. 149.

[2] Delane would have noted that the electorate counted 5,000 more women voters than men.

The risks of uninstructed democratic voting were less well observed after 1923 than they had been a century earlier. In the time of Croker, and of Lowe the risks were new. The increase in the electorate between 1831 and 1833 that startled Croker was 49 per cent. ; bringing the total to 652,777. In Lowe's time, between 1866 and 1869, there was an increase of 88 per cent. ; between 1883 and 1885, 67 per cent. The votes cast in 1885 amounted to 4,380,540. In 1918 the number was five times as great, and a representative section of this was the mass, for the most part uninstructed, that voted at East Fulham. So far from any challenge to security being recognized as implicit in large scale enfranchisement, or a danger to be guarded against by educational or other means, in 1928 the second Baldwin Government accorded the vote to a new class, called the "flapper vote" on account of the large number of young women whom it enfranchised. The act that brought the number of voters at the 1929 election to 28,500,000 was unaccompanied by any move to instruct them in issues of national significance. No such machinery existed ; no Croker, nor any journalist substitute was at hand. Obviously, if public opinion in 1831 needed in Croker's opinion to be " regulated," and in 1866 in Lowe's opinion to be " educated," it needed in 1929 at least to be given a lead. And this was no easy matter at the time either for statesmen or publicists.

In formulating foreign policy a modern British democratic government has to do more than attract the support of the electorate conceived as a mass of isolated individuals. It also has to secure the backing of organized economic interests and vigorously supported philanthropic societies powerful in the Prime Minister's own party councils. A Government has to be careful not to press the loyalty of its own party members too far. It has also to remember that its pledges may have to be carried out by the opposing party. If its foreign policy requires considerable rearmament it has to be sure of the support of both sides of industry for the reorganization of national economic life which rearmament entails. These difficulties, well enough understood in the days of Delane, became greater with the later expansion of industry and of the electorate. The balance between economic interests, philanthropic societies, and the power of the State to " educate," " lead " or " regulate " public opinion was altered. The power of the Press as a whole to exercise these functions was diminished. It was possible for *The Times* under Barnes, with a circulation which dominated that of all other newspapers combined, to create a public opinion hostile to the Government, and to risk a Government " war with *The Times* " in 1835. Delane could afford a second Government " war with *The Times* " in 1855. But though these " wars " strengthened the paper in its moral vigour, its circulation became relatively less in the new epoch of a cheap Press.[1] John Walter III's decision in 1865 not to compete for circulation with the " New Journalism " but to maintain the influence of *The Times* over the already educated and politically effective element in the country necessarily confined the paper's influence to an elite, and even this influence needed to be sought at an enhanced price in comparison with its competitors.[2] The sale of Delane's last issue, November 9, 1877, was only 60,886. The competing newspapers with higher and rising circulations did not succeed in making themselves financially stable, and were, for the most part, compelled to accept party subsidy and direction. It was the second Walter and Barnes who put an end to the eighteenth-century system of managing the Press through Government and party subsidy ; it was Northcliffe who organized his own system of the " management of politicians " by his own Press. In his " management " of politicians (whose company he was careful to avoid) and of public opinion (which he strove to dominate) he had the enormous and unique advantage of controlling the *Daily Mail*, the *Evening News* and the *Weekly Dispatch*, as well as *The Times*. After Northcliffe the power of the Press sensibly diminished.

No journalist before Northcliffe or since had ever brought so formidable an engine of publicity to bear upon political events and personalities. He was at all times ready to stand up to uninstructed public opinion. As Northcliffe died without securing the continuity of his system, politicians have not since had reason to fear " Fleet Street." A nationally important corrective to ministerial inertia and democratic sluggishness disappeared in the period of regrouping and competition in the news trade that began after the death of Northcliffe. No comparable journalistic force, or other national agency, showed itself capable of resisting the prevalent trend towards isolationism and pacifism. As to international affairs, the Press for the most part since Northcliffe, so far from attempting to organize a popular basis for a strong

---

[1] How the Whigs in 1835 and in 1855 discriminated against *The Times*, and succeeded in creating a cheap metropolitan and provincial press is told in Vol. I, Chapter XVIII, " The Whig Offensive " ; Vol. II, Chapter X, " The Second War with *The Times*."

[2] See Vol. II, Chapter XVII, " Price Threepence."

foreign policy, was content to win support in the country for policies already shaped by political parties in conjunction with those preferences and interests on which the parties largely depend. While, therefore, the refusal of statesmen of both parties to face the facts placed squarely upon the Press the responsibility, formerly claimed and exercised by the " Fourth Estate," of " conducting public opinion " in Barnes's sense, the journalists were not strong enough, numerous enough, or well-informed enough to discharge that duty. *The Times* itself was not as concerned in 1933 as it had been in 1866 to instruct, inform and energize the nation by reporting the true state of the facts ; to " brace " the will of a people enervated " by peace societies and false economy " ; or to convince it " of the truth that we have now a dangerous and faithless neighbour."

It is fair to allow that years of depression had not failed to make their mark upon journalism. How difficult it was for a newspaper to win effective support for a policy of its own was indicated by the failure of Lord Rothermere and Lord Beaverbrook, who were agreed upon isolation and also upon the urgency of rearmament, to make the right impression on British foreign policy. They succeeded in strengthening the policy of isolation but failed to reverse the policy of disarmament. In consequence, at the critical time of 1936 even the more responsible sections of the electorate were confused by a fundamental conflict over the purposes and nature of foreign policy. There were those who took the traditional view that it should be primarily directed towards maintaining British interests and preserving the balance of power, and others who held that it should be directed to the maintenance of international law and to the support of liberal, and democratic régimes everywhere. This conflict over doctrine, however, was not so serious as the conflict over practice. A few took the old-fashioned view of British policy and believed in resisting German and Italian aggression on the ground that they threatened Britain's survival, while most stood for collective security but were unwilling to contemplate military resistance to aggression anywhere at any time. In such a confused state the intelligent part of the community drifted with the rest, and the Government and the most part of the daily Press with it. In sum, Imperial isolationism, British pacifism and industrial depression had proved too much for the policy-makers, whether statesmen or journalists. They proceeded to place totally unwarranted faith in the good neighbourliness of a rearmed Germany and the moral authority of an unarmed Britain. Finally, Ministers who were so weak in the face of public opinion proved all too strong for the great metropolitan daily Press. *The Times* was no exception. The paper was ill-fitted to challenge ministerial policy even had it wished.

*   *   *

The Editor accepted unhesitatingly—it might be an exaggeration to say enthusiastically—the reports of the Empire Prime Ministers that their respective electorates were positively opposed to war with Germany. Dawson's other friends, chosen with circumspection, were like-minded. Although, as far as the office was concerned, he was careful to maintain and wherever possible extend the Editor's personal power, he saw no need to organize and to preside over an inquiry into the facts upon which a realistic policy towards Germany might be based. Rather he was a man of subtle intuition, and great loyalty, naturally sensitive and willing to respect the consensus of opinion among his approved friends. These formed in his mind, and in his writing, the body of " thoughtful Englishmen " and Dominion friends to whom was due, he believed, a respect greater even than the foreign Correspondents of *The Times* could claim.[1] Mr. Menzies' words, spoken in Melbourne, might have been those of Dawson and his friends. "Britons should uphold their reputation for fair play " for " Germany might never have had a dictatorship if the Western Powers had shown more sympathy and understanding." (See *The Times*, September 11, 1938.) This, too, was a sentiment that would have been echoed by Mackenzie King. Had there been any doubt in Dawson's mind, Menzies' latest utterances and King's earlier statements would have disposed of it. It was a governing consideration ever present to Dawson and B.-W. that Imperial and national unity were absolutely essential before going to war could even be thought of. Dawson was old enough to remember not only the dissensions of August, 1914, but of the enduring division of opinion over the South African War. Moreover, Dawson, like the " thoughtful Englishmen " of his select acquaintance, did not believe that it was their business, or that of *The Times*, to challenge the trends prevailing in the Dominions or the British Isles. He was not convinced that Germany was determined to dominate Europe and defy Britain

---

[1] *Cf.* the leading article (Dawson writing) in *The Times* on the German march into Austria : " In the immediate matter of Austria they [the readers of *The Times*] will not depart from the view, which has been common to most thoughtful Englishmen, that she [Austria] was destined sooner or later to find herself in close association with the German Reich." This being so, " There would have been no British protest if this process of attraction had developed naturally through growing confidence and mutual goodwill." Such a view of the situation did not represent the consensus of opinion held by the Berlin, Paris and Vienna Correspondents.

and bring down the Empire. Thus *The Times* made no contribution to a strong British foreign policy, no effort to influence the Dominions.

The consequence was that Great Britain in 1938 had to face the responsibilities of a world Power in the knowledge that her ability to participate in a world war depended on the support of a number of distant States, bound to her by intangible ties which, however powerful in an emergency, were not strong enough to make a consistent Commonwealth policy easy to formulate. The point where Britain was immediately threatened, *i.e.*, in Europe, was of less obvious importance to the Dominions, and Britain's instinct of national self-preservation was constantly checked by the far slower reactions of other members of the Commonwealth.

Great credit is due to the men whose careers are set out in this work, principally in the third volume, for the degree of thoroughness, unsurpassed in journalism, with which they surveyed the problems of Australia, Canada, India, Ireland and South Africa beside those of Europe. At no time after 1887 did *The Times* disregard the problems set by these divided communities, some large, some small, some old, others young, but all evolving into many nations, yet united by sentiment and language to a distant parent who was under pressure from a European neighbour. After all this study, the theory of British Empire relations developed in the epoch begun by separate Dominion representation at the Peace Conference proved inadequate to the European strains set up in the ensuing two decades of revisionism. Whether it would have been possible for Great Britain and France, without Dominion support, to tackle the German armed forces of 1938, whether Imperial unity would have survived such a campaign had it been waged, and whether Imperial unity was more important than the maintenance of the integrity of Czechoslovakia, are questions which will probably never be answered. For Dawson, opposed to theorizing about the relations of the Dominions with each other and all of them, separately or together, with Great Britain, improvization on an empirical basis seemed the only " theory." It was likely to produce the best results in the present because it had done so in the past. An awkward fact was glossed over : the German realization that the time to apply pressure to Britain was before any such consolidation of Empire strength could occur. Thus the basic problem of the post-Versailles epoch—how to use the machinery of Dominion consultation as a means of securing an effective policy towards aggressive Powers, and of strengthening

British and Commonwealth defences in accordance with it—was left unsolved until the outbreak of war forced it upon those who had been unwilling to face it.

The immensity of this basic problem is illustrated in the affectionate letter Dawson wrote to Neville Chamberlain, then desperately ill. A letter written in such circumstances is not to be looked at as a political document but it cannot be doubted that Dawson's second paragraph accurately represents his view and recounts his experience, though he might, in other circumstances, have expressed himself in other terms.

8th November, 1940.

My dear Neville,

I was grieved indeed to hear from Edward [Halifax] with whom I have been lunching, that he had found you so stricken when he went to see you yesterday. I had hoped that before long you would be back in your place in Parliament and seeing this appalling conflict through to its only possible conclusion.

You did your best to avert it—far more than any other man would have dared to do. As I told you when I last saw you—how short a time ago it seems—I shall always be an impenitent supporter of what is called the " Munich policy." No one who sat in this place, as I did during the autumn of '38, with almost daily visitations from eminent Canadians and Australians, could fail to realize that war with Germany at that time would have been misunderstood and resented from end to end of the Empire. Even in this country there would have been no unity behind it. We know now that it was inevitable sooner or later ; but we owe it all to you that it was later rather than sooner and that we are assuredly going to win it.

I don't know where you are—I didn't ask Edward any questions —but your faithful Hendriks tells me that he sends you letters, and I feel moved to send you a line of cheer and sympathy to-night.

Bless you for all that you have done for this country.

Yours ever,

[GEOFFREY.][1]

The Right Hon. Neville Chamberlain, M.P.

* * *

The recognition by the Editor that war " was inevitable sooner or later " came after it had broken out. Dawson's instinctive respect for Commonwealth opinion apart, his attitude towards the possibility of war after 1933 had two main causes. First, the Editor's habit of centralizing his authority over the newspaper

[1] Printed from the copy in Printing House Square papers.

was so strong that he abstained from reappointing a Foreign Editor and a Military Correspondent at the effective time; and the same habit made him underrate the value of the reports of his European Correspondents. Secondly, the degree to which the Editor shared the confidences and intimacies of Ministers led him to connive at Baldwin's subservience to party expediency and his indifference to State security. This, more than any other factor, created the situation in which Chamberlain had and could have no policy other than that of continued British concession after persistent German aggression. Dawson, like Baldwin's successor, is necessarily involved in the discredit attaching to the inevitable collapse of such a policy, or rather, substitute for policy. It is just to add that the paper, possessing a degree of freedom higher than any Minister's, incurred a correspondingly greater degree of discredit. Every Editor has the duty to see Ministers and runs the risks of becoming intimate with them. Dawson was apt to ignore these risks. It will be seen from the accounts given of the Anglo-German policy of *The Times*,[1] and of the Abdication policy,[2] that Dawson gave an extreme interpretation to his often expressed doctrine of using his freedom to support any statesman with whose policy he chose to agree. The constitution of 1922 under which the Editor, once chosen and appointed, was responsible for the political direction of the paper so long as he held the confidence of the Chief Proprietors relieved the latter of any duty to make a regular inquiry into policy. Moreover, Astor was a " new boy "; and although he had come into the office in order to " secure as far as possible the continued independence of one great journal,"[3] it could not be expected of him that he should quickly and fully understand the means of safeguarding that " independence " which he with Walter had undertaken to secure. He understood the importance of the traditional aloofness of the paper from politicians of all parties, but it was impossible to foresee the full implications of the " free hand " that the new constitution gave the Editor.

Walter's case was different. He had come into the office straight from Oxford in 1898, and was soon immersed in the troubles his father was having with Dr. Sibley and the small proprietors, which culminated ten years later in the quarrel with Moberly Bell and the sale of the paper, as described in the previous volume. By his father's death in 1910 he had become Chairman of the Company and Northcliffe's partner in the

[1] See Chapters XXI, XXIII, XXIV, above.
[2] See Appendix I below.
[3] J. J. Astor, " The Future of *The Times* " in the *Empire Review*. (London, June 1923.)

direction of the paper. Between two such diverse characters no easy cooperation could be looked for and, after twelve years of an association that had proved mutually disappointing, Walter, worn out by Northcliffe's daemonic energy and autocratic temper, was moved to sell him the family interest, thus leaving him the sole master in P.H.S. It was inevitable therefore, as Astor's partner, that Walter should look forward, with him, to a period of tranquillity for the paper under an experienced Editor of precisely the type they both desired. Thus, both Astor and Walter, while conscientiously acquitting themselves of their several duties as Co-Chief Proprietors, felt free to follow their personal duties, Astor at Westminster, and Walter at Bearwood. The preceding chapters prove that this self-effacement of the Co-Chief Proprietors was not to the advantage of the paper. Their detachment encouraged Dawson's tendency towards centralization, and was a contributory cause of the resulting errors of policy.

While it is true that the arrangement that the Proprietors made with Dawson permitted the former as a matter of course to discuss affairs at all times, it is also true that such discussions were in fact too uncustomary to be of use at the effective time. And, had they done so, the Editor could have pointed out that the policy of Ministers was being emphatically backed by public opinions of all parties. Astor was still M.P. (Cons.) for Dover and therefore bound to give general support to Baldwin and Chamberlain. Walter, it has been seen, remonstrated with the Editor on his German policy but did not press his point. The Editor's personal attachment to Ministers remained unchallenged throughout his second innings.

*   *   *   *

B.-W.'s short Editorship was infused by a belief in independence toward Ministers and in a strict sense of justice. With him justice was a principle of individual, national and international obligation ; not an item of his policy, but an article of his creed, loyalty to which in national and international affairs served him in the place of an ideology. That writing in newspapers is a way of getting something done reasonably quickly was his definition of the function of journalism. He was in consequence a firm upholder, first, of the principle of writing to serve the day, and secondly, of the principle of conducting *The Times* on an empirical basis. He had not his predecessor's instinct for politics without policy provided the Conservative party was in power. His objection to " viewyness " was not less strong than

Dawson's, but its less narrow basis gave B.-W. the freedom to support the Labour party in advance of the election that brought them to power. This support was an aspect of the belief in justice that he had made his rule.

It was this rule that led him, when the Nazis took power, to continue his demand for consideration for such grievances of the German people as had won recognition five years earlier. In B.-W.'s opinion, expressed in 1933, those principally responsible for unsettlement in Europe were Clemenceau, Poincaré and Barthou, whose policy of injustice to Germany gave her after 1933 a Government no less offensive to democratic sentiment than that of Russia. Even after 1933 justice to Germany was due because it was right; so was patience, because it was necessary. Hence, B.-W., like Dawson, was eager to support Baldwin and Chamberlain, who were, he thought, as rightly doubtful of German determination to dominate as Churchill was wrongly convinced of it. Again, like Dawson, ready to discuss differences, B.-W. did not go out of his way to seek the company of those opposed by principle, doctrine, or instinct, to the policy of concession to Germany. If the light of history shows both men to have been wrong, it should be remembered that few members of parliament, politicians or journalists saw the issue differently.

Examples of misjudgement as to foreign affairs are acknowledged in these pages with fidelity as to the political facts and candour as to the editorial writers. The organ that has consistently, since the time of the second Walter and Thomas Barnes, upheld the dignity of political newspaper writing, may not, in the writing of its own History, pursue any other course than resolute self-examination; for " We are bold enough," said *The Times* almost a century ago, " to place the duties and power of a man, be he ever so humble, who contributes to form aright the public opinion of this nation not far below the worth of those who have served the State with honour."

APPENDIX I: THE ABDICATION

THE King's matter, referred to in Chapter XXIII, "Appeasement," was familiar in outline to the office; or, to be precise, to the Editor and his Chief Assistant. Dawson was acquainted with it through the Prime Minister, and B.-W. through an informed source, herein referred to as A. The question of newspaper publicity in Britain became urgent by October, 1936, when Mrs. Simpson's petition for divorce was due to be heard. American Press comment and conjecture became an increasingly disturbing factor. The King made up his mind to anticipate an outbreak of sensationalism in the home Press by consulting expert advisers. A consultation with Lord Beaverbrook took place on October 16. Beaverbrook then saw Mr. Esmond Harmsworth (now the 2nd Viscount Rothermere), who called a meeting of the London and Provincial Press at Warwick House, St. James's.[1] *The Times*, the *Morning Post* and the *Daily Telegraph* were not invited, as their discretion was not in question. Beaverbrook and Harmsworth at that time had no suspicion that the King had already decided to marry Mrs. Simpson, whenever she should be free. They simply told their Press colleagues, therefore, of the King's anxiety lest Mrs. Simpson's forthcoming petition should involve unpleasant publicity and announced that their newspapers, when the time came, were pledged to give bare reports of the case, with no hint that it possessed any more interest than the hundreds of other undefended petitions heard each year in the Courts. The meeting responded sympathetically to the suggestion that the King's friendship with Mrs. Simpson, though well known to Fleet Street, was strictly a part of his private life, with which his subjects had no concern. Provincial and Irish papers not represented at the conference were energetically tackled by telephone, and Beaverbrook and Harmsworth received unanimous promises of cooperation. The King's anxiety to avoid scandal was shared by A., for on October 19 a memorandum by B.-W. records that he had

Before dinner a call from A. More about the case and the Press. My advice: don't ask for suppression but for no prominence, and no

---

[1] In *A King's Story* (New York, Putnam, 1947) the Duke of Windsor states (p. 317): "With the co-operation of Esmond Harmsworth and several others he [Beaverbrook] achieved the miracle I desired—a 'gentlemen's agreement' among newspaper editors to report the case without sensation. The British Press kept its word and for that I shall always be grateful."

connexion with H.M. Indeed, in an ordinary case, such treatment would be grossly unfair and would go near libel on the third party.

On October 20 the King received the Prime Minister. The matter raised was the King's friendship with Mrs. Simpson, and the Prime Minister said that the criticisms of the American Press were such as to endanger the position of the Monarchy and that in his opinion it would be well if Mrs. Simpson's divorce action due to be heard on October 27 at the Ipswich Assizes were not proceeded with. The King, however, was not asked whether he intended to marry Mrs. Simpson. Perturbed by Baldwin's intervention, the King consulted Sir Walter Monckton and discussed his present situation and his future with him, including the possibility of his abdicating.

Towards the end of October, 1936, a British subject living in East Orange, New Jersey, wrote to the Editor saying he was much distressed by the " poisonous publicity attending the King's friendship with Mrs. Simpson." He documented his letter with accounts from the American Press, in which the King's private life was the object of sordid muckraking. The writer felt that British prestige must suffer severely and hinted that abdication was the only course that could prevent a passing evil from becoming lasting.

The Editor was deeply impressed by his correspondent's letter. Taken with the pressure of gossip in London it seemed to justify some action on his part. He decided on the morning of October 26 to give a copy of it to an official in close touch with the King at Buckingham Palace and, later in the day, he gave another copy to the Prime Minister who, Dawson noted in the memorandum he wrote at the time, " then told me, more fully than he ever spoke of later events, about his first private conversation at Fort Belvedere on the previous Tuesday, October 20." Next day, October 27, Mrs. Simpson was granted a decree *nisi* from her husband at Ipswich Assizes on the ground of his adultery. Thus she might be free to marry again if she chose at the end of April, a fortnight before the Coronation of the King on May 12. The news was recorded in *The Times* in thirty lines, without comment, and with colourless headings : UNDEFENDED DIVORCE SUIT | CASE AT IPSWICH ASSIZES. The rest of the British Press showed equal restraint.

During the next few days the Editor had conversations with Neville Chamberlain, Mackenzie King and other statesmen but nothing that he heard induced him to change his mind on the subject of Press publicity. Since his return from holiday in mid-September every post had brought him letters and cuttings on the subject of the King and Mrs. Simpson. There were many anxious requests for editorial comment that would put an end to the mischief or bring it to a head. The Editor felt strongly that *The Times* should be the first to speak, and did not overlook the fact that every day's delay increased the danger of an explosion of opinion elsewhere in the Press, or perhaps in the pulpit. But as long as the King had not definitely committed himself to the projected marriage, the Editor did not feel justified in publishing comment that would inevitably embarrass the Royal Family, and might finally wreck the Prime Minister's delicate negotiations. His first discussion on the matter with another journalist occurred on November 10, when Sir Arnold Wilson, editor of the *Nineteenth Century*, said he was prepared " to explode " in his December number. After talking it over with Dawson he changed his mind.

Next day the Editor saw the Archbishop of Canterbury who said he was deliberately standing apart from the controversy. That night (November 11) and the next night, the Prime Minister discussed with the Editor the possibility of appropriate publicity, and the time for initiating it. As demonstrations were likely during the King's impending visit to South Wales and to the Fleet, the Editor felt that newspaper criticism that began before these engagements might be taken as an advance attempt to undermine His Majesty's popularity : if immediately after them, as an attempt to minimize his influence. The Editor noted in his memorandum that

It was a very difficult problem, on which S.B. professed himself quite unable to give advice. The Press is an unknown world to him, and he wondered vaguely, supposing that it should ever become necessary for him to explain the position to the newspapers as a whole, what machinery was available for his use. As things turned out, the necessity never arose, and S.B. was able to keep his confidences for the House of Commons.

The Prime Minister's professed ignorance of newspapers, and his representation of the Press as " an unknown world to him " need not imply that he had at hand no colleague able to render some assistance in this regard. In fact, Baldwin had at call a member of the Cabinet more than ordinarily capable of acting for him with the leaders of the Press. When he found the subject was much to the forefront in the mind of the King, the Prime

Minister appointed Sir Samuel Hoare, then First Lord of the Admiralty, to approach the Press. Certainly the risk of a broad split in the Press, and a huge national debate, was close enough to press Baldwin and Hoare to great energy. The task was no light one, for Churchill was in the field on the King's side. Baldwin, however, succeeded in winning Attlee's support. Thereupon Churchill and Beaverbrook, on the other side, found that Lord Southwood, in consequence of Attlee's intervention, was unable to keep his promise to support the King. However, neither side wished to break silence. *The Times* was still disposed to avoid the subject. But the matter could hardly be allowed to drift. On November 13, the Prime Minister and the inner Cabinet met to discuss possible action in view of the likelihood of a clash over the King's intentions towards Mrs. Simpson. On that day, also, the King's Private Secretary who was in close touch with Baldwin, asked the Editor to call. He said he was drafting what the Editor later described as a " courageous " letter. Hardinge considered it his duty to warn the King of the critical situation in which he might soon find himself. The Press might break silence at any moment and the resignation of the Government in the event of a clash of opinion, might leave the King unable to form a new one. Hardinge further shocked the King by suggesting that Mrs. Simpson should go abroad and immediately. The newspapers were obviously feeling an acute sense of embarrassment. Neither the King nor the Prime Minister could expect Proprietors or Editors to hold their hand much longer. There was a formal consultation in the Office after Dawson had seen the Private Secretary on Friday (November 13) and heard about the letter to the King.

Dawson then went to spend the week-end as the guest of Lord Stanhope at Chevening. Here, too, was Walter Runciman, who assured the Editor that while most of the Cabinet were " sound " the situation was anxious and the Free Churches were getting restive, &c. Baldwin was due to see the King on Monday. On Sunday morning (November 15) an American newspaper correspondent telephoned to Dawson at Chevening to say that an alleged interview with the Editor of *The Times* was a feature of the Press of his country that morning. Dawson was reported as denying that the King would marry Mrs. Simpson, and as stating definitely that he would on the contrary marry " a hand-picked Balkan princess." Other reporters were waiting for the Editor in London, and he explained to them that the " interview " was probably a perversion of one of the soothing letters he had earlier sent to unknown correspondents in the United States and Canada. This simple and truthful explanation was in most cases accepted, and no more was heard of the matter.

It was obvious, notwithstanding, that it was becoming more difficult to maintain silence in England. H. A. Gwynne asked for a talk on November 16, and made it clear that the *Morning Post* would not voluntarily break the silence of the British Press. That was, in the circumstances, a gain. The Prime Minister saw the King that day and at 10.30 p.m. asked the Editor to visit him at the House of Commons. Dawson found Baldwin unusually depressed and worried. At the interview with the King, His Majesty had declared first his intention to marry Mrs. Simpson and, secondly, his readiness to go. The Prime Minister confided neither of these facts to the Editor, though he admitted that his reason for being depressed was that the situation was grave. He made the point that Press comment at this moment might weaken his influence, such as it was, with the Sovereign. The Editor accepted the Prime Minister's judgment, and privately inferred that abdication was not unlikely. No reference to the matter was deemed possible at the earliest until the visit to South Wales was over. On Tuesday evening (November 17) G.-W. discovered from a certain source that, first, the King seemed to be determined to marry Mrs. Simpson and that she was unlikely to " retire," and secondly that publicity at the moment would turn the probabilities into certainties.

The procedure if an objection to the King's marriage formally came, as it had not yet done, before the Cabinet, was a difficult question in view of the absence of recent precedent. The Prime Minister helped to clear his mind by discussing the problem with the Editor. He saw him on Friday, November 20, with particular reference to the reaction in the country. Next week brought the crisis to head. There were premonitory signs in the Press. On Monday (November 23) the *Daily Mail* revealed its sympathies by contrasting the King's solicitude for the unemployed in South Wales with the indifference of his Ministers. A leader on the impropriety and danger of this attitude appeared in *The Times* next day (November 24). The article emphasized that both Ministry and public were fully alive to the imperative necessity for inducing new industries to settle in the Special Areas; it was right that the King's contribution should be applauded. The Editor thus proceeded :

But it is a wholly mischievous suggestion, and one altogether alien to the spirit of the Constitution, which would set his well-known sympathy with the distressed against the measures taken by the Government, and which by implication would drive a wedge between the Monarch and his Ministers. The King's Ministers are His Majesty's advisers, and to contrast his personal and representative concern for the well-being of a section of the people with the administrative steps of his advisers is a constitutionally dangerous proceeding and would threaten, if continued, to entangle the Throne in politics To write of the King's visit, as one newspaper wrote yesterday under the heading " A Contrast " :—" He went to see for himself, personal investigation being the basis for every job of work the King touches Then, once he had settled in his own mind the extent and urgency of the dilemma, he called for all the evidence available. . . . The contrast to the way in which national questions are customarily approached can escape nobody. . . . How often does a Minister go boldly forth to see for himself and measure a problem by independent judgment, following this with immediate action ? . . . Surely those who have recently confessed that they dared not tell the people the truth . . . will realize the gulf between their conduct and the King's methods in Wales." —to write in that way is to strike at the very root of the Monarchy ; for if the Monarch is to be dissociated, for the purposes of political argument from some actions of his Ministers, then by inference he must bear a more direct responsibility for all the rest. The King's constitutional position is above and apart from party politics, and those who cherish the institution of the Monarchy will always strive to keep it so (November 24, 1936.)

The Prime Minister and the Editor had had a long talk on November 23. It left the Editor with no more real information but he gathered that the Prime Minister hoped there would be no public comment before his next interview with the King which was fixed for November 25. Dawson therefore finished a leader (for the issue of the 25th) on Mr. (later Sir) Patrick Duncan's appointment as Governor-General of the Union of South Africa, and took the occasion to introduce some passages on the importance of keeping the Crown and its representatives remote from " glaring personal scandal " and above " public reproach or ridicule." Whatever significance was read into these remarks at home or abroad, silence was maintained in the British Press.

The Editor learnt from the Prime Minister on the 26th that on the previous day the King had broached the subject of a

morganatic marriage[1] and had asked the Prime Minister to refer
the idea to the Cabinet and the Dominions. This was being
done. The Cabinet met specially on the 27th to pursue the
King's request, three members having to cancel provincial
engagements. The Government let it be thought in the Lobby
that this hurried summons was due to a new turn of events in
Spain, and several newspapers enlarged on that topic. The
Manchester Guardian of the 28th, however, hinted that the
Cabinet had been called to discuss domestic rather than foreign
problems. On Friday evening, knowing that consultations
were proceeding with the Dominion Governments and their
High Commissioners in London, Dawson visited Mr. (later
Viscount) Bruce, who was ill in bed, and discussed with him
the likely reaction in Australia. It became known to the
Editor during the day that the King had recalled Beaverbrook
from his transatlantic holiday (he was going to Arizona) and
that he had spent only four hours in New York between boats.
This news inclined Dawson and B.-W. to think that the leading
article held in storage would be required on Monday or
Tuesday.

Events were, in fact, moving swiftly. Anxiety was felt in Royal
circles, and Dawson received a confidential note on Saturday
from one of the King's entourage urging silence. Mr. Arthur
Mann, Editor of the *Yorkshire Post*, visited Printing House
Square on the Sunday evening, but after learning from Dawson
that an impasse had been reached between the King and the
Prime Minister, did not offer different counsel. Beaverbrook
arrived at Southampton on Friday, November 26, and went
forthwith to Fort Belvedere. On that evening Beaverbrook was
visited by Hoare, who had been sent by Baldwin to say that the
Government were solid with the Prime Minister. Hoare once
more laid stress on Baldwin's desire that there should be an
unbroken Press front—against the marriage. But the visit, the
first of several, failed in its purpose to detach Beaverbrook from
the King. The Editor of *The Times*, in view of the Prime
Minister's interview with the King due to take place as soon as
the Cabinet's decision was known, refrained from direct
comment in Monday's issue of *The Times*. A leading article,

[1] The Duke of Windsor (*A King's Story*) reveals (pages 340-2) that before this interview
Mr. Esmond Harmsworth (now the second Viscount Rothermere) suggested the plan
of a morganatic marriage to Mrs. Simpson, and also told the King that the idea
originated with his father (Viscount Rothermere). Harmsworth had been to see the
Prime Minister privately about it and been told that it would be referred to the Cabinet.
The Duke of Windsor makes the point that he was entitled to deal directly with the
Dominions, through his Governors-General, but felt that the matter of his proposed
marriage was too delicate to allow him to undertake personal negotiations.

however, dealt with the essential unity of the present House of Commons, and prophesied that it would prove itself " a Council of State, which is able to demonstrate its solid strength in any crisis that may arise, whether foreign or domestic." Dawson looked in on Baldwin at the House of Commons after dinner that evening (30th) and learnt that all the Dominion replies which were coming in confirmed Baldwin's view : morganatic legislation was unacceptable.

It was now recognized that it would not be possible much longer to keep the matter out of the Press. Neither the Prime Minister nor the Editor, however, suspected how, and how soon, silence would be broken. When Dawson returned to the Office after dinner on December 1, he found on his table an agency report of an address delivered during the day by the Bishop of Bradford to his Diocesan Conference which expressed the hope that the King was aware of his need for God's grace at his coronation and added a wish that " he gave more positive signs of this awareness." To this agency report, a long quotation from the leading article due to appear in next day's *Yorkshire Post*, edited by Mr. Arthur Mann, was appended. The quotation had been sent early in the evening by the Editor of the *Yorkshire Post* to the Press Association for general circulation, on the assumption that most of the newspapers of the country would next day comment on the Bishop's admonition to the King, and that the London Press might wish to quote the article in the Provincial Press. While not mentioning the King's supposed matrimonial intentions, the leader referred to American rumours and endorsed the Bishop's remarks on the King's need to dedicate himself to his duty. As the night went on, this article was supplemented from other northern papers which, following Dr. Blunt's lead, expressed doubts as to the strength of the King's character but did not enlarge on the reasons for apprehension.

For three months *The Times* had kept silence in the face of pressure, criticism and even ridicule from both sides of the Atlantic. For some time the Editor had been preparing notes for a leader to meet the emergency that had now been created by Dr. Blunt's speech. The Editor now saw that the floodgates had been opened. He had to decide quickly whether *The Times* should comment that night, or leave the initiative in the hands of the Northern Press. Before deciding to publish anything Dawson sounded two other London journals. The *Morning Post* said it was withholding comment that night. The *Daily*

Telegraph was similarly inclined. Dawson and Lord Camrose believed that Lord Rothermere and Lord Beaverbrook[1] would do the same. Meanwhile the King, after he heard of Hoare's visit to Beaverbrook, was convinced that a Press "bombardment" was imminent.

And because of the intimate association of Mr. Baldwin, Archbishop Lang, and Mr. Geoffrey Dawson, editor of *The Times*, we had instinctively braced ourselves for an opening salvo from the "Thunderer." In fact, rumour had reached us that *The Times* already had prepared a powerful and unfavourable editorial and was only waiting a signal to publish it.[2]

The "Thunderer," however, was so slow to "bombard" the King that it decided to publish the Bishop's Address simply as an item of news. On Wednesday, December 2, the paper gave the Address in full and extracted the important reference to the King for the Bill page. A leading article emphasized the cordiality of the reception given to the Duke and Duchess of York in Edinburgh, and referred to the Duke as the Heir Presumptive to the Throne. No other reference to the matter was made in *The Times*; or, in the event, by any other London morning newspaper. For varying reasons, they had all come to the same decision. The Northern papers were thus allowed to give the country the first public intimation that all was not well with the Monarchy. The London evening papers followed the same cautious line.

That Wednesday proved an arduous day for the Editor. He spent much time in redrafting and polishing next day's leading article and saw the Prime Minister twice—briefly in the morning and again at about 5 p.m. He noted in his memorandum, written shortly after these events, that

He [Baldwin] was going to see the King at 6, and had nothing much to tell me yet beyond reporting a solid front in the Dominions and the House of Commons. He seemed indeed to be nearly at the end of his tether and sat with his head in his hands on the table, probably just glad to have someone with him till the time for his interview came.

[1] The Duke of Windsor states (p. 349) that Lord Beaverbrook telephoned him about the Bishop of Bradford's speech on December 1, late in the afternoon, and informed him that the *Yorkshire Post* would comment on it:
"What are the London newspapers going to do?" I asked Max Beaverbrook.
"They will report Bishop Blunt's speech."
"With editorial comment?"
"No," he answered, "that will be reserved until the results of tomorrow's Cabinet meeting are available."
[2] Windsor, *A King's Story* (p. 348).

The Prime Minister saw the King, and informed him that neithe
the Government in London nor the Dominions was prepare
to pass legislation for a morganatic marriage. When the Prim
Minister told the story to the House of Commons on December 1
he did not say whether the King had commented that Wednesda
evening on the conduct of the Northern Press.[1] Dawson'
memorandum, however, proceeds to say that

In the late evening [December 2], as I was struggling with the pape
he [Baldwin] rang me up twice himself—the only time, I think, that
ever heard his own voice on the telephone—to say that His Majest
was worrying him to find out, and if necessary stop, what was goin
to appear in *The Times*. He understood that there was to be an attac
on Mrs. Simpson and "instructed" the Prime Minister to forbid i
In vain S. B. had explained that the Press in England was free, an
that he had no control over *The Times* or over any other newspaper
When he spoke to me, full of apologies, the second time, it was t
say that the King would now be satisfied, and leave the Prime Ministe
alone, if the latter would read the leading article for him. Could
possibly let him see it for the sake of peace ? By this time, as I tol
him, the paper was just going to press : but towards midnight I sen
a proof of the leader by messenger to Downing Street and heard n
more about it.

The leading article "King and Monarchy," contained som
account of the American Press campaign and admitted its soli
basis of fact. Mrs. Simpson was not mentioned but referenc
was made to the suggestion of "a marriage incompatible wit
the Throne." The previous silence of the Press was briefl
referred to : "If it has not hitherto been the subject o
comment in the English Press, that is due neither to lack o
public anxiety nor to any form of pressure upon the newspapers
official or collusive, but simply to a common self-restraint
inspired by the hope that some authoritative act or statemen
would enable them to put an end to it once for all." Th
article ended with the conviction that the institution wa

---

[1] Barrington-Ward, who had seen his friend earlier in the day (Wednesday
December 2), learnt of the King's displeasure at the critical tone of the Press. Hi
Majesty considered that this tone had been "organized" by the Prime Minister, th
Archbishop of Canterbury and the Editor of *The Times*. The Assistant Editor wa
forced to assure A. that, despite his Majesty's apprehension, the paper did no
intend to publish the full life of Mrs. Simpson in the next issue. The King'
apprehension was intensified by a telephone call which he received on Wednesday
evening (2nd) from Beaverbrook, who warned him that the Cabinet decision agains
morganatic marriage was known in Fleet Street and that the London Press would com
out with "sensational disclosures" on Thursday. The Duke of Windsor was the
certain that "*The Times*, under the fluent and pitiless pen of Geoffrey Dawson, woul
lead the attack." He says that he felt the newspapers were treating him as a commo
felon. It was probably his first experience of unrestrained comment on his privat
life in the British Press.

greater than the individual, but that the time had come for a reassuring act or statement from the Monarch if the Monarchy itself were not to be damaged. The Editor left no room for doubt where *The Times* would stand in any coming trial of strength between Monarch and Government.

The other London morning papers exercised similar reserve in regard to Mrs. Simpson's name, and expressed with varying degrees of conviction the belief that a grave constitutional crisis had arisen through a difference between King and Cabinet over the Sovereign's proposed marriage. The *News Chronicle* alone defined its opinion as being that while the King can choose his own wife, Parliament chooses the Queen and regulates the succession. If, suggested the *News Chronicle*, the King had chosen a wife whom public opinion considered unsuitable as Queen, then His Majesty could marry her in his private capacity as Duke of Cornwall, but she would only be his consort and her issue could be excluded from the succession. There was no consensus of opinion among the London Press, and the evening papers of December 3 showed similar uncertainty as to the public reaction to the news. The *Evening News* devoted much space to Mrs. Simpson and hinted that opposition to the marriage was based on her nationality. The *Evening Standard* said correctly that morganatic marriage was unknown to English law, and indicated the three choices facing the King :

1. Marriage in face of opposition, relying on public support, although newspaper comment that day gave little sign of any such support ;
2. Renunciation of the marriage project ;
3. Abdication.

There was no attempt to judge the issue, which must be left to the King. As the *Evening Standard* put it : " He alone knows whether he can sustain the opposition of Mr. Baldwin and the other Ministers of the Crown." The *Star* could see no insuperable objection to the marriage.

The Prime Minister stated in the House that Thursday that no constitutional difficulty yet existed, but Dawson knew it might be only a matter of hours before Monarch and Government were in open conflict. The King, alarmed for Mrs. Simpson's safety, sent her out of the country late Thursday evening. The National Press remained hesitant, even unsure of its facts. At Printing House Square there was no uncertainty. Friday morning's leading article went straight to the point :

Now that the pressure of events has ended by common consent a tacit and public-spirited agreement to protect His Majesty and the national interest from the embarrassments, or worse, of precipitate comment and discussion, it is of the first importance that the ground should be swept clear once for all of irrelevant contentions and misunderstandings. (December 4, 1936.)

The article then faced the insuperable objection to the proposed marriage : the lady had two former husbands living, from whom in succession she had obtained a divorce. That she was a commoner or an American was entirely irrelevant. By English law the Sovereign is free to choose his own wife, who shares his life as Queen Consort, and their issue are in the direct succession to the Throne. He may choose any woman of Protestant allegiance. There was, therefore, no need for legislation to enable His Majesty to make the proposed marriage. The objection to it, conscientiously held by millions of the King's subjects, was not remediable by law. The Parliamentary Correspondent noted in that issue that the relation of the King and his Ministers was admirably set out in the *Daily Herald* of the day before (December 3). This article, " Crown and Cabinet," written by Harold Laski, defined the constitutional monarchy as at present established in Great Britain. The salient fact was that the Cabinet, not the King, had control of policy-making. That being so, the King must accept the Cabinet's advice in everything, as they were responsible for his acts. Royal opposition to the established Government, if carried to a logical conclusion, could only end in abdication or monarchical dictatorship.

While the *Morning Post* and the *Daily Telegraph* remained opposed to the idea of the marriage, there were signs of a swing-over on the part of the Beaverbrook and Rothermere newspapers. They appealed for delay, for reference to the people, for anything that would keep a popular Sovereign (and, it was not obscurely hinted in some quarters, remove an unpopular Prime Minister). The *Evening Standard* harassed its readers with prophecies of the difficulties to be encountered in the search for a successor to Edward VIII : " Would the people be consulted on the choice of a new Monarch ? If so, how ? " *The Times* was criticized for representing criticism of the King as the voice of the people and for suggesting that the " City " was disturbed by the crisis. The Provincial Press almost unitedly supported the Government. The *Manchester Guardian* of December 4 repeated that there had been no Press censorship or instructions from above. The Press had for weeks realized the impending gravity of the situation :

They did their duty by reticence while reticence could be maintained ; this week, beginning with the newspapers of the country rather than with the papers of the capital, they have done what they conceive to be their duty by speaking out. They have done so in no spirit of sensationalism ; their long and remarkable silence is proof of that. They have spoken now with a deepening sense of responsibility as organs of public opinion and because, by so speaking they hold that they are serving the best interests of the country, the Monarchy, and the British Commonwealth of Nations.

Baldwin did his utmost to stem the development of support for Rothermere and Esmond Harmsworth's idea of a morganatic marriage. His plain statement to a crowded House of Commons that such a marriage was unknown to English law, and that neither the British Government nor the Dominions were prepared to introduce special legislation was supremely effective and Colin (now Viscount) Davidson told B.-W. that an Abdication Statute was being drafted. The announcement of this decision next morning (December 5) in *The Times* carried five double-column headings. The Parliamentary Notes ominously discussed the meaning of voluntary abdication, and the leading article, headed " King and Parliament," cleared the Government of responsibility for a crisis which the King had initiated, and insisted that the nation and the Dominions were solid behind a united House of Commons.

But it was by no means certain yet that the country as a whole would preserve the unity upon the value of which Printing House Square insisted. Saturday's *Daily Express* came out more strongly against the Government. It published a selection of readers' letters to prove that nine out of ten favoured the marriage and opposed abdication. A national ballot was suggested, the personal value of the King was emphasized, and the Archbishop of Canterbury was referred to as " key-figure in the current crisis." The *Evening Standard* contributed a cynical and irresponsible skit by Bernard Shaw of a conversation between the King, the Prime Minister and the Archbishop of Canterbury. The *Evening Standard* also insisted that the Government were pressing the King to renounce his marriage or to abdicate. The *Daily Mail* was equally pro-King and anti-Baldwin. It condemned the Prime Minister's statement on morganatic marriage as " stiff and uncompromising," and said the King's abdication would be " an unspeakable calamity." The Provincial Press continued to support the Prime Minister.

The *Yorkshire Post* considered that his remarks on morganatic marriage correctly interpreted the feelings of the majority in the North of England, for a special bill would ask Parliament to approve an example of moral weakness in the highest quarters, and thus provide a deplorable example for the whole country.

Outside the Press there was confusion of opinion. That Saturday (December 5) Churchill issued a statement pleading for delay and denying that there was any conflict between King and Parliament, because Parliament had not yet been consulted. He pleaded for " the utmost chivalry and compassion " towards a " gifted and beloved King torn between private and public obligations of love and duty," and hinted that the Government were exerting all their power and influence to get rid of the King, who was forced to remain silent. The Sunday papers were also divided in their allegiance. The *Observer* decided that the King must make a hard choice between renunciation of the throne or the marriage, and the *Sunday Times* and *Reynolds News* spoke out roundly against any suggestion of the creation of a " King's Party." The *Sunday Express*, however, saw no cause for abdication but favoured a change of Ministry to promote legislation for a morganatic marriage. A gossip writer in the *Sunday Dispatch* suggested that the " old gang " feared " too strong a man arising for life to be pleasant for them " and that the King had been stirring up the Foreign Office. During the week-end there were a number of small processions in London, some spontaneous and some promoted by Mosley's British Union, who took the occasion for further attempts to divide opinion between the Government and the people.... But there is no evidence that anything as concrete as a party or movement, under any recognizable leader, emerged. There was little unity among the King's declared supporters—the Beaverbrook and Rothermere Press, a group of Conservative M.P.s whose personal loyalty to the Sovereign was voiced by Churchill, and a few Liberals and Left-Wing intellectuals who saw the issue as a fight against Puritanism or clericalism. The Duke of Windsor himself allows that by Monday the " King's Party " was dead.

In Monday's issue the Editor threw the whole weight of *The Times* against the mischief-makers. The first leading article, headed " King and Empire," disposed of criticisms that the Government had been forced by a campaign of scandal abroad to interfere in the King's private concerns or that the Prime Minister and his colleagues had artificially fomented in the Dominions an opposition to His Majesty's known intent. Another leading article, headed " Making Mischief," dealt with the charge levelled against the Cabinet and the Prime Minister of presenting the King with an ultimatum. It asserted and emphasized afresh that the initiative lay with the King, as it had done throughout. Other morning papers kept to the lines they had already developed. The *News Chronicle* condemned the idea of a "King's Party," though it did not see that its own appeal for delay was likely to further its formation. On Monday the *Daily Mirror*, which had shown great hostility to Baldwin on Saturday, published an article to the effect that forty-five million people demanded to know the truth behind the Prime Minister's statement to the House. An attack on the Archbishop of Canterbury as " The Man Who Objects," insinuated that he sought to extend his personal power. The *Daily Mail* contained a letter to the Editor from Lord Rothermere, the paper's pro-prietor, asking the whole country whether Britain could afford to lose a Sovereign of superlative qualities—" In the foreign relations of Great Britain he is worth all our Embassies, Legations, and Foreign Office staff put together "—and claiming that without the King the system of voluntary recruiting would fail and conscription would become inevitable. Lord Rothermere continued his campaign for the King in the *Evening News*, addressing another long letter to its Editor on the advantages of a morganatic marriage, which only needed to be explained at home and in the Dominions to win overwhelming acceptance. He hinted that the Government were encouraging the King to abdicate because they resented his strong words about the depressed areas in South Wales. *The Times* and the *Daily Telegraph* were rated in the *Evening Standard* for their " lack of restraint " and for describing all opposition to the Government as taking part in controversy.

But the newspaper controversialists had little effect on the House of Commons, which gave the Prime Minister whole-hearted approval and sympathy when he explained on Monday that, except for giving an opinion on the King's inquiries regarding morganatic marriage, no advice had been tendered to him by the Cabinet and the Prime Minister's conversations with him had been strictly personal and informal. His Majesty had first raised the subject himself some weeks before when he informed the Prime Minister that he intended to marry Mrs. Simpson whenever she should be free. Churchill was shouted down when he requested an assurance that no irrevocable steps would be taken.

The news on that Monday was a message from Mrs. Simpson in Cannes, protesting her " unchanged attitude " of readiness

" to withdraw forthwith from a situation that has been rendered both unhappy and untenable." The *Daily Express*[1] hailed this announcement next morning as the " End of the Crisis," but elsewhere it was generally viewed and printed just as a mere item of news. *The Times* (B.-W. writing) on Tuesday again rehearsed the facts against a morganatic marriage :

It is the more incredible that within the past twenty-four hours this distasteful device should have been exhumed and offered to the public again upon the strength of stale and discredited arguments. In one of the letters which he addressed to successive editions of his own evening newspaper yesterday, Lord Rothermere, desisting from an earlier attempt to clarify the present issue by bringing conscription and Soviet Russia into the reckoning, advanced, almost as though it had newly occurred to him, the alternative of the so-called morganatic marriage.

The article pilloried the idea by describing it as a demand for statutory recognition of the fact that the woman the King desired to marry was not fit to be Queen. " The Constitution is to be amended in order that she may carry in solitary prominence the brand of unfitness for the Queen's Throne,"[2] which appeared a foolish and deplorable product of misguided ingenuity. Another leading article, " Confused Controversialists," criticized the attitude of the *Evening Standard*, the *News Chronicle*, and the *Evening News*. An article on another page defended the Archbishop of Canterbury from charges of seeking to influence the decision, and referred to the Archbishop's " known friendship with King Edward's father, whose closing days were clouded by anxiety for the future." That morning B.-W. could note that " we have undoubtedly disposed of Rothermere. Opinion pretty solid now. Abdication inevitable."

By Wednesday, December 9, there was a lull in the newspaper accounts of the crisis, while behind the scenes tension was heightening. Abdication did appear inevitable, and some of the " King's Friends " began to come round to the support of the Government. There was little fight left in the Press. Dawson organized an analysis of the vast mass of correspondence that

[1] The Duke of Windsor (*A King's Story*) suggests (pages 394-5) that Beaverbrook influenced Lord Brownlow, who accompanied Mrs. Simpson to Cannes, to approach her and persuade her to issue this statement. The Duke says that Mrs. Simpson really thought she was renouncing the marriage, but Beaverbrook believed she was merely postponing the crisis.

[2] It was probably this article which led the Duke of Windsor to refer so bitterly (*A King's Story*, page 273) to *The Times* which, " once again the ' Thunderer,' turned its wrath against the woman of my choice."

had poured into Printing House Square—the largest ever received—in order to have the basis for the following day's leader.[1]

The Act of Abdication was signed and announced on Thursday, December 10. Of the scene in the House of Commons the Editor wrote : " I only record my personal impression of S.B.'s almost conversational manner, of the characteristic untidiness of his scrap of notes, of the skill with which he told the whole story without a word that could give offence, and of the simple sincerity of certain memorable phrases." The public would read and think of one subject only next day, and the Editor devoted the three subsidiary leaders to offshoots of the main theme. He had spent much time on the first leader, " King Edward's Choice," which he intended to be the paper's last word on the subject. Opening with regret for the King's decision, he paid warm tribute to the Prime Minister and repeated that the initiative, throughout the crisis, had come from the King.

It is well (he went on)

to remember these things, for they complete the picture of dignity with which the King, no less than Parliament and people, has comported himself throughout this sorry business. But let them be remembered in their true perspective against a background which can be nothing but dark. Above all let us have no talk of " romance " about what is indeed a drama, but a drama of the deepest tragedy. King Edward had most of the qualities that would have made a great Constitutional Monarch. He had shown himself brave, completely free from pompousness, chivalrous where his affections were engaged, conscientious in his everyday public duties, attractive to a crowd, genuinely interested in the condition of the poor as he went about among them. He was unfortunate, no doubt, in some of his intimates ; but he also had advisers who served him with courage and prudence, and it would have been well if he could have brought himself to prefer them to the others. . . . They profoundly misunderstood the earlier signs of division in this country who represented it as an issue between " the people's King " and a hide-bound set of aristocrats and ecclesiastics. It would be far more accurate to say that His Majesty's circle was too largely composed of men and women, some of them of high birth and all of them remote from " the people," who cared far less for his welfare than for their own amusement. The real clash was between the thoughtlessness of an exotic society and the hard core of

1 None of these letters to the Editor was ever published but they were studied for the indication they gave of the progress of public opinion. The earliest letters, following the shock of the first newspaper comments, mainly reflected an unquestioning loyalty to the occupant of the Throne, which gradually wavered and gave way to a more critical approach with much legal argument. Mingled with moral doubts, this attitude ended in marked hostility to the King : he was judged as one who had failed to put his public duty before his private inclinations.

a British tradition of conduct which is common to all classes in this country ; but it must also be said in fairness that none of us can realize how hard is the path of a King in choosing good friends.

That, amid all his great qualities, there was also something lacking in himself is sufficiently shown by the unprecedented decision recorded this morning ; for it is proof of obstinacy rather than of strength that it must have been reached in the face of a very human reluctance to abandon a position which afforded him so many proofs of success. For those of us who are more humbly and happily placed there is assuredly nothing but relief in being able to avoid the burdens of a Crown. What seems almost incredible is that any man who was born and trained to such high responsibilities, who had clearly the capacity to undertake them, and who had in fact begun to exercise them with the complete good will of the nation, should sacrifice it all to a personal preference for another way of life. *Omnium consensu capax Imperii nisi imperasset*—the well-worn quotation from Tacitus is irresistible. It can hardly have been a better verdict upon the Emperor Galba than it is upon King Edward that all men would have judged him worthy of the Throne if he had never ascended it. (December 11, 1936.)

And there the crisis was brought to an end so far as *The Times* was concerned. The paper's final contribution to the episode was a suggestion made by B.-W. that the title of the new King should be George VI.

The criticisms current at the time against the Press may be summarized as :

1. That the long silence of the newspapers was due to some censorship or muzzling from outside.
2. That it was due to collusion—an arrangement between themselves for common action.
3. That this arrangement was shared by the Government, who used the Press for their own purposes.
4. That it included the heads of the Church, who deliberately selected the Bishop of Bradford to break the silence.
5. That *The Times*, and subsequently the Archbishop, were guilty of " hitting a man when he was down."

The first charge is easily disposed of. There was no official or unofficial censorship of the British Press, nor any attempt to muzzle Dominion or foreign correspondents. The nearest approach to interference from high quarters was probably the customary request from Buckingham Palace (the precedent having originated in Victorian times) that the Sovereign's privacy should be respected by the Press during his annual holiday. This request was not observed universally, but was generally respected in England.

It can no more be said that there was any general collusion except in regard to the reporting of the case of Simpson *v.* Simpson. The unbroken silence observed by British newspapers and periodicals until the Bishop of Bradford's speech was a voluntary and (since Victoria) traditional discipline, springing from several causes. First and foremost, there is the customary restraint and reserve that obtains in the British Press towards the Sovereign and his immediate family. It is recognized that, through no choice of their own, they are compelled to live their lives in the glare of publicity and to undertake endless public engagements of a fatiguing and tedious kind. In return, they have a right to expect every assistance from the Press in preserving their dignity, for they have no means of defending themselves from public criticism. For this reason the British Press does not publish caricatures of the Royal Family, as it does of politicians and ecclesiastics, who are free to answer criticism or ridicule. Apart from any question of popularity, there is a strong feeling that it is unsporting to hit someone who cannot hit back. Responsible proprietors and editors, therefore, were united in considering that the King's friendship with Mrs. Simpson, or with any other woman, did not offer a suitable topic for newspaper comment or gossip as long as it was only part of his private life. The temptation to imitate the scandalous articles in the American Press was also offset by the fear of incurring the censure of indignant readers, who might vindicate their loyalty by changing to another newspaper.

Moreover the King's marriage was a very serious question, involving constitutional issues of great importance. But it was not an issue to be debated in the Press until the King's intentions were indisputably established. When it appeared to the well-informed that the King did mean to marry Mrs. Simpson, and that the intention had become the subject of disagreement between the King and his Ministers, responsible journalists hesitated to aggravate the situation. As has been shown, Dawson gave great thought to this matter and was consulted by several of his fellow journalists. He knew that *The Times* was expected to give a lead, but there is no evidence that he ever went out of his way to influence the rest of the Press. When other journalists sought his opinion, he gave it, but they were as free as he was to act independently. Nor was any action ever taken by the Newspaper Proprietors' Association or other professional body. The only occasion on which Dawson showed anxiety about the behaviour of other newspapers was on the day of the Bishop of Bradford's speech, when he consulted the

Morning Post and the *Daily Telegraph*. He had no communication with the Rothermere or Beaverbrook Press, whose abstention from comment next morning was in no way due to the influence of Printing House Square. The very fact that the northern papers prepared their leading articles on the Bishop's speech, and so ended the silence of the Press, without reference to their colleagues in London, shows that there was no arrangement between them for common action.

The third accusation—that the Government used the Press for their own purposes—was brought against *The Times*. It has been said that the Editor received his instructions from Baldwin, together with confidential news of the progress of negotiations, or alternatively, that the Editor was consulted by Baldwin and influenced his decisions to an improper degree. This influence, on either side, has been deduced from the fact that the Prime Minister saw more of Dawson at that time than he did of any other journalist. They were old friends, members of the same Club, and for years had been accustomed to discuss public affairs together. But the Prime Minister committed no impropriety whatever in his talks with the Editor. Neither did the Editor. Dawson notes in his memorandum that : " He [Baldwin] never in fact told me any secrets, nor did I ask for them," and this is supported by the fact that, except for their talk on October 26, the Prime Minister never revealed to Dawson what was said at any of his private interviews with the King. He was glad to discuss with Dawson questions of procedure and constitutional correctness, but on the whole seems to have refrained from giving his opinion on the value of Press publicity. When his duty compelled him to approach the Editor on the King's behalf on the evening of December 2, he obviously did so with the greatest embarrassment and with full understanding of the enormity of his behaviour. The Editor, for his part, had made no attempt to get into touch with the Prime Minister when he had to decide whether to comment on the Bishop's speech or remain silent. He saw Baldwin twice the next day but obviously was not invited to divulge the contents of the coming leading article, or it would have been unnecessary for Baldwin to ask for a copy after seeing the King. Baldwin, during the crisis, had the benefit of wholehearted support from *The Times, Daily Telegraph, Morning Post, Daily Herald* and practically all the Provincial Press. But that support cannot be proved to have been due to any personal exertion on his part to win them over—it was given because they understood the nature of the crisis, and realized that it was the supremacy of Parliament over Monarchy that was being challenged. The most that can be said is that the Prime Minister made attempts, rather belated, to detach Beaverbrook from the King's side and failed. But had he succeeded he would undoubtedly have left Beaverbrook to support the Government in his own way. There is nothing to suggest that Baldwin at any time had a defined Press policy or programme, or that he understood then, or at any time, the nature or value of advance propaganda. Nor is there any evidence that Baldwin ever " inspired " anything printed in *The Times* or any other newspaper.[1]

The fourth accusation, that the heads of the Church were included in the conspiracy between Press and Government, was soon abandoned for lack of evidence. The Editor of *The Times* was on friendly terms with the Archbishop of Canterbury and enjoyed his confidence, but Dawson never doubted for a moment that the Bishop of Bradford's speech was made entirely on his own responsibility, and that its results surprised him as much as it did the rest of the Anglican Hierarchy. It is a fact that the Archbishop told Dawson on November 11, when he explained his reasons for keeping entirely apart from the crisis, that George V had had many distressing talks with him about his successor's infatuation, which the Archbishop thought had definitely shortened his life. This was the source of the reference in *The Times* of December 8 to " King Edward's father, whose closing days were clouded with anxiety for the future," which was considered unfair by many supporters of the King.

The paper's share in giving point to the last accusation— " hitting a man when he was down "—is largely based on the leading article of Friday, December 11. The Editor gave full weight to King Edward's good qualities, but he felt compelled also to attempt some estimate of the defects of character which had led to the crisis, and he did not mince his words. His condemnation of the King's unworthy friends, " who cared far less for his welfare than for their own amusement," exposed him to bitter attacks. But the Editor was writing with a keen awareness of the dangers to which the crisis had exposed the institution of the Monarchy. King Edward had enjoyed an overwhelming personal popularity while his successor was comparatively unknown. It was therefore essential to destroy any idea that the retiring King was a romantic figure, who might

---

[1] It may also be asked, in this connexion, why Baldwin did nothing to influence the B.B.C., which throughout published colourless official statements. The ordinary citizen gathered his information from the newspapers.

retain the sympathy of many of his subjects and even perhaps inspire a party bent on his restoration. In the event, largely due to the dignity with which the Duke of Windsor faced the situation, the danger of divided allegiance never materialized, but it was undoubtedly in the forefront of the Editor's mind when he wrote what many considered a harsh and ill-natured valedictory article.

APPENDIX II: SOURCES

The principal manuscript authority for this volume is provided by the collections in Printing House Square, which are more extensive than for any previous period. For the early chapters on foreign affairs which cover the same territory as Volume III, the same sources have been used. The papers at Printing House Square comprise letters by the several Proprietors, Editors and Managers, and from Foreign Correspondents. The latter are filed in the office under the heading of the relevant country. All letters are now being filed in chronological order, and a guide thereto is in preparation. The practice of using letter-books was discontinued after 1915.

The Walter Papers include a mass of correspondence; legal, financial, and other memoranda of importance to the property, and to certain principal appointments on the staff. These are kept in separate deed boxes.

Northcliffe Papers. By the permission of the late Sir George Sutton, Bt., and Mr. Henry Arnholz, Literary Executors of the late Lord Northcliffe, *The Times* has been given access to the whole of the documents relating to the paper kept at Coutts's Bank in the Strand, and enabled to publish from the Northcliffe Papers in Printing House Square. The day-to-day memoranda, or " communiqués " as they were called, sent by Northcliffe to Printing House Square and Carmelite House have been used. These are described below at Sources, Chapter IV.

The Astor Papers comprise a large number of letters, notes and documents relating to the purchase of the control from the Northcliffe estate, correspondence with Mr. John Walter and important colleagues.

The Ralph Walter Papers amount, in effect, to a diary of the proceedings in the summer and autumn of 1922, the year in which J. J. Astor and J. Walter acquired the property ; also a mass of detailed financial abstracts. These are kept in separate deed boxes.

The Times Publishing Company Limited Papers include minute books, share ledgers, balance sheets, circulation figures and costs of production.

Editors' Diaries: Dawson, Steed and Barrington-Ward continued the practice of entering in a diary the names of the writers of leading articles and of certain other " special " contributors. These diaries have been consulted for the present volume. The successive Editors also wrote for their own guidance, and that of others, memoranda, all of which have been used, and a number of letters. Dawson's correspondence, relating principally to his second term, is of value. He had the habit of writing memoranda, sometimes long, of events and interviews. These provide a dependable statement of his views and actions in controversial situations, e.g., the Abdication. In addition, his office correspondence illustrates his relations with public men. These Papers are kept in Printing House Square.

Steed's Papers. In his capacity as Foreign Editor, and Editor, Steed was a vigorous correspondent with an exceptionally wide range. A large amount of this remains at Printing House Square. A considerable volume of Steed's papers relating to his terms as Correspondent in Rome and Vienna has been deposited in the office.

Barrington-Ward's Papers include engagement books, private memoranda and letters, many of which are of some length. They are of value to those interested in the period 1928-1938. Mrs. Barrington-Ward has given access to private Papers.

Printing House Square Papers. The general mass of office papers, filed under subjects and writers, and consisting of the available written exchanges between the office and its representatives abroad, is full for this period, though in some respects inadequate. It provides evidence of what Correspondents thought noteworthy when they had time to write letters, but is less informative about events during crises, when the office and the Correspondent alike were under pressure. Notes of telephone conversations rarely remain. The confidential *résumés* of the affairs of the country occasionally sent by a Correspondent from the capital to which he was accredited, were circulated to a varying list of members of the editorial staff, to ensure that leading articles were written with an adequate background in the writer's mind. A number of these remain. It is worth noting that very few of these confidential Papers were written by the paper's Berlin staff, who had too much other work on their hands. The office correspondence, for this period, is preserved in the form of carbon reproduction of the typewritten original, and is filed in boxes, the letter-book system having been abandoned in the interests of " efficiency." These carbons are to be used with caution as the carbon is frequently, and not always obviously, left uncorrected.

Among manuscript sources not collected by Proprietors and Editors are :

Milner Papers. By kind permission of Lady Milner and the Librarian at New College, Oxford, these have been consulted and on occasion copied. They are listed in Chapter VI below.

Certain Papers in the hands of collectors who prefer to be anonymous.

Principal printed works used, besides those diplomatic archives which need not be listed (see Vol. III), include the Dictionary of National Biography and:

British and Foreign State Papers. (H.M. Stationery Office.)

Council of Foreign Relations, U.S.A.: The United States in World Affairs. Intended as an annual publication.

Department of State, U.S.A.: Peace and War, United States Foreign Policy, 1931-1941. (Washington, 1943.)

Documents on German Foreign Policy, 1918-1945. (Series D. 3 Vols., H.M. Stationery Office, 1949-1951.)

Gooch, G. P. and Temperley, H.: British Documents on the Origins of the War, 1898-1914. (H.M. Stationery Office, 1927-1938.)

Royal Institute of International Affairs. Yearly surveys and documents. (Oxford.)

Temperley, H. W. V.: A History of the Peace Conference of Paris. (6 vols. London, 1920-1924.)

Ward, A. W. and Gooch, G. P.: The Cambridge History of British Foreign Policy, 1783-1919. (3 vols., Cambridge, 1922-1923.)

Woodward, E. L. and Butler, Rohan: Documents on British Foreign Policy, 1919-1939. (3 series, the first two consisting of three volumes and the third of two, H.M. Stationery Office, 1946-1950.)

World Peace Foundation: Documents on American Foreign Relations. (Annual volumes, Princeton University Press.)

P.H.S. Publications

In addition, reference has also been made to the special publications of Printing House Square, i.e., books, pamphlets, supplements, etc. The most complete and accessible list of these, far too numerous to be listed in this Appendix, is that of the Library of Congress which may be referred to at Vol. 145, pp. 311-317, of The Catalogue of Books Represented by the Library of Congress Printed Cards (Ann Arbor, Mich., 1945).

For many years before 1906 it was the custom in the office to compile a manuscript index to The Times, but neither this, nor the unofficial indexes (e.g. Mr. Palmer's) which were published, fully met office requirements. Beginning in January, 1906, a monthly index was published from P.H.S., the twelve-monthly parts being amalgamated and re-edited in an annual volume. This production continued until July, 1914, when it was decided to abandon the monthly and annual issues and publish instead a quarterly volume. In effect the index to The Times is also a guide to the date of the appearance of important home and international news in every other newspaper. Now that The Times has been microfilmed the index forms a valuable aid to researchers throughout the world.

Newspapers

The principal contemporary daily newspapers read include the Manchester Guardian, Morning Post, Daily Telegraph, Daily Mail, Daily News, together with, in some instances, their evening publications. The files of the Sunday Observer, the Spectator and the New Statesman have also been consulted. For the proprietors, editors, prices and policies of the journals for the period 1884-1950, see the table printed in this appendix.

The files of The Times have been used in both microfilm and volume form, together with the Official Index.

German newspapers have been utilised for the eve-of-the-war Chapters.

Parliament

The Official Reports (Hansard) for the period have been read.

The estimate of public men general in the office is reflected in Buckle's articles in the Encyclopaedia Britannica (12th edition, supplement, 3 vols., London, 1922).

He contributed biographies, or additions to biographies already given in the 11th edition up to 1910, of the following statesmen : Asquith, Balfour, Carson, Lord Hugh Cecil (Lord Quickswood), Lord Robert Cecil (Viscount Cecil of Chelwood), Winston Churchill, Cromer, 4th Earl Grey, Viscount Grey of Fallodon, Haldane, Henderson, Lansdowne, Bonar Law, Lloyd George, Long, Alfred Lyttelton, McKenna, Milner, Morley, Rhondda. At two points under Asquith the Press is mentioned, and credited with having peremptorily called for Kitchener to be War Minister in August, 1914 ; and The Times is said to have revealed the disastrous shortage of munitions in 1915. Buckle also wrote on English History, 1910-1921.

I. THE NEW IMPERIALISM

Manuscript

Unpublished autobiography of L. S. Amery.

Correspondence of Moberly Bell with Amery, Buckle and Dawson.

Printed Works

[Amery, L. S., editor] "*The Times*" *History of the War in South Africa*.
This work had been originally intended as a collection of the articles contributed to the paper by Flora Shaw, Amery and others, supplemented by chapters written in the office, the whole to consist of one or two volumes, and published under the supervision of the Manager. The suggestion had been made by Amery originally as a jest when the Manager lamented the cost of the body of correspondents (at one time twenty) which *The Times* had maintained in South Africa. The appointment of Amery as Editor increased the scope and seriousness of the work, and eventually six volumes and an index appeared. H. A. L. Fisher, who reviewed the last volume in the *Literary Supplement* (July 1, 1909), declared that " in his (Amery's) hands ' *The Times*' *History of the War* is a history with a mission. Its aim is to defend Imperialism in the past, to make Imperialists in the present, and by displaying not only the virtues but also the faults of British organization to strengthen the Empire against the perils of the future." The production of six volumes containing over three thousand pages, eighty-five maps and plans, and eighty-seven plates and reproductions, was, in itself, no small task, but was performed scrupulously, down to the decoration of the bindings with the obverses and reverses of appropriate medals and medallions. Lionel James was Amery's principal collaborator, responsible in particular for the provision of maps. Basil Williams edited Volume IV in which Lord Roberts' campaign was described, and Erskine Childers Volume V which covered the operations of the " guerilla war." Correspondents of the paper, in addition to Flora Shaw, e.g., Perceval Landon, Alsager Pollock, Bron Herbert and Repington, all assisted Amery, together with many others both in the office and outside. An index completed the set, which was published by Sampson, Low, Marston & Co.

The work occupied Amery for nine years. He delivered slowly, for other commitments demanded an increasing share of his time. The public impatiently awaited the appearance of each volume, relieving their feelings by corresponding with the Manager so frequently and fiercely that he was forced to stereotype his replies, an unusual concession for that keen writer of the *Bell-lettre*. In consequence, he chided Amery, who tells, in his autobiography, a characteristic story. On one occasion, to justify himself, Amery sent to the Manager a letter from a senior army officer, warmly commending the latest volume and adding that his wife read the work daily to him while he was ill. " Moberly Bell's only rejoinder was to send me back that day's *Times* with a blue cross against the obituary column which recorded the death of Colonel —' after long sufferings heroically endured '." As an inducement, Bell later made Amery a partner with *The Times* in the enterprise. There were good reasons for the delay. Amery was concerned to produce an accurate narrative of events; but, in addition, he wished to place the South African War in historical perspective. As he began his labours in the belief that " the South African War has been the greatest political event in the history of the British Empire since the conclusion of the Napoleonic wars " (Vol, 1, p. 1.), he was not chronicling merely the suppression of a couple of small Republics in a remote part of the world. Even in 1900 he foresaw that the war would have far-reaching effects upon " the organization of the British army, the political and economic development of South Africa, the relations between the various self-governing parts of the British Empire, and the the position of that Empire among the nations of the world." During the nine years that followed much occurred that justified this belief. In 1909 he confessed that had he known in 1900 the magnitude of his task—largely self-imposed—" I should probably not have had the courage to embark upon it. I have grown very weary of it at intervals. But now that the work is done I regret none of the labour which it has cost. To me it has been a wonderful lesson not only in the supremely interesting business of war, but in the whole Imperial problem of which the struggle in South Africa has been but a single phase." (Preface to Vol. 6.)

The " supremely interesting business of war " was inevitably the chief pre-occupation. The campaigns were described in careful detail, and from friends who took part in the Boer campaigns he received accounts of the enemy operations, which were incorporated. Bell recounted that a practice of Amery's when information was scanty was to write an abusive chapter on a general, send it for approval to the general concerned, and then to re-write the chapter in the light of the angry flood of information he received in reply. Bell may have humorously exaggerated, but, whatever his methods, Amery succeeded in presenting not only the plans and strategy of the various battles, but also the details of the fighting. His revised version was never abusive, though he did not abstain from criticism, often unfavourable. He admitted this; his intention was " to try and help towards the solution of present and future needs by the study of our past mistakes." (Preface to Vol. III.) Until 1905 he was Military Correspondent of *The Times*.

Throughout the work he believed the war to be " the first serious test of the strength of the growing sentiment of Imperial Unity." (Preface to Vol. VI.) In the first part of Volume VI, written largely by himself and completed in 1909, he reviewed events since Milner began his reconstruction until 1909, the year before South Africa received Dominion status. He defended Milner and found much to criticize in the activities of the Liberal Government since 1906.

At the beginning of the work he defined his own position. Although he wrote convinced of the essential justice and right of the British case, he wished to do no injustice to that of the Boers, to whose side he had been attached for a period of the war. The only attitude with which he had no sympathy was that of the " pseudo- " or " pro-Boer." " Those who believe in progress, in honest government, in political liberty and equality, must, upon a true statement of the facts, be on the side of England. Those to whom nationalism is all in all, who hold that the creation of a national state, with racial and linguistic characteristics of its own, is the one supreme object of political development—an object justifying every means taken for its attainment—will naturally tend to be on the side of the Afrikander Republics. But for the former class to share the sympathies of the latter can only be due to a misconception of the real situation. . . . No one who has studied the history of the relations between Great Britain and the Republics, or the lifelong policy of the old President, can have convinced himself that the Transvaal was a peaceful, unaggressive, unambitious, well-managed state, or that President Kruger's only object was to preserve unaltered the independent status guaranteed him by the Convention of London." (Preface to Vol. 1.) In this conviction lay the root of his objection to the policy of the Liberals.

Amery, L. S. : *Days of Fresh Air.* (London.)

Bell, E. Moberly : *Flora Shaw.* (London, 1947.)

Bell, E. Moberly : *The Life and Letters of C. F. Moberly Bell.* (London, 1927.)

Halpérin, Vladimir: *Lord Milner et l'évolution de l'impérialisme britannique*, précédé de Lord Milner. Impressions et souvenirs par Paul Mantoux. (Paris, 1950.)

The writer of this well-documented and most useful biographical and political study had the advantage of conversation and correspondence with L. S. Amery and other friends of Milner and his group. M. Halpérin, as the title of his book and the series in which it appears (" Colonies et Empires," edited by C. André Julien) implies, is interested above all in Milner's Imperialist doctrine, but he provides in Chapter III an account of Milner's career between 1914 and 1925 which touches upon his attitude to Zionism but passes over his achievements as a Minister in the Coalition Government.

Hewins, W. A. S. : *The Apologia of an Imperialist.* 2 vols. (London, 1929.)

[Repington, Lt.-Col. C. à C.] *Imperial Strategy, by the Military Correspondent of " The Times."* (London, 1906.)

[*Idem*] *Essays and Criticisms by the Military Correspondent of " The Times."* (London, 1911.)

The writer argues for Dominion navies and for an Imperial General Staff between 1905 and 1910.

Schulze-Gaevernitz, G. von : *Britischer Imperialismus und englischer Freihandel.* (Leipzig, 1906.)

The Round Table. A quarterly review of the politics of the British Empire. Volume 1. (London, November, 1910 to August, 1911).

" The aim of the *Round Table* is to present a regular account of what is going on throughout the King's dominions, written with first-hand knowledge and entirely free from the bias of local political issues, and to provide a means by which the common problems which confront the Empire as a whole, can be discussed also with knowledge and without bias. For that, in the opinion of the promoters, who reside in all parts of the Empire, is what is most needed at the present day ". From the first the review gave space to the discussion of continental questions and it presents, therefore, an authentic statement of the Imperialist attitude towards Europe. In this first volume the following articles are specially important : No. 1, for article " Anglo-German Rivalry "; No. 2, " Anglo-Japanese Alliance "; No. 3, " Imperial Defence "; No. 5, " Britain, France and Germany "; No. 6, " Balkan Danger and Universal Peace "; No. 9, " Balkan Crises "; No. 11, " Balkan War and Balance of Power ".

Schuyler, R. L. : *The Fall of the Old Colonial System. A study in British Free Trade,* 1770-1870. (New York, 1945.)

Skelton, O. D. : *Life and Letters of Sir Wilfrid Laurier.* 2 vols. (London, 1922.)

The New Canada. (London, 1921.) The Ottawa Correspondent's articles in the 1921 Empire Supplement published in book form.

Various Writers : *The Empire and the Century.* (London, 1905.)

A series of essays on Imperial problems and possibilities by various writers, including *The Imperial Ideal*, by W. F. Monypenny; *Imperial Defence and National Policy*, by L. S. Amery; *The Prospects of a United South Africa*, by G. G. Robinson [Dawson]; *The Tropics of the Empire*, by Lady Lugard; *Our Imperial Interests in Nearer and Further Asia*, by Valentine Chirol.

II. "REVOLUTION" AT HOME

Printed Works

Chamberlain, Sir Austen : *Politics from Inside*, 1906-1914. (London, 1936.)

Dawson, W. H. : *Social Insurance in Germany*, 1883-1911. (London, 1912.) A scientific and historical comparison with the Insurance Act of 1911.

Gwynn, Stephen (Editor) ; *The Anvil of War*. Letters between F. S. Oliver and his brother, 1914-1918. (London, 1936.)

Newton, Lord ; *Lord Lansdowne*. (London, 1929.)

Shadwell, Arthur, M.D. : *Drink Legislation and Temperance*. (London, 1902.) Also by Shadwell :

Industrial Efficiency. A Comparative Study of Industrial Life in England, Germany and America. (London, 1906, 2 vols.) A new edition was published in 1909.
London Water Supply. (London, 1909.)
Coal Mines and Nationalisation. (London, 1919.) Reprinted from *The Times*.
The Revolutionary Movement in Great Britain. (London, 1921.)
Problems of Dock Labour. (London, 1920.) Reprinted from *The Times*.
The Engineering Industry and the Crisis. (London, 1922.)
Drink in 1914-1922 ; A Lesson in Control. (London, 1923.)
The Socialist Movement, 1824-1924. 2 vols. (London, 1925.) Covers the meaning, progress and prospects of Socialism and intended to be uncontroversial.
The Communist Movement. (London, 1925.)
The Breakdown of Socialism. (London, 1928.)
Typhoeus ; or the Future of Socialism. (London, 1929.)
Trade Union Reform. (London, 1927.)   Reprinted from *The Times*.

Thompson, Laurence : *Robert Blatchford. Portrait of an Englishman.* (London, 1951.)

" I will go as far as to say that during the first ten years of *The Clarion*'s (1891) life it had more influence on public opinion in this country than any other English journal, *The Times* included." Blatchford, writing in his autobiography (p. 130) . . . " Early in 1909, a special correspondent of *The Times* [Shadwell] surveyed the world of Socialist activity with the amused distaste of an Alexandrian philosopher examining the goings-on of primitive Christians." (p. 191.) " It was noticeable that, though *The Labour Leader*, *Justice* and *The Clarion* all lined up to cock their atrabilious or cheery snooks at the equator, they all printed more or less of what the equator had to say about them, with an evident air of pride that the equator should notice them at all. And they were right to do so, for *The Times* articles were, as *Times* articles tend to be, an indication of a changing attitude." (p. 192.)

III. THE EUROPEAN EQUILIBRIUM

See Appendix to Vol. III, Chapters XI, " Saunders at Berlin " ; XII, " The End of British Isolation " ; XV, " The Accord with Russia " ; XXII, " The European Equilibrium, 1909-1912."

IV. PRICE ONE PENNY

A primary source for Northcliffe's journalistic policies is the large collection of notes headed " Communiqué," " Memoranda " or " Message," on the day's issue of *The Times*, which began in 1912 in the form of private typewritten letters to Dawson. In the next stage the notes became fuller. The papers were read and analysed generally from 6 a.m. and his observations were dictated to a secretary who telephoned them to another secretary at Printing House Square. They were then circulated in copies, as many as 25, typewritten on quarto paper, duplicated by carbon on flimsies, to the principal members of the staff. In addition copies were always sent to G. A. Sutton and R. Hudson. Occasionally the " Memoranda," or " Communiqués " touched on politics and, as such, reached the hands of persons outside the office whom Northcliffe considered undesirable. Hence after 1916 (?) the legend " Private and Confidential " appears over the date-line. Later instructions were issued that all the copies were to be returned to one of Northcliffe's secretaries. A complete collection has not been available and perhaps does not exist.

The available collection covers all the aspects of journalism, ink, paper, typographical composition, printing, advertising, editing, sub-editing, circulation, the economics of newspaper production, the recruitment and remuneration of staff, for his eager eye watched every department of the paper. They vary in length; often Northcliffe tackled the paper page by page. Appreciation is as regular as criticism. " An excellent *Times* this morning " and " I wish to congratulate our Manchester man on his reporting of the Armstrong case " are as frequent as " Enquiry ought to be made into the slovenly writing of the Guildford Show." Individual members of the staff are regularly singled out for praise or the reverse. "Considering the paper was only twelve pages, that the staff is depleted by influenza, and that the Advertisement Department put in too many advertisements, Lloyd Evans did remarkably well in the make-up." "I looked with a good deal of anxiety at *The Times* leader this morning because I know that the whole American party here, from the President downwards, will read and re-read it. I was unable to telephone owing to bronchial trouble last night. The leader could not have been improved. I have no idea who the author is, or whether it was a joint effort; but I was very pleased with it." (December 27, 1918.)

Northcliffe's interest included the style of writing. From 1910 at least he was firmly opposed to the introduction of unnecessary Americanisms: "I have lately seen such words as 'draft' (for 'conscription') and 'peace drive' introduced into *The Times*. Somebody should stand at the entrance to Printing House Square with a coke-hammer and smash every American and other foreign word that tries to get into the building. Our own language is quite good enough. American is very amusing to talk, but it should not be allowed to be printed in *The Times*. . . ." Northcliffe had, indeed, a good command of the American vernacular and was ready to use it. In July, 1918, he writes of a certain noble Lord that " he worked this racket on a previous occasion," which is ten years earlier than its first appearance in print (the *Daily Express* used it, in quotes, on September 14, 1928). The word "racketeers" appeared in *The Times* of January 11, 1930. Northcliffe's puritanical dislike in print of American and any other slang moved him even to insist upon quotes for " slump " in the City article.

Throughout this period Northcliffe sent, with equal regularity, to Carmelite House his "communiqués," in which the *Daily Mail* and the *Evening News* were examined. Copies of these were regularly sent to Steed and Stuart at Printing House Square from the spring of 1919, in accordance with the intention to co-ordinate the policy of the newspapers.

The circulation in 1914 was : February, 48,676 ; April, 147,589 ; August, 278,000 ; September, 318,000. The make-up of the average 24-page paper (with Financial Supplement) was six columns to every page and remained unaltered till 1916. The subject arrangement normally was : Shipping, Law Reports, Home News, Imperial and Foreign Intelligence, Main News (to left of Leader page), Court and Society, Obits, Entertainments, Parliament (if any), Sporting Intelligence. Correspondence was printed on various pages according to topic.

There was no issue for Christmas, 1913, the first weekday (Thursday) missed in the history of the paper.

Northcliffe's demand of January 25, 1914, for a light leader daily, resulted on the 26th in " Anticipation and Memory " (A. Clutton-Brock). There has been others in similar style. January 27, " The Fear of the Pedagogue " (B. Darwin), and 28th, " Blue Hair and Gilded Faces " (H. Child), were more frivolous in title and treatment.

V: THE COMING OF WAR

The Marconi Inquiry, 1912-1913

On March 7, 1912, a tender from the English Marconi Company, to erect six long-distance stations for an Imperial wireless scheme, was accepted by the Postmaster General, Herbert (later Viscount) Samuel, for the British Government. These stations were to be in London, in Egypt, and at Aden, Bangalore, Singapore, and Pretoria. Though the German Telefunken scheme and that of the Poulsen Company were not without supporters, most experts were satisfied that the Marconi Company could most effectively carry out such a programme, and a contract was signed on July 19. Room could not be found in the Parliamentary programme for a motion of approval until just before the summer recess, and even then various objectors required that discussion be held over until the autumn session.

Meanwhile the Attorney General, Sir Rufus Isaacs (later Marquess of Reading), had during a luncheon at the Savoy Hotel with his brother Godfrey on April 9, 1912, been offered shares in the American Marconi Company, an off-shoot of the English Company but connected therewith only by the circumstance that Godfrey Isaacs was the moving spirit behind both enterprises. It could not be said that this financier had been outstandingly successful; later it appeared that various undertakings of his had been registered not under the Companies Act but under the less exacting Industrial and Provident Societies Act. Sir Rufus declined the offer, partly because he thought the American Company over-capitalized, but also deeming it wise not to associate himself with a business under the direction of a relative who was then hoping to secure a Government contract. But on April 17, when the offer of shares was renewed by another brother, Harry Isaacs, who had also been at the luncheon but held no position in either Marconi Company, Sir Rufus purchased 10,000 of the American shares at £2 per share. To two friends, Lloyd George, Chancellor of the Exchequer, and the Master of Elibank (later Lord Murray of Elibank), Chief Liberal Whip, he passed on a thousand shares apiece. All three politicians were satisfied that such investment could not conflict with their official duties; for the English Marconi Company had practically secured its contract already, and its prospects and those of its American counterpart were not mutually affected. When the shares were publicly offered in London on April 19 they were dealt in at some £3 ; Sir Rufus at once sold £5,000 of his holding, and subsequently disposed of a further £2,000. Lloyd George sold his packet next day at $3\frac{9}{32}$; he later explained that his purchase had been meant as an investment and the sale was an unpremeditated action suggested by a broker. Lloyd George, however, on his own account bought a further 3,000 American shares on May 22.

While these transactions were in progress there occurred the great boom in Marconi shares in both countries. No doubt a contributory factor was the manner in which news was received of the *Titanic* disaster, which impressed public opinion mightily with the value of wireless telegraphy at sea. *The Times* in its Finance Supplement on April 23 wrote of " excessive speculation " in Marconis. After the shares had soared and then in the summer slipped back, there were rumours that Ministers were mixed up in market dealings in their private capacities; the Marconi contract was jobbery; people were making fortunes out of a public need; the country was on the verge of revelations which would hurl the Government from power. W. R. Lawson in the *Outlook* led off with a series of insinuations, beginning on July 20, against the integrity of Samuel and Isaacs. Cecil Chesterton in the *Eye Witness* (later *New Witness*) began those articles on " The Marconi Scandal " which were to involve his prosecution and fine in May, 1913, for criminal libel upon Godfrey Isaacs. Leo Maxse, editor of the *National Review* and always a bitter assailant of the " International Jew," though denying that he was anti-Semite, started to thunder monthly from September, 1912, in which month the *Spectator*, while refusing to listen to any charge of trickery, urged that there should be a Parliamentary inquiry into the Marconi contract. The *Morning Post* on October 2 wrote of a " taint " in the air.

These allegations, passing from the vague to the specific, never substantiated yet not withdrawn, were thought sufficiently serious for Ministers to make statements in the House of Commons on October 11, when it was resolved to set up a Parliamentary Committee to inquire into the Marconi agreement. Sir Rufus Isaacs denied that he had been a party to negotiations between the English Marconi Company and the Government, or that he had ever trafficked in shares of " that company." Literally accurate though these words were, it was unfortunately, though not unnaturally, assumed that they covered all Marconi enterprises everywhere. Not for five months did Sir Rufus's and his colleagues' speculations in the American shares become public knowledge. To *The Times*, when on May 8, 1913, it came to recapitulate all the incidents, this want of candour was the crucial point.

A plain admission of the truth in October, when there was a direct invitation to make it, would have revealed the origin of the current rumours, killed a host of malicious gossip, saved an immense amount of time and trouble, and set the public mind at rest.

In his biography (vol. I, p. 249) the 2nd Marquess of Reading allows that his father here made a mistake, but explains it thus: a Select Committee was about to be set up, and the accused Ministers might assume they would go before it immediately instead of being kept waiting for months ; moreover a technical discussion of the nature and extent of the transaction would have demanded time and more familiarity with the Stock Exchange than most M.P.s possessed. " That the omission was deliberate, no one can doubt; that it was designed to be permanent, few can suspect; that it was an error of judgment, subsequent events proved with overwhelming force." Proceedings of the Committee began on October 24, 1912. Northcliffe took a personal interest in it.

No comment on rumours about gambling in shares was offered at any stage by *The Times*, nor was the Parliamentary Committee noticed editorially until February 13, 1913, after Maxse, summoned before it, had refused to divulge the source of information which satisfied him that there was ground for the suspicions concerning Samuel, the Isaacs brothers, and Lloyd George being voiced in his monthly fulminations. As the position of an editor depended much on his confidential informants, Maxse held that he would not be able to carry on after betraying any confidence. On this point of journalistic principle, which was later to be seconded by Hilaire Belloc to the discomfiture of the examiners, *The Times* observed:

> The position taken up by Mr. Maxse is one which it is essential to maintain, if the power of newspapers for good from time to time is not to be impaired. Much information and criticism beneficial to the public will necessarily be suppressed if those who communicate with editors are no longer assured that the confidence reposed in them will in all circumstances be respected. It is to the honour of English journalism that the implied promise given to correspondents has rarely been broken. We do not doubt that it will continue to be kept.

After all, parallel practice in extracting and keeping confidence was usual among physicians and Roman Catholic clergy. As to journalists, " the chief sufferers from breaches of the present practice would, in the long run, be the public themselves."

Next a libel action was brought by Herbert Samuel and Sir Rufus Isaacs against *Le Matin* of Paris, whose London Correspondent had set down as facts what Maxse had quoted in the *National Review* as typical rumours. Though the suit on March 19, 1913, was undefended, Carson as their counsel contrived to give the plaintiffs the opportunity of rebutting in Court such suggestions as they had already faced in the House of Commons.

It was then that the purchase of American Marconi shares came to light. Next day *The Times* congratulated the Ministers on the outcome, speaking of the " sincere satisfaction to all right-minded men " that unqualified denial had been given to charges inadvertently made that Ministers, being in possession of official knowledge of a Government contract, bought shares in a company at a low price in order to profit by the rise. The paper remarked that " it might have saved a good deal of trouble if Sir Rufus Isaacs had made in October in the House of Commons the statement he volunteered in Court about his purchase of shares in the American Company. Counsel for the *Matin* very properly disclaimed all idea of using that statement to relieve their clients of legal liability." The paper concluded:

> It still remains for the House of Commons Committee to investigate the slanderous charges that have been circulated. We are of opinion that more delicacy might have been shown by the Ministers involved in the selection of their investments. But mere lack of judgment is a very different thing from the monstrous offences that have been imputed to them.

To Maxse this leader was a " lamentable article," but he charitably excused it on the ground of the Editor's holiday. The *Observer*, bringing in on April 6 its earliest reference to the Marconi case, was more tart:

> It is, unhappily, certain that a grievous mistake has been committed in public life by those who ought to have been the last to make it. It is certain that the failure to make a clean breast of that mistake last autumn was a blunder of the first magnitude.

The attitude of *The Times* differed from that of the *Morning Post*, the *Daily Express*, the *Globe* and the *Spectator*. It was known by some of the Editor's friends (hence Maxse's reference to his being on holiday) that opinion in Printing House Square was divided. From the beginning Northcliffe, for motives that remain obscure, decided upon a relatively neutral course. Dawson was absent recuperating for a fortnight or more after March 5, during which period Northcliffe intervened on more than one occasion to alter leading articles. On March 20 he told the Editor that " In the matter of the Marconi case, I was in the devil of a difficulty. Pressed on the one side by Unionists in high places, and their organizations, to take it up as a good opportunity to attack and perhaps defeat the Government; on the other by my conviction that there is nothing worse than indelicacy or want of judgment and foresight, I asked Reggie [Nicholson, Manager of *The Times* in succession to Moberly Bell], to see that a moderate article on this line was written ... " When read to him the leader was disapproved as seeming to be libellous, and Northcliffe " patched one together " himself; and " a very poor patch it was " (Northcliffe to Dawson, March 20, 1913). Capper, who was in charge, was instructed by Nicholson to substitute Northcliffe's leader for the original written by Ross which represented the views that the Parliamentary Correspondent reported as generally prevalent in all parties. The occasion had been a debate in the Commons that traversed the apparently complete frank and candid statement made to the House by Sir Rufus Isaacs on October 11, 1912, in which, however, he made no mention of his purchase of American shares and the avowal was only now made under pressure. This concealment under the guise of candour made a bad impression on the office, but Northcliffe's mind was not easily altered. The Editor kept in close touch with him on the subject without, however, bringing him into line with what the office believed to be the state of public opinion as revealed, for instance, in all parts of both Houses.

When the Parliamentary Committee adjourned to sort out its conclusions, *The Times* on May 8, 1913, took the chance of summarizing facts in " what has come to be known as the ' Marconi scandal,' which has nothing to do with the merits of rival wireless schemes." The paper said that a climax could no longer be avoided, but dreaded the prospect of a debate in which the radical question of Ministerial propriety would be buried under the " promiscuous irrelevances of a purely party struggle. That, indeed, has been the essential weakness of the working of the Committee itself." There followed this judgment by the Editor upon the evidence collected:

> Nothing which has come out in the course of the evidence affords the slightest ground for believing that the Marconi Contract was not concluded with a single eye to the public interest. There is no question whatever of " corruption," in the sense that Ministers made a bad bargain in their public capacity for the sake of private advantage. Their personal integrity is not in dispute. The real case against them is happily of a different order altogether, though in our opinion it is sufficient to justify the fullest discussion in Parliament.

First, for Ministers to speculate at all was indiscreet; next, the securities chosen were closely associated with the stock of a company with which the Government was dealing.

> There are forms of indiscretion—and we hold this to be one of them—which are frankly breaches of the rule (in Mr. Lloyd George's own admirable words) that " an officer of the State should not merely be incorruptible but that he should have no association with companies which would make him open to suspicion." Sir Rufus Isaacs' original refusal of the shares showed plainly enough that he had

serious doubts about the propriety of taking them; and though the conditions were different in the following week, they were never sufficiently different to justify his change of front.

Above all other considerations the Editor placed the want of candour with which the House of Commons had been treated throughout. Meanwhile the *Pall Mall Gazette* had run a series of five front-page articles, to which the *Observer* alluded with pride on May 11, when it declared: " We acquit the Ministers involved of corrupt action, motive and intent. But things have happened which the unwritten code of our private life was supposed to render impossible." A Cabinet despotism was seen by Garvin to have resulted from " ruin of the House of Lords." The Ministers " could not have realized that they were trying to make money out of ' one of the worst gambles that the City has ever seen,' as a direct consequence of the *Titanic* disaster. But to say that is to convict them of an utter want of right thought and right feeling at that moment." It had been wrong to speculate at all; to unload part of the purchase on a gambling market; to act in circumstances of calamity; to gamble in any wireless shares; and to associate with Godfrey Isaacs, the brother of a Minister. Finally, the whole Cabinet was blamed by the *Observer* for the failure to tell all in October.

Northcliffe remained unaffected by these or the Editor's arguments. A long letter to the Editor signed " Ever attached Chief " and dated May 7, 1913, needs to be reproduced (incidentally the characteristic paragraphing should be observed).

I should be very sorry to have any difference of opinion with you, especially at the present juncture, when the paper looks like emerging from its forty-year slough of despond, and after so magnificent an issue as that of this morning, but have thought carefully over your conversation of last night, and have since waded through the greater part of 200 pages of Maxse's garbled story and Garvin's outrageous *Titanic* insinuations.

I had previously read much of that which has appeared in the *Morning Post, Daily Express, Spectator* and *Globe.*

I do not agree with you or with them.

I have no intention of being part and parcel of an attack upon a man because of his brothers' faults. I have been so attacked myself. Nor have I any intention of being associated with an ascription of grave imprudence as roguery.

I am quite willing to stand sponsor, as I should have to, to an impartial, if strongly worded article on the subject, for I agree that there is much to be said.

Even if public opinion were as you say, which I entirely doubt, I am not the least afraid of public opinion. I stood up against it here in the Dreyfus case. I took my life in my hands prior to the Boer War, and in connexion with Mr. Rhodes, when a pamphlet was placed in every seat in the House of Commons accusing me of being paid by Mr. Rhodes. History has justified me in both cases. Rhodes was grievously indiscreet, but he was not corrupt. I am not comparing a Welsh solicitor and Jew barrister with C.J.R., but I see around me exactly the same malevolence from exactly the same kinds of minds as that with which I was faced before.

I do not see why we should not plainly ask Isaacs and George for their defence and publish it in *The Times,* for if the Committee meets to-day and adjourns over the Whitsuntide Recess there are three more weeks for Leo, Garvin, the *Morning Post,* etc., etc., to continue their insinuations, and there is every reason to believe that they will do so.

I quite agree with you in regard to the attitude of the Liberal Press, and, as you know, I wished an article in *The Times* long ago on the deportment of Ministers, which would have bridged what looks to me like a curious or careless silence.

Please do not think that I am like one of those judges who object to their decisions being reversed. Late at night, and very speedily, in the midst of much work, I decided on certain lines with regard to these men which may not have been strong enough. It was what I thought, and still think to be fair, though a bad article technically. I am not speaking of the conduct of the two Isaacs brothers at all.

May I say I was really surprised to hear you suggest that Cabinet Ministers connived at a put-up action between themselves and an obviously hostile foreign newspaper. If you have watched this matter you will see that *Le Matin* has reported this thing most malevolently, with many scraps of insinuations and attack which have not been used here.

You told me that the Bar were hostile to Isaacs. Some of them are; some of them are not. The enclosed [now lost] should, I think, have been printed in *The Times* this morning, especially as we affect to be the lawyers' organ, and print all sorts of little legal *faits divers.*

I was surprised too not to see the oil matter, which I had taken so much trouble to verify, and which I could have used elsewhere.

I do not want to come to Printing House Square to-day because I am hoping to get away to-morrow, and have much to do, but I would like to see you at St. James's Place at three thirty to-day.

Clearly Northcliffe had sided with Rufus Isaacs (for additional comment on their relations see below). The Editor and the Office needed to be circumspect if they were to avoid a repetition of the incident occasioned by the Declaration of London (*see* vol. III, p. 747). Northcliffe's papers contain no hint of any personal connexion with the scandals. At least once he insisted to the Editor that he wanted the whole truth to come out, but " my talk with Bonar [Law] showed me that whatever our hot heads may think, there are other serious considerations in overdoing the attacks on the Government." As for himself, he said " It will involve me in directly critical relations with highly placed personal friends for which I know neither you nor I care a 2d. dam " (*sic*). (Northcliffe to the Editor, undated.) Northcliffe as man and journalist despised scandal and the Marconi scandals were either tragic or negligible; the inquiry was either nationally necessary or partisan spite. Moreover, at this time Northcliffe was on pleasant terms with Churchill. In a letter undated (obviously sent between Easter and Whitsun, 1913) Northcliffe is to be found writing :

My dear Winston,
I shall be very glad to go in a submarine at the end of the Whitsuntide recess, if that would be convenient, but please do not trouble to come yourself. I presume Portsmouth is the nearest? If anything goes wrong with the submarine with *both* of us in it I am sure it will be the cause of much satisfaction to many.
Your Marconi friends stage manage their affairs most damnably. The system of making mysteries of pieces of evidence in the inquiry, and doling them out like a serial story, has a bad effect on the public, though, as a matter of fact, the whole Marconi business looms much larger in Downing Street than among the mass of the people. The total number of letters received by my newspapers has been exactly three, one of which was printed—the other two were foolish.
The method of dragging the thing out really does make some people think that there is something behind it all, though I personally, as I had your word for it that there is not, know there is not. If they had only taken the trouble to refer to [Machiavelli's] *The Prince* they would have issued a twenty-line paragraph in the Political notes of *The Times*, giving all the facts, and little more would have been heard of the subject. My own belief is that both of them throughout the whole matter have greatly lacked sense of proportion and foresight. Ever sincerely,
NORTHCLIFFE.

By June 3, *The Times* understood that three different reports were to be submitted by the Parliamentary Committee. The draft of Sir Albert Spicer, as Chairman, took the view that Ministers who bought shares in the American Marconi Company were guilty of an error of judgment but that no charge of corruption could stand. James Falconer, on behalf of the Liberals, put forward an alternative, which ultimately became the Majority Report, brushing aside the American issue altogether and confining itself to relations between the Government and the English Marconi Company, in which of course, there was no ground for censure. Lord Robert Cecil and the Unionist minority on the Committee wanted to condemn for impropriety Sir Rufus Isaacs, Lloyd George, and Lord Murray (as the Master of Elibank had become). When sittings were resumed on June 9, immediately after the Chesterton trial—defendant had been found guilty on five counts out of six, but was fined only £100 and cheered by a small crowd—there was fresh and startling evidence. Murray, unknown to his colleagues, had made a later purchase of American Marconi shares, " for his own account or for that of some mysterious trust," as *The Times* observed. Was the business never to be cleared up? The paper gave way to its exasperation about " the totally unnecessary difficulty which has been placed in the way of getting at the truth." Ninety-nine readers out of a hundred, it thought, must have believed after the debate of the previous October that no Minister had ever dealt in any kind of Marconi share. Only after the action against *Le Matin* could opinion adjust itself—" somewhat painfully, it must be admitted "—to the American purchase. Then came the disclosure of Lloyd George's second investment, and now the revelation about Murray. " The unfavourable impression is deepened by the manner in which the facts have been arrived at—little by little, and in the face of a fire of recrimination, protest, and objection." These again were temperate words beside those of the *Observer* on June 8: " There has been nothing in our time more humiliating, grotesque, inept, suicidal than this tale of shabby dabbling exposed by driblets "; and a week later: " First, these Ministerial transactions and tactics have shaken confidence and destroyed respect. Secondly, though they were not corrupt, nothing short of corruption could be much worse."

A leader on June 13 referred to the perplexity in many minds that Carson and F. E. Smith, trenchant Unionist critics of the Administration, should have appeared as counsel for Samuel and Sir Rufus Isaacs against *Le Matin* and for Godfrey Isaacs against Chesterton in cases almost inseparable from issues to be debated in the Commons. Was professional etiquette a principle strong enough to outweigh the possibility of hands being tied in a matter of national significance? Many people, it was said,

believe the purity of public life is involved in some of the questions lately discussed in the Courts of Law and before Sir Albert Spicer's Committee. It matters not that there are no charges of corruption. Those who disclaim any intention of making or insinuating such charges . . . desire the assistance and guidance in such debates of all members who speak with authority and experience. They believe it would be lamentable, and would give rise to misunderstanding in the country, if men of eminence were constrained at some turn of the discussion to say, " We cannot speak freely; our mouths, for professional reasons, are sealed " . . . To the man of ordinary intelligence there is something inexpedient, if not impossible, in the attempt to fill two irreconcilable parts, and no appeal to rules of etiquette will convince him of the contrary.

Amid the correspondence which developed, Smith on the 17th was allowed 1½ columns of crisp rejoinder, in which the following is a specimen paragraph:

> May I without incivility add that, if upon a matter requiring some degree of enlightenment and cultivation for its adequate comprehension, the " ordinary man " is uninstructed upon the function which every civilized country in the world has assigned to the advocate, *The Times* would be better employed in informing his mind than in appealing to his judgment ?

All three sections of the Report were given as a Supplement to the issue of June 14, accompanied by a leader headed " A Partisan Report " and expressing general condemnation of the method, the conduct, and the outcome of the inquiry. " The Chairman's draft report was treated with contempt and left derelict. The first six paragraphs were amended at Mr. Falconer's instance; the remaining twenty-four were simply cut out and replaced by Mr. Falconer's. In short, the Committee adopted Mr. Falconer's draft instead of the Chairman's. But when we say the Committee we mean the Ministerial majority on it, for everything was determined by strict party voting. . . . The effect will be to condemn the Committee. The substitution of Mr. Falconer's report is a piece of pure party business."

The measured censure of the Unionist minority evoked this summary in *The Times* (of the 14th):

> If the Committee had adopted the firm and fearlessly judicial method of Lord Robert, it would have inspired general respect and in the end have done the Ministers better service than the transparent attempt to hush up the whole thing. The general public, as every one knows, have made up their minds that, though nothing corrupt or dishonourable was done, several mistakes or indiscretions were committed, which would have been avoided if the gentlemen who committed them had not been thinking more about making money by a promising speculation than about the responsibility and dignity of their office. That opinion will be confirmed rather than shaken by the present Report; and the part played by Mr. Falconer in its adoption is likely to stimulate speculation on the reasons why he and Mr. Booth behaved through the inquiry in the curious manner to which Lord Robert briefly refers in his draft report. They kept to themselves knowledge which the Committee ought to have had, and they checked inquiry into matters which the Committee ought to have investigated. If they suppose that the public cannot see through these proceedings, or will be satisfied with the result, they are greatly mistaken.

The leading article on June 14 pleased the Chief, who on the same day thus expressed himself to the Editor:

> I have written the *Daily Mail* leading article for Monday, taking as its text:

> The general public, as every one knows, have made up their minds that, though nothing corrupt or dishonourable was done, several mistakes or indiscretions were committed, which would have been avoided if the gentlemen who committed them had not been thinking more about making money by a promising speculation than about the responsibility and dignity of their office.—*Times*: June 14.

> I hope you will get a really fine writer to deal with the matter in a detached and dignified way. The *Times* leading article is likely to be looked at again and again when you and I have long been forgotten. I would suggest that it be absolutely free from any Party suggestion.

> I should have liked the Minority Report a good deal better had it not been drawn up by such fierce Party men. One or two of them have come under the headline of " the limit."

It remained for Parliament to debate the Report on June 18-19. Commenting on the original Unionist motion put down, which regretted both the Ministerial transactions and the want of frankness in later accounting for them, *The Times* said the credit of the House of Commons was at stake. With Ministers exonerated from grosser charges, the vital thing was achieved already; but if the House were to find nothing to regret, then it would deliberately set up a standard lower than that demanded by public opinion. Another danger lay in undignified behaviour should the affair be reduced to a party question. The paper itself proposed a way of averting that: while approving the terms of the motion, it simultaneously asked for some words of congratulation to the gentlemen who, " lying for months under the harrow of baseless rumours," were acquitted of mischief. Apologies from Sir Rufus Isaacs and Lloyd George during the first day of debate left *The Times* rather unsatisfied. The Attorney General acknowledged that he had been mistaken both in buying the American shares and in saying nothing about them during the October debate, but strenuously denied that there was anything dishonourable about the deal; that it ever crossed his mind he might be suspected of corruption; that he misled anyone intentionally. " If he had known all that he knows now he would never have bought them; but here, too, he protested the excellence of his intentions." The Chancellor of the Exchequer, while admitting his error of judgment, likewise defended himself ethically by pointing out that the company in which he invested had no contractual relation with the Government, and that he purchased at the market price. Yet, said *The Times:*

> Neither Minister seems to understand how their conduct strikes the public. It may be put by way of a metaphor. A man is not blamed for being splashed with mud. He is commiserated. But if he has stepped into a puddle which he might easily have avoided, we say that it is his own fault. If he protests that he did not know it was a puddle, we say the he ought to know better; but if he says that it was after all quite a clean puddle, then we judge him deficient in the sense of cleanliness.

In the end it came to a party division, an amendment from Sir Ryland Adkins being carried by 346 votes to 268; this accepted the Ministers' regrets, absolved them from acting otherwise than in good faith, and reprobated false charges of corruption. *The Times* on June 20 disliked the division but was proud of the debate, especially of speeches by Asquith and Balfour. What everything came back to was that men of sense and honour had never credited the extreme rumours, and if only Ministers had been entirely candid in October, 1912, the incident would have closed itself.

> Formal censure would be a punishment heavier than is called for, and we should be sorry if, as a result of this wretched business, either Sir Rufus Isaacs or Mr. Lloyd George were driven from public life. After the present severe lesson there is reason to hope that they will be far more useful public servants than before. Mr. Lloyd George, in particular, will be much improved by a chastened ambition, a less exuberant self-confidence, and a less venomous tongue.

The paper returned to this topic once more on July 2, 1913, when it considered Lloyd George had given direct provocation in an address to the National Liberal Club. It reminded him that dignified silence would go further than too much protesting towards his rehabilitation. The issue was closed, as far as P.H.S. was concerned on August 9 when there was a leading article in support of the new contract with the English Marconi Company.

It may be added that Rufus Isaacs was one of the few public men with whom Northcliffe had no quarrel public or private. He supported Reading as Viceroy against some of Chirol's criticisms, and years later he sought his mediation with Lloyd George after the feud began in 1918. See below.

The German Press, 1913

The year 1913 was one of close Anglo-German cooperation to prevent the Balkan conflict from spreading all over Europe, and the German official classes were, at this time, satisfied with the attitude of *The Times*. The March articles on the *entente* and the French revanchist campaign were well received. The journal's attitude to the re-organisation of the army is not considered hostile, by some as even friendly, as corresponding to an understanding of the necessity imposed on Germany to adapt her land forces to the situation created by the change in the European balance of power. The end of the year is marked by Bethmann-Hollweg's speech (December 9) and the semi-official comment of the *Norddeutsche Allgemeine Zeitung* which both appreciate the fact that in Anglo-German relations a considerable step forward has been made. The German Press and public took little notice of the critical attitude of the paper towards the Liman von Sanders affair. The German Press at this period would appear to be acting with great reserve towards Russia (cf. Goschen to Grey, December 27 and 30, 1913, Gooch and Temperley XI, nos. 450 and 453, pp. 398 and 403).

> Schiemann hints, as early as January, 1914, rather plainly, that the contributions of the Russian Government to the Russian Supplements issued by Printing House Square, are nothing but a subsidy and that *The Times* is in the pay of Russia. Schiemann and the rest could not understand that the advertisement department of Printing House Square applied the same formula to Russia as to Brazil, and would organize a special Supplement, as a source of revenue, on the basis of a guarantee of so much space being bought by business firms engaged in import and export, banks (official and semi-official) or other agencies. There was nothing " corrupt " about such Supplements on either side, and no political considerations were involved, except those of the most indirect kind, at any time. *The Times* was well able to stand on its own feet and had no need to take advantage of Russian propaganda habits, obvious enough in other countries. But in August, 1914, it is stated over and again in German newspapers and pamphlets that Russian money was behind the strong support of Russia in *The Times*. Yet Sazonov was convinced, in June, 1914, that in the Anglo-Russian conflict over Persia, the journal was used by the British Foreign Office to make trouble; and it seems that even Grey's protest against this allegation, and Benckendorff's emphatic assurance that *The Times* was the best friend Russia had in Britain, failed to convince the Russian Foreign Minister. In sum, while it is true that the incidents during the first half of 1914 confirmed German official circles in their long-held views about the fundamental Germanophobia of *The Times*, they had no definite influence on Anglo-German relations in general, or the attitude of the German public towards England. Taken as a whole, the atmosphere was not unfriendly. During the first weeks after Sarajevo the attitude of *The Times* attracted little attention in Germany and Austria. It was

noted that it was not friendly; but as the pro-Serbian sympathies of *The Times* were known, that, by itself, did not cause much surprise; and as nobody at that time expected the conflict to develop into a European affair, little importance was attributed to it.

Nevertheless, when the Austrians started their Press campaign, they were quick to see the importance of *The Times* with regard to English and international opinion and spared no endeavours to make contact with Printing House Square, whereas the German Embassy apparently considered hopeless any attempt to get publicity for the Austrian standpoint in *The Times*, and did not even try. The article of July 16, the result of Austrian action, caused a certain sensation in official circles, annoying the Serbians and Russians, pleasing the Austrians and, to a lesser degree, the Germans. Many thought it inspired, particularly in view of the almost simultaneous article in the *Westminster Gazette*, which was generally considered as the semi-official paper ; and the advice to Serbia rather than the warning to Austria was noticed. As the British Government never disclaimed publicly their connexion with these articles, the impression that they expressed official views was more or less persistent up to the publication of the Austrian Documents. As the Austrian Foreign Office was aware of the origin of both articles, the Ballplatz, at least, cannot have mistaken them as semi-official, and cannot have been induced to conclude from these articles that its policy would be acceptable to British opinion. Furthermore, the Austrian Foreign Office had noted well before the ultimatum that *The Times* was changing its attitude.

This change had already become apparent in the articles of July 22 and 23; they did not, however, cause much concern to the Press of the Triple Alliance although they were noted by some observers with hardly comfortable feelings. More attention was paid to them by the French papers, especially to the article of the 23rd. Later German writers and historians were to attribute more significance to them. The reaction of *The Times* to the Austrian ultimatum was noted with some optimism by the Austrians, and, with a clearer understanding of its real meaning, by the Russian diplomats; there is no evidence of the reaction of the Wilhelmstrasse. German official opinion knew that *The Times* was not friendly, but there are no signs of a particularly deep impression, perhaps because events moved already too fast. Nor did the first days of the interventionist campaign of *The Times* create much stir in Germany. Only after the articles of July 30 and 31, and perhaps on account of the notice given them in the English non-interventionist Press, was more attention paid to it. Some German publicists took the stand of Printing House Square seriously, others, while not entirely discounting it, comforted themselves and their readers with the notion that *The Times* was, after all, not representative of the views of the British Government or English public opinion. Rather, the paper was the organ of an international anti-German Press organization, a favourite idea of the Kaiser's. He put it to Otto Beit in 1905-6; Moberly Bell, Wesselitzky of the London Office of the *Novoye Vremya*, and Harmsworth were all in it; and in 1917-18 Northcliffe is depicted as the centre of it. Abroad, the greatest effect of the July articles and especially that of July 20, seems to have been made on Russia whose Press seems to have been very active in making use of *The Times* in assuring Russian opinion that it could rely upon British support, and thus influence the British Government. Hence, perhaps, Benckendorff's indignation over the article of July 30 and its effect on British politicians and public opinion. From August 2 to 5, the diplomatic documents are more or less silent with regard to the effect of *The Times* abroad. They merely give some indication concerning cooperation between *The Times* and French and Russian official circles in order to impress British opinion.

It was only after the outbreak of the war that the writings of *The Times* during the critical days up to August 1 became widely known in Germany; the propaganda of the day mocked the paper's description of Russia as a defender of European civilization. In the main the paper's attitude in the final stages of peace is taken as corroborative evidence of a continuous and persistent hatred of *The Times* for Germany, some writers letting it begin with the accession of Edward VII to the throne, others with the purchase of *The Times* by Northcliffe. The older ideas were not forgotten and *The Times* was again denounced as a member of an international organization (*Matin, Novoye Vremya*, New York papers, etc.) and the effort was made to persuade the Germans that there was a journalistic " Einkreisung," working for the political encirclement of Germany. The Crewe House propaganda naturally gave this idea a fillip and the Germans struck a medal in dishonour of Northcliffe, who is shown ruling *The Times*, the *Daily Mail*, the *Novoye Vremya* and other journals. Some German historians discuss the meaning and origin of the article of July 16, but they are out of date, not having seen the Austrian documents. The contradiction between the latter and Steed's *Through Thirty Years* is only noted by Wegerer. More or less all authors agree that *The Times* was hostile throughout to the Central European Powers, but none of them ventures to claim that the paper used the opportunity offered by the murder of the Archduke to widen it into a European affair which must needs lead to a war between Triple Entente and Triple Alliance; all agree that the paper's campaign was not directed at provoking a war on the Continent, but limited to the task of preventing Great Britain from staying out of it should it arise; and, therefore, to prepare for British participation in it only after it had become apparent that war was inevitable.

The influence of *The Times* upon Austria was not great. Between July 16 and 20, 1914, no changes in the general situation are reflected in the Press. It is only after Tisza's speech that interest becomes once more intensified. Lichnowsky (*England before the War*, p. 9) claims that the speech made English opinion uneasy and caused a change of front particularly in *The Times*. He does not say which of several of Tisza's speeches he has in mind, but the probable one seems to be that of July 19. His statement about the impression in England and the change of attitude of *The Times* seems, however, incorrect; at any rate, the echo of the speech in the paper was not considered as meaning or preparing a change towards an unconditionally anti-Austrian attitude. Zimmermann (p. 32) notes that *The Times* has no objection to the speech and that its correspondent points out its caution and reserve. Anrich (p. 105), who incorrectly dates the speech as delivered on the 15th, says that the comments of *The Times* do not convey the impression that it was unfavourably received. At any rate, the comments of other English newspapers (e.g., *Morning Post*, *Westminster Gazette*) were much stronger (Zimmermann, p. 32). The German Press has no criticism to proffer in that respect. It is true that the Austrian Foreign Office seems to have felt somehow uncomfortable about *The Times*. When Count Forgàch spoke to Tschirschky, the German Ambassador, about Mensdorff's campaign (Tschirschky to F.O., July 22, Kautsky, I, no. 128, p. 147), and told him that Steed, " after momentarily having seen reason, seemed to have relapsed into his former Austrophobia," he can hardly have had the article of the 22nd before him, and his opinion was probably based on the general trend of the conversation between Steed and Mensdorff (see below). However that may be, Forgàch seems not to have taken the line of *The Times* as likely to be very serious with regard to English opinion in general, as he apparently thought it could be counteracted by articles from prominent Austrians in the English Press.

More generally, it is the article of the 22nd (" A Danger for Europe ") which is taken as indicating a change in the attitude of *The Times*. Whether this article was the consequence of another conversation of Steed with the Austrians (it is quite possible that there were further meetings after those reported by Mensdorff, for which see below), or whether (which seems more likely) it was caused by the article of the *Neue Freie Presse* (21st) concerning the presumed contents of the Austrian note and the subsequent panic at Continental stock exchanges, is an open question. But even then the article of the 22nd was not generally realized as indicating an anti-Austrian turn; rather it seems to be that the article of the 23rd about Poincaré's visit to Russia caused uneasiness. The *Kölnische Zeitung*, July 22, evening, calls the article of the 22nd " as a whole, very cautiously worded." A London dispatch of 23rd (24th, evening) is slightly more concerned, but apparently with the Poincaré article; referring to *The Times* and *Morning Post* the paper says that the discussion of the Austrian-Serbian tension continues, and gradually the interest of the Triple Alliance and the Triple Entente in the matter is put more and more in the foreground. The *Neue Freie Presse* (July 22, evening) gives some hints concerning inspiration with regard to the article of the 22nd, and the Poincaré article is quoted *in extenso* next evening. The *Hamburgischer Korrespondent* (July 25, see below) is well aware of the hostility of *The Times*, but does not refer to any particular article. Zimmermann (p. 33) comparing the article of the 22nd with the comments of other English papers, sees it as relatively neutral. He slightly contradicts himself when, analysing its contents, he says that *The Times*, though admitting in principle Austria's right to demand effective guarantees against the continuation of a seditious movement within Serbian territory, makes the principle dependent on requirements incompatible with the fundamental status of Austrian sovereignty. Anrich (p. 143) points out the conspicuous likeness between the trend of thought in the article of the 22nd and Grey's overtures to Lichnowsky on the same day, but he discards the idea that the article may have given an inspiration to Grey. He notes, on the other hand, the link with intervention on the part of the Triple Entente. Meinecke (*Internat. Monatsschrift*, April, 1915, " Problem des Weltkriegs," p. 32), sees the article of the 23rd as the expression of fundamental hostility against Austria and Germany.

Le Temps on July 25, sums up the contents of the article of 23rd (Poincaré's journey) as emphasising the point that neither Great Britain nor France can afford to disregard the danger to the balance of power arising from the situation. The link with the Russian note, which would seem to appear from the article, is probably unintended. The *Journal des Débats* (24th) has not the slightest doubt that Russia will intervene and that she will not be the only Power to do so; *The Times* article of the 23rd, " un article magistral, écrit avec une extrême modération," leaves not the slightest doubt about the consequences of an " initiative belliqueuse " of Austria.

In Russian official circles the articles seem to have been received with satisfaction. Sazonov is supposed to have told Buchanan at this time that with the exception of *The Times*, the whole English Press was worth nothing; and Benckendorff hastens to explain to him on July 26 (Hoetzsch, I, 5, no. 91, p. 87) that the other papers are not so bad after all. As Benckendorff can have heard of Sazonov's remark only at the British Foreign Office (" You told, I believe, Buchanan ") and the Foreign Office must have had it from a report of Buchanan, this remark of Sazonov can hardly refer to the comments on the ultimatum, but to the situation before it; and in this connexion the articles of the 22nd and 23rd are the only ones which would enter into consideration. It may be noted that Benckendorff's dispatch was among those documents from the Russian archives which were published by the *Norddeutsche Allgemeine Zeitung* in 1919 (August 28), and was taken, in the early days of the war-guilt discussion, as evidence of the support given to Serbia by Russia before the official intervention (cf. B. von Bülow, *Die Krisis* (Berlin, 1921, p. 99).

It can hardly be said that the policy of *The Times* had any obvious influence on German diplomacy in the critical last weeks. It seems strange, rather, that the storm signals sent up between July 27 and 31 left hardly any trace in the German diplomatic correspondence. On the other hand, as has been said, the influence on opinion was greater in France and still greater in Russia. It does appear to be the fact that participation in the war was made acceptable to most of Britain by *The Times* to a far greater extent than the *Daily Mail, Morning Post* and the other papers of the interventionist group. The paper's argued case against the *Manchester Guardian*, the *Daily News* and the non-interventionist group was a strong one; but, of course, the invasion of Belgium, long expected in Printing House Square, gave the final blow to non-intervention. Yet even so, it is not to be doubted that it would have been impossible for the interventionists to have steered their course successfully if *The Times* had adopted the attitude of the Liberal Press, or that it would have been extremely difficult for them if the journal, though not actively joining the anti-interventionists, had remained, so to speak, neutral. The other side of the problem, viz., the question how far the campaign of *The Times* was intended to, or in fact did, force, or at least encourage, Grey and the British Foreign Office, is a question that may never be answered. There is no evidence that the Foreign Office used *The Times* during the crisis, there is little to the effect that the paper succeeded in inspiring Foreign Office officials though it sought, as it always must seek, to influence that Office by publicly argued presentation of its views. The only evidence of the relations between the Foreign Office and *The Times* at this period, viz., Steed's report of his visit at the Foreign Office before writing the article of July 22, indicates that he was not very welcome there.

Steed's Meeting With Mensdorff, July, 1914

The differences between the accounts of Steed's encounters with the Austrians appear in the following narratives :

H. Wickham Steed: *Through Thirty Years*. (London, 1924, I, pp. 404 ff.). The time-table would have been:

Thursday, 16.7: Invitation by Goldscheider for

Friday, 17.7: Dinner with members of the Embassy.

Saturday, 18.7: Invitation by Mensdorff for

Tuesday, 21.7: Luncheon with Mensdorff and Franckenstein; Steed's visit to the Foreign Office.

Wednesday, 22.7: Article " A Danger to Europe."

According to the *Oesterreichische Aktenstuecke*, VIII (see above, pp. 180 ff.) :

Wednesday, 8.7: Berlin asks for press campaign.

Thursday, 9.7: Instructions to London.

Friday, 10.7: Mensdorff's reply: will try, but very difficult.

Saturday, 11.7: Vienna repeats instructions and asks Berlin for support.

Between 10 and 15.7: Meetings of Mensdorff with Lansdowne and Rosebery.

Tuesday, 14.7: Meeting Steed-Mensdorff.

Wednesday, 15.7: Meeting Steed, Dubsky and Franckenstein. Letter of the Editor to Lansdowne.

Thursday, 16.7: Article " Austria-Hungary and Servia."

Thus Steed's narrative places the meeting with Mensdorff a whole week later than the Austrian Documents, and makes it correspond with the article of July 22, whereas the Austrian Documents establish a time-connexion with the article of July 16. According to Steed, he met the members of the Embassy *before*, according to the Documents *after*, meeting the Ambassador. According to Steed, Franckenstein was present at the meeting with the Ambassador, whereas it almost seems from the Documents that he was not. Franckenstein does not throw light on the matter.

The key to the discrepancy may lie in the absence of personal relations between Mensdorff and Steed or any member of the Austro-Hungarian Embassy between the latter's return to England in October, 1913, and the supper at Goldscheider's house on July 17, 1914. Steed once met Mensdorff in St. James's Street (he had known him quite well at Marienbad in the days of King Edward VII) but they merely greeted each other and had no political conversation. It was impossible for Steed to go to the Embassy after the seizure of his book, *The Hapsburg Monarchy*, in Vienna for " insult to Majesty "; and this was the first point that Mensdorff mentioned at the lunch with him and Franckenstein on July 21. Dawson did not inform Steed of the letter to him from Lansdowne, which was followed by the leader "Austria-Hungary and Serbia " on July 16. No doubt Dawson instructed Flanagan to write it on the strength of Lansdowne's letter. Mensdorff did not mention this leader to Steed or say anything about Lansdowne. He may have felt that this leader was not enough, that its line would possibly not be maintained and that he must get hold of Steed if anything like a pro-Austrian campaign were to be started by *The Times* and kept up. He could not invite him direct to the Embassy or hint what was afoot. Goldscheider was mobilised, therefore, to get up a supper to which all the principal members of the Embassy, except Mensdorff and Franckenstein, were invited, as well as the Consul-

General, Count Sizzo-Noris. It was on the Thursday that Goldscheider telephoned to Steed saying that a number of " friends from Vienna " were coming to supper and asking him to come, too, because they would be glad to meet him at " ein gemütlicher Herrenabend."

There is indirect proof that Mensdorff's dates are wrong. Had he spoken to Steed on the 14th, given him the impression that Austria-Hungary was bent on war and that Germany was behind her, Steed would certainly have criticized the leader on the 16th as incompatible with the message he had left for Grey, and with the warning Steed had given Mensdorff.

There remains the mystery of Mensdorff's two reports to Vienna dated London, July 17. The second report contains the positive mis-statement that " Mensdorff had last Tuesday a long and thorough conversation with the Foreign Editor of *The Times* who also spoke next day to Baron Franckenstein and Count Dubsky." It would seem that the first report was written to show that Mensdorff had impressed Lansdowne—before the Mensdorff-Steed meeting—and the second report was confusedly put together with the wrong date after the luncheon on the 21st.

Another circumstance may bear indirectly upon the question of dates. Maurice de Bunsen told Steed that he had learned on July 15 from Count Lützow that on July 14 the Austro-Hungarian Foreign Office was certain of German backing. On July 16, Professor Kuno Meyer wrote a postcard from Berlin to Mrs. J. R. Green (widow of the historian of the English people), saying that the Austrian Emperor would shortly sign an ultimatum to Serbia after having received from the German Emperor an encouraging letter which Kuno Meyer's friend, Professor Schiemann, had read before it was sent off. Mrs. Green showed this postcard to Mr. George Trevelyan who told Steed of it. He suggested he should call on Mrs. Green and get her to show it to him. He did so. Mrs. Green showed the card the more readily as Steed had dined at her house in the previous April with Kuno Meyer, Schiemann and Haldane.

It would seem that when the Austro-Hungarian decision was finally taken, on or about July 14, Mensdorff was given a hint, either direct or through the German Embassy, that he must intensify his efforts to capture the British press. This would account for Goldscheider's invitation to Steed on the 16th and its sequel. The article " The Danger to Europe " on the 21st was the immediate result of Steed's report to Northcliffe and Dawson upon his talk with Mensdorff. Thus Mensdorff's dates are bound to be wrong.

The Ballin Telegram

There is nothing in the office archives to alter in any way the account published many years ago by Steed. (*Through Thirty Years*, II, 16-25.) The great German shipowner, Albert Ballin, had in Germany a range of acquaintance reaching to the very highest circles, and in England those scarcely less limited. Among the people he knew in this country was the fourth John Walter, who had been entertained by him at the Kiel regatta in June, 1914. Ballin visited London in July, dining on the night of his arrival (the 25th) at Haldane's, where Grey and Morley were present also. Ballin seemed " very anxious," and his anxiety can hardly have been lessened when both Grey and Haldane told him " that if Germany attacked France we could not remain neutral." (Maurice, *Haldane*, I, 353.) By August 2 Ballin was back in Germany, and on that day he tried to exploit his friendship with Walter in his Kaiser's interest. He telegraphed—in German—to the head of the London office of the Hamburg-Amerika Line a letter addressed to Walter which expressed his amazement at the idea that the German Emperor contemplated an aggressive war, and (as transmitted at once in indifferent English) ended " . . . Russia alone forces the war upon Europe. Russia alone must carry the full weight of responsibility." Walter produced this letter at the editorial conference that day, at which Northcliffe presided. On Steed's advice, since the letter conflicted with the apparent trend of events, the Editor decided not to publish.

On that same evening, a fortunate error by a Post Office clerk delivered to Printing House Square a telegram from the Wolff Bureau, the official German news agency, addressed to its London office. It said that *The Times* would publish next day a statement by Ballin, which was to be telegraphed back *verbatim* to Germany. This was thought by Steed, who opened it, to reveal that Ballin's message to Walter had been concerted with, if not dictated by, the German Government. On August 12, as soon as Bethmann Hollwegg's speech in the Reichstag on August 4 had become available in London, *The Times* published both the passage in that speech which admitted German violations of international law and Ballin's letter to Walter (suppressing the sender's and the receiver's names), with the Wolff Bureau message; and left readers to draw their own conclusions.

Eight months later Ballin gave an interview in Berlin to a New York *World* correspondent in which he put the whole blame for the outbreak of war on Sir Edward Grey. *The Times* at once (April 15, 1915) published an account of this interview and repeated with it Ballin's letter of the previous August 2 (now revealing his authorship): this incited Berlin contradiction between the two was rubbed in by a leading article. This incited Berlin to send to the *Kölnische Zeitung*, which published it on April 17, another letter of his to John Walter, dated August 1, 1914, in which nothing at all was said about Russia's responsibility. This letter had never been received by Walter; and *The Times* could only (on April 19, when it next appeared) say so and repeat a reference to what had in fact been sent. (The English original of the letter of August 2 had been destroyed after six months according to the office custom in handling printed copy.)

Another piece of good luck concluded the controversy. A former employee of the Hamburg-Amerika Line happened upon the German original of Ballin's telegram to Count Wengersky, its London head, which he had saved from the offices of the Line and was able to rescue from a fire in his nursery. He brought it round to Steed, and it was published in facsimile on April 23. This made it clear that the letter which Ballin had sent to the *Kolnische Zeitung* had replaced the text which the paper had printed, and established both his bad faith and the reliability of *The Times*.

Printed Works

Barnes, Harry Elmer: *Genesis of the World War*. (New York, 1929.)

The professor's evidence concerning the order to withdraw French troops from the Luxemburg front is the alleged revelation that the suggestion came to the French from London as the result of collusion between Paul Cambon and Grey who, as Benckendorff tells us, understood the importance of preparing English opinion for the coming conflict. This information that the withdrawal order was given at the instigation of England is credited (p. 411) to " Gerald Campbell of the London *Times* " (see below). " The new British documents furnish no confirmation of Campbell's allegation. They do indicate that Grey had probably decided as early as the 30th that war was inevitable and that England must enter on the side of France. At any rate, Grey fully realized that the French withdrawal order was absolutely a diplomatic subterfuge and he co-operated fully with Cambon and Viviani in using this ruse to deceive his own countrymen as to the acts and policies of Russia and France " (p. 411).

Campbell, Gerald: *Verdun to the Vosges*. (London, 1916.)

The writer says that " at the end of July, for some days before the war began, the French had withdrawn their troops to a distance of six miles from the frontier all along the line, from Luxemburg to the point, a mile from Pfettinhausen, which is the meeting place of the boundaries of France, Switzerland and Alsace. They were acting, I believe, partly at the suggestion of the English Government, and certainly with their warm approval " (p. 33).

Haldane, R. B.: *An Autobiography*. (London, 1929.)

Chapter 8 refers to the systematic campaign of attack by the Harmsworth Press and other newspapers. It began when *The Times* discovered that Albert Ballin, the Hamburg shipowner, had on August 1, 1914, sent by messenger a letter to his personal friend Haldane. From that moment Haldane's earlier admiration for some aspects of German society was grossly misrepresented, his motives in going on a mission to Berlin in 1912 were assailed, and every kind of ridiculous legend circulated. " I had a German wife; I was the illegitimate brother of the Kaiser; I had been in secret correspondence with the German Government; I had been aware that they intended war and had withheld my knowledge of this from my colleagues; I had delayed the mobilisation and despatch of the Expeditionary force." The Foreign Office was averse from publishing records of 1912 which would have cleared matters up. Haldane expresses little surprise or bitterness that such a campaign should have developed while there was general ignorance of facts, but shows that from the autumn of 1914 the attacks persuaded him to resign the Lord Chancellorship rather than weaken the Government.

Steed, H. Wickham: *The Foundations of Diplomacy*. (Lecture to the Royal Institution January 30.) (London, 1914.)

Great Britain was far behind other nations in comprehending that apparently small incidents of dispute in the Balkans in 1912-13 might have world-reaching consequences. Diplomacy is foreign policy in being, and for success needs an instructed public opinion and a clearly directed public will. Because they had these supports, Cavour and Bismarck triumphed. Bismarck selected Treitschke to educate opinion in foreign affairs. Among the British, diplomacy has lost prestige because interests rather than ideals are supposed to actuate all framers of policy. It is thought of as a game without rules except that blunders must not be made. Behind the words and gestures of an envoy should lie the will of a united people; but what are the issues today on which a nation would stake its existence ? If statesmen would talk on broader matters than party politics, professors popularise the results of their studies, pressmen appeal to idealism as well as the craving for sensation, all the means of reaching and educating the public would be found available. Steady painstaking propaganda is the way. Historical examples are given of errors which might have been avoided given more enlightened opinion: Polish partititions, Austrian ingratitude to Russia over the Crimean War, neutral complacency over the seizure of Alsace-Lorraine, injustice to the Balkan peoples in 1878—all contributing to the uneasy equilibrium in Europe.

Trevelyan, G. M.: *Grey of Fallodon*. (London, 1937.)

Book II (Chapters 8 and 9) describes Grey's failure to unite the Balkans as his great diplomatic defeat. It could not have been done without military success in the Near East, and he was not responsible for the armies on the Dardanelles Expedition. Grey first intended not to remain in the Government after Haldane's exclusion was certain. He took no significant part in the reconstruction of 1916, and in any event his eyesight was too bad to allow of long continuation in office. There is noted a letter of December 12 (p. 331) to *Chicago Daily News* declining to join in " a campaign of defence of past policy against the Northcliffe press." October 3, 1918: Letter from Northcliffe to Grey quoted. He thinks the Old Gang are trying to drag L.G. down. Northcliffe will not use his newspapers to support in a most critical election any Government unless he knows in writing and can approve of its personnel (p. 366). This letter is of importance in view of the mystery surrounding the great Lloyd George-Northcliffe feud, for which see Chapter VIII.

VI. WAR.   VII. COALITION

Manuscript and Typescript.

P.H.S. Papers. A large quantity of material of unequal value; very few of the correspondences being complete. Incoming letters are occasionally of interest (especially from Adam). Many of the outgoing letters of which typescript copies were kept in the office are useful; but few of these copies (except Steed's) were initialled at the time of writing and their authorship is sometimes uncertain. There is hardly any written record of decisions of importance taken within the office unless they affected some foreign correspondent.

Asquith Papers. Among these papers, now at Balliol College, Oxford, is much of value which at the date of publication of Lord Oxford and Asquith's official *Life* (1932) was not regarded as suitable for the public eye. A good deal of this value occurs in documents, graded " secret " or " very secret," emanating from the offices of the Committee of Imperial Defence and usually from the pen of Colonel (now Lord) Hankey. More light is thrown on the political background of strategy than can be gleaned either from the *Life* or from the official naval and military histories of the war; but it is of little direct relevance to the purposes of this work. Moreover the papers concerned are not at present in any regular order. Rather more material evidence can be found in the surviving political correspondences, which provide more side-lights on the influence of party during the first Coalition than can be seen in the *Life*, and include a number of direct references to the newspaper magnates and newspaper attacks which Asquith despised. Personal letters to him and from him, exchanged with a number of close relatives and friends, are of interest in that they show the workings of his mind and the social background against which he worked; but are naturally unsuitable for direct use in histories.

Dawson Papers. These are not as a rule revealing, but there are exceptionally illuminating flashes in the Editor's correspondences with, for instance, Braham, Fraser and Maxse. The collection was at some time severely winnowed by Dawson himself.

Milner Papers. These documents form a historical source of exceptional importance for the war of 1914-1918, so far unused, since no official life of Lord Milner has yet been written. Accordingly, it may be well to outline their scope. They fall into four classes, the first of which calls for some description in detail.

(i) *Private Letters*, in eight bound volumes. These include much only of personal and family interest, much more of intense political interest and great importance. Their study is indispensable to an understanding of Conservative policy just before and during the war, and they form the core of the collection.

There is little in them that bears directly on *The Times* in spite of Lord Milner's warm friendship with the Editor. No letters to Dawson are here preserved, even as copies (there are none in the accessible Dawson Papers either), and the few notes from him are neither long nor interesting. There are indeed remarkably few letters to or from the members of Milner's " kindergarten," for that close-knit body, membership in which sprang from personal qualities, exercised its influence on British imperial policy more through personal contacts than through distant exhortations. Some letters from L. S. Amery will be noticed below. The only other frequent correspondent in the group with its acknowledged head was the only other member of it who spent much time during the war out of London, F. S. Oliver. A man more of letters than of action, his inclination was to reach for pen and paper at a moment of crisis, and Milner's correspondence was enlivened by many letters from his Border seat which expounded with fluent pungency the current beliefs of the circle to which they both belonged.

A unique source from which to study the circle's activities is Lord Milner's diary, which is in the custody of his widow. It will eventually form part of the collection at New College, and may be mentioned in parenthesis here. Lady Milner has been so good as to allow the compilers of the present work to have access to it, and some of their conclusions are recorded above. For the last thirty-two years of his life Lord Milner made a few notes, every night just before he went to bed, in a duodecimo diary with a page devoted to each day. A normal entry would be some 150 words long, and would include a note of where he had taken luncheon or dinner, and with whom; what meetings he had attended; and who had called on him or received a call from him during the day. A few words might be devoted to the subject of any particularly important conversation or meeting; and he almost always mentioned the time that he retired. These bare and battered volumes, in his rapid manuscript, provide a source of tantalising brevity, yet irrefragable accuracy.

They cannot, however, do more than hint now and again at some of the facets of his character which are illuminated fully in the volumes of private letters now under discussion. It is only to be expected that his faith and interest in the Empire should have been prominent in his correspondence. He was enough of an elder statesman, and commanded enough general respect, to be appealed to as an impartial arbiter in a dispute between the Colonial Office and a Judge in a West African court, about the' fairness of the Judge's supersession (one of the letters to him in this connexion revealed incidentally, that he was a Mason). Within a few days of Joseph Chamberlain's death, the Chamberlain family appealed to him to write that statesman's official *Life*, either in the form of a full-length biography or in that of an introductory volume for a selection from Chamberlain's papers to be edited by Amery. The outbreak of war, with the extra work that it brought him, unfortunately prevented Lord Milner from taking a part in this task, which was also refused by Geoffrey Dawson, was executed in part by J. L. Garvin, and remains at present in the hands of Mr. Amery's son. A glimpse of the imperialist creed of the kindergarten can be got in phrase from one member of it, dated May 25, 1915; " We are not a part of Europe, even if the most important unit of the British community lies off the European coast." The influence of this view of the Continent on Dawson becomes clear in the "Appeasement" period surveyed in Chapters XXI and XXIV.

There are also glimpses of Milner's relations with the men of the extreme Right and of the extreme Left in English politics. An unnamed correspondent deplored in December, 1914, a suggestion in the *Round Table* that democracy might help to win the war, and a year later a staff officer wrote to him that " We want aristocracy, at any rate for ' 3 years or the duration of the war '; the rule of the select instead of the chatter of the elected, decisive government instead of useless and dangerous special pleading." Yet occasional touches show up what might be called the Tory Radical side of Milner : he had read and recommended to a friend G. D. H. Cole's *World of Labour*; on November 3, 1916, he called the author " a very extreme and in some respects very wrong-headed revolutionary young man, but he is not altogether wide of the mark, and I think it is possible to gather from his statement what amount of real reason there is for the Syndicalist movement, and what the new Labour men are—not certainly in the wisest possible way—trying to get at." In the spring of the same year he had told Lady Roberts confidentially that he was " trying very hard, but quietly, to further a purely working class movement, which I hope will knock out the ' Independent Labour Party ' and start a ' Workers' League ' among the Trade Unionists, who will make Imperial Unity and Citizen Service ' planks ' on its platform." All this time, it may be noted, he described himself in Dod's *Parliamentary Companion* as a Liberal Unionist, and not as a Conservative or a Unionist *tout court*.

Suitably to his position both as a London banker and as a founder of Toynbee Hall, Lord Milner interested himself keenly in the economic side of the war. From its earliest months he showed anxiety over the means of reducing Germany's imports of cotton, copper, and petrol; and in July, 1916, he accepted an invitation from Sir Herbert Samuel to coordinate the work of three committees on coal production (though in the same month he refused a joint request from Asquith and Bonar Law to preside over the enquiry into the failures at Gallipoli). At the end of August, 1916, he considered a paper which discussed the oversea payments problem and the impending dollar crisis in terms that are thoroughly familiar to the reader of to-day.

Both before and after he took office himself at the end of that year, Lord Milner's main preoccupation seems, from his surviving papers, to have been the efficient conduct of the war. It was because he thought the voluntary recruiting system inefficient that he was an ardent conscriptionist, because he thought Churchill's touch as a strategist unsure that he was an anti-Churchillian. Because he and his friends thought, as one of the most learned of them wrote, that " Asquith as a political leader is thoroughly untrustworthy," and was not therefore the man to inspire the confidence necessary for victory, Milner was Asquith's devoted and permanent foe. Some of his friends were even more devoted in their dislike of the Prime Minister of the first two years of war, and none of them made any attempt to conceal their dislike in their letters to each other.

Volumes of private correspondence, naturally, are not the place in which a Cabinet Minister's views on strategy are to be found, but there are a few glimpses in this connexion of Milner's shrewd judgement in military matters, including a letter to a close friend written as early as August 21, 1914, in which he forecast exactly what happened a fortnight later at the battle of the Marne. Milner had a particularly high opinion of Sir Henry Wilson, took him on his Russian mission, and no doubt paid attention to his pungently expressed views on strategy, though these were more strictly " western " than were Milner's own conceptions.

On the whole, up to the end of 1916, it was political rather than military strategy that occupied his attention. He had been long enough in politics, and stood high enough in society, to treat Ministers as his equals, and did not struggle hard against the temptation to treat some of them as his inferiors—inferiors in business efficiency and in determination to finish the war (" hopeless wobbling and irresolution," " the unspeakable sloppiness of the administration," " as for the ' supreme direction ' here, it has been just too awfully incompetent and *backboneless*," these were among the phrases that he applied to the government of 1915-16). The need for a small and competent Cabinet to direct the war he took for granted, and the idea that he might himself be a member of it was by no means a strange one to him. Many friends wrote to deplore his omission from the first Coalition, and a few months afterwards one of them—L. S. Amery—sent him a serious appeal. He was the only man, Amery assured him, who was capable of leading the nation at war to its necessary goal, and he ought at once to put himself at the head of a political group which could ensure his accession to the premiership. Lord Milner seems not to have taken this project very seriously, though seven months afterwards—in March, 1916—a paper of his own on the political situation, which has been kept among these letters in MS, glances with some favour at the idea of forming a new party in Parliament with the object of the better conduct of the war.

At the supreme political crisis of the war, in December 1916, the Milner Papers are almost silent : but what they do have to say, in copies of letters to a close friend, is highly significant for the study of the course of the intrigues that secured the fall of Asquith (two phrases from them may give their tone—" I said come out—come out of Sodom and Gomorrah "). There is no formal offer of a seat in the War Cabinet from Lloyd George, and only a passing mention of a summons to its first meeting. Once Lord Milner had attained office, passing in a fashion unprecedented except by the younger Pitt straight to the second position under the crown, he had much less time to write or to read letters, and the interest of this part of his papers is correspondingly reduced. Amery continued to write to him from the Balkans, and to urge on him the need for us to help ourselves instead of relying on some other power to win the war for us: otherwise the letters preserved are not of especial interest. His journey to Russia, in particular, is hardly covered at all.

There are a few memoranda which show his awareness of the importance of other fronts than that in France, and a number of some interest to the military historian, including three long narratives which he wrote at the time. These deal respectively with his visit to France in November, 1916 (the efficiency of Haig's headquarters and the personality of its commander impressed him much), with the resignation of Sir William Robertson in February, 1918, which enabled Sir Henry Wilson to rise to the height of a staff officer's ambition and become C.I.G.S., and above all—perhaps the most important document in the collection—with his celebrated visit to France in the following month and the conference at Doullens that secured unity of command in the west and saved the Channel ports. It is not untypical of the somewhat haphazard arrangement of this collection that it is here, and not among the military papers, that there has been preserved the correspondence between the War Office and the Admiralty about the possible evacuation of the B.E.F. from France, which brings home to its reader how nearly the war was lost eight months before it was won.

(ii) *Cabinet Papers.*—Many more of these than of the private letters, in proportion to the totals, have been preserved. Those of the highest secrecy have, of course, been returned to the Cabinet Offices. Those that remain consist largely of copies of correspondences between the Foreign Office and British representatives abroad. So long as the Foreign Office files remain inaccessible, these copies will be important, though they will eventually be replaced by the full files of minutes and correspondence at the Public Record Office.

(iii) *Military Papers.*—The same is true to a lesser extent of these papers, some of which will retain permanent value even if a distant future sees the opening of the War Office files, for a large number of Sir Douglas Haig's dispatches home bear comments, and the heads of arguments in reply, in Lord Milner's hurried handwriting. There is also material of much military interest on the work of the Supreme War Council at Paris in 1917 and 1918.

(iv) *Press Cuttings.*—The principal interest of these is that Milner bothered to have a secretary paste up in many albums any articles bearing on himself or his interests which happened to catch his eye in the English and South African Press.

Northcliffe Papers. Occasional glimpses of Northcliffe's policy and opinions on matters of significance can be gleaned from the welter of words that he employed in his daily messages to the office throughout the war, and from his long chatty letters to his staff from the United States.

Steed Papers. Little material relevant to these years, but what there is is of value.

Lord Kitchener's Appointment to the War Office

The history of this appointment is not perfectly clear. According to Asquith's biographers, the decision to appoint Lord Kitchener was taken by the Prime Minister, on his own initiative, after a council of ministers and generals (attended by Lords Kitchener and Haldane among others) held at 10, Downing Street, on the afternoon of August 5, 1914. Asquith recorded this in his notes made at the time, and subsequently rebutted any suggestion that either Press or personal influences had affected him. In August, 1914, however, Lord Milner told Lady Edward Cecil (now Milner's widow) that Asquith had in fact appointed Haldane to the War Office on the morning of the day on which war was declared; and that he, Milner, had persuaded Kitchener to call on Asquith and force him to change his mind. The date of this interview is established by the following extracts from Milner's diary—always written up night by night—for August 4:

> Day of great rush & excitement. Amery & Gen. Wilson came to see me early in the morning, then Austen Chamberlain. I went with the latter to see Lansdowne about urging the Govt. to send the " Expeditionary Force " *at once* [this before war had been declared]. Chamberlain went on to see Balfour, then Lovat joined Lansdowne & me. We had an earnest talk about it & I think L[ansdowne] was convinced.

> From Lansdowne House to the City . . .

> At 4.30 to House of Lords. Nothing in the House, but I met Amery & Lovat in the Lobby & arranged with the latter to go & see Kitchener.

> At 5.30 I had tea & a short talk with Lady Edward at the Albemarle Club.

> At 6.30 I went to 17 Belgrave Square to see Kitchener. He & Wingate were together. Lovat joined us & we prevailed on Kitchener to go straight to Asquith.

> Dined alone at Dieudonné's. . . .

According to Lady Milner, during this interview at Belgrave Square Kitchener received a note from Asquith simply suggesting he should stay and help in England. He asked Milner gruffly what answer he should give to so indefinite a proposal; Milner is said to have replied that he should not answer but go at once and see Asquith. *The Times* for the following day recorded Kitchener as one of a number of callers at 10, Downing Street, between 7 and 8 p.m. on August 4. The paper also mentioned that Haldane had been absent from part of the two-hour cabinet meeting which began at 11.30 a.m. on the same day; an absence which would not be inconsistent with his performance of urgent duties at the War Office, where he had been hard at work since the morning of August 3. Neither his *Autobiography* nor Maurice's *Life* throws much fresh light on the incident, though Maurice records (I, 357) how " Asquith agreed with Haldane that Kitchener should be War Minister and at the Prime Minister's request Haldane sounded Kitchener on the subject," apparently on August 4; nor have the present writers been able to find any discussion of it in the Asquith Papers. Kitchener was at work at the War Office on August 5, and kissed hands as Secretary of State and was sworn of the Privy Council on August 6.

Prosecution under D.O.R.A.

On May 21, 1915, *The Times* published a letter from a Major E. H. Richardson on the contrast between the casualties which the French had already suffered and were trying to replace through a stringent system of conscription, and the very large number of able-bodied young men who were still to be seen about the streets and fields of England. The Home Office saw fit to institute a prosecution of him and of *The Times* under the Defence of the Realm Act, for publishing information likely to be of use and value to the enemy, and the case came before the Mansion House police court on May 31. It was adjourned to June 5, when the paper's counsel (later Lord Chief Justice Hewart) was able to show that the German press was fully aware of the matters referred to in Major Richardson's letter; and the magistrate found that there was no case for the prosecution. On June 11 some remaining charges were withdrawn. Freeman pointed out, in a ponderous leading article next morning, that the Government had made itself look foolish and would do better to treat the press as an aid than as an enemy. Major Richardson's costs were paid by the paper.

Sir John Simon and *The Times*, 1915

On October 30 (October 17, old style), 1915, the Moscow *Russkoe Slovo* published a message from its Paris Correspondent which attacked the Balkan policies of *The Times* and the *Daily Mail* on the ground that the enemy had found it worth while to reprint in full some of their articles bearing on the Balkans. On November 19, the *Daily Chronicle* republished this message in London. Five days later the message was read to the House of Commons by the Home Secretary, Sir John Simon, in answer to a supplementary question. A sharp leading article by the Editor in next morning's *Times* (November 25) drew attention to the fact that Simon had quoted a message *to* Russia as a message *from* Russia. *The Times* published tributes to the paper's usefulness from the Tsar himself and from Sazonov. (For the great support given to Anglo-Russian sentiment see below, Section VIII.) This brought an incomplete apology from Simon which was printed next morning, with appropriate comment; below it was a letter from Repington which pointed out that all the articles of his quoted by the Germans had been passed for publication by Simon's " incorrigibly inefficient " censorship. According to a letter from Wilton to Steed of December 2, 1915, based on a talk in Moscow with the *Russkoe Slovo*'s editor, the message did represent Russian opinion to this extent: that some alarm was felt in Russia lest her Allies would not support to the full all her claims in the Balkans; but this could not be said explicitly in a Russian leading article.

On Monday, November 29—a result, it may be conjectured, of a week-end in Oxford—*The Times* printed a column article by the Editor, exposing an intrigue against the paper which Sir Henry Lunn was carrying on in that city. " The dons at Oxford," observed this article, " are an honest and unsuspicious race, not unwilling, as recent correspondence in our columns has shown, to append their signatures to scraps of paper." Nevertheless, the manifesto in denunciation of *The Times* which Lunn was circulating was too much for some of them, and was making little headway. Lunn was characterised as " a prominent figure for years in the party of misguided Englishmen, whose assiduous efforts to cultivate close relations with Germany did so much to blind our people to their greatest danger." The paper called on Sir John Simon to account for the intrigue; and published on the same day a message from Adam in Paris which denied that the *Russkoe Slovo* telegram represented opinion fairly. Next day there appeared a letter from the Russian paper's Paris Correspondent which denied that he had been " inspired " to write as he did; though an editorial note explained that it was known that he had " actually received a request . . . from a British Government official, who was formerly in the service of a Liberal newspaper," that he should publish this denial. The same day's correspondence columns also included an accusation by Leo Maxse that Lunn had stood for Parliament in 1910 " on what may without extravagance be termed ' the full Potsdam ticket '."

By this time the blood of Liberal Ministers was up, and they decided to call *The Times* to order: not in the columns of its contemporaries, but on the floor of the House of Commons. A " one-line whip " to Liberal and Labour members of that House was therefore issued in these terms:

Tuesday, 30th November
The House will meet at 2.45.
Immediately after Questions

Sir John Simon
is expected to make a statement
on matters arising out of
" The Times " strictures on
his recent answer.

Your presence is requested
JOHN W. GULLAND

No such summons was sent to Conservative supporters of the Coalition. Simon spoke for an hour-and-a-half, in a full-dress attack on *The Times* for lack of patriotism and lack of support for His Majesty's Government at a time of national danger. The debate lasted seven hours in all. It was the occasion for much plain speaking but could hardly have been of assistance to the Government or the Home Secretary. It certainly did nothing to conciliate *The Times* or the Northcliffe Press, nor in the course of the debate were there wanting voices who spoke on behalf of *The Times*, the *Daily Mail* and Lord Northcliffe. It was perceived by some speakers that the object of the incriminated newspapers and their Chief Proprietor was to win the war. Dillon, the Nationalist member for East Mayo (who in September had demanded the imprisonment of Northcliffe), now described the evening's business as one of the most serious debates of the war: " You need not flatter yourselves that you have heard the last of it. It is a death struggle between those Ministers I have named [Asquith, Grey, Kitchener] and Lord Northcliffe, and I am not at all sure that Lord Northcliffe is not the greatest power in England to-day." He was echoed by Alden, the Liberal member for Tottenham, who revived Churchill's idea of commandeering *The Times*.

So sharp an attack as Simon's, from so high a quarter, could not go unnoticed; and next morning the Editor replied in an equally vigorous leading article, which suggested that the Home Secretary had spoken for himself and not for the Cabinet. Dawson did his best to account for the venom of Simon's speech by a reference to the latter's dislike of another leading article in *The Times* (also from his pen) of the previous October 11. This had ended " But we warn the Government that they [the people of England] are in no mood to tolerate indecision and mismanagement, and that no belated improvements in machinery will satisfy them if they have come to the conclusion that the men in charge of it are fumblers."

" Plain Englishmen," he went on, " bent on winning the greatest war in history will, we think, be amazed that a Cabinet Minister, summoning only members of his own party, should devote so much time to an attack on newspapers which do not happen to agree with his politics. . . . If Ministers themselves would attack the Germans with half the energy which they devote to *The Times* they would be a good deal nearer to winning the war." A week later, Alden revived again the project of Government control of the paper, and in a written question asked the Prime Minister whether in view of the fact that " *The Times* newspaper is regarded on the Continent as having a semi-official, if not official character, and in view of the importance of preventing the dissemination of news that misrepresents the position of this country and the Allies, he will consider the advisability of taking it over and running it as a Government organ until the close of the war ? " The Prime Minister replied: " No, Sir, I am disposed to think that the Government have sufficient responsibilities without taking over such a serious addition." Within two months the Home Secretary's connexion with the Government ended. He resigned in December, 1915 (Asquith Papers, Balliol College, Box 26; Asquith's *Life*, *II*, 202), though the fact was not published till next month, secure in the belief that his opposition to the Cabinet's proposed measures for conscription would be seconded by Liberal feeling in the country to an extent so overwhelming that he would be swept back to power.

Milner on Intervention in Siberia (1918)

In mid-June, 1918, Milner wrote, but never sent, the following letter to Balfour :

I think the C.I.G.S. is sending you a screed on this subject. *Entre nous*, I feel that No purely military argument is *possible*. The whole question is one in which military and political considerations are inextricably interwoven. If I may put the feelings of the soldiers, *who are absolutely unanimous on the subject*, in my own way I should say their view was this:

Unless something is done, Russia is absolutely at the mercy of Germany. The Bolshevik Government is manifestly *quite powerless* against any organized military force.

But if Germany is allowed to help herself to anything she wants in all Russia —not only supplies, but *ultimately men*—then Germany cannot possibly be beaten.

The only way to prevent Germany overrunning all Russia to the Pacific, as she has already overrun (very easily and quickly despite Bolshevik resistance) the Ukraine and great part of Transcaucasia, is to occupy as much of Russia as can be occupied *by an adequate military force* before the German wave of invasion sweeps over it. At present Germany is establishing her dominion over vast tracts of Russian territory at very small cost to herself. Her political penetration is just like the military infiltration of her machine gunners. She goes boldly ahead, on the chance of meeting with little or no resistance, until she bumps up against something strong enough to stop her. The position then is this:

1. Germany will rapidly establish her dominion over all Russia, unless there is something to resist her.

2. The experience of the last six months proves by demonstration, and every authority in Russia or over here, Russian or foreigner, agrees in affirming, that there is no capacity in Russia at present to resist foreign aggression, and that if ever again Russia is to make headway against German or any other foreign invasion, she must have some external help to give her a start. The absolute helplessness of Russia by *herself* to do anything but lie down and let the Germans walk over her, is the most palpable fact, perhaps the only quite indisputable feature of the situation.

3. But while Germany thus has Russia at her mercy, Germany does not dispose of and—unopposed—does not require any large military force, to overrun the whole of Russia, as far as the Pacific.

4. If only an allied military force even of moderate dimensions could be set up as a bar to the eastward advance of Germany, either (1) that advance, having no weight behind it, would be easily checked, and all Russia east of the barrier would remain outside the domination of Germany, or, (2) if Germany was bent on conquering this portion of Russia also she would have to send a large army, a long way from its home base, in order to effect that conquest, and would thus inevitably weaken herself in other theatres of war.

5. It follows, that unless we are prepared to sit down and watch Germany like a *boa constrictor*, gradually swallowing Russia, the only thing to do is to resort to Allied Military Intervention to stop her. The only Allied Power, which can at present spare any considerable force to send into Russia is Japan. She is also most favourably situated for such intervention from a geographical point of view. Moreover her considerable Army is at present of no use to the Allies. It is not thrown into the scales, nor is it ever likely to be thrown in, except in Siberia. It is, therefore, wasted as a factor bearing on the ultimate result of the war. If engaged in Siberia on the other hand it would either (1) preserve a large and rich territory, full of supplies, from falling into the hands of the enemy or (2) compel the enemy to withdraw a large number of divisions from employment elsewhere in order to fight the Japanese. As a matter-of-fact it would *probably have both these effects*.

The desirability of such intervention would almost seem to have the force of a mathematically demonstrable proposition.

The only real objection ever urged to it is that Japanese intervention is so unpopular in Russia that it would throw Russia into the hands of Germany. I venture to submit that this is entirely a question of the *character* of Japanese intervention, the form it assumes, the declarations of Allied policy, with which it is inaugurated. It would seem easy, the Japanese being willing to intervene as the agents of the Alliance, in the Allied interest, which postulates the resuscitation of Russia as an independent power and her liberation from German influence, to rally a considerable amount [of] Russian support to the Allied Standard, even if carried by the Japanese. Some elements in " Russia " will probably side with the Germans. They will do that in any case, but what is the alternative ? It is that, if the Allies do nothing, practically all Russia, except the momentarily dominant faction [the Bolsheviks] whose power is visibly on the decline, will quietly and indeed gladly accept German control as the only way out of the present intolerable situation. Very likely German domination might not last. It is probable that, sooner or later, Russian national feeling will revive and revolt against the foreign yoke. But if it only lasts a year or two, that will be long enough to enable Germany to bring the resources and probably also to some extent the man-power of Russia to bear with crushing effect against the Allies.

I don't know whether the above are " military " arguments. What I do know is that the recognition or non-recognition of the importance of these considerations is going to determine the result of the war.

Please don't trouble to acknowledge this screed.

Newspapers and Periodicals

Daily News, December 5, 1914: " A Letter to Lord Northcliffe. | The *Daily News*, the *Daily Mail* and the War." | A.G.G.'s answer to " Scaremongerings." These are described as having been collected by one who has spent his life " in an infamous servitude to the changing passions of the hour," and A.G.G. ends by prophesying that the war would " make an end of the most sinister influence that has ever corrupted the soul of English journalism." These were some of the more " unquakerly " remarks that his Lordship liked to remember against the " chocolate millionaires." See below, Sources, XVII.

Daily Chronicle, December 7, 1916: " The Press Vendetta, Tyranny and Torture " on leader page; whole column. It says *The Times* leader of Monday (4th) and the Northcliffe Press were factors in deciding Asquith that, if he had accepted the proposals as presented to him originally and humiliated himself, his troubles would not have ended, and the attacks would have been redoubled. While negotiations were proceeding smoothly, and when an understanding was almost arrived at, *The Times* on Monday published an attack on Asquith. The article, purely destructive, revealed a plan to set the Prime Minister aside—information could have come only from Lloyd George, directly or indirectly—and gave evidence, so it seemed, of a scheme intended to make new conditions impossible for the Prime Minister. Any new Ministry, says the *Chronicle*, will have to deal with the Press menace as well as the submarine menace; otherwise Ministers will be subject to tyranny and torture by daily attacks impugning their patriotism and their earnestness to win the war. Conditions under which the Prime Minister works will have to be revised, without interfering with the liberty of legitimate criticism of Ministers. *Daily Chronicle* emphasizes that *The Times* says that the Prime Minister was not to be a member of the War Council.

Daily Chronicle, front page, December 8, 1916: Lord Northcliffe. No intention of joining the Cabinet, the Central News telegraphs. In view of rumours, published and unpublished, associating his name with the Government now in process of formation by Mr. Lloyd George, Lord Northcliffe was last night asked if he would make a statement on the subject. In declaring that he had no intention of joining the new Cabinet, his Lordship adds : " I prefer to sit in Printing House Square and Carmelite House."

Printed Works

Adam, George: *Behind the Scenes at the Front.* (London, 1915.)

Accurate though cheerful descriptions of life at the front by a partisan of Franco-English friendship.

Callwell, Major-General Sir C. E., K.C.B. : *Field-Marshal Sir Henry Wilson, Bart., G.C.B., D.S.O., his Life and Diaries.* (2 vols., London, 1927.)

During January, 1915, Wilson saw Northcliffe and found him very bitter about the embargo on press correspondents at the front. (Vol. I, p. 200.) Diary for November 16, 1916, when Wilson visited Northcliffe by appointment at *The Times* office:

I could not get him to talk sense. He would not consider my offensive of two Sommes. At one moment he said the Boches were on their last legs, in the next he said they had an inexhaustible supply of men. He thought they were starving because eels had gone up from 4 marks to 21 marks ! He agreed that Bukarest might be taken, that Sweden would attack Russia, that the long-range submarine was a real danger, and said that Ireland would give any number of recruits if there was a settlement, i.e., Home Rule ! Berlin would get hundreds of thousands of men then—and so on and so on. Haig and Robertson were perfect, and had now full power as he (Northcliffe) could " force the Government to do anything ! " (Vol. I, p. 297.)

On November 27, two days before any newspaper spoke of Government changes, Wilson dined with Fred Oliver, Carson, Milner, Geoffrey Dawson and Waldorf Astor. " Carson asked what he should advise Lloyd George and Bonar Law to do, as a crisis was coming. Our unanimous advice was that he should get Lloyd George to smash the Government and get Bonar Law to come out, so that Lloyd George should get the Unionist machinery for a general election, should one come about." (Vol. I, p. 299.)

In 1917 Wilson flatly refused to go on the mission to the U.S.A. if he was to serve under Northcliffe. This " rather irritated Bonar because he said Northcliffe represented the British Government, to which I naturally replied by asking whether we had not got an Ambassador." (Vol. II, p. 11.)

Cook, Sir E. T.: *The Press in Wartime.* (London, 1920.)

Cox, Harold: " The Power of the Press," in the *Edinburgh Review.* April, 1918; pp. 383-391.

Concedes that Lloyd George owes his position and various Service chiefs their dismissal to the action of the Press, principally Northcliffe's. Though the House of Commons naturally deplores it, Press influencing of the Government need be no more injurious to the country than control by the party caucus. The old division of newspapers on party lines lapsed necessarily when a Coalition was formed, and all a paper can do now is criticize in the national interest. The Northcliffe Press has never failed to advocate vigorous warfare with victory as the aim. L.G. can depend on nothing else but Northcliffe's aid, as each party caucus is disciplined by another leader. When the House of Commons controlled ministerial appointments, this did not invariably act for the national advantage. A. Chamberlain, who attacked Press influence, has only the unchecked tyranny of the caucus as an alternative. Destruction of liberty of the Press may proceed equally with growth in its power; the prosecution of Gwynne and Repington for publishing opinions on Palestine is an example. The real trouble is extravagant extension of the functions of government.

Dugdale, Blanche E. C.: *Arthur James Balfour.* (2 Vols., London, 1936.)

Vol. II, Chapters 8, 9 and 12 are important for this work. The author was dining alone with her uncle, Balfour, on December 21, 1915. He said the Government was already " hated, discredited, distrusted. They hate Asquith "—" a splendid chairman of a committee," but one who would never " originate or suggest." Asquith's chief incubus was Kitchener, a man great only in personality, not in ability. (p. 156.) This was twelve months before the Coalition fell. Page 168 contradicts Lord Beaverbrook's statement (in *Politicians and the War*) that Balfour did not attend Bonar Law's Conservative conference at the House of Commons on November 30, 1916. In fact he made a memorandum of it (quoted in full). On the Lansdowne letter, first published in the *Daily Telegraph* on November 29, 1917, Mrs. Dugdale writes that Lansdowne spoke to Balfour on the 26th of his intention to publish, but the first person he showed the letter to was Geoffrey Dawson. Family record of conversation on December 11 shows Balfour saying that he had not read the letter and thought it a mistake (pp. 250 ff.).

Elton, Lord: *The Life of James Ramsay MacDonald* (to 1919). (London, 1939.)

Chapter 9 claims that MacDonald was essentially a moderate throughout the war, as he was before and after it, and his beliefs were travestied by Press and public. These were (1) Great Britain need not have entered the war but for Grey's secret commitment to France; (2) being in, she had to win; (3) the unimpassioned temper of mind must be kept alive so that a sensible and lasting peace might be made.

As an example of " Special concentration of venom upon MacDonald " there is quoted (page 292) a letter by Chirol in *The Times* of October, 1914: " Is it a mere coincidence that the German Chancellor himself . . . invariably bases his denunciations of Great Britain's perfidy on just the same sort of arguments which Mr. MacDonald employs? Is it a mere coincidence that, following Mr. MacDonald's lead, the whole German Press . . .? In time of actual war . . . Mr. MacDonald . . . has helped the enemy state . . . to poison against his country the wells of public opinion . . . in neutral states whose attitude . . . might at any moment . . . decisively affect the issue of the war. Such action . . . cannot properly and safely be disregarded by the British Government and the British people."

Graham, Stephen: *Russia in 1916.* (London, 1917.)

Russia and the World. (London, 1917.)

Gardiner, Alfred G.: " *The Times* " in the *Atlantic Monthly.* (Boston, Mass., January, 1917.)

This study of the career and methods of Northcliffe (rather than of the newspaper) was written before the fall of Asquith. Having captured the masses with his sensational treatment of news, Northcliffe set out to be a dictator of national policy by appealing to the governing classes through *The Times.* That paper had survived the Parnell crisis only to reel on " like an old wooden hulk, labouring under canvas and battling with newly invented ironclads." Northcliffe's treatment of rivals is illustrated. When Lord Burnham reached his 80th birthday (Dec. 28, 1913) Northcliffe headed a deputation of congratulatory journalists. " Within a few weeks *The Times* was brought down to a penny, and the whole Harmsworth artillery was turned upon the *Daily Telegraph*, which was the chief competitor of *The Times* in the new field that it sought to occupy." The war gave Northcliffe his great opportunity, for while Parliamentary criticism of the Cabinet was practically silenced, control of the Press was negligible. Asquith was impervious to Press campaigns, and though he could easily have suppressed Northcliffe, that might have meant, says Gardiner, trouble with Lloyd George, as he and Northcliffe were allied throughout 1915. This, it may be seen from Chapter VII above, was not the case. Hence, too, Simon's attack on the Northcliffe Press for its policy of panic and pessimism was not followed up. A greater danger to the Allies than military reverses was disruption of purpose. That peril was created by Northcliffe's feverish exploitation of the reverses of 1915. His method was " to learn what was contemplated by the Government and then to start a raging demand for it in the newspapers." The agitation over the shell shortage was typical of the panic campaigning which made Allies suspicious of British good faith and Germans welcome the Northcliffe Press as prophetic. Northcliffe succeeded in destroying Haldane, but his instinct was at fault when he attacked Kitchener, who refused to be a tool of the Press. In conclusion Gardiner argues that the French have a better way of safeguarding democracy by controlling the Press and giving Parliament, through its committees, a real authority over the executive. A.G.G.'s persistence in attributing to Northcliffe personal responsibility for all the acts of his Editor, robs the article of any historical value.

Hamilton, Mary Agnes: *Arthur Henderson.* (London, 1938.) Chapters 6-7.

Claims that Henderson's speech to the Labour Party Conference on August 10, 1917, when discussing whether British Socialists should go to the Stockholm Conference, suffered in reporting from " what may in origin have been a mistake of hearing, but was persisted in and used with suspicious insistence. He had said that they should *supplement* military by political effort; ' supplement,' however, was printed as *supplant*. This went on being used against him, for months, nay years." (p. 154.)

The tone of these chapters is distinctly hostile to Lloyd George, who is charged with having engineered the Government crisis of 1916, and as wanting in integrity both in his negotiations of 1917 with Henderson and his statements about them afterwards.

Hewins, W. A. S.: *The Apologia of an Imperialist.* (Constable, 1929.)

Hewins, who was a member of the Unionist Business Committee (to ginger up Asquith) quotes as follows from his diary:

" December 11 [1916]. On Sat. it became clear that a hitch had occurred and I rang up [Sir William] Bull in the evening, to know what had happened (I suspected some development following Asquith's speech but was mistaken) and went to see him at Hammersmith on Sunday morning. It appeared that Balfour, Austen, Long and Cecil were upset by the criticism in the Northcliffe press. Long in his impulsive way said he must insist on resigning, though he was willing to stay on at the local Government Board. However, consultations were held and ultimately they intimated to Lloyd George that if it would ease matters he was free to make other appointments to their offices. This led to the postponement of Saturday and I could not gather that the question was settled yesterday. They left it to Lloyd George to throw over either Northcliffe or them. My opinion was that it was not important, before the appointments were made, to include any of the four in the Ministry, but that it would be unfortunate to give way now to press criticism. . . . I thought it might be a good thing to see Lloyd George and explain the position from our point of view and we tried to make an appointment at the War Office. But Ll. G. was not available. However, the official list of Ministers was published this morning. . . . I have just got on to Bull. After our meeting yesterday he went round to *The Times* as Parl. Secretary of the Business Committee and, using my name as Chairman, he told Geoffrey Robinson [Dawson] that we had 100 members behind us and we were determined to stand no more of these attacks on any of the four. He was with him for an hour and prevailed. He promised there should be no more attacks. We shall see. But the *Daily Mail* was venomous against Bob Cecil as Blockade Minister this morning." (Vol. II, pp. 97-8.)

Lloyd George and the Coup d'Etat. " By a British Observer " in the *Atlantic Monthly.* (Boston, Mass., March, 1917.)

The " ceaseless and reckless attack " by the Northcliffe Press upon the Coalition Government is made equally responsible with Lloyd George's manoeuvres for its fall. *The Times* leader of December 4, 1916, was the critical point. Obviously inspired, " it indicated that the Prime Minister had been practically obliterated." Had the general public been fully informed on events, there would have been no crisis, and had the coup been delayed a week it could never have succeeded, because Asquith's policy was on the point of triumphing in an application from Germany for peace negotiations. The rehabilitation of Milner, thinks the " Observer " (probably A. G. G.), proves how closely Northcliffe is behind Lloyd George in the change of government.

Maurice, Major-General Sir Frederick: *Haldane.* (2 vols., London, 1937.)

Prints letter (vol. I, p. 356) of August 3, 1914, which shows that Haldane himself proposed to Asquith that Kitchener should take the War Office. But the campaign of vituperation in the Press lessened in Kitchener's eyes the value of Haldane's advice and thus contributed to the Territorial Army being pushed into the background. On the general principles of expanding British armed forces Haldane was right and Kitchener wrong.

Prints letter (vol. II, p. 42) from Edmund Gosse to Haldane, October 30, 1916:

> I have some information to give you which is very unpleasant. The hounds of Hell are again being laid on to your track. A friend of mine who is of importance in the journalistic world tells me that a few days ago Northcliffe gave a luncheon at the Aldwych Club to prominent journalists. He made a speech entirely directed against you. After the bitterest diatribes he adjured all those newspaper men to see to it that you never regained political power in this country. He told them that there was a campaign afoot to reinstate you, but that they all must combine by all means known to them to defeat it. He assured them that you were the greatest enemy to the English State.

> One of these journalists, moved by all this, asked him, since he was in possession of all this evidence against you, why he did not rise and expose you from his place in the House of Lords. This took him aback for a moment, but he answered that this would lead to controversy which would be dangerous and unsatisfactory. "What you have to do," he went on, "is perpetually to insinuate into the public mind suspicion and hatred of Lord Haldane, so that the moment there is a question of his re-appearance in public life, public opinion may automatically howl him down."

> I think you should make this odious conspiracy known amongst your friends.

In 1926 *The Times*, reviewing vols. 30-33 of the German Foreign Office documents relating to the war, acknowledged that it had wrongly interpreted Haldane's mission to Berlin in 1912 (Vol. II, p. 204).

Northcliffe, Lord: *At the War*. (London, 1916.)

Reprinted articles reporting visits to France, Italy, Spain and Switzerland.

Petrie, Sir Charles, Bt.: *Walter Long and his Times*. (London, 1936.)

The author notes in the Preface that shortly before his death Long destroyed a great many of his papers. There is an account of the formation on January 27, 1915, of the Unionist Business Committee, with Long as chairman, Ernest Pollock (later Lord Hanworth) as vice-chairman, and Sir William Bull, Bt., as Parliamentary Secretary (p. 188). The important duty of the Committee was enquiring into the supply of munitions, and Long claimed that it was first responsible for directing attention to the shortage, which eventually led to the fall of the Liberal Government. There are several letters from Long to Bonar Law during the first year of the war, criticizing the Government but fearful that a Coalition would eventually destroy the Unionist party. On May 21, 1915, Long writes to Bonar Law "Forgive me for uttering a word of caution. This Coalition business is being very badly stage-managed. The *Morning Post* has just saved the situation but only just. *The Times* had fairly put the 'fat in the fire' and made things very difficult for many of us ... " (p. 193.)

On Dec. 5, 1916, Long became Secretary of State for Colonies in the new Government. The author says: "The Northcliffe Press had, however, complicated the position by a violent attack on Mr. Long, Mr. Balfour, Mr. Chamberlain, and Lord Robert Cecil, and they intimated to Mr. Lloyd George that he must choose between Lord Northcliffe and them. At the same time Sir William Bull went to the office of *The Times* [account given as in Hewins *op. cit. sup.*]." (p. 207.) On April 29, 1919, Long complains of the hostility of the paper, which he considers is trying to create a breach between the Prime Minister and himself (then First Lord of the Admiralty): ". . . I hesitate to refer to a domestic question, and only do so in order that there may be no misunderstanding as to what has occurred. I do not know whether you have seen the article in *The Times* of, I think, last Friday: it is a very bad one—and it is quite clear that the object of the last paragraph is to create a feeling of suspicion and ill-will on your part towards me. Stories *from reliable sources* reach me from Paris, and are also in circulation here, to the effect that you and I have had a serious disagreement over Beatty's appointment [Beatty succeeded Admiral Wemyss as First Sea Lord in October, 1919]; that you favour the attitude of *The Times* towards me; and that there is a movement on foot which has your approval, for bringing the Admiralty under Winston, who already has the War Office and the Air Force.

I need hardly say that I treat these stories with the contempt which they deserve; but I believe myself, from information which reaches me from time to time, that they are deliberately put in circulation by Northcliffe and his agents, and that they are part of his deep-laid schemes for attacking you and your Government . . . I have had careful enquiries made through reliable channels, and I am very much afraid, that, as is often the case, there is a woman at the bottom of all this. . . . This agitation in *The Times* is, I believe, a thoroughly dishonest one, and purely political; and this is confirmed by the evidence which I get, but which I cannot use as it is of a secret character." (pp. 220-222.)

Repington, Colonel C. à C.: *The First World War*, 1914-1918. (London, 1920, two volumes.)

It is difficult to conjecture Repington's motives for publishing a work which can have done nothing but harm to his reputation.

Robinson, H. Perry: *The Turning Point.* (London, 1917.)

A thorough account of the battle of the Somme, based on his messages to the Paper: suffers through its excess of detail from lack of a map.

The Times History of the War. (London, 22 volumes, 1914-1919.)

The Times Documentary History of the War. (London, 11 volumes, 1917-20.) Incomplete.

An even more ambitious project than the *History of the War*, for which it did not prove to be possible to find the permanent staff. It remains a useful collection of diplomatic documents, despatches from the front, etc.

The Times Diary and Index of the War. (London, n.d.) [1921.]

Wrench, Sir (John) Evelyn: *Struggle.* (London, 1935.)

Whereas in the author's *Uphill* Northcliffe is an integral character, in this sequel which covers 1914-20 he is incidental. Letter of Dec. 12, 1915 : " Most people, I am glad to say, are coming round to see that Northcliffe has been right all along and that he has tried to tell the truth when it was v. unpopular to do so." (p. 147.) Letter of Nov. 8, 1917 : " I am told he aspires to be Prime Minister. He thinks he is the only person who can run the country." (p. 265.) Letter of Nov. 16, 1917: " It appears quite definite that Northcliffe is not coming to the Air Board. I understand that he means to be Prime Minister and is going for larger game. I wonder what Lloyd George will have to say." (p. 253.) Sketches of Rothermere and Beaverbrook are given; the latter " understood the political game much better than Northcliffe." (p. 293.) Northcliffe's great secret was concentration: perhaps for a month *The Times* would be his sole concern, and all other compartments of his mind would be partly closed.

Thomson, Malcolm: *David Lloyd George.* (London, 1948.) Chapters 14-17.

The Times leader of December 4 was responsible for the fall of Asquith's Government in 1916, though Northcliffe had been told nothing by Lloyd George or Bonar Law. Balfour's acceptance of the Foreign Office is made the decisive move in Lloyd George's success.

Taylor, H. A. : *Robert Donald.* (London, 1934.)

Robert Donald, editor of the *Daily Chronicle*, was a first-class journalist. Incidentally, he was a first-class shorthand writer, and his reporting, said Northcliffe, was as accurate as a stop watch. Mr. Taylor's biography is particularly valuable for the contemporary records given at pp. 106-142 of the oral accounts received from Bonar Law (December 1, 1916), Bonham Carter (3rd), Riddell (5th and 6th), Asquith (7th), Bonham Carter (20th), Lloyd George (undated), Bonar Law (29th), E. S. Montagu (February 27, 1917). These are the only first-hand accounts of the events of these days that may be put beside Lord Beaverbrook's *Politicians and the Press* (frequently referred to in the text of Chapter VI of this *History*). Chapter VII, " Afterthoughts on Asquith " chronicles Donald's views regarding the clash between Asquith and Lloyd George. The latter, as Prime Minister, requested Donald to make a report on the Propaganda organization as existing and a document was printed: | CONFIDENTIAL. | REPORT ON PROPAGANDA ARRANGE- MENTS | ROBERT DONALD | JANUARY 9, 1917 | 61 pp. fol., printed 18 Feb. 1918 |

In accordance with Donald's recommendations a Department of Information was set up and, also on his advice, the Prime Minister first appointed John Buchan as Director, but soon afterwards named Carson Minister in charge of Propaganda. This, too, lasted only a short time. In February, 1918, the Ministry of Information was set up and Lord Beaverbrook resigned his Chancellorship of the Duchy of Lancaster to become Minister in Charge. On his invitation Donald became Director of Propaganda in Neutral Countries, while at the same time Northcliffe became Director of Propaganda in Enemy Countries. The circumstances in which the Prime Minister and Donald drifted apart are described on pages 170-174.

It is possible to supplement Mr. Taylor's narrative. The *Daily Chronicle's* criticism of Lloyd George's attitude to the Generals was a primary motive for the decision in Downing Street that the Prime Minister needed a completely " loyal " morning Liberal journal, and Frederick Guest was instructed to secure the *Daily Chronicle*. Its sale by Frank Lloyd to a group of the Prime Minister's supporters followed. On several occasions since he became Prime Minister Lloyd George had hinted to Donald that he would like friends of his to acquire the *Daily Chronicle* from the ageing and ill Frank Lloyd, and make it the official organ of his party. Many months were spent in making soundings among wealthy supporters of the Prime Minister. Guest talked to Sir Henry (later Lord) Dalziel, while Sir Howard Frank thought that Sir William Lever (later Lord Leverhulme) might find the money. Lever's accountants investigated the position. By the summer stories were current in Fleet Street. Sir William Lever, some said, was acting in conjunction with Lord Beaverbrook, and it was thought that a merger between the *Daily Chronicle* and the *Daily Express* would result. It had, indeed, been difficult for Guest to apportion the " scoops " between the *Chronicle* and the *Express*, and the latter's proprietor not infrequently complained of favours shown to the former, while others complained of leakages. It was a grievance in certain quarters that the appointments of Lord Milner in succession to Lord Derby at the War Office, and Derby's appointment as Ambassador Extraordinary to the French Government, had appeared in the *Daily Express*.

Lord Beaverbrook, however, was not then minded to buy, nor to help buy, the *Chronicle*. On September 7, 1918, Guest succeeded in interesting Andrew Weir, later Lord Inverforth, as well as Sir Henry Dalziel. When it turned out that Lloyd was not, after all, willing to allow one-third of the capital in the new business in the form even of 5 per cent. Debentures, more cash was required and Guest then turned to Messrs. William and Gomer Berry. They were willing to assist, but their terms included complete commercial control, which Dalziel was unwilling to consider. Guest's difficulties increased when the Berrys disclosed that their proposal to finance their holding in the *Chronicle* had been to sell the *Sunday Times* (which they had purchased in 1915) to Beaverbrook. Guest persuaded the brothers Berry not to sell the *Sunday Times* until he had dealt with the *Chronicle*. The deal was thereupon arranged and, in the event, the Sunday paper remained in their hands.

On October 4, 1918, Lloyd first told Donald that, as far back as the end of July, he had come to an agreement with Dalziel, and afterwards talked with Lloyd George and Guest, when the Prime Minister complained of some criticism of himself that had appeared in the *Daily Chronicle*; and, evidently referring to past criticism, added, " We cannot trust Donald." The transfer took effect on October 5, 1918, when Donald was informed by Lloyd in answer to his question that " the purchasers would take possession tonight at 6 o'clock." Donald resigned the Editorship of the *Daily Chronicle* on the same day that his assistant, E. A. Perris, was appointed Editor, and the paper then gave political satisfaction to Downing Street.

It gave less satisfaction on the commercial side. In July, 1919, as Lord Inverforth had decided to retire from politics he proposed to put real life into the *Chronicle*. Every effort was made by the Government to assist the party paper. This occasionally led to difficulties with Beaverbrook and the *Daily Express*. The *Chronicle* still did not prosper and Dalziel became anxious to retire from it. The Prime Minister agreed to his relinquishing the Chairmanship, and saw in the vacancy an opportunity to provide for Philip Kerr. He decided to arrange for him to become first a member of the Board, and later Chairman. Dalziel retired at the end of the year, and among the consequent changes was the unexpected resignation, in February, 1922, of Kerr. Chapter 16 in Mr. Taylor's book tells the later history of the paper; its passing into the hands of Sir David Yule, Sir Thomas Catto, and Lord Reading; its sale to William Harrison in July, 1928, and its sudden amalgamation, on Sunday, June 1, 1930, with an hour or two's notice to the staff, into the *Daily News* under the new title of the *News Chronicle*, at present in effect.

VIII. PEACE MAKING

The importance to the Entente Cordiale, concluded in 1905 between Britain and France, of the adhesion of Russia in 1907, is fully treated in the previous volume, Chapter XV, " Accord with Russia." Chirol's distaste for the Anglo-Russian agreement is described in " Accord with Russia," and some of its risks, as appreciated in the office in 1912, are set out in Chapter III, " The European Equilibrium, 1912-1913," *supra*. The consequences to British peace aims of the 1907 public accord and the 1915 secret agreement were grave. They so profoundly affected the atmosphere in which the Peace Conference assembled, and the decisions made, that it seems advisable to supplement, rather extensively, the account given in Chapter VIII of the origins and consequences of these accords and agreements.

Russia and the Straits

The mystical ambition to control Constantinople that Russia had long vaguely cherished acquired urgent political necessity when, in the winter of 1913, the German General Liman von Sanders was appointed to command the first Turkish army corps in the Capital (See Chapter III, p. 117). The gaining of Constantinople was the equivalent to many Russians of the regaining of Alsace-Lorraine to many Frenchmen. This is not the place in which to discuss the origins of the war of 1914-18. It is sufficient to say that the Straits question became insistent for Russia when Izvolsky learnt that Austria-Hungary had decided to annex Bosnia and Herzegovina (for which see Steed's conversation with Izvolsky in 1908, Vol. III, Chapter XX). The annexation took place on October 6, 1908, Izvolsky having understood from Aehrenthal that Austria-Hungary would give diplomatic support to Russia on the Straits question. The appointment of Liman von Sanders in December, 1913 (see above, Chapter III, p. 115), gave a decided check to Izvolsky's diplomacy, and Russian anger at the sight of Constantinople being virtually under German domination created a tense situation. (G. P. Gooch, *Before the War*, II, Chapter IV, on Sazonov for an account of Russian protests.) The position of *The Times* remained what it had long been: " Turkey must . . . take charge of the Bosphorus, the Sea of Marmara, and the Dardanelles, not as a concession, not as the outcome of any sympathy, but because it is expedient in the interests of all the nations concerned that she should do so." (November 9, 1912; see Chapter III above, p. 82.) After the appointment of Liman von Sanders the Triple Entente lodged a joint protest. The serious crisis that followed was overcome, but time did not erase the memory or remove the implication. (See R. J. Kerner, "The Mission of Liman von Sanders" in *Slavonic Review*, VI, 1927; VII, 1928-9.) Russia proceeded with measures that, when a favourable moment should come, would make her and not Germany controller of Constantinople and the Straits. In November, 1913, a memorandum concerning the Straits was drawn up by M. Basili, Vice-Director of the Chancery of the Ministry for Foreign Affairs, and laid by Sazonov before the Tsar, who approved. Four months or so later, *i.e.*, at the beginning of March, 1914, a conference, at which were present many of the chief political, military and naval advisers, deliberated upon this memorandum. According to Sir James Headlam-Morley, *Studies in Diplomatic History* (London, 1930, pp. 252-3), the memorandum and the records of the conference at which it was considered (as published by the present Russian Government), "afford valuable indications as to the conceptions" of the Tsarist Government. The main consideration, Sazonov said, was that "if by force of events the Straits should be withdrawn from the dominion of Turkey, Russia could not allow any other Power to establish itself on their shores, and, therefore, perhaps, might be compelled to take possession of the Straits, and to determine the arrangements for the control of the Bosphorus and the Dardanelles. . . . Our historical task [this is the mystical element in Russian politics] in reference to the Straits consists in the extension of our dominion over them." Control over the Bosphorus alone would not be sufficient. Simple neutralization would not be satisfactory [this is the practical element in Russian politics] for there would be no security against its violation, and therefore it would neither guarantee the exit of the Russian fleet from the Black Sea, nor the closing of the entrance against a hostile Power. It was agreed that the main object would not be secured except as the result of a general European war. In such an event the fleet of the Triple Alliance would be held in check by the English and French navies; no support could be expected from Greece; "the dream of Constantinople will probably be a hindrance to a closer approach between us and Greece," but Greece and Bulgaria would probably take opposite sides; Serbia would be fully occupied with Austria. The conference [of March, 1914] therefore proceeded to a discussion of the military and naval preparations by which, in the event of a general war, Russia should seize Constantinople and eject the German mission. Among other measures it was recommended that the Black Sea fleet be quickly strengthened by a strong detachment of modern dreadnoughts. This programme was in full swing in the summer of 1914. Accordingly, says the Historical Advisor to the Foreign Office (writing in November, 1922), "If we are to understand the situation just before the outbreak of war, [in August, 1914] we must always recollect that for Russia the question of the Straits was predominant; to this the interest in Serbia, though it occupied a much larger part in public controversy, was subordinate. In the past the main opposition [to Russian domination of the Straits] had always come from France and England; Germany had been favourable. Now, [since 1912] the situation was changed and it was becoming more and more clear that the road to Constantinople lay through Berlin. If we keep this in mind we shall not be surprised to find that from the very moment that war broke out the Russians began to show extreme anxiety as to the future of Constantinople; when the Gallipoli expedition was proposed, they at once came forward with the demand that the zones of both Straits should be assigned to Russia, and at the beginning of 1915 they secured from Great Britain and France a formal acknowledgment of their claim." Headlam-Morley was a principal reviewer for the *Literary Supplement* of books on international politics and the brevity of his reference to the Straits question is typical of the Foreign Office and of Printing House Square. The importance of the Dardanelles question as a cause of war, its influence on the peace as contemplated before the Revolution, and on the abortive efforts to arrange a peace that were made before 1917 await thorough investigation.

The extent to which Russia pressed alternately the Triple Alliance and the Triple Entente to favour the claim to Constantinople is of great interest. While Russian opinion was united in the desire to make the Tsar paramount on the Straits it was believed by one section of opinion that Britain, for the reasons set out in *The Times* of November 9, 1912, still adhered to her traditional position that Turkey should govern in Constantinople. The speech delivered to the Duma on May 23, 1914, by N. E. Markov (a bureaucrat supervisor of the Government Press Department) is significant. He was a member of the group on the extreme Right which compared unfavourably the vagueness of the existing Anglo-Russian understanding with the solidity of the alliance offered by Germany. His speech was in part a polemic against Miliukov and wholly a diatribe against England, whose only motive was to set Russia to quarrel with Germany. As for the Dardanelles, "All history shows that it is England who has been keeping us out of the Straits, and now it is not Germany alone, not General Liman von Sanders alone, who has been keeping us out, but our own friendly England. . . . but it may be that we can come to terms with Germany; and so to have the Straits offered to Russia, even against the wishes of England." (F. A. Golder, *Documents of Russian History*, pp. 26-7.) The speech was not reported in *The Times*; and in the weeks between Sarajevo and the declaration of war, the paper made no reference to the Straits question. The powerful pro-German set in Russian society naturally put the Straits into the forefront, affirming that if Constantinople was vital to Russia Germany could be trusted to let the Tsar have it. The pro-Entente section naturally replied that Russia's claims would not be obstructed by the Allies. The Government and the pro-Ally Russians, even the Liberals and Cadets, were aware that neither Britain nor France was ready to acquiesce and within a few months of the war the Russian Government found it impossible to avoid making an unequivocal demand.

This claim was put forward to the Allies by Sazonov. The Russian Foreign Minister in his memoirs, *The Fateful Years*, completed in 1927, describes how he responded to popular clamour rather than to his own personal sense of Russian necessities ; and, backed by naval and military opinion, he came to agree that only a fundamental solution of the Straits problem would reconcile the Russian people to the sacrifices demanded by a war which was already foreseeable. Accordingly, Russia must become possessed of the Straits either during the war, or at its conclusion; otherwise she was doomed to years of economic weakness and external danger. It was common ground to both wings of Russian opinion (Witte in favour of a Russo-German alliance; Sazonov in favour of a Russo-French-British alliance) that the burden of land-fighting in war against Germany must fall upon Russia. The same point had been made in February, 1914, in the memorandum of P. N. Durnovo (State Councillor and Minister of the Interior in Witte's cabinet) that England was virtually unable to fight on European soil and France was too weak numerically to hold Germany. The conclusion was that the alliance with France and Britain was useless to Russia (see F. A. Golder, *Documents of Russian History*, No. 1). This was the doctrine, with all its inferences, that lay at the root of the problem faced by Sazonov, Grey and Delcassé in the summer of 1914 : Britain and France unbacked by Russia could not face Germany. But there were other factors. Germany could not abandon the Hamburg-Berlin-Vienna-Constantinople-Baghdad prospect, which naturally led Russia towards France. On the other hand, Britain and France did not want either Russia or Germany in Constantinople. The problem was rendered urgent by the murder of the Austrian Archduke and the Archduchess on June 29, 1914. Sazonov, still not really an enthusiastic supporter of the Straits policy, had not only to deal with Witte and the pro-German section of Court and Society. Miliukov, the historian, was the leader of the Cadets (the equivalent of the French Radical Socialists). Sazonov needed his support and he was supremely interested in the Straits. Sazonov had to sponsor a firm pro-Straits policy. It is beyond the scope of this note to discuss the possible influence that the Sazonov-Miliukov line may have exercised on the diplomatic and military moves in St. Petersburg during the last weeks of July, 1914. It is necessary only to emphasize that on his own responsibility (mentioning it only to the Naval Minister), Sazonov opened negotiations on the Straits with the Allies, adding that he would resign if agreement failed. It should be remarked also that *The Times* evaded the subject with great deliberation until it reported and commented upon Trepov's speech in the Duma on December 4, 1916 (see below).

The moment was awkward for Russia's allies. Witte's pro-German propaganda had been active in St. Petersburg long before July, 1914. He had even gained space in the *Novoye Vremya*, the leading St. Petersburg anti-German daily. Inevitably, the pressure of pro-German circles created the need for a response from the West. If Russia was to be kept faithful to the Triple Entente, a supreme task of Entente diplomacy, it must soon become necessary for Britain and France to promise her Constantinople, and this meant a complete reversal of British and French policy. *The Times*, for all its sense of the importance of the Russian alliance, gave it no encouragement or even mention. Had Britain and France been confident of their ability to beat Germany alone the response to Russian pressure would certainly have been different. But German influence over Turkey and the passage through the Straits of the Goeben and the Breslau procured the entry into war of Turkey on the side of the Central Powers. Turkey's closing of the Straits against Russia, effected in October, 1914, was a paralysing blow. The emergency forced London and Paris to reconsider the political aspects of the war, and Petrograd to announce war aims that would be nationally acceptable. Soon after the recall of the allied Ambassadors from Constantinople, the Russian Emperor, addressing his people in a manifesto, said that " Turkey's unwarranted intervention would but prepare the way for the solution of the historic problem bequeathed to us by your forefathers on the shores of the Black Sea." Shortly after this the British Ambassador, Buchanan, in view of the Russian wave of patriotic emotion, was instructed to say that in the event of German defeat (the words should be noted), the question of Constantinople and the Straits would be decided in conformity with Russian needs. During the winter the patriotic movement gained in strength, and early in the new year Sazonov told Buchanan that the Emperor desired a more precise and definite assurance that Constantinople would belong to Russia when the war was won.

Already by the second half of October, 1914, Britain knew that Russia's demand, however little sympathy there was for it (see Grey, *Twenty-five Years*), would need to be recognized. Sazonov's new demand was that Constantinople should be an outright Russian, and not an international, city, as he had asked earlier. Inevitably there was delay over the form of the diplomatic documents. But by February 1, 1915, the British Ambassador was able officially to confirm to Sazonov the British Government's abandonment of the Straits to Russia, and agreement with Russia to make the necessary territorial acquisitions to ensure the safety of the Black Sea. Thus (1) Turkish power would be abolished in Europe; (2) the Enos Media line uniting the Aegean with the Black Sea was to be the frontier with Bulgaria; (3) on the Asiatic shore, the frontier was to run along the River Sakaria and (4) the southern shore of the Sea of Marmara. How strongly some Russians felt in the first week of March is indicated by the message from G. Trubetzkoy, Russian Minister at Nish (in Serbia) to Sazonov urging the need to abandon illusions. " If we can reach our goal [the Straits] in agreement with France and England against

Germany so much the better. If not let us reach it in agreement with Germany against them." (G. P. Gooch, *Recent Revelations of European Diplomacy*, London, 1940; p. 170.) The pressure on Buchanan was intensified.

But Buchanan could pledge only Britain; Sazonov needed French agreement. He foresaw difficulties and at once contacted Delcassé's personal friend, Izvolsky, who was hopeful of bringing round French governmental and public opinion. The position, long accepted in Paris, was that a neutral Straits was desired; but that, under pressure an internationalised Constantinople would be accepted. This, Sazonov thought, was worse for Russia than Turkish control. He conferred with Paléologue and Buchanan, and offered to guarantee French financial and cultural rights in Turkey. Negotiations continued smoothly and quickly, up to the Gallipoli landing at the end of 1915. This Sazonov greatly disliked, and said so; but while not ceasing to press Russian demands, he expressed readiness to concede all the allied demands elsewhere in Turkey. On Witte's death *The Times* described him in a leading article as a man who nearly became " great " but, as a strenuous supporter of the Dreikaiserbund, failed to make his policy good. " He was a type of the superior Russian bureaucrat permeated with German ideas and with German sympathies " (March 15, 1915). Witte's removal from the scene did little to lessen pro-German influence for he had himself not been playing an active part for some time before his death. By now pro-German pressure in the Russian Capital was intense. An unequivocal announcement on the part of the Allies that Russia was to have Constantinople and the Straits was demanded. But although the negotiations with the Allies were accelerated, Buchanan on March 12, 1915, writing to Sazonov said that " Until the Allies are in a position to give to the Balkan States, and especially to Bulgaria and Rumania, some satisfactory assurance as to their prospects and general position with regard to the territories contiguous to their frontiers, to the possession of which they are known to aspire, and until a more advanced stage of the agreement as to the French and British desiderata in the final peace terms is reached, Sir Edward Grey points out that it is most desirable that the understanding now arrived at between the Russian, French and British Governments should remain secret." This insistence on secrecy was later maintained until it became the cause of the Liberal British and American objection to " secret diplomacy " and the Wilsonian demand for " open Covenants openly arrived at." (Golder, p. 62.)

Buchanan's message on secrecy arrived simultaneously with fresh activity on the part of Rasputin and his friends, all of whom had been against the war from the first, and were now conscious of their power. As they were aided by the Left, it was urgent that in order to keep Russia in the war the Allies could no longer avoid making their undertaking explicit.

By March 17, 1915, negotiations with London and Paris had so far proceeded that Petrograd could send a telegram to the English and French Governments stating the Russian claims, and expressing the hope that they would be favourably received. The text of this statement served as the basis for an agreement between Russia and her allies. By the end of March, all that remained to be done was to write a formal accord, leaving the precise formulation of claims and guarantees as to freedom of navigation, pilgrimages, etc., to be drawn up at the peace conference.

Hence, on March 27, 1915, Buchanan handed over a memorandum which confirmed British consent to Russian annexation of Constantinople and the Straits on condition that the war should be brought to a victorious issue, and Great Britain and France should satisfy their claims at the expense of the Ottoman Empire, and certain regions outside of it. The memorandum explicitly laid down the governing condition of " war till final victory "; it was obvious, indeed, that without victory there could be no question of acquiring any part of Turkish territory. The memorandum also laid down the following points :—(1) Constantinople to include a free port (warehousing and transport); (2) Arabia and the Muslim Holy places to be under Muslim independent rule; (3) The Anglo-Russian treaty of 1907 was to be revised, and the neutral zone of Persia was to pass to the British sphere of influence. The closer definition in April, 1916 of the allies' Ottoman acquisitions after the Sykes-Picot Treaty was intended to remove the possible causes of misunderstanding between the members of the Triple Entente.

Sazonov was then able to inform the allied ambassadors in Petrograd by letter that the Imperial Government understood the arrangement to include the annexation by Britain of Mesopotamia, by France of Syria and Cilicia, by Russia of Erzeroum, Trebizond, Van and Bitilis, and the Black Sea coast as far as the point to be determined when the frontier was drawn. Russia was also to take over Kurdistan south of Van and Bitilis ; and, in exchange, France was to acquire a considerable portion of Asia Minor including the town of Kharput.

The first anniversary of the British declaration of war against Germany elicited the expected messages, including one from Sazonov who praised the pioneer work of *The Times* in promoting Anglo-Russian concord. But in the same month the *Novoye Vremya* confirmed rumours of German overtures for a separate peace. These synchronized with the great Russian reverses, and were probably seriously meant by Germany. It was alleged that Germany had offered Russia Galicia, the Dardanelles and a guarantee of the integrity of her frontiers. Germany stipulated for Egypt on the pretext of compensating Turkey, and for a free hand with Russia's allies. (*The Times*, August 12, 1915.) The *Novoye Vremya* called the proposals cynical but Petrograd swarmed with peace rumours throughout the month. (That there was substance in these rumours may be verified in Adamov, *Die europäischen Mächte*, etc.) *The Times* Special Correspondent (Stanley Washburn) dealt with these in a turnover article on

August 28, headlined WILL OF RUSSIA | NO SEPARATE PEACE | which comprised a denunciation of peace "fables" authorized by Sazonov for publication. Russia, obviously hard-pressed, was in retreat all along her vast line. "Acute Tension in Russia "; " Russia at Bay," were some of the headlines that appeared in *The Times* in September.

The Special Russian Supplements that had been begun three years before continued. The fifteenth issue, published on December 17, 1915, was introduced by the veteran Mackenzie Wallace with a sage article comparing British and Russian ideas of the " dogma " of the balance of power. Wallace had contributed anonymously to many of the numbers and some of these reappear with the other contributions in " *The Times* " *Book of Russia* (London, 1916, with an Introduction by Wallace). The paper worked mightily to preserve the alliance and the year 1916 opened with a special message to *The Times* from Sazonov, Kokovtsev and Guchkov. The expected success of the Gallipoli landings created an opportunity for the pro-German Russians to sow suspicion. Britain was accused of plotting to occupy Constantinople. France, Russia and great Britain then drew up an advance project for the administration of Constantinople for the duration of the war by both civil and military authorities. Russia maintained that the civil authorities should not be subordinate to the military. Hence, six departments for the administration of all civil affairs were to be created, Russia reserving to herself Law and Internal Affairs. Thus the possibility of disagreement between the Allies was guarded against. The risk was not negligible. As General Zhilinsky put it in November, 1915, at the Inter-Allied Military Conference at Chantilly, " in the event of evacuation it must be complete, Russia not wishing to give the English a permanent port—a new Gibraltar—at the entrance to the Mediterranean." (R. J. Kerner, " Russia and the Straits Question " in the *Slavonic Review*, VIII, 1929-30, p. 591.) The new Convention did not remove the suspicion in all Russian parties regarding Britain's ulterior motives and calculations. They originated, said many well-intentioned Russians, in respect for Muslim feeling, above all in India.

In the event, it was disagreement in Russia that became the difficulty. Fear of revolution, if the war continued for long, encouraged " reactionary " circles to revive hints that Britain had never intended to let Russia have the Straits and never would. In March, 1916 Miliukov found it necessary to declare in the Duma that though Russia did not begin the war for the Straits and Constantinople she should not end it without them. It cannot be doubted that practical politicians under the autocracy needed to take into account a strong feeling for Constantinople and that the feeling was shared by all classes. When Sazonov, at the intervention of the Empress, was suddenly dropped in July, 1916, the Foreign Ministry was placed in the hands of Stürmer, Prime Minister in succession to Goremykin since the previous February. The dual appointment was a sensation of the first order. The retirement of Sazonov greatly shocked *The Times*, but loyalty to the alliance compelled the paper to say that the extruded Minister had, in fact, suffered from ill-health, etc. " But it was peculiarly unfortunate that his skilled hand should be withdrawn from the management of Russian diplomacy at this juncture. There is little reason to fear that M. Stürmer, upon whom this task now devolves, will not be able to gather up the strands of Russian and Allied policy and weave them to good purpose. . . . His devotion to the Allied cause is not open to doubt." The paper laboured its confidence that " the changes involved no alteration of policy." Opportunity to say a word on the career of the former Minister came when Russia was known to be drifting dangerously. A translation of Miliukov's article (laudatory but not uncritical) on Sazonov in the *Retch* of July 25 was given in the Russian Supplement No. 22 of 26th August, 1916. There was emphatic need to reassure Russian opinion. Still the Constantinople question had not been settled. The Tsar telegraphed late in August to King George V that " a brief official declaration on the part of the Russian Government announcing that England and France regard the acquisition by Russia of Constantinople and the Straits an unchangeable condition of peace, would calm all minds and dissipate all suspicions." (R. J. Kerner, " Russia," etc. in the *Slavonic Review*, VIII, p. 592). Whether to publish the Anglo-Russian-French accord of March, 1915, to which an annex might now be drafted, was discussed but rejected as embarrassing to all parties. There existed in the Russian General Staff a party in favour of a separate peace with Turkey, and their programme included the abrogation of the 1915 accord on the Straits. Thus the matter was left in debate in August and September, 1916.

During October and November, 1916, *The Times* makes many references to a food crisis, and the sufferings of the working class. Miliukov and others are recorded as demanding ameliorative measures. The Petrograd Correspondent's message of November 2 (4 November, 1916) quoted the Labour Group of the Central War Industrial Committee as insisting that : " It is easy to throw a spark among the inflammable popular masses, exasperated and disorganized by the present state of affairs, but any outbreak, which the enemies of the country will endeavour to convert into a general *pogrom*, will merely play into the hands of the foe." So argued the Labour Group's manifesto.

The British Government signified its displeasure at the supersession of Sazonov by demonstratively bestowing the Grand Cross of the Order of the Bath upon the extruded Foreign Minister, while the German Press emphasized that Stürmer had never shown any enthusiasm either for the war or for the acquisition of Constantinople. Many in Petrograd believed that Stürmer was about to negotiate a separate peace. But, if so, he did not last long enough to accomplish it. Blatant use of State power for personal advantage drew upon him the incessant attacks of Miliukov. That Russia was now moving towards a major crisis was clear to all the world on 25 November when *The Times* announced the appointment of Trepov as Prime Minister, and mentioned grave charges that had been preferred against Stürmer.

At last, on 4 December, 1916 the Russian claim to the Straits, as made by Sazonov, Miliukov and others, became for the first time the subject of a direct statement in *The Times*. These were the circumstances. Trepov, in his proclamation from the tribune of the Duma repeated the statement that Asquith had made to the deputation of the Duma visiting London, that the Allies and Russia were in complete agreement on Eastern questions. The new Minister made his statement in the face of fierce opposition. This had been duly reported in *The Times*, and also a fortnight later, Sazonov's statement to *The Times* Correspondent in Petrograd that Asquith's statement, implicitly settling the question of the Straits in Russia's favour, heralded the dawn of a new day in world politics and world diplomacy. He meant that opposition to the Allies and to the war was thus deprived of any basis. It was Trepov's task to justify Sazonov's estimate of the situation. He sought to do this by giving Asquith's statement explicitly clearer definition. But Trepov was not given due support. His appearance alone inspired the extreme Left to demonstrate and for an hour they prevented his rising to speak. The Minister was forced three times to mount the tribune before he could make his statement. That twelve Socialists were suspended, including Kerensky and Tchkeidze, proves that opposition to the war was far from quashed by the renewed promise of Constantinople. As to the political aspect as it was seen in England, *The Times* leader of December 5 was cool. The paper thus commented upon Trepov's declaration : " This explicit statement reveals nothing new to those who have followed the process of the diplomatic consideration of the aims and interests of the Allies during the war ". The passage was unenthusiatically worded and was in fact typical of the reserved attitude that *The Times* had taken towards the Straits question from the beginning. None of the long series of monthly special Russian numbers had discussed, or even mentioned the question.

It was still believed in Petrograd (and in London) that the promise of the Straits and Constantinople to Russia would suffice, if anything could, to keep Russia in the war on the side of the Allies. On Christmas Day the Tsar followed Trepov's statement with a message to his army describing the acquisition of the Straits as a war aim to be achieved before peace was restored. It remained highly questionable whether the Russian contribution to the acquisition of the Straits would be significant. While talk of the possibility of a Russian expedition to take Constantinople revived the drooping spirit of Russia, alarming rumours from Petrograd culminated in the news (at last authentic) of the murder of Rasputin on January 3, 1917. There was one more political change: Prince Golitzin was named as Trepov's successor on January 11, Pokrovsky remaining at the Foreign Ministry.

Trepov's statement made on December 2, 1916, represents the most explicit statement ever made of the settlement by the Allies of Russia's claim to the Straits. As has been seen, it was reported on December 4 and endorsed by *The Times*, without enthusiasm in a leading article next day. The matter thereupon was taken in Britain as having been dropped. But the paper unexpectedly returned to the topic on January 27, 1917 by presenting a translation of the full Russian text of Trepov's governmental declaration made more than six weeks before :

> For more than a thousand years Russia has striven southwards, to free egress into the open sea. The keys to the Bosporus and Dardanelles, the buckler of Oleg on the gates of Tsargrad [*i.e.*, Constantinople]—such are the immemorial, sacred dreams of the Russian people for all the time of its being. And this striving is now near to realization. At the beginning of the war, sparing human lives, we employed all our efforts, together with our Allies, to restrain Turkey from insensate participation in military operations. France, Britain, and Russia did not try to draw Turkey into participation in the war; they merely insisted that in her own interests she should remain neutral. In this connexion Turkey was given formal assurances and promises that for her neutrality she would be guaranteed integrity of territory and independence, and also granted various privileges and benefits. But all efforts proved vain. Blinded by the flattering promises of the Germans, Turkey treacherously attacked us, and thereby signed her own death-warrant. The vital interests of Russia are also understood by our loyal Allies as they are by us, and conformably therewith, an agreement concluded by us in 1915 with Great Britain and France, to which Italy also adhered, finally establishes the right of Russia to the Straits and Constantinople. The Russian people must know for what they are shedding their blood, and according to the now existing mutual stipulation, our agreement with the Allies is to-day proclaimed from this tribune. I repeat, complete unity in this cause among the Allies has been firmly established, and there is no doubt that Russia, having acquired supreme possession of free egress to the Mediterranean sea, will grant free navigation to the Rumanian flag, which not for the first time is unfurled in battle side by side with the Russian standard. . . .

The reason for the reproduction of this speech only became obvious when it was announced that a Conference (the first) of the Allies was due to open in Petrograd.

On January 29 the Allied delegates arrived. Milner, Henry Wilson and Revelstoke represented Britain, with the Ambassador, Buchanan; Doumergue, Castelnau and Paléologue; Scialoja, Ruggieri and Carlotti; represented France and Italy respectively. The Conference separated on February 21, 1917. Pokrovsky, the last Foreign Minister of the old régime, who was deeply suspicious of the Allies, agreed, after the Conference, in a memorandum addressed to the Tsar, dated March 6, 1917, that " if Russia did not acquire the Straits and Constantinople before the peace conference neither our actual Allies nor our enemies would ever forget [the intensity of Russian feeling] and would never pardon us for desiring to have Constantinople and the Straits." Pokrovsky, therefore, was among those in favour of an expedition (Kerner, *op. cit.* p. 561). Within a week of Pokrovsky's signing this memorandum the Revolution began. Prince Lvov became Prime Minister of a Provisional Coalition Government and Miliukov was given the Ministry of Foreign Affairs, to the great satisfaction of Buchanan (see " *The Times* " *History of the War*, vol. XIII, p. 108).

The internal controversy over the Straits and Constantinople now entered a new phase. At first the Petrograd Left, including the Bolsheviks, though holding to the formula of " no annexations and no indemnities," and recognizing the right of " self-determination " with readiness to make peace, accepted the fact that " Russia is bound by alliances to England, France and other countries. It cannot act on the questions of peace without them. This means, however, that revolutionary Russia, freed from the Tsarist yoke, must directly and openly address itself to its Allies proposing to them to reconsider the question of opening peace negotiations. What the answer of the Allies will be we do not know, neither do we know what will be the answer of Germany should this proposal be made. . . ." (L. Kamenev in *Pravda*, March 8, 1917, reprinted in the *Collective Works of Lenin*, XX, II, p. 380). Kerensky argued that Russia did not need the Straits; what was important was access to the Mediterranean. The Socialist leader, according to V. V. Shulgin (quoted by Bernard Pares, *Fall of the Russian Monarchy*, London, 1939, p. 460) was in the Duma when [? March 14] a man delivered a packet to him. " Kerensky, throwing it on the table, says: ' These are our secret treaties with the Powers; hide them!' and off he goes in the same dramatic way. As the Duma is crowded out and there is no chest available, the secret papers are hidden under a table." There resulted in the next week or two more open and unprecedented discussion of Constantinople, and of the question whether an expedition should secure the position in advance of the peace conference and thus revive Russian patriotism. The possession by the Duma of the " secret treaties," as they were to be universally known, did nothing to allay Russian suspicions of the real intentions of the Western Allies. The immediate political importance of Kerensky's argument lay in the fact that Miliukov had taken up the discussion of an expedition with Denikin, the new Chief of the General Staff (Kerner, p. 597). But many of those formerly in favour of an expedition now rejected the idea as impracticable, and recommended rather that a separate peace be made with Turkey, on condition that Russia obtained military and naval control but leaving the Turks in Constantinople and the Straits region. Bazili of the General Staff informed Miliukov to this effect on April 24, 1917 (Kerner, *op. cit.*, p. 398). Miliukov compromised having, as he thought, active support from all the bourgeois parties at least and from some of the Left. This was the opportunity for him to realize the ambition of a life-time, and himself secure Constantinople for Russia. On May 1, 1917, he addressed a note to the Allied Governments reaffirming strict regard for the engagements entered into with the " Allies of Russia," which Britain, France and Italy understood as requiring them to keep the arrangements made in 1915. Miliukov's note (text in Golder, pp. 333-4) also laid stress upon the will to continue the war. The note produced an instant storm. He seems not to have appreciated the significant fact that the Bolsheviks, after many zigzags since March, had straightened out their line, or had had it straightened out for them, soon after April 3 when Lenin arrived, some 18 days after Stalin and Kamenev had come to Petrograd. The Committee of the Bolshevik Party's resolution adopted on May 3 described the note as proving that the Provisional Government " is a thoroughly imperialist government bound hand and foot by Anglo-French and Russian capital," and therefore unable to give up annexations. (*Collected Works of Lenin*, XX, II, p. 392.) Stalin's article in *Pravda* described Miliukov's aims as " Imperialist. . . . Russian soldiers are shedding their blood on the battlefield not to ' defend their fatherland,' nor for ' liberty ' as the venal bourgeois Press assures us." The Mensheviks were equally opposed to " imperialist " war aims; there was a general and widespread war-weariness. The note was fiercely attacked as lacking authority, as opposed to proletarian aspirations, etc., and the denunciation from the right also, entailed Miliukov's downfall. The upshot was the acceptance by the Provisional Government of peace based upon " no annexations and no indemnities," a policy to be forwarded immediately by Miliukov's successor, Tereshchenko. Miliukov's speech to his (Cadet) Party on May 22, 1917, ranks as the last Russian stand for Constantinople: " I admit quite frankly, and stand firmly by it, that the main thread of my policy was to get the Straits for Russia. I fought, unfortunately in vain, against those who favoured the new formula [no annexations, no indemnities and the right of self-determination] that Russia should free the Allies from their obligation to help her secure sovereign rights over the Straits. I would say, and I say it proudly, I regard it as a distinct service to the country, that until the last moment that I was in office I did nothing which gave the Allies the right to say Russia has renounced the Straits." (Golder, p. 334; *The Times*, May 28, 1917.) So ended the last public demand on behalf of Russia for the Straits by Professor " Miliukov-Dardanelsky," as the Bolsheviks nicknamed him (R. P. Churchill, " Paul Nikolayevich Miliukov," in Bernadotte E. Schmitt, *Some Historians of Modern Europe*, Chicago, 1942, p. 327.)

The British Government's acknowledgment of the Russian Provisional Government's note, *i.e.*, Miliukov's, was guarded. ("If our reply to Miliukov's note is published in the present form there is certain to be friction, and the Soviet will try to force our hands." Buchanan, *My Mission to Russia*, II, p. 129.) The opinion of the British Foreign Secretary was that the treaties which it had concluded from time to time with the Allies, in the general features, were in accord with the declaration of the Provisional Government; " but if the Russian Government wishes, the British Government is quite ready to examine these treaties with its allies, and if necessary revise them." (*Collected Works of Lenin*, XXII, II, p. 327.) The Bolsheviks made the expected capital out of it, and explained that neither Britain nor France did, or would, accept the policy of no annexations, etc. The Bolsheviks did not for that reason cease to demand the liquidation of the war, and their success inevitably carried with it the renunciation of the Straits. Miliukov's successor, Tereshchenko, pressed by the Left to publish all the secret " treaties " (the word was used irrespective of its technical meanings), took up Kamenev's earlier position and argued that such an act would isolate Russia, and proposed to establish mutual confidence among the Allies.

On July 25 *The Times* reported a statement made by Arthur Henderson on his return after six weeks in Russia. He was accompanied by four members of the Council of Workmen's and Soldiers' Delegates and, among other things, he said that the future in Russia was largely in the hands of the Council, whose delegates were likely to become the dominant party in the Constituent Assembly: " People in England should clearly distinguish these more moderate, though distinctly revolutionary, Socialists, from what were known as the Maximalists (or Bolshevists). They hold decided views regarding the settlement of the war, and consider it essential that the organized democracies of the Allied Countries should influence an immediate restatement of Allied War Aims, " with " a complete renunciation of all intentions inconsistent with their own declarations. They said frankly that they were determined, keeping Constantinople in mind and having doubts as to Mesopotamia, not to leave the settlement of the paramount issues of the war to the chance decision of a meeting of diplomatists." Meanwhile, Tereshchenko was proceeding with an Inter-Allied Conference with the object of revising the arrangements for existing treaties with the exception of the London Agreement of September 5, 1914. As a preliminary to re-establishing Russia's diplomatic position, the July offensive was ordered. The Bolsheviks seized power the day before Tereshchenko had planned to leave for the Inter-Allied Conference in Paris.

Suspicion of Western motives was increased by the circulation in Petrograd of reports of a meeting in Switzerland of a group of allied " bankers," who planned a peace with Germany at Russia's expense. *The Times* printed a Foreign Office communiqué dated September 15, 1917, which said that the British Government were without knowledge of the meeting. But the atmosphere of suspicion and distrust of allied motives continued to prevail. It was equally current in London, and the secrecy that surrounded the agreements everywhere led Liberals and Socialists to agitate against secret diplomacy. Mr. Brailsford's article in *The Herald* of December 6, 1917, was entitled " Those Shameful Secret Treaties." There were leakages in Russia, and in America also, that embarrassed the West. On December 12, 1917, the *Manchester Guardian* published an agreement between France and Russia dated February 24/March 9, 1917. " We are prepared to allow France and Britain complete freedom in drawing up the Western frontiers of Germany in the expectation that the Allies on their part would allow us equal freedom in drawing up our frontiers with Germany and Austria. It is particularly necessary to insist on the exclusion of the Polish question from the subject of international discussion, and on the elimination of all attempts to place the future of Poland under the guarantee and the control of the Powers."

The publication of the " revelations " in *Izvestia* during November (see p. 343 above) was calculated to prove that even if Russia continued to fight with the Allies she would not get Constantinople or the Straits, and so the " secret treaties " would prove of the greatest agitation and propaganda value against the middle-class parties using patriotism, the Bolsheviks would say, as a " smokescreen " for counter-revolution, or, counter-Bolshevism. The attitude compelled the Bolsheviks to take the " unpatriotic " line. Promptly after the Bolshevik *coup d'etat* on November 7, 1917, a proclamation signed by Lenin and Stalin demanded that Constantinople remain in the hands of the Muslims. They renounced all Russian claims on the Straits (December 7, see Louis Fischer, *Soviets in World Affairs*, I, p. 399), a policy to which they remained faithful at Lausanne in 1922-3 and since.

The Russian Revolutions of 1917

Liberal and Conservative estimates of the Revolutions in March and November, and their effect upon peace proposals and settlements, may be compared with that of *The Times* by reference to the following table, which makes no pretension to completeness, of the editorial opinions and correspondents' despatches in the *Daily Mail, Daily Telegraph, Daily News and Leader* (London), *Manchester Guardian, The Nation* and *Observer* :

Daily Mail.

Leader of March 16 refers back to Hamilton Fyfe's forecast on February 1 of a " benign revolution." " The whole nation has made it. This earthquake would have been impossible were not all Russia solid for reform. ... The reformers and the great and glorious Russia for which they stand have always been loyal to the Alliance." The paper emphasizes that German influences in Petrograd are being cleared out. March 24: The paper on finding order restored in the capital and discipline at the front pleads for moderation towards the Tsar. March 27: Petrograd Correspondent states that the Republican idea is gaining strength daily. May 17—Isaac Marcosson writes: " Alexander Kerensky is the Lloyd George of the Russian Revolution—and when I say that I say everything. If ever an individual in a great crisis was a man of destiny, Kerensky is that man."

The July revolt is attributed to the Ukrainians with German assistance. July 19 —Alexander Thompson, Petrograd Correspondent: " With the utmost wish to do justice to the sublime achievement of the Russian Revolution, one must respectfully submit to the members of the Council of Workmen's and Soldiers' Delegates who participated in it that liberty, justice, and peace were not altogether invented by M. Tchkeidze and that the world's democratic ideals are not summed up in any three-headed formula." July 25—Thompson: " It does not look a one-man job, but if one man can pull Russia through, Kerensky, now practically Dictator, will do it."

September 12—Leader: " General Korniloff undoubtedly acted as he has done because he believes, with most educated Russians, that Russia can only be saved by a temporary military dictatorship." September 17—Petrograd Correspondent: As an instrument of the counter-revolution, Korniloff failed " because the base upon which he built his plans proved rotten."

November 9—Leader: " Russia's part in the war has been a small one for the past eight months, and it can hardly be said that this *coup d'état* makes very much difference to the other Allies." On November 10 Lenin is called a proved traitor and Trotsky a sheer Anarchist. But the real Russia is not represented by the Soviets, and will ultimately prevail.

Daily Telegraph.

March 16: The Revolution will not affect Russia's determination to carry on the war to the finish. It represents a great popular movement, having on its side the nobility, Zemstvos, Assembly of People, and Labour Party. " The Duma appears to be establishing its indubitable rights against a powerful, though not necessarily numerous, party of bureaucrats, who have tried to stifle the true voice of Russia." Expressions of sympathy and respect for the Tsar. Next day the paper is against Stürmer, Protopopov, Sukhomlinov, but in favour of Lvov, Rodzianko, Miliukov. Pen pictures are given of the new appointments, the only deprecatory one being of Kerensky. " His oratory is rather of the Hyde Park than the Parliamentary type. It is all delivered in one tone, and that is the very loudest. It would be more correct to say that he shrieks than that he speaks in the Duma. The substance of his orations is quite to match. Everything is always for the worst, in the worst of all possible worlds. He invariably leaves the tribune in a state of physical exhaustion." March 19: " A chief element of success is the moderation of the leaders and the absence of wild schemes of retribution and vengance." Much is hoped from " the wise leaders of the Duma " and " the magnificent assistance of a regenerated people." March 21: " The mere fact that M. Kerensky is Minister of Justice qualifies the possible peril from the side of the Extremists."

The Petrograd Correspondent is strongly in favour of events and clear that the Revolution is not a dictatorship, neither is it atheistic or Nihilist. April 20: Petrograd Correspondent makes first mention of Lenin, whose acceptance of a passage from Germany through Switzerland " arouses intense indignation here." " At the meeting of the Social Democrats yesterday [17th] his wild rant was received in dead silence " and he " was left absolutely without supporters." On April 24 the Correspondent states that Lenin is condemned almost unanimously by the Labour journals.

May 19—Petrograd Correspondent: " The responsible leaders of Russian democracy are coming to see that loyalty to the Allies is essential to the consolidation of the newly gained Russian liberty. It only remains for the formula ' No annexation or contribution, and the right of all nations to decide their own fate ' to be given precise definition."

On July 20 a leader castigates " fanatical visionaries " who propose to lay down arms: " the dupes of Germany when they are not her direct agents." Petrograd Correspondent says that a strike, probably of German origin, has direct connexion with the Government crisis, of which the majority of the people are unaware. Next day the Correspondent gives his version of the rising. A meeting on the 15th of Leninists and Anarchists resolved on a big effort to overthrow the Government. " I hear that a statement was issued to the Press last night [17th] charging Lenin and his associates with acting as German agents in Russia, and with receiving money from German sources. . . . At the last moment the executive of the Council of Workmen's and Soldiers' Delegates requested the Press not to publish the document. One little paper disobeyed the injunction, and the document was read by thousands."

On September 17 the Petrograd Correspondent gave his verdict on the situation to date: The net result of Kornilov's activities is that the Soviets are stronger. The Bolshevists are more prominent in Committees and their influence all round has increased. September 18: The Republic was the only logical outcome of the Tsar's abdication and the Moscow Conference. Kerensky's chief danger may lie in yielding to extreme Socialists.

The paper put up the headline " Russia's Crisis " as early as November 5, and that day printed a Petrograd message dated October 31—" The Soviets have reached a crisis." On November 9 the leading article opens: " Civil war is added to the misfortunes of the Russian people." The paper claims to have foreseen some time ago that the Maximalists might attempt a coup—" the most dangerous and reckless body of anarchical extremists in Europe "—" a handful of anti-national political desperadoes, who have placed themselves outside what law there is in Russia." " The people of Great Britain are aware that the chief authors of this insane crime are their proclaimed and bitter enemies." Petrograd Correspondent: " Civil war seems the lesser of the only two alternative evils. The other is the rule of Lenin, Trotsky, & Co. That would be a disaster to Russia even in times of peace. If Lenin is not a deliberate traitor, he is a crazy visionary. The question which he is may still be left open, though his record is a bad one." November 10—Petrograd Correspondent: " From the very outset the Leninite propaganda has had an emphatically anti-British character." Trotsky has proved himself " the most persistent and embittered enemy of this country." The paper's view was that " M. Kerensky, in his fall and flight, may now regret too late that he denounced as a traitor to the Revolution the general who had the courage to say that only by military dictatorship and the suppression of these fatal committees could Russia and the Revolution be saved. The incurable fault of democratic revolutionaries is that they refuse to take warning by the beacon lights of previous revolutions. The Russian Revolution, which was to have been the salvation of Russia and a winning stroke for the Allies, has proved instead the salvation of Germany and Austria during the campaign of 1917." November 12: Headline is " Bolsheviks Collapsing." The paper still sees hope that the Cossacks may save the day.

Daily News and Leader.

Entire front page was devoted to Russia on March 16. At Petrograd was Arthur Ransome, who continued for months to cover affairs admirably, even if he showed a propensity for finding a fresh " crisis " every month. The first leader said:

" We stand in the presence of perhaps the most momentous event of the war. . . . There has been no blow delivered against Germany so crushing and so far-reaching as this. . . . The Russian people have been fighting for their life on two fronts— against the enemy without and against the enemy within. . . . We are not concerned now with the internal affairs of Russia. But we cannot forbear the expression of the belief that in this respect also an event of good omen for the world has come to pass." March 17: An interview at Brighton is recorded with Prince Kropotkin, who gives his opinion that this defeat of autocracy is final. A.G.G. explains that the Revolution succeeded because the people allowed the Government to strike first by trying to suppress the Duma. " Refusal to be suppressed gave the signal to the nation and the revolt of the Guards turned the current of revolution against the enemy. . . . If the Duma, the nation, and the Army are firm behind the Govern- ment of Prince Lvov, who represents all that is best in the cause of Russian freedom, there is no reason to fear the morrow." On March 20: Ransome begins lyrically, " It is impossible for people who have not lived here to know with what joy we now write of the new Russian Government."

In May A.G.G. and Ransome wrote of suspicions sown in Russia by recent events in England and by the utterances of certain Parliamentarians and newspapers that England had no sympathy with the Liberalism of her ally; that she was seeking help from Russia to beat Germany but not to end Prussianism.

On May 11 the paper thus appraised the position: " The body directly representative of the authority of the revolution, the Council of Workmen's and Soldiers' Delegates, is essentially democratic, or 'Left.' The Provisional Government, which forms the temporary Executive, leans, both in respect of social and political tradition, much more towards the Centre. The difference is undoubtedly accen- tuated by the fact that the outstanding figure in the Government is M. Miliukov, whose Imperialistic views do not correspond with the will of the democratic Council, and whose declarations on Russia's war aims cut directly across the Council's official pronouncements." The paper thinks it would be a good plan to call in more popular representatives to support Kerensky in the Provisional Government and to transfer Miliukov to another post.

On the open letter from the Petrograd Society of Journalists to the Union of English Journalists, accusing The Times Petrograd Correspondent of writing false- hoods, the Daily News, while acknowledging that it lacks evidence on which to judge, observes on May 12: " There is no doubt that the general course of the policy pursued by the reactionary Press in this country has estranged probably fatally advanced opinion in Russia." May 21—Leader: " The real hope of the situation which no changes or chances can utterly quench again, is the spirit which breathes in M. Kerensky's great speech. It is the right voice of heroism. There has not been quite such an utterance heard in the modern world, from a man of M. Kerensky's eminence, since Garibaldi's famous order of the day to the garrison of Rome."

On the resignation of the Cadets over the granting of home rule to the Ukraine, the leading article of July 18 says:

Technically, the Cadets were right; on practical grounds, they were deplorably wrong. They acted with the doctrinaire perversity that has characterized them throughout. . . . In destroying the Coalition, they have flung Russia back into the peculiar phase out of which it had seemed to have passed, and have revived the activities on the one hand of the Extremists who clamour for the downfall of the Government and on the other of the pro-German elements who are working through the Press and every corrupt channel to preach disorder in the Army. . . . Against that we put the firm attitude which has been taken up by the Council of Workmen's and Soldiers' Delegates. This body, as our Petrograd Correspondent has insisted throughout, is the real driving wheel of Russia.

Ransome said on July 20 that: " It is stated also that Lenin was entrusted with the task of destroying the faith of the Russian nation in the Temporary Government, and that the money for the agitation was received through a certain Svendson employed in the German Embassy at Stockholm." July 23—Ransome: "The suggestion of immediate proclamation of a Republic is not so sensational as it seems" and the leader of 24th still believes Kerensky will prove the saviour.

On September 11 the leading article is entitled " The Russian Abyss." From the moment Kornilov entered Moscow, it says, " we feared the worst and the worst has come." " Russia is faced with a combination of horrors on a scale unprecedented in history." There is another retrospective attack on the hostility displayed by " our own Prussian Press " towards a friendly Government. Next day's leader grants that Korniloff may be sincerely devoted to the Revolution and quarrelling with Kerensky not as to purpose but only upon immediate steps. September 14— Ransome: " Such a crisis as this may end in civil war." September 15—A.G.G.: " I do not think anybody who believes in the Revolution can have watched the attitude of this country in regard to Russia, as reflected in the Press this week, without indignation and concern. With a few exceptions, the newspapers have declared definitely for Kornilov and against Kerensky." He adds, characteristically, that " The Northcliffe organs have fed their readers with slanderous ridicule of the Soviet and of Kerensky."

November 9—Leader partly blames Kerensky's fall on the Allies. In Great Britain Henderson was thrown over at the time of the Stockholm Conference, and Kornilov's effort at dictatorship was approved by the Press. Reactionaries notably assisted the advance of the Leninites. Kerensky's eclipse, however, was not necessarily final. November 10—Ransome: " It is folly to deny the actual fact that the Bolshevists do hold a majority of the politically active population." A.G.G. is still not expecting Russia to make a separate peace. " The Revolution in Russia, whatever happens, will remain the one glorious episode of the war. Mr. George, Northcliffe, and the *Morning Post* have made safe the counter-revolution, but the victory is not the Autocracy's; it is the Extremists'." November 19—Leader points out that the Bolshevists are in theory the party least likely to favour peace with the Prussian autocracy. " As for the suggestion that German influence and German money are at the root of all Russia's distresses, the best answer to that groundless charge is the complete security which Allied Ministers and Allied subjects still enjoy in Petrograd. The effect of such assertions of Russian opinion is, of course, disastrous. Unhappily, they are of a piece with the whole of the Allied diplomacy through the recent crisis." November 24—the leading article agrees there can be no recognition of the Lenin-Trotsky Administration; and the Bolshevist Government, " with its extravagancies and its quixotic follies," is doomed.

Manchester Guardian.

March 16: " The sympathy of every man in this country will go out to the Russian people in this supreme hour. If they win and establish their liberty upon an impregnable basis, then they will have given a new aspiration to civilization. . . . The revolution in Russia is the deadliest blow to the war morale of Germany that has been struck. . . . It is the reactionaries who have now been struck down who worked for a separate peace and an alliance with Germany." March 17: The Revolution was made by forces of the Left. March 21: Paper deplores the tendency in the English Press to take sides over the future Government of Russia and to abuse the Republicans. That kind of newspaper clamour which makes or unmakes Ministers in England will have no effect on the Russians. March 23: Bonar Law was not equal to the occasion when congratulating the Duma and the people on the Revolution; but Asquith made good the defect.

May 14—Leader: " Bad friends of Russia, of England, and of civilization are trying to create the conviction that because democratic Russia repudiates Imperialism it is aiming at a separate peace." Even an Extremist like Lenin does not propose such a thing. Michael Farbman, Special Correspondent in Petrograd, foresees a Coalition for the revision of war aims. May 16: Farbman announces that the Executive Committee of the Council of Workmen's and Soldiers' Delegates have decided to join Coalition. May 18: " The repudiation of annexation and indemnities is not quite so simple as it appears. None the less, it expresses the spirit of democratic policy."

On the armed demonstrations in Petrograd in July, David Soskice, Special Correspondent, writes for the paper of 19th: " I have the positive assurance from the Government that all their troops were forbidden to leave barracks. The only possible explanation is that *provocateurs* started shooting to intensify the rebellion and ruin the revolution." Next day: " Circumstances prove that German agents participated in the rebellion." September 11—London Correspondent: The fall of Riga and consequent menace to the capital were exploited by Kornilov's party as a weapon for seizing power, but Kerensky's courage and promptitude saved the Revolutionary Government. Civil war is now extremely unlikely, for Kornilov is not unpatriotic, while Maximalists and Leninites are likely to quit their Extremist positions if it is a case of uniting to preserve the Revolution.

For the principal set-piece attack on *The Times* over its attitude towards the Revolution, see the leader of September 15:

And how has this great transaction, this struggle of a nation for its life, been viewed in this country ? So far as the Government is concerned, in silence: so far as the Press is concerned, unhappily, with scant sympathy. *The Times*, which is still taken abroad as a semi-official organ of our Foreign Office, so recently as the day before yesterday took upon itself to scold those newspapers, ourselves included, who differed from it in not desiring the ruin of the established Government of our great ally and the triumph of the military revolt against its authority. *The Times*, in the course of its long and distinguished career, has committed many indiscretions and many follies, but none perhaps so great and so gratuitous as this. At the very moment that it wrote the revolt was already doomed, and its own columns bore testimony, could it but have recognized the facts, to the ruin of the cause which it vainly advocated. This unhappy incident would of itself be of comparatively small consequence were it not for the misunderstanding and resentment which it must necessarily cause in Russia, and the rather deadly use which can, and no doubt will, be made of it by German propaganda. If we were to suppose that the attitude of *The Times* did in truth represent the views of our Foreign Office, let alone of the War Cabinet, the matter would of course be infinitely more serious. It would mean that at the head of affairs in this country we had men without vision, and whose understanding of the most critical events affecting one of our chief allies was warped by narrow and reactionary views. The country desires to think a good deal better of them than this, and will certainly refuse to accept *The Times* as their mouthpiece.

The paper of September 17 is reminded by Kornilov of Dr. Jameson. It regards Kerensky as the only man capable of maintaining unity. Leader of September 18 will not allow that the Kornilov venture was a " regrettable misunderstanding "; it was an attempt to overthrow the Revolution. Its frustration is to be credited to the Soviets. As Kerensky's new directorate of five is without a representative of these democratic organs there is danger of a serious conflict.

November 9—Leader: Russia's allies should be concerned only with the foreign policy of the Maximalists (*i.e.* the Bolsheviks). Any peace terms they put out must pass beyond such vague generalization as " no annexations and no indemnities " before they can give satisfaction abroad. November 10: Leader rubs it in that it is now too late for Great Britain to affect events in Russia at all. There was a time when she might have done had the Government, the official classes, and the Press sincerely hailed the Revolution as a democratic movement. A Government that understood Russia would have examined her proposal for peace without annexations and redrawn its war aims in regard to Turkey and Austria-Hungary. The Stockholm Conference might have kept genuine Socialists in Russia in touch with British Labour. The London Correspondent reports talk with a Russian official recently in Petrograd. " His chief point was that the English and still more the French newspapers attach an altogether exaggerated importance not only to the Maximalists as a democratic power, but to the importance of the Soviets themselves. Most of those who instigated the Revolution would refuse to follow Lenin, while the Cossacks would prove a rallying point for the vast forces against the Maximalists." November 12—short leader: " Litttle news comes from Russia, but what there is points to the early collapse of the Maximalists. . . . Lenin, like Kornilov, seems on the point of being overthrown chiefly by the spontaneous uprising of the democracy itself." November 20—M. Philips Price from Petrograd: " The Government of M. Kerensky fell before the Bolshevist insurgents because it had no supporters in the country." November 24—David Soskice from Oslo: The Bolshevists must fall, for all educated Russians are against them, while their followers begin to discover the emptiness of their programme. " The Allies should not despair of Russia. She will soon get rid of her new tyranny." The *Guardian*'s editorial view was that " It is not the Bolshevik Government and its peace policy that count. The serious matter is the disorganization of Russia supervening upon economic distress."

The Nation.

Paper on March 17 opens: " The greatest tyranny in the world has fallen. The glorious news of the successful Russian Revolution will send a thrill of joy through democratic Europe." " A London Diary " for same day: " Liberalism has won its first great victory on the moral battleground where all along the true conflict was going on. . . . Association with the Tsar was a curse and an incubus. Alliance with the Russian people is a glory." On March 24 appeared a Russian Number, whose theme was that the Revolution was a Parliamentary movement.

" *The Times* may deliberately desire the return of the autocracy, and with it the loss of the war, but, unless it does, it is an act of political madness to try and rest the Revolution on the Progressives and Cadets alone." Later the paper says: " There has been too much carping, panic-stricken writing in our Conservative papers about the danger from the supposed ' anarchists ' of the Petrograd movement." March 31: " Nor must we allow *The Times* to lure us into the belief that Imperialism is in the saddle at Petrograd." April 14: Paper sees *The Times* pursuing the Workmen's Council with " consistent animosity." It cannot confirm the story that the Council tried to arrest the Provisional Government. The danger in the attitude of *The Times* is that Russia will feel British Imperialism is trying to use the Revolution for its own ends; perhaps to supporting the Cossacks against the Socialist movement. On the refusal of the British Government to let Lenin return to Russia by sea, the paper writes on May 5: " The policy of imposing continued exile on Russian Socialists of whom our Government disapproves, is not likely to improve our very delicate relations with the Russian proletariat."

By June 16 *The Nation* is beginning to wonder if after all there may be a separate peace. The Allies must convince Russia of their own sincerity in disclaiming aggrandizement and must work for the triumph of men like Kerensky, who desire peace by negotiation but not to leave Prussia dominant.

July 28: Lenin's " crime against the Revolution is gross enough " without need of the assumption that he was in German pay. Lenin's career suggests the fanatic rather than the traitor. " The salvation of Russia depends on an early general peace. It is a witless levity which pretends that the demand for an early peace comes only from a handful of venal extremists. . . We hope for a rally which will make a defensive stand before any vital loss has been sustained. That is the gigantic task before the heroic personality of Kerensky. It lies with Russia's Allies to do the rest." August 11: " We do not believe in the triumph of any kind of authoritative reaction in Russia, ' bourgeois,' military, or royalist. The Tsar has disappeared, and there is no Pretender. But the Russian temperament is subject to depression, to epidemics of apathy, or even to contagions of despair, and if one of these fits were to set in, or the winter brought famine after the hope of peace had gone, the chaos might be irremediable, and accident might throw up a dictator." September 1: The result of the National Congress in Moscow seems to have been negative, and there is some dread of counter-revolution.

September 15: Paper opens : " The counter-revolution, which everyone expected, has broken out in Russia, played its gambling stroke, and failed. The man of destiny was General Kornilov." *The Times* is abused for having assumed that Lenin or anybody rebelling against the Provisional Government must be in German pay, and then gleefully hailing Kornilov's reaction as highly patriotic. " The only difference perceptible to us is that the July rebellion was made by soldiers and workmen, while the September rebellion was the work of generals and the propertied class." Kornilov allowed Riga to fall so as to discredit the Kerensky Government; in short, he committed treason before rebellion. " Kerensky and the Revolution have come brilliantly out of this trial." *The Times* has for weeks tried to cover the Revolution with odium, turning on Kerensky its full battery of sneers, ready to applaud " any first murderer in uniform." September 22: " The General's revolt stands out as one of the most frivolous and criminal actions in history! "

At this stage *The Nation* was all in favour of a Russian Republic being proclaimed. It was several weeks before *The Times* was allowed to hear the last of Kornilov. The paper which, however, supported the Workmen's Councils now sounded a different note. October 13: " There is no doubt that the new Government will be pursued by the implacable hostility of the Bolsheviks. Forcible suppression of their anarchic activities may well be necessary." November 10: The new Revolution is explained by the fact that, though the Maximalists were never a strong party, behind them stands the big " war-weariness party." Russia might never have arrived at this pass had Henderson been listened to in his advocacy of the Stockholm Conference and new definition of Allied war aims. Hardly was a Revolutionary Government installed in Petrograd than such papers as *The Times* set out to destroy it. The key to the future is that the people of Russia will demand peace and bread.

Observer.

Earliest reference is on the main page on March 18: " An example is given to the Kaiser's subjects—political slaves now by comparison with emancipated Russia—which will shake to its foundations the German governing system which caused the war. . . . The triumph won by the Duma and the Army together for freedom and modern government is one of the greatest and best things of time. The breath of a new morning is felt not only by Russia but by all mankind."

On April 8 the Petrograd Correspondent says that a counter-revolution is felt there to be most unlikely, while all signs of the old regime are disappearing. On April 22 he foresees no danger of a separate peace. He reports that Lenin found himself quite out of touch with most Russian Socialists when making an inflammatory speech calling for immediate peace and establishment of the Commune. It is incorrect, says the correspondent on April 29, to lump the Councils of Soldiers and Workmen together with Extremists among opponents of the Government. Only in Kronstadt has the situation looked ugly, because there Extremists among the soldiers and workmen gained control.

Petrograd Correspondent, May 6: "Even the extravagant Lenin declares himself opposed to a separate peace, though his agitation, if it had any success, would tend that way." Most of the people and the Army desire neither a separate peace nor Miliukov's type of Imperialism.

May 13 main page: People in England must not label as reactionaries all Russians who are not Extremists. A good compromise may be reached in the formula that "decisive victory does not mean conquest." Petrograd Correspondent says that though the country as a whole is for fighting on, the Council of Workmen's and Soldiers' Delegates is the most powerful organization in it.

July 22: Petrograd Correspondent explains rebellion as an effort by Extremists, though in a minority in the Council, to force the Council to take over full power. The Executive Committee could not do this without disobeying the mandate of the entire country. Lenin is said to have made for Kronstadt disguised as a sailor; Zinoviev, "one of the most notorious of the Maximalists," has been arrested. July 29—Petrograd Correspondent: Russian troops are beginning to see that Extremists and Germans are working together.

August 12, main page: The Soviet, which has monopolized power and thereby paralysed Russia, has now lost it again. Kerensky and Kornilov are political and military dictators respectively. "Either the Soviet will henceforth be powerless or the old lesson of the French Revolution will be repeated and only the military dictatorship will survive."

September 16: Main page is given entirely to Russia, the first time since March 18. Argument is that Kerensky has rallied the Jacobins and at the same time kept in touch with Cadets and Liberals. Russia must determine her own form of government and exact confidence and support from the Allies. Kornilov was not a traitor, but may have thought the fall of Riga would be good to awaken the country and discredit a Government that did not break with the Soviet. Kornilov failed to bring off his coup because he omitted personally to lead troops to Petrograd. Kerensky stands out above all competitors, "the man of genius and the man of Russia." Allied prospects are better than they have ever been. On September 23 the Petrograd Correspondent diagnoses class conflict and sees the start of a swing to the Left.

October 28—Main page: "By common consent the Soviet is weakening." There must be no suggestion after the war that the Allies should abandon Russia —unless of course she prove unable to do anything to help herself. On November 11 judgement is reserved on "the new Russian Revolution," and the story of the Bolshevist coup is taken from Reuter's Petrograd Correspondent. Next week there is still no comment and practically no news given of Russia. On November 25 a short leader still appeals for postponement of judgement and comment, but, admits the outlook to be black. "The Leninites, with a culminating frenzy of mingled treachery and madness, propose a separate peace." But "nothing is more certain than that Bolshevism will perish."

The New Europe

On October 19, 1916, the first number appeared of a new weekly review of foreign politics, *The New Europe*, with the sub-title "Pour la Victoire Intégrale," published by Constable, price 6d. The editorship was not disclosed, but the list of "Collaborators" included Ronald M. Burrows, Émile Cammaerts, André Chéradame, Sir Arthur Evans, H. M. Hyndman, Take Ionescu, Thomas Masaryk, Ramsay Muir, Alison Phillips, Paul Sabatier, R. W. Seton-Watson, Wickham Steed, André Tardieu, Paul Vinogradov, A. F. Whyte, H. Spenser Wilkinson, C. Hagberg Wright, and Sir Francis Younghusband. Bernard Pares and Harold Williams wrote on Russia, Madariaga on Spain, George Saunders on Germany, Mario Borsa on Italy, George Young on the Foreign Office and the League of Nations. Seton-Watson tirelessly put the case for the Southern Slavs, while Masaryk wrote on a wide range of subjects including Pan-Germanism, the history and constitution of the Austro-Hungarian Empire, and the forerunners of the Russian revolution. Steed contributed to Vol. I an article on "Britain and the Spirit of France" (p. 65) and a short obituary of the Emperor Francis Joseph (p. 203). Vol. V contains Steed's lecture on "Austria and Europe" delivered to L.C.C. teachers at King's College, London, on December 8, 1917 (pp. 359 and 388).

The first issue gave the aims of the review: "to provide a rallying ground for all those who see in European reconstruction, on a basis of nationality, the rights of minorities, and the hard facts of geography and economics, the sole guarantee against an early repetition of the horrors of the present war." It would try to unmask German war policy, provide the historical, racial and strategic background to current problems, and emphasize the need of an allied counter-plan for victory. Its methods would be "frankly critical and vigilant, reading the meaning of history out of the brutal logic of facts." The Pan-German project of "Central Europe" and "Berlin-Bagdad" must be answered by an "integral" allied victory, bringing the vindication of national rights and public law, and the emancipation of the subject races of Central and South-Eastern Europe from German and Magyar control. To this end the review would work for the creation of an " alert, organised and eager " public opinion, which would support statesmen in their difficult task of peace-making after victory.

The articles were brief, vivid and authoritative, full of information but not tediously so, and outspoken in criticism of those who disagreed with the editorial policy. The *Morning Post* suffered the humiliation of having the " notorious forgeries " of its " Budapest Correspondent " exposed. Some time later the *Post* published a leading article (April 23, 1918) in which *The New Europe* was compared to " an Ethnological Museum " in which " a guiding principle " was missing. The Editor reminded the *Post* of a forlorn but wealthy spinster who adopts " a whole menagerie of strange little pets " to comfort herself. *The New Europe* published a brisk comment : " The *Morning Post* is a typical product of that state of insular ignorance and prejudice against which the foundation of *The New Europe* was a protest; and its displeasure is our justification." (Vol. VII, p. 72.) The *Post* then accused the review of having as its chief aim the propagation of Bolshevism in Europe—a charge which was emphatically denied. In fact, while the review welcomed the Russian revolution of March, 1917, as likely to strengthen Russia's contribution to the war, it deplored the overthrow of the " liberal " government and the subsequent Bolshevik control. The Vatican was viewed with considerable suspicion as a reactionary, monarchical and unneutral influence, bent on conserving the Austro-Hungarian Empire in order to preserve the Catholic equilibrium in Europe. The Papal Peace Note provoked bitter criticism of Benedict XV for preaching " an unneutral homily of which the pious accents scarcely avail to mask the unmoral substance." The writer of the article saw in the Note the work of Father Ledochowski, General of the Jesuits, Father Galen and Father Zabeo—all champions of the Hapsburgs—and remarked that " in Jesuit hands the Sovereign Pontiff is as wax." It was emphasized that there must be no Papal representative at the Peace Conference. (Vol. IV, p. 161.)

Special supplements were published giving the text of important documents, as in Vol. II, No. 14 (January 18, 1917)—the Peace Movement; Vol. V—the Russian Secret Documents; and Vol. VI, No. 66 (January 17, 1918)—the Secret Treaty with Italy (April 26, 1915), " not yet published in this country "; and No. 72 (February 28, 1918)— the text of the Ukraine Treaty (Brest-Litovsk, February 9, 1918). Vol. IX, No. 105 (October 17, 1918), contains the review's peace terms, some points of which are : 1. Germany to remain united, though inhabitants of Alsace-Lorraine, Schleswig and Posen to resume their former allegiance if they wish, but German provinces of Austria also to be free to unite with German Empire; 2. Free and independent Poland; 3. Russia preferably to be reconstituted on a federal basis; 4. Austro-Hungarian Empire to be broken up, with a free Bohemia, Jugoslav State, Hungary, etc., and the border peoples to join their neighbouring states; 5. Conference to be set up to delimit Balkan frontiers and promote a Balkan Confederation.

With the victory of the Allies, the review threw itself whole-heartedly into organising public opinion towards a sane, lasting peace settlement. Vol. IX, No. 110 (November 21, 1918), bore on its cover the slogan—" We have won the War: We must not lose the Peace," which appeared until the middle of May, 1919. The League of Nations was supported and vengeful reparations regretfully abandoned as impracticable. But with the end of the war public interest in foreign affairs and the fate of small nationalities slackened. The last number appeared on October 28, 1920, when rising costs compelled the Editors to cease publication.

For a note on Self-determination see below, p. 1094.

Interview with Lord Milner. (*Evening Standard*, October 17, 1918)

On the origins and circumstances of the interview, Mr. A. H. Mann, C.H., Editor of the *Evening Standard*, 1916-1920, writes the following memorandum:

I had lately started in the *Evening Standard*, which I edited, the feature that I christened " The Londoner's Diary." I made a round of calls each morning upon " key " people so that the day's issue might contain the most up-to-date background intelligence of the war situation and the home front. On October 15th, 1918, I was calling at No. 10, Downing Street, when William Sutherland, the Prime Minister's Private Secretary, made the suggestion that Lord Milner, then Secretary of State for War, and a member of the War Cabinet, would like to see me. When Sutherland threw out his suggestion I said I would be ready to wait upon Lord Milner at any time convenient to him.

Later in the day I heard from Downing Street that Lord Milner would receive me at 11 o'clock the next morning. When I arrived, he sat down opposite me, and started to talk very earnestly and deliberately. Except for an occasional comment or question from myself he propounded the theory that though the military situation had changed dramatically in the past few weeks in favour of the Allies the German armies were not absolutely broken. Shortly they were likely to be driven back across their own frontiers; already they had been driven out of vital positions in France and Flanders. But in Germany they would retire behind very strong prepared positions and, fighting in defence of their Fatherland, their resistance would almost certainly become stouter. He (Lord Milner) had no doubt that in such a struggle ultimate victory would be ours, but at very heavy cost in men. The Allies had already suffered very grievous losses in manpower. Heavy fighting in Germany would increase those sacrifices and create in Central Europe a state of chaos, confusion and desperation congenial to the spread of Bolshevism. Would it not be far better for an armistice to be concluded as soon as possible, so long as its conditions guaranteed the military supremacy of the Allies ?

Naturally I made the comment that the British public were at the moment looking with eager expectancy to the invasion of Germany and a peace dictated in Berlin; such a peace as would leave no doubt as to the complete destruction and humiliation of Prussian militarism.

Lord Milner then proceeded to give his views as to the German people's attitude to militarism. They did not, he thought, like the Junker and the Jackboot. They tolerated Imperialism because these forces had, under Bismarck, welded several puny States that had been the sport of greater powers into one strong State, and given its people a sense of prestige, prosperity and of strength. But as soon as the wreckage of the Prussian military machine was demonstrated before their eyes, as it would be if peace terms were dictated by the Allies, militarism in Germany would be utterly discredited. So, proceeded Lord Milner's argument, an armistice concluded without delay would give us all we had fought for and prevent fruitless bloodshed. The Allies hoped for reparations from Germany and these could be better obtained from a country under a stable government than one suffering civil war and chaos. Changes were already taking place in the character of the German Government. In fact Lord Milner held that a " complete transformation of the system of government was already in progress." We should not be in too great a hurry to denounce these changes as a sham.

When Lord Milner had concluded his argument, of which I have indicated only the main points, I asked whether he had any objection to the publication of his views. I had not taken a single note, but the force and earnestness with which he had spoken had made such an impression upon my mind that I had no doubt I could reproduce his argument with accuracy. He replied that he had no objection at all provided that he could see the interview in proof before publication. I went back to the *Evening Standard* office, and while the conversation was fresh in my memory wrote the interview at the length of an *Evening Standard* column and a half. Lord Milner read the proof carefully, altered two words, made a reference to the accuracy with which his views had been set down, and confirmed his wish to see the interview published.

It occupied the main position on the front page of the *Evening Standard* next day, October 17th, accompanied by a leading article headed " Lord Milner on Victory."

The interview, which was the main front page feature, is textually reproduced below with the italics of the original but without the headlines and crossheads.

At the outset (writes the interviewer) I would express Lord Milner's tribute to the wonderful valour of our armies in France and Flanders, and to the skill of the British generals, that have contributed so largely to the complete change in the military situation during the last few months. As head of the British War Office, Lord Milner gladly seized the opportunity of expressing, through the *Evening Standard*, his hitherto unspoken feelings of admiration for the Army, which, undismayed by the serious reverses of the spring, had gone forward to the offensive with even greater dash than ever before, and had been most brilliantly led. The spirit displayed by the troops, the skill and the leadership, and the efficiency of the rear services were beyond mere words of praise, but would live for ever in the nation's memory.

Lord Milner takes the view that it is the duty now of the Allied statesmen and the peoples at home to do and say nothing likely to retard or render more difficult the task of the armies in the field. Complete victory is in sight. *How can it best be reached in the shortest possible time and with the lowest cost of life?*

What constitutes complete victory? In Lord Milner's view this question is best answered, as most of us would answer it, in the familiar phrase, " *the destruction of Prussian militarism.*" All other aims fade into insignificance in comparison with this primary object. The punishment of the men who made the war and were responsible for its crimes, the questions of reparation for wrong and damage done, even territorial readjustments, are all secondary to *the one object of rendering Prussianism impotent for evil.* Achieve the one aim, and the rest naturally follow.

In Lord Milner's opinion, there is a danger at present of the destruction of Prussian militarism being postponed by the ulterior questions being raised in such a fashion as to strengthen the resistance of the German armies and people. I will endeavour to state, in brief, Lord Milner's argument.

It is a *serious mistake*, Lord Milner thinks, to *imagine that the German people are in love with militarism.* They have submitted to it partly from security, partly owing to the glamour of its hitherto unbroken success. But especially of late years, until it was submerged by the war, there was a rising tide of revolt against the Junker and the Jackboot.

Lord Milner was in Germany at the time of the Zabern incident, and then the people were so incensed that a *revolt* against the brutality of the system *was with difficulty restrained.* The German people tolerated Imperialism and militarism because these forces had bound together several puny and helpless States, that had been the sport of greater Powers, into one united whole and given their peoples prestige, prosperity, and the feeling of strength.

Lord Milner draws the natural conclusion that when the people of the German Empire actually see the complete and ignominious defeat of militarism, and realise that the system has brought them ruin and humiliation, they will be as eager to do away with it as are the Allies. So the main task of the Allies is *to hasten the day when the utter wreckage of the Prussian military machine is demonstrated before the very eyes of the German people.*

This may be achieved in one of two ways—either (1) by a complete and decisive victory leading to the enemy's unconditional surrender. or (2) by an armistice under such conditions as to guarantee that the military supremacy of the Allies shall not be weakened, but rather strengthened, by the cessation of hostilities. The guarantees might take various forms, according to what the High Command of the Allied armies regarded as necessary.

Of these two alternatives Lord Milner thinks *the second would be as successful as the first in bringing about the utter collapse of Prussian militarism.* The Allies would be in the position of dictating terms of peace on the general lines already accepted by the German Government. Militarism would be powerless and utterly discredited.

Lord Milner, regarding an armistice in such conditions as certain to be attended by the realisation of our full war aims, is anxious, as I have already suggested, that nothing shall be done to postpone its accomplishment. He is *inclined to think that if the Allies at the present time attempt to dictate to Germany certain drastic changes in their own government both as regards constitution and personnel, the resistance of the German armies and people, already waning, may be stiffened.*

After all, Lord Milner points out, there must be a German Government to negotiate an armistice with, and it must not be overlooked that the Germans have put up " new men." *A complete transformation of the system of government is already in progress.* In Lord Milner's opinion we *should not be in too great a hurry to denounce it as a sham.*

The present holders of power are responsible to the Reichstag, and the Reichstag is the only popularly elected national assembly in Germany. It is in the interests of the Allies to see a stable Government of some sort maintained in Germany. As reparation has to be obtained, we do not wish to see Bolshevism and chaos rampant there.

It will thus be seen that in Lord Milner's view all thoughts should be concentrated upon the task of pressing on to a complete military victory, *which will cause the Germans either to surrender unconditionally or be forced to enter into an armistice the conditions of which will reduce Prussian militarism to virtual impotency.* When that is achieved, and the German people are faced with the bill of costs, they may be relied upon to put Kaiserism in its place. Meanwhile, says Lord Milner, *there is need to think more of victory and less of vengeance.*

But we must not forget Justice. At the same time, if the war can be concluded with the conversion of the German people to the view that the Allies had right on their side, and that Prussianism was Germany's enemy as well as our enemy—well, so much the better. But the German people will have to give ample proofs of their conversion before they are believed. (*Signed*) A.H.M.

There was little international reaction visible in the newspapers. The leading article in *Le Temps* observed incidentally that " Lord Milner nous invite à croire qu'une Allemagne démocratique abjurerait nécessairement le militarisme prussien." The *New York Times* merely summarized the interview in a quarter of a column.

Hansard, *Parliamentary Debates*, November 7, 1918 (col. 2354).

Sir Edward Carson : I am quite alive to the fact that it is almost high treason to say a word against Lord Northcliffe. I know his power and that he does not hesitate to exercise it to try to drive anybody out of any office or a public position if they incur his royal displeasure. But as at my time of life neither office nor its emoluments nor anything connected with Governments, or indeed public life, makes the slightest difference, and the only thing I care about is really the interests of decent administration, I venture to incur even the possibility of the odium of this great trust owner, who monopolises in his own person so great a part of the Press of this country, and has always for himself a ready-made *claque* to flatter him and to run any policies for him that he thinks best in his own interests.

Within the last few days there has been an attack made by this Noble Lord's papers upon Lord Milner. Lord Milner is Secretary of State for War, and if Lord Northcliffe is not a Minister—as I believe he says he is not a Minister—he is at least an official of one of the Government Ministries. Lord Milner seems to have given an interview to a rival paper, or another paper, with the merits or demerits of which I would not be in order in dealing, except so far as to say this, that, having read it and having read the criticism of some of Lord Northcliffe's papers upon it, I believe that it has been purposely and intentionally misrepresented and mis-understood. But whether that be so or not, all I can say is that it seems to me to be nothing but indecent that the gentleman engaged in foreign propaganda on behalf of His Majesty's Government should make part of his propaganda an attack upon the Secretary of State for War in the Government, under which he purports to serve. But it is really worse than that, because he professes to do it upon the ground that Lord Milner's interview was an indiscretion which was likely to do harm in France, and yet day after day he repeats Lord Milner's words in order that the indiscretion may be more and more rubbed into the French people. I noticed yesterday, or the day before—indeed, I would not have seen it, only somebody brought it to my attention, because I do not read those papers—that he quoted, or that the paper quoted in its leading article, what purported to be a telegram from the French correspondent who, I have no doubt, is either Lord Northcliffe himself, who happens to be there, or is somebody with whom he was in immediate contact, calling attention to the great damage that had been done, now many days ago, by this interview of Lord Milner's.

I think it is really time to put an end to this kind of thing. The Government may imagine that they gain power and support, but I do not believe it for a moment. I believe that all the best elements in the country resent this kind of thing. Everybody knows who has been in public life or in public office that the moment Lord Northcliffe's displeasure is incurred from that moment onwards a kind of manhunt commences until he drives anybody whom he looks upon as an adversary out of office. I have a strong suspicion myself in this case that he is anxious to drive Lord Milner out of office, and, indeed, he does not cloak it because he heads his articles " Will he resign ? " " What is the way out ? " and all those other, I suppose we will call them popular, headlines in the midst of a crisis like this, when every moment of Lord Milner's time and his brains must be concentrated upon events of the greatest magnitude in this world—he does not cloak it that he wants to drive him out of office, and for what purpose ? Is it because he has been inefficient ? Not at all, Sir, because I think everybody will admit that since Lord Milner went to the War Office there has been an immense improvement in the whole management and organisation of the War Office. No, Sir; at the present moment, when Lord Milner is in France, and has been in France, I am told, as I have not seen him for a long time, dealing with these matters at the Versailles Conference and everything of that kind and with matters of vital importance to this country, to which he is devoting his whole time day after day, come these attacks from an official of the Government upon Lord Milner to drive him out of his office. For what ? In order that Lord Northcliffe may get it or may get into the War Cabinet so that he may be present at the Peace Conference, whenever it comes. The whole thing is a disgrace to public life in England and a disgrace of journalism. I know perfectly well how difficult it is to ever criticise the Press. I know perfectly well the reward you reap for it. Thank God, I never cared what they said about me. I have never cared, but I do hope that Members of this House, whether they agree with Lord Milner, or whether they agree with any other Minister, will see that, at all events, at a crisis like this fair play, fair criticism, honest dealing, and decent life are necessary.

Mr. Mann recalls that at the Lord Mayor's Banquet on November 9 he met Milner again for the first time since the publication of the interview. " As I stood in the cloakroom about to recover my hat and coat I saw Lord Milner struggling in a narrow passage outside with a mass of men moving in the same direction. Leaning towards him and stretching my hand over the heads of the intervening people I said ' Lord Milner, having done you a disservice may I do you a service ? ' He handed me his cloak-room ticket and I recovered his hat and coat with my own. As I helped him on with his coat he said ' I do not consider you have done me any disservice: quite the contrary '." [A. H. Mann to the present compiler.]

Lloyd George on the Risks of Self-determination, 1919

The memorandum of March 29, 1919, circulated to the Peace Conference and published as a Command Paper three years later was printed in *The Times* of March 25, 1922. The following extracts should be read in conjunction with the note on *The New Europe* (above p. 1090) and the references in the text at pp. 321, 497. " You may strip Germany of her colonies, reduce her armaments to a mere police force and her navy to that of a fifthrate Power; all the same, in the end, if she feels she has been unjustly treated in the peace of 1919 she will find means of exacting retribution from her conquerors. . . . The maintenance of peace will then depend upon there being no causes of exasperation constantly stirring up the spirit of patriotism, of justice, or of fair play." He was ready to be " severe," " stern," and " even ruthless," but the terms must be " so just that the country on which they were imposed will feel in its heart that it has no right to complain. But injustice, arrogance, displayed in the hour of triumph will never be forgotten or forgiven."

For these reasons, therefore [Lloyd George proceeded], I am strongly averse to transferring more Germans from German rule to the rule of some other nation than can possibly be helped. I cannot conceive any greater cause of future war than that the German people, who have certainly proved themselves one of the most vigorous and powerful races in the world, should be surrounded by a number of small States, many of them consisting of people who have never previously set up a stable government for themselves, but each of them containing large masses of Germans clamouring for reunion with their native land.

Lloyd George then urged the drafting of terms which a responsible Government in Germany could expect to carry out.

Steed, if he saw this document, made no reference to it in his messages (see p. 497). But he did note, during the first week of April, that Lloyd George was anxious to rebut French Press accusations that he was pro-German, and to prove he was France's greatest friend.

The Revolting M.P.s (1919)

The interest taken at home principally concerned Lloyd George's abandonment, it was alleged, of essential Allied peace aims including the presentation to Germany of the bill " in full " for the cost of the war. One of the incidents which brought Lloyd George back to England from the Peace Conference was receipt on April 8, 1919, of a telegram from 370 M.P.s. This telegram referred to " persistent reports " from Paris that British delegates " instead of formulating the complete financial claim of the Empire, are merely considering what amount can be exacted from the enemy." The signatories wished to tabulate a full bill, secure Germany's acknowledgment, and only thereafter to discuss ways and means of obtaining payment. Included among the " persistent reports " was a dispatch in the *Westminster Gazette* on March 31, recording as " the authentic British view " of " a high authority " the outline of a " sensible peace." The writer was Sisley Huddleston, its Correspondent just appointed by J. A. Spender. What Huddleston and his informant postulated as " sensible " was not to press for indemnities beyond reparation for actual material damage; not to ruin Germany industrially and so weaken the European fabric; not to take so much of her output that British workers would lose their livelihood; not to waste money on a huge occupying force. It so happened that Northcliffe, then in France, had sent to Lieut.-Col. Lowther, M.P., a message on what he regarded as the Prime Minister's weakening, and this rather than what the *Westminster Gazette* said, was the proximate cause of action by the 370 members.

On April 1, 1922, the *Westminster Gazette* printed a statement by Huddleston that the authority he had quoted for the so-called " moderation interview " of 1919 was Lloyd George himself. The Correspondent was now able to make this disclosure because Lloyd George had publicly issued a memorandum (see above) he had circulated to the Peace Conference in that year, expressing strikingly similar views and some of the very phrases used in the dispatch to the *Westminster Gazette* on March 31, 1919. This proved that " whatever has been done since the early days of the Peace Conference, which has prolonged the period of hatred in Europe, and has prepared other wars, has been done against the better judgement of Mr. Lloyd George." Huddleston believed the identity of his informant was an open secret, and had wanted to name him at the time.

> Not only have I no patience with the incognito statesman as such, but in this case my impulse was to cry the truth from the housetops. The truth was that an impossible treaty had been imposed upon Europe, and that at least two of the treaty makers— Mr. Wilson and Mr. Lloyd George—knew it. I wanted the process of education of the public to be accelerated. Since, however, the *Westminster Gazette* was in some way involved in any action I chose to take on this matter, I was bound to accept the advice given me by a man whom I regard as one of the three ablest journalists of my time—my friend and my master—and I carefully took Mr. Lloyd George's name out of the publisher's proofs. But no one has been deceived.

The episode, as Spender commented, raised questions both of journalistic ethics and of the ethical standards of public men.

In his memoir *In My Time*, Huddleston observes (p. 140) that Lloyd George in his speech to the Commons on April 16, 1919, was able to create the impression that the dispatch in the *Westminster Gazette* was of no great weight, thereby disowning his personal conviction when it was becoming awkward, to draw off discussion from the interview; and while assailing Northcliffe in a savage speech, quite convincingly since the two were known to have quarrelled, he then " surrendered to those who strove for a vindictive peace." The sequel to Huddleston's disclosure in 1922 was that " the defence of Mr. Lloyd George was of the lamest. He ' did not remember '; there were ' inaccuracies '; but he virtually admitted the facts. . . . Nobody came to the rescue of Mr. Lloyd George, while there was almost unanimous support for me." Sir John Simon claimed that if the Prime Minister had boldly avowed what he secretly wrote, Wilson would have been fortified and calm judgement vindicated. " History will attribute no small part of the ruin and desolation, the loss and suffering that are visiting the world to-day, to this tragic error." The Editor of the *Westminster Gazette* appended his observations on the journalistic aspects of the episode in the issue for March 31. The whole was reprinted in *The Times* of April 3, 1922. In the debate on the Peace Situation in the House of Commons on April 14, 1919, the Prime Minister, having asked his famous question " How many members have heard of Teschen? I do not mind saying I had never heard of it," proceeded to give the assurance that there need be no recognition of the Bolsheviks, and no military intervention. " We have had quite enough bloodshed." Passing to the general question of Peace and its nature Lloyd George announced that the delegates were unanimous in believing that to publish the terms before discussing them with the enemy would be " a first-class blunder." He then referred to the telegram from the 370 members. " I did not object to that telegram but let me say a word to my pen friend (Mr. Kennedy Jones, Hornsey, C.U.). I object to the information on which it was based." At this point Kennedy Jones gave his reference to the *Westminster Gazette*'s " reliable service" whereupon Lloyd George skilfully drew Colonel Lowther into the debate and immediately made the attack on Northcliffe, " the threepenny edition of the *Daily Mail*," as chronicled in Chapter XI, pp. 499-501.

The Lloyd George—Northcliffe Quarrel

A surviving letter from Steed to Dawson is relevant:
... I have asked Ll. G. about it and he never mentioned N.'s alleged ambition to be an official delegate to the Peace Conference. He said that " N. wanted to dictate," and that he (Ll. G.) would not be dictated to. The proposal N. meant to make to Ll. G. was something quite different; and when I explained it to Ll. G. some years ago, Ll. G. said he had never understood it. [S. to D., August 15, 1938.]

Newspapers

Daily Telegraph, November 29, 1917.

Co-ordination of Allies' War Aims. Letter from Lord Lansdowne. Column on main page turned over to page 6; Leading article: " We do not say that Lord Lansdowne, in his letter, does not take some of the ground of which many thinking and patriotic men may disapprove," and instanced his reference to Freedom of the Seas. November 30, long letter from T. Gibson Bowles against; C. A. McCurdy for; It would give Russia the assurances and ultimate purpose. Two letters from Gilbert Murray in favour.

Izvestia, November 28, 1917.

The Italian Treaty published.

Manchester Guardian, January 18, 1918.

The Italian Treaty published. The signatories were J. Cambon, Imperiali, Benckendorff, Grey.

Marchand, René: *Un Livre Noir. Diplomatie d'avant guerre d'après les documents des archives russes.* (Paris, 1922-1927, 2 vols.)

The second volume summarizes the documents on the Straits question.

See also the *Manchester Guardian*, February 24, March 9, December 12, 1917.

The Herald (Brailsford), December 6, 1917, on " Those Shameful Secret Treaties."

The Great Anti-Northcliffe Mail, No. 1, March—April, 1917. (Zürich, Jean Frey. Blanket folio, 10 pp., one issue only.)

Criticisms of the *Daily Mail* and other constituents of the Northcliffe Press. *The Times* is only slightly mentioned. A paragraph of some interest to students of propaganda is the one that rejects the allegation commonly made in Germany that Northcliffe was a renegade German Jew, from Frankfurt-on-Main, named Isaak Stern. The correct statement is made that two of Northcliffe's mother's sisters married Germans. There is good fun in Bart Kennedy's squib beginning " O Thou Great Northoleon." Some of Kennedy's squibs had been printed earlier in London.

The Paris *Daily Mail*.

The title of the newspaper is DAILY MAIL CONTINENTAL EDITION. A legend at the head of the paper reads :

The Northcliffe Press. The *Daily Mail* (Paris Editions) is controlled by Lord Northcliffe and is a member of the Northcliffe Press. Several editions, including an American issue, are published each morning for the various fronts, for Paris and its environs. The paper is on sale daily, etc.

The headlines to the main features of the issue for October 23, 1918, are UNITED DIPLOMACY. NO HAGGLING WITH THE HUN. SPEECH BY LORD NORTHCLIFFE. LORD MILNER'S LANSDOWNEISM. The issue for November 2 records that " Lord Northcliffe, accompanied by Lieut.-Col. Campbell Stuart, has arrived in Paris, and is staying at the Hotel Ritz."

Printed Works

Adamov, E.: *Die europäischen Mächte und die Turkei während des Weltkrieges. Konstantinopel und die Meererungen. Nach dem Geheimdokumenten des ehem. Ministeriums für Aswärtige Angeletenheiten.* (4 vols., Berlin, 1930-1932.)

German translation of a portion of Adamov's work on the documents in the Tsarist archives, begun in Moscow in 1924. The first volume is a general introduction to the question from the general international standpoint 1908-1917. Vols. II-IV comprise the documentary section August 20, 1914—October 1, 1917, some 368 telegrams, dispatches and memoranda, etc., dealing with the Straits question; the whole of key importance to the strategic considerations applying to the Powers great and small. The complete collection printed in the Russian edition was used in the article in the *Slavonic Review* mentioned, *s.v.* R. J. Kerner, below.

It is unnecessary to tabulate here the works of M. N. Pokrowsky, F. Stieve, and others as these are all set out and commented upon in G. P. Gooch, *Recent Revelations of European Diplomacy*, the fourth edition (London, 1940), of which has been used.

Baker, Ray S. : *Woodrow Wilson and World Settlement.* (3 vols., London, 1923.)

The extent of official American knowledge of the London Agreements, *i.e.*, the so-called " Secret Treaties," is dealt with in Vol. I, Chapter II, p. 34 ff. The terms of the principal secret treaties are outlined in Chapter II and a number of documents given, e.g., Sazonov's telegram to Benckendorff, May 20, 1915, on Grey's assent to the settlement of the Straits Question and Constantinople in accordance with Russia's design, and the compensation to Britain.

Bemis, S. Flagg : *First Gun of a Revisionist Histriography for the Second World War* in *The Journal of Modern History.* (Chicago), XIX, No. 1, March, 1947, pp. 55-59.

Mr. Bemis introduces his argument by tracing revisions after the First World War to the publication of *Die grosse Politik der europäischen Kabinette*, 1871-1914, which began publication in 1922. " Within five years some American historians were relieving Germany of any principal responsibility for the terrible conflict. Some of them [Michael Cochran] actually published a book called *Germany not guilty in* 1914. . . . This disillusionist histriography resulted in the complete repudiation of Wilson's foreign policy and in the neutrality legislation of 1935-37. As everybody now can see, that legislation assisted the rise of Hitler's power and his onslaught on Western civilisation." Mr. Bemis proceeds to deal critically with George Morganstern, *Pearl Harbor ; the Story of the Secret War.* (New York, 1947.) The publication of diplomatic documents by Gooch and Temperley on behalf of the British Foreign Office began four years after *Die grosse Politik* had been initiated:

Clarke, Tom : *My Lloyd George Diary.* (London, 1939.)

The narrative opens in 1926, when Mr. Clarke went to the *Daily News* as Managing Editor.

The entry for March 7, 1929, records that " When Mr. Lloyd George's attention was called to Mr. Churchill's implication that Mr. Asquith was refused a place on the Peace Delegation, because Mr. Lloyd George feared Lord Northcliffe's anger, Mr. Lloyd George laughed. ' Why,' he said, ' when Northcliffe asked me to put him on the Peace Delegation I told him to go to Hell.' . . . ' I refused absolutely to have him at the Peace Conference '." (p. 45.)

May 9, 1929: [Lloyd George] " said of Northcliffe, ' Yes, I put up with him for four years. It had to come—the row—when he wanted to dictate to me. As Prime Minister I could not have it. Max (Beaverbrook) tried it, too, once. Northcliffe thought he could run the country. I could not allow that. It was a good thing for me that I didn't get turned out while he was alive, or he would have claimed he had done it. I was with Poincaré when news came of Northcliffe's death. It was a great blow to him. It moved him. It was as if a big support had been swept away. Northcliffe was a great man, but one could not allow him to dominate the Prime Minister '." (p. 50.)

Under June 8, 1933, Mr. Clarke explains the rift between Riddell and Lloyd George. Riddell went to the Peace Conference against the wishes of Northcliffe, who had quarrelled with the " Old Gang " and thought Riddell was being made a vehicle of propaganda for them. Northcliffe told Riddell not to assume that, though Chairman of the N.P.A., he spoke any longer for the Harmsworth Press, and Riddell, being a newspaper man first, perceived that Northcliffe meant more to him than Lloyd George did. (p. 217.)

Cockerill, Sir George : *What Fools We Were.* (London, 1944.)

Sir George Kynaston Cockerill, Director of Special Intelligence, 1915-1918, gives on pages 60-79 the best available account of the activities of Crewe House. The leaflet war was, he says, initiated by the Directorate of Special Intelligence in March, 1915, " long before the Ministry of Propaganda [*sic*] was even thought of, and conducted thereafter under my direction until September 1, 1918, on which date and not a day earlier, Lord Northcliffe became responsible." He proceeds to give the story of the leaflet war, and of his decision to appoint, towards the end of 1916, Captain (afterwards Sir) Peter Chalmers Mitchell to the task of making an analysis of materials for the purpose of counter propaganda. Mitchell produced the *Report on the Propaganda Library* in April, 1917, which, according to the introduction by Sir George Cockerill, would be " invaluable in the future as a guide to historians, who, in the leisure of peace, may devote themselves to the intensive study of German literature relating to the war." (p. 64.) See below *s. vv.* Mitchell, Northcliffe.

APPENDIX II: SOURCES

Cocks, F. Seymour : *The Secret Treaties and Understandings. Text of the available documents with introductory comments and explanatory notes.* (London, 1918.)

The 1915 agreement was known as the result of a statement by Trepov in the Duma on December 2, 1916. Salandra made his reference to " sacro egoismo " on October 18, 1914.

Dickinson, G. Lowes: *Documents and Statements relating to Peace Proposals and War Aims.* (London, 1919.)

A record of the armies of the belligerents as set forth in their own diplomatic documents, speeches, etc., put forward between the first German peace note of December 12, 1916, and Wilson's note to Germany of November 5, 1918, with an introduction and a chronological table.

Gathorne-Hardy, G. M. : *A Short History of International Affairs* (London, 1950), 1920-1939.

Golder, F. A.: *Documents of Russian History.* (New York, 1927.)

A comprehensive and valuable collection beginning with P. N. Durovo's Memorandum of February, 1914, and ending with Lenin's land decree of November, 1917. The book has a good index which enables the reader to gain a clearer idea of the development of war aims in Russia than is available elsewhere.

Graves, Philip: *The Question of the Straits.* (London, 1931.)

The former *Times* Correspondent at Constantinople gives at pp. 161-3 a useful account (supplementing Sazonov) of Miliukov's policy towards the question, the Secret Treaties, etc.

Howard, Christopher: *Historical Revision*, No. XCVI. *The Treaty of London*, 1915, in *History*. (XXV, No. 100. London, March, 1941.)

An account of the Italian and Russian negotiations, etc. The accompanying critical bibliographical note is of value. The study is, by definition, chiefly concerned with the Italian war aims.

Harris, Wilson : *J. A. Spender.* (London, 1946.).

This admirably perceptive biography chronicles incidentally a chance encounter between Northcliffe and Spender in 1920 or 1921. The date is significant, for the conversation touched on the Northcliffe v. Lloyd George quarrel. Northcliffe denied to Spender that his quarrel " was due to the refusal of his request for a seat at the Peace Conference. The originators of the report, he said, knew perfectly well that in the early months of 1919 he was threatened with a serious operation, and required by his doctor to submit himself to complete rest in preparation for it. Whom he regarded as the originators of the report Northcliffe apparently did not say, but it may be noted that in his *Truth about the Peace Conference* Mr. Lloyd George wrote, etc." (pp. 143-144.)

Kerner, R. J.: " Russia, the Straits, and Constantinople," in *Journal of Modern History*, I, No. 3. (Chicago, September, 1929.)

Kerner, R. J.: " The Mission of Liman von Sanders " in *Slavonic Review*, VI, VII. (London, 1927-29.)

Kerner, R. J.: " Russia and the Straits Question " in *Slavonic Review*, VIII. (London, 1930.)

Professor Kerner's articles are indispensable.

Laloy, Émile: *Les documents secrets des Archives du Ministère des Affaires Etrangères de Russie publiés par les Bolcheviks.* (Paris, 1919.)

Luckau, Alma: " Unconditional Acceptance of the Treaty of Versailles of the German Government, June 22-28, 1928," in the *Journal of Modern History*. (Chicago.) XVII, No. 3, pp. 215-220. (September, 1945.)

Luckau, Alma: *The German Delegation at the Paris Peace Conference.* (New York, 1941). With a Preface by J. T. Shotwell.

Seventy documents, an Introduction and Bibliography. The German Note " On the Responsibility of the Authors of the War," addressed to the President of the Peace Conference (Clemenceau) by Brockdorff-Rantzau under date May 28, 1919, was compiled by Hans Delbrück, Albrecht Mendelssohn-Bartholdy, Max Montgelas and Max Weber. They quote Repington's statement in *The Times* of July 30, 1914: " And in a very short time after a Russian mobilization is announced it will be a miracle if Europe is not aflame." (p. 292.) The covering letter to the German counter proposals forwarded next day (May 29, 1919) contrasted what they called the peace of justice they expected with the peace of power they were faced with; related their grievances about Danzig and Czechoslovakia; adduced the principle of self determination; statements of war aims by Asquith, Grey, Lloyd George, Wilson and others. " Millions of Germans in German Austria are to be denied the union with Germany which they desire and that further, millions of Germans travelling along our frontiers are to be forced to remain part of the newly created Czechoslovakian State (p. 319).

Mez, J.: *Peace Literature of the War.* (New York Association for International Conciliation, 1916.)

PEACE MAKING

Mitchell, Sir Peter Chalmers: *My Fill of Days.* (London, 1937. Chapters 13-14.)

The author had been reviewing scientific books for *The Times Literary Supplement* since 1902 and contributing zoological notes to the paper since 1911. He worked with Steed at Crewe House and on the Press side of the Peace Conference, and became a leader-writer on *The Times*; but withdrew from the editorial conference when Dawson returned to the chair, to write only occasionally on his special subjects. On pp. 266-7 he sketches the office routine in 1919-22: Steed, " pale, elegant and ambassadorial, gave us what he called his *Child's Guide to Knowledge.*" Brumwell, " silent and polite, but a little impatient to return to his duties " [the make-up]; " there was an Intelligence department beyond all praise." Mitchell's leader on November 7, 1919, on the verification of Einstein's theory by observers of a solar eclipse, started world-wide discussion. Mitchell himself suggested that Northcliffe should send him as an independent observer on an air route from Cairo to the Cape in 1920. Instances of warm-hearted actions by Northcliffe. " In politics, national or international, he was an idealist, and I know that the stories as to his having coveted government office for himself are untrue."

Northcliffe: *⁎⁎⁎ Die Geschichte des englischen Propagandafeldzuges.* (Berlin, 1921.)

Largely based on facts in *Secrets of Crewe House* by Sir Campbell Stuart. Shows little feeling until the conclusion. " We certainly cannot withold from Northcliffe our highest esteem; for the deeds of this man were mighty, full of consequence, even gigantic . . .Yet from the methods of a Northcliffe a whole world separates us. His methods have for much the greater part no relation to the first requirement laid down by himself for all propaganda, the requirement of veracity for its foundation." But the best account of propaganda work in enemy countries is in " *The Times* " *History of the War*, vol. XXI, Chapters CCCVI, " British Missions in America," CCCXIV, " British Propaganda in Enemy Countries."

Northcliffe, Lord: " From War to Peace " in *The Times* and the *Daily Mail*, Monday, November 4, 1918.

The complete text is as follows:

This Article is appearing to-day in the leading papers in Canada, Australia, New Zealand, South Africa, Newfoundland, India, the British Dependencies, United States, South America, France, Italy, Spain, Switzerland, Holland, Norway, Sweden, Denmark, Japan, and elsewhere.

It will be circulated in Germany during the present week.

Now that peace is at last in sight, I hear the question being asked on all sides: " How are we to pass from war conditions to peace conditions? " This cannot be done by a sudden and dramatic declaration like the declaration which in August 1914 changed peace into war. It must be a slow and laborious process—a process with, as it seems to me, at least three distinct and successive stages. Out of these stages will be formed the organic whole which will constitute the machinery for replacing war conditions by peace conditions.

It is important to get these three stages clearly outlined in our imaginations, and it is important also to bear in mind that each stage will smooth the path for its successor precisely in proportion to the sincerity and thoroughness with which it has been completed. There is but one goal for those who are honest and far-seeing. That goal is to create a condition of the world in which there shall be opportunity and security for the legitimate development of all Peoples. The road is long and difficult, but I believe that its course is already clear enough to be described, in the same words, to those who are our friends and to those who are now our enemies.

I.

The first stage is the cessation of hostilities. Here, whether they cease on account of an armistice or by reason of surrender, there can be no question as to the " Honour " of the German people, or as to any adjustment of the conditions to any supposed strategical or actual strength of the Central Powers.

If they feel humiliated, they must blame those who brought humiliation upon them; and as to military strength, the semi-official organ of the German Government, the *Norddeutsche Allgemeine Zeitung*, has admitted that our reserves are such as Germany cannot compete with. " It is clear," said this newspaper on October 12, " that if we systematically continued the war in this way fighting might go on for a long time. The annihilation of the German Army is still a long way from attainment; we still have a quantity of unspent forces at our command in the recruit depots behind the front, in the reserve battalions, and at home. *But doubtless there are certain limits to all this on our side, whereas our enemies—chiefly America—are in a position to replace men and materials on an ever-increasing scale.*"

Another equally important admission I found in the *Münchner Neueste Nachrichten*, the leading South-German organ, on October 25. " A German retreat beyond the frontier," this journal said, " and especially an advance by the enemy to the frontier, would render the German situation much worse, as it would expose Germany's industrial territory to the Entente's artillery fire, and particularly their air attacks, while the danger to the enemy's industrial districts would be correspondingly removed. *This condition alone would not only secure the enemy's military preponderance, but would increase it.*"

Thus it is clear that Germany, deprived now of the help of her allies, recognises her hopeless situation. The conditions upon which hostilities can cease must be laid down by the military and naval leaders of the Associated Powers and accepted by the Central Powers in such form that no resumption of hostilities is possible.

And this I will say: The spirit in which Germany accepts these stern and necessary conditions will do much to determine the course of future events. If she haggles over the conditions, or is sullen and obstructive in her mode of carrying them out, then our profound distrust of her spirit and motives will survive into the subsequent stages and still further delay that re-establishment of tolerable relations which must be our object. But if Germany by word and deed makes plain her abandonment of that belief in Might which her rulers, supported until recently by the majority of her people, have used as a menace to the power of Right, the greatest obstacle in the path of equal justice will have been removed.

By a stroke of the pen, in accepting the conditions of armistice, or by a mere gesture of unconditional surrender, Germany can cause fighting to cease. Naturally, the business of evacuation and of reoccupation will have to be conducted in concert between the military and naval leaders. The first governing condition in these operations and detailed arrangements will be the safety of the peace. The second condition will be the security of civilian life and property. The emotional background to all this will be a daily increasing desire on the part of all to get back to normal conditions of life. Co-operation and agreement will be required, not so much to secure that demobilisation and disarmament shall be forced sternly on those who have surrendered as to secure that each side takes its fair share in the burden of maintaining order and in facilitating the change from military to civilian organisation.

II.

The second stage of the passage from war conditions to peace conditions will begin as soon as it is certain that security has been obtained for the permanence of the first stage. It will consist in the acceptance by Germany of certain principles as indisputable. The security provided in the first stage ought to be sufficient to enable us to pass through the second stage quickly. With sufficient guarantees there need be no waiting to see whether the transformation of the German Government from irresponsible autocracy to responsible democracy is as genuine as it is represented to be, or whether the changed professions of those who speak for the People represent a change of heart.

The indisputable principles which Germany must accept in this second stage have been stated in different forms at different times, but the consensus of opinion among all classes of the Associated Powers seems to me to be so clear that it is not difficult to state them objectively in a form very close to that which they are likely to assume in their final enunciation.

The first is the complete restoration, territorial, economic, and political, of Belgium. In this there can be no reservation, no bargaining, no attempt to raise counter-claims or offsets of any kind. By her initial violation of International Law, and by her subsequent treatment of Belgium, Germany has forfeited all right to discussion. Reparation is impossible, but she must undertake restoration in such form and measure as shall be indicated to her.

2. The freeing of French territory, reconstruction of the invaded provinces, compensation for all civilian losses and injuries. Here again reparation in any full sense of the word is beyond human power, but Germany must accept the full burden of material reconstruction, replacement, and compensation, again in such form and measure as shall be laid down.

3. The restoration to France of Alsace-Lorraine, not as a territorial acquisition or part of a war indemnity, but as reparation for the wrong done in 1871, when the inhabitants of the two provinces, whose ancestors voluntarily chose French allegiance, were incorporated in Germany against their will.

4. Readjustment of the Northern Frontiers of Italy, as nearly as possible along the lines of nationality: the Eastern and Adriatic Frontiers to be determined in accordance with the principles embodied in the Italo-Jugo-Slav Agreement and ratified by the Rome Congress of April 1918.

5. The assurance to all the peoples of Austria-Hungary of their place among the free nations of the world and of their right to enter into union with their kindred beyond the present boundaries of Austria-Hungary. This involves the creation of independent Tchecho-Slovak and Jugo-Slav States, the reduction of Hungary to the ethnographic limits of the Magyar race, and the union of all Rumanians with the present kingdom of Rumania. In the same way the Poles and Ukrainians of the Dual Monarchy must be free to unite with their co-nationals across existing frontiers, and it is obvious that the same right of self-determination cannot be denied to the German provinces of Austria should they desire to enter Germany as a federal unit.

6. The evacuation of all territory formerly included in the boundaries of the Russian Empire; the annulment of all Russian treaties, contracts, or agreements made with subjects, agents, or representatives of Enemy Powers since the Revolution and affecting territory or interests formerly Russian; and the unimpeded co-operation of the Associated Powers in securing conditions under which the various nationalities of the former Empire of Russia shall determine their own forms of government.

When Russia offered a peace of reconciliation without annexations or indemnities, the Central Powers, taking advantage of the military position, rejected all considerations of justice and imposed terms that were brutal and selfish. Thus they forfeited the right to aid Russia and the various nationalities of the former Empire of Russia in their efforts to establish self-determination and their own form of government.

The seventh indisputable principle concerns (a) the formation of an independent Polish State with acccess to the sea, which State shall include the territories inhabited by predominantly Polish populations; and (b) the indemnification of Poland by the Powers responsible for the havoc wrought.

This condition is indispensable for the reign of justice in Europe. Germany has ruthlessly oppressed the Poles within her Empire. Justice and stability demand the restoration of the predominantly Polish parts of the present German Empire to the new Polish State.

8. The abrogation of the Treaty of Bucarest; the evacuation and restoration of Rumania, Serbia, and Montenegro; the Associated Powers to aid the Balkan States in settling finally the Balkan question on an equitable basis.

The Balkan question must be settled, and it follows from that principle of self-determination to which the Associated Powers adhere that the Balkan States must be encouraged to agree among themselves and given what advice or assistance they may ask in coming to an agreement.

9. The removal, as far as is practicable, of Turkish dominion over all non-Turkish peoples.

The complexity of the distribution of nationalities in the present Empire of Turkey makes the details of the problem difficult, but the failure of the Turks, in act and in intention, to rule justly has been so disastrous, and the acquiescence of the Central Powers in Turkish misdeeds so complete, that no departure from this principle can be considered.

10. The people of Schleswig to be free to determine their own allegiance.

The case of Schleswig is a fundamental instance of the fashion in which Prussia and Austria used their might to override the principle of self-determination. The wrong done must be redressed.

11. As reparation for the illegal submarine warfare waged by Germany and Austria-Hungary, these Powers shall be held liable to replace the merchant tonnage, belonging to the associated and neutral nations, illegally damaged or destroyed.

In spite of repeated warnings, and in defiance of the pledges which they had given to the Government of the United States, then a neutral Power, the Central Powers have persisted in operations which, by their nature and by the fashion in which they were conducted, outraged both International Law and common humanity. The question of punishment must be dealt with separately; that of restoring the ships or their equivalents, and of material compensation to the victims and their families, cannot be subject to discussion or negotiation.

12. The appointment of tribunals before which there shall be brought for impartial justice as soon as possible individuals of any of the belligerents accused of offences against the laws of war or of humanity.

While I regard this condition as an essential preliminary to peace, as a just concession to the outraged conscience of humanity, I admit freely that its practical application is full of difficulty. I foresee the extraordinary difficulty of assigning responsibility; I recognise that during the actual conduct of war there are reasons why belligerents should hesitate to punish adequately those whom in normal times they would unhesitatingly condemn. I offer my own solution of the difficulty. It is that the appointed tribunals should act as Courts of First Instance. They would hear the evidence brought against the accused, and, if they found a *prima facie* case established against them, would refer them to their own countries for ultimate trial, judgment, and sentence. I believe that more stern justice will be done if nations which desire to purge themselves condemn their own criminals than if the punishment were left to other nations which might hesitate to be severe lest they should invest the individuals punished with the halo of martyrdom.

13. The former Colonial possessions of Germany, lost by her in consequence of her illegal aggression against Belgium, shall in no case be returned to Germany.

Germany's possession of her Colonies would have been inviolate but for her illegal aggression against Belgium, which brought England into the war. She has proclaimed that the fate of her Colonies would be decided on the Western front;

it has been so decided. She has proclaimed the uses to which, if victorious, she would have put her Colonies; such uses must be prevented for ever in the interest of the peace of the world. Furthermore, there is this consideration; that, after what has happened, it would be as intolerable for Australasia to have New Guinea in German hands as it would be for the United States to have Germany in possession of Cuba. The Colonies therefore cannot be returned to Germany, but their assignment as possessions, or in trusteeship, together with the fashion in which they shall be administered in the interests of their inhabitants and of the world generally, are matters for future decision.

These are the indisputable conditions of peace which must be accepted in the second stage of the negotiations.

I have dealt with the first two stages as logically separate and successive. In actual fact agreement on them might be coincident in time. In any event, acceptance of the indisputable conditions would be made before the guarantees required under the terms of surrender or of armistice had become accomplished facts.

The conclusion of the first two stages, whether concurrent or consecutive, will be the end of dictation. They form the preliminary to co-operation. They will be an earnest of a complete break with the past on the part of Germany. They will go far to satisfy the natural desire of those who demand that the guilty should be punished, and yet I believe that they contain nothing that is not imperative for a just and lasting peace. And I hope that their imposition and acceptance will, in the subsequent stages, make it possible to take advantage, for the benefit of the world, of those powers of discipline and organisation which Germany has perverted to the great harm of the world.

III.

The third stage should, I consider, consist in the appointment of a large number of Commissions to study and work out the details of the principles which I have enumerated. These will report ultimately, some of them quickly, some of them after months or years, to the Central Peace Conference. For my part I see no reason why the members of the Commissions, if the principles on which they shall act are settled beforehand, should not be selected chiefly from among those who have the greatest interest in the matters to be settled. I do not see, for instance, why a Commission consisting largely of Poles and Prussians should not be asked to work out the future frontier of Prussia and Poland. This may be thought the suggestion of an idealist. But I claim that in this instance the idealist is the realist. If our goal be lasting peace, then let us give every opportunity for arrangement and mutual accommodation before we resort to compulsion.

So far I have said nothing of the future government of Germany. The Germans assure us that the transformation of autocratic government to responsible government is taking place. I should like to believe them. I am certain that its accomplishment is necessary to Germany itself and to the final attainment of a just and lasting peace. I frankly admit that the perfect form of government does not exist, and that the genius of Germany may evolve some form as good as, or even better than, existing Constitutions.

But Germany must understand that it will take time to convince the world, which has so much reason to distrust her, that this sudden change is to be a permanent reality. Fortunately the stages which I have described do not require for their accomplishment more than the hope that Germany has set out on the right path. While the last stage is in progress there will be time, and more than time, to see whether Germany realises our hopes and what I believe to be now the wishes of the majority of her own people.

For this last stage will mean nothing less than reconstructing the organisation of the world, and establishing a new policy in which a League of Free Nations shall replace the old system of the balance of rival Powers.

The accomplishment of a change so gigantic as the adjusting of national organisations to fit into new super-national machinery must be difficult and slow. Fortunately, the very steps necessary to make it possible are steps that will slowly make it actual. Let me select a few simple examples. The cessation of hostilities will leave the world short of food, short of transport, short of raw materials. The machinery that has regulated these during war will have to be kept in action beyond the war. Food will have to be rationed, transport will have to be rationed, raw material will have to be rationed. It is a world problem that can be settled only on a world basis, and there will be every opportunity, in the years of transition, to transform those economic relations which are forced upon us by necessity into a system which will meet with free and general acceptance.

Intimately connected with these matters will be the problem of the returned soldier, whether wounded or otherwise, the problem of pensions, the problems of wages, housing, hours and conditions of work, regulation of child labour, female labour, and so forth. The equalisation of those in different countries will be necessary to fair rationing, and from this necessity will arise international conferences of workers which may be able to settle some of the most difficult questions of super-national organisation. When the question of disarmament arises, some will demand as a fundamental necessity that their nation must have a large army or a large navy. Some will advocate, as an act of punishment or of justice, the disarmament of other nations. In the consequent negotiations it will soon be found that to insist on an unduly large army or navy is to saddle one's country with a huge expense; to insist on the disarmament of another country may be to present that country with a huge annual income that can be used in commercial rivalry. And so we may come to a condition in which, if there be international security, there will be a contest, not as to which country shall maintain the largest navy and the largest army, but as to which country shall most completely disarm.

I foresee international Commissions at work for a long time, trying to establish frontiers, conditions of Parliamentary responsibility, canons of international law, rules of international commerce, laws even of religious freedom, and a thousand other conditions of national organisation. In the very act of seeking the foundation for a League of Free Nations, and in slowly building up the fabric, we shall get rid of the passions and fears of war. By the mere endeavour to find the way to a better condition of the world, we shall bring this better condition about.

Oxford and Asquith, 1st Earl of: *Memories and Reflections.* (2 vols. London, 1928.) Vol. I, Chapter 27; Vol. II, Chapters 1-2, 5-10.

Notes in diary form interspersed with narrative chapters. July 13, 1914. Asquith had an interview with Northcliffe at Lord Murray of Elibank's flat and " tried to impress on him the importance of making *The Times* a responsible newspaper." (Vol. II, p. 4.) Mention of a letter from Northcliffe (November, 1914) pointing out that he uses his newspapers to stimulate recruiting in face of apathy. Asquith doubts if the diagnosis of affairs is just, but admits that the communication was a real service to the national cause. (Vol. I, p. 234.) Comment on French's claim to have started the agitation for a Coalition Government in 1915: " He ' furnished evidence ' to *The Times* Correspondent, Colonel Repington; and he sent over his A.D.C., Captain Guest, to lay this ' evidence ' before leading statesmen of the Opposition." (Vol. II, p. 79, *note*.)

Paléologue, M.: *An Ambassador's Memoirs.* (London, 1925.) Vol. III.

On Thursday, May 3, 1917, the Ambassador wrote: " Yielding to the pressure of the Soviet, Kerensky and, unfortunately, Albert Thomas too, Miliukov has bowed to the necessity of informing the Allied Governments of the manifesto issued on the 9th April to enlighten the Russian nation about the views of the Government of Free Russia on the subject of war aims, a manifesto which can be summarized in the famous expression— ' No annexations, no indemnities '." (p. 328.)

Rodd, Sir James Rennell: *Social and Diplomatic Memoirs,* 1902-1919. (London 1925.)

For a sympathetic account of Sonnino, see Chapter X. Chapter XIV devotes some disgruntled paragraphs to the " authoritative " foreign editor of *The Times,* (pp. 353-356), whose activities in Italy he wholly disliked.

Sazonov, Serge: *Fateful Years.* (London, 1928.)

Essential for a study of Russian war aims, but requires to be handled with great caution. The author states (p. 245) that personally he was interested in the Straits and not in Constantinople, " which the Russian people had named ' Tsargrad ' " in 1914.

Scheidemann, P.: *Memoirs of a Social Democrat.* (London, 1929, 2 vols.)

In the Reichstag on May 15, 1917, Scheidemann said: " If the English and French Governments should now renounce annexations, as the Russian Government has done, and the German Government, instead of ending the war by a similar renouncement, should intend to continue it for the purpose of self-aggrandisement, then, mark my words, gentlemen, you will have revolution in this country." (Vol. I, p. 292.) By July a peace resolution was debated in the Reichstag, and Scheidemann used the phrase " peace without annexations and reparations." (Vol. II, p. 361.) *The Times* leader of July 10, 1917, attributes this programme and phrase to Erzberger, and adds: " Such Potsdam theatricals should not for a moment divert the Allies from their vigilance, or lead them to suppose that Germany is approaching collapse."

Steed, Henry Wickham: " A Programme for Peace," in the *Edinburgh Review,* April, 1916, pp. 373-392.

Advocates " the kind of peace which a strong frontier police dictates to marauding tribesmen " as the safeguard against German danger, but it must be thought out in advance. Great Britain, having suffered least among the Allies, must exert its whole strength to ensure permanent peace. Germany must be remembered not for her treatment of Austria in 1866, but of Denmark in 1864 and France in 1871. Neutrals must be placed in various classes according to their attitude during the war. Essential postulates of peace are:

(1) The Allies must win the war so thoroughly as to be able to dictate terms.

(2) Great Britain must entrust management of the war to a few men determined to conquer at all costs.

(3) Franco-British co-ordination should be developed; if Great Britain is accorded first place in naval enterprises, France should be in military.

(4) Policy of economic alliance within the British Empire shall be drafted.

(5) Economic defence against the Central Powers both during and after the war, beginning with a tighter blockade.

(6) European reconstruction to include:

    (a) Restoration of Alsace-Lorraine to France.
    (b) Belgium.
    (c) A united Yugoslavia.
    (d) A self-governing Poland under the Russian sceptre.
    (e) Autonomy for Bohemia, Moravia and Slovakia.
    (f) Rumania to be given Rumanian regions of Hungary and Bukovina in return for helping to liberate them.
    (g) Freedom of shipping in Bosphorus and Dardanelles, with Russia in Constantinople.
    (h) Completion of Italian unity in Alpine and Adriatic regions.

[As to (6), (a) is Point 3 of Northcliffe's article of November 4, 1918 (see above); (b) is Point 1; (c) and (e) are covered by Point 5; (d) omitting mention of the Russian sceptre, is Point 7; (f) is covered by Points 5 and 8; (h) is approximately Point 4.]

It is important to have conditions of peace worked out, because there may be a period of armistice, in which the exhausted belligerents might seek a rapid settlement with too little regard for safety. Germany will be ready with political and psychological manoeuvres to cloud the issue unless a minimum is insisted on. Reconstruction will be a hard task and diplomats too little trained in political understanding to carry it out in detail quickly. Steed is specific about Constantinople: " Our duty to Russia . . . is to aid Russia in securing the possession of Constantinople and to place the economic freedom of the Straits upon unassailable foundations. . . . In our attitude towards Russia, as towards our other Allies, any hint of egoism . . . would be fatal." (p. 390.) These words were written after the London agreement with Russia, for which see below.

Temperley, Harold: *A History of the Peace Conference of Paris.* (London, 1924.)

Incidentally of great use in connexion with the London agreement, or so-called " Secret Treaties."

Vol. I: Chapter V.: " The Public and Official War Aims of the Belligerents " by H. W. V. Temperley.

Vol. I. Chapter VI.: " The War Aims of Labour " by C. Delisle Burns.

Vol. IV. Chapter V.: " The Treaty of London " by H. W. V. Temperley.

Vol. VI. Chapter I.: " The Secret Agreements affecting the Near and Middle East," (1915-1917), by H. W. V. Temperley.

Vol. VI. Chapter III.: " The Bolsheviks and Diplomacy " by H. Wilson Harris.

Washburn, Stanley: *Field Notes from the Russian Front.* (London, n.d.) [1915.]

The Russian Campaign April to August, 1915. (London, n.d.) [1915.]

Victory in Defeat. (New York, 1916.)

The Russian Advance. (London, 1917.)

Plentifully illustrated with photographs by G. H. Mewes of the *Daily Mirror* who accompanied the author on his journeys.

Subsequent events revealed many of Washburn's assertions of Russian discipline and unity to be misguided. The books, which are principally his reprinted long articles for *The Times,* are evidently the work of a lover of Russia and, as evidently, were written under severe pressure of time. They also reveal that their author was seldom actually under fire.

Wilton, Robert: *Russia's Agony.* (London, 1918.)

A hurried narrative of a personal character, useful if read with care. This book has few claims to objectivity, but is of interest, if only as a portrayal of its author's decided views on a number of subjects. It brings out his admiration and friendship for Kornilov, his distrust of the effects of Soviet propaganda on discipline, and his belief that Soviet control over life in Russia was considerable even during the period of the Provisional Government.

Wilton was generous in acknowledging help in the preparation of his work; it is not without significance that he did not bring up in this connexion the name of Miliukov, the foreign minister of the Provisional Government, who " practically dictated " his dispatches according to the allegation of the *Vossische Zeitung*'s Stockholm correspondent in March, 1917. Nothing in such of Wilton's letters and messages as survive at Printing House Square suggests that he knew Miliukov at all well, and the German correspondent evidently made a mistake. The preface is dated January 13, and was published on March 1, 1918. The author's articles on Russia in " *The Times* " *History of the War* in Vols. viii-xiii, abundantly illustrated, repay the trouble of reference.

Winkler, Henry R.: " The Development of the League of Nations Idea in Great Britain," in the *Journal of Modern History*, Chicago XX, No. 2, June, 1948, pp. 95-112.

Includes a useful summary of British Liberal, Labour and Socialist opinion as expressed in the London Newspaper Press and the reviews. The writer's belief is that the idea of a League was first presented to the British Cabinet by Haldane in a memorandum of April 8, 1915, a few weeks before he left office.

IX. THE PROBLEM OF AMERICA

As it was necessary to bring forward into Vol. IV material dealing with Anglo-American relations the Chapter to which these notes refer opens with affairs that called for comment in *The Times* during Buckle's period.

The South American *Supplements*

The first special South American *Supplement* appeared on December 28, 1909. It was a full-size venture, issued as pages 17-88 of the paper and was reproduced on January 18, 1910, in Spanish, price 3d., and a Portuguese translation was promised. Each republic was dealt with particularly, apart from general articles on the continent and its foreign relations. The *Supplement* gave, in fact, a comprehensive account from every aspect, of what then was to the general public a *terra incognita*.

The monthly South American *Supplement* began publication on July 30, 1910, and was edited by Porter, who had previously been to South America as a special correspondent. The usual *Supplement* size was adopted, and the contents comprised special articles, notes of a general character, and a trade and finance section, with a number of minor features and notes. It also contained news. A leading article was added on September 27. The minor articles and notes were later replaced by correspondence and book reviews. Full-page advertisements with photographs, paid for by the several Governments, provided the *Supplement*'s financial basis. The initiation of the South American *Supplement* was dictated partly by the financial necessity of tapping a new source of advertisement revenue.

When Porter took charge of the *Supplement* Department, Alison Phillips, who had been Chief Assistant editor of the *Encyclopedia Britannica* since 1908, was appointed editor of the South American *Supplement*. Like Porter, he spent six months in South America before beginning work on a part-time basis. But Phillips found it a full-time job, and was hampered by the conflict between the thriving financial section of the parent paper and the struggling monthly trade and finance section of his *Supplement*. Also, since the *Supplement* had to be ready for press days before publication, the news could not always be kept up to date. These were difficulties inherent in the production of a regular *Supplement* where the subject overlapped to a great extent with the parent paper. At that time the only other *Supplements* appearing regularly were those devoted to special interests, such as literature, education and engineering.

After a run of forty-four numbers, the *Supplement* was discontinued when the price of *The Times* was reduced in 1914 to one penny. But editorial interest in South America did not lapse. McClure was sent out in the summer of 1914 to make preparations for the improvement of the news service. The general policy of Printing House Square is outlined in a memorandum from Dawson to Steed dated August 23, 1914 : " Without knowing the country at first hand, I am strongly convinced that it has a great and most important future, and that *The Times*, which after all was first in the field, must continue to be well represented there."

The pressure on space, and the deflection of public interest during the war inevitably made the South American venture uneconomic. McClure was recalled, and the project abandoned.

The Fourth of July Numbers

After the War, the instruction of British public opinion regarding the United States, which was an essential element of editorial policy after Versailles, was carried forward in the City pages and trade *Supplements*. Particular attention was paid to the country's increased industrial development. American films were reviewed and the industry described, while the reporting by special correspondents of important yachting and golfing events was revived. On July 4, 1919, a special American Number was published. In May, 1920, began a series of articles on the United States and world trade. The writer, a " special commissioner ", had been, it was announced on May 8, " sent out last autumn to investigate the trade position," and his reports were published weekly. On July 4, 1920, the second special American Number appeared under the inspiration of Perry Robinson. A letter to Lints Smith at the end of August, 1919, expresses the spirit in which Robinson had undertaken the first special Number:

The biggest thing in the world now is the encouragement of friendly relations between Great Britain and the United States, and " *The Times* " *must take the lead in it*. Not only must we take the lead in it, but *the American people must be made* to know that we are taking the lead. . . . It was imbued with this conviction that, last April, I turned my back on the War, asked not to be sent back to the Rhine, said I did not want to go on Royal tours, but begged to be allowed to do the Fourth of July Number. That Number did some good as a first blow; and while I was engaged on it, I became more than ever convinced that my view is right.

The contents of both numbers were comprehensive, the contributors were authoritative, and, equally, the pivot was the importance of true information about American policy in the post-war world. Significantly, the 1920 special Number printed one article not devoted to America : a contribution by Lord Bryce on Ireland intended for the enlightenment of Americans. Perry Robinson's hope was that such a " lucid and impartial document " would be taken to heart in the United States. In the letter to Lints Smith already quoted, he had proceeded to say that

English friendship (or enmity) is going to be the pre-eminent topic in American politics in the near future. It is almost so now—inextricably mixed up with the Irish question. Our work on the Irish question, in connexion with the American Number, has placed us in a commanding position in America, *so far as that position is known over there.* But we must make it universally known, especially in the West. We must do it, first, because it is just one of those great Causes, which it is the business of *The Times* to champion. We must do it no less for our own profit.

During 1921 *The Times* printed several articles based on Lansing's *The Peace Negotiations* (" a frontal, flat-footed, right, left and centre attack on pretty well everything that Mr. Wilson said and did—or did not say and do—during the peace negotiations in Paris ") (March 29, 1921). The Fourth of July Number was prefaced with a special message from the President (Harding), and good wishes from Taft, Lansing and many other political figures.

As Willmott Lewis was fully occupied in Washington, the disadvantage of sharing Bullock in New York with the *Daily Mail* (*The Times* had the minor share) was apparent. A remedy was found by the appointment of L. E. Hinrichs from January 1, 1923. The change in the scope of the service from America since Moberly Bell's day is emphasized by an undated memorandum in the autumn of 1922 from the Foreign News Editor:

A satisfactory service of correspondence from the United States of America will need to embody the following:

1. Occasional political dispatches. Normal length about four hundred words but Correspondent should know when we can take briefer or longer political messages.

2. Occasional political letters by mail. Frequent during periods of crisis, less frequent when U.S. politics are less problematical.

3. Political routine news. That is, prompt brief telegrams recording actual events in U.S. politics. Fifty to 150 words in length.

4. A summary of the non-political events of the day. Varied but *Times*-worthy news.

5. Occasional articles by mail on non-political phases of American life. Articles of four to 800 words most in demand.

6. Economic and financial reports by cable.

This outline may have preceded the visit of Lints Smith to the United States in the autumn of 1922, when he met Lewis and discussed the service.

Later, Harold Williams wrote to Lewis, whom he did not know personally, endeavouring to bridge the gap created by the infrequence of Lewis's correspondence. The outstanding subject of policy, which Lewis had raised with Lints Smith, was thus tackled by Harold Williams. It was an acknowledgement that the paper's policy must be formulated from Washington rather than London:

We have become accustomed to relying very largely on your own judgment as to the tendencies of American policy. At this end there was nothing to do. America would not move for reasons that we could understand, so we simply had to wait. Frankly, we did not like it. We often get very impatient with America on this side but we feel that America had to go through her own evolution and we had a certain curious and sometimes rather bitter interest in watching the process. At the same time we know that we are lonely in the world now and that the only foreign people who are ever likely to understand us and sympathise with our ideas are the Americans. So, we are patient.

Printed Works

Baker, R. S. : *The Public Papers of Woodrow Wilson*; *The New Democracy*. 2 vols. (New York and London, 1926.)

On February 10, 1915, Bryan instructs Page to protest to Grey against the use of American flags by British vessels to escape enemy attack. On March 30 he tells Page that the recent British Order in Council upon blockade appears to claim unlimited belligerent rights over neutral commerce within the whole European area.

THE PROBLEM OF AMERICA

On November 4, 1915, Wilson, speaking at the Manhattan Club, N.Y., said that " It has been American policy time out of mind to look to the Navy as the first and chief line of defence," and hinted at increasing the pace of building and recruitment.

Speaking at Milwaukee on January 31, Wilson emphasised the point that the Navy is fourth in the world by size and fighting force (but he would put it higher by quality). He wants to bring it in five years to a strength which might otherwise have needed eight-ten years. At Chicago the same day he gave figures : three years ago there were in commission 182 vessels, now 238; three dreadnoughts and 15 other craft will be added; 6,000 more sailors have enlisted; expenditure has risen to $44 millions annually. Three days later (February 2, 1916), he asked a Kansas City audience : " Do you think that a Navy that ranks only fourth in the world in force is enough to defend the coasts and make secure the territory of a great continent like this ? " It was next day (February 3) that at St. Louis he said : " America apparently has never been jealous of armed men if only they are at sea. America also knows that you cannot send volunteers to sea unless you want to send them to the bottom. . . . We are going to give them ships enough." He followed with the phrase that the United States must have " incomparably the most adequate navy in the world." [H. & M. Sprout : *The Rise of American Naval Power*, 1776-1918. (Princeton, 1939.) Claims that Wilson actually said " greatest " and not " most adequate," as in the official version (p. 336).]

Baker, Ray Stannard: *Woodrow Wilson: Life and Letters* (8 vols., London.) *Woodrow Wilson and World Settlement*. (3 vols., London, 1923.)

Bartlett, Ralph J.: *The Record of American Diplomacy*. (New York, 1948.)
Documents from 1686-1947. A collection of great value in the study of the evolution of American foreign policy.

Chirol, Valentine: *Fifty Years in a Changing World*. (London, 1927.)
Chapter XVI for the account of Chirol's meeting with Theodore Roosevelt.

Clinard, O. J.: *Japan's Influence on American Naval Power*. (California, 1947.)

Council on Foreign Relations: *Survey of American Foreign Relations*. (New Haven, 1928.)
Useful account of the genesis of the Anglo-American naval controversy before 1923.

Croly, Herbert : *Willard Straight*. (New York, 1925.)
English readers who find it difficult to understand the interest taken in China by American capitalists are advised to read this lively life of the brilliant young Rhodes-like character, who spent many years in the East in securing railway concessions and endeavouring to forward the great Harriman scheme of a trans-world railway. Straight later founded the *New Republic* (of which his biographer became the first Editor) and he died on active service in France in 1919 at the age of 38. This is a remarkable work.

Daniels, Josephus : *The Wilson Era*. (New York, 1944.)
" Having felt themselves neglected by the Navy for many years, the people on the Pacific Coast appreciated the first recognition given them and welcomed a day when they could fittingly show their appreciation in an impressive way. Their opportunity came in 1916 when by giving the electoral votes of California and Washington they could show their gratitude. The election returns showed that Wilson carried every part of both States where Naval expansion had been made or was in the making. Except for the big change in the vote in San Diego, Los Angeles, and Mare Island districts, Wilson would have lost California. The change from Republican to Democratic votes was revolutionary in the districts most affected by the New Naval Policy." (p. 472).

Garvin, J. L.: *The Life of Joseph Chamberlain*. (3 vols., London, 1934.)
Vol. III for some account of the Venezuelan controversy.

Gwynn, Stephen: *The Letters and Friendships of Sir Cecil Spring Rice*. (2 vols., London, 1930.)
See *History of The Times*, Vol. III, p. 837 for reference to Spring Rice's letter to Roosevelt in reference to Chirol's interview with the President.

Knox, Dudley W.: *A History of the United States Navy*. (New York, 1936.)

Lodge, H. Cabot: *Selections from the Correspondence of Theodore Roosevelt and Henry Cabot Lodge*. (2 vols., New York, 1925.)

Millard, T. F.: *America and the Far Eastern Question*. (New York, 1909.)
The possibility of war with Japan, as influenced by the building of the Panama Canal.

Reading, 2nd Marquess of: *Rufus Isaacs, First Marquess of Reading*. (2 vols., London, 1942-45.)
Vol. II, Chapter 2, covers Reading's experience as High Commissioner to the United States, in which post he succeeded Northcliffe in September, 1917.

The Demand Loan, nicknamed by Northcliffe the " Sea-Serpent " because it appeared suddenly in unexpected places and was always increasing in size, had reached £80 millions just after the U.S.A. entered the war. Balfour and Lord Cunliffe having interviewed McAdoo, U.S. Secretary to the Treasury, understood him to say the sum necessary to pay off the Demand Loan would be advanced to the British Government out of the first U.S. public loan. McAdoo said later he merely agreed to reckon the £80 millions in the total of British financial requirements. Confusion followed. On July 12 McAdoo writes to his Ambassador in London, Page :

" Am I to understand that Lord Northcliffe has been designated financial agent of the British Government, and that he will conduct all negotiations ? I am really confused by the number of people who undertake to speak for the British Government." The Memorandum of July 20 from Bonar Law to McAdoo confirms this appointment but adds : " Lord Northcliffe has, however, suggested that the United States Government would themselves prefer that someone with political experience, such as an ex-Cabinet Minister, should be asked to cross to the United States for the purpose of dealing with the financial situation."

This suggestion was the origin of Reading's appointment. McAdoo regarded him as peculiarly fitted for the mission (p. 61). At p. 63 appears a statement from Northcliffe (no date or reference given): " In my opinion, anyone not possessed of Reading's charm, ability and tact in dealing with these difficult people could not have brought off this achievement. By his frankness and lack of concealment, his sympathy and understanding for their worry over the daily Allied demands for money and trouble with politicians and the Press, Reading will, I am convinced, do all that any man can do for us."

Reischaur, E. O.: *The United States and Japan.* (Harvard, 1951.)

Reuter, B. A.: *Anglo-American Relations during the Spanish American War.* (New York, 1924.)

Seymour, Charles: *The Intimate Papers of Colonel House.* (4 vols., Boston and New York, 1926, also London, 1926.)

Whelpley, J. D.: *British-American Relations.* (London, 1924.)

X. NORTHCLIFFE *v.* THE EDITOR

The Times and the General Election, 1918

On December 11, 1918, Lloyd George's six points were set out in *The Times*: Trial of the Kaiser; Punishment for atrocities; Fullest indemnities from Germany; Britain for the British; Rehabilitation of War Victims; A happier country for all.

The Parliamentary Correspondent said that every estimate took it for granted that the Coalition would have a sweeping majority. There was little life in the election; what there was had been contributed by Labour. The main burden of the leading article on the next day was " Vote for Lloyd George." The following paragraphs eloquently urge the electorate to vote for the Prime Minister as the architect of victory:

Mr. Lloyd George is fully entitled to all the credit of being the statesman who was not merely fortunate enough to be at the head of the nation during the noblest triumph in British history, but himself played as large a part in securing that triumph as any living man. . . . Mr. Lloyd George does provide for the moment the one hope of averting relapse into the dreary unreality of our pre-war politics. He has gradually combined in his programme—perhaps he has tried to combine too much—the main ideas of thinking men and women on a progressive social policy. (December 12.)

XIII. THE PROBLEM OF IRELAND

The Idea of Federation

In 1885 Joseph Chamberlain put forward a scheme for a National Board or Council for Ireland to replace the " Castle " administration. Under this system, which he proposed might eventually be extended to Scotland, Wales and England, the Council would control local and municipal matters, such as education, while an Imperial Parliament at Westminster would deal with national affairs. This solution was revived by some of the " New Imperialists " of the Milner " kindergarten," F. S. Oliver, Lionel Curtis (adviser to the Irish Conference in 1921), and Philip Kerr (Lloyd George's Secretary). Under the pseudonym of " Pacificus," Oliver had already been an active letter-writer to *The Times* in Buckle's period, and his letters had attracted considerable attention. In 1910 Oliver had contributed two groups of letters. The first group of three (May 23, June 6, 8) advocated a conference of party leaders to settle the question of the Constitution; the second group of seven (between October 20 and November 2) expounded Federalism. In 1912 three letters criticizing the Home Rule Bill were published (April 30, May 8, 9). The seven letters on Federalism were republished by John Murray in December, 1910, under the title of *Federalism and Home Rule.* Shadwell's notice which appeared in *The Times* on December 9 thus described the book.

It covers a good deal more ground than is implied by those terms in [the title] and perhaps the most valuable part of it is not specially or directly concerned with Federalism or Home Rule. It is rather a general plea for settlement by consent of the present political perplexities, which include, but are by no means confined to, the Irish question. So far as that is concerned the attitude of " Pacificus " has been rather misunderstood, and the republication of his letters as a connected series, with the additional observations in the introduction, will serve to remove misapprehension. He does not exactly advocate Federalism, but rather explains it and pleads for consideration.

Healy's plan for a settlement was the creation of four councils for Munster, Connaught, Leinster, and Ulster, with control of such local affairs as education, and responsible to an Irish Parliament at Dublin. He believed that Ulster, though in a technical minority, would become the most powerful party in such a Parliament within ten years. This belief, however, was only a personal conviction. Fraser had gone to Ireland with an open mind on the Federal devolution scheme, and found at first little enthusiasm for what he called " glorified county councils." A visit to Ulster made him agree that such a solution was possible, provided that no control was exerted from Dublin. Healy, Fraser and Dawson argued that a general election was the primary necessity, and for this the Editor pressed throughout November, 1913. Also, since a general election would be fruitless unless the English electorate appreciated Ulster's reasons for resistance to the Bill, their exposition was part of his policy. Dawson agreed with Oliver's contention that no Irish settlement could be permanent until the question of the House of Lords had been settled by general consent; but the Editor's immediate purpose was to use Ulster as a means of securing a general election. On its result depended all future plans. Meanwhile, Dawson suspected that the Cabinet was not in agreement among themselves. He wrote to Healy on November 10, 1913:

> I am inclined to think, but without any special knowledge, that the result of to-morrow's Cabinet may be an offer from the Government, conveyed sooner or later, and by means which may not be decided, to exclude Ulster from the operation of the Bill. What form the offer may take, and how much of Ulster it may be prepared to exclude, I do not know. But that things are tending in this direction I am tolerably certain. If Asquith exerts his great authority he will have little difficulty in getting his own party to agree. There remain two sources of opposition. In the first place the Unionists, puffed up with the triumph of recent by-elections, may refuse to consider any compromise at all. This in my opinion would be absolutely fatal, because Asquith would certainly put the thing in such a way as to throw all responsibility for a subsequent breach of the peace on to his opponents. That is the purely party argument. On broad national grounds I feel that the refusal to listen to such an offer would be even more disastrous. In the second place the Nationalists may jib (though I imagine Asquith will do his best to make certain of them before moving in the matter at all). Feeling as I do at present about the exclusion of Ulster, I am not sure that a Nationalist revolt against compromise is not the best thing to hope for. However we shall see.

On November 15 Churchill spoke separately of " Nationalist Ireland " and " Protestant Ulster." Dawson found in this subtle distinction confirmation of what he had suspected: that at least one member of the Cabinet favoured exclusion, and he directed his leader-writer to emphasize this aspect. The interpretation caused some sensation, for Fleet Street had found little untoward in the First Lord's speech. It was apparent, however, that he had not yet persuaded Asquith to go so far.

Dawson was correct, nevertheless. Lloyd George had a scheme: that Ulster should accept exclusion for six years and then be automatically included. A series of secret meetings took place between the Nationalists and members of the Government. Plunkett's proposal, that Ulster should accept immediate inclusion, with the option of voting herself out later, and which was known to Dawson, was also mooted, but overridden by Lloyd George. Redmond finally agreed to exclusion for six years, provided the Government would enforce the Home Rule Bill without regard to protests from Ulster. Asquith, thus assured of Nationalist support, put forward the plan when the Home Rule Bill was read for the second time on March 9, 1913.

" Irish Peace," 1919

The ten articles on " Irish Peace: A Test of Statesmanship " from the pen of R. J. H. Shaw appeared on June 28 and 30, July 1 to 5 and 7 to 9, 1919. The main points made may thus be summarized:

I. The Accepted Time.

> The Empire cannot wait for a solution of this urgent problem. In Ireland there is a militarized government, justifiable only on the ground that the authorities fear rebellion. Speeches by the Chief Secretary have given dissatisfaction and the Government is profoundly distrusted. What one Irish party calls firmness, the other calls coercion. Present methods must be put to this test: are they helping towards some form of self-government? Sinn Fein and Republicanism have a hold on three of the four provinces. Irish Americans who formerly followed Redmond have gravitated to de Valera.

II. Is it Possible?

Redmond having been more moderate than his supporters, the leadership has passed to de Valera. Easter, 1916, is seen by the idealists to have been in the tradition of 1641, 1798, and 1803. Many adherents of Sinn Fein are those who in normal times would have emigrated, and it would be a mistake to overestimate their number. Sinn Fein is not a practical movement and needs some external stimulus. Now that peace has returned to Europe it may be more amenable to reason. "The Irish people are quicker to appreciate facts than to admit them." The growth of Labour in Belfast has cut across the old division between Unionists and Nationalists. Ulster is rather hoping for than fearful of an eventual settlement. Unobtrusive traders and farmers would welcome nothing so much as a restoration of peace and quiet.

III. The Failure of the Convention.

This article traces the course of deliberations among 94 Irishmen called together by the Government as a war measure in 1917-18. Sinn Fein was not represented, and the proceedings had the disadvantage of being neither secret nor public. There was a scheme to establish a single Irish Parliament, but on a crucial question whether or not it should have power to vary customs and excise, the Nationalists said yes and Ulster no. Nationalists held out for virtually Dominion status The Prime Minister undertook that, if the Convention failed to arrive at a settlement by consent, his Government would be bound to act.

IV. The Basis of Settlement.

Both countries must forget to use the Irish question as a party matter at Westminster; Asquith is trying to revive it as such. What Irish members now need is an authoritative definition of the limits England must impose in granting any kind of independence. There cannot be a Republic; few Irishmen indeed believe it has the smallest chance of being conceded. Sinn Fein would probably accept Dominion Home Rule. But equally a legislative Union is doomed in a world not peopled entirely by economic man. Compromise is inescapable.

V. A Great Opportunity.

The scope of industrial reconstruction is sketched. During the Union Irish industry was held back partly by the multiplicity of Government Departments with which Chief Secretaries—a new one assuming office on an average every two years—had to accustom themselves. There was neglect or mismanagement of local railways, canals, harbours, and possibilities of electrification. Future prosperity may lie in placing all communications under single control.

VI. Materials of Contentment.

Though agriculture must always be Ireland's premier industry, the country has been reduced rather to a kitchen-garden of the British Isles. Much can be done by drainage and afforestation; the flax-growing area might be extended; mineral resources are far greater than they are usually reckoned. The earliest appearance of Sinn Fein under such men as Griffith was as an economic movement. But the weakness of Sinn Fein economics remains in its obsession with anti-British impulse.

VII. Ulster.

The Ulster Unionists' objection to a Dublin Parliament is "based on racial, religious, political, and economic grounds, and it is not lessened by a distinct trace of civic jealousy." Carson's demand for the partition of Ireland "was the natural evolution of the militant policy of the province, and it established a case which could be very speciously supported by argument." A principal obstacle to partition is the fact that Ulster and the six counties are not synonymous, and the proportions of Protestants and Roman Catholics in the six and in the nine counties are not identical. Ulster must stay part of Ireland; justice to her claims does not require obedience to her dictation.

VIII. The Risk of Exclusion.

In matters of trade the six counties have greater need of Southern Ireland than the latter has of them, for an agricultural country can find more ready markets than a manufacturing centre. The economic soundness of a policy of exclusion would depend on rigorous limitation of the powers of an Irish Parliament. Is Carson satisfied that this can be quickly guaranteed?

IX. The Lines of Settlement.

Three chief considerations are underlined: the provisions of any proposed measure should be compatible with the idea of federalism within the United Kingdom; in view of the Convention's failure, any degree of self-government must be imposed by the British; the eventual settlement may come about most easily by evolution. The key to the whole puzzle is reconciliation of Ulster with Sinn Fein. This might be achieved by a system of Provincial or State legislatures in specific relationship to an Irish Parliament.

X. A Wider Prospect.

The Island is only the nucleus of a greater Irish community and its discontent therefore is a world force. This finds expression in religious conviction and political idealism. But "there is a constant undercurrent of warfare between the spiritual and the material," which means that those leaders succeed who have an eye to both, as Sinn Fein had when it opposed conscription and demanded a Republic. Now, while Ulster is prepared to take economic risks for Protestantism, " Sinn Fein subordinates everything to the fulfilment of a hopeless ideal." From the Dominions and the United States comes back the echo of the Irish clamour for settlement. " Britain will be judged by her intentions; Ireland by her reason." The British democracy will support the Government in taking immediate action.

The Press on *The Times* Proposals

Carmelite House ranged itself beside Printing House Square on July 25, 1919. The *Daily Mail* leading article concluded with the restrained paragraph:

What does the Government propose to do ? The duty of framing the terms of a measure of Irish self-government is theirs. It is very doubtful in view of the unsatisfactory statements which have recently been made in the House of Commons whether they possess any definite scheme. If this be so, *The Times* patriotically accepts the odium of suggesting one. There will be criticism of its provisions from many sources, but there can be no just criticism of the motives which inspired the production of so definite a proposal at the present juncture. It is for Mr. Lloyd George to accept the scheme or produce a better. The situation as regards Ireland permits of no evasion or delay.

The *Daily Telegraph* had nothing to say, for on July 24 the paper had hastily published its own proposals which pronounced that " all this loose talk about Dominion Home Rule is mischievous in the extreme." The *Daily Telegraph* would not desert the Unionists, and American opinion of Nationalist agitation was discounted in Peterborough Court. The *Manchester Guardian* had put its views before the public on July 23, before they could know what Steed was planning, and they had nothing to add, believing that Ulster must give way. The *Daily Express* ignored the subject. In Ireland, however, the plan was received with interest, though not enthusiasm, and the *Daily Mail* devoted much space to reporting the attitude of the Irish papers. The *Irish Times* reserved judgement; the Dublin *Daily Express* (Unionist) rejected the plan; the *Independent* (Nationalist) denounced it as " an insidious plan for permanent partition." More reasoned was the comment of the *Freeman's Journal* (regarded as favourable to Redmond and Dillon).

Whatever opinions Nationalists or Sinn Feiners may form upon the principles and details of the plan which *The Times* puts forward for the settlement of the Irish question, they will agree that the publication of these periodicals is an event of the greatest importance in the history of the Irish question. Those who continue to hope that a peaceful settlement may be found will frankly recognize the invaluable services rendered by the journal in the recent articles which prepared the ground for the proposal now made and by the temper in which the settlement is advocated. Those articles are well worth the study of even the best informed of every section.

The Nation believed in the plan but it could only have had a chance of success if it had *started* (italics of *The Nation*) from an all-Ireland parliament, with Dominion powers. The weekly's correspondents had assured the Editor that the scheme had little chance.

On the 26th an editorial paragraph in the *Spectator* expressed approval:

The Times on Thursday published a scheme—in certain respects not a new one—for the solution of the Irish difficulty. So far as we have examined it, we cannot pretend to be sanguine of its prospects. At the same time we naturally desire to give every consideration to an attempt at a solution which is evidently sincere and has been carefully thought out. The plan is quite rational in that it really tries to meet the difficulties. In fact it is so rational in its effort to stop all the gaps that it is extremely complicated, and it would be impossible for us to discuss it on Thursday when we go to press, and have no space at our disposal. . . . The objections of North-East Ulster to a Dublin Parliament are frankly recognized, and it is suggested that there should be two Provincial Assemblies, one representing the whole Province of Ulster, and one representing the rest of Ireland. There would also be an all-Ireland Parliament. But would Sinn Fein accept that solution, even if Ulster did ? We fear that Sinn Fein would not look at it. Of course the trouble is that the Sinn Feiners want to rule North-East Ulster but not to win her acquiescence. How the Sinn Feiners might win the heart of Ulster if they really wanted to do it we have explained in our first leading article.

The Editor of the *Spectator* promised to examine *The Times* plan if it proved to be important. He did not, however, think it necessary to do so the following week. The *Sunday Times* was silent. On the 27th the *Observer* devoted an editorial column which began:

No newspaper has ever put its hand to a better work than that of *The Times* in working now soberly and boldly for an Irish settlement, while facing both sides of the contrasting realities. Our contemporary has followed up an admirable series of articles by bringing out the other day a full constructive plan. The plan is obviously enough in itself the result of recent and independent thought, of dispassionate investigation and deduction; but we may be excused for not welcoming it the less warmly because it confirms in its main features the *Observer's* policy formulated on October 30, 1910.

Stephen Gwynn, a regular contributor, also discussed the plan with approval. Thus party allegiance tended to dominate the newspapers of England and Ireland. It was party allegiance and even rank prejudice that *The Times* hoped to break. Abroad, comment in American newspapers and those of the Dominions was more free, but appreciation of the gesture rather than of the details of the plan itself was general. Both *The Times* and the *Daily Mail* reported these comments during the following week. The *Observer* summed up the effect the next Sunday in a leading article.

> We believe that the scheme for an Irish settlement which *The Times* has propounded has already done good service. For the British public it has marshalled again, most opportunely in the new light which the war is directing upon old problems, the facts, hopes and contradictions of the Irish situation. In the Dominions and America it has been received with the utmost sympathy by the mass of temperate thinkers. It is accepted as evidence that opinion in Great Britain is disturbed and unhappy about Ireland and is ripening for an honest and patient attempt to end an age-long trouble in a generous and non-partisan temper. (*Observer*, August 3.)

The support given to *The Times* by the *Daily Mail* undoubtedly influenced Fleet Street's reception, and also that of Lloyd George: the plan became associated with Northcliffe who, it has been seen in the text, had nothing to do with it, and such an association damned it. The *Morning Post* dismissed the scheme in verse on this account:

> For statesmanship Northcliffe's the man,
>   Have you heard of his wonderful plan ?
> 'Tis born of aversion for Irish coercion
>   And designed disaffection to ban ?
>
> It's as simple as simple can be;
>   Irish Parliaments, one, two, and three,
> By instant creation you give to that nation,
>   And afterwards let them run free.
>
> If Irishmen dare to object,
>   Lest their charter of freedom be wrecked,
> At the point of the rifle their murmuring stifle,
>   Such is Home Rule. What *did* you expect ?

(*Morning Post*, July 26, 1919.)

The reception of these articles by the great die-hard Conservative daily was not enthusiastic. The *Morning Post* printed a considerable number of passages on *The Times* policy towards Ireland in the summer of 1919. All bore heavily on the alleged " quackery " of the proposals, their " audacity," " hypocrisy " and what-not. The following are a few samples:

> August 2: " Who are the syrens who sing so alluringly of ' Dominion Home Rule ' and the ' settlement of Ireland '? They are *The Times*, the *Daily Mail*, the *Sunday Pictorial*, all trained to a chorus by that syren choirmaster Lord Northcliffe...

> " When the wounds of Ulstermen are not yet healed, and the grass has not yet grown on the graves of her dead, *The Times* has the audacity to say: 'Neither Sir Edward Carson nor Mr. De Valera has the right to preach rebellion in Ireland.' So there is no difference between Sir Edward Carson and Mr. De Valera? "

> The powers *The Times* proposes to give Ireland are said to amount practically to independence in the realm of trade. As Ulster Protestants would be in the minority in an All-Ireland Parliament, *The Times* proposes " to get over that difficulty by a little hocus-pocus."

> " These quacks imagine that by ' various devices ' they can evade the solid facts of life and of history."

> August 6: " *The Times* has run up the Home Rule ensign, and, accompanied by all the frigates, cutters, corvettes, wherries, and ketches of the Northcliffe Press, is pouring broadside after broadside into the Union. The *Fighting Temeraire*, as we might call her, makes a great deal of noise, which is caught up and reverberated by the swarming craft around her; but whether or not the old seventy-four is doing any real execution is a question at least open to doubt."

> August 9: On the gratification of *The Times* at finding that a settlement is to be imposed, it is asked whether this means imposed upon one section and accepted by another. " That would explain all the abuse of Sir Edward Carson and the people of Ulster." ... *The Times* is reappearing as an advocate of coercion—in Ulster.

> August 16: " We feel a sense of shame in the spectacle of *The Times* openly urging what is nothing less than surrender to blackmail."

> October 9: " According to the Political Correspondent of *The Times* (which now shares with the *Freeman's Journal* the literary leadership of the Home Rule cause), the Home Rule Act comes into force when the Treaty of Peace with Turkey is signed."

October 10: " Even *The Times* (now the English organ of the Irish Home Rulers) demands as a condition of the new Bill ' The essential unity of Ireland '."

December 24: " It would almost appear that the only elements to be appeased by this scheme are not Irish elements at all but the Northcliffe elements."

The same die-hard tone was manifested in the *Post* in 1920.

March 12: " When the dotard King Lear propounded his Home Rule policy for Ancient Britain he was very much annoyed by the protests of an honest courtier and the silence of a dutiful daughter. In the same spirit, if we might venture upon the comparison, our contemporary *The Times* denounces Ulster and Sir Edward Carson for their attitude on the Home Rule policy of His Majesty's Government. If, then, Sir Edward Carson has now suffered a defeat, one of the reasons is that *The Times* has now gone over, bag and baggage, to the enemy. It is a defeat, possibly a terrible defeat, but we deny that it is humiliating."

The paper this day prints in parallel columns under the heading " Then and Now " extracts from *The Times* leaders on Carson of September 19, 1912, and March 11, 1920.

March 13: Carson writes to the *Morning Post* on " hypocrisy and inconsistency " in *The Times* : " In 1916 Lord Northcliffe, at Mr. Lloyd George's request, urged me to press the Ulster people to accept a settlement—' this most reasonable settlement '—eliminating the six counties from the Parliament set up by the Home Rule Act of 1914! "

March 15: " Both the Prime Minister and Sir Edward Carson have publicly said what they thought about the Northcliffe Press. Their indiscretion was most unfortunate, because it suggests that journalism is being used as a weapon of revenge."

September 30: " As for the Northcliffe Press, they are enthralled by an illusion called Dominion Home Rule. We would not condemn the idea until it has been made intelligible; but it seems a little hard that in the meantime the Royal Irish Constabulary are to be sacrificed."

December 13: " *The Times*, which at one time valued law and order, says that ' armistice appears to be the necessary preliminary to any agreement.' Armistice with whom ? Are we to have an armistice with the people who murder police and manufacture bombs in cellars to blow up public buildings in their own cities ? Are these the people with whom *The Times* suggests we should negotiate an armistice?"

December 14: [*The Times*] " used at least to wait for the evidence, when something injurious to a British cause was alleged, and its habit has not always been to blame the police the day or the second day after a crime."

1921.

February 28: " Mr. Asquith, Sir John Simon, *The Times*, the *Westminster Gazette*, and all the other politicians and newspapers engaged in making a meal of the police in Ireland, always begin by invoking a curse upon Sinn Fein. It seems to give an air of respectability to their repast. But we notice that while the fare gets hotter the curse gets shorter and more perfunctory. Thus, for example, *The Times* devoted a whole leader to the denunciation of police methods and Government policy in Ireland, but had brought the ceremonial denunciation into the space of a single phrase: ' No party in the State is in sympathy with the methods of Sinn Fein '."

March 16: [*The Times*] " actually changed the wording of a Press Association message from Ireland so as to drive home a charge against the police. Changed days! Mr. Piggott [*sic*] now seems to have got inside *The Times* office."

March 28: " Since that exposure our contemporary has modified its note, and has been condemning the Sinn Fein ambushers with a quite refreshing robustness. Whether, however, the change is diplomatic or sincere remains to be seen." There follows an attack on Northcliffe, in which his Irish sympathies are accounted to his origin, and his assertion that Ireland does not really want a Republic is said to be meaningless. Carson's speech to the Orangemen on July 12, 1919, was provoked by a reference, in Northcliffe's message of congratulation to Alcock on his Atlantic flight, to " the future . . . Dominion of Ireland," and a series of articles in *The Times*.

July 14: " *The Times* and the *Daily Mail*, for example, are so enchanted by the visit of De Valera to London that they have omitted to mention the terrible series of murders which signalize his triumphant entry."

September 17: [*The Times*] " had been dallying with the idea of a ' Dual monarchy ' and the Irish principle of harnessing a Republican jennet with a Monarchist horse; but De Valera's claim to a ' Sovereign State ' is too much for our contemporary."

Lloyd George on the Proposals

The Parliamentary Correspondent of the *Manchester Guardian* only wrote what other correspondents were thinking when, reporting Lloyd George's remarks on Ireland, he added, " Incidentally, the proposals put forward in what has been called the Northcliffe scheme were gently derided, with a passing sarcasm at the expense of their putative author." (August 8.) Lloyd George's actual words were " There is a great journal which is not particularly friendly to me—I am not sure that I have been particularly friendly to it—which has joined the ranks of those who say that ' something must be done.' But it did not confine itself merely to that statement. It began to say exactly what should be done; it proposed a great scheme, and I watched the result. It is a scheme which every party in Ireland has joined in condemning. That is the experience of everybody. It is very easy to say ' you must do something; you must do it at once; there should not be any delay in putting forward your proposals; why do you not do it ? ' But the moment you do it, you find that the experience which this great journal has had during the last few days is the experience of everybody who comes forward to propose a scheme." (Hansard, col. 654, vol. 119.) That Lloyd George was not quite accurate when he described the reception the plan had received had already been proved —by *The Times* itself, by the *Daily Mail*, and by the *Observer*. The latter paper again came to the support of *The Times*:

> He [Lloyd George] described it [*The Times* scheme] as a scheme which every party in Ireland has joined in condemning. That is not altogether a just estimate of its reception. It has received a critical, but still a friendly, welcome from that large body of opinion which lies between the separatists and the Orangemen. He himself went on to declare that Irish condemnation would be the fate of any scheme propounded, and that the Government—very wisely—would produce the solution which it thought to be right and just and accept responsibility for its passage into law. The scheme which *The Times* has put forward has attracted all the more comment to it because it has been more ambitious than such schemes usually are. It has attempted more in the way of detail. There is no reason for complete adherence to the details of this or any other scheme. What is involved is not the credit or *amour-propre* of any newspaper. The point is that the basis of a scheme has been submitted, and that any one may improve on it who will. (*Observer*, August 10, 1919.)

The Debate on the Ratification of the Irish Treaty 1921-2

Parliament was summoned for a new session to be opened by the King in State on December 14, 1921, and de Valera convened a meeting of the Dail Eireann for the same day. In Ulster there were signs of alarm. Ulstermen already resented the financial proposals and also that of a Boundary Commission; published correspondence between Craig and the Prime Minister showed that throughout the discussions they had solidly insisted on their claims. In Southern Ireland the de Valera section let it be known that they were against the action of those whom the Dail had appointed as plenipotentiaries. The debate on the Treaty in both Houses of Parliament lasted for three days. In the Upper Chamber Carson bitterly attacked the Government; in the Commons, Bonar Law, whose attitude had been doubtful at an earlier stage, powerfully supported them; the Prime Minister hailed the Treaty as marking the end of an age-long conflict. The result was a triumph for the policy which might be said to have been inaugurated by the King's speech at Belfast. Both houses ratified the agreement by large majorities. The Ulster Unionists voted against the Government.

Dail Eireann took longer to decide. At first it sat in private; but on December 19 the Press was admitted and the public debate showed a marked divergence of opinion between the supporters of Griffith and Collins and those of de Valera. The delegates back from London fulfilled their promise and stood by their signatures. Their opponents attacked them mainly on the ground that the Oath of Allegiance embodied in the Treaty involved complete abandonment of the Republican position. De Valera himself further alleged that the document had been signed under duress. On December 22, after four days' discussion that seemed to leave the issue of ratification uncertain, the debate was adjourned until January 3.

Meanwhile peace had by no means been brought to Ireland. Representatives of *The Times* with those of other newspapers and of news agencies remained there to watch the development of events.

The Irish Free State, Northern Ireland and the Six Counties 1922

When Dail Eireann resumed the discussion of the Treaty on January 3, after bitter opposition from the Republican party, the motion approving it was finally carried by the slender majority of seven. Thereupon de Valera resigned his office as president, and the motion for his re-election was defeated by a majority of only two. Griffith was almost immediately elected president of the Dail, with Collins, Cosgrave, and Mulcahy as Ministers of Finance, Local Government, and Defence, respectively. *The Times* could no longer refrain from comment on these developments. The leading article of January 6 thus stated the position :

> It has seemed to us until now that the division of opinion they [the proceedings in Dail Eireann] have disclosed has been primarily a matter for Irishmen themselves,

and we have felt that even the most discriminate words might have seemed an interference with their natural preoccupation with their own affairs. The fact that the subject of discussion was the acceptance or rejection of Dominion status in our eyes entitled this Irish Assembly to be treated with the same consideration and respect that Englishmen show to the duly constituted Legislatures of the self-governing Dominions. This self-imposed obligation of reticence has, however, been removed by the publication of Mr. de Valera's suggested alternative to the Peace Treaty, and it would be impolitic if we hesitated to express a definite opinion upon it. . . .

They [Mr. de Valera and his supporters] seem to ignore the definite announcement of the Prime Minister that it would be impossible for his Government to reopen discussion. Mr. Lloyd George may from time to time have made statements to which he has subsequently found it impracticable to adhere ; but we can scarcely think that, if he is put to the test, this will prove to be one of them. (January 6, 1922.)

This salted support to the Prime Minister was in accordance with the policy announced in the paper the previous August: that Ireland had received the utmost the Government could offer, and no further concessions could be won. When, on January 15, a provisional government (which was promised the support of the Unionists of the south and west) was formed under Collins, *The Times* prepared to support the efforts made to carry out the terms of the Treaty. It was soon apparent, however, that de Valera was ready to resist. Violence was general. There were daily reports of ambushes, kidnappings, murders, and pillage and destruction. Some of the Southern Irish, finding in fuller measure than they had thought possible the realization of their forefathers' dreams of political independence, were allowing internal anarchy and faction to ruin the prospect. At the end of January there began a succession of railway strikes, followed by Sinn Fein raids across the border into the Northern provinces. Craig, too, with his Ministers was faced with a state of affairs calling for the exercise of much courage, statesmanship and resolution. From the border the campaign of violence spread to Belfast, where for several weeks factional disorder poisoned the life of the city.

In Parliament at Westminster, the debate on the Free State Agreement Bill began on February 16, with the object of strengthening the hands of Griffith and Collins by giving the new state the opportunity to elect its parliament. On February 21, Ard Fheis, the Sinn Fein convention, accepted the agreements made by the leaders of the rival parties that there should be no election for three months. The month of March ended with a meeting in London between delegates from Northern and Southern Ireland to discuss the disturbances on the Ulster border and the outrages in Belfast, in the interest of the restoration of internal peace. On the following day the Bill received the Royal Assent but it was already plain that the north as well as the south was dissatisfied.

Collins, as the head of the provisional government, had a difficult task. Ulster was dissatisfied with the boundary settlement, de Valera had refused to acknowledge any government but the Republic he claimed was already set up. Craig made several efforts to come to an agreement on the boundary, meeting Collins on January 21, and again at the end of March in London. The meetings were on both occasions abortive, but *The Times* approved the principle: that Irish leaders should settle Irish affairs, of which the boundary controversy was one. De Valera resorted to force. A long letter written by Craig to Northcliffe on March 6, 1922, had expressed "most hearty thanks for the courteous reception you accorded to me and for your kind promise to give information to your Leader writers on the question on Ulster's boundaries."

The letter continued bluntly: "This is the danger point in the present position, and the state of feeling respecting it is so acute that any attempt to interfere at large with the boundaries laid down by the 1920 Act of Parliament would lead at once to civil war."

After reciting the terms of the several pledges given on behalf of the British Government respecting the position of Ulster from the time of Lloyd George's visit of conciliation to Ireland in 1916, Craig declared: "The danger of civil war on the boundaries of Ulster is aggravated by the recent public admission by Mr. Collins that Mr. de Valera had a majority in favour of a republic. This means that if a Boundary Commission transferred Loyalists from the area of Northern Ireland it may be transferring them not to a Free State nominally within the Empire, but to a Republic outside the Empire flying a foreign flag. You will be doing the right thing and will be conferring a great service upon the Loyalists of the Imperial Province if you will support a policy of ' Amendment of boundaries by agreement only; no compulsion on either side '."

Across the first page of this letter Northcliffe wrote: "I agree with Craig. I know the border country well. Chief. Show to T. M. [Thomas Marlowe, Editor of the *Daily Mail*] and E. N. [*Evening News*] people."

On April 9 a new constitution was drawn up for the Republican Army by which it was pledged to support the Irish Republic. This divided its ranks, and throughout the summer Collins and de Valera were in conflict. On April 13, 1922, the Four Courts were seized by the Republicans, in whose possession they remained until the end of June. The Free State party, however, achieved triumph in the parliamentary election on June 16. In London Field-Marshal Sir Henry Wilson was assassinated by Irish gunmen on June 22, and then in Dublin the Four Courts were stormed and re-captured by

Free State troops and some violent street fighting followed. There was fighting in other parts of the south too. With Michael Collins as Free State commander-in-chief, Limerick, Waterford, Tipperary and Cork were successfully retaken from the occupying rebels and also, in August, Dundalk and Greenore. But the sudden death from illness of Arthur Griffith on August 12 and the fatal shooting of Collins in an ambush near Bandon ten days later removed the two chief members of the new Irish government at the moment when the fighting in the south had reached its climax.

The places of the two dead leaders were taken by Mulcahy and Cosgrave, and the latter was elected president of the Dail on September 9 at the first meeting of the Irish Parliament. Under these two a fresh outbreak of rebel terrorism was met by a stern policy of military repression. At Westminster, Parliament was occupied in passing two Irish Acts giving effect to the Treaty and to the Free State Constitution. These received the Royal Assent on December 5, and on the next day Mr. T. M. Healy was sworn in as Governor-General. In Ulster, where the Duke of Abercorn was sworn in as Governor-General on December 12, 1922 (the Northern Parliament having voted the Six Counties out of the Free State five days earlier), the year ended with a substantial promise of peace and prosperity.

The Kidnapping of a Special Correspondent

When the year 1922 opened the two Special Correspondents, Northend and Kay, were in Dublin together. On January 6, *The Times* published a dramatic message from " Our Special Correspondent " in Dublin reporting that his colleague, A. B. Kay, had been kidnapped by armed men and taken in a motorcar to a destination then unknown. One of the kidnappers at the time had referred to an article sent by Kay from Cork in December as being the reason for the outrage.

It appeared that, on January 4, Kay had been removed at pistol point from among a group of six journalists sitting over some refreshment in a room behind a shop in Dublin during a luncheon adjournment of the proceedings of the Dail Eireann which they were attending as reporters. Northend's account of the incident mentioned that his colleague's bearing under the trying conditions was admirably cool and collected. After Kay's enforced departure from the room under escort the third of the trio of kidnappers held back. He assured the journalists that no personal harm was intended but warned them not to raise an immediate alarm, and also indicated that offence had been caused by an article written by Kay from Cork, which the gunman said contained untrue statements which must be refuted. Kay already had warning that some of the displeased members of the " Irish Republican Army " were looking for him, and had been in touch with the liaison officer of that force in Dublin.

On the morning of January 5, before the Dail met, the correspondents of the world's Press in Dublin gathered at University College and signed an emphatic protest against the outrage perpetrated on one of their colleagues. They also called upon the Dail to take action for his release and the public punishment of the culprits. In the meantime the affair had been made known to officials of the " I.R.A." in Dublin—though their intelligence branch had made them aware of it before the journalists could report it—and prompt measures were taken to deal with the situation. So prompt, and effective, in fact, that a late additional message from Northend included in the same issue of *The Times* of January 6 stated that Kay had left Cork by road in the evening of January 5 and should reach Dublin about five a.m. next day. Michael Collins and the I.R.A. Chief, the message said, had worked hardest to have him released. Collins was up for most of the night. Also included in that issue of January 6 was a reprint of the article from Kay dated Cork, December 27, in which the Correspondent stated his opinion, based on talks with various persons, including members of the I.R.A., that certainly in County Cork there was a general desire for peace and a disposition to accept the Treaty and the obligations implied in it.

The leader on January 6 on the Irish issue and the debate then proceeding in the Dail made incidental mention of the kidnapping of Kay. The writer (Shaw) commented:

> In other circumstances we might have attached more importance to the insult offered to the Press by the treatment accorded on Wednesday to one of our Special Correspondents in Ireland. As it is, we neither enlarge upon it nor upon the moral of so short-sighted an attempt to hide the true state of Irish feeling from the outside world. From the first it was unthinkable that any responsible body of Irishmen could have lent themselves to an act of such patent folly. . . . Had there been a settled administration in Ireland capable of exercising the normal functions of government there would at least have been shoulders to take a direct share of the blame. As things are, however, we must in justice indict the past follies and delinquencies of this administration and of Sinn Fein rather than the present inability of either to maintain the decencies of civilized life in Ireland. We also note that the responsible Irishmen seem to have realised the disrepute into which this attack on an impartial representative of an impartial journal has brought their country, and to have acted promptly and successfully to obtain his release. . . . Our Correspondents are in every corner of the globe. They discharge their duties without hindrance even among peoples commonly regarded as savage. It would be truly strange if newspapers were compelled to consider the dispatch of a representative to Ireland as no less hazardous an undertaking than exploration in unknown Africa. (January 6, 1922.)

Next day's issue (January 7) published a " turnover " article of two columns from the released victim himself, to whom was given in the heading the rare distinction for a staff reporter of *The Times*, i.e., " From Our Special Correspondent, Mr. A. B. Kay." The first headline, very properly and succinctly, was " Kidnapped." The article told how the Correspondent journeyed by motor-car across Southern Ireland in company with three armed men who, after a call at a wayside hostelry, where captive and escort together " got fortified to meet the rigours of the night," warmed towards him and arranged a procedure for the rest of the journey. " They threw their guns into the bottom of the tonneau of the car and I gave them my word that I would not attempt to escape."

At a farmhouse some miles from Cork the party spent the night and the following evening a " court " was established in the sitting room and the charge formulated against *The Times* Correspondent. The charge was that he had published news concerning the " Army " which had not been authorized, and put forth views that did not represent the view of the " Army " in Cork. After witnesses and the Correspondent himself had been heard he was asked to withdraw while the " court " considered its verdict. When, after some time, he was recalled he was told that if he chose to give a statement that he did not interview officers and men of the " Republican Army " he would be allowed to go; otherwise he would be deported. He made a statement and was allowed to go, and the whole party motored into Cork, where they met a deputation from Dublin highly incensed at the action of the Cork men in carrying out a coup in the metropolitan area. After mutual recrimination, the Correspondent left Cork with an escort of Dublin men and after a night's journey arrived in Dublin where he placed on record his testimony to the courtesy shown him by his captors, and by his escort back, and expressed his thanks to the chief liaison officer of the I.R.A., Emett Dalton, who, he learned, had proposed to offer himself as hostage to the British Government on Kay's account.

The Boundary Commission

Joseph Fisher, an Ulsterman who practised both law and journalism, had been, after an apprenticeship in Fleet Street, the Editor of the *Northern Whig* until 1913. His support of the Unionists had made him a valued friend and adviser of Carson and Craig. After 1913 he had returned to England and ceased to take part in Irish politics. He came into contact with Printing House Square when he contributed to *The Times* " History of the War." In 1924 the Boundary Commission provided for in the Treaty was set up. Craig, supported by the Northern Ireland Parliament, refused to recognize the authority of the Commission and, consequently, to appoint a representative. Ulster was determined on " Not an Inch." His Majesty's Government was empowered by a special Act to make the appointment themselves, and Fisher was the nominee, a choice eminently satisfactory to Ulster. Special attention to the circumstances was drawn in a footnote when the announcement was printed in *The Times* on October 29, 1924.

> Mr. Fisher's acceptance will be generally welcomed in this country and on both sides of the Irish border. In Northern Ireland Mr. Fisher's name is well known as that of a stalwart champion of her rights and liberties, and among Nationalists he is respected as an honest and honourable opponent. He has a triple qualification for his task, for he is a publicist, a lawyer, and a historian who knows the difference between propaganda and impartial judgment. Ulstermen will feel confident that by Mr. Fisher the case of Northern Ireland will be fairly and squarely put.

This piece minimized the formal statement in the concluding paragraph that " We understand that the Government of Northern Ireland has had nothing to do with the appointment of Mr. Fisher, and will be in no way responsible for anything he may say or do on the Commission."

The powers of the Commission were eventually revoked as the Free State representative, Professor O'Neill, resigned in the following October. An agreement, signed on December 3, 1925, left the extent of Ulster as it had been provisionally fixed in the Treaty.

Printed Works

Brennan, R.: *Allegiance*. (Dublin, 1950.)
Brennan was a Sinn Feiner acquainted with most of the leading figures of the period. In this autobiography he describes how in London in 1920 he met a friend, one Frank Carney, engaged on a mission for the I.R.A.:

> Next day Frank told me he was to meet John Chartres, whom he did not know, and he asked me to go with him. I had, years before, met Chartres several times in Griffith's office in Dublin. He was in charge of the Index to the London *Times*, and he was a very valuable under-cover agent for Sinn Fein.
>
> We went along to a very select and conservative club in the vicinity of the Houses of Parliament. Here, in a cloakroom, Chartres opened a bag and showed us a very serviceable-looking machine gun.

The statement regarding Chartres's association with Printing House Square is misleading. He was in the office from 1903 until February, 1914, and during the latter part of his service was in charge of the Intelligence Department, responsible for the production of the

Index. He was not, however, to the knowledge of the office, involved at that time in Irish affairs. During the reorganization of the staff preliminary to the reduction of the price to one penny, Nicholson dismissed him, in circumstances which precluded any continuance of relations. A barrister by training, Chartres had worked for the *Daily Graphic,* and had spent some time in America attempting to repair heavy losses incurred at Monte Carlo. During the war he was at the head of the Intelligence Section of the Labour Department of the Ministry of Munitions. At some time he became acquainted with Arthur Griffith, and Brennan is probably correct in stating that by 1920 Chartres was a valuable under-cover man.

In the office he may have met Erskine Childers, with whose career his ran parallel to some degree. Childers was originally a member of the Milner kindergarten, which led Amery to introduce him to Printing House Square. He assisted in the compilation of *The Times History of the War in South Africa,* for Volume V of which he was mainly responsible. Childers early turned his energies to the Irish problem, and in 1911 published his *Framework of Home Rule,* which advocated settlement on Dominion lines. In 1914 he first took an active part in the spectacular gun-running at Howth. In 1917 he was secretary to the Irish Convention, and in 1921, together with Chartres, secretary to the Irish Treaty team. By this time he was firm that the establishment of a Republic was the only possible solution and he was already attached to de Valera. Differences between himself and Arthur Griffith led him to break with the moderates and to do everything in his power to defeat the Treaty in the Dail. In November, 1922, he was arrested for the illegal possession of a Colt revolver, and sentenced to death. His trial and execution were fully reported in *The Times.* The following judgement was passed in the obituary notice:

Ever since the peace negotiations in London in 1921, Childers had been one of the most intelligent and subtle opponents of the Irish Free State. He was the real author of the famous Document No. 2, which was attributed to de Valera, and which contained the alternative oath; and to his cool, calculating brain and knowledge of the art of war were chiefly due the organization of the Republican forces and their persistence in the policy of destruction. . . .

The failure of the Convention undoubtedly hastened the development of a mind attuned to extremist policy. Childers belonged to the type of man who, accepting premisses without sufficiently careful examination, pursues them rigorously to their logical conclusion. (November 25, 1922.)

Chartres died in 1927. Before his death he was editor of the *Irish Trade Journal,* the official organ of the Free State Ministry for Industry and Commerce.

Spender, J. A.: *Life, Journalism and Politics.* (London, 1927, 2 vols.)

" The campaign which, with Wickham Steed's aid, he [Northcliffe] conducted against the Irish policy of the Government, was one of the most powerful efforts in the journalism of my time, and it was, I am sure, inspired by a generous impulse in which the Irishman within him came to the top." (II, p. 170.) It has been seen in Chapter XIII how Northcliffe was embarrassed by the efforts of Steed, Shaw and Stuart.

XI. A NEW EDITOR
XIV. THE NAVAL TREATY

Grey's visit to Washington, 1920

Steed told Grey on January 7, 1920, that he was "entirely at your disposal from the moment of your arrival." They met on January 14 for two hours' conversation, at the end of which Grey supplied a statement which he desired Northcliffe and Steed to criticize, amplify or shorten, as they thought fit. It was to be published under his name. " He says," Steed wrote to Northcliffe on January 14, " you have done so much for Anglo-American understanding, have so keen an appreciation of the American point of view and are so popular over there that he is very eager to have your advice on, and approval of, anything he may write." The points chiefly discussed by Steed and Grey were the " six to one " vote and the British policy towards Bolshevist Russia. In a second letter to Northcliffe on January 16, Steed described Grey's impression of Americans:

They say in effect: " For you who have had experience of Alliances, this League of Nations business means a big departure. For us who have had no experience of Alliances it means a revolution. Wilson defied us when he said last March that he would bring back the League of Nations so interwoven in the Treaty that we should never be able to disentangle it. We are bound, if not to disentangle it, to make such reservations in regard to the application of it as to enable us to look before we leap. We do not want to remain outside the peace settlement. We want to do our bit, but you must let us do it on our own terms and trust us to play up like gentlemen when the time comes." Grey thinks this attitude not unreasonable, and he is inclined to go as far as possible to meet it.

On the 18th Steed informed Northcliffe that Grey would not publish his memorandum at the moment " because he does not wish to seem to play into the hands of Lodge and the Senate before the Senate has 'put up' some compromise to the President."

Grey was referring to a bipartisan conference of senators held between January 15 and 30, which met to discuss a possible compromise. Borah, however, learned of the proceedings, which threatened to be successful, and used his influence to prevent agreement between Lodge and the Democrats. This was known when on the 28th Steed wrote that Grey had returned the statement " modified in accordance with our suggestions, which he thinks have improved it considerably. He has put it in the form of a letter to the Editor, and says that if you and Willert agree, it might be better to publish it without waiting. . . . My feeling is that the sooner we publish the better." Northcliffe, and also Willert, were of the same opinion. Before publication the statement was also shown to Lord Robert Cecil who suggested the sentence : " It is therefore possible, I think it is even more than probable, that, in practice, no dispute will ever arise," and Grey added a concluding sentence: " Our object is to maintain the status of the self-governing Dominions, not to secure a greater British than American vote; and we have no objection in principle to an increase of the American vote."

The letter was published in *The Times* on January 31 as an unofficial statement of the desirability of the kind of announcement that *The Times* had urged. Grey's analysis of the position was that made familiar by the Washington Correspondent. He pointed out that the Senate was only exercising its constitutional right, that there was no question of bad faith in rejection, and he agreed with *The Times* that the participation of America, if it could only be obtained on her own terms, necessitated compromise; and he had the fewer objections since the eventualities contemplated might never materialize. Although written by a private person, as Grey then was, the letter introduced a new element into the situation. A supporting leading article pressed home the main points. The only disagreement was over eventualities, it was not enough to dismiss them in the belief that they might not materialize. Otherwise the paper was in agreement with what it hoped was, or would be, in effect, the Government's policy. However, lack of unity in the Government was soon apparent. A succeeding leading article (February 2) referred to a British newspaper, " which is supposed to be connected with the Prime Minister," as having charged the United States with selfishness and bad faith. No official statement supported Grey's letter.

In the United States the letter won wide approval. The Washington Correspondent described it as having had " as great an effect here as the utterance of any statesman of one country ever had upon the Parliamentary and political situation in another." The Correspondent saw a chance—" most observers at present think a good chance "— of ratification with reservations tantamount to those of Senator Lodge, for the Democrats showed every willingness to vote for the reservations. But their allegiance on the final vote on ratification lay with their leader. It seemed certain the President could not refuse what the British, and possibly also the French, Government would accept. Willert added, however, the warning that, even if the United States did ratify, her tendency to isolation would continue (February 6). The President's reaction to Grey's letter was reported to be one of annoyance, natural to one who held, as he did, that any reservations would destroy the League (February 7). *The Times* was dubious even of the possibility of his conversion: " Mr. Wilson has often shown a disposition, bordering upon obstinacy, to adhere to his own views" (February 7). The risks to harmonious relations were not negligible. A letter of Steed's to Northcliffe describes an incident where, by the intervention of the office, the Government was prevented from endangering Anglo-American relations. The President had sent a stiff memorandum on the Adriatic question which concluded that, if his advice were not taken, the United States would completely withdraw from the Treaty. Steed heard that the Council had drawn up a " pretty vigorous " reply. Alarmed, he consulted with Campbell Stuart, and they both went to the American Ambassador (Davis). He was in agreement with them that any reply likely to irritate Wilson and lead to a breach between Europe and America should be modified. Steed wrote a leading article for the following morning (Monday) and Stuart invoked the help of Grey. He refused to intervene with Lloyd George but agreed to approach Austen Chamberlain. A redrafted reply was sent on Tuesday: " I hear it has been completely rewritten and that, under our pressure and that of the warnings of Grey, Lloyd George has veered round completely and has insisted that there must be nothing in the form of the Note that could ruffle Wilson in the least. So we have scored considerably and, if we may judge from the comments of the New York papers, our leader on Monday has had the best sort of effect on the other side." (Steed to Northcliffe, February 17, 1920.)

Steed, H. Wickham: *British Policy in the Pacific.*

This memorandum is dated September 22, 1921. After a preamble describing the circumstances and background of its conception, the text thus continued:

It is possible, but by no means certain that the Washington Conference may lead to a settlement between the United States and Japan. If no settlement is reached there may be war in the Pacific as early as next year. But Japan and the United States may not be able to reach a settlement unaided. Efficient aid can only be given by the representatives of the British Imperial Government. British policy seems likely, therefore, to dominate the Conference, however little its decisive influence may appear on the surface. The framing of British policy is thus a matter of the utmost moment. Upon its character and application the question of peace or war in the Pacific, if not, indeed, of the maintenance of the British Empire in its present form, may depend.

Two main lines of policy are, theoretically, conceivable:

(*a*) A policy based on the consideration that the British Empire as the ally of Japan—though not technically her ally against the United States—and as a great Asiatic Power, ought to strive for peace in the Pacific by holding the balance even between Japan and the United States; that, to this end, the British Delegation should maintain an attitude of lofty, albeit friendly, neutrality towards each of them so that its impartiality may not be open to question should British good offices be needed in any dispute, or clash of interests, that may arise between Japan and the United States; or

(*b*) a policy based on the consideration that, since the British Empire could not side with Japan, in arms or diplomatically, in the event of a Japanese-American war, and since—as will appear later—it might not be possible for some portions of the British Empire to remain neutral in regard to such a conflict, no room for doubt should be left in any quarter that, if Japan provokes a conflict in the Pacific, all the English-speaking nations will stand together.

The arguments advanced in support of an (*a*) policy are too well known to need recapitulation. The political dislocation that might follow the abandonment of the Anglo-Japanese Alliance is not lightly to be faced; while the danger of any action on the part of the British Imperial Government that might be susceptible of interpretation as implying hostility towards an Asiatic nation, *because of its Asiatic character*, is obvious. Such action might entail serious embarrassments in India and elsewhere—though such embarrassments might be diminished were it clear that any change in British policy had been inspired by a desire to protect another Asiatic people, the Chinese, against the encroachments and exploitations of Japan. Were this motive prominent and were practical proof of its existence to be given—as for instance by the return of Wei-hai-wei to China—it would be difficult even for Japanese agitators and agents to represent the issue as a struggle between the white and the yellow races.

Nevertheless, there is, in theory, strong ground for arguing that the best and safest policy for the British Empire to pursue would be to maintain the Anglo-Japanese Alliance if only because its maintenance for a term of years might stave off an armed conflict in the Pacific and give time for such a readjustment of political and military forces as might render the situation, a decade hence, less unfavourable to the British Empire and to the United States than it now is. It should not, however, be forgotten that Japan is quite capable of appreciating this contingency and of drawing her own conclusions from it.

Against the arguments and considerations which militate in favour of an (*a*) policy there are others which tend to show such a policy to be perilous if not impracticable. Starting from the assumption that the prime interest of the British Empire is peace in the Pacific and elsewhere, it follows that the object of British policy should be to secure peace and, with it, a resumption of trade and of normal economic life throughout the world. A war in the Pacific, such as the Japanese have cogent naval reasons to wage not later than next year, would disastrously handicap a revival of trade and a return of international confidence. The chief naval experts in the United States and in Great Britain are believed to incline towards the view that, with their actual and prospective naval superiority, the Japanese could, in a few months, sweep the American Navy off the Pacific, capture Hawaii, the Philippines, Guam and Yap, establish, with a comparatively small military effort, their political and economic control over China, and make themselves the masters of Eastern Asia.

There is reason to believe that this, or something like it, has been for years the settled aim of the Japanese General Staff whose pan-Asiatic ambitions are no less certain than were the pan-German ambitions of the Prussian General Staff in 1914. Such ambitions are incompatible with British interests either in the Far East or in Asia generally; but, by itself, the British Empire might not be in a position to counter them or even to place a serious check upon them.

Into the difficult question whether the moderating influences which undoubtedly exist in Japan are strong enough to control the General Staff, it is needless now to enter. The balance of informed opinion appears to tend towards the view that, in a crisis for which the ground had been carefully selected in advance so that a point of national or racial honour might seem to be involved (such as the immigration question), the General Staff would be able to sway Japanese policy even more easily than the Prussian General Staff swayed German policy in 1914.

One consideration alone seems likely to cause hesitation among the pan-Asiatic elements in Japan—the consideration of ultimate risk. Were it certain that the British Empire would be ranged against any aggressive Japanese tendencies, the influence of the wiser and more moderate elements in Japan might be greatly increased, since they would be able to urge that, however sweeping her initial successes might be, Japan could not, in the long run, hope to prevail against the active hostility, naval, financial and economic, of the United States and of the British Empire, coupled with the passive resistance of the Chinese people. The way might thus be opened for a saner policy on the part of Japan, a policy with which Great Britain and the United States might be able to cooperate.

Apart from these considerations of a general order, contingencies might arise within the British Empire such as to affect a policy of neutrality towards an American-Japanese conflict. As a result of some inquiry, of which I have since verified the conclusions wherever feasible, it seems to me a matter of grave doubt whether British Columbia could or would remain passive in the event of a war in the Pacific. The bare possibility that so important a province of Canada as British Columbia might be compelled by local circumstances to take up an attitude at variance with that of the British Government, or even with that of the Ottawa Government, is a matter that needs to be the more carefully weighed because British Columbia is, in all other respects, the most pronouncedly British of all the provinces of the Dominion of Canada.

Nowhere have I found the Japanese so aggressive or so unpopular as in British Columbia. Though they number only 15,180 out of a total population of 450,000, and though the Chinese are more than twice as numerous as they, the Japanese have incurred the suspicion and the dislike of the bulk of the British population. They possess a practical monopoly of the fishing rights, and are rapidly increasing their grip on the land both along the coast and near the important waterways of the interior. It has been stated—and the accuracy of the statement has not been contested by any person of authority with whom I have discussed it in British Columbia—that should the Japanese, in the event of a conflict with the United States, consider British Columbia to be potentially hostile, they could isolate the province absolutely by land and by sea within twenty-four hours. They are in a position to extinguish every coast light, to sow mines if necessary in every navigable current, and to blow up or otherwise damage every important bridge on the Canadian Pacific, Canadian National and Grand Trunk Railways. Many of those bridges span deep gorges or torrents between the Rockies and the sea. If this were done, the only railway communication between British Columbia and the outside world would be by a line that passes through American territory and would, therefore, not be available for the transport of troops, except in the event of an Anglo-American Alliance. The provision for local defence in British Columbia is, I believe, inadequate.

Though there is little intercourse between British Columbia and California, the probability that similarity of feeling towards the Japanese might bring about similarity in action cannot be overlooked. Should it, however, be found possible to maintain the neutrality of British Columbia, the activities of the Japanese population there might cause complications. Moreover, there might be a stampede of Japanese into British Columbia from the Northern Pacific Coast of the United States. The Japanese are highly organized, and all able-bodied males are subject to Japanese military discipline. British Columbia would probably become the centre of Japanese espionage against the United States—a circumstance that might lead the United States Government to demand the expulsion of the Japanese if they had not already been spontaneously expelled or suppressed beforehand by the British Columbians themselves.

In either case the neutrality of British Columbia and, indeed, of Canada, might be exposed to a severe strain. As regards opinion in Canada generally, I am inclined to think that Manitoba, Saskatchewan and Alberta would support at once the standpoint of British Columbia. The attitude of the rest of Canada is harder to judge because the Oriental question is little understood in Ontario and Quebec. But I am inclined to think that Eastern Canada would stand by Western Canada as soon as the importance of the issues were appreciated.

Leaving out of account the repercussion of a Japanese-American conflict in Australia and New Zealand, it seems, therefore, desirable that the effect of possible developments in Canada should be fully considered in the light of the fullest available or obtainable information, before the instructions to the British delegates at the Washington Conference are finally framed. A policy of aloofness from American-Japanese disputes might encourage the more militant Japanese to think that in no circumstances could the United States rely upon British support, and, therefore, lead Japan to be more uncompromising in her demands than she would be if she felt Great Britain and the United States to be in substantial agreement upon the terms of a peaceful settlement in the Pacific. No position could well be less dignified or more dangerous than that of a British Delegation which, after endeavouring to remain benevolently neutral, should be compelled to take sides by care for the cohesion of the British Empire.

Other considerations of vast importance to the future of the British Empire seem likely to arise, directly or indirectly, in connexion with the Washington Conference. Of these the chief is the future relationship between the English-speaking peoples. Assuming that an Irish settlement has been achieved (at least in principle) by the time the Conference meets, the future attitude of the United States towards Great Britain (as distinguished from the British Dominions) may be influenced favourably or unfavourably by the attitude of the British Delegation. (It need hardly be said that, in the event of a resumption of hostilities in Ireland before or during the Conference, the position of the British delegates would be unenviable, inasmuch as they might have to live and work under police protection.) The people of the United States are averse from subtle distinctions. Should a crisis arise at Washington between their

Government and that of Japan, the question instinctively asked by the vast majority of Americans would be: Are the British with us or with the yellow men? However unreasoning and unreasonable such a question, and however much individual Americans might appreciate British difficulties and make allowances for them, the broad fact is that the attitude of the bulk of American people would be that which I have indicated.

Another danger may arise from lack of discrimination on the part of the American public and even of American public men. Their minds are simple, almost childlike; they have not yet learned from international experience the value of pains-taking discernment. For this reason they are apt to be at once trustful and very suspicious. I believe that, if the Conference is to be safely steered through the delicate situations which will undoubtedly arise, the steering will have to be done, unobtrusively, by British hands. But I believe also that it will not be possible for British hands to touch the helm effectively unless complete confidence has been established in advance between the British and the American Delegations.

To sum up: If the Washington Conference is to succeed, and to avert the danger of war in the Pacific which might imperil the British Empire, it can only succeed through the intelligent and self-sacrificing efforts of the British Delegation which, working for higher ends than the Americans are yet able to perceive, would leave the prestige of success to the American Government and be satisfied with the quiet substance of success for the British Empire. No hostile or even chilly attitude towards Japan would be necessary on the part of Great Britain. It would suffice that the Japanese Delegation should perceive that the British Imperial Government fully realize the possible implications of a Japanese-American conflict, and should understand that, in working for a settlement, the British Delegation was seeking to serve the lasting interests of Japan herself.

The Washington Naval Conference, 1921

The main cause of the French opposition was that the U.S. had refused to ratify the Anglo-American Convention of June 28, 1919, which promised support to France against any fresh German attack, and Great Britain, shortsightedly, had then repudiated her part of the Convention. There was little prospect of an improvement in the European situation, particularly as regards War Debts and Reparations, unless France and Britain went to Washington hand in hand, and by helping the Conference to succeed, revived American interest in a European settlement. These were the circumstances in which the Editor, having obtained an outline of the probable British policy at Washington, went to Paris in October.

The Editor saw Millerand (President of the Republic); Viviani, the Prime Minister; and Briand, the Foreign Secretary, as well as a number of influential Senators and deputies. But it continued to be taken for granted, on the authority of Jules Jusserand, French Ambassador at Washington, that the U.S. would propose naval reductions far too sweeping for Britain to accept, and that a grave Anglo-American dispute would be the result. Thus France would be able to get something for herself and " get level " with Britain, by taking the American side in this prospective quarrel. In the sequel Sir Auckland Geddes told the Editor that Hughes, the U.S. Secretary of State, had informed him that on the morrow of Briand's arrival in Washington, some days before the opening of the Conference, Briand had said to the Secretary that, as America was going to have trouble with the British, if it should come to blows some excellent French harbours, notably Brest, were at his disposal. Secretary Hughes rounded on Briand sharply, and promptly informed Auckland Geddes to whom he expressed surprise and indignation. Briand's stock at Washington never recovered from this initial *gaffe*, which may possibly have induced Hughes to humiliate the French by bracketing France with Italy at only 1.75 capital ship strength as compared with the 5-5-3 ratio for the U.S., G.B., and Japan.

The French were very sore at this treatment. Viviani, eager for a personal success, delivered a single magnificent harangue to the Conference, and went home. Briand followed suit by getting the Four-Power Pacific Treaty concluded before the Naval agreement was tackled, and left the tougher job to Albert Sarraut and Admiral de Bon. The Admiral opposed the 1.75 ratio for France, and objected to the abolition of sub-marines which Balfour wanted. A deadlock ensued, and the Conference seemed likely to break down. The Editor, who was still in Washington, tried unsuccessfully to patch up some kind of British understanding with Sarraut. So far, the British delegation had scored heavily until Balfour seemed to appeal to American public opinion against the U.S. delegation to support the British view on submarines, and his stock fell rapidly. Lee of Fareham, First Lord of the Admiralty, also blundered. He had secured an article by the French naval captain, Castex, in the official naval review, *La France Maritime* (not *La France Militaire*) which set forth the views of the pro-submarine school in the French navy, and went on to argue that these views were mistaken because only superiority in capital ships could prevail in the long run. Instead of using this article to support the British case against submarines, Lee of Fareham—misled perhaps by imperfect knowledge of French—saddled Castex of *La France Maritime*, with respon-sibility for supporting and approving of German submarine warfare. The French had no difficulty in pulling American opinion round to their side and from these two blunders British prestige at Washington did not recover.

Debts and Isolation, 1922-3

Hope of settlement was destroyed by the failure, bluntly described as such on August 14, 1922, of the London Conference. The negotiation of the Anglo-American debt was not resumed until Bonar Law's Government came into power. In the New Year the Debt Funding Commission went to Washington in an atmosphere of good will. The American proposals were that the rate of interest should be 3 per cent. for ten years, and 3½ per cent. thereafter, a considerable concession since the original agreement was for 5 per cent. interest. The Conference was adjourned while Baldwin took these proposals back to London for discussion. Although the paper thought 2½ per cent. would have been a fair rate, it acknowledged that the Americans had shown generosity, and advised a speedy and grateful acceptance. (January 29.) The terms were accepted (February 1) and ratified by Congress (February 22). The leading article of February 23, while admitting that, on the dark side of the settlement lay a heavy financial burden on two generations, stressed the moral repercussions: " We can . . . hold up our heads, alone in Europe," and the hopes it gave for the future: " As time proceeds, the influence of America is not likely to become less powerful on the Continent of Europe; and we now have better ground than hitherto for assuming that in many issues we shall have America with us."

Meanwhile it had become clear to all that Germany was nearing a financial abyss and that France was threatening to give her the final push. The Reparations Commission lacked the power or the incentive to provide a rapid solution. The need for an official American representative was obvious enough but Lewis was compelled to deny the rumours current in December that the United States was contemplating intervention.

It cannot too often or too strongly be insisted that without a radical change of policy it would be impossible for the United States to do more than has been done since March, 1921, towards the adjustment of the European situation, and that nothing 'has so far happened which justifies the belief that such a change in policy is in sight. (December 13, 1922.)

This was accepted in the office, yet

we have long believed that the whole problem of German reparations and of inter-Allied debts can only be settled in the last resort with American cooperation. (December 18.)

The problem, the leading article said, was to organize the conditions in which the United States could act. Lewis's later suggestion was that France should call a conference on reparations. (December 21.) Two days afterwards, he reported that Borah had proposed the President should call such a conference. Harding demurred because he wanted the Debt Funding Commission to be given a free hand. (December 29.) A second proposal of a conference of experts came from Hughes. (December 30.) Another hopeful sign was Harding's own suggestion to Congress that the United States should enter the Court of International Justice. (February 27, 1923.)

The Congressional term ended in March and these projects remained in the air. Harding would do nothing without Congress, and Lewis, summing up four months later, was inclined to believe that Britain had been wrong to expect the little she did. Each time hopes had run high of United States help disappointment had been the result: " it is as though Mr. Harding had once or twice tested the water of European affairs with a timid toe, had found it too cold, and had withdrawn "—but then he was not a Roosevelt or a Wilson. He believed in discussion and advice—advice had been freely given to Europe, and in fairness Lewis added, generous financial help—but there was a very definite limit. (July 28.) This long message proved a prescient summing up of the Harding Administration; within a week Harding was dead. (August 4.) This unexpected event made little difference to Anglo-American relations. The late President had, the paper admitted, done something to encourage American participation in international affairs (August 4); Coolidge, Lewis prophesied, would maintain the Harding policy and certainly nothing more: " The United States will in all probability be more widely separated from Europe in the months to come than at any time during the past year." (August 4, 1923.)

This proved to be the fact. Coolidge (Lewis described him on October 12 as " an incarnate monosyllable ") was reticent. His watchword was " Stability " as Harding's had been " Normalcy." Lewis forecast " one half-pennyworth of membership in the World Court, with an intolerable deal of reservations," as the new President's policy. (October 12.) Politically, this was dictated by the need to preserve unity in the Republican Party. (October 27.) Coolidge fulfilled Lewis's prophecy in his first Message. It was a clear statement on the theme that " Our main problems are domestic problems." (December 7.) Lewis wrote: " Europe must save itself for all that Congress will do, and without Congress the Executive can do little. Nor does the President intend to do much."

XVI. THE COALITION STANDS

Mr. Ward Price's Telegram from Genoa to the *Daily Mail*, April, 1922

The telegram recalled that Mr. Lloyd George and M. Barthou had both denied that the former had threatened to abandon the Entente Cordiale; said that their denials had been fully accepted as far as they went; but affirmed that the denials did not go all the way.

After seeing M. Barthou on Saturday, and using that significant phrase that "we have reached a parting of the ways," Mr. Lloyd George on Sunday saw M. Philippe Millet. M. Philippe Millet is probably the best-known and the most responsible international journalist in France. Not only is he the foreign editor of the *Petit Parisien*, the most widely circulated newspaper in France, but he is the founder and editor of the *Europe Nouvelle*, one of the ablest diplomatic weeklies of the world, and he was long the correspondent of the *Observer*. He is an old acquaintance of Mr. Lloyd George.

It was to this man that Mr. Lloyd George unbosomed himself without restraint and without any pledge of secrecy. In talking to Philippe Millet, the British Premier knew that he was talking to France unofficially but more effectively than if he had chosen official channels for his statements.

[Millet's statement to Ward Price then followed.]

" I saw Mr. Lloyd George on Sunday and had a long conversation with him —one that will always remain deeply impressed upon my memory. The Prime Minister exacted from me no pledge of secrecy. I had the impression indeed that he intended his words to go beyond myself to the French public. But I am a firm partisan of the Entente Cordiale and when the conversation was over I remarked to Sir Edward Grigg that I did not intend to use the British Premier's words as an interview. I have not done so, though I have written several articles in the *Petit Parisien* which reflect the gravity of the statements he made to me."

Mr. Lloyd George said that he considered the Entente Cordiale at an end. I replied, " On the contrary, I am a firm believer in the Entente Cordiale,[Mr. Prime Minister, and I refuse to believe that it is at an end."

The Prime Minister went on to say that he had long been urged to abandon France and seek an understanding with Germany. He stated that Lord Birkenhead had especially pressed this course upon him. " I have had letters from Royal circles recommending me to bring the Entente to an end " said the Premier. " In fact, I am almost the last partisan of the Entente in England. Only the other day I received a letter from a colonel of the Black Watch, a regiment that used to be particularly fond of the French, urging me to drop France. And now I am compelled, to my great regret, to do so. I shall have to hold myself free to make new international attachments for England. France has chosen between us and Belgium. After all that England has done for her, she has preferred Belgium. I cannot help it. I am forced to yield to the pressure brought to bear on me, and I regard the Entente Cordiale as ended by the choice that France has made." This conversation depressed me greatly. I related the purport of it, of course, to M. Barthou, and to several influential compatriots of mine. I am only too glad to learn from Mr. Lloyd George's *démenti* yesterday that he has abandoned the intention he held on Sunday; and I look forward to a closer cooperation in the future between England and France, to both of which countries I am deeply attached. (From a contemporary copy of G. Ward Price's telegram in Printing House Square Papers.)

XVII. END OF THE NORTHCLIFFE REGIME

Manuscript

Steed, H. Wickham: *Notes of my Intercourse with Lord Northcliffe.* (June 11 to 14, 1922.)

Quarto, typescript, 44 pp. " Dictated June 17, 1922, H. W. STEED. Taken from dictation and typewritten, June 17, 1922, Eileen Dickie."

Price, G. Ward: *Fifty years of the " Daily Mail,"* 1896-1946.

This history of the paper, which has remained unpublished, contains much of value to the historian of the Press. It consists of 456 folio leaves and 16 leaves of appendices and index. A copy is available in the Library of the *Daily Mail*, Northcliffe House, E.C.4.

Printed Works

Northcliffe, Alfred Viscount: *My Journey Round the World,* 16 *July* 1921-26 *February* 1922, edited by Cecil and St. John Harmsworth. (London, 1923.)

Essential to the estimator of Northcliffe. The book omits much of value to the biographer, *e.g.*, there is no mention at pp. 82-3 of the visit to Manila on October 21, 1921, where he spoke against Philippine independence. At the same place and time Northcliffe delivered a warning about Japan, the Pacific questions, the next war, armaments, the " so-called scientific weapons that would be developed still further and on a more devastating scale," and declared that Britain and America would again be found standing together. (See the *Philippines Free Press*, October 29, 1921, report, with half-tone of Northcliffe speaking to the Rotarians of Manila.) Northcliffe then proceeded to Canton, *en route* for Tokyo.

Blumenfeld, R. D.: " Lord Northcliffe, 1865-1933 " in *The Post Victorians*, with an Introduction by W. R. Inge, pp. 427-442. (London, 1933.)

A tissue of errors.

Clarke, Tom: *My Northcliffe Diary*. (London, 1931.)

Mr. Clarke is clear that on December 3, 1916, Northcliffe went to the War Office intending to see L.G., but cannot be positive that any interview took place, and L.G. states that there was none. (p. 106.)

Clarke, Tom : *Northcliffe in History ; an intimate Study of Press Power*. (London, 1950.)

The book gains its " intimacy " from the fact that Northcliffe's younger brothers, Cecil and Leicester, favoured Mr. Clarke with their memoirs, which enables him to document Northcliffe's first meeting with Lloyd George in 1909 (see p. 87). Mr. Clarke repeats the account given him by Lloyd George in 1929 and printed in the author's *My Lloyd George Diary* (London, 1939, p. 50) of Northcliffe's demand in 1919 that he be made a delegate to the Peace Conference (p. 145). It is shown in Chapter VIII that this was not Northcliffe's demand.

Spender, J. A.: *Sir Robert Hudson*. (London, 1930.)

There is an account of the anxiety felt in 1922 on account of the state of Northcliffe's health, and of his dependence upon Hudson whom he first met in 1914.

" Lord Northcliffe " by J. St. Loe Strachey in *The Outlook* (New York, weekly) September 13, 1922, pp. 69-72.

An ignorant and pompous attack. " Lord Northcliffe was not a great Editor. He was not a great publicist. He was not even a supreme organizer and collector of news, nor a great purveyor of publicity. He was something totally different." The highest praise Strachey can give is that " he was a great man of business, a great money-maker accidentally engaged in the work of journalism."

" Lord Northcliffe. A character study of the man who is more fiercely attacked than any other personality." By Andrée Viollis, the well-known French Journalist, in the *London Magazine* [a Harmsworth property] August, 1919, pp. 439-450.

An abbreviated translation of the writer's *Lord Northcliffe* (Paris, Grasset, 1919) illustrated with excellent photographs not published elsewhere, collected by the author, who was a visitor to Elmwood, and had exceptional opportunities to observe and please Northcliffe. " The portrait of the young proprietor of the *Daily Mail* strongly recalls some of the pictures of Bonaparte as First Consul." The article was advertised in a half-page display in *The Times* of July 18, 1919, as " The man the Germans feared most."

Wrench, Sir (John) Evelyn: *Uphill*. (London, 1934.) Parts 3-4.

The author held high executive positions with the Northcliffe Press from 1904 until in 1912 he decided to give chief attention to his Over-Seas League. Northcliffe never understood the development of the author's mind. " The misfortune in our relations was that he built his plans for the future on the Evelyn Wrench of 1909, his enthusiastic admirer and the ambitious young man whose only desire was to push the firm's wares. He reckoned without the human factor, despite his great knowledge of human nature. . . . The bulk of his fortune came from these publications which I appeared to despise. It was not that I despised them in reality. " A " psychic upheaval " had taken place in Sir Evelyn (p. 257). Certainly this was a factor that Northcliffe might have overlooked even in lesser men, but he emerges from the early part of Sir Evelyn's record as the kind of man a younger colleague could idolize. A deterioration in his character, the author thinks, may have dated from 1909 (p. 225). " Northcliffe in later life never had much respect for Parliament. He thought the real power in the realm lay in Fleet Street." (p. 192.) " In 1908 he was already talking about the Anglo-German struggle as a certainty." (p. 198.)

There is a character sketch of " the Chief " at pp. 197 ff. : personal magnetism; flair for coming events; no time for religion; wonderful will power, but often consecrated to unworthy objects; wrong tactics towards men devoted to him; best traits, love of mother, of children and of youth; he could be entirely absorbed in one project at a time, thus " He said,' 1908 was my *Times* year and 1909 will be my periodical year (that means my Sales Department) '." (p. 219.) Already in 1911 the main difference between Northcliffe and the author was plain, *i.e.*, the increasing egoism of " the Chief." " He considered that he and the *Daily Mail* largely ran the country. He thought the best thing that could happen to Great Britain was to increase the power and influence of the *Daily Mail* " (p. 243).

Northcliffe's Break with the Newspaper Proprietors' Association

" Newspapers and their Millionaires," by Viscount Northcliffe in the *Daily Mail*, May 8, 1922.

I shall be glad if everyone before reading this article will realize that the wages question in Metropolitan daily newspapers in no way resembles the wages situation in Agriculture, the Mines . . . The London daily newspapers each controlled by a number of very rich people who are merely competing with *each other*, and not with foreigners as are our coal-owners, shipbuilders and engineers. Good wages to printers of daily newspapers do not mean loss of trade to Great Britain, but *low* wages mean the disappearance of skilled printers to the United States where, I regret to say, I have met hundreds of them.

There follows the attack on capitalists:

> We journalists have no objection to capitalists owning newspapers and thus creating employment. But I object to being a member of a Combination in which capitalists ignorant of Fleet Street dictate terms to those who have spent their lives trying to understand the complex questions of a newspaper.

XX. THE NEW PROPRIETORSHIP

Changes in Newspaper Ownership after the death of Northcliffe

Astor, J. J.: "The Future of *The Times*" in the *Empire Review*, September, 1923. (pp. 944-951.)

For a time " the individuality of Lord Northcliffe " obscured in the public eye the individuality of the paper itself (p. 945). At his death the majority of the shares in *The Times* came on the market under John Walter's option to purchase. It was, since " no political party is nowadays content unless some important organ of the Press is enslaved to its service . . . . . surely, a wise object to secure as far as possible the continued independence of one great journal, and through it the perpetuation of the highest standards of British journalism. It also seemed that *The Times* could best fulfil this purpose if it stood aloof and free from the necessity of having to consider any interests external to Printing House Square. Such at least were the considerations that actuated the writer to join with Mr. John Walter in exercising his option and in purchasing the bulk of the shares in *The Times*." (p. 946.)

The new Proprietors intended to follow a policy of " enlightened conservatism," which, while favouring the principle of continuity, was neither insensitive nor necessarily hostile to the inevitable processes of political development. (p. 950.)

The Times as a National Institution

Spectator, September 22, 1922, contains the following :

An interesting article by Mr. Garvin in the *Observer* of last Sunday alluded to the intention expressed by Lord Northcliffe to make arrangements in his will that the *Times* should become a permanent national institution.

In the summer of 1908, Lord Northcliffe several times talked to me on the subject and asked me to give him my views. He seemed to think it would be very difficult to carry out any such plan. I pointed out to him, however, that he might quite easily make a trust, though, if he did so, he must be careful to avoid the petrifaction which so easily falls upon endowed bodies. After our conversation I grew warm with the subject and threw my proposals into the form of a letter. This I think it may be of interest to print at the present moment :

" *Confidential*.   Monday, August 10th, 1908.

" MY DEAR NORTHCLIFFE,—I have been thinking very carefully over the points on which you wanted my advice, that is, in regard to the best way of establishing the *Times* by your will as a national institution. Clearly, the main point to be aimed at is the vesting of the *Times* in a body of independent trustees, who shall from time to time appoint the editor and manager, and who shall generally control the paper in accordance with your desire that the *Times* shall remain an impartial, judicial and national organ of public opinion.

" I will begin my suggestions with the trustees, who shall hold in trust the proprietary shares which carry the control of the paper. I suggest that these trustees should be :

" The Lord Chancellor (or if for any reason he cannot act some person of high legal position and standing named by him, as, for example, the Lord Chief Justice or the Master of the Rolls).

" The Speaker of the House of Commons.

" The Archbishop of Canterbury.

" The Vice-Chancellor of the University of Oxford.

" The Vice-Chancellor of the University of Cambridge.

" The Editor of the *Times* and the manager of the *Times* for the time being.

" Such a body would represent all the elements of the national life with which the *Times* is specially concerned. The selection of Oxford and Cambridge alone among the universities may seem unfair, but the *Times* has always been specially representative of those two universities. It would be the duty of the trustees to appoint an editor and a manager whenever those posts were vacant, and to appoint for ten years, of course with possibility or, indeed, expectation of renewal. After his appointment the editor should be irremovable, except on the ground that he was for physical and mental reasons incapable of fitly conducting the paper. In fact, his tenure should be very much that of an English judge. The editor should have complete power and responsibility over everything written in the paper, and should be at liberty to oppose any policy or movement which he considered contrary to the interests of the nation. His conduct of the paper, however, would have to be consonant with the general aims and objects laid down by you in your will. These, I take it, would be something like the following :

"The essential object of the *Times* should be publicity in regard to all that concerns the national and imperial life and interests, so long as publicity can be obtained without injury to good morals. In order to obtain such publicity care must be taken to give the views of those opposed to the policy of the *Times*, as well as the views of those in agreement with the *Times*. In other words, the speeches, writings and letters of those from whom the editor of the *Times* differed would be as fully reported and printed as those with whom he was in agreement. The general aim of the paper should be to secure what may be termed ' judicial journalism.' Speaking generally, the editor would put public affairs of all kinds before his countrymen, as a wise and impartial judge lays a case before the jury. While putting both sides to the jury a judge, however, can rightly make it clear which view he considers the true one. In the same way a judge, though he puts both sides impartially, does not hesitate to denounce strongly and sternly that which he thinks of evil report, or, again, to give proper praise and commendation to what he thinks is right. The *Times*, in a word, though judicial, need not in the least be flabby or invertebrate. It would hear both sides, but would say fearlessly what it thought to be best. So much for policy.

"In addition, it might be laid down that in its pursuit of a wise publicity the *Times* must take special care as to the adequate reporting of Parliamentary proceedings, and also of all legal proceedings, and further, that it must pay special attention to foreign affairs, its object being to let the country understand the development of political affairs throughout Europe and the rest of the world.

"The financial question is a little hard to settle. In the first place no doubt the profits should go to accumulate a large reserve fund in case there might be a period when the paper had to be carried on at a loss. Assuming, however—as I suppose one may assume—that there would generally be a considerable profit, I think the best plan would be, first, to have a moderate and reasonable profit-sharing scheme for the staff, and after that to use the profits in the way the Royal Literary Fund is used, except that the fund in question would be distributed amongst members of the journalistic profession rather than on literary men in general. The trustees might appoint a committee of three persons who would make grants from the fund, after the manner in which grants and pensions are paid out of the Civil List.

"I hope you will not think these ideas very crude. At any rate, I send them to you for what they are worth. The question has interested me very much. We hope to come over at tea time next Sunday, and I daresay by that time you will have found a great many holes in my proposal and many practical points which I have overlooked.—Yours very sincerely.

J. St. Loe Strachey."

Changes of Proprietorship in the Metropolitan Press

On the newspaper changes of the period, see Lord Burnham's statement as President of the Press Club. (*The Times*, October 15, 1923.)

In proposing the toast of " Fleet Street," Lord Burnham remarked how wonderful it was that when they turned from political coalitions to Press coalitions no variety of policy was the smallest obstacle to a hearty and profitable union. There was no doubt that coalitions of the Press added to the financial strength that they enjoyed, and, he had no doubt, to the efficiency of the news service. They welcomed Major Astor into the fraternity of Fleet Street, and were certain that his coming augured nothing but well for the character and reputation of the newspaper Press. Major Astor had already set a great example by constituting his paper a public trust. The *Times* newspaper was a national possession of which they were proud. Major Astor did not mean to be merely a spectator of his own machinery. On the contrary, he threw himself with the greatest keenness and with the fullest appreciation into the work of his great newspaper. If Major Astor made any change, he was more likely to desert the House of Commons for Printing House Square than Printing House Square for the House of Commons. He (Lord Burnham) had never recognized the antagonism between the Press and Parliament which some people assumed. On the contrary, it looked as if they would have to stand united in the future against destructive policies which, in his opinion, if pursued to the end, would only lead to the ruin, not only of our Parliamentary, but of our newspaper life. All wanted to preserve the independence of the Press, and they were just as keen—those of them who had been Parliamentary men—on preserving the independence of Parliament. He thought that an alliance frankly recognized, and, to the best of their ability, carried out, to maintain the honour both of the Press and of Parliament was likely to produce the best fruit for the future welfare of the State.

Major Astor, replying, said that he personally was not concerned with any coalition, either political or journalistic. Fleet Street, as they knew, was the street of adventure; but from a brief connexion with the neighbourhood he was inclined to think that the adventure did not end at Ludgate Circus. At any rate, he was quite sure that Printing House Square would like to take its share in any compliments that might be floating round. He had only recently joined the great world which was so importantly represented that night. The Press extended a warm welcome to the newcomer and made the first impressions of its neophyte very delightful and very vivid. It was just about a year ago that he woke up one morning to find himself a member—and a very proud member—of this fraternity. He woke up rather suddenly, feeling keenly that something very big had happened to him. He still had that feeling, and he hoped he should always have it.

During the year there was much comment and discussion devoted to the Press. Lord Beaverbrook, speaking at Brighton on "Newspapers" on October 17, 1923, drew in the *Globe* :

"The newspaper that is given to you is always a very dangerous possession. I once had a newspaper given to me—or very nearly given to me. It was the *Globe* newspaper in London. That newspaper was given to me—at least the man who sold it to me said he was giving it to me (laughter). He took several thousand pounds of my money as he went out. Well, this newspaper was a wonderful possession. I had quite decided that I was going to make it the foremost London journal: in fact that was part of the headline title. I was prepared to live up to it. But shortly afterwards I went out to Canada, and when I came back again I looked into the accounts, and I said ' In God's name get rid of it.' The journalist who represented me said: ' Oh, certainly; I will get rid of it at once.' He came back when night fell. I said ' Have you disposed of the newspaper ?' He said ' Not yet.' I said ' To-morrow.' The next day passed, and when it was over I said ' Have you sold the newspaper ? ' ' No; I haven't sold it.' And so it went on for six or seven days, and at last I parted with that newspaper. I parted with it on novel terms—I, at that time a stranger within your gates, a Colonial from Overseas, unacquainted with English conditions, I disposed of that newspaper, and do you think I got a price ? Not at all. I had to pay a man £5,000 in cash to take it (laughter). I paid him that sum in exchange for a covenant that he would run it for the next six months." (Report in *Sussex Daily News*, October 18, 1923.)

Lord Beaverbrook's views on newspapers as political agencies in 1923 are to be found in the *Daily Express* of November 27. Here he gives his opinion on the *Morning Post*, *Observer*, *Daily Herald*, and his own daily, as to which he had been accused " without the shadow of proof or justification, of being animated by the lowest kind of personal matters, *e.g.*, complicated schemes and plans which never entered my mind because I shall stick to the Imperial policy with which I won Ashton-under-Lyne in 1910 and to the flag which I refused to haul down in December, 1911."

Political Changes in the Press

The political situation in the Press at that time may be gauged from a paragraph in the *Manchester Guardian* of November 28, 1923 :

CIVIL WAR IN THE TORY PRESS.

The indignation and perplexity of London Conservatives over the antics of the main part of the Conservative Press in London moves even Liberals to sympathy. Nothing remotely resembling the present state of things has ever been known in London before. No evening paper is supporting the Government. Of the daily papers the Rothermere group of the *Daily Mail*, *Daily Mirror*, and *Daily Sketch* are all conducting a feud with Mr. Baldwin, Lord Beaverbrook's *Daily Express* goes even further in its opposition, while Messrs. Berry's the *Daily Graphic* has no lead to give.

Briefly, the position is that the readers of the big circulation Tory papers in London are without guidance even from their Press mentors that have told them what hat to wear and whom to take it off to, and have instructed them generally on every other subject. Nor does the malevolent neutrality of the papers stop there, for both the *Daily Mail* and the *Daily Express* have opened fire on *The Times*, the latter paper not scrupling to bring in the fact of Major Astor's American birth, while the *Morning Post* pours broadsides into both of them, and they accuse the high Tory organ of inconsistency. Lord Beaverbrook to-day ends his attack on the *Morning Post* with this delightful metaphor: " There is one person against whom the rat has a deadly venom—the man who has stood to his guns."

Mr. Baldwin's support, then, is reduced in London to *The Times*, the *Morning Post* and the *Telegraph*. How different from the days when the newspaper posters and caricatures of the popular Tory Press furnished the chief ammunition of the party ! It is small wonder that the Liberal spirit is reviving all over London, and the spectacle of the Tory Press vigorously whacking one another on the head every morning is a healthy stimulant. (November 28, 1923.)

Printed Works

Camrose, Viscount: *British Newspapers and their Controllers*. (London, 1947.)

This book sets out the history of the ownership, finance, class, circulation, price, etc., of the morning, evening and Sunday newspapers of London and the Provinces. The author became Proprietor of the *Daily Telegraph* in 1928. The names of the

Proprietors and directors of their Companies are given. For the names of the staff and their functions, reference should be made to *Newspaper Personnel and Data* published periodically by the *World's Press News* (London), and to the *Newspaper Press Directory* (London, Benn Bros.).

Hindle, Wilfrid: *The Morning Post*, 1772-1937, *Portrait of a Newspaper*. (London, 1937.)

The *Morning Post* was edited by H. A. Gwynne from 1910. In 1924 Lady Bathurst (daughter of Algernon Borthwick, Lord Glenesk, who died in 1908) was succeeded by the new Proprietors, *i.e.*, the Duke of Northumberland and others. There was another change, and " In its last years *The Morning Post* was under the control of a group in which Sir Percy Bates, Chairman of the Cunard Line, and Major J. S. Courtauld, M.P., were notable figures" (p. 240). On June 15, 1928, the *Daily Mail* described the *Morning Post* as " a parasite in the advertising business," which was a harsh rendering of Northcliffe's judgement given in 1914 (see Chapter IV) that London could not support *The Times*, the *Morning Post* and the *Daily Telegraph*. The war delayed the verdict of the economic process, but on October 1, 1937, the *Daily Telegraph* absorbed the *Morning Post*. From that date " class " journalism in the London morning Press was limited to the productions of Printing House Square and Peterborough Court.

Honours for the Press

The following list of honours conferred upon prominent personalities in the newspaper trade during the period 1914-1929 may be noted and compared with the table in Vol. III, Appendix, Sources, p. 782. It reveals a greatly accelerated rate of promotion to and in the peerage, especially during the Lloyd George Ministries.

1914	Sir Harold Harmsworth, Bt. (Baron Rothermere).	Asquith
1916	Wm. Waldorf Astor (Baron Astor).	,,
	W. Maxwell Aitken (Baronet).	,,
	Cyril Arthur Pearson (Baronet).	,,
1917	Lord Astor (Viscount).	Lloyd George
	Sir Maxwell Aitken, Bt. (Baron Beaverbrook).	,,
	Lord Cowdray (Viscount).	,,
	Lord Northcliffe (Viscount).	,,
	John Ritchie Findlay (Kt.).	,,
1918	Robert Leicester Harmsworth (Baronet).	,,
	George Riddell (Baronet).	,,
	James Henry Dalziel (Baronet).	,,
1919	Lord Rothermere (Viscount).	,,
	Lord Burnham (Viscount).	,,
	William Sutherland (Kt.).	,,
	Walter Layton (C.H.).	,,
	George Sutton (Baronet).	,,
	William Thomas Madge (Baronet).	,,
	Malcolm Fraser (Kt.).	,,
	Sir Clement Kinloch-Cooke, Kt. Bach. (K.B.E.).	,,
1920	Sir George Riddell, Bt. (Baron Riddell).	,,
	David Hughes-Morgan (Kt.).	,,
1921	Sir James Henry Dalziel, Bt. (Baron Dalziel of Kirkcaldy).	,,
	Wm. Ewert Berry (Baronet).	,,
	Hon. Gervase Beckett (Baronet).	,,
	Sir Malcolm Fraser, Kt. (Baronet).	,,
1922	Sir William Sutherland, Kt. (P.C.).	,,
	Hildebrand Harmsworth (Baronet).	,,
	Edward Iliffe (Kt.).	,,
1925	Sir John Ritchie Findlay, Kt. (Baronet).	Baldwin
	Sir David Hughes-Morgan, Kt. (Baronet).	,,
1926	Sir Clement Kinloch-Cooke, Kt. (Baronet).	,,
1928	J. Gomer Berry (Baronet).	,,
1929	Sir Wm. Ewert Berry, Bt. (Baron Camrose).	,,

THE METROPOLITAN PRESS. 1884-1947.

A. MORNING.

Founded	Title	Proprietors	Editors	Policy	Price
1794	Morning Advertiser	Incorporated Society of Licensed Victuallers	Capt. Thomas Hamber 1876-1886 Thomas Wright 1886-1894 F. G. Doney H. Hamilton Fyfe 1902-1903 Geo. W. Talbot 1903-1913 H. C. Byshe 1913-1924 A. E. Jackson 1924-1927 F. H. Atkins (Night Editor) F. W. Milman (Day Editor) W. E. Hopwood (Associate Editor) H. R. Bennett (Managing Editor)	Defence of the interests of the Licensed Trade	1d.
1772	Morning Post	Sir Algernon Borthwick (Lord Glenesk) 1876-1908 Lady Bathurst 1908-1924 Absorbed in Daily Telegraph 1937 as " Daily Telegraph and Morning Post ", (Lord Camrose)	William Hardman 1872-1890 A. K. Moore 1895 Oliver Borthwick 1895-1897 Algernon Locker 1897-1905 James Nicol Dunn 1905 Spenser Wilkinson 1905-1911 Fabian Ware H. A. Gwynne 1911-1937	Conservative	1d. 1882 2d. 1916 1d. 1926
1846	Daily News	Daily News Limited 1901 (Chairman George Cadbury 1901-1911) Amalgamated with Morning Leader as Daily News and Leader 1912 Amalgamated with " Westminster Gazette." 1928 Amalgamated with " Daily Chronicle " 1930 and continued as " News Chronicle "	F. H. Hill 1870-1886 Sir Henry Lucy 1886-1887 Sir John Robinson 1887-1896 E. T. Cook 1896-1901 Rudolph Lehmann 1901 Alfred G. Gardiner 1902-1919 J. S. Hodgson 1920-1931 J. Hugh Jones (Managing) 1924 Tom Clarke 1926-1933 (Managing till 1930) Aylmer Vallance (Managing) 1933-1936 Gerald Barry (Managing) 1936-1947 R. J. Cruikshank 1948-	Liberal, Social Literary Progressive, Social reform. Betting and Turf news excluded	1d. ½d. 1904 1d. 1918

Year	Newspaper	Ownership / History	Editors	Political	Price
1855	Daily Telegraph	Lionel Lawson Sir Edward Levy Lawson (Lord Burnham) Lord Burnham (second) Sold to Sir William Berry (Lord Camrose), Sir Gomer Berry (Lord Kemsley) and Sir Edward (Lord) Iliffe, 1928 Absorbed Morning Post as Daily Telegraph and Morning Post, 1937. Same year Lord Camrose acquired Lord Kemsley's and Lord Iliffe's interests.	Thornton Hunt 1873-1885 Sir Edwin Arnold 1885-1923 Sir John M. le Sage 1923-1924 Fred J. Miller Arthur E. Watson 1924-1950 Lord Camrose (Editor in Chief) 1950 Colin R. Coote 1950	Conservative	1d. 1½d. 2d. 1d. 1½d. 2d.
1857	Standard (Morning)	Bought from Johnston family by C. A. Pearson November, 1904 Sold to Davison Dalziel (Lord Dalziel) 1910 Ceased 1917	W. H. Mudford 1874-1900 G. Byron Curtis 1900-1904 H. A. Gwynne 1904-1911 Herbert A. White 1911-1917	Conservative Opponent of Tariff Reform	1d.
1869	Daily Chronicle	Edward Lloyd 1871-1918 Frank Lloyd and family trading as United Newspapers Limited Lloyd family parted with their interest, 1918 Incorporated with Daily News as News Chronicle June 2, 1930	R. W. Boyle 1876-1889 A. E. Fletcher 1890-1895 H. W. Massingham 1895-1899 W. J. Fisher 1899-1904 Robert Donald 1904-1918 Ernest A. Perris 1918-1930 See Daily News	Unionist Gladstonian Liberal Govt. Left Wing Liberal	1d. ½d. 1904 1d. 1917 1½d.
1884	Financial News	Harry H. Marks 1884-1916 Financial News Limited 1898 Incorporated with Financial Times 1945	Harry H. Marks 1884-1916 Dr. Ellis 1921 H. C. O'Neill 1921 W. H. Doman } William Lang } Sir Laming Worthington-Evans 1924 Sir Edward Hilton Young 1925 Oscar Hobson 1929 Maurice Green 1934 Hargreaves Parkinson 1938	Finance, Independent	1d. 2d.

Year	Newspaper	Proprietorship / Notes	Editors	Politics	Price
1888	Financial Times	Financial Times Limited. Incorporated Financier and Bullionist. Incorporated with Financial News 1945	D. G. Macrae 1901; W. R. Lawson 1909; Arthur Murray 1924; C. H. Palmer 1938; D. S. T. Hunter 1940; A. H. T. Chisholm 1945-1949; A. G. Cole (acting); Hargreaves Parkinson 1950; L. G. Newton	Finance, Independent Monetary and Economic Affairs Commodity Markets Trade, Industry, World Security	1d. 2d. 3d.
1890	Daily Graphic	Founded by William L. Thomas. Owned by H. R. Baines and Co. Amalgamated with Daily Sketch 1946. Kemsley Newspapers	T. Heath Joyce 1890-1891; Hammond Hall 1891-1907; Holt White 1907-1909; W. A. Ackland 1909-1912; A. S. M. Hutchinson 1912-1917; A. W. Netting 1917-1919; Harold E. Lawton 1919-1922; E. G. F. Tebbutt 1923-1925; H. N. Heywood 1925-1926		1d.
1892	Morning. Became London Morning (1898) and Morning Herald (1899). Merged with Daily Express 1900	Morning Newspaper Company	David Christie Murray		½d.
1892	Morning Leader	Colman family of Norwich. (Chairman: Professor the Rt. Hon. James Stuart, M.P.) Merged with Daily News as Daily News and Leader 1912 and later with News Chronicle	Ernest Parke 1892-1912	Liberal	½d.
1896	Daily Courier 98 issues	Sir George Newnes	Earl Hodgson	Social Chat of the Nineties	½d.
1896	Daily Mail	Alfred Harmsworth (Lord Northcliffe) Associated Newspapers, Limited	Alfred Harmsworth 1899-1926; Thomas Marlowe 1926-1929; W. G. Fish 1929-1930; Pulvermacher 1930-1931; W. A. McWhirter 1931-1935; W. L. Warden 1936-1938; A. L. Cranfield 1939-1944; R. J. Prew 1944-1947; S. F. Horniblow 1947-1950; Frank Owen 1950-; Guy Schofield	Independent, Right Wing Cons.	½d. 1d. 1½d.

Year	Newspaper	Proprietor / Company	Editor(s) and Dates	Politics	Price
1900	Daily Express	C. Arthur Pearson — Daily Express (1900) Limited — London Express Newspaper Ltd. 1915 — Controlling Shareholder Lord Beaverbrook	C. Arthur Pearson (Editor-in-Chief) 1900-1903; S. J. Pryor 1900-1901; B. Fletcher Robinson 1901-1902; R. D. Blumenfeld 1902-1929; A. Beverley Baxter 1929-1933; Arthur Christiansen 1933-; H. S. Gunn Managing Editor 1943-1944	"Patriotic rather than Party" Independent	½d. 1d. 1½d.
1903	Daily Mirror	Alfred Harmsworth — Sir Harold Harmsworth (Lord Rothermere) 1914 — Pictorial Newspaper (1910) Co. — Daily Mirror Newspapers Ltd.	Mary Howarth 1903; H. Hamilton Fyfe 1904-1907; Alexander Kinealy 1907-1915; E. F. Flynn 1915-1919; Alexander Campbell 1919-1930; L. D. Brownlee 1931-1934; Cecil E. W. Thomas 1934-1949; Silvester Bolam 1949-	Independent	½d. 1d. 1½d.
1904	Daily Paper 32 Issues	W. T. Stead	W. T. Stead	"A paper for the abnormally scrupulous"	1d.
1906	Tribune Ended 1906	Franklin Thomasson	William Hill; S. J. Pryor	Liberal	1d.
1906	Majority a few issues	Majority Limited		"The organ of all who work for wage or salary"	½d.
1908	Daily Sketch (Printed in London 1911) Changed to Daily Graphic 1946	E. Hulton & Co., Ltd. — Daily Mirror Newspapers Ltd. and Sunday Pictorial Newspapers (1920) Ltd. — The Daily Sketch and Sunday Herald Ltd. (name changed to The Daily Sketch and Sunday Graphic Ltd., 1927. Changed to The Daily Graphic and Sunday Graphic Ltd. 1946) (Subsidiary of Allied Newspapers Ltd. now Kemsley Newspapers Ltd.)	James Heddle 1909-1914; W. S. Robinson 1914-1919; H. G. Lane 1919-1922; H. L. Gates 1922-1923; H. G. Lane 1923-1928; A. Curthoys 1928-1936; A. F. W. Sinclair 1936-1939; S. W. Carroll 1939-1942; The Hon. Lionel Berry 1942-1943; A. R. Thornton } joint 1943-1944; M. H. Watts 1943-1944; A. R. Thornton 1944-1947; N. F. Hamilton 1947-1948; H. E. Clapp 1948-	Independent now Conservative	½d. 1d. 1½d.

Year	Title	Ownership	Editor	Dates	Politics	Price
1912	Daily Citizen to January 1915	Labour Newspapers Limited	Frank Dilnot	1912–1915	Official Labour	½d.
1912	Daily Herald	Daily Herald Printing and Publishing Society in association with Odhams Press Ltd. Formed Daily Herald (1929) Ltd. (Chairman, Lord Southwood).	J. S. Elias (Lord Southwood) Chairman and Managing Director W. S. Seed Sheridan Jones Rowland Kenny Charles Lapworth George Lansbury W. P. Ryan Hamilton Fyfe William Mellor W. H. Stevenson F. Williams P. Cudlipp	1929–1946 1912 1913 1923–1926 1926–1931 1931–1937 1937–1940 1940–	Official Labour	½d. 1d. 1½d.

B. EVENING.

Year	Title	Ownership	Editor	Dates	Politics	Price
1803	Globe	Sir George C. H. Armstrong 1871–1907 Sir Hildebrand Harmsworth 1907–1911 Sir W. T. Madge 1912–1914 Absorbed by Pall Mall Gazette 1921, and incorporated with Evening Standard, 1923	R. E. Francillon Sir George C. H. Armstrong Ponsonby Ogle W. Algernon Locker J. P. Harrison Charles Palmer Wadham Peacock	1886 1908–1912 1912–1915	Conservative	1d.
1827	Evening Standard	Bought by C. A. Pearson from Johnston family, 1904. Absorbed St. James's Gazette, 1905. Davison Dalziel (Lord Dalziel), 1910. Owned by Hulton and Co., 1915–1923. Incorporated with Pall Mall Gazette and Globe, 1923. Bought by Lord Beaverbrook, 1924	Sidney Low S. J. Pryor William Woodward J. A. Kilpatrick D. M. Sutherland A. H. Mann D. Phillips E. R. Thompson G. Gilliat P. Cudlipp R. J. T. Thompson F. Owen M. Foot S. Elliott H. S. Gunn P. Elland	1888–1897 1906–1912 1912–1914 1914–1915 1916–1920 1920–1923 1923–1928 1928–1933 1933–1938 1938 1939–1942 1942–1943 1943–1945 1945–1950 1950–	Conservative	1d. 1½d.

Year	Newspaper	Proprietors / History	Editors	Dates	Politics	Price
1865	Pall Mall Gazette	George M. Smith H. Yates Thompson W. W. Astor (first Lord Astor) 1892 Sir Henry Dalziel 1917 Sir John Leigh 1923 Incorporated with Evening Standard, 1923	Frederick Greenwood John Morley W. T. Stead Sir E. T. Cook C. Kinloch Cooke Henry C. Cust Sir Douglas Straight F. J. Higginbottom J. L. Garvin D. M. Sutherland	1865-1880 1880-1883 1883-1889 1890-1892 1892-1896 1896-1909 1909-1912 1912-1915 1915-1923	Conservative Liberal 1880-1892 Conservative 1892	1d.
1868	Echo, ended 1905	Bought by Baron Grant, 1875. Sold to J. Passmore Edwards 1876. Sold 2/3rd share to Andrew Carnegie Syndicate 1884. Passmore Edwards rebought and retained till 1897. Sold to syndicate including Thomas Lough, M.P., and John Barker. Later sold to Consolidated Newspapers. F. W. Pethick-Lawrence, M.P., in control 1901-1905	Aaron Watson W. M. Crook T. Cox Meech Percy (later Sir) Alden, M.P., F. W. Pethick-Lawrence, M.P.	1883 1901-1902 1901-1905	Radical Progressive	½d.
1880	St. James's Gazette	Edward Steinkopff 1888 W. Dallas Ross 1903 C. A. Pearson 1905 Amalgamated with Evening Standard	Frederick Greenwood Sir Sidney Low Hugh Chisholm Ronald McNeill, M.P. (Lord Cushendun) S. J. Pryor Gerard Fiennes	1880-1888 1888-1897 1897-1899 1903 1904	Independent and Progressive Conservative	1d.
1881	Evening News	Coleridge Kennard and Harry Marks Alfred Harmsworth (Evening News Limited) 1894 Associated Newspapers Limited 1905	Martin Fradd Augustus Daly Charles Williams Frank Harris Louis Tracy W. Kennedy Jones Walter J. Evans Charles I. Beattie F. L. Fitzhugh Guy Schofield John N. Marshall	1881 1894-1896 1896-1921 1922-1924 1924-1944 1944-1950 1950-	Unionist	½d. 1d. 1½d.

Date	Paper	Proprietor	Editor	Politics	Price
1887	Star	Star Newspaper Company	T. P. O'Connor 1887-1890 H. W. Massingham (a few months) 1891-1908 Ernest Parke 1908-1920 James Douglas 1920-1930 Wilson Pope 1930-1936 Edward Chattaway 1936-1941 R. J. Cruikshank 1941- A. L. Cranfield	Liberal	½d. 1d. 1½d.
1893	Sun, ended 1906	T. P. O'Connor, M.P. ? Horatio Bottomley 1900	T. P. O'Connor Theodore Dahle	Literary and non-political	½d.
1893	Westminster Gazette	Sir George Newnes 1893-1908 Liberal Syndicate (Chairman: Sir Alfred Mond, M.P.) 1908-1915 Last issue as evening, Nov. 5, 1921 First issue as morning, Nov. 7, 1921 Incorporated with Daily News, February 1, 1928	Sir E. T. Cook 1893-1896 J. A. Spender 1896-1921 J. B. Hobman 1921-1928	Liberal	1d.
1910	Evening Times, ended 1911	London Evening Newspaper Co. Major J. A. Morrison, M.P. Sir Samuel Scott, M.P. John Cowley	Charles T. Watney Edgar Wallace	Conservative	½d.

XXI. DAWSON'S SECOND INNINGS
XXIII. APPEASEMENT

Manuscript

Dawson's Memoranda.
Barrington-Ward's Notes.

Geoffrey Dawson and Lloyd George, 1918, 1923

For Dawson's view of the General Election at the time, see *The Times* leading article, December 12, 1918, noted above, p. 457. The view he later adopted is expressed in the following:

[By a Former Fellow-Worker.] "Lord Milner Goes. The End of a Great Partnership." The *Yorkshire Post*, February 5, 1921.

> Geoffrey Dawson's comment on Milner's resignation from the Coalition Government. "From the middle of the war down to its final triumph these two [Lloyd George and Milner] were in effect the executive Cabinet, working in intimate partnership and with mutual respect. . . . We are just beginning to realise what we owe for those critical months to the Lloyd-George—Milner combination, and especially to Lord Milner's typically self-effacing side of it. But the possibilities of such a partnership were almost limited to the war. The General Election that followed, that orgy of unnecessary vote-catching, was almost a familiar incident to one of the two, but it must have been sheer torture to the other. Lord Milner knew—the demagogues of the day denounced him for telling them—the real value of the pledges to 'hang the Kaiser,' to 'make Germany pay the cost of the war,' and all the rest of the current cat-calls. It is not unreasonable to believe that he would gladly have withdrawn at that earlier stage if he could have done it without seriously weakening the British case at the Peace Conference."

The comment is interesting for the light it throws upon Dawson's progress towards revision of the Treaty, two years before he returned to *The Times*. The peg in 1923 was the subject of reparations.

> The French public have, to our minds, an almost fantastic notion of what Germany can pay now and in the next few years. . . . There was a time when they were not alone in their error. It was Mr. Lloyd George who first demanded these huge amounts; who insisted, against the terms of the Armistice, on the inclusion of pensions in the bill; who left to the French Government, with their vast devastated areas before their eyes and with priority refused to them, no option but to make claims even more extravagant than at one time were our own. (June 11, 1923.)

Lloyd George's reply was printed on June 13, accompanied by the specific contradictions of a leading article:

> We are bound to say we are not greatly impressed by the statement in which Mr. Lloyd George attempts this morning to refute the charge that he began the fatal process of setting hopes of reparations far too high. He begins his record in 1921 and narrates with sufficient accuracy from that time onward his part in the gradual process of "scaling down." But the crime of which he stands accused was committed not in January, 1921, but just two years earlier. It was in the winter of 1918-19 that the Prime Minister of England was pledging himself to "demand the whole cost of the war from Germany"—to say nothing of "hanging the Kaiser" and performing a number of other feats which had never even occurred to serious brains on the Continent. The French themselves, by all accounts, were amazed at the magnitude of the British election programme. Still, it was not for them to fall short of it, and from that time onwards began the period of competition in fantastic claims from which Mr. Lloyd George, as he truly says, was constantly endeavouring to extricate himself in his later days. When every allowance has been made for an uninstructed and overheated public opinion in this country, there can be no question about the deplorable effects of those election pledges in postponing the peace of Europe. (June 13, 1923.)

The correspondence provoked by this broadside led the Editor to thunder again on the subject.

> These were the battle cries ["fullest indemnities from Germany" and "till the pips squeak"], repeated without any qualification from a hundred platforms, with which the Prime Minister went to the polls the following week. It was amid their echoes that he crossed triumphant to Paris for the Peace Conference. No amount of quotation, either from his own speeches or from *The Times*, can dissipate the essential memories of that disastrous and wholly unnecessary campaign. It was the beginning of all his difficulties in what he curiously regards as the successful achievement of "keeping the Allies together." It remains, and must remain, a blot on his great career. (June 15, 1923.)

Harold Williams

Letters to the Editor of *The Times* on his death.

Sir,—You rightly say that *The Times* has suffered an irreparable loss by the death of Dr. Harold Williams. The brilliant linguist who spoke more than thirty languages, the sensitive student of affairs who knew by instinct the significance of European movements, the lovable colleague whose wide knowledge meant sympathy and not superiority—how will you find another to combine these varied and remarkable talents?

So also is it with his many friends in the world at large. We also have suffered a loss that cannot be made good. If I may take my own as typical of the experience of friends, there must be many circles both in England and on the Continent where the gap left by his death will never be fully filled. I had the good fortune to touch his life at many points that never failed to give a vibrating response. I knew him in Russia in the dark days before the Revolution. I worked with him in many fields of foreign politics when the War was over, and it was due to his insistence that I carried out a mission for the Russian refugees in Eastern Europe. If any Russian issue arose, he was always at hand to plead for the people that he loved so passionately and to testify to the ultimate and inevitable recovery of a great country.

By his death *The Times* has lost an incomparable Director of its foreign service, his many friends a companion of great knowledge and equal charm, and thousands of refugees a steadfast upholder of an anti-Bolshevist Russia, and a friend who never failed them in the hour of their country's distress.

Your obedient servant, SAMUEL HOARE. (November 20, 1928.)

A colleague wrote:

Few men can have been so easy to work with as Dr. Harold Williams. Even when he was most deeply immersed in his own work, with little time to spare, he was always ready and willing to answer a query or give helpful advice. His answer, too, was always prompt, as were all his actions, and invariably right, for, though his mind was wonderfully stored with knowledge on the most abstruse subjects, the material was all so well arranged that he had never any occasion for hesitation or doubt or reflection about his reply. His unfailing good temper and his cheery smile always made it a joy to go and converse with him, and his talk would cover a wide variety of subjects that was simply amazing.

His knowledge of Russian and the other languages which people generally learn was taken for granted, but he could pick up any foreign newspaper and read fluently. Even the Egyptian newspapers, with their difficult and ill-printed characters, he could read without effort. Yet, apart from newspapers and current magazines, his reading must have been tremendous, and where he found the time is difficult to imagine. One would sometimes tell him of a newly published book, almost unheard of, and find he knew all about it already. But his interest reached out far beyond the present, and he was thoroughly familiar, to take just a few instances, with the Arabic historians, with medieval history and literature, with the most recent theories of the prehistory and early history of mankind, and with a great deal of modern European thought.

Still, books and ideas alone did not satisfy him, and he had a genuine interest in men. He had friends in almost every corner of the world, and he would often speak of them—men he had known at the University of Berlin, where he studied for some years, and elsewhere, men whose work had carried them to such distant parts of the world as Swatow in China or the University of Wisconsin in the United States, and with whom he was constantly in touch.

Yet, above and beyond all these remarkable gifts and accomplishments, Dr. Williams was a most lovable man. He made the stranger feel wholly at ease in his company. He gave freely of his confidence and gained the same readily in return. Without being religious in any narrow or formal sense, he was truly religious, for there radiated from his personality inspiration and kindness and love. He was a loyal friend, and those who knew him and worked with him will always be able to treasure a pleasant memory and be thankful for the privilege of having known so true a man. (November 21, 1928.)

Upon the bread and salt of Russia fed,
His heart with her high sorrow soared and bled.
He kept the bitter bread and gave away
The shining salt to all who came his way.—MAURICE BARING. (November 21.)

Sir,—We have to-day returned from seeing, but not of feeling, our last of Harold Williams. Of his gifts of thought and knowledge I will say nothing; they spoke for themselves to all who knew him and to many who did not. But, if ever in a long and loving friendship I had been able for a day to believe that I had a character like his, it would have been a happy day for me; and if many of us could have or hold that illusion, even for a day, the world would be a happier place.

Yours truly, ROBERT VANSITTART. (November 21.)

F. B. Riley

Frank Basil Riley, born in 1893, spent his early years in Western Australia where his father was Archbishop of Perth. In 1912 he went as a Rhodes Scholar to New College, Oxford, and distinguished himself for qualities of initiative and leadership. He joined up in 1914, but had the misfortune to be captured within three months. While in prison he came into contact with captured Russian officers and studied Russian. After the war he returned to New College to read Economics and then entered the educational service of Iraq. Occasional contributions to *The Times* so impressed the office that when Riley visited the United States in 1924 he became a permanent member of the staff as assistant to Louis Hinrichs, the New York Correspondent. His ambition was to return to Asia, and when the confused civil war in China and particularly the anti-foreign demonstrations in January, 1927, made the appointment of a Special Correspondent desirable, Riley, with his experience and abilities, was an obvious choice. He reached China early in May and visited Hankow just before the end of the Borodin-Chen régime, Borodin being at that time under orders to break up the Left wing of the Kuomintang and to replace its members by Communists. Riley went north on his own initiative to find out the truth about Feng Yu-hsiang, " the Christian General," whose position, according to a letter of Fraser's to the office, dated June 23, 1927, was equivocal. Fraser's own opinion was that Feng was too jealous of Chiang Kai-Shek to support the Kuomintang, but that he would be dependent on communist connexions. Riley disappeared from Chengchow on July 23. An intensive search failed to reveal any clues and, since local report was unanimous that he had been attacked by Feng's soldiers, it was assumed that he had been murdered. The fact that Borodin was due to arrive at Chengchow, a railway junction, where motor cars had been ordered to meet him on July 28, may or may not be relevant.

Printed Works

Adler, Selig: *The War Guilt Question and American Disillusionment*, 1918-1928, in the *Journal of Modern History* XXIII, 1 (Chicago, March, 1951), pp. 1-28.

Emphasizes the connexion in the mind of American liberalism of American treaty revision and the Secret Treaties revealed by the Bolsheviks. Mr. Adler cites articles in *The Nation* (N.Y.), on " Some Outstanding Diplomatic Revelations " that appeared in 1919. He regards it as " one of the major blunders of Anglo-French policy after 1918 " that so long an interval occurred after the publication by the Germans of *Die grosse Politik* (40 volumes published between 1922 and 1927) and the beginning in 1926 of *British Documents*. British " pioneer revisionists, representing a small fragment of opinion, had tremendous influence upon the American revisionists." The " liberal " journals of opinion, Mr. Adler says, almost always used the war-guilt question to preach isolation. The article includes annotation on the work of the professional historians, H. E. Barnes, Charles Beard, S. B. Fay, B. E. Schmitt and the controversies between the schools. Mr. Barnes's reply to Prof. Adler should be read in the *Journal* for September, 1951.

Bassett, R.: " Telling the Truth to the People " in the *Cambridge Journal*, November, 1948.

This important article disposes in a dozen well-reasoned pages of the popular myth about the " Baldwin confession " on November 12, 1936, and deserves to be better known.

Beaumont, M.: *La Faillite de la Paix* (1918-1939) Paris, 1946, second edition : volume XX in the *Peuples et Civilisations* series of MM. Halphen and Sagnac.

The indispensable work of reference on matters of fact for the period it covers.

Beloff, M.: *The Foreign Policy of Soviet Russia*, two volumes. (London, 1947 and 1949.)

The most recent scholarly guide to Russian foreign policy between 1929 and 1941.

Churchill, W. S.: *The Gathering Storm*. (London, 1948.)

This book compels admiration and needs no praise.

Ciano, G.: 1937-1938 *Diario*. (San Casciano, 1948.)

Ciano, G.: *Diary* 1939-1943, ed. M. Muggeridge. (London, 1947.)

Ciano, G.: *Diplomatic Papers*, ed. M. Muggeridge. (London, 1948.)

Documents and Materials relating to the Eve of the Second World War, two volumes. (Moscow, 1948.)

These were issued by the Ministry of Foreign Affairs of the U.S.S.R., with the object of lessening the bad impression of Russian foreign policy produced by the State Department's damaging publication, *Nazi-Soviet Relations* 1939-1941 (Washington, 1948), through diverting attention to the foreign policy of Russia's recent allies when almost comparably disgraceful at an earlier period. The first volume consists of some twenty extracts from the German Foreign Office file, captured by the Russian Army in Berlin, on

Anglo-German relations from November, 1937, to November, 1938, buttressed by another score of documents from Polish, Czech and Russian sources. The texts of the Munich agreements are included. Much of this material is discreditable to British policy and to some British personalities, and it is all authentic, but so manifestly incomplete, as well as one-sided, as to lose the force that might have been attached to a complete publication of the German file. The second volume consists principally of excerpts from the private papers of Herbert von Dirksen, German Ambassador in London in 1938-39.

Documents on British Foreign Policy, 1919-1939, third series, ed. E. L. Woodward, two volumes. (London, 1949.)

" Problem of Germany " in the *Round Table*, Vol. XXVII, No. 107. (London, 1937.)

The harmony of ideas between *The Times* and the principal organ of the Imperialists is illustrated in this article. " Modern Germany is nationalist, not Imperialist, and is quite prepared to recognize the rights of other nations and their title to live. She knows what modern war means. Her people, indeed, are opposed to war. But Germany is dissatisfied, etc." (p. 497.)

Documents on German Foreign Policy 1918-1945, series D, ed. J. W. Wheeler-Bennett and others, two volumes. (London, 1949 and 1950.)

A ponderous collection, of general value in depicting the period (September, 1937-September, 1938) with which these volumes deal, but with very little of particular relevance to *The Times*.

Feiling, K. G.: *Life of Neville Chamberlain.* (London, 1946.)

This suffers from the usual defects of an official biography, lenience towards its subject and a presentation of great affairs on a narrow front, but it has its advantages also, for the Prime Minister's family papers were made available to Professor Feiling, who used them with revealing freedom. This most interesting book deals to better effect with home than with foreign policy; on the former, subject and author alike seem to feel themselves to be on surer ground.

François-Poncet, A.: *Souvenirs d'une Ambassade à Berlin.* (Paris, 1946.)

François-Poncet, A.: *De Versailles à Potsdam.* (Paris, 1948.)

Straightforward accounts of Nazi Germany from the French point of view.

Gedye, G. E. R.: *Fallen Bastions.* (London, 1939.)

The account of a very angry man, formerly a *Times* correspondent in Central Europe, of the extension of Nazi rule over Austria and Czechoslovakia. As a picture of the life of a serious correspondent in a police state, this book has much value.

Hadley, W. W.: *Munich, Before and After.* (London, 1944.)

A gallant attempt to defend the Munich policy at the moment of its greatest unpopularity.

Hitler, A.: *Mein Kampf,* tr. J. Murphy. (London, 1939.)

The importance of this almost unreadable book does not need to be stressed.

Kennedy, A. L.: *Britain faces Germany.* (London, 1937.)

Kennedy's book is a good example of the thinking on international politics that was common in England and in Printing House Square when he wrote it: lucid on some points, full of good intentions, but not following out logically the necessary conditions of their fulfilment.

Kennedy, A. L.: " Munich," in the *Quarterly Review*, October, 1948.

Kogon, E.: *Der SS-Staat.* (Stockholm, 1947.)

Dr. Kogon was a founder-member of the Buchenwald concentration camp, and has described the organisation and methods of these places of torture with remarkable moderation and veracity.

Kordt, E.: *Wahn und Wirklichkeit.* (Stuttgart, 1948.)

The only attempt made so far in Germany at a scholarly study of Hitler's foreign policy, by the brother of the German Chargé d'Affaires in London in 1938, who himself attended the Munich Conference. It is worth remark that there is no evidence among Dawson's papers, which provide a very full and detailed account of the abdication of Edward VIII, to substantiate in any way the illusion from which Hitler and Ribbentrop appear (p. 84 of Kordt's book) to have suffered: " that Great Britain might under the rule of the ' social King ' Edward have moved on to the side of the Axis."

Mussolini, B.: " Fascismo," in *Enciclopedia Italiana*, Vol. XIV. (Milan, 1932.)

In this brief and brilliant article, not a hundredth part of the length of *Mein Kampf*, the nature and doctrines of a totalitarian state are set out a hundred times more clearly.

Namier, L. B.: *Diplomatic Prelude* 1938-1939. (London, 1948.)

Namier, L. B.: *Europe in Decay*. (London, 1950.)

The first of these books is indispensable.

Nuremberg: *The Trial of German Major War Criminals: Proceedings of the International Military Tribunal sitting at Nuremberg, Germany*. (London, in progress since 1946.)

The determination of the Germans to leave none of their bestialities unrecorded, in writing or at least by word of mouth, has made the proceedings at this trial and their accompanying documents into a historical source of unusual amplitude on the nature of Nazi Government.

Oakeshott, M.: *Social and Political Doctrines of Contemporary Europe*. (Cambridge, 1938.)

Rauschning, H. : *Germany's Revolution of Destruction*. (London, 1939.)

This is in some ways a muddled book, but it has one important thing in it that needed saying: that the Nazi revolution was not a revolution " for " anything, it was essentially destructive and not constructive.

Saint-Chamant, J. de: " Les contactes germano-russes " in *Revue des Deux Mondes* for July 1, 1938.

An accurate forecast of the events of nearly fourteen months later, based on analysis of the Russian state trials of 1936-7.

Seton-Watson, R. W.: *Britain and the Dictators*. (Cambridge, 1938.)

Seton-Watson, R. W.: *From Munich to Danzig*. (London, 1939.)

The first of these books was a sequel to the same writer's authoritative *Britain in Europe*, which had surveyed British foreign policy from 1789 to 1914. The second, a further sequel, originally appeared under the title *Munich and the Dictators*. It reviewed the dismemberment of Czechoslovakia with the scholarly ferocity that was to be expected of an old friend of T. G. Masaryk, Edvard Benesh and Wickham Steed. Events, however, moved so fast that it was impossible to publish this account of the Czechoslovak crisis before the Polish crisis of August, 1939, with which it also dealt, had involved Europe again in war.

Spender, J. A.: *Between Two Wars*. (London, 1943.)

This short account is interesting because of the information which was available to its author about the armaments position, often the critical factor in the formation of British policy.

Wheeler-Bennett, J. W.: *Munich*. (London, 1948.)

The passage in this book which deals specifically with *The Times* has been fully discussed on pp. 930 ff. above. It also contains a valuable account of British foreign policy between 1933 and 1938, as well as many necessary documents.

The Spanish War

This war produced an astonishing effect upon the intellectuals of the Left in the non-belligerent countries. The revolt of the Generals against the legally elected Spanish Government, with the rather more than tacit support of the Church, naturally evoked strong criticism from the British Secularist and Protestant ranks. But the almost immediate discovery that the revolt, far from being a purely domestic affair, was backed by considerable Italian forces and equipment gave it a significance which many besides Leftists and Liberals felt to be personal and urgent. Strategists considered its implications in terms of the Mediterranean; Constitutionalists regarded it as a struggle of law and order against banditry; Catholics saw it as a crusade; Liberals saw it as a struggle of the " common people " for elementary rights menaced by their native and age-long tyrants— Church, Army, Landowners and Bankers; Doctrinaires were impressed by the unfavourable prospect of the growth of Fascism. In the view of many intellectuals of the younger generation, the heroic Spanish people were the first to stand up and defy Totalitarian Capitalism. There was little understanding of the exact nature of Spanish politics, or the credentials of the Republican Government but there was a feeling, not only in extreme Left-Wing circles, that Chamberlain's and Daladier's policy of non-intervention did not represent the views of the mass of the people of England and France. Their policy was alleged to reflect a covert support for Franco and fear of victory by the forces of " democracy." Militant idealism roused in the bosom of this minority educated, if not born, since the Armistice, contrasted sharply with the supine pacifism of the country generally. Some of these militants volunteered from several countries to go to Spain and fight for the Government against the Spanish rebels and the Italian Fascists. The motives of the British volunteers are set forth in the introduction to the *British Battalion XV International Brigade Memorial Souvenir*, published on the disbandment of the Brigade (London, 1938). It is claimed that the men of the Brigade had fought for the principles of John Ball, Wat Tyler, John Wycliffe.

The support for the Republican Spanish Government revealed a development in public opinion. It was becoming understood that pacifism by itself was useless opposed to a determined, ruthless and well-armed foe. But in the judgement of this, and other sections of opinion, the chief foe of what, at this time, began to be called " the British way of life," was not Germany but Italy, and in particular Mussolini who, between 1936 and 1937, was regarded by the broad British public as the dominant personality in the Axis. The indignation of the British Left was spent more liberally against him than against Hitler. *The Times* was no exception, on this point, as Dawson's " Corridor for Camels " witnesses. The paper, however, was rigidly disinterested in the Spanish War.

Mackenzie King and *The Times*, 1928

The Editor's Memorandum dated June 10, 1928, referring to the Chanak crisis in 1922 throws light on the feelings of the Dominion then and later.

In a telegraphic summary of a speech by the Prime Minister [Mackenzie King] on March 26 [1928] our Ottawa Correspondent wrote : " He claimed the credit for averting a serious European war by his stand over the Chanak affair in 1922." In a debate in the House of Lords on March 29 [1928] Lord Parmoor quoted this sentence, which he interpreted as follows : " In other words, what he says is that had the Canadians been prepared at that time to send their forces in connection with the Chanak affair, in his view there would have been another European war. We know, of course, that they would not do that, and that they stood out against it. But the claim he makes requires very deep consideration—that because they stood out, and in consequence of the attitude of Canada, the danger of what he calls a European war was prevented." On May 28, in a further debate in the Canadian House of Commons, the Prime Minister made the following statement : " I wish to say, after looking at the Press reports which passed from this country with respect to a certain debate which took place here, and which gave rise to this discussion in the House of Lords, that I am convinced that particular discussion would never have taken place in the Lords had a correct report of what took place here been sent to the paper I have in mind by its correspondent in this country."

Later in the debate Mr. Bennett, Leader of the Opposition, challenged this statement and read Mr. Mackenzie King's original speech, which in his opinion completely justified the summary sent to England. Mr. King, it appears, had spoken as follows on March 26 : " What are the facts as they have come to be known to the world ? In brief, they are that the British Cabinet as a whole had never considered the communication which was sent to the Government of Canada and which was published broadcast in the Press at that time. Not only the British Cabinet as a whole had not considered that appeal, but leading members of the Government and leading public men in England took the position that it was one of the most dangerous appeals that had ever been made by any Government in any part of the world. More than that, we were told that but for the action of Canada in taking the position which she did at that time in asking that the facts be first brought out and that the parliament of Canada should have its say before contingents were sent abroad, a second great European conflict might have taken place." He proceeded to fortify this view by quotations from speeches of Bonar Law and Asquith and from *Maclean's Magazine*. From this latter he read the following extract : " . . . had our Premier succumbed to the Lloyd George-Churchill demands, preceded as they were by propaganda and scheming for Canadian participation, the British Empire would undoubtedly have been at war now with Turkey, Russia, and perhaps India, Afghanistan, Persia, and God knows who else or what the end would have been." And he added : " That was the opinion at that time of Colonel Maclean, and he had sources of information which I do not hesitate to say from what I have since learned were pretty reliable. The view which he there expressed I have been told in Great Britain on very high authority was not far from the mark as to what might have followed had Canada not taken the position which she did."

This last sentence seems to me [Dawson] to be of considerable importance, and to confirm the view that our Correspondent's condensed report did not give an unfair impression of the Prime Minister's attitude as a whole. Later in the debate of May 28, the following passage occurred :

Mr. Bennett : I do not think it is quite in keeping with the traditions of the great office which he now occupies that the right hon. gentleman should vent his personal spleen against *The Times* correspondent by making the observations he made this evening. I do not think it adds either to the dignity of the office or the greatness of the right hon. gentleman himself.

Mr. Mackenzie King : I am venting no personal spleen. I never had any.

Mr. Bennett : Those of us who know have a clear understanding of that. So far as the right hon. the Prime Minister is concerned, that gentleman would not be the correspondent of the London *Times* if he could help it.

Mr. Mackenzie King : I suppose he was appointed at the instance of my hon. friend.

The Prime Minister, of course, is well aware of the circumstances of the Correspondent's appointment, which was communicated to him before it was made with a full statement of the reasons for it. He knows that Mr. Bennett had nothing whatever to do with it, and that the one objection which we all felt was his own old feud with the Correspondent. G.D.

XXII. IMPERIALISM; A NEW PHASE

The Ottawa Conference, 1932

The Times, pursuing its policy of general support of the National Government, gave fullest publicity to the Imperial Conference at Ottawa, convened at the suggestion of the Canadian Premier, R. B. Bennett. The paper regarded the Conference, with the talks at Lausanne, as the beginning of an attempt to break the economic depression. Dawson attached so much importance to the talks that he determined to visit Ottawa himself, though he did not expect to see the Conference through, unless it was unexpectedly brief.

In addition to ensuring the best and fullest reports of the Conference, the Editor saw other important advantages in his presence at Ottawa. It would afford him " an unusual opportunity for meeting people from Australia, New Zealand, South Africa and other parts of the Empire. It would be easy also to go to New York, where there was an impending change in the staff, and to see the Washington Correspondent at the same time. Above all, I felt that it was a good thing from time to time to get away from England and to look at the paper from a distance."

Having provisionally settled the problem of *The Times* representation, Dawson turned his attention to the composition of the British delegation. It was, in his view, impossible for J. H. Thomas to be entrusted with the leadership, and he wrote to a Correspondent at Montreal on March 14: " I think we have pushed Baldwin into going to Ottawa as leader of the British delegation. I realised some time ago that Jim Thomas and Neville Chamberlain would be an impossible combination without someone else of obviously higher rank, and eventually floated this notion in *The Times*. It had a very good response, though J.H.T. himself seems to have exploded in all directions and denounced me on the telephone with many strange expletives for spoiling his position." The Ottawa Correspondent in a despatch of March 11 confirmed Dawson's view, though for rather different reasons. He wrote " I suppose Jimmy Thomas must come on the British Delegation but he did not go down well here chiefly owing to his penchant for Rabelaisian stories and telling them to decent Catholic ladies." In fact, J.H.T. proved a great success at the Conference. " Baldwin himself," Dawson continued, " is quite prepared to go if his colleagues wish it and Parliament is up early, which was another of my bright suggestions; and the P.M., with whom I had a talk yesterday on his return, seemed disposed to clinch the matter to-day." The matter was clinched to Dawson's satisfaction, and Baldwin headed the delegation.

The British Government was apparently uncertain of the views of the Canadian Government and people on the Conference, for on March 14 Dawson wrote to ask the Ottawa Correspondent for information on this point, as " Our Ministers here seem to be quite in the dark about their attitude." A friend had already sailed for Canada and would return to England in April with, it was hoped, " some information and hints for the guidance of our Government in dealing with Canada. Owing to the peculiar position of Ferguson (Canadian H.C. at London), who is at daggers drawn with Jim Thomas and apparently confers with Beaverbrook, who is anti-National Government and particularly anti-Baldwin, I doubt whether the intelligence which reaches Mr. Bennett is either accurate or impartial."

In the months preceding the Conference *The Times* devoted much attention to Imperial problems. The May 21 issue of *The Times Imperial and Foreign Trade and Engineering Supplement* was an " Empire Products Number." It was an excellently produced survey of the Empire, designed fully to inform the public of the problems which the Conference would be called upon to solve. Leaders and articles in both *The Times* and the *Supplement* continued to lay stress upon the urgency of the situation.

Dawson sailed for Canada on June 24, three weeks before the delegation was due to leave. Brumwell was left in charge of *The Times*, with Braham to write the Ottawa leaders. Dawson spent Dominion Day (June 30) at Montreal, and then left for Ottawa. Sir William Clark, British High Commissioner in Ottawa, having mentioned the prospect of the Editor's journey to the Governor-General, Lord Bessborough, Dawson was invited to stay at Government House. Although Dawson wrote on March 29 accepting the invitation, he stayed at the Chateau Laurier at first, but took a small flat when the Chateau, where all the delegations were based, became too noisy.

The Ottawa Correspondent, meanwhile, was taking every opportunity of meeting Bennett and Stevens, of whose repeated assurances that the Canadian preparations were progressing favourably he was sceptical. Bennett later deprecated too high hopes for the Conference: Canada was right alongside the U.S.A. and, he said, it was " difficult to beat geography." The Ottawa Correspondent's belief was that Bennett was afraid to antagonise the powerful manufacturing interests which had supported his " Canada First " election campaign. The history of the Conference proved the correctness of this view.

Bennett invited Dawson to luncheon to meet practically the whole of the Cabinet. The Premier and the Editor had then " spent the whole afternoon driving slowly around and around the parks of this most beautiful capital in the most intimate conversation." He had shown Bennett the record of that " intimate conversation " before cabling it and the Canadian Premier had suggested only a few small amendments. Dawson believed that though the cable had been vague, it had at least committed Bennett to a definite attitude towards the Conference. Most of the time the Editor spent in New York was devoted to the affairs of the office. In Washington his host was Sir William Wiseman, the link with Colonel House during the first World War. He met Averell Harriman, L. F. Force, F. Polk and others at a dinner party at which the chief topic of discussion was War Debts.

The British delegation, with some other Colonial and Dominion representatives, sailed on July 13, and comprised nearly half the Cabinet, Baldwin, Neville Chamberlain, J. H. Thomas, Lord Hailsham, Cunliffe-Lister, Runciman and Sir John Gilmour. *The Times* Parliamentary Correspondent accompanied them, and reported the preliminary discussions which took place on the voyage.

The Irish delegation, whose presence at the Conference had at one time seemed very doubtful, had arrived in Ottawa the day before. The main body of delegates arrived in Ottawa to find that " Newsboys wearing the uniform of *The Times* and selling copies of that journal, have now become familiar figures in the streets of Ottawa and are attracting general attention." (July 19.) The paper for July 21 printed a long account from its Special Correspondents of the preparations for that day's opening of the Conference, together with an excellent description of the history and geography of Ottawa by the resident Correspondent. The leader for that day's issue held out high hopes of " the most momentous Conference in the history of the British Nations." On July 22 the paper printed the full details of the opening of the Conference by the Governor-General. The Special Correspondents sent their reports of the proceedings from a small office that Bennett had given the Editor. It was near the one which Baldwin occupied, so that, as the Editor wrote to Brumwell, " I see all these people constantly."

Dawson sailed for England at the end of the month, confident that, between them, the resident Correspondent and the Parliamentary Correspondent could continue the reporting of the Conference on the scale he had initiated. The later stages were marred by disputes between the British and Canadian delegations. They almost broke up the Conference and were partly responsible for the summary eviction of *The Times* representatives from their very convenient office to make way for Bennett's brother-in-law, Herridge, the Canadian Minister at Washington.

The paper never doubted the eventual success of the Conference, and its leader of August 20 was able to declared AGREEMENT REACHED. *The Times* then stated that " The success of the Ottawa Conference is now not only assured; it is an accomplished fact. The final plenary session will be held this morning, when the agreements will be signed and some of their contents disclosed."

On August 22 *The Times* gave a full report of the agreements between the various delegations. The leader for that day ended by congratulating the Conference on " a great work achieved and a firm foundation laid for future progress." Both the paper and the *Supplement* which had published admirable weekly reviews of the progress of the Conference, extended cordial congratulations to the British delegation when it returned to England on August 27, 1932.

XXIV. A NEW WORLD WAR AND A NEW EDITOR

The 150th Anniversary of *The Times*, January 1, 1935

The anniversary, which occurred in the same year as King George V's Silver Jubilee, was kept with no private celebration. *The Times* marked the occasion by a special number of thirty pages, and by the publication of Volume I of the *History of The Times*. The paper was able to make the proud claim that it had appeared continuously since January 1, 1785, a performance equalled by no other daily register of news. (With the exception of *The Times*, no daily newspaper maintained publication during the General Strike of 1926. A volunteer force in the office brought out an attenuated sheet.) As the first leading article remarked : " To-day's anniversary is more than domestic. It may rationally and not immodestly be taken to commemorate the rise of the Fourth Estate." The achievement of Thomas Barnes, the full extent of which was revealed for the first time in the *History*, was given prominence in the special number. The number recognized that no editorial staff, however superlative in quality, can alone guarantee the survival of a newspaper, and a substantial section was devoted to the other departmental activities, past and present, necessary and consequent to newspaper production.

Prominently displayed was the message of congratulation from His Majesty. Flanking the facsimile of the King's letter was a philosophical reflection on the nature of news *per se*, a subject which, in the midst of his daily task and turmoil, the journalist has little time to consider. The remaining article on the front page attempted some observations on that figure seldom encountered in Printing House Square, the " Reader of *The Times*." He was, as he still is, " the omnipresent Englishman. ' This is he :' the great arbiter to whom this journal for 150 years has submitted its service so that he shall know ' elder truths, joyful truths, fearful truths, grand truths.' "

APPENDIX III

Corrigenda : Volume III, Chapter III " Parnellism and Crime "

(published in 1947.)

THE TIMES is indebted to Captain Henry Harrison, O.B.E., M.C., Parnell's surviving colleague and biographer, for drawing attention to errors, of which two require more than conventional acknowledgment.

(a) The chapter omits the name of Captain W. H. O'Shea, which is written within the " Stationery Office " stamp affixed to official files and clearly seen on the two letters reproduced at pp. 44 and 76. O'Shea was called very early in the Commission's proceedings to give evidence for *The Times* (QQ 101-1019) ; he personally brought the alleged Parnell letters to the notice of the Commission, and vouched for them all as genuine. Captain Harrison's works, *Parnell Vindicated*, *The Lifting of the Veil* (London, 1931), *Parnell, Joseph Chamberlain and Mr. Garvin* (London, 1938) and *Parnell's Vindication (Irish Historical Studies*, V, No. 19, March, 1947), cite abundant evidence to show that it was Chamberlain who arranged with Buckle for O'Shea to be available to *The Times*. O'Shea's evidence was made the foundation for the only personal charges against Parnell—four in number—all of which were discredited by express findings in the Commission's Report. J. L. Hammond's *Gladstone and the Irish Nation* demonstrates conclusively O'Shea's worthlessness as a political figure and the harmful effect that he exercised on Chamberlain and Parnell in particular and on Ireland in general. It is necessary now to admit, first, that the paper's association with O'Shea proved by Captain Harrison is not creditable ; secondly, that the fact should not have been ignored in the *History of The Times*.

(b) It is hinted (p. 79) in the Chapter under notice that some of the letters may, after all, be genuine, whereas they were all formally withdrawn both in Court and editorially in 1889. In the circumstances, the Chapter should have quoted the unqualified finding of the Special Commissioners :

We find that all the letters produced by Pigott and set out in the Appendix (also in the Appendix to Vol. III, pp. 775-6) are forgeries, and we entirely acquit Mr. Parnell and the other Respondents of the charge of insincerity in their denunciation of the Phœnix Park murders.

There are other points in the Chapter that should also be noted in this connexion and corrected :

Page 44. " . . . to buy letters whose contents were known only by hearsay from a person whose identity was undisclosed. . . ." " By hearsay " is too strong a term : Houston brought copies of the letters with him to this interview (see Vol. III, p. 64).

Pages 45-6. The possibility should be taken into account that Buckle's share in the paper's attack on Parnell is minimized, although the evidence is insufficient to prove whether this was so or not. But it is true (*a*) that Buckle personally asked Joseph Chamberlain by letter for O'Shea's services and that he established personal touch with O'Shea both directly and through the medium of Ernest Caulfield Houston before the Commission sat, and (*b*) that though he took a prominent part in the earlier stages of the preparation of Vol. III, no letters (sent or received), no diaries, notes, memoranda or other personal papers of his relating to the Chamberlain-O'Shea association with him in the attack on Parnell were made available as part of the sources of Chapter III, and (*c*) that Houston was regarded by O'Shea as representing Buckle, and as such prepared the proof of O'Shea's evidence, after receiving from him, by Chamberlain's permission, all the Chamberlain-O'Shea documents " save two of Mr. Chamberlain's letters."

Pages 47 *and* 57. Parnell is stated to have " applied to the Home Secretary for police protection " in May, 1882. Application was made, but by O'Shea who pretended without authority to be acting on Parnell's behalf. Parnell, on oath before the Commission, denied that he had made or authorized any such application (QQ 58,824-7). This should have been stated and accepted. The story, however, had had wide currency (see *Standard*, May 12, 1882) by a calculated indiscretion of Sir William Harcourt. The best contemporary evidence — apart from the evidence given by Parnell and O'Shea to the Commission — is the account recorded by Mr. Justin McCarthy in 1887 and published in 1912 in *Our Book of Memories* which conflicts with the re-written diaries (*ca.*, 1891-92) of Joseph Chamberlain and Sir Charles Dilke. McCarthy accompanied Parnell in his visits on May 7, 1882, to both Dilke and Chamberlain, and heard both severally warning against the danger of violence from Londoners and *not* from Irish Invincibles. He records that Parnell was not impressed and, on leaving with McCarthy, refused to adopt suggested precautions. Chamberlain, even before this, had warned O'Shea of the possibilities of British anti-Irish violence. (See letter, Chamberlain to O'Shea of April 17, 1882, in Barry O'Brien's *Life of Parnell*, Vol. I, p. 338.) And on May 8, 1882, Joseph Chamberlain, on approaching Parliament, had to be protected by the police from imminent molestation by a London mob. (*Standard*, May 9, 1882.) The legend of Parnell's abject fear on May 7, 1882, was first born in the Chamberlain-O'Shea letter (signed by O'Shea) for which Buckle gave special facilities and a supporting leading article in *The Times* of August 2, 1888, and was an essential element of the help sought and obtained by Buckle from Chamberlain and O'Shea. (See *Parnell Vindicated*, Appendices B and C, where it is examined and disproved.)

Page 48. It is an error to state that (lines 8-12) " Accordingly Walter . . . agreed to accept the letters as genuine, and purchased them for *The Times* at Houston's previously mentioned price of £1,780. This point was reached in the middle of January, 1887." In fact, the agreement to purchase occurred three months later and the final instalment of the £1,780 was not paid until several months after that. The text thus incorrectly states that the agreement and purchase *preceded* the consultation with *The Times* Counsel (Sir Henry James, Q.C., later Lord James of Hereford) when he disclosed his previous knowledge of the letters and of Pigott's implication in their procurement, and how he had advised that the whole matter should be handed over to Scotland Yard.

Page 56. The special and leading articles accompanying the publication of " letter No. 2 " in facsimile on April 18, 1887, are said to have been " written in the ordinary course of the night's work." It is fair to mention, however, that the day chosen for publication was also the day of the division on the second reading of an important Coercion Bill. The facsimile letter and the articles sought to influence this Bill.

Page 61. The Bill to set up the Special Commission is said to have been " bitterly opposed by both the Home Rule Liberals and the Irish." Although this was true of the committee stage, which was drastically closured, it passed its second reading without a division at Parnell's urgent instance. (Morley, *Life of Gladstone*, III, 400.)

Page 63. There is a suggestion that in 1885 Gladstone and " the Liberal Party were at daggers drawn with the Parnellites." This was believed for many years, in spite of the hints to the contrary in Morley, but has now been exploded, at least as far as Gladstone personally is concerned, by R. C. K. Ensor's *England*, 1870-1914, Appendix A, and in much greater detail by J. L. Hammond's *Gladstone and the Irish Nation, passim*. The latter work traces Gladstone's belief in Home Rule which Parnell adopted back as far as 1871, four years before Parnell himself entered Parliament.

Page 63. A statement is made that " to young Houston his (Pigott's) name was as yet quite unknown" in 1885. Houston told the Commission (Q. 49,992 ff.) that he knew Pigott by name as a Nationalist journalist already.

Pages 69 *and* 71. According to Soames's evidence before the Commission (QQ. 49,009-11) Houston had been paid " for all purposes " £30,000, not £1,780 only.

A possible source of error in the text and in its implications is the close association of E. C. Houston with the conduct of the original transactions in 1886-89 as well as with the ultimate recording of them in Chapter III. Soames, solicitor to *The Times*, testified that Houston assisted him in the conduct of *The Times'* case, and Houston has told of some of the tasks which thus came his way. Chapter III opens with an elaborated version of the earlier dealings of Buckle with Houston in 1886-87 when the affair started, and of their consultation (pp. 48 *ad fin.* and 49) which gave rise to the articles on " Parnellism and Crime." Houston's continuous co-operation as to the latter is seen in his lengthy written report, addressed to Buckle, Oakley Street, Chelsea, in 1935, and later in the passage (p. 83, lines 11 and 12) " Houston, as we have seen, asserted, and still asserts . . ." etc.

APPENDIX IV

PRINCIPAL MINISTERS 1910-1940

1. *January*, 1910-*May*, 1915—*Liberal*

Prime Minister : H. H. Asquith

Lord President of the Council : Lord Wolverhampton (1910) ; Lord Morley (1910-14) ; Lord Beauchamp

Foreign Secretary : Sir E. Grey

Chancellor of the Exchequer : D. Lloyd George

Lord Privy Seal : Lord Crewe (1910-11) ; Lord Carrington (1911-12) ; Lord Crewe

Home Secretary : Winston Churchill (1910-11) ; R. McKenna

Colonial Secretary : Lord Crewe (1910) ; L. Harcourt

Secretary for War : R. B. Haldane (1910-12) ; Col. J. E. B. Seely (1912-14) ; H. H. Asquith (1914) ; Lord Kitchener

Secretary for India : Lord Morley (1910) ; Lord Crewe (1910-11) ; Lord Morley (1911) ; Lord Crewe

First Lord of the Admiralty : R. McKenna (1910-11) ; Winston Churchill

Chief Secretary for Ireland : A. Birrell

2. *May*, 1915-*December*, 1916—*Coalition*

Prime Minister : H. H. Asquith

Lord President of the Council : Lord Crewe

Foreign Secretary : Sir E. Grey

Chancellor of the Exchequer : R. McKenna

Lord Privy Seal : Lord Curzon

Home Secretary : Sir J. Simon (1915-16) ; H. Samuel

Colonial Secretary : A. Bonar Law

Secretary for War : Lord Kitchener (1915-16) ; D. Lloyd George

Secretary for India : Austen Chamberlain

First Lord of the Admiralty : A. J. Balfour

Minister of Munitions : D. Lloyd George (1915-16) ; E. S. Montagu

Chief Secretary for Ireland : A. Birrell (1915-16) ; H. E. Duke

Minister without Portfolio : Lord Lansdowne

3. *December*, 1916-*January*, 1919—*Coalition*

Prime Minister : D. Lloyd George

Lord President of the Council : Lord Curzon

Foreign Secretary : A. J. Balfour

Chancellor of the Exchequer : A. Bonar Law

Lord Privy Seal : Lord Crawford

Home Secretary : Sir G. Cave

Colonial Secretary : W. H. Long

Secretary for War : Lord Derby (1916-18) ; Lord Milner

Secretary for India : Austen Chamberlain (1916-17) ; E. S. Montagu

First Lord of the Admiralty : Sir E. H. Carson (1916-17) ; Sir E. C. Geddes

Minister of Munitions : Dr. C. Addison (1916-17) ; Winston Churchill

Chancellor of the Duchy of Lancaster and Minister of Information : Lord Beaverbrook (1918)

Chief Secretary for Ireland : H. E. Duke (1916-18) ; E. Shortt

Ministers without Portfolio : Lord Milner (1916-18) ; Sir E. H. Carson (1917-18) ; A. Henderson (1916-17) ; Austen Chamberlain, Lieut.-Gen. J. C. Smuts, G. N. Barnes

4. *January*, 1919-*October*, 1922—*Coalition*

Prime Minister : D. Lloyd George

Lord President of the Council : Lord Curzon (1919) ; A. J. Balfour

Foreign Secretary : A. J. Balfour (1919) ; Lord Curzon

Chancellor of the Exchequer : Austen Chamberlain (1919-21); Sir R. S. Horne

Lord Privy Seal : A. Bonar Law (1919-21) ; Austen Chamberlain

Home Secretary : E. Shortt

Colonial Secretary : Lord Milner (1919-21); Winston Churchill

Secretary for India : E. S. Montagu (1919-22) ; Lord Peel

Chief Secretary for Ireland : J. I. Macpherson (1919-20); Sir H. Greenwood

Ministers without Portfolio : Sir E. C. Geddes (1919) ; G. N. Barnes (1919-20) ; Sir L. Worthington-Evans (1919-21) ; Dr. C. Addison (1921)

5. *October, 1922-May, 1923—Conservative*

Prime Minister A. Bonar Law
Lord President of the Council: Lord Salisbury
Foreign Secretary: Lord Curzon
Chancellor of the Exchequer: Stanley Baldwin
Home Secretary: W. C. Bridgeman
Colonial Secretary: Duke of Devonshire
Secretary for India: Lord Peel

6. *May, 1923-January, 1924—Conservative*

Prime Minister: Stanley Baldwin
Lord President of the Council: Lord Salisbury
Foreign Secretary: Lord Curzon
Chancellor of the Exchequer: Stanley Baldwin (May-August, 1923); Neville Chamberlain
Lord Privy Seal: Lord Robert Cecil
Home Secretary: W. C. Bridgeman
Colonial Secretary: Duke of Devonshire
Secretary for India: Lord Peel

7. *January-November, 1924—Labour*

Prime Minister: Ramsay MacDonald
Lord President of the Council: Lord Parmoor
Foreign Secretary: Ramsay MacDonald
Chancellor of the Exchequer: Philip Snowden
Lord Privy Seal: J. R. Clynes
Home Secretary: Arthur Henderson
Colonial Secretary: J. H. Thomas
Secretary for India: Lord Olivier

8. *November, 1924-June, 1929—Conservative*

Prime Minister: Stanley Baldwin
Lord President of the Council: Lord Curzon (1924-25); Lord Balfour
Foreign Secretary: Sir Austen Chamberlain
Chancellor of the Exchequer: Winston Churchill
Lord Privy Seal: Lord Salisbury
Home Secretary: Sir W. Joynson-Hicks
Colonial Secretary: L. S. Amery
Dominions Secretary: L. S. Amery (from 1925)
Secretary for India: Lord Birkenhead (1924-28); Lord Peel

9. *June, 1929-August, 1931—Labour*

Prime Minister: Ramsay MacDonald
Lord President of the Council: Lord Parmoor
Foreign Secretary: Arthur Henderson
Chancellor of the Exchequer: Philip Snowden
Lord Privy Seal: J. H. Thomas (1929-30); V. Hartshorn (1930-31); T. Johnston
Home Secretary: J. R. Clynes
Colonial Secretary: Lord Passfield
Dominions Secretary: Lord Passfield (1929-30); J. H. Thomas
Secretary for India: W. Wedgwood Benn

10. *August-November, 1931—National*

Prime Minister: Ramsay MacDonald
Lord President of the Council: Stanley Baldwin
Foreign Secretary: Lord Reading
Chancellor of the Exchequer: Philip Snowden
Lord Privy Seal: Lord Peel
Home Secretary: Sir H. Samuel
Colonial Secretary: J. H. Thomas
Dominions Secretary: J. H. Thomas
Secretary for India: Sir S. Hoare

11. *November, 1931-June, 1935—National*

Prime Minister: Ramsay MacDonald
Lord President of the Council: Stanley Baldwin
Foreign Secretary: Sir J. Simon
Chancellor of the Exchequer: Neville Chamberlain
Lord Privy Seal: Lord Snowden (1931-32); Stanley Baldwin (1932-33); Anthony Eden
Home Secretary: Sir H. Samuel (1931-32); Sir J. Gilmour
Colonial Secretary: Sir P. Cunliffe-Lister
Dominions Secretary: J. H. Thomas
Secretary for India: Sir S. Hoare

12. *June, 1935-May, 1937—National*

Prime Minister: Stanley Baldwin
Lord President of the Council: Ramsay MacDonald
Foreign Secretary: Sir S. Hoare (1935); Anthony Eden
Chancellor of the Exchequer: Neville Chamberlain
Lord Privy Seal: Lord Londonderry (1935); Lord Halifax
Home Secretary: Sir J. Simon
Colonial Secretary: Malcolm MacDonald (1935); J. H. Thomas (1935-36); W. G. Ormsby-Gore
Dominions Secretary: J. H. Thomas (1935); Malcolm MacDonald
Secretary for India: Lord Zetland
Minister for Coordination of Defence: Sir T. Inskip (from 1936)
Minister for League of Nations Affairs: Anthony Eden (1935)

13. *May*, 1937-*May* 9, 1940—*National*

Prime Minister : Neville Chamberlain

Lord President of the Council : Lord Halifax (1937-38) ; Lord Hailsham (March-October, 1938) ; Lord Runciman (1938-39) ; Lord Stanhope

Foreign Secretary : Anthony Eden (1937-38) ; Lord Halifax

Chancellor of the Exchequer : Sir J. Simon

Lord Privy Seal : Lord De La Warr (1937-38) ; Sir J. Anderson (1938-39) ; Sir S. Hoare (1939-April, 1940) ; Sir H. Kingsley Wood

Home Secretary : Sir S. Hoare (1937-39) ; Sir J. Anderson

Colonial Secretary : W. G. Ormsby-Gore (1937-38) ; Malcolm MacDonald

Dominions Secretary : Malcolm MacDonald (1937-38) ; Lord Stanley (to October, 1938) ; Malcolm MacDonald (1938-39) ; Sir T. Inskip (January-September, 1939) ; Anthony Eden

Secretary for India and Burma : Lord Zetland

Secretary for War : L. Hore-Belisha (1937-40) ; Oliver Stanley

First Lord of the Admiralty : A. Duff Cooper (1937-38) ; Lord Stanhope (1938-39) ; Winston Churchill

Secretary for Air : Lord Swinton (1937-38) ; Sir H. Kingsley Wood (1938-40) ; Sir S. Hoare

Minister for Coordination of Defence : Sir T. Inskip (1937-39) ; Lord Chatfield

Minister of Information : Lord Macmillan (September, 1939-January, 1940) ; Sir J. Reith

INDEX

Printed by Burrup Mathieson & Co., Ltd., at their London Factory